A Note from the Publisher

Psychology: Exploring Behavior examines the major areas of psychology by combining theory with a variety of practical applications related to student interests now and in the future. Its coverage extends from ways we use psychology in daily life to the research process used by professional psychologists. In the units of study—which discuss development, the bases of behavior, learning and language, motivation and emotion, personality and testing, social psychology, research, and careers—the text involves students in the practice as well as the content of the discipline. A comprehensive visual program of colorful photographs, diagrams, charts, and illustrations helps students develop their skills of analysis and observation. Specific features of the text are listed below. Page numbers refer to examples of features.

- A chapter outline opens each chapter (page 148).

- "What's the Answer" is a series of vignettes or questions that appear at the beginning of each chapter. They spark interest in the topics to be discussed (page 116).

- Important concepts and terms are italicized in the text (page 204), defined in the margin (page 150), and included in a glossary (page 555).

- "Think about it" features pose a stimulating thought question, and then provide the answer. They are interspersed throughout each chapter (page 408).

- "In review" features, which appear throughout each chapter, provide brief summaries of important content (page 372).

- Boxed features describe experiments or present other items of high interest (page 328).

- A wide-ranging graphics program illustrates, reinforces, and supplements the text (page 280).

- Chapter Application and Review at the end of each chapter includes the following: "Using Psychology" (page 177), a practical application of chapter content; "Review Questions" (page 452), a set of questions about each section; "Activities" (page 210), suggested activities that give firsthand experience in the methods of psychology; and "Interested in more?" (page 359), a bibliography of recommended readings.

- Research processes in psychology are treated fully in Chapter 17 (page 512).

- Psychology and Careers, an epilogue, describes careers in the field (page 532). Special activities at the end of each chapter, called "Career Search," also take a close look at careers in psychology (page 45).

- Capsule biographies of significant psychologists (page 543) supplement the text.

- A glossary defines key terms italicized throughout the text (page 547).

- A "References" section cites the many studies and readings that document the text (page 560).

- A comprehensive index provides a useful tool for finding specific information and reviewing broad topics (page 570).

To assure a highly readable book, the content for this text has been selected, organized, and written at a level appropriate for high school students. The Fry and Dale–Chall readability formulas were used to control reading level. These scores are available on request from the Educational Book Division of Prentice-Hall, Inc., Englewood Cliffs, New Jersey 07632, or from your local Prentice-Hall representative.

love
true
Thankyou.

PSYCHOLOGY

EXPLORING BEHAVIOR

PSYCHOLOGY

EXPLORING BEHAVIOR

Richard A. Kasschau

Department of Psychology
University of Houston

Consultants

Virginia Amos Trimble Technical High School, Fort Worth, Texas

John Christiano McQuaid Jesuit High School, Rochester, New York

James Divine De Kalb High School, De Kalb, Illinois

Carol Meszaros N.B. Broughton High School, Raleigh, North Carolina

Robert Shreve Palo Alto High School, Palo Alto, California

Jean La-Yvonne Valetta Deputy Commissioner of Education, St. Paul, Minnesota

PRENTICE-HALL, INC., Englewood Cliffs, New Jersey

Dr. Richard A. Kasschau is Professor of Psychology at the University of Houston. He has advanced degrees in experimental psychology and psycholinguistics, and has conducted research at Massachusetts General Hospital. He has taught at both the undergraduate and graduate levels and has participated in many high school curriculum workshops and projects in psychology. He is a member and has been chairman of the American Psychological Association's national Committee on Psychology in the Secondary Schools. He has also served as head of the APA's division for the teaching of psychology. His writings include numerous papers, pamphlets, and television programs, as well as authorship with others of the books *Psymple Psych: A Complex Introduction to Psychology; Language and Communication; and Exploring Psychology.*

SECOND EDITION

Auxiliary Materials

Teacher's Guide with Tests
Student Handbook: Experiments and Quizzes

Front cover photographs:
Row 1 Peter Arnold: Bruce Curtis; r Lou Jones **Row 2** J. Gerald Smith **Row 3** Woodfin Camp: Michal Heron; r Larry Lawfer **Row 4** Lou Jones; r International Stock Photo: Mimi Cotter **Row 5** Woodfin Camp: Michal Heron; r Leo de Wys: Bill Hurter **Row 6** Woodfin Camp: Howard Sochurek; r Photo Researchers: Susan Kuklin

Back cover photographs:
Unit 1 The Stock Market: Roy Morsch Unit 2 Woodfin Camp: Howard Sochurek Unit 3 The Picture Cube: C.T. Seymour Unit 4 Woodfin Camp: Jeff Lowenthal Unit 5 The Stock Market: Barney Elz Unit 6 Taurus Photos: Lenore Weber Unit 7 Woodfin Camp: Michal Heron

PRENTICE-HALL INTERNATIONAL, INC., London
PRENTICE-HALL OF AUSTRALIA, PTY. LTD., Sydney
PRENTICE-HALL CANADA INC., Toronto
PRENTICE-HALL OF INDIA PRIVATE LTD., New Delhi
PRENTICE-HALL OF JAPAN, INC., Tokyo
PRENTICE-HALL OF SOUTHEAST ASIA PTE. LTD., Singapore
WHITEHALL BOOKS LIMITED, Wellington, New Zealand
EDITORA PRENTICE-HALL DO BRASIL LTDA., Rio de Janeiro

Acknowledgments

Graph p. **103** adapted from J. Botninick *Cognitive Processes in Maturity and Old Age*, Figure 21, p. **179**. Copyright © 1967 by Springer Publishing Company, New York. Used by permission. Graph p. **142** adapted from Figure 2.5 (p. **27**) from *Drugs and Alcohol*, 2nd Ed., by Kenneth L. Jones, Louis W. Shainberg, and Curtis O. Byer. Copyright © 1967, 1973 by Kenneth L. Jones, Louis W. Shainberg, and Curtis O. Byer. Reprinted by permission Harper & Row Publishers, Inc. Graph p. **306** adapted from Hebb, *Textbook of Psychology* 3rd Ed., © 1972 W. B. Saunders Company. Used by permission. Graphs p. **315** adapted from Schachter and Singer, ''Cognitive, Social and Physiological Determinants of Emotional State,'' *Psychological Review*, 1962, 69. Example from Faces Inventory Test, p. **449**, Stanford Research Institute, the U.S. Office of Education, and Jack Frymier, School of Education, Ohio State University. Drawings p. **461** and p. **466**, adapted from Raven and Rubin, *Social Psychology; People in Groups* copyright © 1976 John Wiley and Sons, Inc. Used by permission.

Photo Credits

Key to position of photographs: *t*—top; *b*—bottom; *c*—center; *l*—left; *r*—right; *tl*—top left; *tr*—top right; *tc*—top center; *bl*—bottom left; *br*—bottom right **photographs:** American Optical Corp. **156.** Animals, Animals: H.S. Terrace **264.** Billy Barnes **62, 183.** The Bettman Archives **25, 352, 354t, 433l.** British Tourist Authority **237b.** Bruce Coleman, Inc. **192l;** H. Reinhard **55;** Jonathan T. Wright **138.** Culver Pictures **23, 368br.** Jay Dorin **184, 281.** Enrico Ferorelli/DOT **7t, 149.** Helena Frost **67l, 155, 196t.** George W. Gardner **468.** Charles Gatewood **61l, 97.** Joel Gordon **134, 364.** Granger Collection **172, 347, 348.** Great America, Marriott Corp. **326b.** Guttmann Maclay Collection, Institute of Psychiatry **382, 383.** Harry F. Harlow, University of Wisconsin Primate Laboratory **328.** Harold Lambert Studios: Frederic Lewis **213.** Grant Heilman: **171l;** Runk/Schoenberger **119, 152.** Michal Heron **54, 88, 95, 157, 239** (both), **259l, 296, 309r, 317** (both), **319, 326t, 380, 387, 473, 479l, 499, 519, 538.** Ken Heyman **67r, 248, 460r.** Richard Howard **349.** Drawing by Sam Hunt: ©1967 The New Yorker Magazine, Inc. **268.** Inmont Corp. **153.** International Stock Photo: Mimi Cotter **2 row 3r.** Walter loose, Jr. Sports Illustrated ©Time, Inc., **338.** Lou Jones **2 row 1r, 2 row 3l, 245.** Kristin Kasschau **450r.** Drawing by Koren: ©1978 The New Yorker Magazine, Inc., **403.** Susan Lapides **399.** Larry Lawfer **2 row 2r, 33, 427.** Leo de Wys: Bill Hurter **2 row 4r.** Drawing by Levin; © 1977 The New Yorker Magazine, Inc. **168.** Drawing by Lorenz; ©1977 The New Yorker Magazine, Inc. **132.** Magnum Photos, Inc.: Boris Erwitt **74;** Leonard Freed **196b;** A. Heyman **327;** Inge Morath **450l;** Alex Webb **41, 259bl.** © by Bill Maul, first published in Esquire Magazine **195.** Thomas McAvoy, Life Picture Service **64.** Joan Menschenfreund **60t, 469.** Monkmeyer Press Photo Service: **351;** Mimi Forsyth **42, 57l, 410, 431, 478;** Hugh Rogers **535;** Sybil Shelton **22, 214, 406, 495, 522;** David Strickler **494.** National Library of Medicine **344, 368l.** NASA **10c, 354bl, 354br.** New York Times Picture Service **122.** Omni-Photo Communications: Ann Hagen Griffiths **10t, 335;** Dannielle B. Hayes **5b, 26;** Ken Karp **535b;** John Lei **535t;** Lenore Weber **49.** Nancy Palmer Photo Agency, Inc.: Rita Freed **5c, 21, 60b, 463r;** Kenneth Murray **309l;** Bill Powers **171r;** Peter Arnold, Inc.: Bruce Curtis **2 row 1l;** Barbara Pfeffer **288.** Pfizer, Inc. **192r.** Harvey R. Phillips/PPI **443r.** Photo Researchers, Inc.: Susan Kuklin **2 row 5r.** Photo Unit New York City Fire Department, **460l.** The Picture Cube, Boston: Betsy Cole **337;** Sharon Fox **278, 463l;** Dave Johnston **275;** Terry McKoy **444;** Julie O'Neil **305;** Jaye Philips **101;** Dave Schaefer **393;** C.T. Seymour **181;** James H. Simon **7c, 185;** Frank Siteman **322, 395;** Richard Wood **513.** Bill Powers, Corrections Magazine **487.** J. Gerald Smith **487.** Sotheby Parke-Bernet/Art Resource Sale 4373, **361.** Stock Boston: Fredrik B. Bodin **57r;** Donald C. Dietz **259br;** Bohdan Hrynewych **43, 448;** Peter Menzel **7b, 267;** John Running **284;** Peter Vandermark **5t, 19.** Cary Wolinsky **479r.** The Stock Market: Barney Elz **333;** Roy Morsch **17;** Vince Streano **457.** Taurus Photos: Alex Duncan **416;** Pam Hasegawa **50;** Dan Vessel **490;** Lenore Weber **90, 337, 455.** Herbert Terrace, **10b, 533.** Arthur Tress **323.** Copyright © 1975 United Feature Syndicate, Inc. **501.** U.P.I. **257, 386, 476.** Walter Reed Army Medical Center **435r.** Drawing by Weber; ©1977 The New Yorker Magazine, Inc., **108.** Woodfin Camp & Associates: Jim Anderson **514.** Dan Budnik **170;** Daily Telegraph Magazine **435l;** Timothy Eagan **289, 353;** Michal Heron **2 row 2l, 2 row 4l, 85, 117, 511.** William Hubbell **236;** Jeff Lowenthal **273;** Ellen Pines **61r;** Howard Sochurek **115;** Bob Strauss **294l;** Arthur Tress **325;** Adam Woolfitt **237t.**

CONTENTS

Features

What you always thought you knew about
psychology 20   Operationalizing a
definition 28   Apes of wrath? 35
"Many a tear has to fall" 36

10

FOCUS ON CAREERS

GRAPHS, CHARTS, DRAWINGS

TABLES

TO THE STUDENT

The opportunity is at hand to introduce you to psychology. In this book we draw upon the research and theories of a wide range of scientists and practitioners. We aim to bring you an over-all picture of the field, which has grown to be known as the science of human and animal behavior and experience.

What follows are seven units, or topical areas, starting with developmental and physiological psychology, where psychology overlaps most with biology. We then move toward the most complex social psychological behaviors, where psychologists' interests overlap those of sociologists. Along the way we study sensation, perception, remembering, language, learning, motivation, emotion, testing, personality, mental disorders, and therapies. We conclude with a view of the future of psychology and of how psychology can serve you now and in the years to come.

The book has many aids and features to help you in your learning.

1. **Chapter Outline.** Each chapter starts with a topical outline. Scan it so you'll have an idea about where we're going and how we'll get there.

2. **What's the Answer?** is a series of questions and brief sketches. They are meant to tease your curiosity. All concern topics that will be discussed in that chapter.

3. **Sections.** Chapters are divided into numbered sections to help you organize your thinking about the topics discussed.

4. **Think about it.** We interrupt each chapter at a point where you'll have gained just enough information to discuss a thought question. Before you read our answer, see if you can answer it yourself, from your own experience or from the reading you've just completed.

5. **In Review summaries appear throughout each chapter.** They give you the gist of the topics just covered. They stress facts without qualifications and are intended to give you practice in going through the material. The more times you review this material, the better you'll know it.

6. **Boxed human interest features** point out the incredible array of activities in which psychology operates. Each is meant to illustrate a point about behavior.

7. **Marginal definitions.** In the margins we define most new terms as we introduce them. We also list these terms and others in a complete glossary at the back of the book.

8. **Italicized words** act as cues to concepts, help to clarify and emphasize, and aid in the process of review.

9. **Using Psychology.** Each chapter concludes with a page or so of practical applications of psychology to areas important to you in your life today.

10. **Review Questions.** Each chapter has sets of questions about the sections in the chapter. These review questions provide one more opportunity for you to review the content of the chapter.

11. **Activities.** At the end of the chapter we include a variety of suggested activities. These are intended to give you firsthand experiences in the methods we've discussed. At least one of these activities is a career search, to give you an indepth look at a career using psychology.

12. **Interested in More?** lists books that apply to the material in each chapter. We hope you'll find the subject so interesting you'll want to pursue it further on your own.

13. **Research Processes and Careers.** The last unit describes research methods in greater detail. You will learn how psychologists go about adding to the store of psychological knowledge. You will also read about careers in which psychology is useful.

14. **References.** Several hundred different sources have been used in writing this book. They're listed by chapter number in the References at the end of the book.

15. **Some Significant Psychologists** lists many of the important contributors to the field and gives brief biographical sketches and titles of their major works.

So, with the clues and cues above, you're now ready to begin your studies. Happy reading!

Richard A. Kasschau

PSYCHOLOGY

EXPLORING BEHAVIOR

UNIT ONE

HUMAN DEVELOPMENT

Although individual differences are vast, almost all humans pass through the same stages of development.

In Chapter 1 we introduce you to the intriguing part-science, part-social-science field of psychology. We sketch a brief history of psychology's different strands and survey some of the many issues and varied methods of psychology today.

In Chapters 2 and 3 we concentrate on one of the major content areas of psychology: the developmental changes that take place in humans as they progress through the life span. For each of the major age periods—infancy, childhood, adolescence, adulthood, and old age—we'll describe changes occurring in the body, in motor skills, in language ability, and in self-concept. And, as we move through this developmental analysis, we'll touch on many topics discussed in greater depth and detail later on.

Psychology: Its Nature and Nurture

CHAPTER OUTLINE

WHAT'S THE ANSWER?

"Ahm gowa gega ped dawp."
"Ahm ink thasa dawp's ta on."
"Eir, dawpy, dawpy, lokame."
"Es, dissa ma ped dawp na." *What's going on here? Does this speech reflect logical behavior?*

☐ *Are psychologists today interested in studying the "mind"?*

☐ *"Intelligence is what an intelligence test measures." Does this make sense?*

☐ *Will psychologists learn how to control behavior? If they do, will they have too much power over our lives?*

1 What Is Psychology?

As you read the unfamiliar syllables in the introductory paragraph above, you exhibited certain behaviors. You may have made a quick decision: that part of this book is written in a foreign language. Or you may have decided that psychology was

The influence of peers becomes especially powerful during adolescence.

more complex than you'd thought. Or perhaps you looked at the quotations and realized that they fit the normal rules for language. The "words" seemed to occur in logical order. In short, you have decided that this material reflected some sort of normal human behavior, but you just didn't know the rules. In any case you began to wonder about psychology.

Now, as part of your introduction to this subject, read Box 1-1, which contains many statements about psychology. Which ones are true? After you've quizzed yourself, you might discuss them in class and then try again. You may know more about psychology than you think. Information about each of these topics will appear throughout the book.

Feature 1–1 WHAT YOU ALWAYS THOUGHT YOU KNEW ABOUT PSYCHOLOGY

Following are some beliefs people have that are related to the field of psychology. With which ones do you agree? Discuss each of them in class. After each statement is the number of the chapter that will give the facts.

1. It is very easy to demonstrate your "body sense" even with your eyes shut. (Answer in Chapter 5.)

2. People are either introverted (inward-looking) or extroverted (outgoing). (Answer in Chapter 11.)

3. After you learn something you forget more of it in the next few hours than in the next several days. (Answer in Chapter 7.)

4. The main factor determining whom a teenager is likely to ask for a first date is the person's physical attractiveness. (Answer in Chapter 16.)

5. If you must punish a child, it is best to do it immediately after the misdeed. (Answer in Chapter 6.)

6. All people in America are born equal in capacity for achievement. (Answer in Chapter 14.)

7. Teaching a child to roller skate very early in life will give the child a permanent advantage in this skill. (Answer in Chapter 2.)

8. The number of people in mental hospitals, per 100,000 population, has been declining steadily since 1946. (Answer in Chapter 13.)

9. Animals lower than humans are not able to reason. (Answer in Chapter 8.)

10. Modern psychologists don't study animals. (Answer in Chapter 1.)

11. One of the major reasons you turn and face the front when you get on an elevator is that the other riders have already done so. (Answer in Chapter 15.)

Definition of psychology

Perhaps you're impressed (or worried?) by the wide range of topics that may be studied by psychologists. In fact, while the topics are many, they all involve behavior. Psychology is defined as *the science of human and animal behavior and experience.*

Let's discuss each part of that definition. First, consider the word *science.* When we refer to psychology as a science, what do we mean?

The term "science" is really used in three different ways. It may simply identify a *frame of reference*—a set of values, customs, and attitudes that make up a certain approach. In this sense it is only one way to study the events of nature. Religion would be another. Philosophy might be a third. Sometimes "science" identifies *procedure.* Scientific methods, or sets of established procedures, can be used when studying or trying to prove a theory. Lastly, "science" sometimes refers to everything we've

frame of reference: *a set of values, customs, and attitudes that make up a particular approach to a subject*

scientific method: *a formal, orderly series of procedures used to arrive at facts and laws, classify things, and test hypotheses (educated guesses)*

already learned by applying scientific methods. Thus science is also a *body of organized knowledge* that has already been confirmed. In studying behavior, psychologists use science as a frame of reference, as a procedure, and as a way to accumulate and apply knowledge.

Now, consider the words *human and animal* in our definition of psychology. It *is* true that psychologists study both humans and animals. Why? For several reasons. Obviously, animals also behave, and they are interesting in their own right. But, more importantly, processes such as motivation and learning may be easier to study in lower animals. Moreover, there are some experiments that simply can't be performed on humans—for instance, studies of the effects of hunger on behavior.

Perhaps the most important word in the definition is *behavior*. We all "behave," but what do we mean by that? In order to interest a psychologist, behavior must be *observable*. How to make behavior publicly observable is a problem all psychologists face.

Finally, even when you are absolutely still, not moving anything, you may still be experiencing dreams (or nightmares!), itches, and urges. Whereas some psychologists once discouraged the study of internal *experience*, today many examine the total mental processes involved in any given activity.

These, then, are aspects of psychology as a science. Psychology was only formalized as a scientific discipline a little more than 100 years ago—in the late 1870's. However, many of the

"Behavior" can refer to almost any activity. We all constantly "behave." Psychologists concern themselves with behavior in hopes of understanding why we act as we do and predicting how we may behave in the future. Among their interests are the emotions, such as love.

→ Think about it

The **question**: On the first page of this chapter are these words in a nonsense language: "Ahm gowa gega ped dawp." That doesn't seem to make any sense, but what's going on here? Is the "conversation" from which this is drawn a logical one?

The **answer**: The answer to the first question is that what's occurring is communication—as you suspected. Your own past experience probably led you to think that a logical conversation was taking place. More than likely you assumed that the behavior *was* logical, but that you simply didn't understand the rules of the language. However, for those who did it was intelligible.

You probably assumed that since you're reading a psychology text, we must be demonstrating something about human behavior. You also may have assumed, since books usually explain what they're about, that we're going to explain to you now exactly what we are demonstrating. No such luck. We're going to come back to this demonstration in our discussions of perception, of language and thought, and of person perception. By then you'll be better able to translate this "foreign language" into understandable English.

For now, simply rest assured that some of your assumptions about our purposes are correct. Take our word for it: Both *your* assumptions *and* the conversation are logical. As you read the book, you'll find out why.

Psychologists use scientific methods in the study of behavior. Many experiments in motivation and learning have been conducted by observing lower animals.

topics and concerns of psychology have been of interest to thinking humans for centuries. What are some of the early roots of the subject? What are the origins of the existing trends and theories we study today?

2 The History of Psychology

Since the times of the ancient Greeks, the brain has been recognized as the seat or location of the mind. On the other hand, religious views maintain that humans have souls. "Mind" is a concept very similar to that of "soul." And, like soul, it's not an easy concept to isolate. One of the oldest arguments of the philosophers concerns what has been called the "mind-body" problem.

Part of the debate has concerned the question (still unresolved), How are the brain (body) and the mind related? One possibility is that they interact. They are separate, but equal. They may experience the same thing, but they are separate and distinct entities. A second possibility is that mind and brain are operating in parallel. Maybe they experience the same thing, but the brain is part of the physical world whereas the mind is part of another (separate, or dual) universe. A third possibility is that there is simply one underlying reality, or essential identity. Whatever the brain experiences, the mind also experiences.

In recent years the importance of this difficult issue has faded. Science today, including psychology, leans heavily toward physical explanations, which can be measured by scientific means. (We'll be discussing these later.) For now we'll just note that while the mind-body problem hasn't gone away, the great increase in the types and varieties of problems studied by psychologists has directed their attentions elsewhere.

The 1800's

Rarely did the debates of the ancient philosophers question the importance or worth of the human being. However, by the late 1800's, humans' views of themselves had undergone two severe blows. First, over three centuries earlier, Copernicus had dared to suggest that the earth was not the center of the universe. We're simply hurtling through space, occupying a planet that is not even at the center. Second, in the latter half of the 1800's, the English naturalist Charles Darwin had suggested that humans might not even be the supreme beings they had thought they were. He suggested that humans were simply the latest in a continuing series of changing—evolving—organisms.

Although human self-esteem was lowered by these advances in thought, in the name of science all kinds of scientific efforts continued. Biologists were busy developing a classification system for animals. Chemists were busy studying elements already discovered, and pushing toward the discovery of additional elements predicted to exist by their Periodic Table. Physicists were making great strides in their studies based on the atomic theory of matter.

But, also about this time, there were a number of interesting problems that were not being studied by any existing sciences. These included: (1) the old mind-body problem, (2) individual differences in abilities of humans, (3) reaction times of individual humans, and (4) the perception of sensory information such as light waves and sound waves. These problems were now taken over by a group of scientists, often trained in neurology (sometimes as part of medical training) or in philosophy. In 1879, Wilhelm Wundt established the first psychological laboratory at a university in Leipzig, Germany.

1879 is identified then as the year when psychology organized itself as a science. Over the next 50-60 years—into the early 1900's—a series of "schools" of psychology developed. These were not "schools" such as a high school or college is a school. Rather, they were schools of thought. They were attempts to organize the problems being studied, the techniques of study being used, and the means of analyzing the experimental results. These schools had a large impact on the development of psychology as a science.

Structuralism. The first school of thought resembled the other sciences in the reasons and ways it developed. Remember, biology, chemistry, and physics were making advances by subdividing their content into ever-smaller units. The structuralists did the same for psychology. They relied on *introspection*. This is a technique in which a person (even today still called a *subject* in any psychological experiment) reports his or her thoughts. For example, in viewing a brick wall, the subject would be asked to analyze the experience. A report on the color of the wall would include an analysis of the basic colors apparently blending to make the color perceived. The texture of the wall, the distance from it, its perceived size, and so forth would all be analyzed. The structuralists were interested in each part that combined to make the total experience. Do you see the parallel to the chemists' studies of elements?

The structuralists formalized the split from physiology and philosophy. They introduced scientific methods to the study of human behavior, and, as we said before, used them as a procedure and a way to accumulate knowledge.

Copernicus was among the first scientists to deflate the view that humans had of themselves as all-important inhabitants of an earth at the center of the universe.

structuralism: *a school of psychology in which subjects use introspection and analyze their experiences*

introspection: *in psychology, a technique in which the subject reports his or her thoughts*

Functionalism. The functionalists, who made up the second school of thought, tolerated introspection, but were more concerned with what experimental subjects were introspecting *about*. They felt the internal nature of the experience was not nearly so important as the *purpose* being served by the experience. *Why* was the organism behaving as it was? What was the function, the purpose, or the goal of the behavior?

The functionalists broke down some of the early restrictions on what could be studied. They increased the emphasis on directly studying behavior itself. Their early concern with the goals of behavior led to the interest we have today in applying psychology to everyday experiences.

The value of these early schools was not in the rightness of their assumptions. Rather, they presented their views in such a way that others could see the problems and offer better theories or explanations. That's the advantage of a theory.

The 1900's

By 1900 psychology had established itself as a separate discipline. It had made a couple of theoretical attempts to organize itself, but much work remained. Whereas the first two schools followed one another, the next three schools developed more or less at the same time.

Behaviorism. John B. Watson, an American psychologist, followed through on a trend started by the functionalists. Watson threw out all the introspective data; he eliminated any concern with "consciousness" and "mind," insisting that they were only products of behavior. To Watson, the *only* thing to be studied by psychologists was behavior.

The behaviorists further increased the variety of behaviors that could be studied by psychologists since they included animals as well as humans. They also narrowed the field of study to include only behavior that could be observed, and they simplified the subject matter.

Gestaltism. Along with behaviorism, another approach was developing—that of Gestaltism. A demonstration of Gestalt principles is seen in the drawings. The Gestaltist school basically was concerned with perception. They didn't analyze things into smaller and smaller parts. Instead, they concentrated on how the brain achieves a "whole" (the "Gestalt," or pattern) from all the bits of information the senses perceive. Gestaltists provided many challenging problems for the other theoretical views, but offered little by way of explanation themselves.

functionalism: *a school of psychology in which the function, purpose, or goal of a behavior is stressed, and behavior is studied directly*

behaviorism: *a school of psychology that studies only observable behavior, omitting any concern with "mind"*

Gestaltism: *a school of psychology that concentrates on the study of total figures, or whole patterns of experience*

Psychoanalysis. From the late 1800's onward, another intellectual movement was gathering force in psychology. This movement grew from the thinking of Sigmund Freud, a Viennese neurologist who started treating abnormal personal behaviors he found in his patients. What evolved was viewed by some as the third great challenge to the self-centered views we humans tend to hold of ourselves. We'll discuss psychoanalysis in more detail in Chapter 13. For now let's just note that the psychoanalysts continued to study unconscious behavior even though the behaviorists attempted to throw out such concerns. Freud awakened interest in sex and in the developmental processes of childhood in understanding adult behavior. Perhaps most important of all, Freud called attention to the newly developing discipline of psychology. He caused controversy, and that gained attention. He challenged humans' views of themselves. He suggested that we may not be aware of some of the forces influencing our behavior.

Sigmund Freud (1856-1939) was founder of the theory and discipline of psychoanalysis. His discoveries about the unconscious, revolutionary in their day, were basic contributions to the science of psychology.

By the mid-1930's the major schools of psychology were well established. Their principles dictated what could be studied and what could not. Data were interpreted in terms of these theories. But the golden era of master explanations passed gradually. By 1960 psychology could best be described as an *eclectic* field. A theory was chosen mainly in terms of how well it explained the particular behavior at hand. With the arrival of the 1980's, several more new trends had developed.

First, the *mind*, rejected from psychology since the early days of John Watson, suddenly became a topic of interest again.

psychoanalysis: *a school of psychology, founded by Sigmund Freud. As theory it stresses unconscious conflicts. As part of a therapeutic technique it stresses bringing these conflicts into consciousness.*

eclectic: *as applied to psychology, using ideas and techniques from a variety of different theories*

Figure 1-1 The drawings illustrate the Gestalt principle that "the whole is greater than the sum of its parts." Although the lines within each box are the same thickness and length, we perceive them differently because of the way they are arranged.

Self-growth theories of psychology are based on behavior performed by humans and not shared with animals. These theories emphasize development to the maximum of your potential.

Behavior was no longer regarded as the simple phenomenon the behaviorist thought it was. Second, as research machinery was improved, studies of the brain and the physiological bases of human behavior increased markedly in importance. Third, *humanistic* psychology (see Chapter 11) kept growing in popularity, even though it was of relatively little interest to the major research centers. Humanistic psychology emphasizes growth, with the goal of helping individuals achieve the fullest measure of their human potential.

So as psychology entered the 1980's it was not blessed with a single overriding theory or principle that could integrate its many different findings. Yet it remains a very popular discipline. One former president of the American Psychological Association suggested that psychology is popular because of the questions it asks, not because of the answers it has so far offered. Keep that in "mind" as you read this book. We have studied some very interesting questions, but we have a long way to go toward providing all the answers.

In review . . .

We all constantly observe behavior, assuming that human and animal behavior follows certain psychological "laws." The word "science" may be used to mean a frame of reference, a procedure, or knowledge that is already known. Five distinct "schools" of psychological thought emerged in the 50-60 years after the first psychological laboratory was founded in 1879. The *structuralists* tried to break experience down into its parts. The *functionalists* were concerned with *why* behavior occurred. In the 1900's the *behaviorists* studied only observable behavior and ignored internal processes. The *Gestaltists* and *psychoanalysts* were more generous in the effects and behaviors they would study—including "mind" and the unconscious. Since about 1950 psychology as a whole can be described as eclectic.

→ Think about it

The **question**: Are psychologists today interested in studying the "mind"?

The **answer**: In the early 1900's—even up until about 1930—they were. Between 1930 (as Freud's influence began to decline) and 1970 they were not. In fact, during the heydays of behaviorism the mind was essentially ignored and, to some extent, so was the brain. Psychologists simply studied behavior without worrying about what went on in the brain. Since 1970 physiological psychologists and linguists have begun making intellectual break-throughs in the study of the brain and brain functioning. This has led to some renewed interest in the mind, even though the mind is not directly observable. New experimental procedures have markedly increased the range of behaviors and phenomena that psychologists can study.

3 Problems and Methods Today

As you've seen, psychology, starting from a limited set of problems, has now grown to become the science of human and animal behavior and experience. Let's return now to a discussion of the scientific methods we mentioned earlier.

Operational definition

It is very important to all scientists that their work be objective, and that events being studied be observable—by you, by me, by anyone else who's interested. It makes it easier to specify what is being studied and how. These events must also be repeatable. That assures that you can study an event whenever you want. Events must also be testable and measurable.

Feature   **1–2   OPERATIONALIZING A DEFINITION**

The scene is a March Sunday morning in the Emergency Ward of the Massachusetts General Hospital. At 3 a.m. Ralph Tieball has staggered into the hospital to have a serious cut on his right arm treated. The smell of liquor is on his breath. When questioned by the doctors, he admits he fell ("No, I just tripped!") while walking near the hospital. All this is recorded on the Emergency Ward Admission Sheet that is filled out on each patient admitted for treatment.

All might have been forgotten, except Ralph happened to qualify for a study conducted several years later. Some psychologists were interested in whether or not alcoholics tend to be more isolated from society than other citizens. To study this the researchers sought the Emergency Ward log for MGH and collected a sample of 200 "alcoholics." How did they define an alcoholic? Very simple. If the word "alcohol" or "liquor" or any products normally associated with drinking ("whiskey," "bourbon," and so forth) appeared anywhere on the Emergency Ward Admission Sheet, that person was defined as an alcoholic.

In Ralph's case words qualifying him as an alcoholic appeared in two places. In the general observations section it was noted that "the smell of liquor could be detected on his breath" and later, "Patient admitted falling, apparently due to excessive alcohol consumed earlier in the evening."

For each of 200 people who qualified as "alcoholics," a number of additional facts were sought from that admission sheet. Did the patient have medical insurance? Who was listed as next-of-kin? Was the patient employed? Doing what? How did the patient

come in—by self-admission or with a family member? By public authority, such as police or hospital ambulance? About 20 such facts were gathered for each of these "alcoholics."

When the data from the "alcoholics" were compared with similar data gathered from people admitted to the Emergency Ward whose record contained no mention of alcohol, some interesting differences showed up. For example, the "alcoholics" were much *less* likely to have medical insurance. They were *less* likely to list a parent or child as next-of-kin, and *more* likely to list an aunt or uncle or cousin, if they listed anyone at all. The "alcoholics" were *less* likely to have a job, and those who did tended to hold *less* important (lower-paying) jobs than the average job held by the other (nonalcoholic) group. Moreover, the alcoholics were more likely to come by public means (police or ambulance), whereas the comparison group were more likely to be brought in by a member of their immediate family.

These researchers concluded that alcoholics (defined as they defined them: people admitted for treatment, and on whose Emergency Ward Admission Sheet the word "alcohol" appeared) were more likely to be socially isolated. You might quarrel with the operationally defined definition of "alcoholic," but once you agree with that you can't disagree with these researchers' conclusion. In short, once we've agreed on an operational definition, it's much easier to specify what it is we may still want to argue about. Operational definitions lend precision to research and scientific arguments based on that research.

The easiest way to achieve all this is to define events operationally. An *operational definition* means simply that any concept is identical to its operations. For example, if you talk about the length of your father's mustache, how are we going to measure it? To find the length of an object we must perform certain physical operations with a tape measure or yard-stick. The concept of length is thus fixed when we specify the operations by which length is measured. If we use a yard-stick, we know your father's mustache will be measured in inches, feet, or yards. If we use a meter stick, it will be measured in centimeters, decimeters, or meters—assuming he'll let you get close enough to measure it. This seems trivial, but it's an important matter. Box 1-2 suggests some uses of operational definitions.

What do you mean when you say "I love you" to your boyfriend or girlfriend? Many things are involved in that statement, but if a psychologist is to study "love," the term must be operationally defined. If you're in love, it is likely that (1) you will seek the company of that individual before anyone else, (2) you will give gifts, such as birthday presents or valentines, (3) you will date that person, and (4) you will do many other such things. Maybe this is just describing the obvious, but it should also be obvious that if those behaviors aren't there, you probably aren't in love. The operations, then, define the concept.

operational definition: *a definition in which the concept is identical to the operations used in measuring the concept.*

→ Think about it

The **question**: "Intelligence is what an intelligence test measures." Is that a logical statement?

The **answer**: Yes. Although you might argue about the nature of intelligence, that statement is an operational definition. (An English teacher might call it a circular definition.) Someone who scores high on an intelligence test is considered to be "smart" or "very intelligent." But what determined how high that person would score on the test? The intelligence test itself! In the chapter on Testing (Chapter 14) we study such tests in more detail, but for now just realize that this may not be a bad definition. It *does* emphasize the *operations* that are performed in testing one's intelligence.

Variables of interest

Let's suppose you're a psychologist and you're interested in answering a question that has been posed to humans all over North America (at least since an advertising agency created it): Is it true blonds have more fun? In order to collect some data on this matter, we might set up an experiment. For instance, we might decide to watch two types of humans—blonds and non-

Table 1-1 Number of observed smiles (one-hour time period)

BLONDS				NONBLONDS			
S #	# SMILES	S #	# SMILES	S #	# SMILES	S #	# SMILES
1	71	11	38	21	25	31	39
2	55	12	20	22	36	32	56
3	60	13	48	23	57	33	40
4	83	14	22	24	11	34	43
5	51	15	53	25	47	35	68
6	19	16	46	26	16	36	18
7	47	17	30	27	62	37	53
8	42	18	37	28	46	38	48
9	59	19	12	29	71	39	21
10	6	20	44	30	23	40	51

blonds. In your experiment you would then need to measure the fun had by all the people you were studying. But that's not so easy. What usually happens when people are having fun? We could just assume that the more often these things happen, the more fun such a person is having. So, we could measure the number of smiles. Or, if we wanted to study people for a longer time, we could keep track of the number of dates they had, or the number of different people they talked with on the telephone each week, or the number of times they were invited to parties or other social affairs. But counting smiles is probably easiest.

In order to keep it simple, you might decide to limit your study to 40 people, 20 blondes and 20 nonblondes, with 10 of each sex in each of your two groups. And you would probably decide to collect all the data at the same time, maybe by finding 40 people (with the help of a lot of your friends!) at a Saturday night rock concert. For one hour—say, from 8:30 to 9:30—you would simply count how many times each of the 40 people in your group smiled. At 9:30 you would eagerly start collecting the reports from your helpers, and you might get a series of numbers such as those listed in Table 1-1. Totalling your data you find that blonds smiled 843 times, or 42.15 times per person. The 20 nonblonds smiled 831 times, or a total of 41.55 times in that hour. You conclude that blonds do have more fun—but not by any significant amount.

Independent variable. In conducting this experiment you've used a number of basic scientific procedures and concepts. One of the important concepts you've used is that of the *independent variable*. This is a factor that is selected by the experimenter. You chose to study blonds. The independent variable is changed or varied to find out what effects or behaviors it may be causing. You compared blonds with nonblonds to see whether blondness influenced how much fun people have.

independent variable: *the factor, chosen by the experimenter, that is changed or varied; the cause (in a functional relationship) of change*

Dependent variable. You also had a *dependent variable*, which is a factor that is also selected by the experimenter. However, the actual value of the dependent variable is determined by the subject being studied. Your dependent variable was smiling—a response that *you* selected. But it was each of your subjects who decided how many times he or she would actually smile during the hour you were watching.

Intervening variable. Finally, although you may not have known it, you also had an *intervening variable*. We invent this concept for what must be occurring inside our subjects. The intervening variable identifies any relation we find between our independent and our dependent variable. What is our intervening variable here? Fun! We assumed that blonds might have more fun. So we identified two levels of blondness—present and absent. Since we couldn't measure fun directly, we measured what we *could* see, namely smiles. In your experiment, smiles were used as the operational definition of fun. Anyone having fun would smile. What we've done is summarized in the drawing.

Using intervening variables may sound a bit confusing, but there are actually quite a number of intervening variables that would fit our definition. *Love* is an intervening variable. *Hunger* is an intervening variable. As we'll see later, *learning, personality,* and *intelligence* are all intervening variables. For instance, we know many things that will cause you to be hungry—you haven't eaten, you've been very active, or you're growing. All of these cause an internal state we call hunger. When people are hungry, we know what they'll do. They'll eat if food is given to them. They'd be willing to do some work for us if we'd give them food, and so forth. So intervening variables are really just scientific shorthand. They summarize a lot of relations that exist

dependent variable: *the factor, chosen by the experimenter, that may or may not change when the independent variable is changed. Its actual value is determined by the subject being tested.*

intervening variable: *a nonobservable process within the subject suggested to explain the relationship between the independent and dependent variable*

Figure 1-2 Independent, intervening, and dependent variables involved in the question "Is it true blondes have more fun?" See text for an explanation of how these factors are determined.

VARIABLES		
INDEPENDENT	INTERVENING	DEPENDENT
	FUN	
Blondness		Smiles
Physique		Conversations
Popularity		Friends

between independent variables (or causes) and dependent variables (or effects).

And why do we run experiments? Mainly to study *functional relationships*. An *experiment* is an organized attempt to study a functional relationship between an independent and dependent variable. A functional relationship simply states how changes in an independent variable influence the value of a dependent variable. Chapter 17 talks more about functional relationships, especially how we show them statistically. For now, all you need to know is that in most graphs in this book the independent variable is along the horizontal (or *X*-) axis, and the dependent variable is along the vertical (or *Y*-) axis.

The need for control

The procedure for deciding whether blonds have more fun would qualify as an experiment. But, if that's what we're interested in, why on earth did we also study the fun that was had by nonblonds? The main reason is the "more" used in the question "Is it true blonds have *more* fun?" *More* than whom? The nonblonds, meaning all the rest, serve as a very important reference point. We *all* have a certain amount of fun. We were interested in finding out whether blonds have more fun then most other people. So, a group of nonblonds was found to serve as a *control group*.

This principle of *control* is probably the single most important feature in scientific experiments. By control we mean isolating the impact of the cause (independent variable) on the dependent variable that is being studied. We knew that *people* have fun, but we were interested in finding out whether blond people have *more* fun. So we set up an experiment in which a large number of nonblond people would have fun. That was our *control* group. They established how much fun the average *person* would have at the rock concert as measured by the number of smiles. We also placed 20 subjects who were *people* in that same situation, but they were also *blond*. Blondness was our independent variable. By comparing the nonblond (control) group's smiling rate with the blond (experimental) group's rate of smiling, we could determine whether blonds had more fun than a comparable group of nonblond people.

Creating a good control group is one of the skills in running a good experiment. To have a good control group you must be sure that two things have happened. First, everyone (whether blond or nonblond) must have an equal chance of being selected to be in the experiment. Otherwise we would have a biased sample. Second, we must control what some people call "nuisance" variables. Nuisance variables are uncontrolled variables

functional relationship: *the manner in which changes in an independent variable influence the value of a dependent variable*

control group: *in an experiment, the group of subjects exposed to the same conditions as the experimental group except that the independent variable is not applied*

experimental group: *in an experiment, the groups of subjects to whom the independent variable is applied*

that might cause the same change in the dependent variable as the variable we are actually studying. Both the experimental *and* the control group must be treated identically throughout the experiment *except* for the independent variable that will be experienced by the experimental group. In that way if there are any differences in the behavior of the experimental and control group subjects, we will be able to conclude that the differences were caused by the independent variable.

Collecting data

Applying the use of operational definitions to everything they study, psychologists still use a wide variety of techniques in collecting data. The same behavior may be studied in many different ways. Let's look at the three most common techniques.

Experiments. The *experimental method* refers to any data collection technique in which control is exercised over many variables that might influence the behavior being studied. It is frequently conducted in the laboratory. In fact, the term "experiments" usually refers to procedures in which the effects of one or two independent variables are being studied in a well-controlled (laboratory) situation.

experimental method: *any data collection technique in which control is exercised over as many variables as possible that might influence the behavior being studied*

Psychologists use many different techniques in collecting data. A one-way mirror provides a method for undetected observation.

The experimental methods are good for several reasons: (1) When accurate operational definitions have been used, you can repeat other people's experiments if you question their results. (2) The laboratory-based experiments are usually well controlled so that nuisance variables are not a big problem. (3) The laboratory allows for very precise presentation of independent variables. But, as you probably suspected, there are also some problems. For one thing, you can't always measure something in the laboratory. If we wanted to study the social process of falling in love—as we were talking about earlier—it would be almost impossible to do it in a laboratory setting. Also, the laboratory situation *is* artificial. Sometimes by bringing a behavior into the laboratory to study it we may interfere with the behavior as we try to measure it. So there are some limits on what we can study in a purely scientific laboratory. (Box 1-2 showed you one example of such research.)

Naturalistic observation. Another often-used method is that of naturalistic observation. Here the researcher goes out "into the field" and observes behavior in the environment where it naturally occurs. The subject doesn't need to cooperate in order for such research to be done. Sometimes the observations may be more true-to-life if the subject doesn't know he or she is being observed. Observing or measuring behavior is less likely to interfere with the behavior being studied, as sometimes happens in the laboratory. Yet, there are problems here, too. Since the observer doesn't directly influence the behavior being observed, it sometimes requires great patience to wait for the expected event to occur. Moreover, we humans sometimes tend to become overly generous with our own attributes as we observe subhuman animals. Have you ever heard someone talk about a "sly" fox? What *is* a sly fox? At best, what people are talking about is a fox who behaves as *if* it were sly in the human sense. But granting human characteristics to subhuman animals (called anthropomorphism) must be avoided. Box 1-3 relates some of the observations of a researcher who lived in the African jungles for several years in the late 60's. She has recorded some never-seen-before behaviors of jungle apes.

Case history (interview). The third technique has probably been applied to you many times already: the *case history*, or *interview*. Perhaps it was in your doctor's office. Or, if you have ever been treated by a psychologist, you were probably asked about your personal history. So it's a method that can be well fitted to the individual. Relying on the traditional, trusting, doctor-patient relationship, it is a very efficient way to gather

anthropomorphism: *attributing human characteristics to animals*

Feature 1–3 **APES OF WRATH?**

At the corner of three African nations—Rwanda, Uganda, and the Democratic Republic of the Congo—lie the Virunga mountains. The wooded slopes are the remote African highland home of the mountain gorilla.

These are not small animals. The largest males may stand six feet tall and weigh as much as 400 pounds (181 kilograms). Using a variation of naturalistic observation, Dian Fossey has lived in these mountains for thirteen years since the late 1960's. Not content simply to sit and observe, Ms. Fossey started acting like a gorilla. The more she learned about gorillas, the more like them she was able to act.

Ms. Fossey reports that gaining the gorilla's confidence was a long, slow process. She states: "I imitated their feeding and grooming, and later, when I was surer what they meant, I copied their vocalizations, including some startling deep belching noises." When trying to gain the gorillas' confidence, Fossey used to beat her thighs with her open palms to mimic their chestbeating. She reports that the "sound was an instant success in gaining [their] attention. . . . I thought I was very clever but did not realize that I was conveying the wrong information. Chestbeating is the gorillas' signal for excitement or alarm, certainly the wrong message for me to have sent as appeasement!"

But by waiting for the gorillas to come to her and by imitating the gorillas' actions, Ms. Fossey gradually became accepted by them. Some of her observations were surprising. In fiction the gorilla is portrayed as a savage, highly aggressive animal. Not so, reports Ms. Fossey. Of a total of some 2,000 hours of close observation, she reports only three instances of aggression started by the gorillas. They'll fight back when threatened, but, being vegetarians, they almost never attack humans.

Such observations result from a technique in which the experimenter becomes "part of the scenery."

data. On the other hand, such a method yields data that apply to only one person or subject. Will it hold true for others? Only more interviews will tell us. An interview always relies on the subject's memory of past events, and under certain situations such memories can't be trusted. In addition, trying to put such verbal reports into numerical terms for analysis may be difficult, if not impossible. Finally, there may be many different interpretations of a person's responses to interview questions. So, although this is a valuable source of data in dealing with individuals, it is not often used in studies involving large numbers of people. Box 1-4 contains an interview with two parents whose daughter began behaving in unusual ways. The information the psychotherapist gained through the interview helped her identify how to solve the parents' problems with their children. Yet this information may not apply to the unique problems of other parents.

Feature   1-4   "MANY A TEAR HAS TO FALL"

MOTHER: My son, Cary, was throwing temper tantrums when I dropped him off at nursery school on my way to the university. But we've corrected his problem.

DR. MARTINEZ: How did you do that?

MOTHER: We set up a chart at home. Cary got a gold star every day he went to school without crying. Five stars and we took him to his favorite restaurant. But now Katie, my daughter, has become so upset. . . . I just don't understand it! She's been perfect for five years, and now this!

DR. MARTINEZ: What's happened?

MOTHER: She's started throwing temper tantrums. She doesn't want to stay with her babysitter while I'm at school. She doesn't want to visit friends, and she doesn't want me to leave.

DR. MARTINEZ: That sounds like a really dramatic change. As I think about it, it seems to me your son's crying was related to his anxiety about being separated from you. He was in school—a new and stressful situation for him. He missed the consolation of knowing you were home when he left and would be there when he returned. Why do you think your daughter is suddenly acting this way?

FATHER: I don't know. I think it's because Katie doesn't like to leave Kim.

MOTHER: No, I think it's because Katie saw Cary crying about school.

(As you can see, even direct participants in the event couldn't agree on the impact the mother's absence had had on their daughter. From this fact, what would you conclude about this family?)

DR. MARTINEZ: I suspect that's part of it, but it may not be the whole story. Yes, Katie misses you, Kim, and she saw Cary doing the same thing a month ago. The difference is that she later saw Cary being rewarded for not crying any longer. I suspect we should deal with it in exactly the same way. I'd suggest you try giving Katie a gold star every time you can leave to go to the university without Katie shedding a tear.

In review . . .

Psychology is the science of human and animal behavior and experience. It relies heavily on operational definitions of its terms and procedures. Psychology seeks to discover functional relationships between independent and dependent variables. Intervening variables are a concept invented for what must be occurring inside a subject. They identify relations between independent and dependent variables. Any experiment requires a control group, which is a group exposed to exactly the same conditions as the experimental group *except* for the independent variable. Creating a good control group is one of the skills required for running a good experiment. Data are usually collected in psychological experiments through the experimental methods, naturalistic observations, or case histories (interviews).

Goals of psychological study

At this point you may be asking yourself a very simple question: "So what?" Why are psychologists going to all this trouble? What are their goals? It's a good question, and it can be answered in several ways. We'll answer it one way now, and add more information at the end of the book—after you've read more about psychology. Most psychologists have two major goals when they study behavior. These two goals imply certain other goals.

Understanding. When you understand something, there are several things you're able to do. First, you can describe it. If you show up two hours late for a date to an important dance, your partner (if he/she *is* still waiting for you) will be very mad. You understand why and can explain why in terms of (1) the importance of the dance to your date, (2) the social embarrassment your date may expect unless there's a logical reason why you were so late, (3) the fact that the flowers he or she has bought for you are now wilting, and so forth.

If you understand a behavior, you can *identify and describe* the independent variables which influence it. Second, if you identify something and can describe it, then you can *measure* it. Third, if you can describe and measure something, then you can *explain* it. This means that you can identify the important independent variables and how they influence the dependent variables you are measuring or observing. Psychology as a science is an effort to understand human behavior.

Utilization. If we understand something, there may be an even more important goal that follows from that understanding—*use* of the knowledge. If we've gone to the trouble of studying a behavior so as to understand it, that understanding is of little benefit unless it is put to use. Good salespersons "understand" human behavior. They may not be able to tell you what cues they're using in selling a product to their customer, but cues are being used.

There are roughly two ways in which we use the understanding of human behavior that we've already achieved. One use is the *prediction* of future behavior. If you go on to college, you're very likely to take one or more aptitude tests. These measure what you already know, and the results will be used to predict your probable success in college. If we understand the important independent and dependent variables in any situation, then we can use this understanding to predict when and where and how and why a behavior will occur.

Now think a moment. Wouldn't it be nice if you could predict how the stock market was going to react? You could be rich! It's but a short step from predicting behavior to attempt to *control* it—the second use of understanding. The fear that psychologists might be striving to control human behavior has made some members of the public very nervous in recent years.

Two counterpoints should be noted. Psychology as a science is very young. We simply do not yet know enough about many human behaviors to be able to control them. Moreover, many of our behaviors are already controlled. We are told how fast we can drive on the highway. We are expected to respect our elders. We sit in a large group facing the front of the room in most high school and college classrooms. We're already controlled.

But the advantage of a public search for greater understanding of the principles that control human behavior is good. People who worry about psychologists controlling the world give psychologists a great deal more credit for their knowledge than the facts you are about to study will warrant.

Think about it

The **question**: Will psychologists learn how to control behavior? If they do, will they have too much power over our lives?

The **answer**: To a limited degree, yes, they may learn how to control behavior. But the answer to the second question is no. The main goal of scientists who are psychologists is to understand behavior. It is true that they wish to utilize that understanding to predict and control behavior. But, as scientists, psychologists are no different from physicists who are gaining understanding of and utility from the atomic structure of matter.

Science is the most powerful tool yet invented that can give humans some sort of understanding of and control over their environment. This does cause problems sometimes in that science delivers products that political, social, and religious institutions don't know how to govern or control. As science makes advances (for instance, the artificial heart installed in Barney Clark in 1983), the results are constantly challenging society to reassess itself. Society is forced to appraise the value of the discovery.

Will psychologists ever gain absolute control? That's very unlikely. Society would not allow it to happen. Psychologists are not likely to want it to happen. Behavior is too complex and our understanding of the laws and principles of behavior too elementary. If control of behavior becomes possible, the governmental institutions of society as a whole will have to develop legal mechanisms for controlling the products of scientific laboratories.

Central issues and why they are

We spoke earlier about the *mind-body problem* that was "left over" when psychology became a formal science. Why, exactly, did interest in this issue wane? First, scientists began to follow the concept of operational definitions more closely. Trying to separate mind from body or brain was not a problem that could be easily operationalized. Second, as scientists continue to learn more about brain function, they tend to believe that *all* mind functions—whether we speak of perception or thinking or "the mind"—are directly related to brain function. Some even suggest that everything studied by psychologists will eventually be explained by the research and findings of physiological psychologists. (We discuss the biology of behavior in Chapter 4.)

The nature-nurture problem.   What causes you to behave as you do? Did you *learn* how to behave? Did you *learn* how to speak? Or are you just somehow responding to inherited messages passed on from your parents?

This is a debate that you will see reappearing again and again in the chapters to follow. Nature is sometimes called "inherited inclination" or heredity or inheritance, but the terms mean essentially the same thing. "Nurture" is sometimes called learning or "environmental influences" or experience, but all these terms identify the same processes.

The mistake that is often made is to pose this as an *either-or* question. In fact, very few of our behaviors can be traced strictly to environmental *or* inherited causes. More often both factors are influencing our behavior, as you will see.

Level of explanation.   You're riding in the back seat of your family's car on a vacation trip with your parents. Your older (or younger) sister (or brother) is "sharing" the back seat with you. You've been driving for hours in hot, sticky, dusty country. You're fed up. The person riding with you in the back seat puts something on "*your*" side. You push it back. He/she pushes it over—slowly, subtly, but he/she definitely inches it back onto *your* side. You *shove* it back. He/she *jams* it back. You *slam* it back. He/she literally *throws* it back. You are just arming yourself for all-out war when one of your parents looks back and asks, "ALL RIGHT! WHO STARTED IT!?!"

Indignantly, and of course full of innocence, you reply, "He (or she) did!"

Your brother (or sister)—just as indignantly, and also just as innocently, interrupts and shouts, "NO! He (or she) did!"

Resolving this may take hours (and miles). But this little story illustrates a point. At one level your brother or sister started the fight by encroaching on your territory. At another level you were responsible (especially if you were the older child) for starting the fight by insisting on your share of seat even though you didn't need it at the time. At another level your parents were at fault for driving the "southern" route—which they knew would be hot—instead of a more northern route on the vacation.

Psychologists face somewhat the same problem. To "explain" something at one level may mean ignoring facts at another level. For instance, some would argue that all of sociology will ultimately be explained by the principles of psychology. Biologists would insist that psychology can be explained by biological principles. The series continues back through biology and chemistry to physics—the *basic* science. This is a process called *reductionism*. It involves reducing the principles and explanations of any discipline to a science that is in some way considered more "basic."

Yet, the same process goes on within psychology itself. If we take a complex abnormal personality problem—such as disorganized schizophrenia (discussed in Chapter 12)—we can "explain" it in terms of the *social* environment from which the person came. At another level we might offer an explanation in terms of the learning experiences and potential of the person. At yet a third level for some of the psychotic personality disorders, we can offer a physiologically based explanation in terms of blood chemistry or basic biological malfunctions. This problem of the level at which to assume we have sufficiently "explained" something is constantly with psychologists.

How is the problem resolved? The family doctor explains to the children at one level when their father is about to die. Yet, he or she will usually speak at a different level to the mother and wife. Thus the problem of choosing the appropriate level of explanation of any behavior rests primarily on judging the purpose to which the answer will be put. We can explain many psychological effects at a number of different levels. Watch how that level will shift as you read the remaining 16 chapters.

Theoretical views. As we start our study of the science of psychology, you should be warned in advance that psychologists often disagree in explaining a particular behavior. The argument is generally based on the fact that there are many different theories that equally well explain what is going on. *Learning* or *social-learning* explanations are usually derived from environmentally based principles. We'll examine these in detail in Chapter 6.

Other explanations focus on *psychodynamic* or *psychoanalytic* concepts. These theories trace their origins to the pioneering work of Sigmund Freud. They place great emphasis on how the conscious and unconscious parts of the mind are organized.

Some *cognitive* theories can be traced to the work of Jean Piaget. Piaget was a Swiss psychologist whose work has begun to have an impact on psychology only in the last 15 years or so.

reductionism: *reducing the principles and explanations of any discipline to some science that is considered more "basic"*

cognitive theories: *explanations stressing mental operations, mainly in the fields of language and development*

Cognitive theories stress the importance of mental operations. We'll see such theories mainly in developmental and language areas, but they'll also show up elsewhere.

Finally, *humanistic* theories are mainly concerned with attributes and abilities that are human—not those we share with animals. Theorists in this camp tend to reject much of what is assumed by other theorists. These theories focus on the self, stressing the importance of our perception both of ourselves and of the world of which we are a part. The emphasis is on growth, achievement, and the positive aspects of human behavior.

The human potential movement stresses the self and the importance of awareness of our true feelings in relation to ourselves and to the world around us.

These theories are not all present when we try to explain *any* given human behavior. However, keep your eyes open as we move through the next 16 chapters. You'll see when we have competing explanations that they are usually drawn from one of these four types of theories. Psychology is still a very young science, and some disagreement among its theories is to be expected.

Research vs. application. Other arguments are based on the immediacy of goals. Is this psychologist pursuing immediate answers to current problems? Or is he or she a basic researcher trying to understand the fundamental principles of behavior? This "battle" may take many forms: The clinician *versus* the experimentalist. The practitioner *versus* the theoretician. The field of psychology is full of people who like to argue, but the arguments aren't as serious as they appear.

Some psychologists say they're clinicians, others call themselves researchers. The "researcher" may be pursuing "pure" research—for instance, a problem such as learning in what form words are stored in our memory. The clinician is trying to use the current level of understanding—however incomplete or partial it may be—to offer solutions to today's needs.

It is sometimes tempting to pose the problem as research *versus* application, but the more important issue is: How soon do we need the ultimately correct answer? *That's* all that separates researchers from those psychologists applying the principles of the discipline now.

In review . . .

Psychologists have two major goals in studying behavior. They want to understand it—meaning identify/describe it, measure it, and explain it. They also wish to *utilize* that understanding to predict and control behavior. The study of behavior has long dealt with four major issues. The *mind-body* problem concerns the relationship between the mind and the brain. The *nature-nurture* issue involves whether human behavior is inherited or learned. The *level of explanation* concerns how far we must reduce a phenomenon to simpler units to say we have explained it. *Theoretical* views of modern psychology include learning, psychoanalytic, cognitive, and humanistic theories. Differences between research psychologists and those seeking practical applications are limited to differing needs for immediate answers.

A research psychologist may be pursuing a long-range goal by accumulating statistical data (here, an experiment in hypnosis). The clinical psychologist may use the same scientific methods, but the goals are more immediate.

4 Psychology as Art and Science

We've defined psychology as the *science* of human and animal behavior and experience. But how scientific is it? Let's examine it in terms of the definition of science offered earlier.

Science involves *observation*. Psychology clearly qualifies. Psychologists do experiments the results of which can be confirmed by any observer.

Science implies *measurement*. Again, psychology clearly qualifies. As we'll see, psychologists use a wide range of measures of behavior in order to quantify (or measure) dependent variables.

Science implies some form of *organization* to allow the various facts to be treated logically. Here psychology falls a bit short. Psychology doesn't have a single theory—or even a small or limited number of theories—that can organize large numbers of facts. There are many laws that have side applicability, but there is no single all-encompassing theory. Psychology doesn't yet have its version of a Periodic Table such as organizes most of chemistry.

Finally, science also implies *communication*. Here psychology qualifies very well. In fact, you are reading one effort at communication. Many books are published; innumerable journals and experimental reports are printed each year. So psychology does share its information. It *is* communicating its findings.

In summary, then, by a vote of three to one, psychology seems to qualify as a science. Yet, is it something more?

Psychology an art? Defining "art" is a bit more difficult than defining "science." Is psychology an art? Yes . . . and no. It depends, once again, on how broadly the term is used. "Art" can refer to the refined techniques or skills of an able person practicing his or her profession. A psychiatrist who is sensitive and intuitive in helping a patient solve emotional problems is practicing an art. We will never bring human relations, with all their vast complexities, to the same degree of scientific reliability as elements in chemistry or physics. The part of psychology that is not based on scientific method alone but on creative insight— that's what we can call an "art."

A psychologist who is intuitive and skilled in listening, interpreting, and communicating may not only be applying scientific methods but also practicing an art.

Art often involves the ability to take common materials and create uncommon effects. In that sense, the creativity shown by a psychologist can be called an art. Designing a good experimental procedure is an art.

Psychology vs. common sense. One problem remains. Have you ever heard someone suggest that *everyone* is a psychologist? Docs your mothcr think she is a psychologist? Do you think you are? This problem is almost unique to psychology as a discipline. We all "study" behavior. We all watch each other behave. We organize our own behavior according to how we expect others will behave. Aren't we all psychologists then? The answer is no. Psychologists use common sense to identify what behavior ought to be studied. But after that first step, the scientific processes of psychological research and the principles derived through them separate psychology from common sense knowledge.

Chapter Application and Review

REVIEW QUESTIONS

SECTION 1 (pages 19–22)
1. What are some of the meanings of the term "science"?
2. Is psychology a science? Why or why not?
3. What are some of the basic assumptions of psychology?

SECTION 2 (pages 22–27)
1. What were the earliest schools of psychology, and how did they differ?
2. Has psychology as a field become more unified since its early days? Explain.

SECTION 3 (pages 27–42)
1. What is an operational definition? Why it is used in psychology?
2. Think up an experiment and then identify the independent variable(s), dependent variable(s), and any intervening variables. Give the purposes of each variable.
3. Did you include a control group in your experiment? What is the importance of a control group?
4. What goals do psychologists have in studying behavior?
5. How do research psychologists and clinical psychologists differ, if at all?

SECTION 4 (pages 42–44)
1. Describe ways in which psychology is a science and ways in which it qualifies as an art.
2. How does psychology differ from common sense?

ACTIVITIES

1. One of the hardest things to do is to gain control of your time. How you spend (or waste) your time is a key factor in determining your success—as a student, on the job, indeed in life itself. Students are often heard to complain that they "just don't have time for . . ." this, that, or the other thing. You can check your behavior by finding out how you spend your time. Create a sheet of paper for yourself with seven days of the week written across the top, starting with today or tomorrow. Down the left side of the sheet put time in 30-minute intervals from when you get up until when you usually go to bed: 7 a.m., 7:30 a.m., and so forth. For one week keep track of how you spend your time, putting down just enough information so you can remember next week what you were doing: eat, sleep, study psych(??), babysit, team practice, whatever. After your schedule is finished, analyze it. Are you making the best use of your time? Could you change your behavior in certain ways so your time would be spent more effectively? Compare with your friends' schedules.

2. Career Search. Interview a psychologist in your community. There are several places you might find one: check the Yellow Pages, under "Psychologist"; seek out a professor at a local college or university Department of Psychology or Behavioral Sciences; or see if your school district, or even your own school, has a counselling or school psychologist (about whom we'll talk more later). Find out his or her job title, whom he or she works for, what the hours are, what is actually done on the job, and how he or she likes the work. In terms of the material in this first chapter, did you interview a researcher or a practitioner? Does this type of activity appeal to you? Why?

3. Try conducting an experiment to understand the difference between independent and dependent variables. Locate some public building that has an elevator. With four friends get on the elevator and ride facing the *back*. When the door opens and someone you don't know starts to get on, record two things:

a. Did he or she get on or not, and
b. If he or she got on, which direction did he or she face while on the elevator: frontwards (ignoring you), sideways, or backwards (conforming with you)?

You'll also need to collect some data while you ride facing frontwards with the same arrangements. Again, record the behavior of the people who get on the elevator alone. Your independent variable is the position of you and your friends: front-facing (control) or back-facing (experimental condition). Your dependent variable is the response of the person waiting for the elevator—did he/she wait or get on and face the front, side, or back? If you compare the number of people doing each of those responses in your experimental and control conditions and they differ, what can you conclude about the effects of your independent variable?

4. Conduct a simple experiment using naturalistic observation. How slow do you suppose most people go when they reach a stop sign? Find an intersection that has a stop sign and a clearly marked crosswalk. Most state laws say a driver is to stop at a stop sign behind the first stripe of the crosswalk, so mark off a distance ten feet behind that first stripe and ten feet in front of it. Now record one of two things for each car going straight ahead (not turning) at the intersection: Did it stop within the 20 feet you marked off? If so, indicate its "speed" at the stop sign as 0. If it did *not* stop, then use a stop watch (or count as best you can) to find how long it takes the front bumper of each car to pass from the first to the second stripe. Use the following data to record an estimated speed through the stop sign:

SEC.	MPH	SEC.	MPH	SEC.	MPH	SEC.	MPH
0.1	136	0.7	19	1.4	10	3.4	4
0.2	68	0.8	17	1.5	9	4.5	3
0.3	45	0.9	15	1.7	8	6.8	2
0.4	34	1.0	14	1.9	7	13.6	1
0.5	27	1.1	12	2.3	6	27.3	½
0.6	23	1.2	11	2.7	5	54.5	¼

Refer to Chapter 17 for help in developing a frequency distribution, but based on the data you collected, what would you say is the behavior most often seen at a stop sign?

5. Career Search. Volunteer some time after school to work in the emergency ward of a local hospital, or in a nursing home or home for the retired. Keep a diary of your experiences. Record your observations on aging, on the reactions of people in emergencies, or on the reactions of families to death. You might also be able to add your experiences to later discussions on the use of psychological principles of learning, or on therapy, or on other topics covered in the remainder of this book. Write down your expectations before you start and then tuck them away so you can't see them. Check after a month of volunteer work. Are your expectations being met? Would you define "psychology" after a month as you did when you started this class?

6. Try another experiment in observing human behavior. As you change from one class to another in school one day, try smiling at every person whose eye you catch. Count how many of them smile back at you. The next day at the same time look at about the same number of people in much the same way as you did the day before, but this time do not smile at all. Again count how many people smile at you. Would you say that smiling is a reflection of a person's internal state, or is it simply a response to stimuli offered by other people? Basing your conclusions on the data you've collected, you should be able to agree with one or the other of these possibilities. Another way to conduct the same experiment is to keep track of how many people say back to you exactly what you say to them when you first greet them. If you say "Good morning" (afternoon or evening, as appropriate), or "Hello" or "Hi" or whatever, do people mimic you, or respond with a different greeting? If you change your greeting, do the greetings that people say to you tend to change? What does this tell you about who "controls" what people say to you?

INTERESTED IN MORE?

As we introduce you to psychology, we recommend that you consider doing some additional reading and study on any topics of particular interest to you. We have chosen a variety of appropriate sources—some easy, some difficult—which we list after each chapter. For the most part, they are books that you should be able to locate somewhere in your community—perhaps at your town library or in a bookstore—or obtain by ordering from the publisher.

Since this chapter touches lightly upon a wide range of subject matter, we've included here some recommendations for general resources, such as textbooks, that may help you delve more deeply into the various topics that are introduced later in the course. We've also included the names of a few general magazines in the field. To help you make your selections, the bibliography for this chapter is divided into topical areas.

History of Psychology

WATSON, R.I. *The Great Psychologists,* 3rd ed. Lippincott, 1971. Traces the major works of important psychologists over the last 100 years.

WERTHEIMER, M. *A Brief History of Psychology.* Holt, Rinehart & Winston, 1970. Covers the major schools of psychology and places them in the context of science and philosophy.

Research and Psychology

DEESE, J. *Psychology as Science and Art.* Harcourt Brace Jovanovich, 1972. Challenging reading, this book analyzes psychology as both art and science. Suggests how our knowledge of behavior mixes myth with scientific facts.

DOHERTY, M.E. & SHEMBERG, X.M. *Asking Questions About Behavior: An Introduction to What Psychologists Do,* 2nd ed. Scott, Foresman, 1978. Opens with the kind of questions that you're probably interested in right now and then guides you in the formation of scientific questions. Shows how to design experiments to answer such questions. Gives special attention to the study of stress.

How to Study

ROBINSON, F.P. *Effective Study,* 4th ed. Harper & Row, 1970. A classic book in this field, it emphasizes the application of psychological principles in the development of effective study skills. Includes checklists of work behavior

and a full description of the Survey, Question, Read, Recite, and Review (or SQ3R) study technique.

Magazines

Human Behavior. A more subdued version of *Psychology Today,* covering topics at somewhat greater depth. A good source, although it was only published from 1972 through 1979.

Psychology Today. A monthly magazine that stresses broad coverage of contemporary topics more than in-depth analysis of behavior. Colorful and readable.

Scientific American. Almost every month, this lavishly illustrated magazine contains at least one article written by a nationally known psychologist on a topic of current interest.

General Introductory Texts

ATKINSON, R.L., ATKINSON, R.C., & HILGARD, E.R. *Introduction to Psychology,* 8th ed. Harcourt Brace Jovanovich, 1983. A richly illustrated text by a well-known team of authors. Covers a wide variety of psychological phenomena in a highly readable style.

BOURNE, L.E. & EKSTRAND, B.R. *Psychology: Its Principles and Meanings,* 4th ed. Holt, Rinehart & Winston, 1982. Includes many newspaper articles and cartoons relating psychology to issues of current concern.

HOWARD, G.S. *Basic Research Methods in the Social Sciences.* Scott, Foresman, 1985. A very readable introduction to the most modern research methods used by psychologists and other social scientists.

2 Early Development

CHAPTER OUTLINE

WHAT'S THE ANSWER?

☐ "Last summer I served as a senior counsellor in a summer camp up at the lake. Late one evening I was writing a letter to my girl friend when the biggest spider I've ever seen in my life dropped into view. I decided to play a dirty trick on him. The spider was weaving the circular part of his web, so I un-hooked that first strand from the porch floor and part of the web shriveled up. You know what that spider did? He started all over again!—when all he had to do was anchor one more support and go right on." *Why did the spider start its web from the beginning?*

☐ "Marcia's parents both have brown eyes," she said.
    "That's not possible," he said. "Marcia has *blue* eyes! Brown-eyed parents can't have blue-eyed children." *Who's right? He or she?*

☐ "My sister and brother-in-law had a baby girl about a month ago. Last night when I was playing with their baby I put my index fingers in her hands. When I moved my fingers, she didn't let go. In fact, I lifted her right up off the blanket! My sister was there to catch her if anything had happened. But I really don't understand it. That baby can't even hold her own bottle, but she's strong enough to hold herself up in mid-air!" *What did happen here?*

All humans need social experiences in order to develop properly. Loving parents help young children gain a positive image of themselves.

1 Observing Behavior

Suppose you're waiting for a bus. At the bus stop with you are a very heavy woman, burdened with packages, and a mother with her two-year-old child. When the bus arrives with standing room only, the child pipes up loudly "Is that fat lady going to get in the bus?" Although the mother is no doubt embarrassed, probably neither you nor any of the other adults are surprised by the child's tactless question. You show little concern.

Suppose you're waiting for a bus. This time waiting with you are the heavy woman and a woman accompanied by her twenty-two-year old daughter. When the crowded bus arrives, the daughter asks loudly "Is that fat lady going to get on the bus?" How do you react? You probably look shocked. You expect a person of that age to keep her thoughts to herself or even offer to help the burdened woman.

Now suppose you're waiting for the bus, but this time waiting with you and the heavy woman are an eighty-two-year-old woman and her daughter. When the crowded bus pulls up, the elderly woman asks, "Is that fat person going to try to get on the bus?" What is your reaction? You are probably tolerant of the outspoken old woman. You may understand that she could feel threatened at the thought of being crushed in the crowd and is unable to conceal her anxiety.

From this simple example we can note several points about human behavior: (1) We all constantly observe the behavior of those around us. (2) We often base our own reactions on very limited information. (3) We often make assumptions about other human beings based on these limited observations.

developmental psychology:
the area of psychology that studies changes in human behavior as they relate to age

In all three scenes at the bus stop, only one independent variable differs: the age of the person speaking. Yet *your* behavior, the dependent variable, probably differs in each case. Your reactions demonstrate that as humans age, the behavior ex-

Developmental psychologists describe and try to explain changes in behavior related to age. We expect different behavior of people as they reach different stages in the life cycle.

Figure 2-1 Maturation is largely responsible for sequential motor development, but learning is also involved. The ages indicated here are averages. Wide variations are possible since each individual is unique.

1 month — Chin up

2 months — Chest up

4 months — Sits with support

7 months — Sits alone

8 months — Stands with help

9 months — Stands with support

10 months — Creeps

11 months — Walks when led

12 months — Pulls self up to stand by furniture

13 months — Climbs stair steps

14 months — Stands alone

15 months — Walks alone

pected of them changes. What is appropriate behavior at one age is inappropriate at another.

That's the essence of *developmental psychology:* the study of human behavior as it relates to age. Developmental psychologists are concerned with the *lawfulness*, or predictability, of human behavior. With enough scientific information about a person, they try to predict how the person will behave at certain ages and in certain situations.

2 Goals and Methods of Developmental Psychology

The earliest studies of age-related changes in human behavior date back 2,000 years or more. Yet, only in the last 50 years or so have we begun to make real progress. All of the earliest studies of human behavior were descriptive.

Scientists observed behavior as it occurred and then described it precisely. The drawings in the margin, for example, are only descriptive. They are based on careful observation of changes occurring as an infant begins to coordinate muscles and, eventually, to walk. Today, developmental psychologists seek not only to describe behavior but also to explain it—a far more difficult goal. Psychologists do this by trying to identify the important independent variables that influence changes in our behavior as we grow older. Watch carefully as you go through this chapter. See if you can identify for yourself when a behavior is being described and when it is being explained.

If you think about it, you'll realize that when studying developmental changes the presence of age as a "nuisance" variable is inevitable. Older people didn't grow up in the same environment as younger ones. For example, it is likely your grandparents didn't eat food of the same quality and variety that you do. They probably had poorer schooling and fewer medications with which to treat diseases. In short, the environment of many elderly people during their childhoods was probably not as good as the typical environment of most children or adolescents today. So if a psychologist found in a study that older people differed from young people, what should we say was the cause?

Age? Or was it the different environments of childhood? We've got a confounding variable here. Controlling for it is usually accomplished in one of two ways.

Longitudinal study

One way to collect data is to continue to observe one group of subjects over a long period of time. Perhaps you might repeat your measurements at regular intervals. This is called a *longitudinal* study. It does allow us to study the effects of early factors on later behavior. It also gives us good control over such things as intelligence and personality. But there are also problems here. Any errors in selecting our subjects at the start remain in the data for the entire experiment. Moreover, such experiments take a long time to conduct. Psychologists age just as rapidly as anyone else. It almost seems that the only way a good longitudinal study can be conducted is for a young psychologist to have a good idea for an experiment early in his or her career!

Cross-sectional study

Another way to gather data is to conduct a *cross-sectional* study. This involves a one-time-only period during which two or more groups of different age are observed. In such a study we would usually use the same measures for each group. Obviously, such studies have some advantages. The time to conduct the study is usually quite short. And the findings are likely to be more immediately useful. We wouldn't conduct such a study if we didn't have a need to answer questions that are important right now.

Yet, there are also difficulties. Any time you try to compare groups of people who differ in age, you have a very complex problem. Trying to choose subjects for each group who are similar is not easy. The problem, as we discussed earlier, is controlling all the confounding variables.

In addition, we may not be able to study the effects of early experience on later behavior. Why? The main reason is that record-keeping was not always good in years gone by; therefore the only record of what happened to our parents and grandparents is often their own memory. Memory is helpful, except for some problems we'll discuss in Chapter 7. However, you wouldn't let a player for the Washington Redskins serve as referee in an NFL contest between the Redskins and the Los Angeles Rams, would you? For the same reasons we are each poor observers of the events influencing our own lives. We are not impartial.

longitudinal study: *a study in which one group of subjects is observed over a long period of time*

cross-sectional study: *a study in which two or more groups of different age are observed for an identical, one-time-only period using the same measures for each group*

→ **Think about it**

The **question:** If you and your parents and their parents all graduate(d) from high school at the top of their (your) class, who will know the most: You? Your parents? Your grandparents?

The **answer:** You should now know enough to understand that this is a very hard question to answer. It's neither a cross-sectional nor a long-itudinal study: The age of the people involved is different, yes, *but* the quality of the schooling received by each of you is also different. What if we were able to give a test of knowledge to you at graduation, as well as to your parents and grandparents when they had graduated? We'd still have the problem of the differing quality of schooling. Who's smarter? In some ways, that's almost impossible to answer.

In review . . .

Developmental psychologists study changes in human behavior as they relate to age. Most studies of developmental changes in human behavior are trying to describe the behavior and to explain it. The usual research techniques don't work too well due to the changing environments of youth during the past century. To control this problem developmental psychologists use longitudinal and cross-sectional studies, taking care to select groups at each age that are as comparable as possible.

3 What Influences Our Development?

Developmental processes influence almost everything psychologists study—from seeing to talking, from eating to sleeping. So, as we said in our unit introduction, we're going to take what is best called a life-span approach. And we're going to limit our discussion of developmental processes mainly to four areas: (1) physical changes or growth, (2) motor and sensory development, or changes in performance skills, (3) development of language, and (4) development of the self-concept, which includes an awareness of things such as emotions, intelligence, and social skills.

What is development?

Development refers to the changes organisms experience as they live. Though this may involve either gaining or losing abilities or qualities, it emphasizes orderly, systematic change, as we'll see.

development: *the systematic, orderly changes organisms experience as they live and either gain or lose abilities*

Development should be contrasted with another important word: maturation. *Maturation* involves only those changes in behavior that can be directly traced to physical growth. Learning to ride a bike or to drive a car provides a good example of the difference between maturation and development. To master control of a bike or car you must be big enough physically to handle the controls and developed enough personally and socially to appreciate the responsibilities that are involved. Development refers to the quality of your behavior; maturation refers to the state of your body and its readiness for a behavior.

If you've been reading carefully so far, you are aware that there are *two* major groups of factors that influence human behavior: heredity and environment. Now, before we look at the effects of each group of factors, we must clarify some issues. First, the environment in which we live has a direct influence on both our behavior and our development. Any child raised by a family that is abusive, or that fails to meet the child's needs, is more likely to have psychological problems. Such a child is less likely as an adult to be as well-adjusted as one raised in a family that is loving and responsive. Different environments can cause changes in behavior. The quality in human beings that allows such changes to take place is called *malleability*.

But then there's heredity to consider. There are limits to how much we can change anyone's environment and expect it to show up in his or her behavior. To be malleable does *not* mean that all individuals raised in the same environment will develop identical skills. Think a moment. If a fire occurred in your classroom, some students would be too scared to move. Others

maturation: *those changes in behavior of an organism that can be traced directly to physical growth*

malleability: *the quality in humans that allows changes in environment to cause changes in behavior*

Specific genetic information yields the human form when processes of maturation occur. It also allows us to see similarities through several generations.

would scream. Some would act to put out the fire; others would rush for the exits. And the same is true of most situations in which we humans may find ourselves. Some of us are active, some passive; some happy, some sad; some tall, some short; some smart, some not so smart. Part of what accounts for these differences is inherited capabilities.

Unfortunately, many people think about inherited characteristics only in terms of simple things such as eye color. We all know that no amount of *practice* is going to turn blue eyes into brown. But many people also assume that *any* characteristic that is inherited—or known to be genetically caused—can't be changed. They assume an inherited characteristic isn't subject to the whims and changes of the environment. That's not so. It is important to realize that genes do not define your behavior absolutely. At best your genes create what some psychologists have called a "range of possible experiences." Your environment, then, determines what your actual experience will be.

Heredity

Two kinds of information. Inherited "information" is of two kinds. One is *general* information that yields humans or dogs or giraffes as the information dictates. The other is *specific* information. It passes on patterns that cause you to mature into a being who can be identified as part of your own family. Such patterns include your hair and eye color, your skin tone, the shape of your hand and head and body. But such information also includes more complex factors such as your general level of excitability, your intelligence, and even certain aspects of your personality.

How do we study inherited factors? Many things determine how we study the impact of heredity. There are values such as religion, morals, and love which prohibit using humans in research on the effects of heredity. In addition to these ethical issues there is a practical one: If humans were studied, the experimenter would be outlived before his or her subjects had had a chance to demonstrate all their behaviors! For these reasons, scientists have turned their attention to other living things—including plants and animals.

One of the most frequently used techniques for studying inherited characteristics is the process of *selective breeding*. The work of Gregor Mendel was the original in this area. Mendel worked with the garden pea, but the basic principles he developed have since been applied to both humans and animals. These same techniques have also been applied to the study of behavior.

A Burmese cat. When the first cat bearing what are now called Burmese markings showed up on a ship in Boston harbor several decades ago, that cat was bred with a Siamese cat. Through selective breeding the Burmese strain was "purified" for, among other things, eye color (golden), temperament (very pleasant, nonaggressive), and muscle (quite strong). If a trait is influenced by heredity, then selective breeding will influence its appearance in later generations. Ability to alter the Burmese cats' temperament testifies to the impact of inheritance on behavior.

Feature   2–1   PARDON ME, YOUR BREEDING IS SHOWING

In the late 1920's one psychologist gathered up 142 rats. In addition to reducing the local rat population, this also yielded a random sample of rats. The psychologist had all 142 rats run through a maze from start to finish 19 times. If they reached the correct goal box, they earned a piece of cheese. For all 19 trials the number of errors each rat made was recorded. As you might suspect, the rats got smarter with practice. In fact, some rats ran more than half the trials without making any wrong turns at all.

When the experiment was done, the performance of each rat was plotted, as you can see in Figure 2-2(a). In this random sample the total number of errors in 19 trials ranged from 9 to 214. Some of the rats making the least number of errors—called the "maze-bright" rats—were selected to mate. In addition, some of the rats that made a lot of errors learning the maze were selected for breeding. These were called—surprise— the "maze-dull" rats.

Figure a

All of the children (they're called *progeny*) of the maze-bright and maze-dull rats then tried to learn the same maze in 19 trials, the errors again being recorded. The experiment was repeated through a total of eight generations. Each time only the brightest and the dullest of a generation were bred to produce the next generation—bright breeding with bright and dull with dull.

Figure 2-2(b) shows the performance of the third-generation—the grandchildren. Notice that already the performance of the

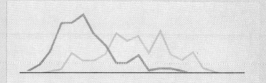

Figure b

progeny of the brightest rats is beginning to separate from that of the progeny of the dullest rats. And Figure 2-2(c) shows the performance results from the progeny of the eighth generation. By now the maze-bright rats' performance is almost so good that it doesn't even overlap with that of the maze-dull rats.

Figure c

What these rats demonstrated, of course, was that it was possible to breed for behavioral characteristics. This was among the first times this was demonstrated in the laboratory. But don't be misled. Don't assume the maze-bright rats in this experiment were bright in everything they attempted. Far from it. Another psychologist took the eighth generation rats and put them in an alley where they had to swim. Here you couldn't distinguish their performance from that of the maze-dull rats in the previous experiments. So, although the experiment produced rats that were very "bright" in one kind of experiment, it did not produce a breed of Albert Einstein-like rats.

Box 2-1 presents one of the classic studies of selective breeding of animals. As you can see from this study of rats, one procedure involves selecting two animals to breed, both of whom are good examples of whatever trait is being studied. The breeding is then used to "purify" that characteristic.

In the study of inherited factors in human behavior, two techniques are most frequently used. One is the study of twins. Here we can examine the similarities and differences in the behavior of two humans. We know more about the genetic information than we would about any two people selected at random. *Identical* twins are created from a single fertilized egg—of which we'll talk later in this chapter. Their heredity is identical. *Fraternal*—non-identical—twins are created from two separately fertilized eggs. We can compare identical and fraternal twins who have been raised together or separately—as might happen if twins are separated shortly after birth and raised in adopted or foster homes.

Such studies have suggested that inherited factors do seem to influence intelligence, some personality characteristics, susceptibility to schizophrenia (which we'll discuss in Chapter 12), as well as shared interests and attitudes toward authority. There are, of course, a number of problems in isolating the effects of environmental factors from those of inherited factors. These problems are well-illustrated in the other technique used to study the influence of heredity on human behavior—the family tree.

Identical twins are created from a single fertilized egg. Since their heredity is identical, they have been used in studies of hereditary similarities and differences. Fraternal twins are created from two separate fertilized eggs. Comparative studies have been made of identical and fraternal twins raised separately or together. Results indicate that inheritance does seem to influence many behavioral factors, including some personality characteristics.

Look at the family tree illustrated here. This shows seven generations of the ancestors and later relations of Johann Sebastian Bach, one of the most famous classical musician/composers ever to live. As you can see, from 50 to almost 90 percent of the people related to J. S. Bach in each generation gained the main part of their livelihood through music—playing it, writing it, or conducting it.

Yet, there's a problem. Are we to credit this love of and predominance in music to heredity or environment? If it's true that to be a classical pianist you need a finger span from the tip of your little finger to the end of thumb that will cover 13 white keys on the piano keyboard, then perhaps we should argue that heredity was the critical factor. But don't you suppose the children of J. S. Bach heard good music in their home? And don't you suppose that the Bach children—if they showed any skill in music—would've been encouraged, maybe even *forced*, into musical activities? So separating the influence of heredity and environment isn't always easy. We'll have more to say about this later.

Environment

Now we've got a problem. Deciding exactly what qualifies as an "environmental" factor is a bit hard to do. In one sense, environmental influences include *everything* that is not inherited. Perhaps the best way to simplify this problem is to distinguish between physical and social environmental factors.

Physical Environment. Up until birth, your *physical environment* literally surrounds you. It surrounds you more loosely after birth, but there are still a number of important influences. These include, first, the ecological factors surrounding you, such as the quality and the temperature of the air you breathe.

A second physical factor is the food you eat. Our diet in the 80's is generally better than in the 70's, the 60's, and earlier, yet it's far from perfect. For example, a battle has long raged about whether saccharin does/does not cause cancer. If it does, how much does it take to make the danger of getting cancer something worth worrying about?

Food additives—for color, for flavor—may also influence the quality of our food. And, surprisingly, whether or not we cook our food and how we do it may end up subtracting from the raw food elements that would be good for us. Vitamins and some nutrients can be lost in the processes of manufacturing and cooking certain foods.

Third and finally, *chemicals* are a very important contributor to our physical environment. As we'll discuss in more detail in

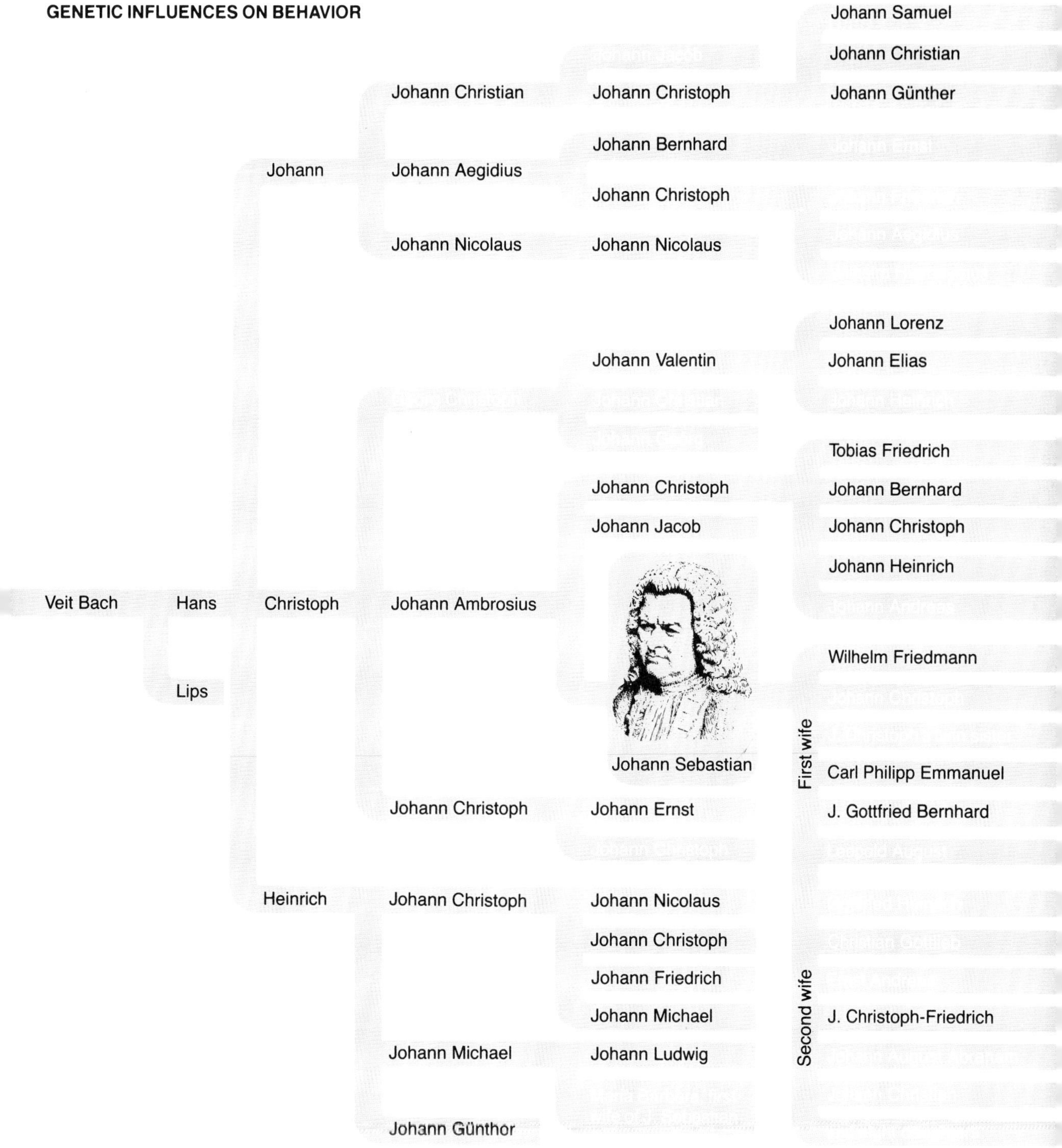

Veit Bach

Hans

Lips

Johann

Christoph

Heinrich

Johann Christian

Johann Aegidius

Johann Nicolaus

Johann Ambrosius

Johann Christoph

Johann Christoph

Johann Michael

Johann Günthor

Johann Christoph

Johann Bernhard

Johann Christoph

Johann Nicolaus

Johann Valentin

Johann Christoph

Johann Jacob

Johann Sebastian

Johann Ernst

Johann Nicolaus

Johann Christoph

Johann Friedrich

Johann Michael

Johann Ludwig

Johann Samuel

Johann Christian

Johann Günther

Johann Lorenz

Johann Elias

Tobias Friedrich

Johann Bernhard

Johann Christoph

Johann Heinrich

First wife

Wilhelm Friedmann

Carl Philipp Emmanuel

J. Gottfried Bernhard

Second wife

J. Christoph-Friedrich

Figure 2-3 This family tree shows the unusually high number of musically talented people in the Bach family. All those listed in black type are known to have been musicians. Which do you think was most responsible for their ability, heredity or environment?

Parents make a major contribution to your social environment. The attitudes they have toward you, their love, values, and expectations, all greatly influence the kind of person you will become.

Chapter 4, many drugs serve only to "pollute" our body with chemicals that can be dangerous in large amounts. Each of these physical factors is an important influence in our lives.

Social environment. Your *social environment* is made up of family members and of social elements beyond or outside your family. Their relative contribution depends directly on your age and the restrictiveness of your parents. Let's look at each social factor.

Within the family. Three elements are important here: your mother, your father, and your siblings (brothers and sisters). Your parents play several important roles (defined in Chapter 15). They usually provide financial support and supply the emotion (love) that ties a family together. They also teach cultural values: It's not nice to litter. You should respect the police. Be honest. Finish any job you start. Brush your teeth twice a day. You *know* what these "cultural values" are!

But your parents also play a major role in shaping your personality. They reward you for getting up on time. They instill good (or bad) manners in you. They influence your views of members of other races, communities, and nations. In short, they shape a lot of the values you hold at least up through high school. (We'll discuss later in Chapter 3 how some of this early training changes once you leave your parents' home.) Finally, your parents also decide (and enforce?) who does what jobs and when—very important decisions if a family is to operate effectively.

Now, while these are things your parents share, there are also some marked differences in the roles played by your mother and by your father. Probably some contributions are almost always made only by one or the other.

Brothers and sisters play an important role as you develop. Until elementary school, a child is most strongly influenced by the social environment supplied by his or her family.

There are also the social contributions made by your siblings. We'll discuss their importance in more detail in Chapter 15, but notice they *do* have an impact on your own childhood and early adulthood. The social environment within your family is most important until you enter elementary school. From that time on, most of your influences come from outside the family group.

Beyond the family. Of the major sources of social influence beyond the home, probably the most powerful is television. One source suggests that the average high school graduate of the 80's has spent more time in front of a television set than in a classroom since entering first grade. And what are the effects of that much television viewing? The *catharsis theory* suggests that watching aggressive acts on television reduces the likelihood a person will act aggressively. By contrast, the *social learning theory* suggests that if children learn by watching, then seeing acts of aggression on television should increase a child's aggression rather than lessen it.

A report summarizing a decade of research on the effects of television was released by the National Institute of Mental Health in 1982. It concluded that violence on television does lead to aggressive behavior by children. Researchers are only beginning to study whether television also influences children's thought and emotional processes. Can children's social beliefs, behavior, and relationships—even their health—be influenced by television? Pressure to smoke is greatest in junior high school. Can television be used to blunt those pressures? All sorts of possibilities abound.

Television has become a potent force in a child's environment. Many people have voiced concern about the crime and violence portrayed and the possible influence such programs may have on behavior. Do you believe a child's actions might be affected by such "observational learning"?

The second outside social factor, obviously, is school. We should note that schools are intended mainly to achieve two purposes. One is to teach the intellectual skills that citizens will need to succeed in society. These are the old "readin', writin', and 'rithmetic." They are the means to communicate the content of society's progress so far.

There is less agreement about the other purpose. Many people feel that school should improve a student's self esteem. It should provide opportunities for and guidance in developing social skills. It should, in short, help students learn about how to live and enjoy life, how to play, how to think logically, and how to enjoy esthetic beauty, whether that be art or music. The relative emphasis to be placed on "the three R's" and social skills tends to be controversial.

The third major source of influence outside the family affecting the behavior of children and adolescents is the peer group. That is the friends and schoolmates of generally the same age. It may be the child next door, a boy- or girl-friend, or just members of one's classes in school. The influence of the peer group doesn't really develop until school age, but it becomes extremely powerful during high school years. Many parents worry about their children's choice of friends. What your parents (and you, for that matter) may not know is that most children and youths tend to choose friends of whom their parents would approve anyway.

Teenagers, in particular, are influenced by classmates, but tastes and interests may differ widely among different teen peer groups.

Another social factor, more directly controlled by your parents, is the degree to which your peer group will have influence over you. This tends to be in inverse proportion to the amount of influence your parents exercise. If your social, emotional, and other needs are met by your parents, you will have less need to turn to your peers for support, for experience, for anything.

New research has revealed a final point. Some psychologists have noticed that peer groups serve as "levelers." Such groups provide a low-threat means for you to find out whether the training you've received at home works correctly "out in the real world." If your parents are too conservative, your friends are likely to seem wild to your parents. If your family life is quite liberal, your friends may perceive you as a "wild" person.

So the combination of friends (and foes), television, school, and family educates you in the ways of the world. But now we are getting ahead of our original discussion. So far we've talked of hereditary and environmental influences as separate, but equal. Are they?

Heredity and environment

As we discussed in Chapter 1, the old nature-nurture argument is often posed as an either-or kind of debate, but it isn't. Rather, it should be concerned with "how much of each?" In the behaviors of interest to psychologists, your inheritance (your genes) sets a range of possible reactions that you might make. The environment can provide a range of possible experiences, but yours will be a *particular* environment. What occurs in each of us is a reaction uniquely determined by our heredity to the particular environment in which we find ourselves.

Some people feel that we humans tend to consider ourselves passive lumps of clay, moldable in any way by the environment to which we are exposed. Actually, we play a vital role in choosing our own environments. We often select environments that we like and reject those that we dislike.

Look at the Figure 2-4 to see what can happen if we combine nature and nurture in one specific example. Suppose your genes had given you a large frame—big bones and a stocky build. Think about the differences that environments offering (1) too little, (2) adequate, or (3) too much food would have on such a body. Now compare the impact of these same food conditions if the original genetic message had been to create a small frame—small bones and a slight build. What is the difference between a genetically stocky frame raised in a food-poor environment and a genetically slight frame raised in a food-rich environment? The differences tend to disappear, don't they? *Both* heredity *and* environment influence biological and psychological factors.

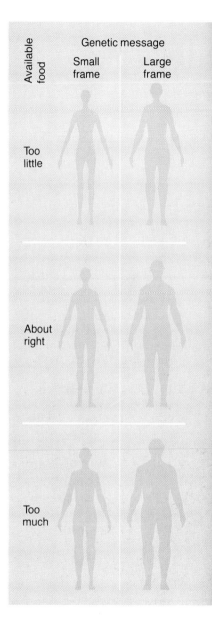

Figure 2-4 A cartoon conception of how differences in heredity can be affected by environment. The amount of food available may be instrumental in lessening genetically determined differences in body build.

━━━━━━━ In review . . .

Maturation involves changes in behavior due to physiological growth. Development includes all changes in behavior related to aging. There are two major groups of factors that influence our behavior. One is the environment, which provides a certain range of experiences. The other source is heredity. Our physical environment and social environment combine with hereditary factors to influence our behavior.

A famous picture of Dr. Konrad Lorenz, followed by goslings that had imprinted upon him. They saw Dr. Lorenz, rather than their mother, a few hours after they were hatched. Consequently, they attached themselves to him.

4 The Study of Development

At this point let's pause a moment for one more look at research techniques. Since some of the facts about human development were first suggested from the study of animals, we will start our examination there.

From the study of animals

Forms of behavior. In studying the range of animal behaviors—from the simplest one-celled amoeba to the most complex multi-celled primates and humans—one thing becomes obvious. As you move from *simple* to *complex* structures in the animal world, you also move from *automatic* to *rational, controlled* patterns of behavior. Let's look at five such forms of behavior, starting with the simplest.

A *taxis* (pronounced TACK-sis) involves the response or orientation of a whole animal either toward or away from some physical stimulus. We humans have a negative *geotaxis*. That means that in relation to gravity we orient ourselves away from it. In short, we stand *up*.

A *reflex* is an unlearned response to a stimulus. However, unlike the taxis response, which involves the whole organism, a reflex usually does not. If you've ever visited a doctor's office, more than likely your doctor has tested your knee-jerk reflex by tapping your knee gently with a rubber mallet. Your foot responds involuntarily by kicking upward. This is the knee-jerk reflex.

A third form of behavior is the *instinct*. An instinct is a complex pattern of response that is unlearned and present in all normal members of a species. Unlike reflexes, which are fairly simple, instinctive responses may last for some time after the first stimulus that starts them.

The last two forms of response will be mentioned here, but we'll spend whole chapters discussing them later. One is *learning*, which we'll define for now simply as instances where experience modifies or alters behavior. If you're still reading this far into Chapter 2, that's an example of a learned skill. The other and most complex form of behavior is *reasoning*. This involves the use of abstract symbols, such as a written language or a system of numbers. Using such a system to solve problems, communicate, or educate illustrates the use of reasoning. An example? How many words can be made from the letters in TEXAS? Answering that question involves reasoning.

As you move up the hierarchy of animals, you find more and more reliance on higher response forms and less and less reliance on simple, automatic responses. For the simplest animals, such as protozoa, all responses are automatic. At the other end of the scale, our human behavior involves only a very few taxic responses. We have a few reflexes and instincts, but we rely strongly on learning and reasoning for most of our behavior.

Think about it

The **question:** The summer camp counsellor we quoted at the start of the chapter was surprised to find that the spider he interrupted started web-building from the very beginning again. Are you?

The **answer:** You shouldn't be. Weaving a spider web is an instinctive response. The spiral weaving response is probably set off by the existence of the main supports of the web. When the web lacks those main supports, the spider starts again by first spinning the main supports for his web.

Ethology

Among the most skillful studies of animals' behavior has been the work of the ethologists. *Ethologists* are zoologists who apply the principles of naturalistic observation to the study of animals' behavior in their natural environment. Work of this kind was so good, so new, and so challenging that three of the first ethologists earned the Nobel Prize in 1973 for their contributions.

The photograph shows a number of greylag geese following ethologist Konrad Lorenz. In fact, they have *imprinted* on him, a process that involves an interesting combination of learning and maturation. There are three necessary elements in imprinting. These elements are timing, the presence of an object to be imprinted on, and young organisms at the particular age of imprinting. It happens in many animals, but especially in birds.

imprinting: a process in which the young of an animal, at a particular and limited time after birth, form a strong attachment to any moving person or object

When birds hatch, the first living, moving object they see is usually their mother. They imprint on her and will follow her anywhere. But what if birds are raised in an incubator, and the first moving object they see is a decoy? If this happens, the birds will imprint on the decoy. In fact, the farther those birds have to follow the decoy, the stronger will be the imprinting that results. In Lorenz' case, he had been the first thing the goslings had seen.

It has been suggested that imprinting takes place because of (1) an increasing fear of strange objects, and (2) a decreasing inclination to approach anything that moves or attracts attention. The combined effects of these two processes yields what is called a *critical period*. It is a period of time during which the events that will cause imprinting *must* occur if it is to result. Early enthusiasm surrounding the discovery of the imprinting process lead investigators to think that once the birds were imprinted to a decoy (as the goslings were to Lorenz), the process couldn't be reversed. Not so.

More recent work has shown that imprinting on an incorrect object is less stable than if an organism is imprinted correctly. Ducks imprinted to humans—when later exposed to their own mother for a period of time—will stay with her rather than returning to the person on which they had originally been imprinted.

How about humans? Are there critical periods in humans? The evidence so far suggests that we do have some critical periods—perhaps quite a number of them—during which we need certain kinds of experiences. We need exposure to other humans in order to learn to speak and to learn various social skills during the early years of infancy and most of childhood. And we need the handling, attention, and care of a mother or father in the earliest years of infancy. People denied these opportunities seem to suffer from slow learning of the missing skills when the opportunity finally presents itself—if they are able to learn the needed skills at all. Clearly, delaying some experiences beyond these ill-defined "critical periods" can have very unhappy effects.

A final concept, important to both humans and animals, is that of *maturational readiness*. This identifies the first time an organism is physically ready and able to respond correctly in a particular situation. With humans, for instance, there has long been an argument as to the best time at which to start training a youngster to read. Certainly, many children started at the age of three or four can do very well if given constant attention. Yet others not trained at all until the age of six or so seem to catch up quite quickly. Purely as a matter of efficiency, is it necessary

critical period: *a period in maturation during which particular events or behavior must take place in order for certain skills to be accomplished properly*

maturational readiness: *the first time in which an organism is physically ready and able to respond correctly in a particular situation*

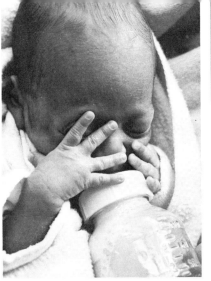

A   B

to start children as soon as they can hold a book up? Apparently not. It seems that the point of maturational readiness to learn to read is reached when a child—no matter how old he or she actually is—can do what the average six- to six-and-one-half-year-old can do.

The illustration describes in some detail how principles of maturation operate in all humans in definite, predictable sequences. You might also refer back to where we showed the various stages taking place as children learn to walk.

The ability of an infant to grasp something and pick it up (known as *prehension*) follows a predictable sequence of development. Gross motions become more and more refined, or *differentiated*. Figure A shows an infant's random movements. Figure B shows a later stage when the infant can control arm, wrist, and fingers in an organized way.

In review . . .

From studying animals, psychologists have identified a number of forms of behavior, ranging from simple to complex. These include taxic, reflexive, and instinctive responses as well as more complex responses based on learning and reasoning. Ethologists have identified a number of processes in animal behavior that also apply to humans. Maturation and development proceed in humans in definite sequences. Human behavior changes from mass-action to differentiated, and from simple to more complex.

5 Toward the Study of Humans

With all of this preparation behind us, let's now pay attention to the developments that take place within the individual human from the time he or she is conceived on through infancy and childhood to adolescence. Just a few words of caution before we begin: In much of the chapter to follow we'll be talking about when the first word is spoken, when an infant can stand and walk, and so forth. The figures we'll cite and the graphs and figures we'll look at show average figures, or norms.

It has been noted that knowing the norm is like knowing the average shoe size of an army: It's descriptive, but useless in equipping personnel. Keep in mind that there are wide variations among humans in the rate at which they mature and develop.

Human procreation

Genetics. As you probably already know from your biology courses, the process of creating a human begins when the *sperm* from the male unites with the *egg* of the female. The *chromosomes* within the fertilized human egg (or *zygote*) are composed of bead-like strands called *genes*. Genes contain the genetic code. This code is the order in which molecules transmit *genetic information*, or all the characteristics that are passed on through the generations. It has been estimated that there may be 10,000 to 50,000 genes in each fertilized egg!

The genetic code itself is embodied within structures of DNA, or *deoxyribonucleic acid*. The DNA is the master key determining the genetic portion of the physique and the potential behavior of every soon-to-be-born infant.

Dominance and recession. Each of us was created by a mixing of many genetic messages—about hair, skin, and eye color, about physique and abilities, about everything. However, we do not result from a mixing of our parents' characteristics as when you mix paint. Let's say the genetic codes of a man and a woman have been combined. What happens if one message says "blue eyes" and the other says "brown eyes"? A *dominant* gene, such as the gene for brown eyes, exerts its full effect over the effect of a *recessive* gene, such as the gene for blue eyes. Thus, any mixed genetic message will be expressed in the individual child in accordance with the dominant gene. The effect of a recessive gene will be expressed only if paired with another recessive gene. Our bodies or abilities may show the effects of a dominant gene even while we carry recessive traits and may transmit them to our children.

The theory suggests that we, the carriers, do not influence the genes we carry. We simply pass them on to our children. The Bach children whom we discussed earlier may well have become interested in piano through their parents' interest. But they could not know how to play a Bach concerto through a genetic message. They had to learn.

genetic code: *the form in which molecules transmit genetic information. Those characteristics within the genes that are passed on from one generation to the next.*

DNA: *deoxyribonucleic acid, the master key to the genetic code*

dominant gene: *an information code that exerts its full effect over the effect of a recessive gene with which it is paired*

recessive gene: *an information code that exerts its full effect only if paired with another recessive gene; its full effect will be masked if it is paired with a dominant gene*

The **question:** Well, what's your verdict? *Can brown-eyed parents have blue-eyed children?*

The **answer:** Yes. You can construct a table as follows, where B = brown (the dominant eye color) and b = blue (the recessive eye color). In short, if Marcia's parents are both of the Bb type themselves (with brown eyes but carrying recessive blue genes), the chances are that 25 percent of their children would have blue eyes (bb). As for the others, 25 percent would have brown eyes (BB), and 50 percent would have brown but be carrying recessive blue genes (Bb).

```
                Father
                 B    b
         B  BB   Bb
Mother                    children
         b  Bb   bb
```

Prenatal life

A human embryo is generally most susceptible to the effects of a poor environment during the first three months (called a trimester) of growth. As organs and life systems mature, there may be times when some pollutants have a higher than normal likelihood of causing certain abnormalities. Diseases, drugs, and various medical treatments, such as x-rays, may have bad effects. Poor eating habits of a mother-to-be take their worst toll during this time. Unfortunately, a woman may not be aware that she is pregnant during this critical first trimester.

During the last trimester the infant is already beginning to react to events outside its mother. One researcher placed a small block of wood over the abdomen of mothers in the latter part of the eighth month. When these researchers hit the board lightly with something that emitted a loud noise, about 90 percent of the *fetuses* began squirming excitedly and kicking. (See Table 2-1 for a definition of this and other terms we'll be using.)

Table 2-1 **Ages and stages for children**

AGE	NAME	STAGE
0-2 weeks *	Zygote	Germinal phase
2-8 weeks*	Embryo	Embryonic phase
2-9 months*	Fetus	Fetal period
0-2 years	Infant	Infancy
2-7 years	Child	Early childhood
7-12 years	Child	Late childhood
12-20	Teenager	Adolescence

*Age from conception.

Even before birth fetuses show vast individual differences. Ask any woman who has had two or more children. Some fetuses may be active 75 percent of the time, others only 5 percent. Some pregnant women have even reported they preferred not to go to symphony concerts—their babies responded to the music and applause with violent squirming! So the evidence is more and more clear-cut that fetuses can and do respond to environmental stimulation even before birth.

Another thought may have occurred to you. Does the *mental* state of the mother during pregnancy affect the baby before and after it is born? Obviously when any of us get upset, our body chemistry changes. If we are afraid, our adrenal glands pump actively, while our digestive processes stop. And if we're sad or angry? Happy or delirious? The answers here are less easy to provide. One study has been done of the babies delivered to mothers who were suddenly faced with an extreme fear or grief (as in the loss of the father) or anxiety during their last trimester of pregnancy. Generally the unborn fetuses of such mothers tended to show marked increases in their activity—as much as a tenfold increase sometimes—at the time of the shock. After birth these infants were mentally and physically all right, but they tended to be unusually irritable and very active. Some even had feeding problems.

And how about drugs? Women who smoke a lot tend to give birth to smaller and lighter infants. Infants born to mothers addicted to narcotics or alcohol tend to show the same severe withdrawal symptoms their mothers would if they stopped taking the narcotic. On the other hand, there *are* benefits to this blood-linked communication from mother to fetus. Mothers' immunities to diseases such as mumps, measles, whooping cough, and scarlet fever are passed on to the newborn child.

During the birthing process itself, only one kind of injury is likely to occur. This is brain damage caused by the use of forceps (instruments used to aid delivery) or a shortage of oxygen as the baby shifts from the mother to the environment outside. Such difficulties, however, rarely occur.

An interesting theory has gained ground in the past several decades about birth being a major psychological trauma. It's an appealing idea. Leaving a warm environment that was established and designed to meet the infant's every need would seem to be a foolish thing to do by adult standards. But remember the dangers of anthropomorphism—attributing thoughts and motives, and complex ones at that, where none may exist. Suffice to say, there is *no* evidence currently available that the birthing process itself is a traumatic event. It has not been shown that birth serves as the source of serious personality problems that may develop later in life.

In review . . .

DNA-carrying genes combine to convey dominant and recessive characteristics to the new organism. The fetus can already react to stimuli which come from outside its mother. Also, prior to giving birth, a mother may unknowingly injure it by ingesting certain substances. The process of birth itself seldom causes any damage to the infant.

6 Infancy

Body changes

Changes in an infant's body size that occur between birth and age two are extensive. Growth is rapid during the first year of human life. By the end of the first year, an infant triples his or her birth weight and stretches out from a starting length of 48-53 cm (19-21 inches) to a height of 63-74 cm. (25-29 inches).

There are a number of problems psychologists face when studying infant development. For one thing, early physical factors such as the size, agility, and sensing factors, as well as early intellectual abilities, are of no use in predicting a person's childhood and adult levels of such factors. A baby's length and weight at birth, for example, don't allow us to predict his or her adult height or weight. Also, there is the difficulty of knowing how to phrase a research "question" so an infant will pay attention long enough to give us an interpretable answer! By the time a child is two, however, we can begin to make a few predictions with ever-greater accuracy.

Consider the growth rate, for example. Growth rate slows down a bit during the second year. Even so, by his or her second birthday a child may well reach a quarter of the ideal (note, we did *not* say actual) adult weight. And the average two-year-old will be almost half as tall as he or she will be as an adult.

Motor skills

One of the most intriguing things about a newborn infant is the wide range of responses that have already been "pre-wired." These response patterns—some of them quite complex—show up as reflexes.

Right hand or left? A motor skill that is always a worry to parents is the development of handedness—shall he or she be right- or left-handed? World-wide, only about five percent of the people are left-handed, but a clear preference doesn't really develop until the latter part of the infant's first year. Even well into the second year an infant will still experiment a great deal—now eating with the right hand, now with the left, and sometimes with both.

Exactly why we develop a preference for one hand over the other is not clear. It may result from which side of our brain is dominant, called cerebral dominance, which we'll discuss in Chapter 4. But it's clearly the case that society as a whole is set up for right-handers. Everything from school desks to scissors, from hand-shaking to vegetable peelers, is designed for right-handers. Is this a cause of right-handedness, or does it result because of right-handedness? It was the fashion in the past to encourage infants to become right-handed at all costs. The best procedure now is thought to be to let handedness develop on its own. It saves worry and wear and tear on parents, teachers and left-handed children as well!

 Think about it

The **question:** Remember the four-week-old baby girl who suspended herself in mid-air by simply hanging on to two extended adult fingers? Can this be done?

The **answer:** Yes. It's called the grasping reflex. It's present in only about 40 percent of all infants, and it disappears completely by the end of the third month.

Sensing the world. When infants arrive in this world they already have some rather well-developed sensory skills for detecting parts of their environment. Yet, we know that an infant's reactions to the world about him or her are directly related to whether the infant is sleepy or alert, quiet or crying. The best time for studying infants is when they are alert, but quiet—which makes the task a bit difficult with newborns since they sleep most of the time. It has been learned that infants are less alert when they are flat on their backs. In that position they tend to fall asleep. It's interesting that our modern chairs for holding infants while they're being fed tend to position the infants on an incline. Perhaps this same finding is why infants stop crying when they are picked up and put over their father's or mother's shoulder. The smells, sounds, and other things in the world around them now catch their attention.

Yet, many other things also influence an infant. Too hot, and the infant will fall asleep; too cold, and it will cry. Tightly wrapped, infants tend to go to sleep; left naked, they tend to cry. Too bright, and they shut their eyes; too dim, and they'll go to

Feature 　　　　　 **2–2 　 WHAT DO INFANTS SEE?**

When we make statements that an infant can do this or can't do that, a problem must have occurred to you. How can we find out what an infant too young to tell us *can* actually do and see and hear? When infants start crawling, can they detect when they've reached the edge of a staircase? In fact, let's take a specific problem that was important to each of us: Can infants recognize a human face? Can they see at all?

We do know that infants can detect and respond to differences in brightness and motion when they are not even one day old. They prefer, in their first weeks, to look at the edges of stimuli—as if they are learning first the shapes of stimuli. But how about a face? Can an infant detect the difference between a face and an equally complex figure that is just a number of scrambled parts?

To answer this question, the four forms in the illustration were shown to a number of four-month-old infants. Several findings are immediately apparent when we examine what proportion of the total viewing time was spent looking at each object.

First, the most normal human face drew the most attention. Second, the form with the fewest details drew the least attention. Third, when choosing between two forms of equal complexity (Faces b and d), infants gazed longer at Face b. This suggests that the meaning of the form—the face in this instance—may be more important in attracting and holding an infant's attention than the complexity. All this was learned just by showing some infants some forms and watching what they watched!

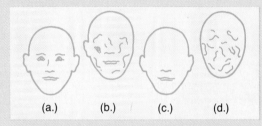

(a.) 　　 (b.) 　　 (c.) 　　 (d.)

Figure 2-5 An experiment performed with four month old babies indicated that they preferred the face nearest to normal. Two-year-olds, however, were more intrigued by the mixed-up face. How would you explain both these results?

---

sleep. Too loud, and they cry; yet with just a calm background noise (remember the use of music boxes?), they fall asleep. So finding out what an infant can do when attentive is no easy task!

In spite of this, we've learned that shortly after birth an infant is already more likely to look at a human face than at a random collection of the same number of features, as discussed in Box 2-2. We know from this that infants can see shortly after birth. Yet, other work has shown that the focal point of an infant's vision is only about nine inches away from his or her face. Interestingly, that's about the distance many women hold their infants from their own face when nursing them.

How about hearing? You'll remember earlier in this chapter we discussed fetuses who become very active if a loud noise is

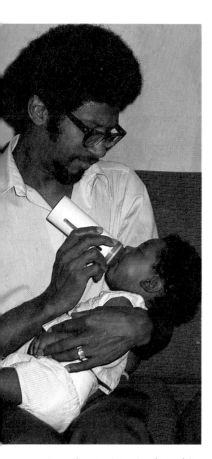

Learning to love begins with the warmth and affection experienced when you are very young.

produced outside their mother's womb. Shortly after birth an infant can be trained to turn his or her head toward a bell if food is given when the infant does so. When held upright between parents who are both speaking to him or her, the infant will turn more often toward the mother, perhaps because the mother is already the more familiar person.

If a change in its environment is detected by an alert infant, several things tend to happen. Its level of activity increases, and its heart rate and pattern of breathing change. We can use this to find out what infants *can* detect. For example, we now know that infants can smell even within two days after birth. First we get them used to smells ranging from acetic acid (a much less concentrated version of which exists in citrus fruit) to anise (which is like licorice). Then, if one of those smells is changed *and* that change is detected, what do we find? Right. The activity level, heart rate, and breathing all change. Taste, as we'll see in Chapter 5, is not as sensitive as smell, yet infants can even distinguish between their mother's milk and a cow's milk!

Language development

During infancy it seems that factors of physiological growth and maturation play a large role in the language skills that develop. This is suggested by several things: First, the initial steps through the first couple of years of language development are remarkably similar world-wide: The same sounds appear first, everywhere. There is the same sequence of increasing linguistic complexity and the same order of use and purpose of word classes. Second, infants have a knack for language. It would be an incredible feat to *learn* enough to be communicating as effectively as two-year-olds do in only two years. By that age a child has usually achieved a vocabulary of 300-400 words!

However, not all psychologists share the same opinion about how language develops. It is an area rich with arguments these days because views are changing rapidly. At birth you had only two choices: You could cry or be quiet. Yet by the time you were four weeks old you were already beginning to "say" different things. When you were uncomfortable, you got tense. As a result your vocal cords were more constricted and narrow. The nature of your crying changed. When you were happy, your vocal cords were more relaxed and you emitted a more open, back-of-the-mouth sound. It may be just an accident of muscle control, but parents can read these cues. Even as a four-week-old infant you were beginning to "speak."

At three months you reached the *babbling stage*. It seems to be enjoyable since infants all over the world do it. We emit random sounds, and we do a lot of it between three and six months of age. In the last half of the first year (6 to 12 months) two things begin to happen. First, infants begin to say the same syllables over and over again. It's in this stage that most proud parents proclaim that they hear their infant's first "word." But who's to say when repeating ma-ma-ma-ma-ma-ma or pa-pa-pa-pa-pa-pa changes to "ma-ma" or "pa-pa"? Nevertheless it *does* occur somewhere around the start of the second year, and who's to argue with proud parents?

The other process occurring in the last half of the first year is *imitation*. Infants are natural mimics. Listen to a six- to twelve-month-old infant, and you'll hear it mimicking many different sounds in its world—some verbal, some not. But during this period the sounds being emitted are getting more and more sophisticated. "Foreign" sounds—meaning those not used in the language the infant is about to learn—begin to disappear. A one-year-old will react to verbal stimuli, and he or she will react very differently to angry and loving voices.

During the next six months (12 to 18 months) there is a steady increase in the number and variety and complexity of sounds being emitted. One-word utterances occur more and more often. They're mostly nouns. In the last part of infancy (18 to 24 months) single-word utterances become two-word phrases. Here two processes can be heard. One is the development of *telegraphic speech*. "Mommy milk!" may mean anything from "Mother, I would like to drink some milk." to "Mother, your elbow just knocked a one-gallon container of low-fat, homogenized and very expensive milk onto the floor." In short, the important words are there, but none of the connectors.

The other process that is heard is *overgeneralization*. Infants try to apply simple rules in complex situations. They may learn that -ed means past tense, but then they apply that rule to too many verbs: "Daddy goed," "Mommy eated," and so forth. It's a mistake, but it's a good mistake, for it shows the infant is thinking about language. He or she is beginning to try to develop rules that will govern the use of this new-found skill called talking.

Self-concept

One of the most fascinating things to watch as it develops is the changing, shifting view of self. Self is a very hard concept to define—even more so for an infant. One way is to define *self* as anything you can touch that will result in two experiences of touch. (Touch your arm with your finger, for example. Your arm will feel the pressure of your finger; your finger will feel the warmth of your arm.) Box 2-3 describes one major source that helps an infant develop a self-concept.

Feature   2–3   TRUSTING BABIES

Crying is a very selfish thing that infants do. Almost everything else is socially oriented somehow: babbling, staring at you, smiling at you—even imitating you. But crying is *very* self-centered. Yet, as with so many things an infant does, the results produced by crying also teach the infant something about his or her world.

The way a parent responds to crying influences the attachment that forms between parents and their child. *Attachment* is the bond of affection that exists between an infant and other individuals—most often the mother and father. One psychologist studied the patterns of behavior that existed between 26 mothers and their children. We're going to look only at the most extreme cases in that study.

For example, suppose you were a parent in the following situation; what would you do? Your child is crying—apparently for food—but you've just fed it an hour ago. Would you yield to its needs and feed it again? Or would you consider your *own* needs and feed it on a schedule? What kind of an attachment would result when either the infant's needs dominate *or* the mother's

needs dominate? We will find some rather surprising results.

First, with a year-old infant, letting the baby's needs predominate led to a better interaction between mother and child—yes, a *better* interaction. Subsequently, when it was put down by the mother and apparently deserted, the infant whose needs had been met as they developed instead of according to the parent's schedule, cried less.

So how are we to explain this? The major factor here seems to be the trust developed by the infant. If it was repeatedly left to cry, it learned that the world was not to be trusted, that its needs would not be met as they arose. On the other hand, infants whose cries were followed by having their needs met, were learning that the world can be trusted. They learned that mother (or father) was a trustworthy person, that that person would show up as needs arose. The result was that by responding to a child's cries during the early months of its life, these parents created a more trusting infant. The more trusting infants eventually cried less, were more tolerant of frustration, and offered a richer variety of communications.

But what are the tasks of the infant here? Table 2-2 lists the components of self-hood that develop during infancy. Perhaps the second task there best shows the difficulty in defining self. For the first several months of its life an infant doesn't distinguish between itself and the environment of which it is a part. There is no boundary between itself and the world. Understanding that boundary is but one of the tasks in developing the sense of self.

All this while, from birth to two, the infant is testing and probing its environment. One theorist (Erikson, about whom more will appear later) has suggested one major task at this age is to form a view of the world—of either basic trust or mistrust. Another is to begin to develop a sense of self-control.

Table 2-2 **An infant's tasks in self-concept development***

AGE	TASK
Infancy (0-24 months)	1) Identify self as able to cause events.
	2) Awareness of boundaries and shape of body.
	3) Awareness of visceral events (such as a stomach ache).
	4) Recognition of self (as in a mirror).
	5) Recognition of self as a constant in a world offering varying experiences.
	6) Naming of self.
	7) Possessiveness.

*Adapted from Newman and Newman, 1978.

▒▒▒▒▒▒▒ In review . . .

During the first two years of life a baby is considered an infant. During this time humans experience one of their most rapid periods of change in body size and proportion. Although possessing a wide range of functional sensory organs, the infant gains much skill in interpreting incoming messages. Hand preference begins to develop, and the infant learns to stand and walk. Meanwhile, starting from random emission of sounds and progressing through babbling, telegraphic speech, and the error of overgeneralization, the infant (by age two) can begin to communicate.

7 Childhood to Puberty

Let's turn now to the events of childhood. What happens along the way from childhood to adolescence? What changes take place, physically and mentally? (As you read about the following skills, be sure to keep in mind our earlier caution about norms.)

Motor skills and body changes

What skills can you expect young children to perform? In terms of motor abilities, two-year-olds are able to walk with an even rhythm, and they can put on their own shoes, but they can't hop on one foot. Their drawing skill is limited to imitating vertical and horizontal lines. Three-year-olds can walk a line on the floor, but their drawings are usually just scribbles. A four-year-old can hop on one foot but often *only* one, walk on a balance beam, and draw crude figures of humans and other objects. By five a child can hop on either foot, tie his or her shoelaces, and draw identifiable animals, houses, and so forth. From six to twelve a child is mainly involved in a general improvement of motor performance. Dancing or tumbling classes may be beneficial to give the child practice in more and more refined motor skills. The child will notice a steady increase in his or her *strength, reaction time*, and *balance*.

You yourself have probably noticed that when you learn any new motor skill, you must at first pay a great deal of attention to the *perceptual*, or mental, aspects. In learning to play any musical instrument, you must concentrate on where your fingers are and how what your fingers are doing is related to what you hear. Mastering any motor skill involves first integrating all the incoming information from your eyes, your hands—in fact, *all* your senses. Then you practice until you have succeeded in moving control of the new skill from the conscious to the unconscious realm. For example, once a person knows how to roller skate, he or she no longer thinks about it. But compare that performance with that of a five-year-old just learning how to maintain balance, see where to go, lean, turn, and brake all at the same time!

The basic senses work quite well in the two-year-old. What continues to develop, however, is the more complex uses to which sensory information is put. For instance, one aspect of this development is what is called *cross-modal transfer*. Suppose we showed you the objects drawn. We then put them in a bag and asked you to pick out, without looking, the red object. If you came up with the right object, you would be performing a *cross-modal transfer*. This means that you'd have taken incoming *visual* stimuli and translated them, interpreting the same object in terms of *touch*. As children grow older, these complex skills are constantly improving—but of course at different rates for different individuals.

There are two final facts that you should note about body changes and motor abilities in children approaching puberty. First, as the quality and general availability of both food and medical services keep improving in North America, children keep maturing at earlier and earlier ages. Second, the age of twelve (roughly) marks the point of greatest difference in the

cross-modal transfer: *taking one form of stimuli and translating it mentally into another form (e.g., sight into touch)*

Figure 2-6 Objects used in a test of *cross-modal transfer.* If you were blindfolded, would you have any difficulty picking out the *red* object?

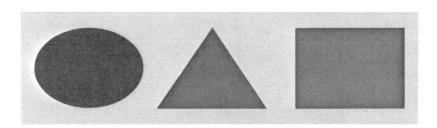

relative maturation of boys and girls. At this time girls are from 18-24 months ahead of boys in the percentage of their adult form they have achieved!

Language development

You will recall that when we left our developing two-year-old, he/she had achieved a vocabulary of 300-400 words. The trends that we saw started in infancy continue into early child-hood. During the third and fourth year many more word classes make their first appearance. A vocabulary that had only nouns and verbs grows rapidly to include adjectives, adverbs, preposi-tions, and even pronouns—the last major class to be mastered. During the fifth and sixth year children simply gain more so-phistication in their language. Some psychologists would argue that by the age of five to six a child knows all of the formal elements of his/her language. The only skill important to the use of that language which continues to develop well past the age of twelve is the size of the vocabulary.

However, one interesting skill does develop between five and twelve—the ability to use language to talk *about* language. That's a skill that is uniquely human, as we'll discuss at some length in Unit Three.

Self-concept

Table 2-3 lists the many and varied events that influence a child's self-concept as he or she progresses through the years two through 12. These factors are divided into early and late childhood. There are marked differences in the concerns for and about the self of young children as compared to those of older ones.

In terms of the theory of Erikson we were discussing earlier, there are several more tasks for the child to master between these ages. The child continues to gain knowledge about control-ling him- or her-self and begins to separate him- or her-self from mother, without feelings of guilt. Other major tasks of childhood are to develop the conscience and to begin to form a sex-role identity.

As these tasks are encountered, the developing language be-gins to be used as an aid. You'll hear a marked increase in "what" and "why" questions as the child ingests more and more information. There is an awakening awareness of the differences between boys and girls, and this too is explored.

So far the family has been the major learning ground, but the last major task of childhood is accomplished mainly in school. It is to develop a sense of industry—the ability and

Table 2-3 **A child's tasks in self-concept development***

AGE	TASK
Early Childhood (2-7 years)	1) Identify internal moods.
	2) Awareness of self as an object analyzed by others ("Isn't he cute?" "Isn't she smart?").
	3) View of self as willful, internally controlled ("Let *me* do it!").
	4) Self as part of family, friendship groups.
	5) Self as a sexual person, fitting certain sex-roles.
	6) Self as a moral person with goals for an ideal self.
	7) Self as (non-) initiator of events.
Late Childhood (8-12 years)	1) Physical changes leading to revision of body image.
	2) Development and evaluation of skills.
	3) Appreciation of multiple-roles for self.

*Adapted from Newman and Newman, 1978.

desire to do things and do them well. Both parents and teachers encourage this skill by achieving a careful blend of challenges to keep the child thinking positively even if experiencing some failure.

So, at this point we have a fully developed child, ready—to the extent anyone is—for adolescence. Before we see how that child's world—almost mastered—turns topsy-turvy again, let's pause for some review.

In review . . .

During childhood, which stretches roughly from two to twelve years of age, a child experiences a moderate amount of external body growth. However, much skill is gained both in motor coordination and in accomplishing more and more refined tasks; strength, reaction time, and balance also improve. During early childhood the remaining classes of words are mastered, while in the latter half vocabulary size is increased. The self-concept undergoes marked development. Social experiences in playing with peers help children learn acceptable ways to behave.

Chapter Application and Review

USING PSYCHOLOGY   *Being a "psychological parent"*

Even people too young or too old to be biological parents are sometimes put in the position where they must care for young children. Do you have younger brothers or sisters? Have you been a camp counsellor or a "baby" sitter? If so, knowing a little about what to expect and how to amuse children at different ages may be of help.

Since we've covered in some detail most stages of development—both physical and mental—here we'll only concern ourselves with play. Various studies have indicated that "child's play" isn't the simple thing the phrase implies. In fact, there's a definite progression in play behavior.

Basically, children play games that get more and more complex as they get older. Knowing about that progression will help you in entertaining children for whom you must provide care. Six forms of play have been identified.

Unoccupied behavior is the first kind of child-controlled behavior we observe. An infant will simply examine his or her own body or look around the room. For you sitters, this can be the easiest "minding" job of all. An environment with interesting (familiar!) things to see, hear, or manipulate can keep a baby happy. Remember the fascination of the human face for an infant.

Onlooker play seems to show an awakening awareness that other children exist. The child talks with other children who are playing—may even make suggestions or ask questions—but does not get into the action. Watching will usually be quite satisfactory for such a child.

Solitary play involves a two- to three-year-old child playing with toys all by him- or herself. None of the actions the child makes are influenced at all by what other nearby children are doing. Now, combining familiar and interesting toys with isolated observing will keep a child happy—still assuming that all bodily needs for food and so forth are met!

Parallel play involves children playing with the same toys, but not really interacting with each other. They will be playing beside, but not *with*, each other. This form is at its peak in two- to three-year-olds. By this age a child appreciates having a friend around, even though he or she may be doing the same thing separately.

Associative play involves the sharing of materials, and some shared interacting behaviors. Here children have similar, but not necessarily identical, goals. This form of play starts to show up in four-year-olds, and by five the younger forms of play are not seen very often. Now group projects with plenty of materials for everyone will be a hit—all painting separate pictures, for instance.

Cooperative, organized play is the last to occur. Now there is a single activity using the same materials and a common acceptable set of rules. Children play many different roles here. The key now is to have an interesting, challenging game with rules.

There is a surprising footnote to these findings. The study that identified these styles of play in the 1930's was repeated in the early 70's. North American youngsters are not now engaging in as many socially oriented forms of play. Certainly the last two forms of play tend to occur later than they did half a century ago. Can this be caused by too much television viewing? It's an interesting question to ponder.

REVIEW QUESTIONS

SECTION 1 (pages 49–50)
1. What do developmental psychologists study?
2. As used by psychologists, what is meant by "lawfulness of behavior"?

SECTION 2 (pages 51–53)
1. What are some of the problems involved in studying development?
2. What are the experimental methods used to avoid the problems?

SECTION 3 (pages 53–64)
1. How does development differ from maturation?
2. What are the major factors influencing our behavior? Give examples of each.

SECTION 4 (pages 64–67)
1. What behaviors have psychologists identified by studying animals?
2. Define *critical periods* and *maturational readiness*. Do these concepts apply to animals or humans or both?

SECTION 5 (pages 67–71)
1. What sequences are followed in the maturation and development of humans?

2. What purposes do genes serve?
3. To what environmental influences is a fetus sensitive?

SECTION 6 (pages 71–77)
1. In the normal human life span, when is the period of most rapid growth?
2. Name some important motor skills developed in infancy.
3. Trace the sequence of human speech development in infancy.
4. According to Erikson's theory, what attitudes toward the world are developed in infancy?

SECTION 7 (pages 77–80)
1. What ages does childhood include?
2. What motor skills develop during childhood?
3. How does the use of language develop during childhood?
4. What changes in self-concept occur during childhood?

ACTIVITIES

1. According to Piaget's theory, during its first eight months an infant learns that objects have "permanence." That is, objects continue to exist even when hidden from one's view. If you can find an infant who is less than eight months old, try to determine whether the child has yet mastered this con-cept. Place a toy in front of the child where the child can see it. Then cover the toy completely with a towel. What does the infant do? Infants under four months of age rarely pay much attention. Infants from four to eight months will look at the towel but probably not under it. Some infants might

duplicate the feat of most eight-month-olds and search under the towel. What did your test subject do?

2. To test the maturity of a child's motor skills, see if you can find a two-, a three-, a four-, and a five-year-old. Ask each child to hop up and down on one leg. What happens? Can a child who can hop on one foot hop on the other? Practice will do very little good until a certain point of maturational readiness has been reached.

3. Career Search. Volunteer to spend some time after school in a day-care center. Record your observations about children's behavior, being sure to record their ages, too. Which principles of maturation and development might explain what you saw?

Discuss your observations with your teacher or a psychologist.

4. At a playground or day-care center listen to the talk of two- to four-year-old children. How does their grammar differ from yours? Did you hear them use telegraphic speech or make any errors of overgeneralization?

5. In order to gain an understanding of children's abilities and limits in thinking, interview a number of children of different ages. You might ask a classic question such as "How does the sun get from where it goes down (in the West) to where it comes up (in the East)?" In analyzing the answers, compare the underlying logic of the children of different ages.

INTERESTED IN MORE?

BRUNER, J., COLE, M., & LLOYD, B. *The Developing Child.* Harvard University Press, 1977. A series of four short books, each of which provides an excellent review and analysis of important findings in its subject area. Subjects include *Mothering, Distress and Comfort, Play,* and *The Psychology of Childbirth.*

FEIN, G.G. *Child Development.* Prentice-Hall, 1978. Focuses on developmental processes in childhood and adolescence, from a life-span view.

FISHER, S., & FISHER, R.L. *What We Really Know About Child Rearing.* Basic Books, 1977. Effectively converts research from laboratory and clinic settings into "how to" advice for parents.

FRAIBERG, S. *The Magic Years.* Scribner, 1968. A well-done description of child-hood from the point of view of an understanding adult. Includes a look at the thinking processes and cognitive world of children.

NEWMAN, B.M. & NEWMAN, P.R. *Infancy and Childhood: Development and Its Contexts.* John Wiley, 1978. A well-illustrated college-level text depicting human development in a variety of contexts: in the uterus; in the family; and in day-care centers, schools, and neighborhoods.

SPOCK, B. *Baby and Child Care.* Pocket Books, 1977. The classic guide on almost any behavioral or physical problem encountered in raising a child.

3 Development: From Puberty to Old Age

CHAPTER OUTLINE

WHAT'S THE ANSWER?

☐ "It happened all of a sudden. My sister just turned 14, but she's really looking mature. One of my college fraternity brothers, who saw her picture, wanted to meet her. When he was visiting me at Thanksgiving, she came breezing through the front door blowing the biggest bubble of bubble-gum that I've ever seen. It covered her whole face—and most of her hair when she saw him. You should have seen the expression on his face! She wasn't what he expected at all, I guess." *What happened here?*

☐ *Why is it that many musicians can begin composing their most famous pieces of music while they're still quite young?*

☐ "Can you believe it? I started playing handball last year. Now my coach thinks I'm good enough for the varsity squad next year in college. Well, my *grand*father challenged me to three games of handball. It's true, he played in college, and he's practiced some since—but still! You know what he did? He *beat* me two games out of three! I don't understand it." *Do you understand it? How could a 71-year-old beat a mature adolescent at handball?*

1 Adolescence

Adolescence—the next period of human development we're going to study—occurs over a period of eight to ten years. The starting point for a boy may be as late as the last part of his

Environment and heredity combine to influence the ways in which we age. Physical and mental activity, and a vital interest in life, can keep people young in relation to their years. Here family members of all ages enjoy a Texas barbecue.

14th year. For a girl it may be as early as the first part of her tenth year. So, while we'll be speaking about average this and average that, keep in mind that the *range* of ages in which these processes occur is far more important than the "average" ages we give.

You should also note that no one is 12 years old, period. A person may be 14 physically, but 10 socially, 11 mathematically, and 12 in his or her skill with language. Keep this variability in mind, too, as we examine the most frustrating, vexing, interesting, complex time in human development—the adolescent years.

Problems of definition

There are two processes that are crucial to this time of life—puberty and adolescence—and defining each of them causes problems. Take adolescence. How are we to define it? It's a period of soaring idealism. Yet, an adolescent often experiences massive feelings of frustration—with self, with family, with friends, indeed, with the world as a whole sometimes. It has even been defined simply as a period between two other periods—childhood and adulthood. We seem to know what *they* are, but we have trouble defining the state between them.

Adolescence is also a time when friends and peers are perhaps more important than at any other period. So, it is characterized by many features.

Defining by body stage. We can define adolescence in terms of biological change. Thus, it is the span of years between the onset of puberty (of which more later) and the completion of bone growth. Staking adolescence to the onset of puberty is a nice way to stress the individual variations in adolescence. Marking the ending by completion of bone growth makes adolescence stretch a bit longer than you might suspect—probably into the 21st or 22nd year of life.

Defining by behavior. Instead of defining it in terms of physical changes, we can do so in terms of social and personal changes. Then we define adolescence as a span of years of increasing, but mixed, responsibilities and skills. During adolescence, human behavior is modified from child-like to adult-like. It can be said that adolescence ends with the achievement of adulthood, defined as self-governance.

Two features of adolescence, defined in either of these ways, have been observed. One is that adolescence seems to make a universal appearance in human development. Moreover, it seems to be primarily a physiologically based event. It is influenced very little by the environment in that its appearance can't be delayed or sped up significantly either by the adolescent or by concerned parents.

Puberty: Another problem of definition. Puberty is derived from the Latin word meaning to grow hairy. That's about all we seem to agree on about puberty.

When puberty is viewed as an *event*, it is usually related to sexual development, completed when the adolescent achieves the ability to reproduce.

Another possibility is to view puberty as a *process*. This lends emphasis to the importance of the joint effects of physical

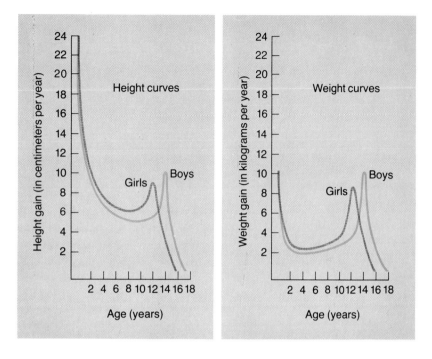

Figure 3-1 Study these graphs of human physical maturation from birth to maturity. Which are the years of most rapid growth experienced by boys? By girls?

changes and psychological events during puberty. Thus, puberty may continue as long as four years—first in preparing for sexual maturity and then in completing it.

Body changes

Structural growth. The illustrations show the pattern of physical maturation experienced by the average human, male and female. When you compare adolescent growth with that of a young child, the "growth spurt" and growing pains of adolescence don't seem nearly as spectacular, do they?

In fact, the *first* year of human life has the highest rate of growth. During adolescence, humans are growing at a much more modest 8½ to 10 percent. Yet, these physical changes may have a major impact on an adolescent's personality and social life if he or she is markedly early or late in maturing.

Maturation by sex. Three parts of the body contribute to starting the process of pubertal maturation. The *hypothalamus* (part of the brain) and the *pituitary gland* will be discussed in Chapter 4. The third part is the *gonads* (the sex glands of both sexes). Together these stimulate the hormones responsible for maturation of the primary and secondary sex characteristics. The illustration shows the differences in physical maturation

Adolescents differ widely in their rate of physical maturation. All of the 14-year-olds here fall within the normal range of development.

possible in both females and males. All fall within the acceptable normal range of development.

Later in this section we'll discuss how these processes of physical/sexual maturation influence our developing concept of self. As you might suspect, the impact is substantial.

Motor skills

In most ways boys and girls have almost the same body build until the start of puberty and the adolescent growth spurt. As the body matures, a number of physical processes also change. Some skills are lost, but many more are gained. In terms of physical ability, boys and girls are very similar in what they *can* do up until about 13 years of age.

When some motor abilities are applied to a particular skill, however, an interesting question arises. Boys can throw a ball farther and more accurately even before the onset of puberty. But think about that for a moment. Throwing a ball is a skill that gets better with practice. Is it possible that girls who have practiced (or boys who have not) would throw a ball with the same skill as those who have practiced (or not) in the opposite sex? How would you test that? It turns out to be very simple. Use the non-preferred arm! Ask right-handed youngsters to throw a ball using their left arm and vice versa. And what happens? The differences—in both accuracy and distance—disappear. There are differences even using the non-preferred hand and arm after the onset of puberty. However, this test again suggests the essential equality of both boys and girls until puberty begins.

Some other facts can be observed when comparisons are made. At about age 13 males start getting stronger. Females, on the other hand, essentially gain no more physical strength than they have at the end of their early adolescent growth spurt. In fact, in some skills they actually lose ground. Body size clearly has an influence in this, but here's a case where social factors—called sex roles—also may have an influence. We'll come back to look at this later in this section.

Males also have one additional change in a "motor skill" that occurs during adolescence—their voices deepen. It happens because of the marked physical maturation of the Adam's apple (the *larynx*). An adolescent male's vocal cords nearly double in length. Following some basic laws of physics, that means the pitch of his voice drops roughly an octave. However, a young man may expect occasional breaks in his voice—when it shifts from low to high or the reverse (without warning)—until he is as old as 16 to 18.

Language development

The development of language is almost complete at the onset of puberty. However, there are some changes that occur during adolescence. For one thing, the vocabulary continues to grow. The first count of the number of words known and used by children was done more than half a century ago—in 1926. At that time six-year-olds were estimated to know about 2,500 words. The widespread use of television and radio in modern society makes it likely that this figure is a serious *under*estimate for youth today.

It has more recently been estimated that most people upon graduation from high school know 30,000 to 50,000 words. Education becomes more and more verbal and abstract in high school. This leads us to suspect that much of the increase in our vocabulary occurs during late junior high and throughout the senior high years. And if you go on through college, you will probably double your vocabulary one more time.

Jargon. Another interesting thing happens to an adolescent's vocabulary. Adolescents often talk in *jargon*—a special vocabulary shared with other adolescents. Most professions (medicine, education, law, psychology, and so forth) also have a jargon. For them it is a technical vocabulary used to communicate complex ideas with a limited number of words. You're learning some of psychology's jargon in this book: *fovea* (Chapter 4), *sensory store* (Chapter 7), *validity* (Chapter 16), *ego* (Chapter 12), and *mean* (Chapter 17). Often the terms invented by adolescents become part of the adult vocabulary, but by that time adolescents have moved on to new terms. People who are popular and well-adjusted in any adolescent's society are usually labeled with some complimentary term in jargon. In the 1950's such people were "cool"; in the 60's "hip"; in the 70's "together." What would you call such people now?

90

Thinking. At the same time as language use is changing, the mental processes and capacities of adolescents also change. At the start of adolescence, thinking is very *concrete*. That means it is tied to the obvious. Remember in junior high school how all your math problems involved apples and oranges, or the number of acres in a field? They were always tied to the material world to fit the thought patterns of pre-adolescents.

By middle adolescence, our thought processes become capable of handling much more abstract material. Finally it is possible to teach theory and logic. Think about your math courses again. You really don't get heavy doses of algebra, trigonometry, and calculus (if that's offered) until the last couple of years of high school. It isn't actually that much more difficult, but it is much more abstract.

In the same time period, adolescent thought also shifts from more self-centered to more other-centered thinking. A seventh-grader may very well think he or she is the *only* one who has ever experienced the terrible problems of adolescence. Twelfth-graders, on the other hand, are much more aware of others. They are quite capable of recognizing human development—even as we're discussing it now—as an abstract process to which all humans are subjected all the time.

In addition, an adolescent's thinking shifts from imaginary thinking and daydreams to thought patterns more related to reality. Logical, abstract thinking ability is gained in the middle adolescent years. Box 3-1 describes one of the most widely cited theories of the development of human thinking. The theory was developed by Jean Piaget (pronounced PEE-ah-ZHAY), a Swiss psychologist, and it is based partly on observations he made as he watched his own children grow up. You can see that the four stages of cognitive development identified by Piaget fit well with our description of adolescent thinking.

As adolescents develop, their mental processes and capacities continue to mature, and they become more involved with social and community issues. For example, the cake sale here is for the benefit of the school athletic fund.

Feature   3–1   PIAGET'S STAGES

Jean Piaget proposed what some call a Stage Theory of Cognitive Development. Piaget's theory is complex, but elegant. It is based on the simple assumption that a child's meaning and understanding of adult words is *not* the same as the understanding of adults. The main intellectual limits experienced by a child are due to immaturity and lack of experience with complex operations. Piaget's Stage Theory assumes that change is continuous and the sequence of change is constant, even though the age of a child at any given stage may vary widely. Piaget was more interested in *how* a child functions intellectually than the age at which he or she does so. He suggested that a child goes through four stages, the last of which is seldom achieved until late childhood or early adolescence. The stages are as follows:

Sensory-motor stage (birth to two years). A major concept that is mastered in this stage is to develop a sense of *object permanence*. Out-of-sight-out-of-mind describes the mental process of an infant early in this stage. Older infants will search for objects that have been hidden under a pillow or blanket. They know the object continues to exist even if they can no longer see it.

Preoperational Stage (two to seven years). More and more use of symbols becomes obvious as the child masters his or her language. The child is better able to separate the symbol from the object it represents. Yet, the thinking of an infant is still self-centered—it does no good when scolding a child in this stage to ask him/her to think how another child feels. It is useless for mother to ask the child to consider how Mom feels about what the child has just done. Thinking is *centered*—it focuses on only one detail at a time. A preoperational child cannot integrate a series of events into

a broader, coherent whole. As a result, seeing Santa Claus in every department store causes most seven-year-olds very little intellectual difficulty.

Concrete Operations Stage (7-11 years). A child's skill with using and manipulating symbols continues to improve. Now children's thinking is no longer self-centered— they can imagine what *your* view of an event or object is like. They master the *conservation* principle—changing the shape of clay does not alter its weight, for example. Now the child can appreciate that a tall glass of liquid may *not* hold more than a shorter, wider glass.

Formal Operations Stage (11 to adulthood). Sometime near the start of adolescence a developing child gains the ability to think abstractly. No longer must the objects be concrete or present. Finally, the child, now adolescent, can think about thought, and education becomes much more abstract and theoretical.

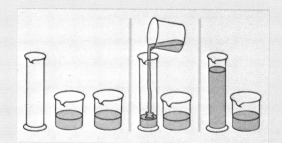

Figure 3-2 The pre-operational child (Piaget's term) is unable to imagine quantities as unchanged if their appearance is different. When asked which container has the most fluid, such a child would indicate the taller one—even after seeing it filled with an identical amount from the smaller container. According to Piaget, the child would not yet have mastered the principle of conservation.

Self-concept

Moral development. This may be called honesty, ethics, or morals, but it is a basic orientation we all must form in dealing with our fellow humans. It involves a complex series of behaviors, including reasoning, feeling or emotion, and action. At birth we are without morals and ethics, so our family is really our first source of values. As children, our moral standards differ quite a bit from those of our parents—we are rather self-centered. However, as our ability to think improves and as we gain experience in dealing with other people, our patterns of moral behavior also develop.

The most complete theory about how we develop our sense of morals is that of Lawrence Kohlberg. He suggests that there are three levels of moral reasoning, each of which has two stages—less, and more sophisticated. Box 3-2 contains a moral dilemma such as any of us might sometime face. Read the situation, and then respond to the question at the end. Be prepared to defend your decision.

According to Kohlberg, we can either agree *or* disagree with the husband's actions, but the *reasoning* we apply in defending our decision determines our level of moral development. Table 3-1 lists the six stages of moral development, along with a brief sample of the logical train of thought that would illustrate each level. Notice how the theory is not *tied* to one's age. Although development of moral reasoning does seem to be *related* to one's age, not all people achieve the highest levels of moral development. Clearly, our skill in thinking is also involved. The higher levels of moral development are much more abstract. On the other hand, the lowest levels are mainly based on whether or not one is likely to get caught!

Feature   **3–2   MAKING A MORAL JUDGMENT**

Suppose you found yourself in the following dilemma. If this were you, would you do what the husband did? Be prepared to justify your answer:

"In Europe, a woman was near death from cancer. One drug might save her, a form of radium that a druggist in the same town had recently discovered. The druggist was charging $2,000, ten times what the drug cost him to make. The sick woman's husband went to everyone he knew to borrow the money, but he could only get together about half of what it cost. He told the druggist that his wife was dying and asked him to sell it cheaper or let him pay later. But the druggist refused to bring down his price. The husband, being desperate, then broke into the man's store to steal the drug for his wife. Should the husband have done that? Why or why not?

Table 3-1 **Kohlberg's six stages of moral judgment**

LEVEL	STAGE	SAMPLE OF REASONING
PREMORAL		
	Stage 1	*Yes*: "If you let your wife die, you will get in trouble. There'll be an investigation of you and the druggist."
		No: "You shouldn't steal the drug because you'll be caught and sent to jail if you do. If you do get away with it, your conscience will bother you."
	Stage 2	*Yes*: "If you do happen to get caught, you could give the drug back, and you wouldn't get much of a sentence. You might have a short jail sentence, but you'd have your wife afterwards."
		No: "He may not get much of a jail term for stealing, but his wife will probably die before he's out, so what good will it do him?"
CONVENTIONAL		
	Stage 3	*Yes*: "No one will think you're bad if you steal the drug, but your family will think you're inhuman if you don't. If you let your wife die, you'll never be able to look anyone in the face again."
		No: "Not only the druggist, but everyone else will think you're a criminal. Afterwards you won't be able to face anybody thinking about the dishonor you've brought on your family."
	Stage 4	*Yes*: "If you have any sense of honor, you won't let your wife die just because you're afraid to do what will save her. You'd have a choice: Do your duty or forever feel guilty for not doing so."
		No: "You're desperate and you know you're doing wrong when you steal the drug. You'll know how wrong you were after you're punished and sent to jail. You'll always feel guilty for your dishonesty and lawbreaking."
PRINCIPLED		
	Stage 5	*Yes*: "You'd lose other people's respect, not gain it, if you don't steal. If you let your wife die, it would be out of fear, not out of reasoning it out. You'd lose self-respect, and probably the respect of others, too."
		No: "You'd lose your standing and respect in the community and violate the law as well. You'd lose your self-respect if you forget the long range point of view because you're carried away by emotions."

Continued on page **94**

LEVEL	STAGE	SAMPLE OF REASONING
	Stage 6	*Yes:* "If you don't steal the drug and your wife dies, you'd always condemn yourself for it. You wouldn't be blamed, but you wouldn't have lived up to your own standards of justice."
		No: "If you stole the drug, you wouldn't be blamed by other people, but you'd condemn yourself. You wouldn't have lived up to your own conscience and standards of honesty."

In review . . .

The adolescent "growth spurt" happens 18-24 months earlier for girls than boys, but both sexes grow eight and one-half to ten percent a year during the fastest period of growth. Until the onset of puberty and early adolescence, boys and girls are very similar in their motor skills and abilities. During adolescence, boys continue to grow stronger, whereas the physical strength of girls stops increasing. An adolescent's vocabulary continues to grow, and the language begins to include jargon. Thought processes become more abstract, as described by Piaget. Moral development as studied by Kohlberg also reflects a growth in feelings and sensitivity toward others.

Social development and sex roles. Many things about adolescence can make a person feel awkward. For instance, because they are so varied in size and shape, boys and girls in this age group find it difficult to get clothes that fit, just at the time when they're becoming more aware of how they look to their peers.

Think about it

The **question:** We described an incident to you at the start of the chapter. A college man visited his fraternity brother's home at Thanksgiving with hopes of meeting an attractive young woman. What he saw was a bubble-gum-blowing child. How do you explain what happened?

The **answer:** Since the girl involved has just turned fourteen, and since the narrator of the incident indicates it "happened all of a sudden," there are probably two things going on. First, the girl has only recently completed a fairly rapid adolescent "growth spurt." And, more importantly, her social skills have not matured as much as her body. The college undergraduate has made the error of equating looks with social maturity.

Certain roles have been traditional for females, such as that of cheering male athletes on to victory. Now many more girls are themselves participating actively in competitive sports events.

Consider the pressures on adolescents. In the past many males in North America seem to have had only two options: They could become what some psychologists have called the cowboy types—they must never cry, always be tough and virile, and show little affection toward girls.

And the other choice? They could become the playboy type, not getting emotionally involved—a woman in every port, a girl a week, love them and leave them. These are extremes, of course, but they point to a problem still faced by many North American males. Males are not encouraged to feel or show emotion, especially in public. Crying is taboo. The result is that many emotions—most profitably released—remain pent-up.

And for the females, until recently, the choices haven't been much more pleasant. As we've seen, from adolescence on, females *are* weaker than males physically, although social pressure and lack of physical training play a major role in this. Despite equality shown on tests of intellect, many girls have not been encouraged to develop their abilities. There has also been a long tradition that encouraged females to be exclusively homemakers. As a result, in the past many females haven't gained the education and skills necessary to be successful wage-earners. They haven't been given equal opportunities, and that has created a strange situation. Almost half of the girls surveyed in one study admitted having played "dumb" or having pretended to be inferior in the presence of boys. (We'll discuss females' fear of success further on.)

All this has been changing dramatically in the last ten to fifteen years. More and more options in education and employment have opened up to women, and along with them have come new attitudes and values. Children growing up today face a variety of choices instead of the relatively clear-cut sex roles of the past.

As an adolescent today you may find that your feelings about work and family life differ from those of your parents. Or, you may feel that nontraditional attitudes are a mistake. Compare the data compiled from polls conducted in 1970 and 1983 and consider where you, males as well as females, stand on the issue of "a woman's place."

Working or Staying at Home: A Comparison of Women's Attitudes

"If you were free to do either, would you prefer to have a job outside the home, or would you prefer to stay home and take care of your house and family?"

	Job	Stay Home
TOTAL	58%	35%
All women	45	47
Working women	58	33
Nonworking women	31	62
Working women with children	50	40
Working women without children	69	24
Women by age		
18–29	56	37
30–44	47	44
45–64	39	51
65 and over	32	63
White women	42	50
Black women	61	30
Women who are professionals and managers	63	27
Blue-collar women	43	49
Women who are teachers or nurses	50	32
Other white-collar women	65	26
Women making below $10,000	53	36
Women making $10,000–$20,000	62	32
Women making over $20,000	62	28

Source: *The New York Times* poll November 1983

WOMEN ON WOMANHOOD

"What do you think are the two or three most enjoyable things about being a woman today?"

Being a mother, raising a family
53%
26

Being a homemaker
43
8

☐ 1970
☐ 1983

Being a wife
22
6

Respect, special treatment
20
12

Career, jobs, pay
9
26

General rights and freedoms
14
32

Sources: 1970 data, Louis Harris and Associates.
1983 data, *The New York Times* poll, November 1983.

Issues: self-image and love

Adolescence is a time when a young person's self-image may be undergoing its most severe tests and revisions. Suddenly he or she begins to experience the natural processes of physical maturation. As a result, the self-image may lag behind what is physically quite obvious to everyone else. Concern with one's own body is perhaps greater during early and middle adolescence than at any other time in life.

This is when information on sex-related processes is perhaps most needed. According to a study in the early 1970s, 85 percent of adolescents want sex education to be taught in school. Roughly the same percentage place the highest level of confidence in information from that source. However, many adults still feel that this responsibility belongs to parents and the home.

Love. Letters are always pouring in to "Dear Abby" and "Ann Landers" from adolescents. The scene varies a bit, but it usually involves several of the following elements: (1) an adolescent is convinced he/she has fallen in love. (2) One (or both) parent(s) objects. (3) Marriage is being considered. (4) There is a difference in ages (or religion or something). What should the writer do? Often the issue is whether or not the two people are in love. Your parents have talked to you about love. Dear Abby has probably written for you about love. You've talked to friends—both boy and girl—about love. Maybe even a minister or your doctor has talked to you. And is there an answer? Can love—or the state (condition?) of being in love—be defined?

Yes, it can. A loving relationship—sufficient to warrant marriage—includes at least three common elements, based on surveys of many hundreds of dating/married adolescent or young adult couples. The elements are, first, *attachment*, a bond based on physical/emotional need.

Second, is the existence of *caring*. This involves a giving of oneself to others. It might even be called total altruism—a placing of the needs of another ahead of your own needs.

Third, is a linkage best called *intimacy*. It's not easy to define, but it is an intense bond between two people that may be seen in a variety of behaviors. One example is the oft-experienced fact that two people who are in love will turn to each other at the same moment and start to ask the same question or make the same observation. This is particularly striking when the question or statement may bear no immediate relation to the current environment or the ongoing situation.

There are other ways to answer the question. If you are asking yourself—in a positive sense—whether you are in love, then some would say you probably are. That's good enough for popular consumption, but it's not good science. We'll be returning to this subject in chapters dealing with emotion and social psychology.

Finally, let's return for a moment to the developmental theory of Erik Erikson that we introduced in Chapter 2. We enter puberty with the issue of industry (productivity) versus inferiority (failure) more or less resolved. The adolescent is then faced with another crisis. We spend much of adolescence—even

Being in love involves caring, attachment, and intimacy. Adolescence is a time when young people develop the capacity to feel and handle emotions leading to long-term relationships.

in our early 20's—resolving what has sometimes been called an *identity crisis*. It focuses on whether or not the adolescent is going to form a positive sense of self. The adolescent may adopt external figures—such as pop stars or groups of friends—as models for behavior. Then dissatisfaction sets in as the adolescent realizes he or she has simply taken on someone else's identity. A sense of "self" cannot be found. Goals and values may change, become less clear, or seem less attainable. Successful resolution may be difficult. Yet, in time, out of this period of "crisis" should come an adult able to respond directly and positively to the question, "Who am I?"

In review . . .

The onset of the adolescent growth spurt may affect both social opportunities and the further development of thinking skills. The adolescent becomes more subject to social pressures—on a boy to become a cowboy- or playboy-type. A girl may still experience social pressures that encourage her toward a role exclusively in the home. Falling in love is said to involve attachment, the existence of caring, and an intense interpersonal bond called intimacy. Adolescents are actively trying to form an identity for themselves.

2 Adulthood

We've spent a chapter and a half discussing just childhood and adolescence. It may strike you as strange that now we're going to do all of adult life and the elder years in half a chapter. The reasons are complex. Essentially, much more research has been done on humans in the first 20 years or so of the lifespan than on any other time period. Then, too, the "baby boom" following World War II created a large number of humans demanding services and encouraging developmental psychologists to try to understand them.

One developmental psychologist phrased the problem very nicely. She said, "Seated under the same circus tent, some of us who are child psychologists remain seated too close to the entrance and are missing much of the action that is going on in the main ring. Others of us who are gerontologists (scientists studying the aged) remain seated too close to the exit. Both groups are missing a view of the whole show."

Today the increasing number of retired senior citizens is the main reason so much more research attention is now being directed to the elderly. So the mid-lifers—adults from 20 or so to retirement—are still being relatively ignored. Yet, we do know quite a bit about them.

Body changes

Most people, if they were asked to draw a chart of human physiological development, would have their curve peak at about age 20 or 25 and drop steadily from then until death. More and more evidence is suggesting that this is not accurate. Of course, there *are* some changes that make this prediction seem true. Wrinkles do occur in the skin, the hair gradually thins out and grays, and the whole frame settles a bit as the bones become less flexible and more brittle. However, the change is not as drastic as most think it to be. From a peak between 20 and 30, the majority of organ systems undergo a general decline in their ability to function—but it amounts to a drop of only about one percent per year.

There are some other changes that may not be so obvious. In any system involving a complex function (meaning many nerve-nerve, nerve-muscle, and nerve-gland connections), there is a greater than average decline. As a person lives longer, the environment in which he or she is living has an ever greater impact on that individual. At 65 differences among people are greater than they have been since puberty—there are wide variations in the aging of various individuals. Perhaps the greatest decline is seen in the ability to react to physical or emotional stress and then return to the level of performance that existed before the stress occurred.

Aging. How is the adult's behavior influenced by the aging process? All of the senses drop somewhat in their efficiency. Most obvious, perhaps, is the gradual loss of accurate vision—reflected in the increasing use of glasses as we age. Generally, there is a decreasing awareness of the external environment, caused by the declining sensitivity of all the senses. We have mentioned that adolescent muscle strength constantly increases, peaking when a person reaches his or her 20's. But by the time a person reaches the early 40's a drop in muscle strength is already becoming obvious.

The *gradual*, but rather slight, loss of general vitality, is coupled with a very simple fact of life: the longer we live, the greater the likelihood that we will have a major accident or develop a disabling or crippling illness.

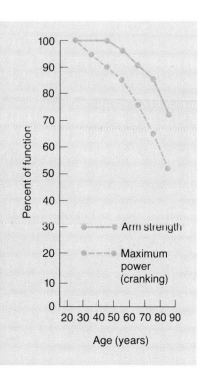

Figure 3-3 Arm muscle strength and other physical powers tend to decrease with age. An active life and exercise can often help to stem the effects of aging.

The impact of such occurrences on an individual may be dramatic. An adult may be healthy, efficient, and productive and then suddenly suffer some kind of permanently disabling accident. The seemingly steep decline in average physical ability shown in the graph may actually result from a series of drastic accidents happening to a relatively few individuals. It's a factor lurking in the statistics that is not obvious when you examine group (or average) curves.

Aged people are not valued in the modern societies of North America. Look at the advertising you see on television and in newspapers. What kind of people appear in the ads? Unless it's an advertisement for a retirement or nursing home, the models posing are almost always in their teens or 20's. Our societies have a strong bias favoring youth. We've even seen it show up in the research subjects chosen by most developmental psychologists. Yet, the times are changing. Starting back in the mid-70's, the not-so-flattering image of older people has been altered slowly. For example, older women are now permitted to be flight attendants, formerly a "youth" profession. Only by applying pressure, however, were women able to make airlines eliminate the under-26 rule long in effect.

Theories of aging. The physiological processes of aging are irreversible. No matter how hard we try to avoid it, we humans do still grow older. *Aging* is the increasing inability of our body to maintain itself and to function at levels typical of young adults.

Why does it happen? We have a number of theories, but rather few firm answers so far. Three types of explanations have been developed. One type emphasizes the combined effects of environment and heredity. Is it possible we simply wear ourselves out through use (meaning through living)? We might accumulate waste products from what we've eaten or inhaled. As these waste products accumulate—from whatever source—they may begin to hinder every normal cell function from digestion to repair.

A second set of theories focuses on the fact that our bodies are constantly manufacturing cells to replace injured or nonfunctioning parts. You see it happen if you cut your skin, scrape yourself, or break a bone. Our cells contain messages (remember the chromosomes we discussed earlier?) by which they reproduce themselves. What would happen if—in the process of making new cells—an error were introduced into the process? From that point forward cell reproduction would be flawed. Aging might just be an accumulation of such flaws over the years.

The third group of theories focuses on what we may have inherited. It is possible that among the genetic messages that combine to form each of us there is a complete life-long program of events. We do reach our peak of performance and efficiency at the time when we are capable of having children and are looking around for an opposite-sexed person with whom to start the process. Or perhaps the speed and course of our life is determined entirely by brain functions—the ultimate "pacemaker." So, we have a number of theories from which to choose. Much research remains before we'll know the answer(s).

Motor skills

The physical skills of adults logically tend to follow—as they must—the changing form and strengths of the body. That is *not* to say, however, that in all physical skills adults reach their peak during their 20's. Why not? Because there are few physical skills that involve only physical strength.

There are also environmental events that influence the physical skills of adults. *Pollution* is one source. It's known, for instance, that if you work (or play, for that matter) for long periods of time in an environment where a loud and/or constant sound is heard, your hearing may become weaker for similar sounds. And, of course, don't forget the bad effects smoking and polluted air can have on the lungs.

Another source of weakening in the adult is the normal *stress* of living. An example of physical stress is the simple act of picking up your children. The first baby is born, say, to a woman who is 25 years old. She's at her peak of health, as is her husband. Picking up a 7-pound infant is no problem. By the time that infant is three years old, a second one has probably arrived. Now the first one is perhaps 30 pounds and continuing to grow. Four years later, the woman will be 32. Her youngest child will then weigh 40-45 pounds, but children still occasionally need to be picked up. The demands on the mother get heavier, not lighter. The last time she will be able to pick up her youngest child will put a great deal of stress on her back.

It is important that you should be left with several general impressions of the effects of time. First, age does not necessarily mean a loss of all physical skills. Second, different parts of the body systems may age at very different rates—depending upon how you and the environment treat them. Finally, third, there are vast individual differences in the aging process within a given adult. You have undoubtedly known some people who were "old" at 55 and others whose views on life and skill in living you'd love to have even though they were 70 at the time.

Physical strength declines with age, but many people can perform well if they make deliberate efforts to maintain their motor skills. This runner, for example, is over 80 years old.

The human body usually achieves its peak physiological form during the 20's. From then until the mid-60's its efficiency gradually declines. Three types of theories have been proposed to explain aging. These emphasize either the combined effects of environment and heredity, or the body maintenance functions, or inherited master plans. Declining physical skills may also be caused by a variety of environmental factors.

Language development

An adult's language changes very little between age 22 and retirement. There are only two exceptions to this. (1) As a young adult achieves a profession—such as medicine—he or she will gain a new jargon (most often a technical or job-related language). (2) During the older years an adult may experience growing difficulties in locating words, but in some senses this is countered by a continuing skill in using a broader vocabulary than the younger adult might use. Maybe those years of experience with cross-word puzzles and Scrabble *do* help! Intelligence, for example, apparently shows no decline with age—although we'll discuss that issue in more detail later. Clearly, once concepts are learned, increasing *experience* in their use may more than offset minor drops in speed.

By contrast, some of the processes in which language plays a central, crucial role do change quite a bit during the adult years. Let's examine two such processes—thought and creativity.

Thought. A basic change occurs—or perhaps we should say is completed—in the nature of an adult's thinking during the early adult years. The shift from concrete to abstract thinking—begun during the adolescent years—is completed in the 20's.

The developmental psychologist Piaget notes that in later adulthood all sophisticated thought processes decrease. Formal thought as well as concrete and abstract thought return to a less mature form. Why? That's not easy to answer, but some informed guesses can be made. In later adulthood, difficulties in recalling specific information may begin. In addition, some responses have been made so many times by the elder adult that they no longer take much active controlling thought. This is what we mean when we describe an older person as being "set in his (or her) ways." Finally, in many of the day-to-day tasks of this world there really *is* little need for formal or abstract thought. It seems that lack of challenge may be a key reason

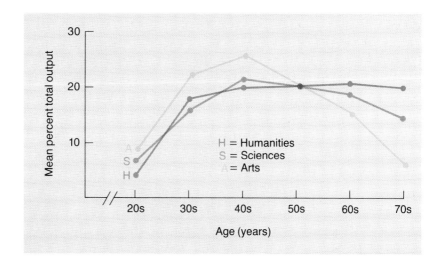

Figure 3-4 In the fields of art and science, most creative work occurs between the ages of 40-49. Work in the humanities seems to continue well into old age. Consult the text for one theory as to why this might be so. What do you think might be the reason?

why older adults no longer engage in higher forms of thought. We'll return to this matter shortly.

Creativity. An interesting alternative view can be made of the last series of conclusions about adult modes of thought. When do you suppose adults make their most creative, original contributions to society? At what age do scientists and humanitarians make their most important contribution? The answers to those questions may surprise you.

Figure 3-4 plots the percentage of total life creative productivity in ten-year intervals for artists (including painters, sculptors), scientists (including chemists, physicists, biologists, psychologists), and humanitarians (including historians). As you can see, in arts and science, the bulk of a person's creative work is done in the early years of adult life—the 30's and 40's. By contrast, in the humanities the major contributions are made in the later adult years—the 60's and even the 70's. Why?

One psychologist has developed a rather fascinating, possible explanation. Think about this: In science, math, and the arts, a person must master only a limited number of details—the principles of mathematics or the principles governing the effective blending of colors. Once these are mastered, one can start to work and make—if one is capable—major contributions. By contrast, history, for example, involves the accumulation and mastery of many, many individual details—facts, dates, and events. It takes longer to master these than the principles of a science or an art. It takes longer to think through and integrate multiple details, and thus it takes longer to develop new, creative views or opinions or theories in such disciplines. It's an interesting possibility.

The **question:** Why is it that musicians—even world-famous musicians—are able to compose their most famous pieces of music while they're quite young?

The **answer:** Composing music requires the mastery of a fairly simple set of physical principles, about which we'll learn more later on. Because the principles themselves can be mastered in a relatively short time with reasonable ease, it is possible for musicians to start applying them quickly when writing music at a young age.

Self-concept

Enumerating the tasks of adulthood would fill a book—they also fill a lifetime. From the early 20's until retirement, most humans find and adjust to a mate, start and maintain a family, manage a home, select and establish a vocation, assume a normal share of civic duties, and find a social group with whom they can relax and feel comfortable. Let's examine some of those tasks.

Emotions and marriage. Most adults get married. The decision to do so is a major one. The results affect life style and happiness, types of experiences, and more often than not the appearance of children. Marriage is most often entered into in the name of love, but are there other factors? Most definitely, yes!

As we'll discuss later in more detail, physical attraction is important. Even more important, however, is the similarity of the two people getting married. Similar ethnic, religious, and social backgrounds all blend to increase the likelihood of a stable family's being formed. To the extent that both members of the couple share interests and values, they have a common background on which to anchor their marriage. A marriage leads to changes in personal freedom, moving the participants more and more toward interdependence. There is a clashing and then a blending of life styles. Whether to squeeze the toothpaste tube from the center or squeeze-and-roll from the end is a classic example of the "battles" that may be fought.

But there are also alternative life styles that have been explored more frequently in recent years. Some people, of course, always choose to remain single; yet this is the exception, not the rule. The alternate forms of living together range widely from simply sharing a home to communal living—both extremes are favorites principally at the late adolescent and 20's age levels. Contract marriages have also been tried, as have group marriages. However, these forms are exceptional, too.

Male-female roles. Traditionally, it has been the male role to get a job and support the family. Today, the roles are changing. Females are three times as likely to have a job now as they were in 1890. The 1980's are the first decade in which more than half the work-age women, including mothers, are in the work force.

Each parent serves as a model of adult male or female behavior. Fathers contribute to the development of their sons' masculinity, aggressiveness, and sex-role behavior. Studies show that a father's absence from home—whether because of death, separation, or long work hours—can result in poorer academic performance for both boys and girls. The effects of the working mother's absence from home is a new research topic of the 1980's.

Issues: sharing and career

Returning once again to the theory of human development proposed by Erikson, we find that adults face two challenges. Having found self-identity, the young adult must make a basic decision: Will his or her adult life be shared intimately with another, or will it be spent in isolation? Erikson presents the outcome of this stage as dependent upon the successful resolution of previous challenges. An intimate—sharing, caring—relationship is likely to develop only between two mature individuals. The close bond of which we spoke earlier in discussing late adolescence can't easily be formed between immature persons, or those who have elected to lead a more isolated existence. Yet, the search for intimacy is still a somewhat self-centered process. It's shared with one other person, yes, but the search is focused on an assurance of our *own* well-being.

Mature adulthood presents yet another challenge. (If you've kept track, we've dealt with six life crises so far.) In some cases this is the most important stage of all—both for the individual and for society as a whole. Why? Well, assuming that close bonds have been established, what follows is a desire to extend the intimacy achieved. This intimacy is shared in several ways. Primarily, more attention is directed toward the establishment and maintenance of a successful career and its relationships. There is also an involvement in community affairs. Choosing between *generation* and *stagnation* provides the crisis of middle adulthood. Adults successfully meeting this seventh challenge are increasing their concern for the next generation—for their children and for other young people.

The mid-life crisis you sometimes hear about is a reflection of this crisis identified by Erikson. It is a concern for keeping in touch with the world and the times, rather than stagnating,

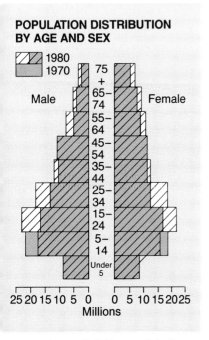

POPULATION DISTRIBUTION BY AGE AND SEX

1980
1970

Male   Female

75 +
65–74
55–64
45–54
35–44
25–34
15–24
5–14
Under 5

25 20 15 10 5 0   0 5 10 15 20 25
Millions

Source: U.S. Bureau of the Census

Figure 3-5 A larger percentage of people in our society are living to more advanced ages. Given the low birthrates of the 1970's (lowest since Depression years), the elderly will soon be exerting an increasing influence.

living on past laurels, and failing to grow. It is a challenge not easily, nor rapidly, met. If your parents are now in their 40's they may—without realizing it—be in the midst of dealing with this crisis even as you are wrestling with establishing your own personal adolescent identity.

In review . . .

Language itself changes very little during the adult years. The vocabulary may grow, but the main gains are in thinking skills. Most creative contributions depend on individual talents. Marriage is by far the most popular living style in North American societies. The major tasks of adulthood are establishing a career and maintaining a productive livelihood while building toward retirement.

3 The Elder Years

A former President of the United States voiced the challenge about as well as anyone. President Kennedy, speaking to the members of the House of Representatives in 1963, said, "Our senior citizens present this nation with increasing opportunity to draw upon their skill . . . and the opportunity to provide the respect and recognition they have earned. It is not enough for a great nation merely to have added new years to life—our objective must also be to add new life to those years."

He touched on a number of important issues related to the problems of growing old—in all North American societies. Let's review some of those problems briefly.

Between 1900 and 1950 the number of people in the United States doubled. During the same period the number of people over 65 *quadrupled!* In the years from 1970 to 1980, the median age in the United States increased from 28 to 30. Some people have taken these statistics to mean that our life span is increasing. New developments—such as modern medicine and medical techniques, greater knowledge of nutrition, and more attention to fitness and health—*are* making it possible for more people to reach old age. Fewer people die in infancy, childhood, or young and middle adulthood. Yet these developments are not substantially increasing our life span. In 1900 anyone in the United States who became 65 could expect to reach 78. Someone 65 in 1980 could expect to live to 81.4—only about a three-year increase after 80 years of progress! See Figure 3-5 for the numbers

Table 3-2 Opinions about the best/worst years of life*

| | AGE GROUP ASKED: | | | | | | | |
| | HIGH SCHOOL | | NEWLYWED | | MIDDLE-AGED | | PRERETIREMENT | |
	MEN	WOMEN	MEN	WOMEN	MEN	WOMEN	MEN	WOMEN
I What is the *best* age?								
Adolescence or the 20's	92	92	70	76	50	35	33	21
Middle age—the 40's	00	00	00	04	19	31	41	59
II What's the *worst* age?								
Adolescence	20	46	45	50	33	44	46	57
Old age	56	27	45	38	37	22	24	17

*Adapted from Lowenthal, Thrunher, Chiriboga, and Associates, 1976.

of people who live to advanced ages today. However, the fact that more and more of us are living past 65 is changing the form of our society. Some of the impact of this population shift is only now beginning to be felt.

One way to summarize attitudes toward these changes is to ask adolescents, newlyweds, middle-aged adults, and adults just prior to retirement what age they consider to be the best. Table 3-2 lists the results of such a survey. It also shows the results of a similar survey asking the same age groups to identify the worst years. The results yield some unexpected findings. Study them carefully. What conclusions can you draw? What are *your* feelings on these questions?

Body changes and physical skill

The pattern of physical change that starts even before we may notice a decline in our skills is clearly a major factor in our adjustment to retirement. However, to describe the typical case is perhaps more difficult for this age than for any since adolescence, for reasons we detailed earlier. At 65 there may be as much as a 30-year span in the apparent agedness of a person.

Think about it

The **question:** Remember the late adolescent about whom you read at the start of the chapter? How do you explain that his 71-year-old grandfather beat him at handball? Since the adolescent mentions only his grandfather's age, we can assume his physical ability was not that different from his grandson's.

The **answer:** Handball is a sport in which cunning and skill go much further than a smashing serve. What probably happened is that the grandfather just outsmarted his grandson—winning not by overpowering him, but by placing his shots smartly—that is, with skill. In this case, skill was more important than youth.

Language skills

Old age represents the only period during which there may be marked losses of language and thinking skills. More than three million elderly in the United States suffer from Alzheimer's disease, a degenerative brain disorder that affects not only speech but reasoning, memory, and time and space orientation. New research seems to indicate that the disease has a genetic origin, but many changes associated with the disease may be related to how often and how well skills were used in earlier years. Even healthy old people with superior verbal skills are unlikely to *add* new words or jargon to their speech.

Self-concept

Clearly, too, inherited characteristics can influence the quality of old age. There are a number of studies (both in the United States and Russia) that suggest we *can* live a long and happy life. These studies agree on four major factors that can help bring this about: First is maintaining a role in society. Second is having a positive self-concept and view of life. Third is having moderately good physical functions—that is, a healthy body. Finally, fourth—probably the most direct way to achieve the third goal—is to be a nonsmoker.

Issue: retirement

Aside from birth, retirement has to be one of the biggest changes we experience during our lifetime. What factors influence how successful a retirement will be? Probably one factor is more important than any other—money. Without income you lose control of your life. As an adolescent you may be experiencing that now—if you're not working or receiving an allowance, you may often stay home whether you want to or not. The same is true of retired adults, except the situation *may* be much worse because they've experienced many years of personal freedom.

One's sex is a predictor of successful retirement. Females in our society have more often than not stepped into and out of the working force more times than males. They've practiced "retiring" and tend to be better at it. For a male, it may be the first time he has ever had extended periods of time when he was responsible to no one but himself and possibly his spouse. This is changing now, since more women are choosing to follow full-time careers.

Attitude is another important factor. Some people you may have met are labeled "workaholics"—for them their job seems to be *everything.* In fact it may be, and they may be hit harder by

Drawing by Weber;
© 1977 The New Yorker Magazine, Inc.

"*I used to be old, too, but it wasn't my cup of tea.*"

Growing old gracefully can be difficult when a society is strongly influenced by its "youth culture."

Feature   **3–4   GOLDEN YEARS OR A GOLD WATCH?**

Retirement as it is usually enforced in North American societies is an expression of bias against old age. There *is* evidence—as we've reviewed in Chapters 2 and 3—that abilities change with age. Yet nothing you've read in these two chapters argues that we all become inept or demonstrably less useful at 65 . . . or 68 . . . or 70 . . . or. . . Many industries simply ignore the later-life needs of older employees, insisting upon an arbitrary retirement age. Give them a gold watch and wave good-bye.

Two types of theories have developed that try to explain what happens to bring about retirement—aside from the laws and rules we've already mentioned. One set of theories, which may be too shallow, emphasizes *disengagement*. This is retirement as controlled by the employer, often proceeding in stages. A worker will notice a change—work assignments will be shifted to younger employees. The person may even go along readily with the change, which will further speed up the shifting of responsibilities.

Other theories emphasize the person's *withdrawal*, retirement controlled by the employee. From a psychological point of view, the ease and stability of post-retirement life can be influenced by how active a person remains. Old roles and friendships are shaken when a steady job disappears. The solution, then, is to find new roles, even though one's options and abilities may become more limited.

retirement than anyone since it requires a total readjustment of living style.

Another attitude that influences the success of retirement is our attitude toward life itself. A feeling of pride in one's accomplishments will lead to a more satisfactory retirement, especially if other interests have already been developed. Remember the first of four "ways to happiness and long life." Maintaining an active role in society is a good predictor of the successful later life.

Finally, the personal history of each of us—our success in living or the lack of it—may be the best predictor of all as to the likely success of our retirement.

The final response: death

You might think that a recognition that death is near would lead those who are older to think more about it. But that is not the case. All humans—regardless of age—think about death, but there is only a very slight increase in the frequency with which older people do so. It's an awkward event to think about anyway. Huckleberry Finn imagined *his* death. Have you ever tried to imagine your own death? We tend to put ourselves in the third person at our funeral—as if we were still alive, observing!

Even defining death isn't easy. It has moral and religious implications. The courts of our land have not been able to define

Table 3-3 **Five stages in humans' emotional reactions to impending death***

STAGE	MOST OBVIOUS REACTION
I	Denial and isolation
II	Anger
III	Bargaining
IV	Depression
V	Acceptance

*Kübler-Ross, 1969.

precisely when a person is dead. Must brain waves be absent? Speech? Unaided or aided breathing? A mind? There is no easy reply, although most of the difficulties come in the gray area between life and death—both at life's start *and* at its conclusion. Interestingly, very few people who have been (or are) close to death report fearing it. Of course, the circumstances in which death will occur have something to do with those views.

Adapting to death. One of the best summaries of the stages of death was developed by a medical doctor from interviews with terminally ill patients. She suggests the existence of five stages. (See Table 3-3.) It is important to note that these stages may or may not actually exist. Some people may be going through two or three of these stages—perhaps denying it, angry about it, and bargaining—all at once. And, of course, even when a person reaches the final stage—that of accepting death—this should *not* be confused with giving up on life. Rather, people in the final stages of their life often engage in what might be called a life review. It seems to be a fairly universal process, perhaps involving a search for the meaning in one's life as much as anything. As that meaning is found, perhaps the acceptance of death does become easier.

In review . . .

The number of people living into retirement has increased markedly. Gradual physical decline continues in the elder years, but problem-solving and language skills decline more slowly. Prospects for a successful retirement can be predicted on the basis of being male or female, one's life history prior to retirement, and one's over-all attitudes. There are many different views about death—both about how to define it and what exactly it is as an experience.

Chapter Application and Review

USING PSYCHOLOGY   *Choosing a marriage partner*

There's an old saying about being "too soon old and too late smart." One of the advantages of the psychological study of life-long developmental processes is that it becomes possible to draw on the experiences of age for the benefit of youth. A big problem for most adults is having to choose a marriage partner—hopefully for the rest of their lives—while they are still in their early to mid-20's.

At some point in the life of 98 percent of us the central question becomes "To wed or not to wed?" It is a subject that has not gone unnoticed by psychological researchers. Yet the results of this research are apparently widely ignored by people having to answer that central question. Divorce rates may be going up due to society's more tolerant attitudes toward divorce or because of less strict religious stances concerning divorce. Perhaps the wider availability of child-care facilities removes concern about the children's welfare as a reason for remaining married. Finally, the fact that increasing numbers of women are joining the work force may account for added strains on some of their marriages.

Are there any bases for predicting what combination of genes, interests, family histories, and dreams will yield a successful marriage? Yes. All of the following factors are in favor of creating a longer-lasting marriage. The greater the maturity of the couple, the greater the likelihood of a successful marriage. The older the couple when they first get married, and the longer they've been dating, the greater the likelihood of a successful marriage. Having a similar ethnic, religious, and social background, more advanced education, and parents who are happily married all contribute toward a successful marriage.

How about the matter of common interests? He likes basketball, she loves soccer—will that cause problems? Common interests *have* been confirmed as supporting successful marriages. Common interests in romantic love, owning a home, having children, and religious activities all lead toward a more successful marriage. Two of the fall-outs of these shared common interests are that the successfully married couple is likely to have friends in common *and* roughly similar attitudes toward sex.

Furthermore, it is not the existence of mutual interests that is so important. It is the *types* of interests that are shared by a couple that are essential to a happy relationship. One of the most crucial "interests" in the successful marriage is the view of each partner on the proper roles for each sex. Is the woman or the man to be superior? Are the burdens to be shared equally? What are the means by which the tasks of each will be adjusted to recognize the family or career demands on the other partner?

These are the interests and views that are crucial to a successful marriage. Establishing that such views are shared by a couple does not happen overnight. Rather, it occurs gradually over months—during shared joys and sorrows, and through experiencing each other in a wide variety of settings and circumstances. Finally, perhaps the most important factor for a happy marriage is the primary motivation behind each person's desire to marry. A person should not marry simply to escape an unpleasant family situation; that can be accomplished without marrying.

Whether or not to marry is not an easy decision to make. Given the length of time to be spent in marriage, however, it is a decision that deserves much careful thought.

REVIEW QUESTIONS

SECTION 1 (pages 85–98)

1. Does the adolescent "growth spurt" begin first in boys or in girls? What effects does the widely varying onset of physical maturation have on personal development?

2. What changes in motor skills occur during adolescence in girls? In boys?

3. How does language use change in adolescence?

4. What are the stages in developing abstract thought proposed by Piaget?

5. What are Kohlberg's ideas about moral development?

6. List some of the social pressures that influence teenagers.

7. What are some characteristics of love?

8. Name one of the major tasks of adolescence.

SECTION 2 (pages 98–106)

1. When is the human body at its physiological peak? What changes take place during adulthood?

2. What are the major tasks of middle adulthood?

SECTION 3 (pages 106–110)

1. The proportion of the elderly in our population has been steadily increasing for many years. How do you explain this?

2. List some of the factors contributing to a successful retirement.

3. List some of the views about when death can be considered to have occurred. What definition of death is most acceptable to you?

ACTIVITIES

1. Have you ever had someone you know find out that he or she was soon going to die? If so, did the person show any or all of the stages suggested by Kübler-Ross? Which ones?

2. **Career Search.** Volunteer to spend some time visiting a nursing or retirement home. Offer to help with the patients there, perhaps feeding them, writing letters for them, helping them with crafts, or any other desired activity. What observations can you make about development that confirm the points made in this chapter? How does the world view of old people differ from your own? Try to get the patients to describe their childhoods, including their education and family life. How do their lives differ from yours? Which differences in their behavior as compared to yours can you attribute to different upbringing and which to different educations?

3. **Career Search.** Interview a personnel officer in an employment agency or local company. Ask whether he or she has seen much evidence of mid-career "crises" in which an apparently successful middle-aged person chooses to try something completely different. Another possibility is to discuss with your parents their views on their own careers. What is their most important goal

now? What subject(s) would they study now, if they had the opportunity, that they didn't study when they were in school? Why?

4. Career Search. If you've never done so before, and if you *are* genuinely interested, why not take some interest tests now, either through your high school counselor or school psychologist, or through a local college testing and counseling service?

5. Interview a freshman in high school. Ask how his or her life has changed since junior high school. Has this person assumed or been assigned more responsibilities at home? Is he or she given more trust by parents? Now find some students who graduated from your high school last year—perhaps one who went on to college and another who got a job. Ask them the same questions (adjusted appropriately, of course). What differences do you find in (a) the views of each person, (b) their ability to express themselves, (c) the responsibilities they now have, and (d) the rights they have gained?

INTERESTED IN MORE?

BRADBURY, W. *The Adult Years.* Time-Life Books, 1975. Richly illustrated, this is but one volume in a *Human Behavior* series. Starts with late adolescence and continues with some fascinating facts and figures bearing on the adult years. Draws data and conclusions from a wide range of social and behavioral sciences.

BUTLER, R. N. *Why Survive?: Being Old in America.* Harper & Row, 1975. Calling aging "the neglected stepchild of the human life cycle," this Pulitzer-Prize-winning author examines the plight of senior citizens. Chapters include "Houses of Death Are a Lively Business" and touch on a wide range of age-related problems, including problems of being caught between declining earning power and rising costs.

FROMM, E. *The Art of Loving.* Bantam, 1956. Asserts that love grows out of maturity, self-knowledge, and courage. Fromm discusses everything from brotherly love to the practice of love. A good exposure to psychoanalytic thought on love, written by a world-famous psychoanalyst.

HORROCKS, J. E. *The Psychology of Adolescence,* 4th ed. Houghton Mifflin, 1976. A topics approach to adolescent development, covering everything from motivation to vocational development.

HURLOCK, E. B. *Developmental Psychology,* 5th ed. McGraw-Hill, 1980. Takes a life-span developmental view of humans, devoting roughly equal space to early-, middle-, and late-life human development, also including dying and death. Discusses behavior patterns at each age.

KÜBLER-ROSS, E. *Death: The Final Stage of Growth.* Prentice-Hall, 1975. Through a collection of essays on death and dying, the author familiarizes the reader with the viewpoints of other people, cultures, religions, and philosophies.

LEVINSON, D. J. *The Seasons of a Man's Life.* Knopf, 1978. It *is* limited to a discussion of men, but this author divides the adult life cycle into a number of specific developmental transitions from the Early Adult Transition (ages 17 to 23) to the Age Fifty Transition (ages 50 to 55).

Moody, R. A., Jr. *Life After Life.* Mockingbird Books, 1975. A paperback book with a religious emphasis. Makes fascinating reading as the author uses interviews with people who experienced "clinical death" and survived.

Newman, B. M. & Newman, P. R. *Development through Life: A Psychosocial Approach,* 3rd ed. Dorsey Press, 1984. Although light on illustrations, this developmental text covers human life from procreation to burial. It includes a good cross section of the recent literature in developmental psychology.

Sheehy, G. *Passages.* Dutton, 1976. A best-selling book about various stages of human experience through adult life. The book's descriptive narration represents a popularized version of the research project reported by Levinson (see above).

Stone, L. J. & Church, J. *Childhood and Adolescence: A Psychology of the Growing Person.* Random House, 1973. Appropriate reading following either Chapter 2 or Chapter 3. Offers a life-span view of human development through the adolescent years, blending laboratory and research findings with "real-world" experiences.

Turner, J. S. & Helms, D. B. *Contemporary Adulthood,* 2nd ed. Holt, Rinehart & Winston, 1982. A well illustrated text that examines the adult years, including physical and intellectual development, family, and issues related to retirement and death. Contains a lot of tables, graphs, and essays, presenting a broad, challenging description of adulthood.

UNIT TWO

THE BASES OF BEHAVIOR

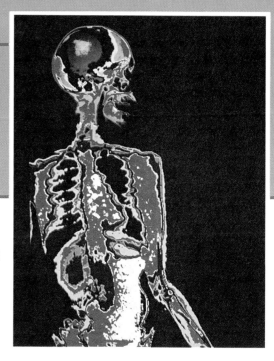

Advanced technology offers computer-enhanced scans of the body that can reveal various abnormalities once difficult to diagnose.

Now that you know how humans develop and mature, you are ready to study the physiological underpinnings of human behavior. In Chapter 4 we'll examine the nervous system, the glands, and the processes they control. We'll discuss sleep, meditation, and hypnosis, as well as the impact of drugs on the body.

In Chapter 5 we'll explore the physical characteristics of our environment—light, sound, heat, and cold—and how human receptors react to these stimuli. You will learn how vision, hearing, taste, senses of smell and touch, and several other senses create your perceptions of the world around you.

4 Physiological Processes

CHAPTER OUTLINE

WHAT'S THE ANSWER?

☐   "I went to see a lady out on old State Highway 711. It was all a big ritual. The room was sort of dark. The only light was provided by candles. She told me she had discovered a technique for telling what people were good at by feeling the bumps on their head. She said bulges projecting from the brain indicated what people were best at. She said I'd be a good dancer and that I'd be able to impress the girls because of my natural abilities." *Is the woman correct? Do bumps on the head indicate a person's abilities?*

☐   Maybe sometime you've overheard a conversation like this one: Aunt Gerda says to Uncle Bert, "Well, I'm glad she finally had that baby. The child looks beautiful! Her head is a little big, but that runs in his family. They're all smart, you know. Amy's a doctor, Jerry's a vet, and Sheila's a pharmacist. All of them in medicine."
Says Bert, "Yup!"
"But you'd expect that. They've all got large heads, and it takes that to hold all the brains you need to do such things. Big head means a smart person. You can count on it."
Says Bert, "Yup!" *Are they right? Is head size or brain size related to intelligence?*

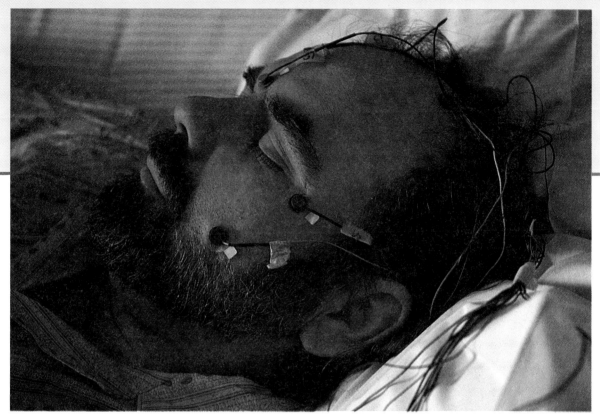

Most people spend a total of about 25 years—a third of their lives—asleep. Psychologists have long been interested in what happens in our nervous system while we sleep. Sleep research has led to tentative conclusions about the purposes of REM, or Rapid-Eye-Movement sleep.

☐ "I met a man on the street the other day who had a small gadget about the size of a pack of king-size cigarettes in his pocket. We were both waiting for the bus. I asked him what it was. He said it was attached to a sensor under his shirt and it monitored his blood pressure. He said he had already had two heart attacks. His doctor gave him the device. Every time his blood pressure gets above a certain level, the machine starts buzzing. His job is to get it to turn off again by lowering his blood pressure." *Was the man telling the truth? Is it possible to monitor and control "involuntary" responses like blood pressure?*

1 The Nervous System

As you start reading this paragraph, tell yourself not to blink your eyes. See how far you can read on this page and the next one before you have to blink. Pay attention, because if you don't think about not blinking, you'll probably do it automatically. You will see later the point we are making with this experiment.

The focus of our discussion in this chapter is the nervous system. It is the part of the body that organizes and coordinates all we think and do. Ultimately all our responses—the emotions, hunger, memories of events long past, the "instant" ability to withdraw our hand after touching a hot plate by mistake— must be explained in terms of the system of nerves, the spinal cord, and the brain. Each of these is one part of that complex whole called the nervous system.

You haven't blinked yet, have you?

As we start our study of the systems that control our behavior, we'll first examine the neurons, the basic cells of the nervous system. Then we'll look at groups of neurons called nerves—how they are organized and how they are studied. We'll examine briefly the structure of the brain itself, to determine how it directs the activities of the body. We'll also consider the glands, which introduce various hormones into our blood stream, and study sleep, one of the most fascinating activities of the nervous system. In conclusion, we'll look at practical applications of our knowledge. How can we influence our nervous system both naturally and artificially? This will lead us into a discussion of biofeedback, meditation, and hypnosis, as well as the use of drugs.

How are your eyes coming along? By this time it is probably beginning to take a great deal of active concentration on your part to keep from blinking. You are overriding a process that your nervous system normally takes care of, but it's getting harder and harder to do so. Keep at it, if you can.

Basic processes–irritation and conduction

neuron: the basic cell of the nervous system; a cell body with one or more axons and one or more dendrites

irritability: the ability of the neuron to respond to stimulation

firing: the process in which chemicals enter and leave the neuron, causing a change in its electrical charge

The simplest part of the nervous system is the individual cell called the neuron. Neurons vary greatly in size. The smallest neurons, probably located in the brain, are less than a millimeter in size. The largest neurons in the system, connecting the brain with the lower legs, may be more than a meter in length.

However, all neurons have two features in common. First, the most basic characteristic is *irritability*. In response to the proper "stimulation," all neurons will fire. *Firing* is a process by which chemicals normally kept out of the neuron are allowed

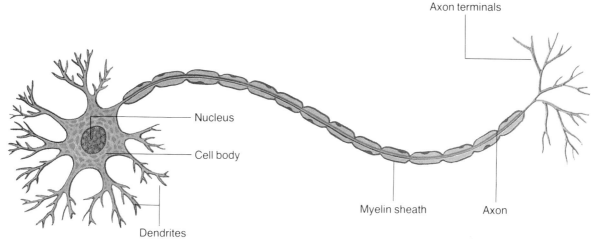

Figure 4-1 Basic features of the neuron, or nerve cell. Neurons vary greatly in size and arrangement. The photo shows an enlargement made by an electron microscope.

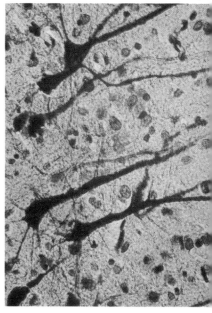

inside the cell boundaries. Likewise, chemicals normally kept within the cell are allowed to escape. The result is that the normal electrical charge (called a *resting potential*) of the neuron is greatly changed for a moment. In response to proper stimulation any neuron will fire.

The other element that all neurons have in common is *conductivity*. That is, once a neuron fires, that complex change sweeps rapidly from the point of stimulation to the farthest ends of the neuron. In a typical case, the neuron is stimulated and fires at one end. The firing impulse (called an *action potential*) is conducted in one direction only, from that end to the far end. These two processes, irritability and conductivity, are the basic life processes that all neurons share.

Have you blinked yet? Well, if not, be our guest and blink now. But remember what you've just been through. We'll talk about it later in a "Think about it" section.

Neurons

The firing process in the neuron completely exhausts its resources. Before it can fire again, the neuron must at least partially restore the resting potential. Certain chemicals must be outside, others inside, and a slight electrical charge must exist between the outside and the inside. The period during which the cell cannot fire again, regardless of how strongly it is stimulated, is called the *absolute refractory period*.

This period is like the exhaustion felt by a long-distance runner just after completing a four-minute mile. He or she would simply be too drained of reserves to attempt another race

resting potential: *the normal electrical charge of the neuron when not firing*

conductivity: *the ability of the neuron to relay impulses or stimulation from one point to another in the body*

action potential: *the reaction of the neuron to stimulation that is above threshold (the point at which it will fire)*

absolute refractory period: *the short time period after firing, during which the neuron can't fire no matter how stimulated*

immediately afterwards. However, without a great deal of rest, the runner could again run a mile—certainly not in four minutes, but he or she could run that distance again. However, with several hours rest, that same runner could run another mile in close to four minutes.

After the absolute refractory period, the recently fired neuron enters a longer phase called the *relative refractory period*. During that period the cell will fire again if stimulated, but it takes more than the usual level of stimulation to fire it. Finally, when the cell has fully recovered, it will fire again when given the same level of stimulation as it received originally. There is one big difference between the neuron and the long-distance runner. The runner takes many hours to recover, but the recently fired neuron recovers fully after only a few thousandths of a second.

If a single neuron is heavily stimulated, it can signal that fact only by firing more frequently per unit of time. It is very much like striking a match. The match, when struck, either lights or does not light. The neuron, when stimulated, either fires or does not fire. That is, it fires according to the *all-or-none principle*—completely, or not at all. Because of that, the only means by which a single neuron can signal severe stimulation is by firing more often.

relative refractory period: *the time period after firing during which a neuron can fire but only if it receives extra strong stimulation*

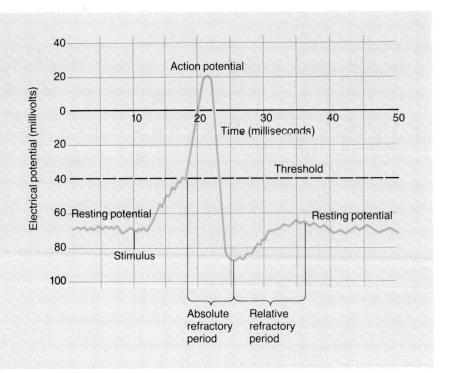

Figure 4-2 The resting potential (normal electrical charge) of a neuron remains quite constant. Any stimulus that boosts the charge above the threshold (which varies from neuron to neuron) causes the cell to fire. The firing neuron has a rapid, large, short-lived change in its electrical charge (its action potential). As the impulse passes along the axon, the change in potential would be as shown.

The junction through which impulses pass between any two neurons is called a *synapse*. When a neuron fires, the impulse usually starts in the *dendrites* of the cell. It passes from there through the cell body and then out along the *axon*. When the impulse arrives at the end of the axon, it releases a chemical, which floods into the synapse. That chemical crosses the synapse and reaches the dendrite of the next neuron. The effect of that chemical on the next cell depends on which chemical has been released. *Acetylcholine* would stimulate the next cell. Any of a number of other chemicals would inhibit the next cell, making it harder for other neurons to fire it. Any one neuron emits only one kind of chemical from its axon into the synapse.

It is perhaps easy to see that transmitting a message across the synaptic gap is the slowest part of the entire conduction process. It is a place at which drugs may influence the nervous system—helping or hindering it.

In review . . .

All cells in the nervous system share two attributes: irritability and conductivity. The neuron is the basic cell of the nervous system. After a neuron fires it enters an absolute refractory period during which it cannot be fired again. This is followed by a relative refractory period during which the neuron needs stronger stimulation than usual in order to fire. Neurons fire according to an all-or-none principle. If the stimulation is severe, they fire more rapidly. The firing of a neuron greatly changes the electrical potential within the cell. However, to stimulate another neuron a chemical must be released and cross the synapse separating one cell from another. Thus, the entire process of neuron-to-neuron conduction is a complex electrochemical reaction.

Nerves

When neurons are grouped together, they form nerves, yet the neurons still fire on an all-or-none basis. However, each neuron has a different *threshold*, or level of stimulation above which it will fire. Thus, when the impulses in one nerve are combined, much more information about the stimulus is passed on than in the firing or nonfiring of a single neuron. More severe stimulation means more neurons within the nerve are firing and each one more frequently. The more severe the stimulation, the greater the total activity within a specific nerve.

synapse: *the junction between any two neurons, through which chemicals relay messages from one neuron to the next*

dendrite: *the branched part of a neuron that carries impulses toward the cell body*

axon: *that part of a neuron through which impulses travel away from the cell body*

threshold: *the minimum level of stimulation at which a neuron will fire*

How nerves are studied. Three different procedures are used to study nerves. These are based on the electrical and chemical nature of nervous activity and on the fact that nerves can't repair themselves.

One way to study the nervous system is to stimulate neurons or nerves electrically and to observe what happens. In the past quarter century scientists have greatly improved their ability to stimulate the nervous system. In fact, they can now reach neurons buried deep within the brain. This is done by operating on an animal (or human), inserting an *electrode* into the brain, and running a very, very slight electrical charge through the electrode. Reaching certain areas of the brain in this way can cause an animal to overeat to the point of death, or to stop eating completely and thus starve. One of the classic demonstrations of electrical stimulation of the nervous system was conducted by José Delgado, as shown in the illustration. We will discuss the behaviors controlled by various parts of the nervous system more fully later in this chapter.

A second way of stimulating the nervous system is through chemical implants called *chemtrodes*. Both electrodes and chemtrodes are of similar size. Both are anchored to the animal's skull so they won't move around after being implanted.

A bull charging directly toward Dr. José Delgado was stopped in his tracks by a radio transmitter held in Delgado's hand. This activated a receiver attached to the head of the bull. Stimulation delivered through an electrode implanted in the bull's hypothalamus caused the dramatic change in his behavior.

However, whereas the electrode is solid, the chemtrode is a hollow tube which permits very small amounts of a chemical to be delivered to a precise point in the brain. It is well known that chemical factors in the blood determine many things, including how hungry and how thirsty we feel. The precise role of chemicals in the nervous system and body chemistry has been investigated using processes of chemical stimulation.

Both of these techniques of stimulation involve very little, if any, damage to the nervous system as a whole. Except for the direct result of the extra stimulation, the normal behavior of the human or animal isn't changed.

A third, more severe method of studying our nervous system involves a process called *lesioning*. This means that a portion of the nervous system is cut or somehow destroyed. For obvious reasons such research is not usually conducted on humans, but we can study humans who have somehow damaged their brains. War injuries, as well as accidents, have produced a large number of humans with various portions of their nervous system or brain destroyed. One famous accident is described in Box 4-1.

lesioning: *cutting or otherwise destroying a part of the nervous system (particularly the brain)*

Feature   **4–1   PHINEAS GAGE**

Phineas Gage, a railroad worker in Ireland during the middle of the 19th century, was a man who made medical history.

Phineas had a job tamping sand around dynamite in drill holes at a construction site. When Phineas was tamping in a charge one morning the dynamite blew up. The tamping iron was forced upward toward Phineas, who was leaning over the hole at the time. The iron entered Phineas' head at about the center of his left cheek just above his left molar teeth. It forced itself up through his head and brain, and it exited from his skull about halfway between his right ear and the center top of his head.

And how was medical history related to that event? Well, in at least two ways. First, Phineas survived. Second, once he recovered, the easygoing, reliable Phineas became the unpredictable, immature, hard-swearing party-goer of the Irish railroad. The tamping iron had destroyed a significant part of the frontal lobe of Phineas' brain, the importance of which is discussed in the brain section of this chapter. His normal living skills—breathing, talking, thinking, eating, and moving about—had not been altered at all. However, it did have substantial effects on his basic personality. Although he did it in an unusual manner, that morning Phineas simply lesioned part of his brain.

Injuries during World War II also yielded knowledge about the brain. A number of soldiers returned with a variety of language difficulties—in understanding or in speaking. It was discovered that most of these soldiers had head injuries. Using x-rays, it was possible to identify two areas of the brain that were always involved when brain injuries caused language problems.

So Phineas Gage was a prophet—100 years ahead of his time.

Tragic as such accidents are, they do at least provide the opportunity to study the behavior of those people who have lived through them. This helps psychologists determine what portions of the brain and nervous system control normal responses. In this way, the areas of the brain that control speech, vision, and a variety of other skills have been identified.

These three techniques—stimulation, either electrical or chemical, and lesioning—all involve actively altering the nervous system in some manner. Another method of study, based on the electrical nature of neuronal activity, requires no such alterations. Using a machine called an electroencephalograph (or more simply, an EEG) it is possible to measure the normal electrical activity of the nervous system. Electrical impulses occur in regular patterns, which change according to the state of the organism. For example, a sleeping human shows a very different pattern of nervous system activity from that of the alert, wide-awake organism. Various EEG patterns are discussed more fully later in this chapter.

These cycles of electrical activity are frequently called "brain waves." In reality they are simply the recording of the changes in electrical activity in the nervous system as the organism performs different acts.

Organization in the nervous system

The nervous system is a complex communications network, controlling the body's internal environment as well as its responses to the world around it. How does this most important system work?

The processes of our nervous system are set in motion by stimuli from the *receptors*. Receptors are a variety of cells—ranging from cells in the eye for vision to cells in the foot for touch and pain. They react to certain aspects of the physical environment. For example, when a mosquito bites you, it is a receptor that detects the bite. (Receptors are discussed in detail in the next chapter, Chapter 5: Sensation and Perception.)

Control of the body is achieved through the *effectors*, muscles or glands to which the nervous system connects. The glands secrete hormones that influence the body's internal environment. Muscles usually respond by action. In our example, it would be the effectors that slap the mosquito.

How are messages carried from receptors to effectors? Basically, three types of neurons are involved: (1) There are *afferent* cells, which conduct nerve impulses from the receptors toward the brain or spinal cord. These are the points in the body where

receptors: *a variety of cells that react to stimuli in the environment (touch, sight)*

effectors: *muscles or glands to which the nervous system connects*

afferent neurons: *cells that conduct nerve impulses from the receptors toward the brain or spinal column*

a decision (voluntary or involuntary) is made as to what the response should be. (2) There are the *internuncial*, or *associative*, neurons (more about these later), which are responsible for many things, including what we commonly call thought. These carry information within the system. Finally, (3) there are the *efferent* cells, which conduct nerve impulses from the decision points to the effectors. Thus, the nervous system—composed of afferent, associative, and efferent neurons—is a network of neurons connecting the receptors with the effectors.

internuncial (associative) neurons: *cells that transfer incoming messages to outgoing neurons*

efferent neurons: *cells that conduct nerve impulses from the brain or spinal cord to the muscles or glands*

If we classify the nervous system on the basis of the location of its parts, the division is quite easy. (See drawing.) The *central nervous system* includes the brain and spinal cord (the portion of the nervous system encased in the backbone). It is the decision-maker. The *peripheral nervous system* is everything else. This includes all afferent nerves bringing messages in to the spinal cord from the receptors as well as the efferent nerves leaving the spinal cord for various organs or muscle groups. It is a relay system.

The peripheral nervous system can also be divided into two groups of nerves on the basis of the function they serve. The *somatic* nervous system controls voluntary muscles and movement. The *autonomic* nervous system controls the glands and organs of the body.

Is that all? Well, no. There's one more division we need to consider. The autonomic nervous system is composed of the *sympathetic* nervous system and the *parasympathetic* nervous system. Both of these systems have connections to the same organs and glands, but for very different—yet related—purposes.

Basically, your *sympathetic* nervous system becomes active when you are in danger or are about to engage in something like an athletic contest. Heart beat increases, digestive processes slow down, and blood flow is increased to the muscles. You are ready for extreme physical exertion—whether that be running away from an enemy, catching the game-winning pass, or what-have-you. Thus, the sympathetic nervous system is focused on using body resources, particularly in times of need.

The *parasympathetic* nervous system is connected to the same organs as is the sympathetic nervous system, but activity of the parasympathetic system has very different effects. It slows the heartbeat, increases the digestive processes, and diverts blood from the muscles toward the stomach and intestines. The parasympathetic system tends to restore body resources in preparation for the next event. Activity of each of these nervous systems has essentially opposite effects. However, together the parasympathetic and sympathetic nervous systems precisely control the organs and chemical balance in the body.

Figure 4-3

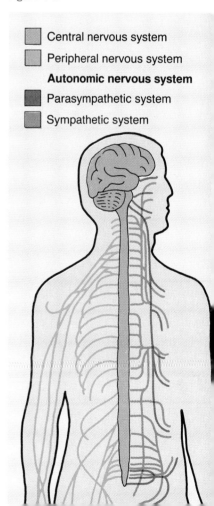

■ Central nervous system

■ Peripheral nervous system

Autonomic nervous system

■ Parasympathetic system

■ Sympathetic system

In review . . .

A nerve is composed of many neurons, and the nervous system is a complex communications network of neurons, activated by receptors. Afferent neurons carry messages toward higher levels in the central nervous system. Internuncial (associative) neurons carry information within the system at any given level. Efferent neurons conduct messages from the central nervous system toward the effectors, which are muscles or glands.

The nervous system can be divided into the central nervous system (brain and spinal cord) and the peripheral nervous system. The peripheral nervous system is composed of the somatic nervous system (controls voluntary muscles) and the autonomic nervous system. Organs and glands are controlled by both the sympathetic and parasympathetic nervous systems, which are subdivisions of the autonomic nervous system. The sympathetic nervous system expends body resources and gets the organism ready to fight or flee. The parasympathetic nervous system restores body resources in preparation for actions to come.

central nervous system: *the brain and spinal cord*

peripheral nervous systems: all neurons in all systems other than those in the brain and spinal cord

somatic nervous systems: *the system responsible for bodily sensation and movement*

autonomic nervous system: *the system controlling the glands and organs*

sympathetic nervous system: *the system that prepares body resources (organs and glands) for strenuous action*

parasympathetic nervous systems: *the system that conserves energy and restores resources after strenuous action*

The brain

Having discussed the message delivery system—the peripheral nervous system—let's now look at the decision-making apparatus: the spinal cord and brain. In simple animals, it's possible that as few as three neurons (afferent, associative, and efferent) may be involved in responding to stimuli from the environment. However, for even the simplest responses in humans, the story is much more complex.

Take the knee-jerk reflex as an example. A tap on the knee activates many afferent neurons. Through them and the afferent

Figure 4-4 These are the areas of the head that were of interest to the phrenologist G. Spurzheim. He associated the regions of the brain underneath these surface areas with specific functions and human abilities.

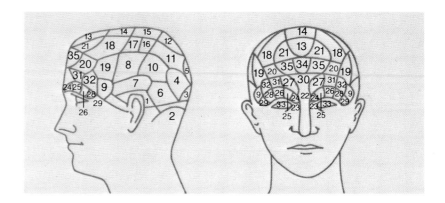

neurons with which they interconnect, the stimulation reaches the lower portion of the spinal cord. There little processing is involved. Through very few associative neurons, the incoming message is transferred to efferent, or outgoing, neurons. These connect to the effectors, in this case muscles in the leg, and your leg kicks out almost immediately. Very few sensory stimuli in humans are processed that rapidly and converted so assuredly into a particular reaction.

In fact, sensory messages are usually relayed to the spinal cord and up to the brain, where active processing is involved before any action takes place. Psychologists have long recognized the importance of the brain in most human decision-making—both voluntary and involuntary. Even before psychology became a formal science, the importance of the head had been recognized, although incorrectly. In the early 1800's the *phrenologists* thought that lumps on the head indicated that a person had unusual ability in skills controlled by the area of the brain under the lump. The "Think about it" that follows describes the assumptions made by phrenologists and how they turned out.

Think about it

The **question**: Do lumps on the head indicate a person's abilities? Is there *any* relation between parts of the brain and specific talents or functions?

The **answer**: Early in the 19th century Franz Joseph Gall (1758-1828) and later G. Spurzheim (1776-1832) developed a process called *phrenology*, to study the mind and its functions. The phrenologists asserted that bumps in the outer skull covered enlargements of the brain beneath them, as shown in the drawing. It was further stated that enlargements in specific areas of the brain meant a person excelled in the abilities controlled by that area.

As it turned out, swellings on the outside of the brain were not directly related to the shape of the outer surface of the skull. Neither could it be proven that enlargement of an area in the brain meant improved capabilities of whatever function was controlled by that area. The phrenologists' assumption that specific body functions are controlled by specific areas of the brain seems to be generally correct for certain skills. Evidence regarding this last point is still being sought and examined. The phrenologists had some interesting ideas about the lumps on your head, but subsequent research did not confirm their theories.

However, we should note that some ideas of the phrenologists were not entirely out of place. Evidence shows that certain body functions are controlled by specific areas of the brain in both humans and animals. All animals require nervous systems that can cope with the same basic physical demands. Thus, all animals are capable of eating, drinking, and moving about without losing their balance. To a lesser extent such processes as sleeping and reproduction are similarly controlled.

What distinguishes humans from other (lower) organisms is not the specific areas of the human brain, but rather the relative development of these specific areas. In humans, as in most animals, the brain is a large group of neurons and nerves in one part of the body. The human brain includes some 10 billion neurons. Yet, it can be divided into a number of areas that are easy to identify. Each controls different responses of the total organism.

The brain is composed of three principal sections: *hindbrain, midbrain,* and *forebrain,* with the hindbrain being closest to the spinal cord. Part of the hindbrain, at the top of the spinal cord, forms the lower part of an area called the *brain stem.* The brain stem relays afferent messages from many of the sensory organs to higher levels in the brain. It also relays efferent messages from those levels to the effectors.

> ## Think about it

The **question**: Aunt Gerda was talking to Uncle Bert about the children of one set of parents. She concluded from her quick analysis that big heads meant smart people. Was she right? How about brain size? Is brain size related to intelligence?

The **answer**: The answer to the first question is no, but the answer to the second question is maybe. As you read, even 150 years ago the phrenologists tried to demonstrate that head size was directly related to intelligence or ability in some direct way. The evidence argues heavily against this idea.

However, during the 1960's it was found that the size of rat and mice brains is related to the kind of environment in which they are raised. The brains of rats raised alone in standard wire-mesh cages were smaller than those of rats raised in an enclosed natural environment that included other rats.

The cortex of the enriched-environment rats grew about five percent more than the rest of the brain. In addition, the cell body of the neurons grew 13-14 percent larger and the number of *glial* cells (which nourish the neurons) increased about 14 percent. Both of these factors probably indicate increased nervous system activity. So we answer with a maybe. Bigger heads do not mean smarter animals or people. But animals with a more enriched environment seem to create larger (not more) neurons and have at least a slightly enlarged cortex. Of course, it is much too early to conclude from this that an enriched environment leads to a larger human brain. That possibility is now being studied by scientists.

The hindbrain performs a number of reflex actions, including such responses as blinking the eyes. In addition, some of the most basic processes of the body, such as breathing and heart rate, are controlled in the brain stem. Another part of the hindbrain, not in the direct line of communication from the

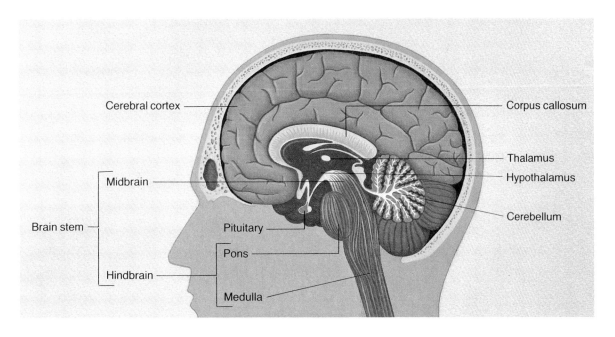

Figure 4-5 The human brain with the left half removed. The *brain stem* is composed of the *medulla* and *pons* of the hindbrain plus the midbrain.

spinal cord to the forebrain, is the *cerebellum*. One of the main tasks of the cerebellum is controlling posture, balance, and the muscle tone of voluntary muscles all over the body.

The *midbrain* is located just above the hindbrain, forming the upper part of the brain stem. Like the hindbrain, it also serves to relay both afferent and efferent messages. The *midbrain* performs some of the same kind of reflex responses that are controlled by the hindbrain. However, the midbrain also controls more complex responses such as walking.

Immediately above the midbrain is the *forebrain*, and it is the most complex and the biggest part of the human brain. It is composed of three parts. The first of these, the *thalamus*, is the last relay station through which afferent messages will pass. It serves as a major "switching point." Messages from all the senses except that of smell are relayed from here directly to a specific area of the highest part of the forebrain, the *cortex*.

A second portion of the forebrain is the *limbic system*, of which the most important part is the *hypothalamus*. The hypothalamus itself has been found to be involved in a huge variety of complex human processes. Many of its activities are unconscious and automatic. It is liberally laced with blood vessels so that it is able to monitor the state of the body by monitoring the blood. The hypothalamus controls eating, drinking, and certain sexual activities as well as more fully automatic adjustments such as temperature.

Through the autonomic nervous system, to which it is directly connected, the hypothalamus controls the operations of the body's organs. Electrical stimulation of the hypothalamus can cause a hungry animal to stop eating, a full animal to continue eating, and a variety of other surprising responses.

Although it oversimplifies things a bit, we can say that the brain stem, thalamus, and hypothalamus are the highest points in the brain at which reflex or automatic responses are controlled. As we move from the spinal cord to the forebrain, we move from areas controlling automatic responses to those controlling more complex, voluntary responses.

> ### Think about it

The **question**: At the beginning of the chapter we asked you to keep from blinking for as long as you could. If you kept this in mind as you read, you probably found you could go for quite some time without blinking. However, the longer you went, the more attention you had to devote to the effort. Since blinking is one of many things you do without thinking about it, how were you able to override that process? What parts of the brain were involved in that process of voluntarily controlling what is usually involuntary and automatic?

The **answer**: We must vastly oversimplify the operation of the brain in order to answer this question. The eyeblink is normally controlled by the hindbrain. It requires no conscious or voluntary thought by any higher portion of the mid- or forebrain. However, a voluntary override of that process can be accomplished by a decision made in the frontal cortex. As the eyes become more and more dry and as dust particles start to bother them, these signals are received in the sensory area at the front of the parietal lobe. As long as the efferent (downward) motor messages from the motor area at the rear of the frontal lobe are blocked by the frontal cortex, you should be able to keep from blinking. But, the moment you don't pay close attention, the automatic response (initiated by the hindbrain) will cause your eyes to blink.

The third and most complex part of the forebrain is the cortex itself. Areas within the cortex are called *lobes*. There are four lobes, three of which are separated by deep valleys, or *fissures*. (See illustration.) The *frontal lobe* is found, as you might guess, at the front of the brain. The back of the frontal lobe contains the motor cortex, which controls body movement. During brain surgery, stimulating this part of the brain may cause involuntary bodily movements.

To the sides of the frontal lobe are the areas of the brain controlling speech. The front of the frontal lobe seems to be used mainly for abstract mental activity. Lesioning large parts of the frontal lobes seems to have little effect on bodily function. However, it may seriously alter more subtle thought processes. (Remember Phineas Gage?)

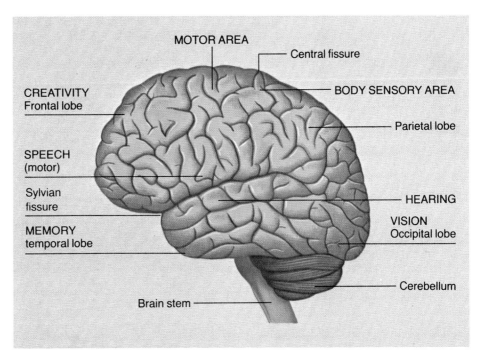

MOTOR AREA

Central fissure

CREATIVITY
Frontal lobe

BODY SENSORY AREA

Parietal lobe

SPEECH
(motor)

Sylvian
fissure

HEARING

VISION
Occipital lobe

MEMORY
temporal lobe

Cerebellum

Brain stem

Figure 4-6 The human brain viewed from the left side. Functions of the different areas are indicated.

The back of the cortex is the center for vision, while the side (separated from the rest by a fissure) is mainly concerned with hearing. The remaining lobe receives messages from the skin receptors and from sensors in the muscles and joints.

When you examine a complete human brain, you note right away that it is composed of two apparently equal halves. These halves are called *hemispheres*. While they look alike, they have some interesting differences in function.

Events that occur to the left side of the body—a pin prick, a feeling of heat or cold—stimulate the right cortex. Events on the right side stimulate the left cortex. Yet, in vision we don't see two different worlds, we see one image. This blending is done by associative, or internuncial, neurons that connect the two hemispheres mainly through something called the *corpus callosum.*

Both monkeys and some humans have had their corpus callosum (and in some cases also connections even deeper down in the nervous system) cut through completely. Thus, the left hemisphere could no longer communicate with the right hemisphere. Some truly amazing results were then obtained, as described in Box 4-2. There can be a lot of truth in the saying that the right hand doesn't know what the left is doing! The corpus callosum insures that each is informed of the other—otherwise you wouldn't be able to clap your hands.

"Foster here is the left side of my brain, and Mr. Hoagland is the right side of my brain."

Feature   4–2   THE SPLIT BRAIN

Since the early 1940's there has been much work on how thinking is influenced when the corpus callosum is cut to create a "split brain." The left half controls language for 92 percent of all right-handed people, but also for 69 percent of left-handers. Thought in this hemisphere follows in a logical way from problem to solution. The right half tends to function much more abstractly, but not always in a logical sequence. This hemisphere coordinates motor behavior and artistic (painting or music) efforts.

Severing the brain's corpus callosum separates the right and left halves and prevents communication between them. However, under normal circumstances that lesion does not alter behavior. To detect what changes may occur, one psychologist asked persons who had undergone the split-brain operation to focus their eyes on a spot. Then he flashed a red or green light in the left visual field. This was received by the right part of the retina (as described in Chapter 5) and relayed to the right hemisphere. The subject was asked to *say* which color had been flashed. But, *language* is controlled by the left hemisphere—the one that did not see the light. So what happened?

Most of the subjects guessed wrong. However, if allowed more tries, they got better and better at correcting themselves. Following an error the subject would frown and shake his or her head—motor actions controlled by the right hemisphere. Then the subject would correct the error!

The left half of the brain that was trying to guess by using language was separated from the half that knew the answer. So the right half, not having control of language, used a motor response (head-shaking and shoulder-shrugging) to signal that an error had been made. A fascinating demonstration of the different capabilities of the left and right hemispheres.

In review . . .

The central nervous system is composed of the spinal cord and brain. The spinal cord controls the simplest reflexes, but serves mainly as a message carrier between the peripheral nervous system and the brain. The brain is composed of three parts: hindbrain, midbrain, and forebrain. Responses controlled at each higher level in the central nervous system become more and more complex, less fully automatic, and involve larger amounts of coordinated, voluntary muscle activity. The forebrain includes the thalamus, the limbic system, and the cortex. Most complex sensory-motor reactions are controlled by the cortex, which is also the seat of thought, memory, and language. The cortex is split into two hemispheres, with each hemisphere controlling responses on the opposite side of the body. The halves can work together on complex activities because connections are made through the corpus callosum (and through other lower-level connections).

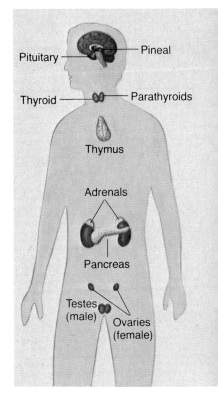

Figure 4-7 The endocrine glands of the human male and female.

2 Glands

Besides the workings of the nervous system, there is another set of processes that affect our behavior. These are the functions of the glands, both exocrine (ducted) and endocrine (ductless).

Exocrine (ducted) glands. The ducted glands produce many different products, including sweat, saliva, and tears, as well as sperm and eggs. They secrete into a duct which carries their product either to the skin (e.g., sweat) or to an internal cavity (e.g., saliva). These glands are not of much interest to psychologists. They tend to be influenced by behavior (when you eat, you salivate), but they do not tend to alter behavior.

Endocrine (ductless) glands. The ductless glands produce hormones which are secreted directly into the bloodstream. They may affect an organ or another endocrine gland, or they may directly influence behavior. These glands secrete hormones upon being stimulated by other hormones or by the nervous system.

There are eight endocrine glands, two of which (pituitary and adrenal) have two parts. All the other endocrine glands are controlled by the pituitary, often called the master gland. The pituitary is controlled to some extent by chemicals released by the hypothalamus. As a master gland it secretes a number of

exocrine (ducted) glands: *glands producing secretions (sweat, tears, etc.) that can influence behavior but don't tend to alter it*

endocrine (ductless) glands: *glands producing hormones that affect organs and other glands, or directly influence behavior*

hormones that influence the glands and organs. Control of the
pituitary gland by the hypothalamus makes good sense, since
the hypothalamus itself responds to chemicals within the blood
stream. So, monitoring the blood chemistry, the hypothalamus
can directly stimulate the pituitary gland through neural connections and hormonal influence. The pituitary stimulates the
other glands.

Men and women have all these glands in common save one
pair, as shown in Figure 4-7. Men have testes, which produce the
male sex hormone, while women have ovaries, which produce
hormones related to female sexual characteristics. Both these
glands (collectively called gonads) respond to *gonadotropin*, a
hormone released by the pituitary gland.

As already noted, three systems—the nervous system, the
glands, and the muscles—are the major factors responsible for
the ways humans and animals react. Psychologists usually do
not study the muscles since they are simply effectors responding
to the nervous system. Thus, from a psychological point of view,
understanding the nervous system and glands is enough to explain the physiological bases of behavior.

3 Sleep

Sleep is one of the most fascinating of all human behaviors.
The average American is actively engaged in sleep—full-time,
doing nothing else—for 20 to 25 years of his or her total lifetime.
Sleep research attempts to relate nervous system activity to
what happens during sleep.

Remember the EEG, or electroencephalograph, that we discussed earlier? That machine is the most important guide to our
understanding of sleep. By attaching the EEG electrodes to the
human scalp, it is possible to record the electrical activity of a
large number of neurons in the brain beneath. These EEG recordings show that cells tend to fire more or less together in the
alert, awake human. The electrical activity, therefore, appears as
"waves" of activity, or cycles of increasing and then decreasing
neuronal firings. The cycles occur very rapidly—as many as 8-12
cycles per second and more when the person is awake.

However, if we continue to record the brain's electrical activity as the person goes to sleep, we find activity in the brain
begins to change. In fact, if we examine the EEG records of
someone going from fully awake to deep sleep, we find four
stages through which we all pass.(See illustration.)

It turns out that a very regular 90 minute cycle of electrical
activity exists throughout the night. We drop fairly rapidly to
Stage Four, the stage of deepest sleep. However, we seem to

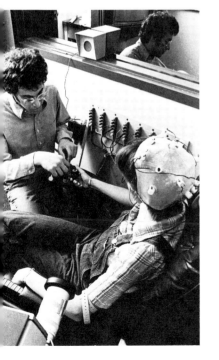

Electrical sensors attached to the skull measure the electrical activity of the brain. The electroencephalograph (EEG) measures very small changes in the electripotential of neurons near the sensor. For a normally alert and wide-awake subject, very high frequency waves are the typical pattern.

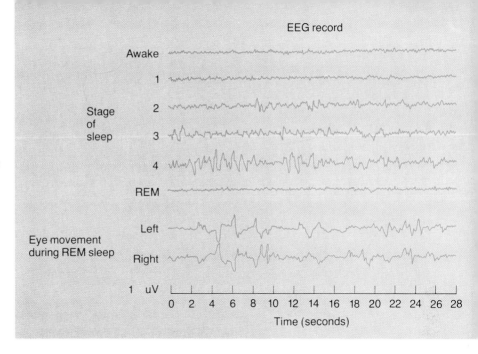

Figure 4-8 Measurement of EEG wave patterns at four stages of sleep, as well as during REM sleep, shows very regular changes. During REM sleep the EEG patterns appear as though the person were awake even though the person is hardest to awaken at that time.

climb out of it into a modified version of Stage One sleep, a fifth stage called *paradoxical sleep*. The EEG record in paradoxical sleep appears as though the subjects were awake, yet they are as difficult to awaken as someone whose EEG record indicates they are in Stage Four sleep.

Someone noticed that during paradoxical sleep subjects' eyes seemed to be moving—almost as if they were open and the subject were looking around. It was soon discovered that these *Rapid Eye Movements* (more simply called REMs) occur at a particular time. What happens if you awaken subjects who are showing REMs and whose EEG records indicate they are in this paradoxical sleep? About 70 percent of the time they will report that they have been dreaming.

This was an important discovery! All sorts of questions pop to mind. Does everyone dream? It turns out that yes, just about everyone dreams. Typically, those who report they never dream have a problem *remembering* that they dreamed. If such people are awakened when they are showing REMs, they too will usually report that they have been dreaming.

Well, then, how important is dreaming? What would happen if we woke people every time they started showing REMS, to prevent them from dreaming? People who are deprived of REM sleep become more short-tempered, more distractable, and less able to concentrate on their everyday responsibilities. In addition, after such people are no longer being awakened when they show REMs, they engage in much more REM sleep than usual. This *rebound effect* suggests that they are making up for lost time or, more precisely, making up for lost REM sleep.

REM sleep (paradoxical sleep): *a stage of sleep in which rapid eye movements indicate that the person is dreaming*

Think about it

The **question:** Is it possible to monitor and control "involuntary" responses like blood pressure?

The **answer:** It is becoming increasingly clear that some responses earlier thought to be involuntary can be actually modified, if not fully controlled. The first use of biofeedback techniques to help someone control involuntary responses involved controlling heartbeat and blood pressure. Early worries have been largely dispelled that other responses (such as breathing or muscle tension) might have been altered, indirectly effecting a change in heart functioning.

Whether or not a heart can be directly controlled is really just a technicality. To the person with high blood pressure, any device that warns him or her when the blood pressure is increasing may assist that person in altering behavior to reduce the demands on the heart. It isn't the direct control, but the necessary effect—less demand on the heart—that counts.

Meditation, such as that practiced in several Far Eastern religions, produces physiological changes. Alpha waves noticeably increase. In research studies done in the United States, some subjects have been able to achieve the same effects when monitoring their own brain wave patterns on the electroencephalograph.

Meditation. The study of consciousness has received much attention in recent years. Consciousness is a concept that is not easy to define. You and I are aware of ourselves. We are aware of our ability to think and experience. That awareness is defined by many as consciousness.

Meditation, a type of deep, concentrated thought, is related to consciousness and focuses on some of these problems. For example, many societies (including our own) offer means by which to "expand" consciousness. There is a marked similarity in the means by which this may be achieved in societies otherwise dissimilar.

In Zen meditation one question (called a *koan*) serves as a point of focused concentration, sometimes over a period of years. Yoga uses one word (called the *mantra*), which is said time and again in the early stages of meditation. This word has or gains great personal meaning. A third kind of meditation has the participant direct his or her attention to an object (called a *mandala*).

It is not easy to define when a meditative state of "higher consciousness" is achieved. All approaches use the same method: they limit the awareness of body feeling and the environment to a single object or concept. Meditation is an altered state of consciousness exactly because of this narrowed attention. However, it is a naturally altered state, requiring nothing more than the will to achieve it.

Earlier in our study of the EEG wave patterns we learned that the alpha wave pattern occurs when the subject is awake, but resting calmly with eyes closed. It has been found that people in meditation often show the alpha wave pattern with their eyes open or shut. This is impossible for the nonmeditator to achieve. Clearly, those who are meditating have their attention so focused that they don't notice anything else. By measuring a number of physiological processes while someone is meditating, it has been possible to study the differences produced during sleep, meditation, and hypnosis. Such comparisons are shown more fully in Table 4-1.

Again, as was true of biofeedback, meditation is of much interest to modern-day psychologists. Meditation seems to allow a person to be aware of stressful situations, yet to control their damaging impact on the body. It also increases the apparent ability of people to "tune-out" nonrelevant perceptions.

meditation: *a state of deep, concentrated thought that aims to expand human consciousness*

Table 4-1 **Comparison of changes in several physiological functions during meditation, sleep, and hypnosis**

PHYSIOLOGICAL MEASURE	MEDITATION	SLEEP	HYPNOSIS
Oxygen consumption	Mixed evidence of a drop	Drops half as much as in meditation, but takes 4 hours or more to do so	No noticeable change from waking state
Carbon dioxide in blood stream	No noticeable change from waking state	Increases	Depends on the suggested state
Rate of respiration	No noticeable change from waking state	Decreases	Depends on the suggested state
Metabolic rate	Decreases	Remains constant	No noticeable change
EEG wave patterns	Alpha waves predominate	No alpha waves	No noticeable change from waking state
Electrical skin resistance	Large increase at a rapid rate	Small increase (half that found in meditative state) at a slow rate of change	Depends on the suggested state
Heart beat	No change or slight increase		Depends on the suggested state
Blood pressure	No change from waking state	Drop	Depends on the suggested state

What happens to the physiology of a meditator? Two psychologists in the early 70's studied 36 people experienced with transcendental meditation, a variety of yoga. Oxygen consumption, carbon dioxide elimination, blood pressure, temperature, skin conductivity, and other functions were measured before, during, and after meditation. During meditation oxygen consumption dropped 16 percent, while carbon dioxide elimination dropped almost 15 percent below pre- and post-meditation levels. Both the rate and volume of breathing dropped about 22 percent, suggesting that basic body metabolism had been slowed.

More recent summaries of research conducted during the late 70's and early 80's contradict these findings. Although meditation is well accepted, there is scant evidence that it effectively reduces somatic (body) arousal any more than simple resting. Learning the actual physiological effects of meditation is important, since it is used both personally and professionally.

How does the physiology of the meditating human compare with that of the other two naturally modified states, hypnosis and sleep? (See Table 4-1.) Generally speaking, the body functions of people under hypnosis measure the same as if the subjects were actually performing the suggested action or thought while they were awake. There is little physiological similarity between the three states.

Hypnosis.   Hypnosis is a third natural means of altering the normal state of consciousness. Is there a separate, identifiable hypnotic state? Can people who are hypnotized be made to do things against their will or against the law? Are superhuman feats possible when hypnotized? Can people actually be made to forget that certain things have happened? Can they be made to do things after they have been hypnotized—things of which they are not even aware? Such questions have formed the basis for many studies of hypnosis. These studies, especially when considered along with recent studies of meditation, are beginning to give some answers.

Experiments have shown, for instance, that hypnosis works equally well with men or women and that even a five-year-old can be hypnotized. They have also confirmed that people vary widely in the ease with which they can be put under. People with unusually high powers of concentration are easiest to hypnotize. They are able to focus their attention on a book, their own thoughts, or even the demands of a hypnotist, and ignore other stimuli.

Some psychologists doubt that the hypnotic state really exists. They explain it as resulting from the "suggestibility" of some people. Others don't question the existence of hypnosis, but are investigating differences in personal attributes, such as the ability to attend to only a limited number of stimuli. Still other recent attempts to explain it have focused on differences in the social environment. The physiological evidence, Table 4-1,

hypnosis: *an altered state of consciousness, the exact nature of which is still in dispute*

argues against the existence of a special hypnotic state. Obviously, more research needs to be done.

Superhuman feats cannot be performed either during or following hypnosis. Feats performed while hypnotized turn out, upon careful analysis, to be well within human capabilities. This is especially true if people are willing to swallow their pride and momentarily "let themselves go."

It is clear that people can behave following hypnosis as though they have actually forgotten a fact, or cannot hear a certain word or see a certain action. This is called *post-hypnotic suggestion*. Even the label itself suggests an explanation for the event. The subject must be a cooperative person, willing to follow the hypnotist's instructions. However, more work is needed here, too, before we can understand what really happens and why.

Will people who have been hypnotized do things against their own will or against the law? The evidence is mixed. In the main it seems to show that no, they won't. *But*, an action may be presented as being required by events of which the hypnotized person has not previously been aware. Then it *is* possible to get people to perform actions which they would not otherwise have performed.

This last point makes the next one particularly important. Can people be hypnotized against their will? The answer is no. Being very open to suggestions and having a strong "capacity for total attention" are important traits in the subject to be hypnotized. However, without his or her active cooperation, no such hypnosis is possible. A person must work actively to place conscious processes under the hypnotist's control.

Artificial changes

So far we have studied events in which nothing other than conscious control is exercised over voluntary and involuntary behavior. In that sense biofeedback, meditation, and hypnosis are natural methods for altering basic body processes. But the nervous system can also be influenced by artificial means. Once these techniques have been applied, the system typically cannot control their effects.

Drugs. The power of drugs to influence the body is easy to demonstrate. As you have read, the most basic function of the nervous system is the electrical-chemical process called neuronal firing. Put simply, one of the most direct ways to influence the body—everything from vision to nerve conductivity—is to introduce chemicals which hinder or help the nervous system. Therein lies the importance of drugs.

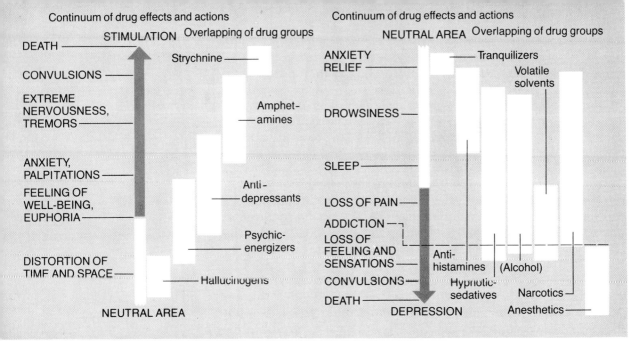

Figure 4-10 Behavioral changes caused by stimulant, depressant, or hallucinogenic drugs. The neutral area represents the normal nondrugged condition. As one moves from that midpoint—either up or down—the drug-related changes in behavior increase. General classes of drugs are listed on the right. The scale on the left indicates the range of effects from using each type of drug. Any drug listed can produce any of the effects noted if taken in large enough doses. Thus, overdoses of either stimulants or depressants may lead to death.

stimulant: *any drug that increases activity in the nervous system or in any function of the body*

depressant: *any drug that reduces activity in the nervous system or slows down some body function*

hallucinogens: *drugs producing changes in the normal senses, particularly hallucinations*

A *stimulant* is any drug that increases activity in the nervous system or in any function of the body. In contrast, a *depressant* is any drug that reduces activity in the nervous system or slows down some body function. The effects of some drugs are difficult to classify by observation. For example, alcohol seems to stimulate, although it is actually a depressant.

Hallucinogenic drugs often produce changes in the normal senses (hallucination), sometimes without altering the person's awareness (or consciousness) of those changes. There is much disagreement as to how these drugs actually function. There is some evidence that they are stimulants. Yet, some of the effects clearly result from depression of normal body processes. The hallucinogens are not just stimulants or just depressants—they produce some of both effects in a series of physiological reactions not yet fully understood.

The nervous system that controls us is very complex. If control of a function is located at a particular point in the central nervous system, then stimulant or depressant drugs that act at that point will affect that function. The chart summarizes the broad range of behavioral effects that may result from various dosages of stimulants, depressants, or hallucinogens.

In review . . .

Long-standing ideas about voluntary and involuntary human behaviors are beginning to change. We can alter our conscious awareness in at least three ways. Biofeedback involves the use of electronic instruments to show the subject the activity of one or more of his or her bodily processes—everything from urine production to brain waves. Meditation is the voluntary production of alpha brain waves by means of concentrated attention. Hypnosis is a more controversial, less understood way to alter the normal state of consciousness. Normal nervous system functions are also altered through the use of drugs: stimulants, depressants, or hallucinogens.

Chapter Application and Review

USING PSYCHOLOGY   *The effects of drug abuse*

Depressants

One of the most widely used depressants, and perhaps the most widely abused, is alcohol. Beer contains the least alcohol, wine has a higher concentration, and distilled liquors have the highest concentration of all. A person must typically drink up to 10 times the volume of beer to equal the effects of one drink of distilled liquor. However, all alcoholic beverages eventually produce the same results in the human body. It is well known that it is the percentage of alcohol in the blood that counts.

What are these results? The main effect of alcoholic beverages on the human body is on the brain. As the percentage of alcohol in the blood rises, the highest levels of the brain—the cortical areas—become depressed. Higher mental processes—thinking, feeling, problem solving—are first to be lost. As more alcohol is consumed, lower areas in the midbrain become affected. Soon a person is increasingly unable to talk and reason clearly.

The person feels relaxed and acts with fewer restraints, but this occurs because the cortex is increasingly depressed by the alcohol. When you lessen the activity of the cortex, you remove controls. With no inhibitions the person may seem more free and active. However, as lower brain centers are affected, even the sense of balance is in time lost. Inability to "walk a straight line" is a traditional (although unscientific) way by which drunkenness is defined.

More extreme depressants include all of the narcotics. These drugs (ranging from opium and morphine to codeine) affect the central nervous system. They depress the functions of the sensory cortex and the thalamus and thus provide a false sense of well-being and relief from anxiety and pain. However, in a short time, as the effects spread, the person may become increasingly drowsy and finally fall asleep. Too large a dose may depress the automatic activities normally controlled by the brain stem, and death can result from respiratory failure.

Stimulants

Stimulants vary greatly in their effects. One group of stimulants—the amphetamines—cause the heartbeat to increase, the pupils of the eyes to dilate, and the organism in general to feel flushed, active, alert and "high."

At the same time the digestive processes are slowed down, so that the body is more active but eating less (thus the use, or misuse, of amphetamines in losing weight). When the person stops taking the amphetamines, the digestive system rebounds and the result is nausea and vomiting. The person may hover between sleep and unconsciousess as the body attempts to restore its chemical balance.

Hallucinogens

As you have read, the hallucinogenic drugs are very difficult to classify as depressant or activating. They may be a little of both.

In small dosages there is little doubt that the hallucinogens produce mild stimulation of the central nervous system. Generally, a person under the influence of one of these drugs is more excitable and alert. This may result from stimulation of the lower brain centers or depression of some of the higher inhibitory centers. However, despite the increased activity, the person is less able to receive and interpret sensory stimuli.

This combination of increased activity and decreased sensitivity to *external* stimulation lends increased importance to prior thoughts and experiences stored in memory. The person may indulge in flights of fancy—immune to outside stimulation and more or less totally at the will of internal thoughts.

One of the most widely recognized drugs of this group is *marijuana*. It is the most widely used. Because of the isolation from external stimuli experienced by marijuana users, the mood or environment in which they originally take marijuana may affect how they will experience it.

At the other extreme is LSD. This drug is extremely powerful—so powerful, in fact, that controlling the effects of the drug is very difficult. Varying even slightly the amount consumed will lead to wide differences in the results. The many changes in behavior resulting from LSD occur because there are many sites that are affected by it. It causes the pupils to dilate and the heartbeat to increase, and it affects the synapses (junctions between neurons) in the central nervous system. The sensory cortex is stimulated but restraints are lost. Information from the senses gains in importance. The mechanisms that normally handle sensory input and processing are so activated that synesthetic experiences ("hearing" a color, "feeling" a sound, and so forth) are commonly reported.

It was at one time thought that LSD might be used to create various personality abnormalities to aid the study of how to prevent or cure them. The drug does produce response patterns very similar to some aspects of abnormal persons. Many hospitals have admitted drug users whose symptoms resembled psychotic behavior. However, the research with abnormalities temporarily created by LSD and related drugs has been very disappointing so far. No insight into illness or clear-cut results have been obtained.

So at this point we can conclude simply by noting that drug usage can and usually does have profound effects on the body, many of which are unpredictable and possibly dangerous. Any altering of the function of the nervous system by drugs will product detectable or even dramatic changes in behavior. The effects of drug use depend mainly on the type of drug involved and the primary site of action of that drug within the nervous system.

REVIEW QUESTIONS

SECTION 1 (pages 118–133)

1. What is the most basic part of the nervous system? What two characteristics does the part have?
2. How does the nervous system transmit information?
3. What methods do psychologists use to study the nervous system?
4. Name three types of nerves and their functions.
5. What are the major divisions of the nervous system?
6. Name the parts of the brain and what they do.
7. What are the differences between the right and left hemispheres of the brain?

SECTION 2 (pages 133–134)

1. In addition to the nervous system, what system controls human behavior?
2. What is the role of the hypothalamus?

SECTION 3 (pages 134–136)

1. What is the relationship between brain activity and sleep?
2. Describe REM sleep and its possible functions.

SECTION 4 (pages 137–143)

1. What are some natural means of altering the operations of the nervous system? What are some artificial means?
2. What are the effects on behavior of the three classes of drugs?

ACTIVITIES

1. Reflexes are among the simplest "built-in" response patterns that humans rely on. Less sophisticated animals (such as your family's pet dog or cat) also rely on reflexes. You may have noticed an unusual one in dogs. If a dog is lying on its side, you can rub its flank—the depression on the side just in front of the rear leg. And what happens? The dog will start moving its rear leg reflexively, as if it were scratching itself. How many of your own reflexes can you name?

2. Career Search. We've talked in Chapters 2 through 4 about heredity *and* environment as factors influencing performance. Invite your school's track coach to come to your classroom and discuss how diet, exercise, and training can influence an athlete's performance. Are there *physiological* limits

to how high humans can jump or how fast they can run? Are there any *psychological* limits?

3. It is *very important* in this activity that you *not* read the last part until you have completed the first part. Find an object that is some distance from you—five meters (16 feet) or more. Focus on it, keeping both eyes open. Line up your index finger so that it seems to be between you and the distant object at which you are looking. Holding your finger steady, and continuing to focus on the distant object, close one eye and then the other. For one eye the finger will block your view of the distant object; for the other your finger will appear to be to one side of the object you're viewing. Now stop and try the demonstration before reading any further.

What did you find? If you are right-handed, then you were probably unconsciously using your right eye to line up your finger with the distant object. In short, you tend to be right- or left-eyed in the same way you are right- or left-handed. Was this true for you? Check with other members of your class. For how many is their dominant eye on the same side as their preferred hand? What is demonstrated here is lateral (hemispheric) dominance.

4. Career Search. *Aphasia* is any physiologically-based brain damage that causes difficulties with language. Invite into your classroom a psychologist, psychiatrist, or medical doctor from a local hospital or a Veterans Administration hospital. Have it be someone who works with older patients who have had strokes or persons who have at some time suffered a head injury in a war or an accident. Ask your expert to describe the differences between aphasias related to the reception of speech (hearing), the production of speech (speaking), the reception of words (reading), and the production of words (writing).

5. We now know that we tend to move our eyes when we dream. If you can find a parent, brother, or sister who will cooperate, encourage this person to take a nap for at least 90 minutes. Watch his or her eyes and—with prior agreement, of course—awaken him or her when you see evidence of eye movement. Ask if the person was dreaming; the odds are high that he or she will have been. You could volunteer to take that nap yourself, *or* ask your parents not to awaken you tomorrow morning until they see your eyeballs moving underneath your eyelids.

INTERESTED IN MORE?

BENSON, H. & KLIPPER, M. *The Relaxation Response.* Avon, 1976. A description of a simple method of relaxation and meditation. Easy reading; accurate guidance for control of anxiety.

CARLTON, P. L. *A Primer of Behavioral Pharmacology: Concepts and Principles in the Behavioral Analysis of Drug Action.* W. H. Freeman, 1983. This is tough reading but important material. Emphasizes problems and methods of analyzing behavior as it is influenced by drugs.

HEBB, D. O. *Textbook of Psychology,* 3rd ed. Saunders, 1972. Written by a Canadian who is a past president of the American Psychological Association, this book is designed to be an introductory psychology text. It is a classic in its field, and it simplifies many explanations of perceptual, learned, and emotional experiences in basic physiology. Excellent reading.

HILGARD, E. R. *Divided Consciousness: Multiple Controls in Human Thought and Action.* John Wiley, 1977. Analyzes a wide range of research on forgetting, dreaming, and hallucinations, as well as on people who suffer multiple personalities. Includes a lengthy discussion of hypnosis and what is meant by "consciousness."

JONES, K. L., SHAINBERG, L. W., & BYER, C. O. *Drugs and Alcohol, 2nd ed.* Harper & Row, 1973. A readable discussion of the effects (and sources) of a wide variety of drugs and alcohol. It includes a comparison of the physiological reactions and behavioral effects of many "popular" drugs.

LAURIE, P. *Drugs: Medical, Psychological and Social Facts*, 2nd ed. Penguin, 1971. The title tells it all.

NARANJO, C. & ORENSTEIN, R. E. *On the Psychology of Meditation*. Viking, 1971. Includes an excellent review and description of various types of meditation.

 ꞈTER, F. H. *The Ciba Collection of Medical Illustrations*. Vol. I., *Nervous System*. ꞈba Pharmaceutical Co., 1958. De-ꞈ ꞈed, large illustrations of the form aꞈ distribution of the nervous system. Beꞈ ꞈiful drawings.

RAY, O. *Drugs, Society and Human Behavio ꞈ* 2nd ed. C. V. Mosby, 1972. Broad ꞈverage of drug use, the basic actions drugs, and even substances not usuaꞈ thought of as drugs (such as coffee)

ROSE, S. *The Cꞈ ꞈcious Brain*. Vintage Books, 1976. ꞈhis unusual book analyzes physiolꞈ as it relates to behavior ratheꞈ ꞈhan the other way around. Memorꞈ sleep, and emotion are among the t ꞈcs covered.

SHAPIRO, D. *Meditation*. Aldine, 1980. Discusses studies of the influence of meditation on subjective and cognitive responses as opposed to the somatic arousal responses discussed in this chapter.

SPRINGER, S. P. & DEUTSCH, G. *Left Brain, Right Brain*. W. H. Freeman, 1981. Looks at a wide array of issues related to split brain; also answers implications of the burning question, "What paw does your dog shake hands with?"

TEYLER, T. J. *A Primer of Psychobiology: Brain and Behavior*. W. H. Freeman, 1975. Free of technical terminology, this brief, readable introduction to structure and function of the brain and nervous system emphasizes behaviors such as learning, language, and consciousness.

WOOLRIDGE, D. E. *The Machinery of the Brain*. McGraw-Hill, 1963. A highly readable book intended for the average lay person interested in the human brain. Describes the major brain areas and their functions.

CHAPTER OUTLINE

WHAT'S THE ANSWER?

☐   Instructors in Driver Education advise their students to look *twice* in both directions before driving across an intersection. *Why?*

☐   "Watch it, Klausman! Watch where you're going! . . . Well, would you look at that. He ran into the goal post!"
   Moments later, "Klausman, how many times have I told you? You've got to look where you're going! What if that had been a defensive player from the opposing team? How do you feel?"
   "I feel OK, coach, but I've got a bad ringing in my ears." *What causes the ringing in your ears that you may hear after bumping your head?*

☐   *How can ice skaters in a dancing routine make high-speed spinning turns without getting so dizzy that they lose their balance?*

☐   Some experimenters have reported frequent successes in transmitting images and thoughts between widely separated individuals. *Does extrasensory perception exist?*

1   Sensation versus Perception

Several years ago a nationally broadcast television show tried to clarify the way in which humans respond to stimuli. The inside of the head was depicted as having a large television

Psychologists Eleanor Gibson and Richard Walk devised an experiment in depth perception using a "visible cliff." A piece of heavy glass covered a yard (about a meter) drop from a platform to the floor. On their own, both infants and animals avoided moving over the "deep" half of the platform. This baby braves the cliff in response to the coaxing of a trusted adult.

screen. On the screen were displayed all of the stimuli viewed by this human. Within the big head lived a much smaller person, who simply pulled levers to make the larger human respond. While this presentation explains nothing (who or what makes the little person respond?), it does point out three basic elements involved when humans react to their environment. The first is the *stimulus*—both its physical characteristics (what it is) and its psychological attributes (how it makes us feel). The second is the *receptor*, which receives the stimulus and sets the reaction in motion. Finally, there is the human *organism* itself—both its prior experiences and its current physiological state. These three elements—stimulus, receptor, and organism—combine to determine the ways in which we respond.

A *sensation* occurs any time a stimulus activates one of your receptors. *Perception* occurs when you apply your experience to interpret sensations. In this chapter we'll be concerned, first, with environmental stimuli and our receptors, and, second, with the more complex processes of perception.

The differences between sensation and perception are more a matter of convenience than importance. In fact, some deny such distinctions can be made. Perception is composed of sensations, which the brain then puts together. For example, a single note from a guitar is a simple event. It can be called a sensation throughout the processes involved in receiving the note and communicating it into the brain. Within the brain, however, combining the notes of the theme and their rhythm so you can recognize a song you know is a much more complex process of perception.

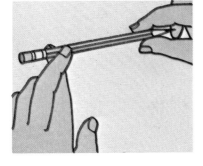

Figure 5-1 An illustration of a simple test of how our perceptions can deceive us. See text for instructions.

sensation: *what occurs when a stimulus activates a receptor*

perception: *what occurs when you apply your experience to interpret sensations*

psychophysics: *the branch of psychology that studies the relations between physical events and the related psychological experiences*

2 Sensory Processes and Techniques

Psychophysics

There is a fairly precise relation between what happens out in the physical world and the internal events to which we react. But the relationship is not perfect. *Psychophysics* is the branch of psychology that studies the relations between physical events and the related psychological experiences. As we examine each of our senses, notice that we'll divide our discussion into two parts. We'll discuss the *physical* (real world) *stimulus*, such as light or gas or cold temperature. Then we'll discuss the *psychological experience*, such as vision or smell or touch.

Look at the illustration for a moment. Now close your eyes and cross the index and middle fingers of your left hand like the hand shown. Rub a pencil or the index finger of your other hand back and forth through the notch formed by your two crossed fingers. What do you feel? Probably you feel as if two pencils or fingers are touching your left hand. You are not perceiving what is actually happening, so there *is* some "slippage" between real world events and our perception of them. This is one experience studied by psychophysicists.

Thresholds

Absolute. The *absolute threshold* is the smallest amount of a stimulus that can be detected by an organism. Your "absolute" threshold may be different from mine. The partially deaf person's absolute threshold for sound is higher than either yours or mine. Thus, though it's an absolute threshold in that it's the lowest amount of a stimulus that can be detected, it is not an absolute threshold in the sense that it's the same for everyone.

Difference. The *just-noticeable-difference* (or j.n.d.) is the amount by which any stimulus must be changed in order for that *change* to be detected. The *difference threshold* is the amount of the change necessary in order for the change to be detected half of the time. *Weber's Law* states that the greater the absolute amount of any stimulus, the larger the amount of relative change that will be required in that stimulus before an observer can detect it. See Box 5-1 for an example of how this works.

How many senses do we have?

The answer depends on how you define a sense. If you do it in terms of different kinds of *receptors*, then we have about ten. These include vision, hearing, smell, taste, the skin senses (pressure, hot, cold, and pain), as well as balance and body sense, or kinesthesis. On the other hand, in terms of the *stimuli* to which we can react, there are about six senses, based on our sensitivity to light, sound, gas, liquids, solids, and body position.

absolute threshold: *the smallest amount of a stimulus that can be detected by an organism*

just-noticeable-difference (j.n.d.): *the amount by which a stimulus must be changed in order for that change to be detected*

Weber's Law: *the law stating that the stronger or greater the stimulus, the larger the amount of change required before an observer can detect any difference*

Feature   5–1   **"I SEE THE LIGHT!"**

A psychologist named Weber was the first to observe that the size of the difference threshold depended on the level of stimulation at which that threshold was being measured. He found that as the level of stimulation increased, the size of the just-noticeable-difference also increased. In other words, the higher (or larger or louder) the stimulation, the more that stimulation must change before you can detect that change.

Using a 50-100-150 watt light bulb, it is very easy to demonstrate this concept. Start with the bulb burning at its lowest—50 watts. As you switch from 50 to 100 watts, the light grows noticeably brighter. Now switch it once more from 100 to 150 watts. This second change involves the same increase in wattage (the physical stimulus), but a much less obvious change in the apparent brightness of the light. Since the level of stimulation was larger, the same physical change (an increase of 50 watts) was perceived to be smaller.

In review . . .

Sensation and perception identify processes that differ only in their complexity. The absolute threshold is the smallest stimulus that arouses a sensation. The difference threshold is the smallest change in any stimulation that can be detected. It is not important exactly how many senses we have.

3 The Sensory Apparatus

Vision

The stimulus—light. The physical stimulus for vision is light. Light from any source has three physical characteristics: wavelength, intensity (or amplitude), and pureness. These characteristics are seen by us as hue, brightness, and saturation (Table 5-1). Changing any of the physical characteristics of light waves makes a difference in our experience of the light.

The source of most of our light—the sun—emits white light, which is a mixture of all light wavelengths. This can be demonstrated by passing sunlight through a prism. A prism spreads light out into the colors of the visible spectrum, as illustrated. *Hue* identifies the perceived color of a particular wave. As wavelength changes, hue also changes.

A beam of sunlight passing through a prism spreads into the colors of the spectrum. The letters of the name Roy G. Biv identify the seven spectral colors — red, orange, yellow, green, blue, indigo, and violet.

Table 5-1 **Light stimuli and how we experience them**

PHYSICAL CHARACTERISTIC OF LIGHT WAVE	WHAT WE PERCEIVE
Wavelength	Hue (or color)
Intensity	Brightness
Pureness	Saturation

As the intensity, or amplitude, of a light wave increases, the result is an increase in perceived *brightness*. As the amount of light waves reaching the eye increases, the apparent brightness of that stimulus increases. Thus, brightness is related to the amount of light present. The light meter in a camera measures the intensity of physical light waves entering the lens.

A totally *saturated* color is a pure light wave, but we don't see these very often. A pure red would have light waves of only one particular wavelength. An *un*saturated light must be black, gray, or white. As you add white light to a pure color, the color becomes less saturated. If you mix all colors together, you recreate white light again. Saturation is also sometimes called *purity*. This refers to the extent to which a particular hue is mixed with white or other light. Hue, brightness, and saturation must all be

The *color solid* illustrates the three dimensions of color: hue, brightness, and saturation. To create the color solid the spectrum—stretching from red to violet—has been bent into a circle. The rectangles at the outer edge of the circle represent the *hue* of any color. (Also included are the purple colors that are not part of the visible spectrum.) *Brightness*, stretching from light at the top to dark at the bottom, is represented by the vertical dimension. Degree of saturation stretches from gray at the center to the most saturated hue located along the midlevel perimeter.

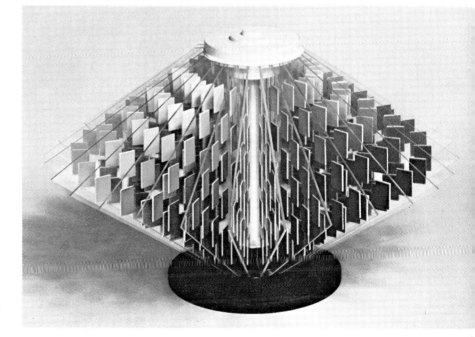

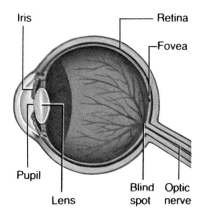

Figure 5-2 A cross-section of the human eye. The iris, or colored portion of the eye, controls how much light enters.

mentioned to describe fully any light source. All three dimensions represented in the color solid can be seen in the illustration.

The *color solid* is used to determine what happens when two colors are mixed. Two colors that are directly opposite one another on the color circle part of the solid are *complementary colors*. If they are mixed together, the result is gray.

We use the color solid only for predicting *additive* mixing of spectral colors. The hue depends on the light waves which are added together. (An additive mixture of several colors yields white.) If we were mixing paints—which is a *subtractive* process, the results of our mixtures would be quite different. The pigment of paint absorbs almost all but one color of the spectrum — as does colored glass. (The subtractive mixture of several colors yields black.)

The receptor—eye. The receptor for visible light is the eye. The eye is in many ways similar to a camera, but it is much more complex. Light enters the eye through the *pupil* and is focused by the *lens*. The light falls on the *retina*, which is similar to the film in a camera. The retina is made up of two receptor elements, called *rods* and *cones*. Rods are more light-sensitive than cones, so they are used to see in poor light, especially at night. Cones are sensitive to color, but they demand more light to function. Rod vision is comparable to black-and-white television; cone vision is similar to color television.

The rods and cones connect with neurons that form the *optic nerve*, which relays visual information to the brain. The point at which these neurons exit from the eye is called the *blind spot*. It is a very small portion of the retina that has no receptor cells. Stimulation on the blind spot will not be received by the brain. Read the Think About It, below, for an example of the effect of the blind spot in each of your eyes.

→ Think about it

The **question**: Instructors in driver education classes often advise their students to look twice in both directions before driving across an intersection. Why?

The **answer**: If you look to the right and to the left only once, it is possible that the image of a car coming from the right might fall on the blind spot of one eye. It might then be obscured from vision in the other eye by the right front roof support. If the car is moving fast enough to hit you, then looking again at the same spot will prevent an accident. This should allow enough time so that the image of that car would not fall on your blind spot both times. The figure shows the location of the blind spot that exists in each of your eyes.

If you look at something, you cause the light rays from that object to fall on your *fovea*—the focal point of your eyes. The fovea is the point of greatest concentration of cones on the retinal surface. At the edge of your visual field, images are sensed only by rods. Thus, color vision is best at your point of focus and absent at the edge.

Function and operation. The difference between rod and cone vision can be shown by testing your absolute threshold for light after you walk from sunlight into a darkened room. We become more and more sensitive to dim flashes of light during the first 30 minutes after coming out of the daylight. This process is called *dark-adaptation*. It explains the kind of awkward experience we've all had in going into a movie theater during the daytime and trying to find a seat. Thirty minutes later, when we want some popcorn, it is no problem to see our way clearly from our seat to the aisle. During that time our eyes have adapted to the darkness, and the rods are now playing a much larger role.

The physical stimuli that are present at sunset are the same as those occurring at sunrise. Yet, if you were asked to paint a picture of a sunset, you would tend to use purples and darker colors. To paint a sunrise you would be more likely to use reds and oranges and yellows. Why? Because each day as you shift (at sunset) from cone to rod vision, you switch to receptors (your rods) that are more reactive to the darker colors. This is called the *Purkinje Shift*. Having lived for many hours with light being interpreted by your cones, you suddenly must rely more on your rods. Rods are relatively more sensitive to colors at the purple and blue end of the color spectrum. As a result, you perceive a sunset as more bluish and purple.

The rods and cones in the eye are responsible for what we call dark adaptation. Cones are more sensitive to color, need more light to function, and, thus, work well during the daytime hours. Rods are used to see in poor light, especially at night. When the sun goes down, you shift from cone to rod vision (the Purkinje shift). Since rods are more sensitive to colors at the purple and blue end of the spectrum, you perceive sunsets as having deeper tones than sunrises. Actually, the physical stimuli are the same.

dark adaptation: *the process of becoming more and more sensitive to dim flashes of light after coming out of the daylight*

Purkinje Shift: *the shift from cone to rod vision at sunset, which makes you perceive more blues and purples*

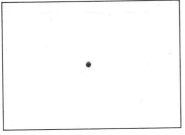

Figure 5-3 Focus both eyes on the spot near the corner of the background field on which the stars are printed. Keep looking at the same spot for 30 seconds or so and then, holding the book at the same distance, shift your eyes and look at the spot in the block. What you will experience is a *negative afterimage.*

One test for "color blindness." The examiner asks the subject to "please read the numbers." No other instruction is given. If you can't see the figures in this circle, you are probably red-green colorblind.

There is yet another visual process you have probably experienced. Look at the illustration for a demonstration of *negative afterimage.*

Positive afterimages don't occur as frequently as negative afterimages. The best example can be achieved if you'll get up at 4 a.m. tomorrow morning. Stumble over to the bedroom light switch. Flash the room lights on and off again instantly. What will remain in your visual field is a positive afterimage. If you turn your head or eyes, the view of your room also turns. It results from overstressing the rods and cones which are fully dark-adapted. It causes no harm, although you may have winced a bit when the lights went on!

A final interesting visual effect is that of color "blindness." It afflicts about eight percent of the men in North American, but less than one percent of the women. A totally color-blind person sees the world only in blacks, grays, and whites, with no trace of color. However, such a person is very rare. Most people who are called "color-blind" are actually just deficient in their ability to see one or more colors.

Red-green color blindness is the most common type. Such people experience the world in terms of black, gray, white, blue, yellow, and any other hues that can be achieved by mixing two or more of these colors. (See the illustration next page.) Yellow-blue color-blindness is a less common form. These people perceive the world in terms of black, gray, white, red, green, and mixtures of these colors. Typically, color-blind people otherwise see quite well.

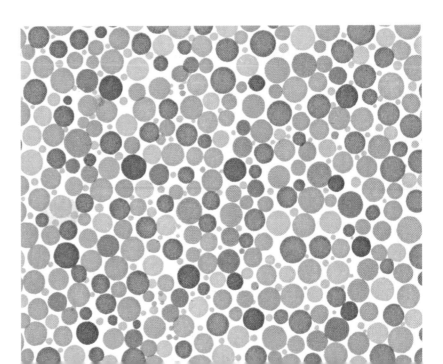

A

B

C

D

The photographs show how a scene is perceived by people with varying forms of color blindness. The totally color-blind person has no cones in his or her retina and sees a scene as shown in Figure A. Figure B represents red-green color blindness. Figure C is the scene as it would be seen by a person with yellow-blue color blindness who could distinguish between red and green. Figure D is the view with normal vision.

Problem—blindness. As you know, there are many physical disabilities to which humans may be subjected. One disability— the impact of which is only now beginning to be understood—is that of total blindness. The problems created by blindness are basically two-fold.

It is now thought that perhaps 80 percent of all the information we learn is first taken in by means of our eyes. Although education and communication are not totally eliminated by blindness, they are made much more difficult. Learning to read braille, the system of raised dots that serve as letters and numbers, is one way the blind can use touch to partially overcome their disability.

There are also the problems of navigation and locomotion. For ease in getting around and solving the problems of education and locomotion, a good and well-trained sense of hearing can also help restore deficits in vision.

In review . . .

The stimulus for vision is light, which has three physical characteristics: wavelength, intensity, and pureness. The psychological attributes are hue, brightness, and saturation. Complementary colors, as well as other colors, may be mixed in an additive or subtractive process. The receptor for vision is the eye, which contains rods for black-white vision and cones for color vision. Vision is poorest at the blind spot and best at the fovea. Dark adaptation and the Purkinje Shift both result from the shift from cone- to rod-vision. Color blindness affects mainly males, but it is a relatively slight vision problem compared to blindness.

Hearing

The stimulus—sound waves. Sound will be detected any time three factors are present: First, there must be a vibrating source, or stimulus. Second, there must be a medium—gaseous (as it usually is, like air) or solid—for transmitting pressure waves from that source. (Remember the old cowboys-and-Indians trick of placing an ear on the rail to find out from many miles away whether or not a train is approaching?) Finally, third, there must be a receptor present.

The physical stimulus for sound, then, is usually airborne pressure waves. These vibrating waves of pressure are known as sound waves. Such changes in pressure are caused by the vibrations back and forth of the sound source itself. As is true of light waves, there are three ways in which sound waves may differ. They may differ in *frequency* (or cycles per second), *amplitude* (or the amount of energy pushing the waves), and *complexity* (or the number of simple frequencies that are represented in a complex wave). To describe a sound source you would need to give all three factors.

These physical qualities of sound are perceived by us as *pitch*, *loudness*, and *timbre*, as shown in Table 5-2. As sound waves increase in frequency, the *pitch* that you hear also increases. As the *amplitude* of a sound wave increases, so does the perceived *loudness* of that sound. Many older radios have a "volume" control instead of a loudness control, but the control is incorrectly labeled. A low note on a church organ has a certain room-filling ability unmatched by any note from a piccolo. What differs between the organ and the piccolo is volume, not necessarily loudness.

Timbre is essentially the complexity of a sound. Were you to pluck middle C on a guitar, the basic note would be the same as one played on a piano. But the various overtones (caused by vibrations of other parts of the instrument) would allow you quite easily to distinguish a piano from a guitar. Too many

Table 5-2 **Sound stimuli and how we experience them**

PHYSICAL CHARACTERISTIC OF SOUND WAVE	WHAT WE PERCEIVE
Wavelength (frequency of vibration)	Pitch (bass sounds to squeaks)
Intensity (amplitude)	Loudness (*not* the same as volume)
Pureness	Timbre (complexity, due to overtones)

tones and overtones all heard at once may sound like noise, as described in Box 5-3 later in the chapter.

The receptor—ear. The stimulus for hearing changes its form several times before stimulating the *auditory nerve*. Examine the diagram of the human ear. Sound waves enter the *auditory canal* and cause movement of the *eardrum*. This changes movement of the air to the physical movement of three bones that connect to the eardrum. These bones in turn are connected to the *cochlea*, where the auditory nerve is stimulated.

Function and operation. As can be seen in the drawing, the cochlea is a tightly coiled portion of the ear. It is liquid-filled, but projecting down into it are very tiny *hair cells* that may be stimulated by activity of the liquid within which they are set. Moving these hair cells sets the auditory nerve in motion. Physical movement is changed into an electro-chemical impulse. As you might expect, loudness is conveyed in the auditory nerve by the number and rate of neurons firing. As loudness increases, so do the number and rate.

Problem—deafness. Deafness is second perhaps only to blindness in the difficulties which it may cause. Obviously, much of the communication between people is verbal, not written (as we'll see in Chapter 8). Until the invention of small, transistorized hearing aids, people with hearing problems were less well-off than those with visual problems.

Figure 5-4 A cross-section of the human ear. The *eustachian tube* prevents pressure that would otherwise develop in the middle ear chamber when sound waves from the outer ear push and pull on the eardrum. The *semicircular canals* are discussed later in the chapter.

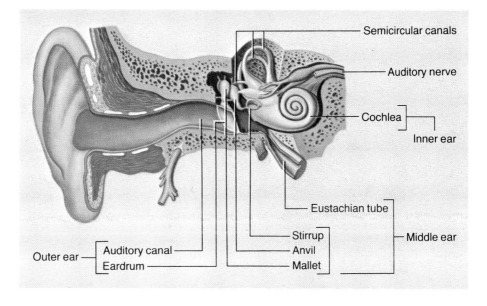

The **question**: What causes the ringing that you may hear just after bumping your head?

The **answer**: The process that changes physical sound waves into the psychological experience of sound is the movement or bending of the hair cells in your cochlea. A blow to your head will sometimes bend these hair cells. You will experience this as a sound or ringing sensation. As long as the hair cells move this way you will continue to hear the "ringing" in your ears.

Examination of the ear drawing suggests two means by which deafness may be caused. Sound impulses are transmitted mechanically from the auditory canal until they stimulate the hair cells. Interfering with any portion of this mechanical process causes *conduction deafness*. Such deafness decreases your sensitivity to tones of all frequencies.

The second means of conduction involves the hair cells and auditory nerve as well as parts of the central nervous system. Interference with, or deterioration of, the nerves causes *nerve deafness*. Nerve deafness usually hinders your perception of high-frequency sounds most, but it also somewhat reduces your sensitivity to low-frequency sounds.

In review . . .

The physical stimulus for hearing is pressure waves, which have three physical characteristics: frequency, amplitude, and complexity. We hear sounds in terms of pitch, loudness, and timbre. The receptor for sound is the ear, within which hair cells in the cochlea stimulate the auditory nerve.

Chemical senses—smell and taste

Think for a moment what your nose may have to go through each morning. First you get up (and that *is* hard!), and if you're a male, there's pre-shave lotion to put on. Then, male or female, you soap your face (say, with a "hint of spring"). Next comes the mouth. There's toothpaste with a mint flavor, and, for good measure, mouthwash to keep your breath fresh. But, you're not finished yet. To that may be added hairspray or tonic and, perhaps, deodorant or cologne. By the time you're ready for breakfast, your nose can be exhausted!

The physical stimulus for our sense of smell is gas. However, to be detected the gas must be soluble in liquid. Even the smell of a solid (such as your desk or your hand or any other nearby "solid" object) results from minute gaseous emissions from the object.

Efforts to identify a small number of basic smells from which others might be composed haven't been successful. Three different theories of "basic" psychological smells agree only on putrid, burnt, and fruity (or musky). There is no universally accepted list of basic psychological smells.

Whereas the receptors for smell react to substances in gaseous form, the receptors for taste react to substances in liquid form.

It is easier to identify tastes than smells. For taste there are four basic qualities: sweet, salty, sour, and bitter. The flavor of most of our food results from a combination of only three basic qualities. But, our sense of taste is nowhere near as varied and interesting as our sense of smell.

The receptor—nose and taste buds. The diagram shows that the receptor site for smell is located on the roof of the nasal cavity. If you detect a new smell in your environment, your normal response is to "sniff." The differences in "sniffs" from one person to another make it very difficult to state definitely how much air has been swirled past the sensing surface. This, and the remote location of the *olfactory-epitheleum*, cause problems in studying the sense of smell.

If you hold your nose and breathe in gently through your mouth, even in a room where there is a pronounced odor, you will not detect it unless air spills into your nasal cavity from the rear. In addition, if you breathe normally and quietly through your nose, you will very quickly adapt to the smells in your environment.

Figure 5-5 A cross-section of the human nasal passages and the mouth.

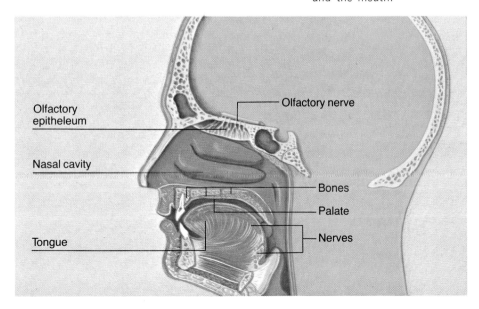

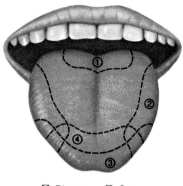

① Bitter ② Sour
③ Salty ④ Sweet

Figure 5-6 A map of the human tongue indicating which areas are most sensitive to each of the four basic taste qualities.

Your tongue is covered with a large number of bumps (called *papillae*). They are not the taste buds. The taste buds are clusters of taste cells concentrated on the papillae and located mostly on the surface and sides of your tongue. The figure in the margin shows those sections of your tongue that are most sensitive to each of the four basic tastes. To swallow a bitter pill with least agony, keep it away from the center back of your tongue.

Functions and operations. There are two aspects of the sense of smell that are remarkable. One is the extreme sensitivity of the sense. You can detect as little as 7 parts per 10 billion of some musky aromas. Second, the sense of smell is also remarkable for its ability to detect specific but very small differences in chemical structure. Any theory of smell must be able to account for both of these abilities.

One of the most successful explanations of smell has come to be known as the *lock-and-key-theory*. It proposes that the shape, not the chemical structure, of gaseous molecules is important in detecting different odors. Much work remains to determine how different-shaped molecules can influence the sense of smell.

In their studies of the sense of taste, psychologists have isolated four cells that are maximally sensitive to one of the four basic tastes. All four of these sensor cells react to any stimulation. However, each is most sensitive to one or a limited number of substances. Thus, the taste that is uniquely associated with an orange, a pepperoni pizza, or an enchilada results from the *pattern* of activity across many taste sensors, not the activity of only one or two kinds of sensors.

Other senses

Skin senses—pressure, temperature, pain. Touch and temperature are actually a collection of several senses sharing enough in common to be called skin senses. Although the skin senses are the first to develop in the newborn (remember Chapter 2?), they are in some ways the least understood of all our senses. They are also the richest in the diversity of stimuli to which they are sensitive. One stimulus for the skin senses is contact; another is temperature. Contact results in our sense of touch. As the force of the contact increases, the sensation of touch becomes the more complex sensation of pressure.

A temperature stimulus is cold if the stimulus is cooler than the surface of the skin (called *physiological zero*). It is experienced as warm if the stimulus is warmer than physiological zero. The same temperature may thus be experienced as hot at one place on the skin and cold at another. If any physical stimulus becomes too severe, the result is pain.

physiological zero: *the temperature of the surface of the skin*

Balance and body position. Both of these senses react to internal stimulation. They need no stimulation (other than gravity) from the outside environment. The physical stimuli for your *vestibular sense* are changes in the rotary movement of your head, as well as its tilt or angle. Any change in the rate of movement produces the experience of rotation. For instance, swinging on a playground swing provides a constantly changing rate of movement. Rotation and the tilt of your head together provide the sense of balance you must have for correct posture, walking, and running.

There are two receptors involved in the sense of balance. The first is a series of three semicircular canals filled with liquid and connected with the inner ear. (Refer back to the drawing.) They are positioned at right angles to one another and filled with a thick liquid. Projecting into the liquid are a large number of hair cells similar to those in the ear. Moving your head in any direction bends the hair cells because of the inertia of the liquid. Any change in rotation thus stimulates the hair cells and causes the feeling of acceleration.

In addition to the semicircular canals, there are two *otolith organs*. These react regardless of the position of your head. Thus, the semicircular canals respond to *changes* in position, while the otoliths respond to *static* position. Together they allow you to maintain your balance.

There is one more sense—body sense, or kinesthesia ("feeling of motion") which is described in Box 5-2.

We have at least four kinds of body-position sensors. Some are located in the muscles themselves. Others are on the tendons that anchor the various muscles, and in the joints where bone meets bone. They react to muscle movements and to changes in the angle of the bones in a joint. Because they are hard to reach, these sensors are not often studied.

Feature   **5–2**   **THE FIFTH CHAPTER STRETCH**

It is very easy to demonstrate your "body sense." Extend one arm out to its full length at shoulder height. With your index finger point out to your side. Look straight ahead and close your eyes. Now, without opening your eyes, touch the tip of your nose with the tip of the index finger of your outstretched arm. You should be fully able to do this even with your eyes shut. What you've just illustrated (if you didn't poke yourself in the eye) is your own kinesthetic sense. You can demonstrate that you know where your body is positioned even without looking.

![arrow] **Think about it**

The **question**: How do ice skaters make high speed spinning turns in their dance routine without getting so dizzy they lose their balance?

The **answer**: The three semicircular canals are what give us our perception of movement. One of those canals is approximately horizontal to the surface of the earth. This canal, then, is most sensitive to left-right (turning) motions of the head. In a high speed spin, a professional tries to keep a fixed point in sight as long as possible. Then the skater spins his or her head around and fixates on that spot again while the body catches up and twists past the head again. Since the head is still most of the time, inertia keeps the fluid in the semicircular canal from spinning. When the skater stops, so does the world around him or her since the fluid is not moving.

Body sense is unusual because it operates "automatically." Without our knowing exactly how, it keeps us informed as to where our body is. In physical skills such as driver-training we benefit from our kinesthetic sense.

In review . . .

The physical stimulus for smell is gas and for taste, liquid. Several systems of "basic" smells have been proposed with varying degrees of success. The four basic tastes are sweet, sour, bitter, and salty. The receptor for smell is the nose, and the lock-and-key theory is the most successful attempt to explain how gases activate our sense of smell. The receptor for taste is the taste buds in the mouth. Specific patterns of taste-bud activity seem to be associated with specific tastes. The common cold shows the extent to which smell is the more important of the two chemical senses.

The physical stimuli for the skin senses are contact and temperature. They give us our sense of touch (or pressure), pain, hot, and cold. The physical stimuli for the vestibular sense are rotation and the position of the head. These give us our "sense of balance." Three semicircular canals and two otolith organs act as receptors. We sense our body position from receptors located in our muscles, tendons, and joints.

4 Perception

At this point we've examined briefly some of the many pieces of sensory equipment that keep us "in touch" with our environment. But these senses are really only equipment. Much more interesting are the processes—the perceiving and misperceiving—by which we interpret the incoming messages.

In our study of stimuli and receptors we touched upon some of the resulting experiences. Now, as we focus directly on those experiences, you should keep two points in mind. First, we never perceive things exactly as they exist in the real world. For example, war veterans with amputated limbs sometimes report "feelings" in the part of an arm or leg that has been amputated. The messages to which they are reacting are coming from nerve endings—perhaps at the site of the amputation. These signals are perceived as if they were coming from the missing limb. This is an extreme example of how the real and the perceived are not the same.

Second, we will now be dealing with internal processes. They are much more complex than the mere act of reacting to (that is, "sensing") an incoming stimulus. If you cut your finger, your finger aches, not your brain. You don't experience a series of sounds, pressures, and colors, you interpret them—automatically—to give them meaning. A mass of confusing stimuli becomes, say, the gamewinning home run.

Perception, then, involves your reaction to incoming stimuli. It also involves your awareness of your reactions. Most simply, perception is your ongoing experience, based on how you interpret incoming messages from your various senses. We'll examine mainly effects in visual perception, because these are the most fully studied. But, in all perception, past experience usually operates, as well as certain principles of organization. Let's examine a few of these principles.

Figure 5-7 What do you see when you look at the illustration? You perceive part as figure, part as ground. But you can shift your attention so that what is meaningless ground can become the figure, while the figure vanishes into formless ground.

Figure-ground

Look at the illustration in the margin. What do you see? You may perceive two faces looking at one another, or it may look like a single vase. But you can't see both at once. This illustrates perhaps the most basic perceptual effect: one thing must be "figure," the other must be background, or "ground." The figure (either one) seems to have a, shape. It seems more substantial, more like an object. It tends to seem nearer and more dominant. By contrast, the ground seems more formless. It seems to extend behind the figure, and is sensed as somewhat further away. The ground is sometimes less easy to remember. Its border is difficult to describe.

The principle operating here is related most directly to visual experiences, but it applies to other senses as well. A mother can hear the sound of her baby's cry over the chatter of guests. The cry becomes the figure, the party sounds become the ground.

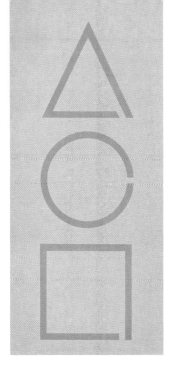

The wholeness of figures

A number of factors combine to determine how we decide what is a "good" figure, or an acceptable whole. Among these is the figure's *symmetry*. In Chapter 7 we'll see that the symmetry of a figure influences both how and how well we may remember it.

A second factor is closure. The illustration shows you a variety of figures. Can you see the circle? The square? The triangle? If you'll look again, you'll see that by the traditional definitions no circle, square, *or* triangle is shown. None of the forms is a completely enclosed figure. Your own brain has closed in the figures to "neaten them up."

Finally, we tend to see as a figure those forms with which we are most *familiar*. You can pick out the alphabetical letters in the drawing even though the other lines are more dominant.

All of these factors—symmetry, closure, and familiarity—operate to determine how we will perceive a figure.

Grouping

In many of our senses, how we will combine individual stimuli can be predicted in terms of rather stable laws of grouping.

Proximity. Objects that are close together tend to be grouped together. We tend to arrange them into familiar patterns.

Figure 5-8 Look at the three figures. What is illustrated is the principle of closure. Although none of the drawings is complete, you fill in the gaps to perceive a whole.

Figure 5-9 Examine the two drawings. The principles of grouping also apply to camouflage.

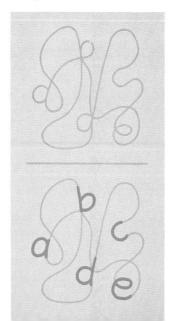

Similarity. Objects that look or feel alike will also be grouped together. As long as there is an obvious basis of similarity, we see them as part of the same pattern.

Continuation. You might have predicted this one, based on the other laws of grouping. In breaking down any complex form into its parts, you tend to group together those parts or lines or elements that seem to make the best "whole." The art of camouflage is simply applying this principle to allow an alien object to blend into its surroundings as much as possible.

Common fate. In any scene, all parts that have similar or common motion will tend to be grouped together. A common defense of animals is to "freeze" in the presence of predators. Thus, only when a camouflaged animal moves, is it easy to detect where it is located.

So, these are the principles that you will see operating in many of the events we'll now discuss. Keep them in mind as we review three factors that influence your ability to perceive.

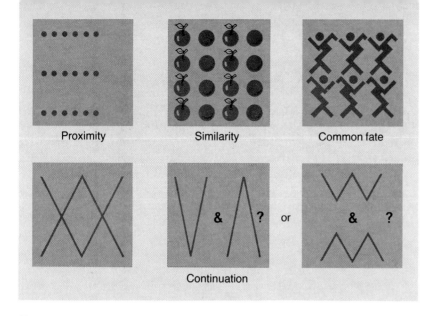

Figure 5-10 Grouping principles.
Proximity: When elements are grouped together, they seem to belong together.
Similarity: When elements are alike, we perceive them as belonging together.
Common fate: When elements seem to be moving in the same direction, they are perceived as belonging together.
Continuation: When elements seem to continue in the same direction, they are seen as belonging together. Which combination of lines seems the most logical way to make up a form similar to the first drawing?

Attention

Attention is our ability to focus on certain aspects of our immediate, ongoing experience while we ignore other aspects of it. At a party, what happens if someone mentions your name? You will manage to hear that conversation even though it may be occurring in a group other than the one in which you are standing. If you look out through a screen door, you ignore the screen to attend to the objects and events outside.

In North America, advertising provides some good examples of the principles of attention-getting. So do the activities you go through in trying to find a date for Friday night. Three groups of factors influence your attention. Let's review them.

Stimulus-bound factors. One way to gain attention is to alter the stimulus itself. The *intensity* or *size* of an advertisement influences whether you will notice it. Likewise, *movement* and *repetition* also attract attention. Finally, *contrast* will catch your interest. Advertisers use all these factors in calling attention to their products.

Now
is the
the time

Figure 5-11 What did you read in the triangle? See text for explanation.

An anthropomorphic view of camouflage. Stimuli are located where they "should" be, and, being motionless, fail to draw attention.

Drawing by Levin; © *1977*
The New Yorker Magazine, Inc.

Organism-bound factors: set (expectancy). You have personal attitudes and ideas that will help determine what aspects of the environment you will notice. *Set* is an adjustment that you make. You are prepared to respond in a particular way. Look at the figure in the margin. How long did it take you to find out what was wrong there? You didn't see anything wrong? Look again. Within the triangle it says "Now is *the the* time"!

Your *prior experience* leads you to expect to see certian things. For instance, did you notice that "certain" in the last sentence was misspelled? You don't expect such things in a textbook, so you're not on guard to find such errors. Your *internal state* can also bias your perceptions. If you're hungry, you are much more likely to perceive food objects in an unclear picture. Remember the last time you were a baby-sitter at night? Every strange sound was a burglar, right? Again, it's your own internal state.

Finally, the *social situation* of which you are a part may influence what you perceive. Experiments have shown that when making perceptual observations, most people will even change their minds to agree with the majority. Social pressure can influence your perception.

Mixed factors. Finally, there are aspects of the stimulus that combine with your own prior experience. Such mixed factors also influence your decisions as to what to attend to in the environment. There are two examples: One is *novelty*, illustrated by the advertising campaign of Braniff International Airlines. To attract attention to their airline, Braniff paints their planes brilliant reds, greens, blues, and so forth. It gains attention only because prior experience suggests that airplanes are usually aluminum-colored or some sky-related color.

Secondly, *familiarity* influences your attention. If you see the local newscaster of the evening news program that you usually watch, you will pay attention. You're familiar with him or her, and you usually associate that person with news events—disasters, wrecks, and various other crises. Familiarity breeds comfort and interest in this case!

Stimulus variation

Attention and set—in fact, *all* normal operations of the perceptual processes—depend on some variety in the incoming stimulation. The ultimate threat for prisoners, short of torture, is to be put in solitary confinement.

Stimulus variation forms a background of experience that allows us to interpret incoming stimuli. It allows us to "anchor" whatever we are attending to. Removing most incoming stimulation is very distressing. Yet, although we may seek height-ened stimulation, such as a ride on a roller coaster, we also tend to limit our exposure to that.

Constancies

Look at the nearest window or door in the room where you are right now. What shape is it? You're probably thinking to yourself that it's rectangular, yet if you held up a piece of glass in front of you and traced the exact outline of the door or window, the shape on the glass you are holding would probably *not* be rectangular. This illustrates one of several *constancies* that operate within us. Although physical stimuli may vary tre-mendously, the objects from which they come are interpreted the same. These constancies aid us in interpreting our world, and at least four of them can be identified.

Shape. The fact that familiar objects can be identified as square or round or rectangular in spite of the angle from which they are viewed is called *shape constancy*. Perception is a "bet" you are constantly wagering with yourself—balancing off your past experience against the specific incoming stimuli of the mo-ment. We'll show you cases later where you bet wrong and misperceive things.

Size. Someone gives you a meter stick to hold at arm's length. Then he or she asks you to pick the matching stick from among a dozen or so sticks, ranging from 0.7 meter to 1.3 me-ters, that are 10 meters away from you. You can do so quite easily. You based your decision on size and shape constancy and the incoming depth cues.

Brightness. Look at the shirt or blouse you're wearing right now. Turn off the room lights and look at it again. In compari-son with other objects in the room it keeps its relative bright-ness. Brightness is related to the relative amplitude of the light waves reaching your eyes from each object in the room. Stress that word *relative*, however, since the effects may differ. For instance, the black squares on the victor's flag waved at a noon-time road race may reflect more light than the white squares of that same flag being waved at sundown. The *relative* brightness seems crucial in determining the brightness of every object we view.

Color. What color is the shirt or blouse or sweater you're wearing right now? If you went outside now, would that color change? Of course you know that wouldn't happen. Likewise, if

shape consistency: *the per-ception of items as square, round, or whatever, no matter what the angle from which they are viewed*

you cast a shadow on part of your clothing, the color in the shadow doesn't really change though it may appear to be different. Your experience and the environmental cues combine to maintain a color constancy and your ability to perceive quite accurately.

━━━━━ In review . . .

The act of perceiving is based on certain factors of organization, including the figure-ground relationship. Another factor is the wholeness of figures (determined by symmetry, closure, and familiarity). A third is the grouping of elements (based on proximity, similarity, continuation, and common fate). Three other factors importantly involved in perception include attention, variations in stimulus input, and the constancies (shape, size, brightness, and color).

5 Visual Perception

Aerial perspective, or bluing, is one stimulus cue for judging distance. The farther away the mountains are, the bluer they look.

These three factors that we've just reviewed—attention, our need for stimulus variation, and the constancies—as well as the various principles for organizing and grouping stimuli, are always operating, especially in visual perception. Now let's have a look at how we judge our environment. In our visual world there are two jobs that are most important—judging distance and judging movement.

Distance

We use a tremendous variety of cues to judge distance. Some cues come from the environment. Other cues come from our own body as we adjust to our environment.

Stimulus cues. (1) One cue for judging distance is based on *size*. (See illustration.) The bigger something is, the closer we judge it to be. (2) We also rely on overlap, or *interposition*. A whole object is closer than any object of which we can only see a part. (3) *Shadows* may give us help, if we know where the light is coming from. (4) We also rely on the *texture gradient*. Look at the floor right where you are. Now look at the farthest piece of floor you can see in the same room. See how much less detail you can see far away? That's the texture gradient.

And there are some other more subtle cues we use. (5) One is called *aerial perspective* or *bluing*. Over long distances, the further away something is, the bluer it looks. (6) *Linear perspective*

Parallel lines seem to come together as they recede into the distance. Linear perspective is another stimulus cue. If an object is too close to us, it will seem blurred, particularly if we are focusing on something in the distance.

is illustrated by what you see looking down the railroad track; parallel lines seem to come together. Finally, (7) if an object is too close to us, it will *blur*. And if we're looking at an object far away, things between us and that object may also seem blurred. All these cues are used in judging distance.

Organism cues. Look at the tip of your nose (without using a mirror!). The pain you feel is caused by the *ciliary muscles*, which are causing your eyes to converge. (1) *Convergence* is a major cue to distance at close range.

Close one eye. Hold your index finger up and focus on it. Now focus on a point on the far wall that is just above your finger tip. Now focus on your finger again. (2) The change in focus is called *accommodation*. It is achieved by the lens in each eye every time you look at anything.

While you've still got that index finger waving around in the air, bring it in to about 10 centimeters in front of your face and look at it with the same one eye you used for the accommodation demonstration. Now close that eye and open the other one. Notice how the view of your finger changes slightly? (3) That's called *retinal disparity*. The different views of your eyes help you judge distance, and also combine to give you the three-dimensional view that you have of the world. This is discussed more in Box 5-3.

All three of these internal cues can be detected as you adjust to your environment. There are some other cues that we also rely on, but this should give you enough of an idea about how complex the perception of distance really is.

Use these pictures for a demonstration of binocular discoupling. You will need a sheet of paper. Directions are in Box 5-3.

Motion

We perceive movement very differently from how we perceive distance. At least two processes are involved. First, individual cells (rods and cones) in the eye either fire or don't fire. Higher up—both in the eye and in the brain—there are cells which are sensitive to the *order* in which lower cells fire. Direction and speed can thus be perceived.

More importantly, second, we don't see movement in an absolute sense. We only see movement relative to the background or another object. Have you ever been in a car on an Interstate highway? When you're going at the same speed as someone you're passing (or *trying* to pass anyway!), you don't seem to be moving at all, even though both of you may be doing 55 m.p.h. So both the context and internal processing are involved when you perceive movement.

Movement where none exists. Two lights are placed side by side. First one flashes and then the other. As the alternate flashing increases, what happens? Although you know you're looking at two separate lights, you sense only one light moving back and forth. By controlling the intensity of the lights, the distance between them, and the delay from one flash to the next, you create what is called the *phi phenomenon*.

A similar example is provided by movies. "Motion" pictures actually are just a series of individual still pictures projected rapidly enough so that your brain fills in the missing information, ignores the flicking, and perceives movement where none exists.

The illustration shows two slightly different views of the same scene with a line separating them. In bright light, place your head directly over the line and hold a sheet of paper along the line between your face and the book. Hold the paper so that each of your eyes can see only one of the views.

Now we're ready to demonstrate *binocular discoupling*. It's not a disease; it's a process. Holding your head, the book, and the helpful sheet of paper as we just described, pretend you are looking at something about half a mile beyond the two pictures. In other words, make your eyes converge on a make-believe distant subject while you are actually looking at the view very close to your face. You should now start to see three or four images—one to the left of your visual field

and another to the right. It's the two that are overlapping in the middle that you want to work on. See if you can adjust your eyes so that the two middle images overlap and fuse into one.

What happens when they do? You see a stereoscopic, three-dimensional picture! In this case we've made the two separate views of the same scene slightly different. Then, by causing your eyes to adjust themselves as if they were converging on a distant target, we've fooled your brain into interpreting the retinal disparity as a full-blown, normal view of the world. All three cues—convergence of both eyes, accommodation of the lenses, and retinal disparity—combine to allow you to perceive three dimensions where only two actually exist.

Induced movement. Have you ever seen the moon on a night when clouds are blowing past it? The moon seems to be moving rapidly the other way. Your perception of motion here is based on the context, your prior experience, and internal processing. Since you can't see the edge of the moving pattern of clouds, your brain doesn't comprehend that the foreground is moving, *not* the object. You make an error. We'll show you more such errors near the end of the chapter.

6 Hearing Perception

Locating sound

Locating a sound relies on three things. First, sounds out to one side always reach the nearer ear first. Onset *time* is a cue. Second, your head casts what is called a *sound shadow*. The ear that is further away will hear a slightly softer sound. Difference in *loudness* is a cue. Finally, when the sound enters each ear, it starts being analyzed by the cochlea. But the ear that hears the sound first has a head start. The sound waves it is analyzing are farther through each phase of their cycle all the time (if the head is not turned). So, *phase difference* is a cue.

Can you tell where a sound is coming from when it originates directly in front of you? It's not easy to do so because the three cues are identical to both ears. The sound waves reach both ears with the same loudness simultaneously.

Noise

Box 5-4 discusses the problem of noise. Any unwanted sound, or a sound that is not understood, or one inappropriate to the situation in which it is heard qualifies as *noise*. A whisper when you're alone with your love is fine, but a whisper at a symphony is noise.

Feature   **5–4   HOW DO WE PERCEIVE NOISE?**

What, exactly, is noise? Noise occurs if the resulting sound waves don't have an identifiable pitch. The illustration shows the difference in sound wave patterns generated by a complex, but meaningful, sound as opposed to a complex and *un*meaningful noise. When too many frequencies all occur at once, the result is noise. The static that is heard on the FM radio dial between stations contains a mix of many frequencies. It is called "white" noise in direct reference to white light, which is a mixture of many light waves.

Noise is also perceived if the person who is listening doesn't understand the sound. Thus, most of us from West European or North American countries might view Chinese music as noise. Such music uses rhythms and sources that are alien to the Western ear.

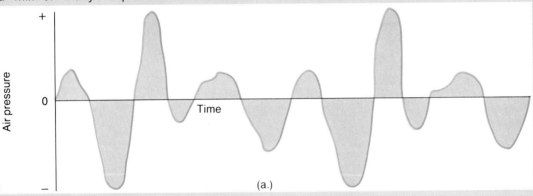

Figure 5-12a The almost perfect regularity of this wave pattern means that the trumpet that made the sound will be heard as a source of constant frequency and loudness.

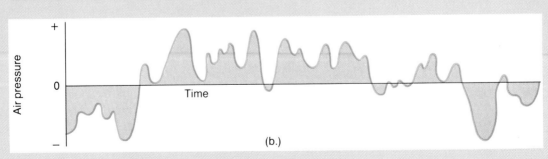

Figure 5-12b The irregularity of this wave pattern means that the kettle drum that made this sound will be heard as a much more uneven source. The loudness of a drum varies considerably from moment to moment, and the frequency is hard to identify since so many individual frequencies combine to produce this sound.

7 "Errors" in Perception

So far we've been explaining the principles of perception. Now, we're going to show you what happens when the constancies fail.

Illusions

Illusions most often happen when the environmental stimulus shares some—but not total—similarity with environmental situations you've experienced before. Your brain will then use your past experience incorrectly to interpret the new stimulus. Look at the illustrations for some common illusions. Related to the illusions we've shown are two other interesting questions.

First, are hallucinations actually illusions? Here the answer is no. Hallucinations result from improper mental activities. They may be caused by drugs or by physical or emotional problems, as we'll discuss in more detail in Chapter 12.

Second, can you photograph illusions? The answer is yes. Illusions result from processing errors. Even mirages can be photographed. Presenting the same physical stimulus pattern—whether in real life, or simply from a photograph—still produces the illusion. In all of the compound and figure illusions the background interferes with your ability to make the judgments required about part of the figure. Much work remains before we can fully explain why we make these perceptual "errors."

Extrasensory perception (ESP)

Parapsychologists ("Para-" means resembling or similar to) who believe in ESP suggest that our response capabilities are not limited only to identifiable, physical, observable stimuli. They speak of communication directly from mind to mind, not using the normally accepted channels and systems of communication. ESP is most frequently studied using a deck of 25 cards with five symbols: circles, squares, triangles, waves, and crosses. There are five cards with each symbol. Table 5-3 lists four types of ESP, including an example of each type.

The obvious question is, does it work? The evidence is mixed, but generally negative. The "you must believe in it to find it" attitude is contrary to the basic principles of science. Very few well-controlled studies have had positive results. In fact, the most interesting thing about the scientific pursuit of ESP is that the better controlled the studies are, the less likely it is the effect will show up. That is exactly the reverse of almost all other phenomena studied using the scientific method: Better control usually gives a *more* accurate picture of a phenomenon.

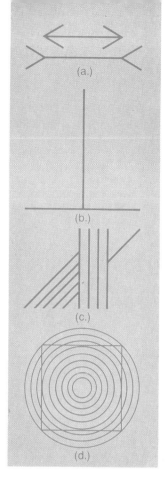

Figure 5-13a The Muller-Lyer illusion. Although the lines between the arrow heads are identical, we perceive them as being different.

Figure 5-13b Vertical-horizontal illusion. Which line is the longest, the vertical or the horizontal? Actually, they are the same.

Figure 5-13c The Poggendorff illusion: The diagonal lines seemingly will not meet if extended through the parallel vertical lines.

Figure 5-13d The Hering fan illusion: The square superimposed on the circles seems as if it has bowed, rather than straight, sides.

Table 5-3 Forms of extrasensory perception (ESP)

TITLE	DEFINITION	EXAMPLE
CLAIRVOYANCE	Sensing a message without an identifiable physical stimulus.	Can you guess which of five symbols is on the symbol card held by a friend?
TELEPATHY	Communication of thoughts from one person to another.	Requires "sender" and "receiver": Can receiver guess card symbol being viewed by sender?
PRECOGNITION	Predicting a future event before it happens.	Can you predict the order of the cards before they are exposed?
PSYCHOKINESIS	Mental control of physical events, things.	Uri Geller alleged* in the mid-70's he could bend keys by exercising his mental powers.

*Evidence was later developed which suggested that Geller may have used skills as a magician, not supernatural powers of ESP, to achieve his effects.

Does it exist? Well, how can we describe those who say they "have" ESP? We know "some have it more than others." We know "only certain people show it." We know "no one has it all the time." And, we know "we can't predict when a person having it will be 'on' or 'off'." When you sum it up this way, what we also know is that the same four statements could also be made of a chance or random event. Don't these same statements apply to your likelihood of finding someone who can toss pennies so that they land "heads up"? ESP is an interesting, challenging notion, but there's little hard evidence to support its existence so far.

In review . . .

There are two important jobs in visual perception. One is judging distance or depth, which is based on stimuli and cues within the organism. The other is detecting motion, which is based on the order in which sensing cells fire and/or movement relative to the environment or another object. In perceiving sound, our ability to locate a sound source is based on onset time, relative loudness, and phase differences of the sound waves reaching each ear.

"Errors" in perception occur when the constancies fail. The resulting illusions are of four types—straight-line, bisecting or orientation, compound straight-line, or figure. Subliminal perception is feared more than is warranted. Extra-sensory perception remains controversial and is still lacking in hard scientific proof.

Chapter Application and Review

USING PSYCHOLOGY   *How does perception affect your "image"?*

As you have read, perception involves a very complex variety of factors. You've seen how our previous experiences can influence the ways in which we respond to stimuli. And there is no doubt that our senses can and do deceive us. But how can you turn this fact to good account? What practical use can you make of your knowledge of perception?

Well, you might ask yourself if you are satisfied with the way people perceive *you* (assuming, of course, you can be objective enough to know). Suppose you want to "change your image"—the image, that is, that meets the eye. There are some simple tips that can help.

Clothing

Are you overweight? Do you want to appear taller and slimmer? Up-and-down lines will help create the illusion. One piece garments of vertical stripes or darker solid colors keep the eye from stopping at your waist where another color begins. Single-breasted jackets will direct the eye in a vertical line. Smooth fabrics are better than fuzzy or textured ones. Likewise, clothes that fit well will make you look less bulky, and more tall and slim.

Suppose your problem is being skinny or extremely tall. To look heavier and shorter, reverse the advice just given. Color contrasts that cut your height in half, and cross-wise lines and stripes will help. Light colors and fuzzy, bulky fabrics add width. Large, splashy prints, distinctive pendants, and belts with fancy buckles will distract the eye. Double-breasted jackets, with their two rows of buttons, also break height.

Color

Colors as well as shapes and lines can play a vital role in projecting an image and creating a mood. Think of the many common expressions that recognize this fact: "seeing red," "green with envy," "feeling blue," "in a brown funk," "purple passion." Some colors are cool, such as blue. Yellow, orange, and red are warm colors. Green is the only color that looks cool in summer, warm in winter. Do you tend to wear brighter colors on a gloomy day? Of course, some colors are simply more becoming to you than others. Your own coloring will make a difference. Wearing blue can emphasize blue eyes. Wearing yellow can make a yellowish skin look sick. You can contrast clothing colors with your own colorations, or choose them to harmonize.

If you're going to wear two colors, it is best to wear two complementary colors, meaning colors across from each other on the color circle. If using three colors, use colors that are about 120° apart from one another on the color circle. So as not to appear too "loud" or flamboyant as a dresser, use less saturated colors.

Blending in with the scenery can pose a safety hazard to humans: yellow slickers are best for visibility on rainy days. Snow skiers are safer not wearing white. Bicycle riders are advised to wear something white at night. (Of course, day-glo and fluorescent colors are helpful too.) You can extend the safety principle to your car as well. What colors would make it more visible in a fog, at night, or on a rainy day?

Analogous color harmony uses colors that are next to one another on the color circle. If you choose these, you should stick to one primary color. Now that you have thought about the effects of color, you can experiment with them to see what works best for you.

Of course the lessons of dressing also apply to the choice of colors in fixing up your room or decorating in general. Again, apply the principles of perception to gain control over how your environment (and you) will be perceived.

REVIEW QUESTIONS

SECTION 1 (pages 149–150)
1. Explain some ways in which sensation and perception are similar.
2. Explain some ways in which sensation and perception are different.

SECTION 2 (pages 150–152)
1. Define the two types of thresholds.
2. What is Weber's Law?

SECTION 3 (pages 152–164)
1. The stimulus for vision is light waves that are received by the eye. Name the three physical characteristics of light and the psychological attributes related to each.
2. Describe the parts of the eye and the functions performed by each part.
3. The stimulus for hearing is pressure, or sound waves received by the ear. Name the three physical characteristics of sound waves and the psychological attributes related to each.

4. What are the two chemical senses and the elements to which they respond?
5. What are now considered to be our four basic tastes?
6. Name and describe the theory that best explains the sense of smell.
7. What is the receptor for taste, and how does it work?
8. What are the physical stimuli for the skin senses? What are the psychological attributes involved?
9. What is the role of the physical organs upon which the vestibular sense is based?
10. Explain kinesthesia and the source of the stimuli that produce it.

SECTION 4 (pages 164–170)
1. What is perception?
2. Name the three organizing factors that help us perceive and the elements involved in each factor.

3. What are three factors that influence our attention as it is related to perception?

4. Describe the role played by stimulus variations.

5. Name some constancies that influence our perceptual accuracy.

SECTION 5 (pages 170–173)

1. What does visual perception involve?

2. Describe the phi phenomenon.

SECTION 6 (pages 173–174)

1. Our ability to locate sound sources is based on what three factors?

2. What is noise?

SECTION 7 (pages 175–177)

1. When do illusions occur?

2. Describe subliminal perception.

3. Describe extrasensory perception. How valid is it? Why?

ACTIVITIES

1. We have discussed how most of the sounds we hear result from the transmission of pressure waves through the air. To demonstrate this process, blow up a balloon to be full but not in danger of bursting. Hold that balloon in front of the bass speaker of a stereo set. (You might try this in a department store if you don't have a system at home.) What happens to the balloon? Now hold the balloon in front of the treble speaker. What happens? What does this show you about the transmission of physical sound waves?

2. A British psychologist suggested an easy way to demonstrate the source of the negative afterimage. Is it in your brain? Is it on the receiving surface of your eye? Touch the outside corner of your eye socket and locate a notch in the bone surrounding your eye. If you apply a steady, moderate pressure to your eye at that spot, you will find your vision will disappear within 30 seconds or so. While continuing to press, turn on a light bulb in front of you. Your eye won't be able to see it. Turn the bulb off and then release the pressure on your eye. As your vision restores itself, you will see a negative afterimage of the bulb you couldn't see before! This demonstration shows that afterimages occur on the sensing surface of the eye.

3. Career Search. Visit the psychology laboratory in a local community college or university. Ask the teacher to explain the nature of any experiments being conducted that relate to physiology. What objectives are being sought? What animals are being used? Have a class discussion about how such animal research can be helpful to humans.

4. One measure of the number of skin sensors that occupy any part of the surface of your body is your ability to detect whether you are being touched by one or two objects at any given point. To measure this, get a friend who will help you. Ask your friend to close his or her eyes. Then, using two sharpened pencils, tell your friend that you are going to touch him or her with one or two pencils, either holding both points together, or separating the points by up to four inches. As you conduct your experiment, make sure that you (a) always touch both points to your friend's skin at the same time, and (b) ask your friend to tell you each time whether the contact was made with one or two points. Gradually increase the distance between the pencils by one half to one centimeter each time you make the contact. In this way you can measure what is called a two-point threshold. When your friend's reports shift from "one" to "two," do not increase the distance again, but re-contact several times. Does the report go back to "one"? Now try this on your friend's arm, cheek, center of the neck, lower part of the leg, and front side of the index finger. Which area is the best detector? Why do you think this is so?

5. Doing this experiment requires some preparation. You'll need a friend with a cold. Prepare half-centimeter pieces of raw, peeled potato, turnip, beet, apple, and the seedless (edge) part of squash. Have the parts of food ready beforehand, and keep the food covered so your subject can't see it before being blindfolded for the experiment. Ask your friend to taste the pieces of food. Allow your subject to rinse a swallow of water around in his or her mouth between tastes of each type of food. Ask your subject to identify each type of food as it is tasted. How rapidly can your subject make the judgment? How accurate is it?

Try the same test with a person who doesn't have a cold. Can someone without a cold make the identification more easily and accurately? What happens to this person's accuracy when you allow him or her to smell a cigarette or a bit of ammonia or an onion just before making the taste judgment?

INTERESTED IN MORE?

GOLDSTEIN, E. B. *Sensation and Perception.* Wadsworth, 1980. A well written, college-level text explaining the basic processes of sensation and perception. In addition to the traditional topics, it includes chapters on perception of music and speech.

HELD, R. & RICHARDS, W. (eds.) *Recent Progress in Perception: Readings from Scientific American.* W. H. Freeman, 1976. A collection of articles from past issues of the magazine, featuring theories and mechanisms of perception. Richly illustrated.

HOCHBERG, J. E. *Perception,* 2nd ed. Prentice-Hall, 1978. A good, tough book greatly expanding the coverage of topics in this chapter. Contains a wide variety of illustrations of sensory mechanisms, illusions, and other current concerns of psychologists interested in perception.

LINDSAY, P. H. & NORMAN, D. A. *Human Information Processing: An Introduction to Psychology* 2nd ed. Academic Press, 1977. Although intended as a general, college-level introductory text, this book is actually an excellent introduction to sensory processes and perception. Well illustrated.

McBURNEY, D. H. & COLLINGS, V. B. *Introduction to Sensation/Perception.* Prentice-Hall, 1977. A book with a little bit of everything: research, "how-to-do-it" advice on simple sensory and perceptual effects, and discussions of various factors that affect our perceptual skills.

WADE, N. *The Art and Science of Visual Illusions.* Routledge & Kegan Paul, 1982. A lavishly illustrated volume containing the most recent theories and research about illusions. Contains hundreds of illusions.

UNIT THREE

LEARNING AND LANGUAGE

Animals, like this killer whale, are trained by operant conditioning, or the process in which the frequency of a response is increased by reinforcement whenever that response takes place.

You now know how fully developed humans receive and respond to signals from the world outside themselves. But what use do they make of these signals? In other words, how do they learn? That's the topic of the next three chapters.

In Chapter 6 we look at three basic kinds of learning: classical conditioning; operant conditioning; and imitation, or observational learning. We also discuss the role of punishment in the learning process. In Chapter 7 we examine other and more complex processes important to learning, such as memory and thinking. And in Chapter 8 we describe one of the most complex skills in which humans engage: using language, the oral and written heart of human progress. Finally, we'll examine communication, including some fascinating studies done by scientists who go beyond human language to "speak" with other species.

6 Learning

CHAPTER OUTLINE

WHAT'S THE ANSWER?

☐ "I was in fourth grade the first time I met up with that 1½-inch rope dangling from the rafters of the school gym. The PE teacher shinnied right to the top and then shouted to me to grab the rope and climb it. I tried my best, but I barely got my feet off the floor. The next time I saw such a rope I was in 11th grade, and now the PE teacher was called 'Coach.' I was afraid I wouldn't be able to climb any better than I had in fourth grade. Imagine how surprised I was when I reached the rafters!" *How do you explain this?*

☐ *Do animals learn the same way humans do?*

☐ "My sister used to have a cute trick she pulled on my father all the time when she was about two years old. When he held her in his arms, she used to suck in a little breath and then blow just a small puff of air into the side of his eye. She always laughed when she saw him blink. A couple of days ago I made a bet with her that it wouldn't happen again. So, she cuddled up next to my father, and then she drew in some air and pretended she was going to blow air at him, and you know what? He blinked! My sister's 15 years old now, and she hasn't done that in a dozen years, I'll bet. He blinked!" *What happened here?*

What role do computers play in the classroom? Educational psychologists are interested in evaluating ways in which learning may be made more efficient—for example, by the use of computers.

☐ "I've been working here at the Resorts National for nineteen years cleaning these ashtrays, sweeping this carpet, and fetching cigarettes for the customers. Some people think I'm in a rut, but I like what I do, and I enjoy seein' other people spend their money. You know who's in a rut? You see that old man in the tan slacks over there playing the slot machine? He comes in here at least once a month with a bag of coins and he keeps putting them into that machine until he runs out. He's been doing it for years . . . long as I can remember. It used to be nickels, but now it's quarters. He's the one's in a rut." *How do you explain this gambler's behavior?*

1 Issues in Learning

Consider how important learning is to you. You learn to find shelter when you see lightning or hear thunder. You learn to swim. You learn how to ride a bicycle. You even learn how to talk with your friends. You gain a lot of skill in your alternating roles of speaker and listener. The examples could go on and on. Some are of life-and-death importance, such as the behavior of heading for the surface when you run short of breath under water. Others are trivial, such as the fact that your index finger fits the holes in a telephone dial more easily than your thumb. All of these examples share one thing in common: they are learned bits of behavior. Examples of learning are present everywhere. Learning controls human and animal behavior.

Definition: learning

Learning can be defined as a *relatively permanent change in a behavioral tendency that occurs as a result of practice or observation*. Learning does not mean just strengthening responses. It may or may not produce an immediate change in behavior.

Is this learning? We have defined learning as *relatively permanent*; it cannot be something that is "here today and gone tomorrow." It must have a continuing effect. In a marathon race you run much more easily at the start of the race than you do at the finish. You don't learn to run more poorly during the marathon. You simply grow tired, but your fatigue will go away with time. This change in your behavior is not learned.

We have also defined learning as involving a *change*: there must be something different about us after we have learned. Notice we have not said it must be a change for better or worse. Learning occurs whether the behavior change is good or bad.

In addition, we have said learning involves a *behavioral tendency*. *Tendency* is the important word here. In watching your girlfriend fix her bike you may notice that she leaves her pliers inside the house when you both go in for a Coke. What happens if you're outside later, and she can't find the pliers? You show her where they are, or get them for her. You learned earlier where they were, but you didn't *behave* as if you had learned until much later.

Finally, we have insisted that learning *occurs as a result of practice or observation*: As is true for a player on a school or major league athletic team, practice, or the opportunity to repeat a behavior, adds to a person's ability to perform it. Children learn how to handle eating utensils in part by observing their parents at mealtime.

The marathon runner becomes tired while running, an unlearned change in behavior.

learning: *a relatively permanent change in a behavioral tendency that occurs as a result of practice or observation*

The opportunity to practice a behavior can lead to the acquisition of a skill. Performance demonstrates that learning has occurred.

Performance is the key.   There is one more point you should keep in mind—the importance of *performance* in demonstrating that learning has occurred. We may say "He learned the poem" or "She learned how to define 'independent variable'," but how do we know he or she *learned*? We find out by watching the person *perform* some act that shows the existence of learning. We talk about learning, but we never see it directly; we only see a performance.

In review . . .

Learning is defined as a relatively permanent change in a behavioral tendency that occurs as a result of practice or observation. Learning cannot be directly observed. Psychologists observe an action and infer from that action that learning has occurred.

instance, our fear of a buzzing bee is a result of classical conditioning. Based on a negative reinforcement (avoidance of pain by escaping the bee), these fears result from only a few childhood experiences.

In review . . .

Classical conditioning, as originally developed by Pavlov, involves four events: (1) an Unconditioned Stimulus (US)—an event that always produces certain response; (2) an Unconditioned Response (UR)—a behavior brought about by a US; (3) a conditioned stimulus (CS)—any event which, prior to conditioning, does not produce any response resembling the UR; and finally, (4) a Conditioned Response (CR)—the response produced by the CS, neutral before conditioning, but resembling the UR after conditioning. Classical conditioning is done by repeated pairing of the CS and US, using a positive or a negative reinforcer.

Think about it

The **question**: Remember the story about the little girl who blew a small puff of air into her father's eye? She was surprised that he blinked when she puckered her lips 13 years later as if she were going to blow into his eye again. What kind of conditioning was involved? What was the reinforcer?

The **answer**: What she had done, of course, without being aware of it, was to condition her father, using a negative reinforcer. The puff of air was the US, and the eyeblink was the UR. Once the conditioning of her father was complete, the inhaling of air and puckering of her lips served as the CS. It produced his eyeblink as a CR—much to the teenager's surprise and delight.

An everyday example. Classical conditioning in Pavlov's dogs is perhaps the simplest type of learning to be studied in the laboratory. We can also see this type of learning in our everyday lives.

One example is provided by the ice cream man who drives around many city neighborhoods ringing a bell to attract attention. He is simply applying the principles of classical conditioning. Ring the bell and feed the children. Pretty soon the children will come running as soon as they hear the bell. This is classical conditioning using a positive reinforcement.

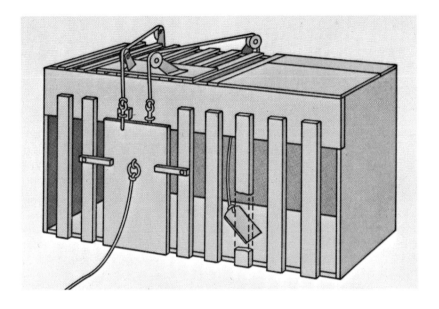

Figure 6-2 A puzzle box similar to the apparatus developed by Thorndike in one of the earliest studies in learning.

3 Operant (Instrumental) Conditioning

Now let's look at a more recent concept—operant, or instrumental, conditioning. There are many research techniques that involve operant conditioning. We'll briefly examine one such technique from which our modern procedures have grown.

Trial and error learning

Pavlov was working out the details of classical conditioning in Russia at the turn of the century. Meanwhile, the American psychologist Robert L. Thorndike was studying another type of learning.

In his experiments, Thorndike put a cat in a puzzle box with a trick door. To escape, the cat had to open the door by pulling down a string, pushing a bar, or some other response. The cat usually tried a variety of wrong responses in attempting to get out of the box. Thus, it was called *trial and error* learning. By accident, most cats finally opened the door. After more practice the cat could reduce its errors until only the correct response for opening the door remained. The animal's behavior operated (was instrumental) in obtaining its release.

In the puzzle box all of the equipment to solve the problem was in sight of the animal. In a maze, which is another form of puzzle box, the decisions must be made one at a time. A maze usually offers only one path as the correct route from a starting point to freedom, food, or some other desirable item.

Figure 6-3 A maze presents a problem that involves decision—whether to turn right or left. At each point only part of the information needed to reach the end is available.

A trained porpoise provides an example of behavior that has been altered by operant conditioning.

A Skinner box. Major features include a bar that can be pressed by an animal as a means of delivering food pellets, a source of water, and a floor of closely placed rods. Light stimuli come from disks on the wall, and sound stimuli come from a loud speaker. (Photo courtesy Pfizer, Inc.)

operant (instrumental) conditioning: *altering the frequency of a response by giving a reinforcement whenever that response is given*

Method of Successive Approximations: *operant conditioning method which results in a final complex behavior achieved through rewarding a series of responses more and more like the desired behavior*

The process

Operant, or instrumental, conditioning is the process in which the frequency or probability of a response is increased by giving a reinforcement whenever that response takes place. For example, the circus trainer often gives an animal small pieces of food after the animal correctly performs a trick. The trainer is using the reward and principles of operant conditioning to increase or maintain the frequency of the animal's doing the trick correctly. This is the Law of Effect in action.

The Skinner box. The basic process is simply a matter of timing a reinforcement so that it immediately follows the response to be learned. To aid in studying the processes involved in operant conditioning, B. F. Skinner developed a piece of apparatus which is now called the Skinner box.

How is it used? One way is simply to place a hungry rat in the box. Set up the box so that every time the lever is pressed a single small pellet of food (about the size of a BB-pellet) will drop into the food cup. Then you can demonstrate trial and error learning in a much more sophisticated piece of equipment—but you really haven't moved past Thorndike.

Method of Successive Approximations. More fun, however, is to use a process called the *Method of Successive Approximations*. This method involves a series of steps. Step One is to train the rat to eat from the food cup. If the animal has been deprived of food for 23 hours, it will explore the chamber actively when placed in it. If the food delivery apparatus is repeatedly operated, the rat will soon start eating when it first hears the sound of the apparatus being activated.

Feature   6–1   **"DON'T WALK UNDER THAT LADDER!"**

Reinforcement leads to an increased frequency of the responses that occurred just before the reward. What happens to *irrelevant*, or random, responses that just happened to occur prior to a reinforcement? Do they increase in frequency? Are these irrelevant responses learned?

For example, suppose you are using operant conditioning to train your dog. Suppose as you reward her for the first time for the complete act of sitting up and barking ("speaking"), your dog touches her nose to the ground at your feet. And suppose that just by accident your dog happens to touch her nose to the ground just before barking correctly the second time.

By now your dog is beginning to learn that sitting up and barking leads to a small piece of food. However, she is also touching her nose to the ground just as often and just as regularly. Yet the nose touching the ground

has nothing to do with getting the food. Your dog has been rewarded for sitting up and barking, but she's also been rewarded for touching her nose to the ground. In short, your dog has accidently conditioned herself in error.

The late Vince Lombardi was a highly successful coach of the Green Bay Packers (and later the Washington Redskins). He always wore a brown suit to the Sunday professional football games he coached. Neither that suit nor its color had anything to do with winning, yet he continued to wear it. Knocking on wood or throwing salt over your left shoulder for good luck are other examples. They are behaviors that are not related to reinforcement, yet they continue to occur anyway. It's probably due to an accidental earlier reinforcement. They are, in short, superstitions—bits of behavior with no demonstrated impact on daily events.

Step Two involves delivering a pellet of food only when the animal is in the general neighborhood of the cup.

Step Three is yet more demanding. Now a food pellet may be delivered only when the rat is close enough to the bar to touch it, even though we are not yet demanding that it do so.

Step Four means that food is delivered to the animal only when its foot is touching the bar.

Finally, in Step Five, food is delivered only when the rat presses the bar itself. That action will close a switch to operate the food delivery mechanism. Now the animal has fed itself and operant conditioning is complete. Steps two to five are called *shaping*.

Reinforcement and punishment. Operant conditioning can also be achieved using negative reinforcement. The procedures are almost the same as those with positive reinforcers that we've just discussed. Of course, there is an obvious change in the nature of the reinforcement. Now the animal is trying to get away from or reduce an undesirable state.

shaping: *in operant conditioning, reinforcing successive steps toward a desired behavior*

One example would be taking an aspirin to reduce a head-ache. The seek-find-and-swallow aspirin response is negatively reinforced by the later reduction in pain. Another example: When walking barefoot in the summertime, you are not likely to stay very long on a heated black highway surface. It's hot—*very* hot. It is negatively reinforcing to step off the highway onto the cool grass.

But this last example raises one other point that needs to be made clear. A negative reinforcer is any event the decrease or removal of which leads to an *increase* in the frequency of the behavior preceding it. Contrast negative reinforcers with punishers. A punishment causes a *decrease* in the frequency of the behavior preceding it.

In review . . .

Trial and error learning involves gradual elimination of errors where cues for the correct solution of a problem are all present at once (puzzle box) or presented one at a time (maze). Operant conditioning today frequently involves use of an enclosed chamber called a Skinner box. The Method of Successive Approximations is an oft-used training technique. It is based on shaping, a process in which an organism is reinforced for performing responses more and more similar to the desired one. Operant conditioning itself involves increasing the frequency of a behavior, either by using a positive reinforcer, or by removing a negative reinforcer or decreasing its intensity.

Classical versus operant conditioning: one major difference

You have now considered two types of conditioning, classical and operant, both of which use positive or negative reinforcement. Although the procedures and reinforcements may differ, the two types of learning are very similar. There is one point of difference, however, and this is in the responses.

In classical conditioning procedures the response is always *elicited*, or forced, from the subject. The subject has no choice regarding whether or not to respond. This is because of the nature of the US-UR pairings that are selected. For the hungry animal food will always elicit saliva; for the thirsty animal water will always elicit drinking. The animal simply has no other choice.

"Have you been waiting long?"

Results of an extended period of operant conditioning.

By contrast, in operant conditioning the response must always be *emitted*, or given, before a reinforcement can be gained. If a rat chooses just to sit in a Skinner box, no responses will be recorded or reinforced. Not until the organism emits a response can anything be accomplished.

4 Observational Learning

For many years learning was analyzed only in terms of classical and operant conditioning. Most of our explanations so far have placed a lot of stress on the role of reinforcement. Gain a reward and learn the behavior. Yet, think for a moment about your everyday life. Do your parents play tennis? If you've started practicing the sport too, it's unlikely you began by holding the racket like a golf club! In short, you had already learned a lot just by watching them play.

observational learning: *learning by imitation*

In the United States television viewing takes up more time than any other waking-hours activity. Do you think that what is learned from television by imitation is mainly for good or bad?

Many sports and physical activities are best learned by imitation.

The process

Since the 1960's more and more psychologists have begun to recognize the obvious: we learn just by watching each other or reading about or seeing pictures of someone making a skilled response. Then—sometimes much later—the observer can try to imitate the model's response. It's called *observational learning, social learning,* or *imitation.*

Albert Bandura suggests that observational learning involves three elements: a modeling stimulus, a matching response performed by the observer (learner), and a reinforcer for the matching responses. There are four processes that control your observational learning: you must pay *attention* to the model, you must show *retention* of the model's behavior, you must be *able to perform* the behavior, and you must be *motivated to perform.* Motivation can be provided by *external* rewards you hope to gain, by the pleasure of seeing someone else rewarded, or by your own *self*-generated reinforcers.

Many of the factors influencing operant and classical conditioning also affect learning by imitation. If the model (the person being observed) is successful, we are likely to follow his or her example. The more similar models are to us, the more likely we are to imitate them. The more similar the environment and stimuli we share with our models, the more likely we are to imitate their actions. But the main advantage in imitation is its efficiency. Once any of us has learned how to perform an important behavior, it can often be passed on best through this method of learning.

████████ In review . . .

Classical conditioning is based mainly on reinforcements that elicit behavior. Operant conditioning involves reinforcing emitted behaviors. By contrast, observational learning or imitation seems to occur mainly because of its efficiency. If an organism sees a behavior and can perform it, then the more traditional classical and operant procedures work much more quickly.

5 Events in Learning

At this point we've looked at the most basic aspects of both classical and operant conditioning and observational learning. It may seem that they are quite different procedures, but in many ways they are, in fact, very similar. Let's review a number of different learning events. Then we can compare their occurrence in classical and operant conditioning.

Reinforcement

In conditioning, reinforcing every correct response is called *continuous reinforcement*. Almost nothing we humans do is reinforced every single time we do it. Continuous reinforcement (or CRF, as the operant conditioners call it) does not occur in the real world very often. Usually, reinforcements occur, or are given, only some of the times a correct response occurs. This is called *partial reinforcement*. It is used in both classical and operant conditioning procedures.

Partial reinforcement can be accomplished in one of two ways. The *schedule of reinforcement* is a statement of the rules governing how and when reinforcements are being given. One partial reinforcement schedule gives reinforcements for either a fixed or average number of correct responses. These are the *ratio* schedules.

The other kind of reinforcement schedule gives reinforcements for the first correct response after a certain fixed or average amount of time has passed. These are the *interval* schedules. Let's look briefly at each of the four possible schedules of partial reinforcement in somewhat more detail.

Fixed ratio. According to this schedule, the experimenter gives a reinforcer for a fixed number of responses. Every second, third, or fourth correct response might be reinforced. It is quite

Fixed Ratio Schedule: *a schedule of reinforcement in which the reward always follows a fixed number of responses*

rigid and predictable, and it produces very stable response rates. The migrant workers who follow the crops up and down the West Coast of the United States each year are often paid on a Fixed Ratio Schedule. They get a certain amount of cash for every basket they harvest.

Variable ratio. Here the organism will be rewarded on the average, or "in the long run," every second, third, or fourth (or more) time it responds. However, for any particular response there is no guarantee there will be a reinforcement. The schedule is based on performance averages rather than a specific number of responses.

Fixed interval. On this schedule an organism is reinforced for the first correct response after a fixed interval of time has taken place since the last reinforcement. It doesn't matter how often the organism responds during the interval following the reinforcement. It won't be reinforced until the first correct response following that interval occurs.

If your teacher gives you a quiz at the end of each week, your studying is being "reinforced" on a fixed interval schedule. The interesting thing about fixed interval reinforcement schedules is that they allow us to "predict" when a reinforcement is due. The response rate picks up just before the end of the interval. And isn't that pattern of behavior exactly the pattern you follow in studying this material? Most likely you study psychology more the night before a quiz than any other night of the week.

Variable interval. Here the organism is rewarded for the first response after an interval of time has elapsed since the last reinforcement—but the precise interval varies. It may average 5, 10, 30 seconds, or whatever. It is unknown until a correct response yields reinforcement.

Does your teacher give quizzes without announcing beforehand when they'll occur? If so, then your studying behavior is being maintained or reinforced on a variable interval schedule. You never know when you'll get your reward. As a result you tend to respond (that is, study) more frequently than you would on a fixed interval schedule. You never know when that next quiz is coming.

Primary and secondary reinforcement. There is one other important point concerning different kinds of reinforcement. Reinforcers can be divided into two broad categories, depending on how necessary they are for the organism's survival.

Variable Ratio Schedule: *a schedule of reinforcement in which the reward is given after a variable number of responses*

Fixed Interval Schedule: *a schedule of reinforcement in which the first response after a definite period of time is reinforced (regardless of the number of responses between times)*

Variable Interval Schedule: *a schedule of reinforcement in which the first response following a changeable, average period of time is reinforced*

primary reinforcement: *a stimulus that is naturally (innately) reinforcing (such as food, water)*

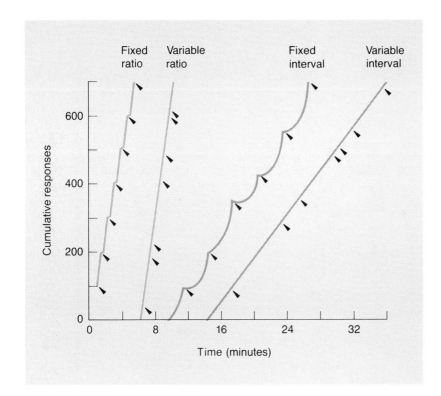

Figure 6-4 The frequency of responses per unit of time under each of four schedules of partial reinforcement. The steeper the curve, the more responses being given per unit of time. Which schedule leads to the highest rate of performance?

What happens if you deprive an animal of food or water or expose it to some kind of pain? Putting it simply, it requires very little learning for that animal (or human, for that matter) to know the benefits which can be gained by certain actions when you reinforce with food, water, or reduction of the pain. These are all examples of primary reinforcers. They gain their ability to reinforce without the need for much prior learning. There are not very many primary reinforcers.

By contrast there is a much larger group of stimuli that *may* become reinforcers. These *secondary* reinforcers gain their ability to reinforce because learning has gone on before. Remember how much you salivated before some holiday dinner was finally put on the family table? Most of the stimuli causing your mouth to water were learned secondary reinforcers. Many times before you've associated a certain time of day, the dishes on the table, the smells of the cooking food, and all the kitchen preparations with eating. These stimuli become classically conditioned, secondary cues that reinforce you. Your response is based on the many times in the past when these cues have been associated with the food you were seeking.

secondary reinforcement: *a stimulus which gains reinforcing properties through prior association with a primary reinforcer*

⟹
Think about it

The **question**: Remember the old man in the tan slacks mentioned earlier? The janitor at a Las Vegas nightclub-hotel said the man arrived once a month or so with a bag of coins. He played the slot machine each time until he ran out of coins. What kind of reinforcement is involved here? What keeps the old man coming back so often to "play the slots"?

The **answer**: It is known, of course, that in the long run the customer will lose money playing the Las Vegas slot machines. The machine must be set to give the "house" a small profit to make it worthwhile to have the machine installed in the first place. However, the man in the tan slacks couldn't care less. He's putting a coin in and pulling the handle. Every now and then he gets a lot of coins back. He is "hooked" on a variable ratio schedule of partial reinforcement.

In review . . .

There continues to be some debate as to whether or not classical conditioning and operant conditioning are identical. However, there is no doubt that they share a number of effects. Reinforcement is one important process involved in many types of conditioning. Continuous reinforcement (giving a reward for every correct response) occurs less often than some form of partial reinforcement. Such partial reinforcement schedules include fixed ratio, variable ratio, fixed interval, and variable interval. Reinforcements are primary (essential to the well-being of the organism) or secondary (learned, and not necessary to survival).

Timing

In classical conditioning the Unconditioned Stimulus is the reinforcer. In operant conditioning the reinforcement is whatever follows the emitted response. In both cases timing is very important and often determines whether a reinforcement has any effect at all on conditioning.

In classical conditioning, the optimal interval between the CS and US is about 1/2 second. The young girl in the "Think about it" puckered her lips and then blew a brief burst of air in her father's eye. Without knowing it she timed her pucker-followed-by-air almost perfectly. It would have been difficult for her to hold her breath for very many seconds. If she had, her father would have had no reason to blink at the sight/sound of the pucker. Conditioning would not have worked.

Figure 6-5 In classical conditioning the response is not under voluntary control. Salivation is an involuntary response. Conditioning occurs as repetition takes place.

Operant conditioning is also more effective if you can give reinforcement right after the response. Suppose you're reinforcing someone every time he or she uses the pronoun "I." Any time "I" is said, you smile and nod in agreement. It will increase the frequency of "I . . ." statements, but not if you delay the smile and nod. Five seconds after starting an "I . . ." sentence your friend may have spoken two dozen words. How could he or she possibly guess which word(s) caused you to smile? Again, timing is critical.

→ Think about it

The **question**: Why is money such a powerful reinforcer for humans? What kind of conditioning is involved in making money into an effective secondary reinforcer?

The **answer**: In terms of classical conditioning, the money is the conditioned stimulus. What accounts for the powerful nature of the conditioning is that the same CS-US pairing occurs many times. That same CS (money) is paired just before people acquire food—a cupcake, a milkshake, or whatever—or when they buy merchandise—a radio or any number of other things people normally desire. Money (the CS) is present time after time just before we get things in which we are interested. So time and time again money is conditioned as a positive secondary reinforcer. It always precedes the reinforcements we need or want.

Figure 6-6 In operant conditioning, the organism actively participates in the learning process. Here the dog learns to wait at the refrigerator and to bring its dish. Extinction, generalization, and discrimination apply to both operant and classical conditioning.

Extinction

Earlier in the chapter we discussed Thorndike's Law of Effect: responses that are reinforced increase in frequency. But, what happens to any response that is no longer followed by the reinforcement that led to its being learned in the first place? If the reward is no longer given, the frequency of the learned response will decrease. This decrease is called *extinction.* Consider the animal in the Skinner box who has been getting a food pellet each and every time it hits the bar. What happens if the animal is suddenly placed on an extinction schedule and never again reinforced? The once-reinforced response is no longer producing the food the animal wants. It makes sense for that animal to quit pressing the bar and to try other responses. Extinction, therefore, comes easily.

On the other hand, think of an animal that is being trained on a partial reinforcement schedule. Neither the precise number of responses nor the exact moment of reinforcement is usually known to the animal. This animal goes for long stretches before it is reinforced. When placed on an extinction schedule (no more rewards are to be given), the animal won't become aware of this for some time. Only slowly will the animal begin to show any decrease in its level of performance. This resistance to extinction is called the *Partial Reinforcement Effect*. It apparently applies to most organisms at all levels of the animal hierarchy.

Generalization

There are two processes that are among the most important aspects of learning. They occur in both classical and operant conditioning. One is generalization, and the other is discrimination.

To illustrate generalization let's look at an event that has occurred at some time to almost all of us. Through years of training, most drivers have learned how to respond when a car with a flashing red light on its roof appears behind them. They pull over to the side of the road and stop driving. It is a highly predictable response for most drivers.

What would happen if a car with a light that was slightly yellower than the traditional police-cruiser red were to appear? Would the driver still pull over? Probably so. What if the flashing light were made more and more yellow, and less and less like the red light to which almost all drivers would respond? We would observe less of the response of pulling over to the side of the road.

The process of responding to stimuli similar to, but not identical with, the original stimulus is called *generalization*. The conditioned response becomes less and less as the similarity between original and test stimuli decreases. This is called a *generalization gradient*.

Generalization is a very important concept for all of psychology. It is easy to see that if an organism had to learn a new response to each stimulus it might ever encounter, it would be dead before it had even learned enough to survive. As a result animals and humans show a marked ability to generalize. They

extinction: *the decrease in the frequency of a behavior until it is eliminated because it is no longer reinforced*

Partial Reinforcement Effect: *resistance to extinction of a behavior acquired under other than continuous reinforcement*

generalization: *in conditioning, responding to stimuli similar to but not identical with the original stimulus*

generalization gradient: *the decrease in the conditioned response as the test stimuli become less and less like the original stimulus*

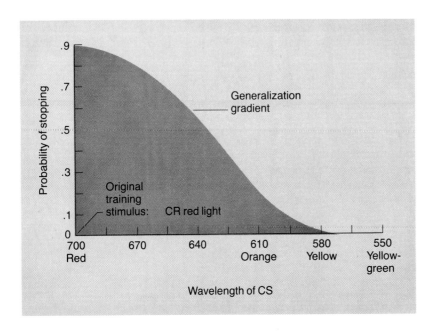

Figure 6-7 A generalization gradient. The graph shows the changing probability of a person's stopping for a car with a flashing red light as the red (CS) varies increasingly to a yellow-green. Within limits an organism will respond to a stimulus similar to a CS with which it has prior experience.

are able to react appropriately to any stimulus similar to ones with which they have had previous experience. How many different ways are there to open a door?

Discrimination

Quite obviously, there must be limits to generalization. Otherwise, once an organism had learned one response, that response would occur to all stimuli! The ability to react differently to similar but distinct stimuli is called *discrimination*. It is an ability equally as important as generalization. Both are critical to the survival of any organism.

How can we demonstrate discrimination? It's easy. Many abilities make a person skilled at "body language" (see Chapter 8). One is the ability to discriminate among cues. A very simple cue is facial expression. If you had a favor to ask of your psychology teacher, you would be more likely to ask it if the teacher was smiling. You'd be much less likely to ask it if the teacher was frowning. In the past you have often been reinforced by people who are smiling, but you have seldom been reinforced by people who are frowning. You rely on your ability to discriminate a smile from a frown to increase your chances of success with the teacher.

discrimination: *in learning, the ability to react differently to similar but distinct stimuli*

The same principle is at work when you encounter a traffic light while driving. If the light is green, you proceed; if red, you stop. Again, it is simply a matter of discrimination.

▨▨▨▨▨   In review . . .

Primary and secondary reinforcement are factors in both classical and operant conditioning. They have other factors in common, including (1) the need to time a reinforcement correctly in order to increase the frequency of a conditioned response; (2) extinction, or the fading away of a response that is no longer reinforced (the Partial Reinforcement Effect suggests that extinction occurs more slowly when reinforcement is not given each time the response is made); (3) generalization, or the response to stimuli that are similar, but not identical, to a previously conditioned stimulus; and (4) discrimination, or the ability to respond to one stimulus and not to another that is similar.

6 Punishment

Decisions about the proper role of punishment in modern society are constantly being made, but those decisions are never easy. When should punishment be used? How effective is punishment in causing a change in behavior? What factors make it most likely to succeed? Applying a punishment should be carefully guided by an understanding of learning principles. The following conditions, related to learning, help determine how effective a punishment is likely to be.

Intensity. Punishment should be severe enough to cause some discomfort. However, it should not be so severe as to hinder the organism from responding at all. For example, new recruits in military training bases use blanks in their first field exercises, rather than live "enemy" bullets. The punishing conditions of battle are there. However, death—the ultimate punishment—doesn't follow if the forgetful recruit gets caught in the line of fire.

Consistency. The response to be altered must be punished consistently. It is much easier to learn what is being done wrong if the punishment for errors always occurs and is always the same. Suppose a child is told she will lose the right to ride her tricycle for 24 hours if that tricycle is not put away properly at the end of each day. That punishment should be applied each time the offense occurs.

Proximity. As you read earlier, the timing of a reinforcement is quite important in learning a response. Timing is also important in punishment. Generally, the greater the time between the response and the punishment it produces, the less the effect of that punishment on the response. What's the favorite threat of frustrated babysitters when the children get out of hand? "Just wait until your parents get home!" It may be the least effective punishment of all.

Strength of punished response. The strength of the punishment must be related to the strength of the response being punished. The greater the pleasure to be given up, the more severe the punishment must be. For instance, people who enjoy smoking say they feel relaxed when they smoke. They say it helps control their nerves. It keeps their hands busy. In fact, they say it generally makes them feel more socially acceptable— or used to, until lately. Such people are not going to be convinced to stop smoking by reading, "Warning: The Surgeon General has determined that cigarette smoking is dangerous to your health." Despite the truth of the warning, the punishment is simply too uncertain.

Adaptation. A punishment may lose its ability to alter a response. What is at first a punishment strong enough to alter behavior may eventually mean little to the persons or animals being punished. They come to view it as an acceptable cost for the benefits they receive.

Rewarded alternative. A punishment becomes more effective if it not only punishes the response to be altered or extinguished, but also reinforces or permits another response. Traffic signals control our behavior in part by "punishing" us. They make us stop on red, but they hold the promise of greater rewards. The reward for waiting at a red light is less interference from cross traffic later.

Response history. How a response is affected by punishment depends on how and why the response was gained. The results of the same punishment applied to responses with different histories will vary widely.

Suppose a child enjoys watching his or her mother make cookies. As a result the child may stick a finger into the batter. A disapproving and stern "No, no" would very likely change this behavior since the fun of watching could be continued just the same. The "punishment fits the crime."

On the other hand, suppose a child is seldom given much attention except for misbehavior. In that case, the punishment serves the child's purpose—getting attention—and bad behavior will continue or even increase!

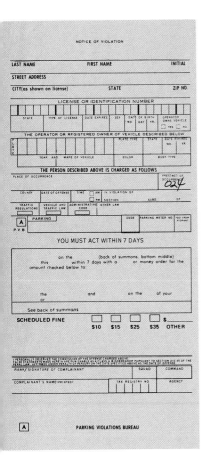

The parking ticket as punisher. Are the rules for effective punishment being followed in your town?

Punishment as a cue. Often, the response being punished is not the only one possible in a given situation. As long as other responses can be made, punishment need not be very severe in order to guide the behavior.

Has something like this ever happened to you? You were taken as a child to your grandparents' home. You started to talk at the beginning of the evening meal when your grandmother was attempting to bless the food. It may have happened only because your parents had foregone the food-blessing tradition. With only a hint from your parents you could easily select silence as a better way to respond. Little punishment was necessary.

There is still a lot of argument among psychologists as to the precise effects of punishment. Clearly, refraining for a while from an action that has been punished doesn't mean that one won't do it in the future. Punishments work better if they suggest a better course of action. To be most effective, punishments should involve learning specific alternative responses. Time in prison is not enough. Time spent learning another set of responses in prison is more effective.

In review . . .

The effectiveness of punishment is related to (1) its intensity, (2) the consistency with which it is applied, (3) how soon it is applied after the offensive behavior, and (4) the strength of the response to be eliminated. It can lose effectiveness if it becomes an acceptable price for the behavior or if the response history creates a special set of circumstances. A punishment works best when it offers or rewards an alternative behavior.

Which should be used?
Reinforcement? Punishment?

The issue of punishment and when to use it is one we all face time after time. Is punishment ever justified as a means of control? It's an oft-debated issue in our society, about which people hold many different views. Is corporal punishment desirable in the school classroom? How about in prisons? The science of psychology offers a powerful set of well-understood learning principles that can be applied to modify behavior. But the scientific view is not the only one to be considered. There are moral and religious, legal, and ethical issues that also must be examined in connection with the modification of behavior.

Prisoners are less likely to return to jail if they have been taught a useful skill. Here men learn how to bake as part of a prison rehabilitation program.

Should we reward the good or punish the bad? There's no easy answer. A punished response is simply suppressed; once the threat of punishment is removed, the unwanted response often returns. A variety of sources indicate that the most effective means of altering behavior—if you must choose between reward or punishment—is to reward an alternative response rather than to punish the undesired response. By rewarding the better, alternative response, you strengthen the possibility it will recur.

Chapter Application and Review

USING PSYCHOLOGY   *Breaking bad habits*

If most of what we do is learned, it would seem that we ought to be able to change our behavior if we want to. Yet some of us still smoke, even though we know we shouldn't. Others of us bite our fingernails—only occasionally, of course. In short, few of us are perfect. How should we go about changing previously learned responses? It is, in a sense, the hardest test of all since we must learn new responses to old stimuli. How can it be done? Let's review four techniques for changing behavior.

(1) *Counterconditioning.* Take drinking liquor as an example. A person may pour a drink in response to a variety of stimuli, including social stress or any situation where he or she doesn't know what else to do. The key in counterconditioning is to develop a new response to the old stimuli. One way you do this is by associating the stimuli (such as stress) that usually bring about the undesired response (such as excessive drinking) with a new, unpleasant response (such as nausea).

For example, the alcoholic who is addicted to alcohol can be injected with a drug called Antabuse. The drug causes no ill effects at all—you can't even tell that it's been injected. That is, you can't until you take a drink of alcohol of any kind. Then a kind of

internal horror is unleashed. You feel nauseous; you want to (and usually do) vomit all that's in your stomach. Generally, the more alcohol you've taken in, the worse you will feel.

Having gone through this suffering once, the alcoholic who continues taking Antabuse very seldom wants to repeat the drinking experience. Thus, whatever were the stimuli that formerly elicited drinking, those same stimuli now begin to elicit thoughts of nausea and sickness instead. The result is that behavior changes—the alcoholic learns new responses to the old stimuli.

(2) *Exhaustion.* Smoking is another behavior that many people say they would like to give up. Rather than changing the response directly by counterconditioning, the response can be elicited so many times as to literally exhaust the person. Many nonsmoking adults can recall the time when they were caught smoking as a child by a parent who showed no anger—in fact, just the opposite: "You want to smoke? Well, here, have one of mine. . . . Done with that one, well, have another. In fact, why don't we have a cigar? Let's *really* smoke!"

What occurs is fairly easy to predict. The child gets so sick of smoke, cigarettes, and smoking that the next time the thought of smoking enters his or her head it is followed immediately by memories of how bad it was the last time. Exhaustion, in a sense, created counterconditioning by using the offending response itself to generate the nauseous feelings.

(3) *Change of environment.* Both exhaustion and counterconditioning involve direct attempts to change the responses elicited by a particular stimulus. Another obvious approach is to prevent the stimulus from occurring. It is very similar to the advice given by a doctor to one of her patients who complained, "Well, doctor, my arm has recovered pretty well. It only hurts now when I twist my wrist around this way and try to reach way up behind my back to scratch." Replied the doctor, "Why not just stop twisting your wrist and reaching way up behind your back that way?" In other words, if it doesn't hurt when you don't do it, why do it? The essential point is a valid one: simply don't present the stimuli that elicit the undesired response.

This is one of several principles underlying the concept of "half-way houses," in which convicts about to be released from prison are aided in readjusting themselves to the outside world. Help is made available to convicts trying to rearrange their style of life. This discourages contact between the convicts and the persons or environment that caused them to get in trouble in the past.

(4) *Increasing toleration.* There is a final method for changing an undesired response—scheduling when that response is to occur. In this way, *you* gain control. We discuss this more fully in the Using Psychology section of Chapter 9.

REVIEW QUESTIONS

SECTION 1 (pages 184–187)
1. How do psychologists define learning?
2. Can you observe learning? How is it measured?
3. What is the Law of Effect?

SECTION 2 (pages 188–190)
1. Who pioneered classical conditioning?
2. What is classical conditioning?
3. Describe trial and error learning.
4. Define positive reinforcer and negative reinforcer. Give an example of each.

SECTION 3 (pages 191–195)
1. What is the difference between trial and error learning and operant conditioning?
2. Are operant and classical conditioning actually the same thing?

SECTION 4 (pages 195–197)
1. What is the main advantage of observational learning?

2. How does observational learning compare with operant and classical conditioning?

SECTION 5 (pages 197–205)
1. Describe the five different schedules of reinforcement and the effect of each on behavior.
2. How do primary and secondary reinforcers differ?
3. Define the following terms: extinction, partial reinforcement effect, generalization, and discrimination.
4. What factors do operant and classical conditioning have in common?

SECTION 6 (pages 205 208)
1. Describe the factors involved in the effectiveness of punishment.
2. Which do you think is better—to punish the bad or to reinforce the good? Explain.

ACTIVITIES

1. This idea is easier to describe than it is to do, but give it a try. When you talk with a friend keep track of how many times he/she says the word "I," or uses a negative word (such as "not"), or uses a plural form. Once you have established a base rate, start reinforcing your friend every time he or she uses the word you want used (let's say "I" for our purposes). What's reinforcing? A smile. A nod of agreement. A mumbled "Mhmm." You are using a positive, secondary, or social reinforcer to influence your friend's frequency of use of a specific word. Does the average use of the word increase? How much? Can you extinguish the behavior by withholding your reinforcement? Try it!

2. You can make a maze using thumbtacks and string or rubber bands. By placing the thumb tacks at every choice point and every end of a blind alley, construct a maze similar to the pattern you see here:

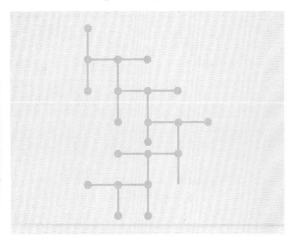

See if you can find some friends who will help you. Blindfold them *before* they can see your maze. Put their finger on the starting point and explain to them that they are to find a path to the goal making as few errors as possible. Make a graph of your results, identifying each attempt (or trial) on the X-axis (abscissa, see Chapter 17) and the number of *errors* (or the length of *time*) on the Y-axis (ordinate). How many trials does it take before your friend can go through the whole maze with no errors? How does your graph show you that learning is occurring? When is learning best? Why?

3. In addition to classical and operant conditioning, we've also discussed observational learning. Complex activities are sometimes learned best by using a *"Watch* me, this is how it's done" approach. Interview a member of your family or a friend who is involved in a trade such as carpentry, plumbing, electrical wiring, or auto mechanics. How much of their training in the trade was achieved by reading? How much was learned simply by watching to see how a senior craftsperson did the job? Would they agree that observational learning was an efficient means of learning their trade?

4. What controls your behavior? Are you punished at home? At school? Make a list of the punishers and the positive and negative reinforcers that are used by friends, family, and teacher to control your behavior. How do you think these punishers and reinforcers influence you? Which would you rather "earn," a punisher or a reinforcer?

5. Career Search. Advertisers employ psychologists to study consumer behavior. You read that we learn to link products with slogans. What else do advertisers hope we'll associate with their products? Pay close attention to the commercials on television for the next few days. What positive themes do you see advertisers pairing with their products? How do the commercials encourage you to associate the positive aspects of some other event or person with the product being advertised? Pool your observations with your classmates.

6. Here's a way to prove to yourself that observational learning is very efficient in some learning situations. Ask ten people you know to take the following brain-teaser: Connect all nine dots in the following diagram with *four* straight lines *without* lifting your pencil from the paper.

When they give up (as we bet they will!), show them how it's done. Then a week later, ask the same ten people to try it again. How many of the ten could solve the problem after seeing the solution just once? What is the solution? That's easy. The answer is as follows:

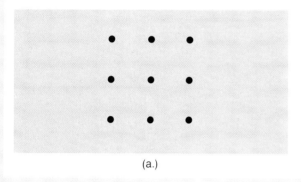

(a.)

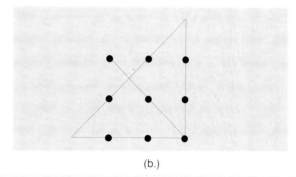

(b.)

INTERESTED IN MORE?

FERSTER, C. B. & CULBERTSON, S A. *Behavior Principles,* 3rd ed. Prentice-Hall, 1982. An advanced introductory text on principles of operant conditioning. A systematic analysis of research studies of human behavior in classroom and clinic and of everyday behavior.

LEFRANCOIS, G. R. *Psychological Theories and Human Learning: Kongor's Report.* Brooks/Cole, 1972. An irreverent look at a variety of traditional theories of learning. Shy on modern learning theory. The man-from-outer-space viewpoint allows the author to poke fun at humans. Nice reading.

MARTIN, G. & PEAR, J. *Behavior Modification: What It Is and How to Do It,* 2nd ed. Prentice-Hall, 1983. The title tells it all. Includes a discussion of basic terms and concepts as well as "hands on" examples of behavior modification principles applied to everyday life.

PAVLOV, I. P. *Conditioned Reflexes.* Dover, 1960. An English translation of the original work in the study of classical conditioning by the Nobel-prize-winning scientist. A treat if you already have a basic understanding of the process.

PETERSON, L. B. *Learning.* Scott, Foresman, 1975. A brief (134-page) review of classical and operant conditioning. Includes an extension of basic principles into more complex activities.

SKINNER, B. F. *Cumulative Record: A Selection of Papers,* 3rd ed. Prentice-Hall, 1972. A wide-ranging collection covering everything from critiques of other theories to the use of operant conditioning in teaching and learning.

_____. *Walden II.* Macmillan, 1948. Can a society be run on the principles of reinforcement, with no use of punishment? Would children raised in such an environment be free from jealousy and envy, or would they lose their individuality? Skinner's program for a utopian society.

CHAPTER OUTLINE

WHAT'S THE ANSWER?

☐ Said June, "Let's invite that new kid who was talking to Patsy to the party this weekend."

Responded Debbie, "Good idea. Give me the phone book and I'll give him a call. Let's see . . . yes, here it is, 739-9267. Where's the phone?"

"Under your bedspread."

"I've got it. All right, here we go . . . seven . . . three . . . nine . . . nine . . . two . . . six . . . seven . . . It's ringing! . . . Wow! Six rings, I hope he's home! Uh, what's that, operator? What number was I calling? . . . Uh, it was . . . uh, six . . . two . . . uh . . ." *What happened? Why did Debbie forget the number she'd just looked up?*

☐ "Both Maria and I had dates Saturday night and Sunday afternoon. We're twins, you know, and we do a lot together. Our grades have been identical in every course we've ever taken together. Well, anyway, I know neither of us had studied for either our English test on poetry or our math test on equations until we sat down Sunday evening. We both had six hours to study and the two tests to get ready for. I spent three hours on English and then three on math. Maria alternated all evening, spending an hour at a time on each subject. And you know what? She beat me! She did better on both tests!" *How do you explain this?*

☐ *Do people who learn things faster tend to learn things better?*

Sometimes the inability to remember something on an exam is not a matter of forgetting it but of faulty input in the learning process.

1 Memory

In the last chapter we studied in detail the most basic learning processes, classical and operant conditioning, as well as observational learning. However, we ignored another significant process—memory. What is the relation of memory to learning?

Obviously, once we have learned something, we have to keep it in "storage" so that we can retrieve it when we need it. How does this work? Psychologists believe that there are at least two

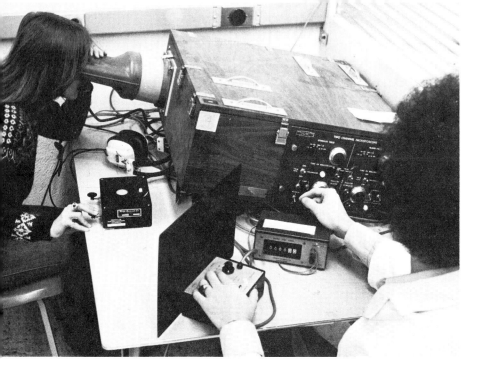

A tachistoscope is a machine used by psychologists to measure the length of sensory storage, or very brief memory.

types of memory, possibly three. We'll examine, first, the ways material is stored in memory, and then, later on, we'll see how it is retrieved.

Sensory store

Look at the illustration, which is a picture of a *tachistoscope*. This is an apparatus that allows a psychologist to present pictures for very short lengths of time, as brief as a few hundredths of a second. Let's suppose we ask a subject to focus on a cross in the center of the screen. In this way we will be assured that our subject is attending to the stimulus we are presenting. (As you recall from Chapter 5, when you focus attention on something, you tend to ignore other parts of the environment.) Then we flash on twelve letters and numbers, arranged in three rows around the cross, for about 1/20 second. (See margin.) Even if the subject pays close attention, he or she will be able to recite correctly only about 4.3 of the letters and numbers shown. That's a little better than one-third.

However, we can provide our subject with some help in retrieval. Suppose we say beforehand that we will sound a high, medium, or low tone to identify which of the three rows we want recited. If that tone sounds within a second after the letters and numbers have been flashed on the screen, it is amazing how accurately any one row can be recalled. For example, if we show the stimuli and then immediately sound the tone, the subject can recall about 82 percent. However, if the tone signal

7 I V F
X L 5 3
B 4 W 7

Figure 7-1 Letters and numbers shown by a tachistoscope, a machine that measures sensory storage. (See text.)

tachistoscope: *apparatus used by psychologists to present visual images for very brief time periods*

is delayed by a full second, accuracy drops to about 38 percent—not much better than he or she would have done without any help at all!

What do we learn from this experiment? (1) We learn that there is a type of memory, *sensory store*, in which information is stored very, very briefly when it is first received. (2) We learn that the information is forgotten if it is not used within the first second or so. (3) We find that nothing a person can do will prevent this loss of unused information.

Short-term memory

Now let's assume that you are the subject being tested by the tachistoscope. We play a middle level tone a short time after the letters and numbers are displayed. We'll assume you are paying attention and that you call them out to us correctly, X - L - 5 - 3. What would you do if you knew we were going to ask you to recite those same letters and numbers again after a minute or so without showing them to you again? Of course, you'd rehearse them, or repeat them to yourself. When we asked you for them again, you'd find you could give them to us without any difficulty. On the other hand, if we asked you for them several weeks later without any warning, it is very unlikely you would remember them. Why? Because you didn't continue to rehearse them.

The figures you were asked to remember were stored for a short time in a second kind of memory, called *short-term memory*. Two researchers named Peterson in 1959 conducted what later became a very famous piece of research on this short-term memory. They asked test subjects to read a three-letter nonsense syllable (any meaningless sequence of three letters) and then right after that to read a three-digit number, as shown in Figure 7-2. The subjects were instructed to remember the nonsense syllable. However, in the meantime they were to subtract three

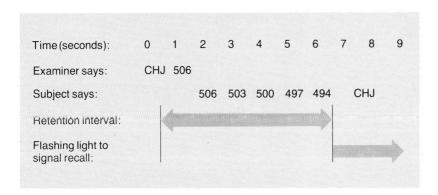

Time (seconds):	0	1	2	3	4	5	6	7	8	9
Examiner says:	CHJ	506								
Subject says:			506	503	500	497	494		CHJ	
Retention interval:										
Flashing light to signal recall:										

Figure 7-2

sensory store: *very brief memory span (0-1 second)*

short-term memory: *memory lasting 1-120 seconds*

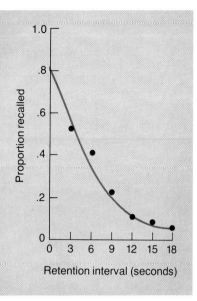

Figure 7-3 The probability of correctly recalling a nonsense syllable without rehearsing it.

216

repeatedly from the number and report out loud each result once a second. They were to keep subtracting three until signaled by a light to recall the letters they had originally read.

What was going on here? If you think about it, what the Petersons did was give the subjects something to remember, but then prevent rehearsal of that information. The results were most interesting, as indicated in Figure 7-3. After as little as 18 seconds, people's ability to recall correctly the original three-letter nonsense syllable had dropped to less than 10 percent accuracy.

Imagine, only ten percent of the time could they correctly recall three letters they had seen for one to two seconds just 18 seconds earlier!

What do we learn from this? (1) We learn that there is a second kind of storage mechanism, short-term memory, in which information can be held for longer intervals of time. (2) We learn that the information disappears if the person is prevented from rehearsing it or fails to rehearse it. These are the characteristics of short-term memory. It is considered an active memory since, to retain information, it requires specific activity on the part of the organism.

Think about it

The **question**: In the story at the beginning of the chapter Debbie and June continued talking after Debbie had looked up a telephone number and dialed it. When the operator cut in and asked Debbie what number she'd dialed, Debbie could not remember even though she had dialed it less than 30 seconds earlier. What caused Debbie to forget the number?

The **answer**: Most simply, she stopped rehearsing it. She looked it up and repeated it just enough to remember it while dialing the number. However, then she stopped repeating it and started talking to June again, thus interfering with rehearsal. Since rehearsal is required to hold information in short-term memory, when rehearsal was stopped, the number was lost.

Long-term memory

Although we understand the sensory storage system and short-term memory, there is much less knowledge—but many theories—about the most permanent storage, *long-term memory*. The active rehearsal used to hold something in short-term memory is necessary to aid long-term retention of new information. Preventing rehearsal, as the Petersons did, causes information to drop from short-term memory and limits its entry into long-term storage.

long-term memory: *memory lasting 120 seconds or more*

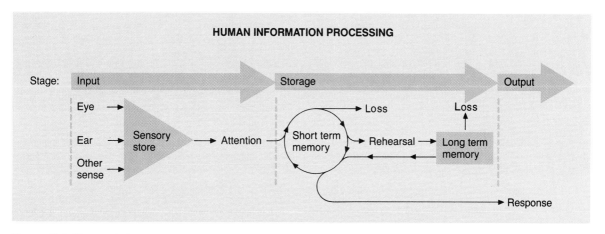

Figure 7-4 Human information processing. Information received through the senses passes from the sensory store into short-term memory, where it may be retained by rehearsal. Some may pass on into long-term memory. Later recall is achieved through return of the information to short-term memory. (See text for details.)

One group of psychologists performed an interesting experiment on long-term memory. They showed yearbook pictures of classmates to people who had graduated from high school two weeks to 57 years earlier. Astoundingly, people retained about 90 percent accuracy in identifying randomly selected high school classmates even 35 *years* after graduating. There is some evidence of increasing loss of these memories among people in their 60's and 70's, although it is not clear why this occurs.

Long-term memory involves at least two sources of information: (1) some kind of trace of the remembered event (this is what most people mean when they talk about a "memory"); and (2) some kind of *retrieval cue*, or information offered at the time an event is to be remembered. This cue allows us to search our memory for the stored trace. (More about cues later.)

Episodic and semantic memory

In 1972, Canadian psychologist Endel Tulving introduced a new way of thinking about memory. He suggested that *episodic memory* stores information about personal experiences, such as *when* particular events happen. Each event is remembered in relation to other events. *Semantic memory* stores knowledge about symbols, including meaning and the rules for using words. Forgetting is more likely to occur in episodic than semantic memory. Having proper cues is very important for recall from episodic memory, whereas concepts in semantic memory are richly interwoven with one another, making retrieval easier.

▦▦▦▦▦   In review . . .

It is generally believed that there are at least two, possibly three types of storage processes by which humans retain information. The sensory store retains information for a very brief interval of time. Rehearsal allows information to be held in short-term memory and helps determine if it will enter long-term storage. Retrieval of information from long-term memory requires some trace of the event and a retrieval cue.

Techniques of study

The study of memory has a long history. While psychologists are still theorizing about memory today, Aristotle, the Greek philosopher (384-322 B.C.), first suggested three bases for memory: (1) contiguity (closeness in time or space of two events); (2) similarity (recall of one event may be caused by the occurrence of a similar event later on); and (3) contrast (opposites will sometimes cause one another to be recalled). Through the long history of studying memory, however, very few methods have been developed for measuring how well a person remembers something. Here are the three most commonly used.

Relearning. Tests of relearning support the common-sense notion that after you've learned something once, it's easier to learn that material again. The less time or effort it takes to relearn something, the greater the amount you have remembered. Even the slightest amount of remembered material will assist you in relearning old material, and the saving can be easily detected.

Recognition. Another measure of memory is based on recognition. You are given a choice of several answers and asked to indicate which you've seen before. A multiple-choice test is a good example. Try this, for instance: In the "What's the answer?" section at the beginning of this chapter, a telephone number was mentioned in one of the stories. Was it 739-9267 or 666-4137 or 851-2600 or 443-4568? The correct answer is 739-9267. Could you have repeated it without having seen it again?

Obviously, there are ways to make such a test harder. A police line-up of suspects can provide a good example. If the suspect is a 17-year-old white male, the police can make the identification harder by lining him up with four other teen-age white males. They can make it easier by lining him up with people who are black, Chicano, female, or old. The similarity of the incorrect choices must be properly controlled. Except for the problems caused by too much similarity between the choices, recognition can be a measure of how much information has been remembered.

Recall. Recall involves simply telling what you know. You either do or do not remember an answer through recall; you get no help from the question or stimulus.

Cues

Relearning uses the material itself as a cue—presumably the best cue of all, since if anything has been retained, the organism will get the benefit. *Recognition* uses the material itself, but sets it with other material more or less similar to the original. Thus, recognizing material as previously learned may be somewhat difficult. *Recall* provides the fewest cues of all and is therefore the least sensitive measure of learning.

Memory and learning

Is remembering the same as learning? Is it possible to demonstrate the existence of memory without using learning? We doubt it. People who study human learning and those who study memory may differ only in the processes they use and the events they study. They are really both studying the same thing. Psychologists studying human learning are most often concerned with stimuli and responses and with the input and retrieval stages we discussed earlier. Those who study memory tend to be more concerned with storage problems and the internal processing of information. But, both learning and memory are always present in any situation where either process is being examined.

Does the speed of learning have an impact on the amount remembered? Does someone who learns material very rapidly remember it any better than someone who takes a long time to learn the same amount of material?

The key phrase in that question is "same amount of material." And the answer is no. Even if the time people take to learn the same amount of material differs widely, there will *not* be a difference in their abilities to remember it. Whether you are a fast learner or a slow learner, if you learn an equal amount of material, your retention will be equal.

However, there is one difference: a fast learner will have more time than a slow learner to devote to "overlearning" the same material. We'll discuss the importance of assuring that all learners have mastered the same amount of material after we've studied overlearning later in this chapter.

▦▦▦▦▦ In review . . .

Three basic methods for measuring the amount that has been learned and remembered have been developed: Relearning is one measure; recognition is another. Recall is the most difficult measure of retention. Although psychologists often say they are studying learning or memory, it is more likely that they are studying different aspects of the same complex process. Moreover, if fast and slow learners learn the same amount of material, there will be no difference in their ability to remember that material.

2 The Three Phases of Memory

The rest of the material in this chapter will describe the three phases of remembering: input, storage, and retrieval. We'll examine each in the order in which it occurs, noting those factors at each phase that influence the process of remembering.

Putting information into memory

The learner. If you are expecting to learn something, there are a number of things that may influence how well you will succeed. The first of these is your *motivation*. Motivation is a topic covered in much greater detail in Chapter 9, but for now we can simply define it as the driving force that guides you toward a goal. Motivation may range from very low to extremely high. The impact of motivation on learning depends directly on the level of that motivation. For maximum learning ability an intermediate level of motivation works best. If motivation is too low, no learning will occur. If motivation is too high, you may be too nervous or so overactive that you react to too many things. The result will interfere with your ability to learn.

However, the complexity of the material to be learned also influences the effect of motivation. If you are learning a very simple task, increasing your motivation will (within limits) simply increase the speed with which you learn.

On the other hand, if you are learning a very complex task, a high level of motivation may very well get in your way. Increasing the level of motivation may speed up your response but make it less likely that your response will be the right one.

A second thing affecting success in learning is *attention*. Remember, we defined attention as your ability to focus on certain aspects of the environment while ignoring others. Your skill at focusing your attention has a lot to do with how much you will learn. Closer attention means better learning. However, psychology has also been concerned with the question of *incidental learning*, that is, learning that takes place without intent. Consider, for instance, learning a foreign language. If your language teacher is attempting to teach you Spanish vocabulary, he or she will present you with English words and ask you for the Spanish. But what would happen if that was the only direction (English into Spanish) in which you practiced? What would happen if you suddenly found yourself in a Spanish-speaking community or in Spain and people were speaking only Spanish? This would demand that you be able to take the Spanish word and supply the English—exactly the reverse of what you practiced in class. Could it be done?

The answer is mixed—some would say yes; some would say no. Basically, the distinction here is between what your instructor told you to do (supply Spanish words) and what you learned incidentally—how to translate Spanish into English.

Therein lies the cue. The major difference between incidental and intentional learning concerns instructions; intentional learning involves learning in response to instructions. Incidental learning involves learning where no instructions have been given. Is the learning gained any different? Probably not. What really determines how well you learn (and thus remember) something is the *number* of responses you make. If you respond as often to incidental stimuli as you do to intentional stimuli, the amount learned will be about the same, whether or not you "intend" to learn.

Another factor that influences learning is *wakefulness*. Now and then you will see advertisements that lead you to think you can learn things while you are asleep. Can this actually be done? The evidence indicates no, it can't. You will remember that we discussed sleep in Chapter 4. We found that sleep, as measured by EEG waves, involves four distinct stages, from Stage 1 (the lightest stage of sleep) through the intermediate stages to Stage 4 (the soundest sleep of all).

Experiments have been made in recent years to see if people could remember facts read to them while they were asleep. Some psychologists thought they had shown that this could be done. Since most people sleep five to eight hours out of every 24 hours, think of the savings in study time!

However, it turned out that in those early studies there was no effective way to detect whether the subjects were or were not asleep. After the EEG measuring device was refined, some of the most basic experiments on learning while "asleep" were repeated. When the EEG indicated Stage 4 sleep, subjects couldn't

incidental learning: *learning that occurs without intent*

Association value

LIST I	LIST II
HIGH	**LOW**
Kitchen	Lozenge
Army	Ferrule
Money	Stoma
Dinner	Grapnel
Wagon	Flotsam
Office	Carom
Heaven	Percept
Jewel	Lichens
Insect	Endive
Village	Tartan

Average number of words thought of per minute

8.26	2.31

Imagery rating

LIST III	LIST IV
HIGH	**LOW**
Hotel	Ability
Pianist	Greed
Goblet	Length
Tweezers	Chance
Acrobat	Style
Dress	Pledge
Corner	Ego
Machine	Theory
Student	Mind
Lad	Honor

Rated ease of obtaining an image

6.32	3.19

association value: *in relation to words, the degree to which a word can bring to mind other words*

imagery rating: *in relation to words, the degree to which a word can bring to mind a concrete picture*

remember anything played to them. It was later believed that those subjects in earlier tests who seemed to have learned while they were asleep were not, in fact, actually asleep. Too bad!

Finally, the last major influence on learning is *intelligence*. We will discuss intelligence farther on. Here we will just mention that level of intelligence is positively related to the speed with which information can be learned. Put most simply, smarter people learn faster.

The material being learned. The nature of the material itself can affect the speed and ease with which it is learned. Some factors are its meaningfulness, its manner of presentation (whether whole or in parts), and its structure (the ease with which it can be organized). Let's look at each factor briefly.

First, meaningfulness of verbal material can be measured in a variety of ways. For example, look at Lists I-II in the margin. Which do you think would be easier to learn? Why?

One measure of a word's meaningfulness, and therefore its easiness, is its *association value*. This can be determined by presenting the word to a group of people. Each of them is asked to write down every word the stimulus word makes them think of in a minute. Some words make the average person think of as many as 10-12 words. Words that can do that are words like KITCHEN (which makes the average person think of 9.61 words) or ARMY (which elicits 9.43 words in a minute). By contrast, words like NAPHTHA (3.64 words in a minute) and FLOTSAM (2.19 words in a minute) are of much lower meaningfulness. Their association value (that is, the number of other words they make people think of) is much lower than words like KITCHEN and ARMY.

Words with high association value are much easier to learn than are words with a low association value. As association value increases, the time to learn a list decreases. List I is also much easier than List II, as proven by using serial anticipation learning (described in Box 7-1).

More recent work has found imagery to be a second important factor influencing the ease with which material can be learned. A word with a high *imagery rating* is one that is easy to picture. For instance, APPLE has a very high imagery rating. Although we may not all be imagining the same apple, there is little doubt in anyone's mind as to what we are referring when we speak about apples. Another way to describe this is to say that APPLE is a very concrete word. By contrast, BEAUTY is a very abstract word. It has a lower imagery rating since it is more difficult to create an image of BEAUTY. There is no single concrete object in the real world to which any of us can point and all agree it represents beauty.

Psychologists who are interested in studying verbal learning processes usually use one of two methods. The first, *serial anticipation learning*, involves presenting a list of words one at a time. Using a piece of apparatus called a memory drum (see illustration), the first word appears in small opening for a short time (usually 2 seconds). Then the drum turns, and the next word in the list appears for the same length of time. The first time through the list the subject simply reads the words as they appear. After that, the subject has been instructed to attempt to guess (or anticipate) what word would show up next. A subject has learned the list when he or she is able to anticipate correctly each word that will appear while the word preceding it is still showing in the opening. The material to be learned is always presented in the same order.

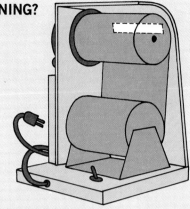

The other procedure used is called *paired-associate learning*. Using the same memory drum, a word (stimulus) appears and shortly afterward (usually 2 seconds) that same word appears again, but now it is paired with a second word (response). Then again, usually 2 seconds later, another stimulus will appear, and likewise this one will shortly reappear paired with another word. There are usually 8-12 such word pairs. The subject is assumed to have learned the list when he or she can correctly anticipate which response word is paired with each of the stimuli. The word-pairs remain the same during any learning session, but the order in which the pairs are presented will vary. The pair that was first might be at the middle or end of the list the second time through.

To measure the imagery of any word we can ask a group of subjects how easily the word brings an image to mind. We can have them rate it from one for "Very difficult—image aroused after long delay, or not at all" to seven for "Very easy—image aroused immediately."

With this procedure we can arrive at a rating of each word's imagery. As words become more concrete in the ratings, they become easier to learn. Thus List III (previous page) has an average imagery rating of 6.32, whereas List IV has an average imagery rating of 3.19. In other words as a word's imagery increases, so does the ease of learning it. A high imagery list is learned much more rapidly than a low imagery list.

A third way words vary is in the *frequency* with which they are seen in print and are used in speech. Thorndike and Lorge counted and listed 18,000,000 words, giving each a number that showed how often it appeared per million words. What do you think was the most frequent word? The answer is THE, which occurs 236,472 times per million words. The frequency of

Frequency of appearance

LIST V	LIST VI
HIGH	**LOW**
Think	Prong
House	Shampoo
Car	Winch
Lady	Lunacy
Right	Coma
Water	Dicker
Smile	Roach
Money	Tangent
Door	Mirage
People	Hobo

Estimated frequency of appearance in print

| 3121/million | 1/million |

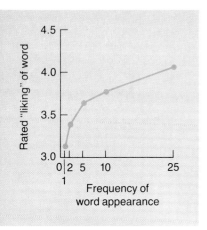

Figure 7-6 Each one of these "meaningless" Turkish words was "advertised" in large print as part of a study on the effects of their frequency of exposure to students who later were asked to rate them on their "goodness." The results of that study are shown on the graph.

appearance of a word is important because the more often you have seen or heard it, the easier it is for you to learn. (Lists V and VI show some high and low frequency words.)

Another reason why frequency is important has been demonstrated as follows. A psychologist placed want-ads in the student newspaper at the University of Michigan and at Michigan State. Each ad was as wide as one column of newsprint and was one inch high. In the center of each space was printed one "word," but the word was in the Turkish language, such as *civadra*. The combination could always be pronounced, but it didn't mean anything in English. A total of 12 words, were "advertised," as listed in the margin. Some words appeared once or twice, while others were "advertised" as many as five, ten, or twenty-five times.

What the experimenter did was to vary the frequency with which students at the two universities were exposed to each of the Turkish words. After the advertising was completed, he asked several classes of students to rate how well they liked the words.

Results indicated that the more often the word had been shown, the more positive regard the students had for it. As frequency of exposure increased, so did the "goodness" of the word. This is happy news for the companies that advertise in magazines and newspapers: the more often they advertise, it would seem, the better their product will be rated!

Another question important to learning is whether it is better to learn material as a whole unit or to break it into parts. Do you play any kind of musical instrument? If so, how do you go about learning a new piece of music? Do you simply "sightread" your way through it the first time, and then gradually improve the quality and timing as you play it all the way through more and more often? Or do you practice the parts one section at a time (paying most attention to any parts that are giving you a lot of trouble) and then gradually add the pieces together until you can play the whole thing?

Table 7-1 **Relation between task complexity and task organization**

TASK ORGANIZATION	TASK COMPLEXITY	
	LOW	HIGH
LOW	Kicking a football	Driving
HIGH	Juggling	Three-dimensional tic-tac-toe

Table 7-1 Examples of tasks of varying complexity that require different amounts of organization in order to be performed correctly.

It is the task itself that largely determines which method is better for learning. Research doesn't provide a clear-cut answer as to whether one should learn parts or the whole on a particular task. So what should we do?

Two major factors are involved: task complexity and task organization. Complexity refers to the demands made by each part of a task on your ability to process and store information. Organization refers to the need to interrelate several task demands all at once. Note the examples of such tasks shown in Table 7-1.

The following advice may help you: For highly organized tasks, the whole method is almost always better, no matter how complex the task. For unorganized tasks of low complexity, either part or whole learning will be effective. However, as the complexity increases, the part learning method becomes the better choice.

Structure is a third attribute of materials that affects how easily they can be learned. Can the material be clustered or organized in some way? For example, look at Lists VII and VIII

clustering: *grouping similar items together to aid in their recall*

Word organization

LIST VII	LIST VIII
CLUSTER WORDS	**RANDOM WORDS**
Tennis	Lake
Joe	Afraid
Banana	Reason
England	Queen
Red	Building
Russia	Valley
Hockey	Ear
Bill	Square
Peach	Truth
Green	Mile
Grape	Price
Baseball	Face
Yellow	Need
France	Day
Tom	Crowd
Brown	Wife
Spain	Judge
Pear	Youth
Golf	Silver
John	Guide
Germany	Ocean
Apple	Hall
Football	Uncle
Blue	Moon
Bob	Kiss

massed practice: *practicing or studying material from start to finish without a break*

distributed practice: *practicing or studying in blocks of time separated by periods of rest or other activities*

(this page). First, read List VII to some friends at the rate of one word every two seconds, then allow them to recall the words in any order. Do the same for List VIII. When you compare the results of learning each list, you should find two things: (1) more of List VII will be recalled than of List VIII; and (2) the material recalled from List VII will tend to be grouped in clusters composed of men's names, sports, fruits, countries, and colors. Related words tend to be recalled together. The ability to organize the material makes it easier to learn and to remember.

In review . . .

The first process in learning and remembering something is to put the information into memory. Certain attributes of the learner affect that input process. These include the learner's level of motivation, level of attention, and intelligence. Aspects of the material being learned influence the ease of putting it in memory. These include its meaningfulness, the manner in which the material is best learned, and the extent to which the material can be organized in some helpful way.

Procedures used in learning. The procedures used will also affect the ease with which material is learned. There are at least four major aspects to be considered: (1) time and how you use it; (2) the activities in which you engage as you learn; (3) the feedback you get about your performance; (4) the "tricks" you know to help organize and retain the information. Let's look briefly at each of these.

First, *time* and how you use it. Obviously some of the time during which you are learning new information must be spent in repeating it. The experiments of the Petersons discussed earlier showed the importance of rehearsal activity. Without it you would forget within a minute everything you had just learned.

However, it turns out that the way in which you engage in that rehearsal is also important. *Massed practice* means that all the practice is done at one time from start to finish. *Distributed practice* means that rehearsal occurs in blocks of time separated by rest periods or intervals during which you do something else.

Which is better? It depends on the kind of material you are trying to learn, and it also depends on how much time you have to devote to the task. If you are learning a list of materials, a serial list or a poem or a speech, then distributed practice is almost always better. Practice a while, but then set it aside and do something else for a time before coming back to it. On the

The **question**: The twins who were described at the beginning of the chapter had performed equally well in school. Both had the same two tests in poetry and equations for which to prepare. One twin spent three hours on one subject and then three on the other; the other twin spent alternate hours on each subject. Both spent a total of six hours studying. Why did the one twin do less well?

The **answer**: The English test required memorizing poetry, and the math test required learning a list of equations. Because of the simple nature of the material, it was likely that distributed practice would prove best. The results of the twins' performances bears this out. The twin who used massed practice on both subjects did less well than the twin who used distributed practice.

other hand, if you are learning more complex materials, the benefits of distributed practice are not so great. The more complex the task, the less benefit there is to distributed practice.

Time and how you use it is also a factor in the process of *overlearning*. Suppose you were given the assignment of learning the following football fight song:

> We've got the team!
> We've got the steam!
> We've got the zest!
> We've got the best!
> We've got a team that's going to fight
> for DEM-AR-EST!

Let's suppose you had to read that verse six times out loud before you could repeat it correctly all the way through without error. Learning took six trials.

Is there anything to be gained by spending any more time studying it? Yes, there is. Six times to learn it means that if you read it three more times, you would overlearn it by 50 percent. If you read it six times after the first perfect recitation, you've overlearned it by 100 percent. So what? Why bother?

Well, you will remember information better if you overlearn it. One psychologist tried this experiment: He asked three groups of students to learn a list of 12 two-syllable nouns. One group read the material until they could repeat it perfectly once. The second group overlearned the material by 50 percent. The third group overlearned the list by 100 percent. Each group was then brought back to the laboratory at varying times after they had learned the material. They were asked to recall it. Figure 7-7 shows the results. It is easy to see that the more overlearning that took place, the better was the recall many days later. If you want to remember something, don't just learn it, *over*learn it!

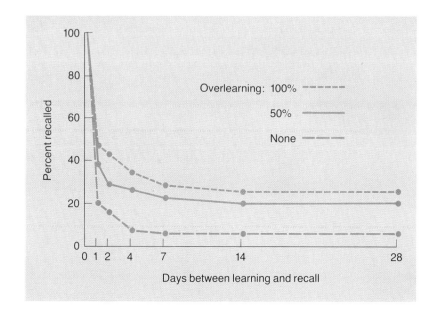

Figure 7-7 The amount of information that could be correctly recalled after varying amounts of practice when recall was delayed 0-28 days.

Think about it

The **question**: Do people who learn things faster tend to learn things better? Earlier we said that the speed of learning does not influence how well information is remembered. We said that fast and slow learners who have learned an equal number of facts will remember those facts equally well. Why might it seem to most people that fast learners do remember things better?

The **answer**: The key issue is overlearning. Both fast and slow learners are usually given an equal amount of time in which to learn information to be remembered. As a result, the speed of the fast learners gives them a great deal of time (not available to slow learners) to overlearn the material. As the graph shows, overlearning results in better retention. Thus, if equal amounts of time are allowed, unequal amounts of learning will occur. When the amount learned is controlled and equal, the retention of fast and slow learners will also be equal.

Second, ease of learning is affected by your *activities* as you learn. Canadian psychologists Gus Craik and Robert Lockhart have suggested that the level at which a word is processed will directly influence how well it is remembered. In one experiment subjects were asked one of three different levels of "yes-no" questions about each word in a list. Is it printed in capital letters? Does it rhyme with another word? Would it fit in a particular sentence? Each question involves more processing than the previous one and more concern with the meaning of the word. After the questioning, the lists were taken away and the subjects tested. Subjects were almost three times as likely to re-member a word if they had answered the last of these three questions than if they had answered one of the first two. Greater depth of processing led to better retention. Others have shown that making information personally relevant redoubles the amount that can be retained. The lesson is quite clear: think about material as you try to learn it.

To master new material, you should recite it rather than just read it, and outline it rather than just underline it. The more times you expose yourself to new material, the more likely you will learn it. When you recite and outline material, you increase the number of exposures. And, if you can make it personally rel-evant, you further increase the likelihood you will remember what you have studied.

A third way you can improve your learning is by finding out how well you're doing. *Knowledge of results* is very important in helping you learn something new. Consider your performance as you drive a car. If the car starts to cross the centerline as you are steering, you tug the wheel slightly to the right so as to stay on your side of the line. If you over-correct and start heading for the gutter, you pull the wheel slightly in the other direction. In short, you maintain a constant balanced position, keeping your car at some point midway between the curb and the centerline. Your ability to do this is based solely on the instant results available to you. With each turn of the steering wheel you can see the effect on the car's motion, and you adjust your actions accordingly.

If there is too much delay between the time a task is per-formed and the feedback about it is received, the feedback is of very little use. The person may have forgotten what he or she was supposed to be learning or how the task was actually per-formed.

The fourth procedure that can have a major impact on how easily material may be learned is a "trick of the trade," called a *mnemonic* (knee-MAH-nick). A mnemonic is any device or phrase or scheme of organization that aids in the learning, storage, and/or recall of information. The skill in developing a successful mnemonic is to create one that is very simple to learn and remember. Time spent learning a mnemonic is time not spent learning the material to be remembered. That fact must be kept in mind so you don't waste time looking for magic formulas to aid your recall. There is no substitute for hard work, but a good mnemonic can organize that work and time in a most efficient manner.

Note that we are discussing mnemonics as part of the input process in learning and remembering. Mnemonics are a means

mnemonic: *any device that aids in the learning, storage, and/or recall of information*

of organizing information for input and output. They don't really improve storage directly—they just aid the input and output processes.

One of the simplest mnemonics is based simply on *clustering* the information that is to be recalled. State license plates are a good example of this. Texas, South Carolina, and California, to name just three, organize their license plates in terms of three letters and three numbers. Telephone numbers are clustered into area code, exchange, and four numbers for a particular phone. When you are spelling your own last name for someone, don't you cluster the letters?

Another mnemonic, requiring more preparation, involves a formal technique called the *method of loci*. You take a series of places or objects with which you are already familiar and in your mind connect each of them with an item you must remember. For instance, you could imagine what you pass when walking from your psychology class to the next class at school, or what you pass walking from your bedroom to the kitchen, or from your house to your best friend's house—any route with a series of objects with which you are quite familiar. To use this as an aid to memory, you must form bizarre (literally, memorable) associations between the items in your mental trip and the items on the list you must remember. See Box 7-3 for an example of how this works.

A final mnemonic is purely cognitive, based on a previously memorized rhyme. The ten-item list in the margin is most frequently used. What you do is form unusual mental pictures connecting the PEG objects with the items you want to remem-

method of loci: *a device to help recall by mentally connecting items to be remembered with other bizarre items, which are often arranged in a series*

PEG system: *associating numbers to be remembered with a familiar item that rhymes with them (eight is gate, etc.)*

Feature   **7–3   "HERE'S THE UMBRELLA FULL OF ICE CREAM YOU WANTED!"**

Let's suppose that on your way home from school you must mail a letter for a friend, stop at the drug store for aspirin for your mother, get some peanuts at the grocery store for a party you're going to have, and pick up your watch at the jewelry store. To remember that list without writing it down, let's suppose you imagine the trip from your seat in the psychology class to your next class. As you pass the wastebasket, you imagine a large letter sticking out of it. As you pass through the classroom door, you imagine that you bump your head and thus give yourself—yes, a headache. Imagine the hose of the fire extinguisher in the hall squirting into a bag of peanuts. Finally, imagine a giant watch band wrapped around the doorknob of your next classroom.

To remember the items after school, all you need to do is to retrace mentally the trip from your psychology class to the next class. You are using the method of loci. Now, shut your eyes and think: What were the four items in the list we just went through?

ber. Of course, the PEG list itself must already be well-known so that all your time can be spent developing associations between those words and the items. You might need a little practice before you get the system down pat.

In review . . .

There are a number of different *procedures* that will have an impact on the ease with which information can be put into memory. These procedures involve (1) how one's time is spent; (2) what activities are used while learning; (3) how resulting information is gained; and, finally, (4) the use of mnemonics in recall.

Retaining information in memory

So far we have discussed putting information into storage; now we are going to study the storage process itself. What processes occur that may help or hinder our ability to remember information until we need it?

Remembering and forgetting: Are they related? Put most simply, yes. The amount of material remembered at any time plus the amount of material by then forgotten (or unretrievable) equals the total amount of information originally learned. One of the first studies of retention and forgetting was conducted in the late 1800's by the experimental psychologist Hermann Ebbinghaus. He learned a large number of nonsense syllables, three-letter combinations that had no meaning—XAC, VIL, and REQ, for example. Ebbinghaus studied the material he wished to remember until he could recite it perfectly. Obviously, then, retention at the time of perfect recitation was 100 percent. Ebbinghaus immediately tested himself again after zero minutes, and then again 1, 8, 24, and 48 hours later. Figure 7-9 shows the results of his studies. It is amazing how much information he forgot in just two days. It is obvious then, that as forgetting increases, the amount of material retained must by definition decrease.

Processes that may cause forgetting. Why do we forget things? Many theories have been advanced about forgetting, based on what is probably happening to the information that has been stored away.

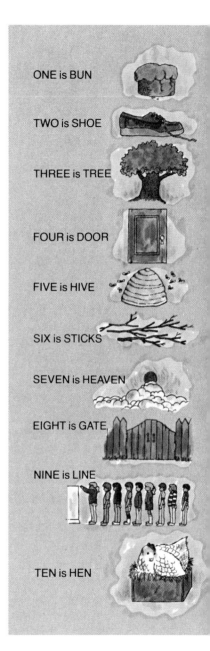

Figure 7-8 The PEG system. A list of ten easy-to-remember and easy-to-visualize images that can be used to form vivid pictures to help in remembering a list of items, numbers, or events.

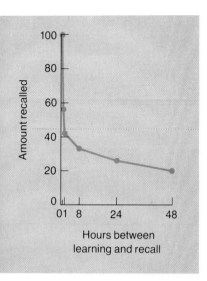

Figure 7-9 These are the results of one of the first studies of human ability to retain information that has been learned once to perfection. Most information is forgotten immediately after learning, but there is a steady additional loss for many, many days.

One possibility involves some kind of weakened memory due perhaps to a process of *decay*. This is a very old and appealing theory of forgetting. It also appears to be quite wrong. According to the theory, with the passage of time and without rehearsal, memory of learned material will gradually fade away. It decays through lack of use. Appealing, but contrary to scientific evidence.

Consider, for example, the old friend you haven't seen for a long time whom you run into quite unexpectedly one day on the street. You can't for the life of you remember the person's name, but either one of two things may very well bring it to mind. If the person gives his or her name, you will recognize it ("Of course, how nice to see you . . ."). It is also true that if given a choice of five or six names, you could successfully pick out the correct one almost every time. If not, it might be just on the tip of your tongue, so to speak, and you'll continue to worry about it. That you *can* in time recall the name is evidence against the decay notion.

Some people suggest that lack of attention when you first learn a name or a fact is an explanation for forgetting, but this also is wrong. Lack of attention when learning is a problem of faulty or partial *input*. It is not a matter of forgetting. We need go no further back than Ebbinghaus to realize that you can't forget what you never learned.

Another explanation for forgetting lies in the processes that *alter* memory in some way. One of these processes is *interference*. When new learning interferes with previously learned information, it is called *retroactive interference* (backward-acting) . On the other hand, when previously learned material interferes with more recently learned material, it is called *proactive interference* (forward-acting) . See Tables 7-2A and 7-2B for an experiment that can be set up to demonstrate both forms of interference. Of these two processes, psychologists believe that proactive interference occurs more often. Forgetting is more often caused by learning that precedes what we wish to remember than it is by learning which follows.

Humans seem to need another process if they are to store information successfully in memory. Evidence about this need comes from a variety of sources. For instance, people involved in automobile accidents, especially those who are briefly knocked unconscious, frequently are unable to report any memory of the events immediately preceding the time of the accident. It is as though the period of unconsciousness in some way wipes out memory of events that took place just before consciousness was lost. The same is true of patients experiencing ECS (electroconvulsive shock, discussed in Chapter 13). They are frequently

Table 7-2A **Retroactive interference**

	ACTIVITY			
	ORIGINAL LEARNING	NEW LEARNING	RETENTION INTERVAL	RELEARNING
TIME	8 a.m.	9 a.m.	10 a.m.	11 a.m.
GROUP				
EXPERIMENTAL	French class	German class	Physical Education	Study French
CONTROL	French class	Math class	Physical Education	Study French

Table 7-2B **Proactive interference**

	ACTIVITY			
	ORIGINAL LEARNING	NEW LEARNING	RETENTION INTERVAL	RELEARNING
TIME	8 a.m.	9 a.m.	10 a.m.	11 a.m.
GROUP				
EXPERIMENTAL	German class	French class	Physical Education	Study French
CONTROL	Math class	French class	Physical Education	Study French

Table 7-2A, 7-2B The tables above are study schedules used in an experiment testing the results of interference in the learning of a language. If the experimental group did worse than the control group during the last (relearning) period, it had experienced either retroactive interference (poor results from learning German after French) or proactive interference (poor results from previously learned German interfering with the relearning of French).

unable to report anything afterward about events occurring as much as 15 minutes prior to the shock treatment. Experiments discussed earlier, such as those by the Petersons, also indicate that interfering with the rehearsal of recently learned material results in a much greater memory loss.

These facts seem to indicate that for us to remember something, there must be a period of time allowed for *consolidation* to occur. Anything—a bump on the head, inability to rehearse, or an electric shock to the head—that interferes with the process of consolidation will lead to reduced memory. The memory has been in some way modified or altered.

Retrieval of information from memory

Remember what happened when you returned to school this fall? Undoubtedly at some point you were walking down the halls and ran into someone you hadn't seen, much less thought about, since last spring. Yet, you knew his or her name—or at least you thought you did. You couldn't quite remember it, but it seemed as if it were on the tip of your tongue. Such experiences offer a number of helpful hints about how information is stored and retrieved.

Box 7-4 describes studies on the tip-of-the-tongue phenomenon. These experiments suggest that words are stored in terms of their features, including the first and last letter, and also, perhaps, by the number of syllables that they have. Sound is more important than meaning. One of the most effective cues

Feature   7–4   **WHAT IS: "A LIGHT-WEIGHT UMBRELLA USED AS A SHADE FROM THE SUN"?**

The "tip of the tongue" phenomenon (called TOT for short) occurs when you cannot quite recall a familiar word, yet you can recall others of similar form and meaning. Reading the definition of a word to people who may be familiar with it results in one of three responses: (1) they know the word; (2) they don't know it; or (3) they tell you it's on the "tip of their tongue."

In one experiment people were read definitions of words like the one in the head above. These "target words" that they defined occurred between one and four times per four million words in print—recognizable as words, perhaps, but hardly in one's active vocabulary. People who said they had such a word on the tip of their tongues were asked a number of questions: How many syllables does the word have? What is its first letter? What are some words that sound like it? Finally, they were asked to list some words that were similar in meaning.

When guessing the number of syllables in the target word, subjects in the TOT state were correct more than 50 percent of the time for words of one to three syllables. Even more amazing, the initial letter was guessed accurately 57 percent of the time! (There may be one to five syllables, but there are 26 letters in the alphabet.) Subjects in the TOT state were more than twice as accurate in their sound-alike guesses as they were in their mean-the-same-thing guesses.

These results suggest that when a word is stored in our memory, its features are analyzed. Features such as the beginning and end of the word are stored first, probably along with the number of its syllables. With this much information, when subjects start trying to think of the correct answer, they are more likely to come up with words that sound alike than with words that have a similar meaning. The TOT state occurs when enough features have been recalled to narrow the choices to only a few words. However, the "I've got it!" experience will not occur until enough features have been recalled to eliminate all the other likely answers, leaving only the correct one.

that can be given as a hint to someone who is trying to recall a word is another word that rhymes with it.

Inaccessible memories. *Inaccessible* memory refers to the *apparent* forgetting of previously learned information. There are perhaps more theories and fewer facts about this process than about any other. It might seem that inaccessibility is a storage problem, but actually it is a problem of faulty retrieval, as we shall see. However, there seem to be two kinds of events in which inaccessibility of a memory takes place.

One comes directly from the personality theory of Sigmund Freud and concerns an active process of *repression*. It's almost as if we told ourselves to forget something. Repression is a basic concept in Freud's theory. According to Freud, repression involves unconciously preventing the recall from memory of any event, actual or imagined, that is unpleasant or threatening. Successful psychoanalysis may allow a person to bring back memories of these disturbing earlier events. Obviously some kind of active prevention of retrieval has been involved.

Another process involves the use of wrong cues in attempting to retrieve stored information. Memory may be inaccessible simply because the organism doesn't know the right cue to use for correct recall. A very simple example will illustrate this point. If you live in Miami Beach, Florida, and meet a new friend at your school who has an address on Collins Avenue, it will do you very little good to try to drive to that friend's house if you only remember the name of the street. Collins Avenue starts at the southern end of Miami Beach and runs north along the Atlantic coast quite a ways towards Fort Lauderdale. Without a street number, it would be a hopeless task to try to find that friend. Without the correct cue for retrieval from memory, it is an equally hopeless task to attempt to recall the information. Much work remains to be done before psychologists can fully explain the importance of cues for retrieving information from memory.

In review . . .

The three important processes in learning and remembering are (1) the putting of information into memory; (2) its storage; and (3) its later retrieval. It is no longer thought that decay takes place during storage because of our failure to use or rehearse information. Forgetting is more likely to be a result of proactive or retroactive interference, or lack of a consolidation period. Retrieving information is based on using a correct cue to locate a memory.

If you know how to water-ski, snow skiing will be easier for you—an example of positive transfer of learning.

3 Transfer—Positive and Negative

Another concept that relates to learning is that of *transfer*. Transfer refers to the effects of past learning on the ability to learn new material or tasks. Tables 7-2A and 7-2B showed a test of the problems you might have if you were studying both French and German during the same school term. The problems were basically those of *negative transfer*, or the hindering of learning of one language because of similar experience with another language. Properly controlling transfer can make learning and remembering an easier task, if the lessons of transfer are well learned. Let's examine the two major kinds of transfer, positive and negative.

There are many examples of *positive transfer* in everyday life. For example: (1) learning to drive a truck or bus after having learned how to drive a car; (2) learning how to use an electric typewriter after having learned to type on a manual machine; (3) learning to fly an airplane after having practiced on a flight simulator and so forth. In each case, the first task helps the person learn the basics of the second task; the transfer effect is positive.

Are there general principles that might help us predict whether transfer is likely to be positive or negative? Yes, because most tasks can be analyzed into the stimuli and responses that go with them. You get the most positive transfer when familiar stimuli from one task are again present in the second or

negative transfer: *hindrance of new learning that results from similar previous learning*

positive transfer: *ease in new learning that results from similar previous learning*

People who learned to drive in the United States may find it difficult to follow the English law of driving on the left—an example of negative transfer of learning.

transfer, task, and especially so when familiar responses are again to be learned. For instance, if you are learning to play the piano, all of your practice prior to today might be viewed as Task 1. Task 2 occurs when you sit down today to practice. Obviously, transfer will be most positive since familiar stimuli (the same piano and the same piece of music) are again being paired with familiar responses (all the motions involved in playing the piano that you've already learned).

Positive transfer will also occur if old responses must be associated with new stimuli. At the start of the 1974 season the National Football League moved the goal posts ten yards further back from the goal line to the ends of the goal zones. The first year following that change, the league's statistics indicated that fewer field goals were kicked (which was the reason the change was made), but the accuracy at each distance *from the goal posts* was unchanged. The same old responses involved in kicking the football were still required of the place kicker, but these responses were simply paired with new stimuli (goal posts ten yards further back than they had been in prior seasons).

If you are expected to learn new responses to old stimuli, however, the result is very likely to be negative transfer. Think about it. If you have a carpool of two friends and yourself driving to school everyday, what happens if the three of you suddenly decide to start giving a ride to a fourth mutual friend? Each morning whoever is the driver is suddenly faced with having to make new responses to the same old stimuli—he or she must remember to pick up that fourth person. Until the new responses are learned, that fourth person had better have another way to get to school. Any negative transfer in the driver's responding means the fourth person is without that ride! Requiring new responses to familiar (old) stimuli usually produces negative transfer.

Finally, and most briefly, if the stimuli *and* responses in the second task are both brand new, then no transfer will occur. How could it? With no prior experience with either the new stimuli or the responses to be learned, no transfer is possible.

All of your education and training in school is based on the premise that you will be able to transfer successfully your experiences in school to the outside world after graduation. Within the limits of its budget, your school attempts to make your schoolwork as similar as possible to the real-life situations you will encounter in the world of work or higher education tomorrow.

In review . . .

Any situation in which two tasks are to be learned offers the possibility of positive or negative transfer. If you want to predict which will occur, you can analyze tasks in terms of the stimuli and responses involved.

Chapter Application and Review

USING PSYCHOLOGY   *Improving your study skills*

Any attempt to improve your skills in studying is simply an attempt to apply the principles of learning. Thus, it makes sense to organize your plan along the same lines as our discussion of memory: (1) input, (2) storage, (3) retrieval.

Input—Most information reaches us through our ears via conversation or discussion (live or recorded), and through our eyes, often via reading. It follows, then, that find-

ing the best way to read is one important factor in effective learning. How can your reading skills be improved? Efficient reading is a matter of encouraging yourself to read as rapidly as possible. Once that pressure for improvement has been established, it then becomes a matter of balancing speed with comprehension. Frequently, negative transfer from earlier experiences in reading is responsible for inefficient reading. Think back

Where you study is almost as important to the art of learning as the methods you use. The desk at the top offers too many distractions; the desk at the bottom has little to take the student's mind off the task at hand. The other important point is to *only* study when seated at your desk. In this way all of the cues at the desk become associated with studying, and it becomes easier to do.

to the first grade, when you were being taught how to read. In order for the teacher (or your parent) to work with you, it was necessary for you to read the words and sentences out loud. You often pointed your finger at each word you tried to pronounce.

Logically enough, most people assume that efficient reading as an adult is nothing more than speeding up these same processes. That's where the negative transfer occurs. In fact, effective silent reading is accomplished not by pronouncing each word, but rather by trying to comprehend contents in phrases or thoughts. The good reader's eyes skip across material, not stopping on each word but pausing only to take in several words at a time. Practice in good reading involves increasing the scope of material you can understand with each pause of the eyes.

There are also other things that influence how effectively you study. First, you must pay attention! We learned in Chapter 5 that humans can attend to only one thing at a time. Some people maintain that they must have noise around them to study—music or people, for instance. The research evidence argues against this. Anything that gains your attention distracts you from the task at hand. Thus, quiet and a simple, uncluttered view provide the best environment for studying.

The principle involved here is stimulus control. It is important that you set aside for yourself a place where all you ever do is study. If you must do other things, do them someplace else. In that way you gradually condition yourself so that all the cues at your desk elicit the appropriate response—studying.

Second, schedule your activities. There are probably many things competing for your time and attention—friends, sports, family affairs. Set aside time for studying, but allot the balance to other activities in a way most satisfying to you.

Studying for storage—Since you can't forget what you haven't learned, our primary concern is to make sure that you really do learn in the first place. Basically there are two requirements: a strategy of attack, and a program. Let's discuss strategy first. Different systems for studying have been proposed, but one that has been widely accepted is the SQ3R approach. This plan of attack involves five steps: *Survey, Question, Read, Recite,* and *Review.*

First, *survey* the material. Skim the material very rapidly, taking only a minute or two. Look at the headings, and read the summary at the end, if there is one. This is to acquaint yourself with the basic content of the reading. What subjects are covered, and in what order? Think back to the mnemonics we discussed earlier. A quick survey will give you a bare-bones outline on which to hang the chunks of information further reading will supply.

Second, raise *questions* about the material. This can be done ahead of time, but is perhaps most effective if done as you read. Changing the section headings into questions will actively involve you with the subject. As you attempt to answer your questions, you will be bringing your own experience to bear. This will also help you understand the material better.

Third, *read* the material. Read actively. What is the answer to the question you just made up at the start of the section? Read to find that answer, and read to the end of the section covered by the question you developed. This is also the point at which to practice the efforts we discussed earlier to speed up your reading. Read rapidly, but read to learn the answer to your question.

Fourth, *recite* the material you've just read. Try to answer the question you developed at the beginning of the section, but try to do it in your own words, without looking at the material. One good way to do this is to attempt to outline your answer in a few key phrases on a sheet of paper. If you can't do it, go back over the section until you can. Don't move on until you understand what you've read.

Fifth, *review* the material once you've completed the reading. You might scan the notes you just wrote, to see if the major points you've listed agree with those in the material you read. Can you now repeat the major points of the material? And with those points exposed, can you list the lesser points under each of them? With this SQ3R method, you have a plan of attack to organize your reading.

Another tip on effective studying relates to our earlier discussion of massed versus distributed practice. All things considered, it is better to spend an hour or so with each school subject every day or two rather than spending four or five hours at one clip once a week. However, we suspect you can see that planning ahead is important. If you've fallen way behind in a subject, you're going to have trouble catching up when you start scheduling your time. Your goal should be to give all your subjects a more equal amount of attention.

Retrieval—If you've done the input and storage processes correctly, you should have no trouble with output, or retrieval. Successful output means being able to answer questions correctly. Massed practice, or cramming, immediately before a test is bad for several reasons: (1) It creates fatigue. (2) It overloads memory with a large amount of information fed into it in a very short length of time. (3) It creates the conditions for a great deal of interference—all the facts tend to become very jumbled up. (4) It greatly increases the likelihood (because of all these other processes) that you will not remember the information when you need it. Finally, it is likely you will forget most of what you crammed shortly after the test—if you're lucky enough to remember it even that long.

One of the few absolute rules in taking a test is that there are very few absolute rules. Scheduling your time during a test is most helpful. Surveying the material on the test before you begin will give you a rough idea of what's coming. Then you can organize your time accordingly.

Finally, a test should always be a learning experience. Even if you completely flunk an exam, you should go over your paper to find out why you failed. Were you misreading the questions? Did you fail to follow instructions? Did you mismark your paper? Or, did you simply not know the material? Finding the answers may avoid future failures.

REVIEW QUESTIONS

SECTION 1 (pages 213–220)
1. Name three different kinds of memory. How are they related?
2. What are three methods used to test the amount of information that is remembered?
3. Is the speed at which information is learned related to how long it is remembered? Support your answer

SECTION 2 (pages 220–235)
1. Name the three steps in the total process of learning and remembering.
2. What aspects of the *learner* and the *learning situation* affect how quickly and well material is learned?
3. What aspects of the *material* affect how quickly and well it is learned?
4. Name three processes that may cause forgetting.

SECTION 3 (pages 236–238)
1. Explain proactive and retroactive interference.
2. Define and give examples of positive transfer and negative transfer.

ACTIVITIES

1. Using a deck of 3″ × 5″ index cards, you can repeat experiments showing the existence of the sensory store. Use a stack of 24 cards; copy letters and numbers onto the eighth card as shown on the left below.

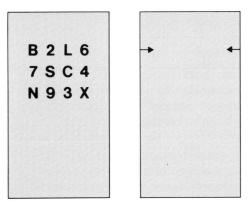

This will now be your new stimulus card. Make one like it for each trial. Also make three cue cards like the right card that have just two arrows pointing at the top, the middle, *or* the bottom row of symbols. By varying how many cards come between the stimulus card and the cue card, you can vary the retention interval for the stimulus letters. Practice until you can hold the cards firmly in one hand and "fan" the other end so that the cards flip past one at a time at a fairly steady and very rapid rate. Now find some friends and try the experiment (always with the stimulus card in Position 8), first placing the cue card in position 9 (zero-second retention), the second time in Position 16 (one-half-second retention) and the third time in Position 24 (one-second retention). Can your friends recall the indicated row correctly? Is their recall better with shorter retention intervals?

2. In order to test the limits of your short-term memory, have someone read you the following list of numbers: 347; 8156; 54921; 607043; 2859610; 92845036; 734196528; 8405396172; 18472943065; 657413298014. Each series should be read in a monotone. After the series is completed, the person reading the numbers should nod his/her head. Then (and *only* then!) write down what you remember. Give yourself credit only if you have recalled all numbers in exactly the correct order. How good is your short-term memory?

3. Using a set of 3″ × 5″ index cards, you should be able to repeat the original experiments on short-term memory for individual letter sequences. For each test, create a deck of cards as follows: Card #1—blank, Card #2—three letters printed, Card #3—three-digit number, Card #4—blank, Card #5—"Recall." Tap your finger once a second while viewing your watch to relay the time. To gather data, place your subject in front of you and indicate that you will flip over the cards in your hand one at a time. He/she is to read out loud the three letters, then read out loud the three numbers, then, once a second, subtract three from the number first read and repeat the result out loud. Use stimuli such as RAK, GUL, HIV, BEC, LOQ, DIZ, YEF, JAT, KUR, MOJ, NAH, PEM, SIL, VOP, and CUW, when making #2 cards. Using the 15 stimuli, randomly assign three to be remembered for 0, 4, 8, 12, and 16 seconds. For each trial, flip over the first four cards, once a second, and then tap your finger once a second for the required interval. Then, flip over the last "recall" card and record your subject's response. When done, calculate the average recall for each interval and plot your results on a graph with seconds on the X-axis and percent recalled on the Y-axis (You may need help with this.) What did you find?

4. Let's demonstrate how much easier it is to learn high imagery items than low imagery items. Place each of the items in Lists

III and IV (found in the margin in this chapter) on a single card. Arrange the cards for List III in a particular order, and sit down opposite a friend who will be your subject. Explain how a serial-learning experiment is conducted and then proceed to flip each of the cards in front of him/her at the rate of one card every two seconds. Starting the second time through the list, ask him/her to guess what word will come next. Simply record the number he/she guesses correctly on each trial (taking as little time as possible to do so) and then repeat the trial, being careful *not* to change the order of the cards!

Using different subjects for each list, how many trials does it take to learn List III? List IV? What can you conclude about the value of high-imagery in learning words?

5. Career Search. Earlier you may have visited a psychology laboratory in a local community or university to investigate areas of research in physiological psychology. The same source may also be conducting animal experiments in learning and memory. If so, write a brief summary of the experimental design used and any conclusions reached.

INTERESTED IN MORE?

LUCAS, J. & LORAYNE, H. *The Memory Book.* Ballantine, 1975. A star basketball player and a renowned memory expert discuss tricks and techniques for learning quickly and recalling correctly vast amounts of information.

LURIA, A. R. *The Mind of a Mnemonist.* Basic Books, 1968. Luria was a famous Russian psychologist who studied a man who could remember anything he wished for any length of time.

MORGAN, C. T. & DEESE, J. *How to Study,* 2nd ed. McGraw-Hill, 1969. Two experimental psychologists apply the principles of their discipline to the task of effective studying. Many helpful suggestions for organizing study space and time.

ROBINSON, F. P. *Effective Study,* 4th ed. Harper & Row, 1970. A classic book for improving study techniques. Contains explanations and exercises concerning the SQ3R method.

TARBY, R. M. & MAYER, R. E. *Foundations of Learning and Memory.* Scott, Foresman, 1978. Includes both animal and human learning concepts. Broad coverage but heavy reading.

Worm Runner's Digest. Univ. of Michigan. Published annually. A sometimes funny, sometimes serious journal. Edited by J. V. McConnell, one of the first psychologists to demonstrate a possible molecular basis for memory.

Language and Communication

CHAPTER OUTLINE

WHAT'S THE ANSWER?

☐ "Ahm gowa gega ped dawp." *We started this book with that quote. Is it language? What does it mean?*

☐ *Do animals have a language? Can they communicate with each other?*

☐ "What're you going to do, Steve? Teresa was the perfect date, but now she's sick. It's only two days 'til the dance. Everybody I know has already got a date," says Jeff to his best friend and fellow senior.

"Well, it's not hopeless yet. Let's go out and 'read the halls,'" replies Steve. Having said it, Steve then moves out to the front entry hall of the school. Classes are out for the day, and many of Steve's and Jeff's friends are leaving school. Steve seems to know everybody and goes out of his way to greet every female who passes. Nobody does more than return the greeting, or pause just a moment for conversation.

As the crowd thins out, Steve turns to Jeff and says, "That was a big help. My guess is that Jessie doesn't have a date. I think I'll give her a call tonight."

"How could you tell? You barely spoke to her!" is Jeff's stunned reply. *How does Steve know?*

Failures in communication have been blamed for many modern ills, from marital unhappiness to international crises. This couple's successful communication involves agreement on the meaning, organization, and form of the signals being transmitted and received.

1 Language

We communicate with each other in all sorts of ways. We try to sell each other soap and cars, real estate and swim suits. We say one thing, but we do so in a tone of voice that may clearly tell our listeners something very different. We sing to each other; we yell; we whisper; we plead. We draw on every skill we've already studied in this book. To sum it all up, when it comes to communicating with others, we rely most heavily on our most sophisticated human skill—language.

Think of the benefits provided by language. In printed form it allows us—even as you are doing now, by reading—to educate ourselves. If your teacher gives you a written assignment, it allows you more freedom than any other animal to express what is unique about you. In fact, language and its related processes may be the most important difference between humans and all other animals.

How is it organized?

One of the most important questions about language concerns exactly how we store and retrieve information so that we can speak and write. There is no easy answer, but two suggestions have been made.

Reappearance. You know from the chapter on remembering that through our life we *do* store certain experiences. If someone asked you right now to recall the first time you gave a talk before a group, you could recall (if you wanted to!) the complete event. In this sense remembering amounts only to stirring up something that already exists. That "memory" simply reappears. This is one means by which language may be stored, but it has some severe limits.

Utilization. There's another possibility. Perhaps we don't actually just "report" on our memory as if viewing from the outside some event stored as whole within us. We may store only a few elements of an event—just the traces of it (as separate "bones," which need to be reunited). If so, we might view memory as a process of reconstruction. There is an easy way to demonstrate this for you. Was the doorknob on the outside of the door you used most often going into the home where you lived three moves back on the right or the left?

Now that's not something you're likely to have bothered to remember. But in recalling the answer—we assume you *were* able to answer correctly!—you probably just "built" a mental image of the entry way. You may have positioned trees or plants, entry steps, railings, and so forth. From this array you logically determined which way the door had to open. From that you deduced where the knob had to be. If that described what you did—as it does for many of us—then you've just experienced memory as an act of reconstruction.

What has this to do with language? Everything! In Chapters 6 and 7 we were concerned with performance limits. We worried about how much we could learn and what conditions lead to the best learning and recall. Here we are more concerned with the actual strategies we use internally as we listen and speak. The problem is easy to illustrate. We learned earlier that our total

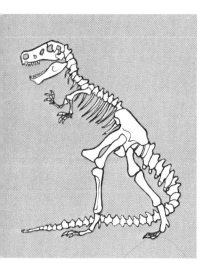

Figure 8-1 A paleontologist uses only the bones found at a digging site plus his or her knowledge of animal structure to reconstruct the complete organism. This is similar to the process by which we may store only a few elements of a total event and then "reconstruct" it if we need to recall some aspect of it.

vocabulary is rather limited—perhaps an adult can recognize 100,000 words. Despite this, we almost never create new words. Most of the sentences we hear (or say ourselves) don't contain new words. Yet we are constantly making up new sentences. Our stock of words is quite limited, but the supply of sentences we *might* generate is almost infinite. You have never before read a sentence exactly like the one you're in the midst of now, yet you understand this sentence with little difficulty. That's the challenge for psycholinguists—those who study language. They must develop a system that will allow us to understand how—even when as young as age five or six—we understand sentences we've never heard before.

What is language?

Defining terms. Let's start by defining *language* as an abstract system of symbols and meanings. This system includes the rules (grammar) that relate symbols and meanings so that we can communicate with each other. The only term in that definition that might give you some trouble is "symbol," but that's easy. A *symbol* is anything that stands for anything else. The dinner bell is a symbol of the food that's available. The scowl of a teacher is a symbol of his or her displeasure. The wink of a friend may symbolize a joke or agreement. Symbols appear constantly in our everyday life.

Competence versus performance. *Performance* is simply an account of what we actually do or say. If we asked you your name, you would respond with some kind of verbal output called speech. *Competence* is a bit trickier. It refers to the ability we each seem to have to generate and interpret sentences according to rules. To illustrate: not proper that Words nonsense are the order in appear do. Said another way, "Words that do not appear in the proper order are nonsense!" You *know* what is correct order in English and what isn't.

This can be further illustrated in another way. One youngster, aged three, hid from her father behind some curtains in the family's living room. She said to her father, "Daddy, I'm behind the KURin."

Her father replied, "Yes, I see you. You're behind the KURin," mimicking her mispronunciation exactly.

She replied, "No! The KURin!" For her, "KURin" when she pronounced it meant "curtain," but not when she heard it. Here, the child's performance has not yet equaled her competence. This last illustration also nicely shows the difference between speech and language.

Figure 8-2 Symbols surround us daily. What do these symbols mean to you?

language: *an abstract system for communication composed of symbols and meanings set down according to certain rules*

symbol: *something that stands for something else (such as a cross symbolizing Christianity)*

Figure 8-3 Reread the "Think about it" on the previous page if you have trouble reading this "language."

Processing language

"Do you know what time it is?"
"Yes." . . .
"Well? . . ."
"Yes. Yes, I *do* know what time it is."
"Will you tell me what time it is, then?"
"Oh. I'm sorry. I didn't realize you wanted to *know* the time. You just asked me if *I* knew the time. It's. . . ."

And there we'll leave our fanciful conversation. Why are we very unlikely to have a conversation like that? Understanding the answer involves a brief explanation of the important elements of language processing.

Sound. We are all used to the fact that our language is composed of series of individual words. But that was something we learned. We didn't know it until we practiced with the language. In fact, when you are speaking at a normal rate of speed, the pattern of sounds coming from your mouth is almost constant. In a simple word association experiment, children were given a variety of simple, single words. They were asked to respond each time with the first word the given word made them think of.

One child, upon hearing ONCE, responded UPONA. It shows the problem. Every fairy tale the child had heard probably started out, "Once upon a time..." And, more than likely, the child had never heard the word ONCE in any other phrase. So we learn how to analyze sound. We gain experience in separating the stream of sounds into individual words. It's important that we be able to do so, yet each spoken word helps us understand the others spoken with it. Box 8-1 discusses some of the ways in which changes in sound may alter the meaning of a message.

Syntax. We spoke earlier about the impact that word order can have on the meaning of a message. There are several aspects of order, of both sounds *and* words, that influence the meaning of a spoken message. When we hear a word, the sequence of sounds determines how we will pluralize the word.

In addition, the order of words themselves in a sentence is also important. Some words seem to be treated with respect, others are pushed around almost at (our) will. Yet we pay attention to the order of words, because it provides us with valuable information. For instance, there are two major kinds of words: content and function.

Content words are an open class—we're always making up new ones. "A-OK" was added to our vocabulary from the moon shots. "Turn on to" was added by adolescents. By contrast, *function* words are closed—we learn all of them by the age of 12 or so. These include pronouns, prepositions, and determiners (such as a, an, the, and so forth), in addition to many other such classes of words. We might think of function words as the mortar holding the bricks (the content words) together. Function words may be deleted in telegrams, but sentences without them are awkward and less well understood.

syntax: *the order of words in a sentence*

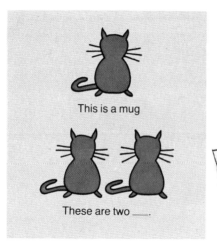

This is a mug

These are two ___.

Figure 8-4 If you call a cat a MUG, then its plural sounds like "Z." When called a MUS, the plural sounds like "IZ." When labelled a MUF, then the plural sounds like "S." The sequence of sounds influences how we pluralize any word.

Figure 8-5 In an old movie about the Air Force the male lead sent this telegram from the frozen north. His wife had just informed him of the birth of his daughter, but she needed a name for the child. His intended message was "I can't think of any name but I hope everything is fine with you." Dropping words caused his wife to misinterpret the message and name the child Hope!

Syntax also has to do with the relationship of words to one another as they appear in sentences. "The man cooked the spinach" is very easy to translate; it follows the rules quite well. But how about "They are frying chickens"? Does that refer to some cooks who are really cooking chickens or does it refer to the type of chicken?

A *psycholinguist* is interested in studying the rules by which we translate sentences and understand the speaker's intended meaning. The distinction between the surface structure of the sentence and the underlying structure or intended meaning is one of the things psycholinguists study. Obviously, in the case of the chickens, the context in which the sentence was spoken would do much to specify the intended meaning.

Semantics. *Semantics* is the study of meaning. What is meaning? You read on page 222 some measures of a word's meaningfulness. Table 8-2, ahead, lists other ways we may understand the meaning of words—but there are still more. A satisfactory definition of "meaning" has to account for a variety of word-related factors. For instance:

(1) Why is "My typewriter has bad intentions" clearly nonsense?

(2) Why is there a *contradiction* in saying, "My sister is an only child"?

(3) Why is it *unclear* to say "I was looking for the pens"?

psycholinguist: *a scientist who studies the psychological aspects of the acquisition and use of language*

semantics: *the study of word meaning*

(4) If we say, "The oar is too short," why do you *know immediately that you can also correctly say* "The oar isn't long enough"?

(5) Finally, if your teacher says, "Many in the class were unable to answer the question," why must it *also be true* that "Only a few in the class grasped the question"?

These are not easy questions, but then, if they were, we wouldn't be listing them! A good theory of meaning has to provide an answer to such questions. Words can be thought of as linguistic *signs,* each of which has an arbitrary connection with the thing to which it refers—its *referent.* That's easy, but then think back to the conversation about time, at the beginning of this section. It illustrated a situation in which a speaker responded literally to a question. Clearly this was inappropriate, as we all know. In asking "Do you know what time it is?" we are really saying "If you know the time, please tell me what it is." There is a conveyed or natural meaning implied in the ques-

Feature   **8–1   SOUND'S IMPORTANT**

In Chapter 7 we spoke about the very shortest-term memory that we have—our sensory store. Most of our examples involved storing visually presented information, but the same sensory storage feature must also be working when we talk with one another. It takes almost a second to say "marshmallow." We have to store and remember the first part of the word until we hear the last part. That way we can be sure the speaker didn't say marshes or marshlands or marshal.

But in addition, such things as emphasis and grouping of words can also affect what we interpret a speaker to mean. For example, read out loud the following sentence: I saw the girl with the telescope. Without knowing how the words are grouped, two interpretations are possible. Re-read the sentence in each of the following ways, but pause between the brackets:

(I saw) (the girl with the telescope.)
(I saw the girl) (with the telescope.)

The location of that pause determines the meaning of the sentence. The first sentence means you saw a girl carrying or possessing or beside a telescope. The second sentence means you used the telescope to see the girl.

Another feature that influences meaning is inflection or emphasis within a sentence. Consider the sentence "I want you to do it." If "I" is stressed, it means the speaker, as opposed to someone else, wants you to do the task. If "you" is stressed, it means the speaker wants you, rather than someone else, to do the job.

These major changes in meaning are one of the reasons why machine translation of spoken language has been so hard to achieve. The wording was identical in our last two examples. Yet the sense of the meaning of each sentence changed markedly as the pauses and emphases were shifted around.

Table 8-2 **How a word may gain its meaning**

SOURCE	HOW IT WORKS	WHAT'S AN EXAMPLE?
CONVENTION	Certain words are directly associated with an object or event.	Any noun serves as an example: arm, road, recital . . .
ASSIGNED	Words not directly associated with an object or event may be combined to generate an assigned meaning.	Describe a zebra to someone who has never seen one: "A stocky white horse-like animal with black stripes."
CONTEXT	The environment in which a word is pronounced often determines what its meaning will be.	"Port" is a wine, a loading/unloading place for ships, and a direction for ships to turn.
INFLECTION	Without changing any word said, the emphasis given to certain words can influence the meaning conveyed.	Pronounce the following sentences emphasizing "ever" one time and "you" the other: "What a pretty dress! How did you ever make it?"

tion even though it is not included in the literal words being used. All these different meanings are what make the meaning of meaning so hard to pin down.

To process language, it is apparent that first sound must be decoded and the syntax correctly understood. The remaining task is to assign meaning to the message. These three processes occur simultaneously, so this doesn't take very long at all. By the time you finish reading this sentence you will have already grasped its meaning. Weren't we right? In trying to identify what goes on when we "comprehend" a spoken message, we find there's little to consider. You either do or do not understand a spoken message. In talking with a friend, by the time he or she is done speaking, you're ready with an answer. If you talk too long, your friend may be so eager to speak and so sure of your message that he or she will interrupt you. One of the challenges for psycholinguists is to explain the rapid and efficient process by which we are able to do these things.

What is required for a (spoken) language?

As we'll see later, there was quite an argument during the 1970s about exactly what was required for a spoken language.

Some people almost seem threatened now that a communication system has been established with chimpanzees and apes. They seem to feel we are somehow less human for the effort. Consequently, a lot of attention has been given to figuring out exactly what abilities separate us as a species from other animals. The ability to think is important, but language, the actual production of speech, seems key. What's involved in language? Four elements are required for speech.

Brain capabilities. Several parts of our brain are involved in receiving, interpreting, and sending spoken words. The *motor cortex* controls our vocal cords, tongue, and mouth movements. Our *auditory cortex* provides feedback from our ears for the words we are speaking. It monitors the speech we are producing. If you pronounce a word wrong or say the wrong word, you catch yourself within a word or two and correct the error quite rapidly.

motor cortex: *the part of the brain that controls vocal cords, tongue, and mouth movements*

auditory cortex: *the part of the brain that provides feedback from our ears to monitor our speech*

Figure 8-6 Areas of the brain involved in receiving and producing linguistic messages. The *occipital cortex* is involved in vision; the *auditory cortex* is involved in hearing. *Wernicke's area* is involved in our awareness of spoken language, and in retrieving and selecting words from memory. *Broca's area* controls muscles in the vocal cords, tongue, and mouth. The *angular gyrus* is involved with vision, hearing, and body sense.

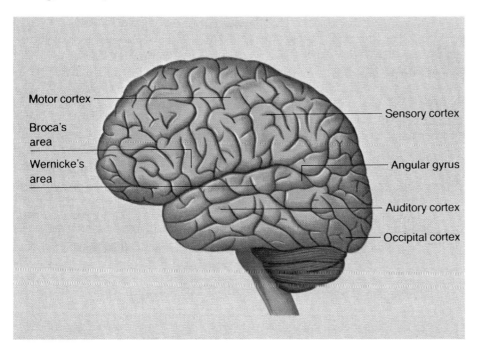

A third portion of the brain is our *association cortex*, which is responsible for storing, processing, and retrieving the words and thoughts we need. Finally, there are a variety—a wide variety—of connections between the temporal (auditory) lobes of our brain and the areas involved in actually processing the spoken word. As can be seen in the illustration, then, many different areas of our brain are involved in speech.

Speech mechanism. Another vital element—but only for *spoken* language—is our vocal cords. The vocal cords are two membranes stretched tightly across a portion of our throat, through which air must pass. They can be made to vibrate with a passage of air going up the windpipe (throat).

For some words, whether or not your vocal cords are vibrating determines which of two sounds you may hear. For instance, place your fingers on your "Adam's apple" (voicebox, or *larynx*, if you want to be technical). Make the sounds associated with F and V. Can you feel your throat vibrating when you say V, but not when you say F? S and Z provide the same effects. Your vocal cords vibrate for Z, but not for S. Notice that your mouth is shaped exactly the same when saying both F and V. Its form is different, but identical for S and Z. The only difference is your vocal cords—a second requirement for speech.

Abstract reasoning. We've already noted that everything in language can be represented by a symbol. For most of us that discovery is made in early life. It occurs almost by accident—we certainly aren't aware of it when the idea dawns upon us.

How important is this ability to manipulate abstract symbols? Consider an example from Helen Keller's life story. Deaf and blind since a very early childhood illness, Miss Keller suddenly learns or realizes that all things have names as she is drawing water at a well. The moment is described by her childhood companion and teacher:

"The word, coming so close upon the sensation of cold water rushing over her hand, seemed to startle her. She dropped the mug and stood as one transfixed. A new light came into her face. She spelled 'water' several times. Then she dropped to the ground and asked for its name and pointed to the pump and the trellis, and suddenly turning round she asked for my name. I spelled 'Teacher.' Just then the nurse brought Helen's little sister into the pump-house and Helen spelled 'baby' and pointed to the nurse. All the way back to the house she was highly excited, and learned the name of every object she touched, so that in a few hours she had added 30 new words to her vocabulary."

Clearly, such an ability to manipulate the abstract symbol is critical to our use of language.

association cortex: *the part of the brain that stores, processes, and retrieves words and thoughts*

larynx: *the voice box, or vocal cords*

Helen Keller lost her ability to see or hear as a result of illness in early childhood. Here she is seen with Annie Sullivan, the woman who helped to bring her the "miracle" of contact with people through the abstract symbols of words.

Inherited urge. Much debate still swirls on the third issue. It's nature versus nurture, heredity versus environment all over again. Evidence suggesting that we *inherit* our tendency to use language is impressive. First, the onset time of the development of language in children is almost constant all over the world. Second, in comparable languages, a fixed sequence of language development exists. Thus, nouns are the first word class mastered and pronouns the last. Third, if something hinders normal language development, it does not alter the step-wise developmental processes of acquiring language itself.

Yet, for those arguing that language acquisition is mainly a *learned* skill there are also some impressive arguments. First, we know that without practice, little language skill and ability to communicate will develop. Second, all around the world children generally remain in the company and care of their parents for many years. In North American societies it may be as long as 18-20 years. This degree of contact assures that a sufficient opportunity for learning a language exists.

We don't have a final answer yet. However, these four elements—brain, vocal cords, reasoning ability, and inclination—seem to be completely represented only in humans.

━━━━━━
In review . . .

In processing language, speakers must share agreement on sound, rules of organization, and meaning. Four capacities are necessary for language to develop as a means of communication: brain capabilities, a speech mechanism, abstract reasoning ability, and also, it seems, an inherited urge to use these capacities.

2 Communication

If you were approaching the group pictured in Figure A, to whom would you most likely say "Hello"?

Which of the dogs in Figure B is mad at you?

These are but two examples of a basic process in which we are all engaged almost all the time—communication. You may be surprised to learn that language is not the only vehicle of communication. It's also true that some animals besides humans communicate, yet they're not using language. How? Let's start at the beginning.

Communication as a process

Defining terms. *Communication* is the passing of information between organisms by way of signals that evoke behavior. We'll see that this may involve a wide range of processes, since the forms of communication vary widely. The wag of a dog's tail, the laid-back ears of a horse, and the sonar beeps of a dolphin all have the common goal of communicating. Among humans, however, the forms have found perhaps their widest diversity.

Native Americans refined one of the oldest means of communication—fire and smoke. Our means of long-distance communication have since expanded greatly. Samuel Morse's code-based telegraph relies on dots and dashes. The telephone, developed by Alexander Graham Bell, relies on clicks, beeps, and voice. Long-distance communication has blossomed even more over the past half-century, and now includes television coverage by satellite. All of these examples share some basic processes. Let's examine them.

A model of communication. The model shown in Figure 8-8 includes the important elements in the process of communica-

communication: *the passing of information from one organism to another via signals*

Figure A (top). We communicate in many ways other than the spoken word. If you wanted to ask a question of the group shown above, to whom would you most care to speak? Why?

Figure B (bottom). Animals also communicate to humans nonverbally in many ways. Which dog would you want to pet?

Figure 8-7 Another use of language is to mark off human territorial rights. What is communicated by the examples above?

tion. Basically, communication has four vital parts. First, there must be a transmitter. This source encodes, or produces, the message. The information source operating the transmitter must follow the rules of meaning, of organization, and of production—whether written, spoken, gestured, or otherwise.

Second, a signal, or message, is produced. This is the spoken word in talking, the dots and dashes in Morse Code, or radio waves in broadcasting. There are many examples of signals.

Third, there must be a channel, the medium by which the signal is carried away from the transmitter. The channel itself has a direct influence on the means of encoding (sending) and decoding (receiving) the signal. The channel may be many different things—wire for electricity, air or liquid or solid for sound waves, or paper for print.

Sometimes the channel itself affects the quality of signal that is received. If you're shouting to someone across a field or a busy highway, you may have problems communicating. Distance allows other sources of sound to make it hard for your friend to hear and understand you. This channel "noise" shows up as static on radio, as "snow" on television, and as a faint signal in direct, face-to-face communication.

Finally, there must be a receiver. This is the intake system for the signal, sometimes called the decoder. Both the transmitter and receiver must operate under the same rules in order for communication to occur. The difficulties you had at the beginning of the book understanding "Ahm gowa gega ped dawp" occurred because you didn't know the meaning of the terms. However, the terms follow the same rules of organization and pronunciation as standard English.

In summary, notice how the four basic elements in this model exist in all of the communication systems mentioned so

Message ▶ Production ▶ Signal ▶ Channel ▶ Signal ▶ Reception ▶ Message

Figure 8-8 A four-part model of communication: transmitter, signal, channel, and receiver.

far. Successful communication in each of these systems depends on prior agreement. The transmitter and receiver must agree on the meaning, organization, and form of the signals being produced and received. The United Nations sometimes flounders because of lack of agreement of this type. Contracts really attempt to spell out an agreement before a deal is completed. Wording and the meaning of the chosen words is thus critical for the forming of a successful contract. To achieve a successful communication, then, requires several steps.

When animals communicate

Do animals have a language? Can they communicate? To find the answers let's study perhaps the most sophisticated analysis of animal communication ever attempted. A Nobel prize was awarded to Karl von Frisch for his work in decoding the communication signals among bees.

The problem is an obvious one. When a bee returns to the hive having discovered pollen, it needs to relay the information to other bees. Your knowledge of geometry should tell you how many pieces of information must be conveyed. What's needed? Distance and direction. Examine Table 8-3 and the illustration to see how this is done.

Table 8-3 Honeybee dances as related to distance separating hive from pollen source

FORM OF DANCE	DISTANCE FROM HIVE
Round dance	3-100 meters
Figure eight and sickle-shaped dances	100-200 meters
Tail-wagging dance	200-300 meters

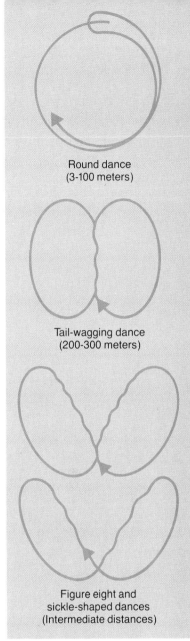

Round dance
(3-100 meters)

Tail-wagging dance
(200-300 meters)

Figure eight and
sickle-shaped dances
(Intermediate distances)

Figure 8-9 Dances of the honeybee. *Distance* is communicated by the form of the dance, the number of times the honeybee repeats the pattern, and the number of body movements. *Direction* is communicated by the overlapping part of the dance, which points directly toward the pollen.

Do the bees have a language? No. Remember how we defined language at the start of this chapter? Two critical issues for language are (1) meaningfulness—the "language of the bees" clearly qualifies—and (2) productiveness—the bees fail here. Their communications use steps and processes that are locked one to one with features of the environment. The dance, the angles, and the speed relay only distance and direction. Those same terms cannot be used to communicate anything else—not even how high above ground the pollen is located. The bees' symbols cannot be used productively.

As we'll see shortly, similar issues rage now that we've established communication systems with chimpanzees, but for bees the issue is clear. They don't have a language. It's less clear with dolphins. Dolphins seem to emit different sonar beeps when they're in a friendly group than when they are faced with danger. In fact, playing audio recordings of each type of sonar beep into otherwise quiet groups of dolphins does seem to alter their behavior. They seem to respond differently to the two signals. Box 8-2 details some of this fascinating research. It remains a question, as yet unanswered, whether these beeps are or can be used productively. Tune in in another decade for a more clear-cut answer.

When animals communicate with humans

About once a decade for the past 60 years one psychologist or another has tried to establish communication based on language with chimps or apes. Most of the early attempts involved just raising the baby animal as a human child, treating it in every way as a member of the human family. No luck. The best attempt after years of effort yielded a chimp that could pronounce three words. However—as with human infants just learning to talk—you had to know the chimp to understand the words.

A chimp "talks" back. Then Beatrice and Allen Gardner, a husband-wife team of research psychologists, made a smart decision. They noted that chimps have a very limited vocal apparatus, but gesture and imitate constantly. Why not try to teach a chimp using American Sign Language (Ameslan)? Ameslan *is* a language that meets all the demands of our earlier definition. The Gardners chose to study *chimps* because they are biochemically more similar to humans than they are to any monkey or ape.

Feature   8–2   "BEEP-BEEP"

The "Roadrunner" of cartoon fame goes "beep-beep" to communicate. Psychologists have discovered that the bottlenose dolphin also emits sounds to communicate, but this time in real life. The sounds have been recorded both in the ocean and also where the dolphin was quite restrained, and presented with specific stimuli. And what has been learned?

The dolphins seem to emit different types of sounds, even though they do *not* have any vocal cords. The sounds are of three types: (1) pure whistles, (2) slow trains of clicks, and (3) complex sound waves (quacks, squawks). Combinations of these sounds seem to be emitted under specific conditions.

For instance, when in distress the dolphin emits two whistles over and over again—one getting gradually louder, the other getting gradually softer. It silences any nearby dol-phins and causes them to search for the source. Once found, that dolphin is pushed to the surface and a complex exchange of signals occurs.

The slow trains of clicks range in frequency up to 80,000 cps. They are emitted to aid navigation—serving as sonar (sound) location to avoid obstacles and find food. When alone, dolphins emit mainly whistles and clicks. Together, they also emit whistles and slow series of clicks—first one dolphin and then the other—though rarely at the same time. When playing violently or courting, all dolphins emit all three sounds. Squawks and quacks then are especially frequent.

There's little doubt these signals are serving as a basis of communication. More work is needed, however, before we'll understand the precise make-up of the messages themselves.

The project started in 1969 at the Reno campus of the University of Nevada. A one-year-old chimp arrived and was promptly named Washoe (the name of the county in which the university is located). Only Ameslan was used in the presence of Washoe, but it was used constantly—for idle chatter, for operant conditioning of Washoe, and for normal give-and-take among the project personnel.

The results were astounding. By the age of four, Washoe could use some 85 different symbols correctly. By the age of five, she had almost doubled that number. As with children, the counting was stopped somewhat after that. Washoe knew too many words for the experimenter to get an accurate count!

By holding up objects that Washoe knew, it was possible to get her to gesture the sign for the object. Another observer (who could not see the object being held up) could identify the sign, and thus the object, correctly. Washoe clearly understood and could communicate the meaning of the words. The Gardners

From his work with Nim Chimpsky, Herbert Terrace of Columbia University concluded that chimps imitate sentences but don't really understand word order. Other researchers, however, maintain otherwise.

were later able to teach four other chimps to use Ameslan. Other researchers at Central Washington University observed in similar experiments using Ameslan that some of the older chimps taught signs to younger ones!

Unresolved issues. Are we actually on the verge of being able to communicate with another species of animals? Some serious questions have developed about Washoe's language. First, does she observe standard rules for ordering single units of language (gestures/symbols) into multi-unit messages (sentences)? The Gardners said yes, about 80 percent of Washoe's two-gesture communications are correctly ordered—well above chance levels of performance. But Herbert Terrace of Columbia University, who in the late 70's raised a male chimp named Nim Chimpsky, reached a different conclusion. After teaching Nim syntax (word order) for signed gestures, Terrace eventually had to conclude that Nim never really understood word order. Terrace asserts that Nim's sentences were largely imitative. Nim signed when he wanted something, making demands but not conversation.

Second, and perhaps most crucially, when children develop language, the increase in average message length grows steadily once they start combining single words into longer sentences. Terrace reported that Nim's average sentence length ranged from 1.1 to 1.6 units as Nim grew from 26 to 45 months old. Sentence length did not continue to increase as it does for humans. Terrace concluded that the chimps are not mastering a language.

The Gardners reply that Washoe was raised for years in a family environment by only a few people, all expert signers in Ameslan. They assert that Nim was raised by a much larger number of researchers, each present for a much shorter period of time. Less skilled in Ameslan than the "family" that raised Washoe, Nim's teachers gestured more abbreviated messages.

Think about it

The **question:** Do animals have a language? Can they communicate with each other?

The **answer:** Animals can communicate with each other, but they use stimuli that do not vary in their meaning. The bared teeth, laid-back ears, and bristling fur of a snarling dog send a message, but these elements cannot be recombined in a different order, or used to mean different things. Thus, most animals do not use a "language" in the usual sense, although chimps, apes, dolphins, and whales may be exceptions.

The Gardners concluded that they observed longer sentences from Washoe because her environment was richer than Nim's.

This is a clash of methodologies. The Gardners use modified naturalistic observation; Terrace uses study techniques much closer to the classic experimental model. The issue of experimental design is a key to resolving the differences of opinion of these researchers.

In review . . .

Communication is the passing of information from one organism to another using signals. Communication involves at least four elements: transmitter, signal, channel, and receiver. The "language" of bees is communication, but its elements are of limited meaning. Communication between humans and chimpanzees has been established using sign language, but some issues are still unresolved. Confirming observations are being sought.

When humans communicate

Use and abuse of language. Let's play with some numbers a bit to see how much language you're exposed to each year. Let's assume that as a student you're carrying a normal class load that keeps you in school and conversing with friends five to six hours a day. That will expose you to perhaps 100,000 words a day—50,000 during six hours of school and a like amount in the rest of your waking hours. That's about 36-37,000,000 words a year if you *don't* listen to the radio or television. Can you read at the rate of 300 words per minute (roughly one page of double-spaced typing with 2½-4 cm [1-1½-inch] margins)? If so, that means you're taking in almost 20,000,000 words a year if you read three hours a day. In total you may listen to or read as much as 60-100,000,000 words a year!

How much output do you produce? That, of course, will vary, depending on whether you're a good listener or a better talker. Most of us talk at a rate of from 120 to 150 words per minute. If we talk—including *everything* we say—five hours a day at that rate and live to 70, we will each produce roughly one *billion* (1,000,000,000) words during our life!

Numbers are fun, but the staggering thing is to consider the accuracy of the entire process. Very seldom do we say "banana" when we mean to say "Excuse me!" Very seldom, in fact, do we ever choose the wrong word for any occasion.

Nonverbal communication. Remember the example of the two young men at the beginning of this chapter? One young man was able to "read" a series of signals, and react to them. Communication from his fellow humans was involved, yet not a word was spoken concerning his need for a weekend date. Learn from this that language is *not* the only vehicle of communication.

In fact, much of what passes for language-based communication is actually information *you* are injecting into a conversation by giving and reading nonverbal cues. In 1927, psychologist Edward Sapir said, "We respond to gestures with an extreme alertness and, one might almost say, in accordance with an elaborate and secret code that is written nowhere, known by none, and yet understood by all."

Nonverbal communication involves transmission of information by means other than language in its spoken, written, or otherwise coded form. Three types of nonverbal messages are most often used. *Factual* messages are involved in requesting or providing goods, information, or services—even in rituals, such as giving a medal for valor. *Idexical* messages contain information about the sender's biological and psychological makeup. How does he or she feel about the other people communicating? What are his or her social and cultural affiliations? Finally, *regulatory* messages help assure orderly management of a conversation. Who speaks? In what order do they speak? How long do they speak? Such communication is accomplished through a variety of nonverbal cues.

Paralanguage. Any time we talk we are offering a verbal signal to be received and interpreted. *Paralanguage* identifies the nonlinguistic aspects of our spoken words. In what tone are we speaking? When do we pause? Do we stutter? All of these are paralinguistic cues that will "flavor" any listener's interpretation of what is heard. For example, even the simple word "Thanks" can be interpreted either as genuine gratitude or as sarcasm, depending on the tone in which it is spoken.

Proxemics. How do you walk with your friends? You don't walk ahead or behind them, you walk beside them, and within a certain distance—not too close, but not too far away either.

Proxemics is the study of the distance between us when we walk, talk, stand, or sit around with one another. We are individually wrapped by our "personal space"—an invisible envelope that we maintain around ourselves into which others cannot intrude without arousing discomfort. We prefer to let only certain people within that space, as you can see in elevators. People don't all crowd next to the door. Rather, they spread themselves out so that each person has roughly an equal share of the available space.

nonverbal communication: *transmission of information by means other than language in its spoken, written, or otherwise coded form*

paralanguage: *nonlinguistic aspects of speech that can affect interpretation, such as tone of voice, pauses, and emphasis*

proxemics: *the study of the distance maintained between humans in the course of daily life*

Proxemics involves the distancing factors involved in human interactions. Although these women are probably friends, each keeps some personal space for herself.

Personal space doesn't exist for us when we first learn to walk—we'll touch anyone or anything. By the age of three, however, we have developed our own personal space, and it increases in size between ages three and twenty-one years.

The distance between two people can be used to predict the nature of the social relationship that exists between them. For example, the further up you go in a business organization, the larger your desk becomes, and, therefore, the farther away from you a visitor sits.

Skin sensitivity. *Skin sensitivity* refers to who touches what parts of what person's body in a conversation. This sounds crude, but some very reliable rules are still operating here. For instance, are you more likely to tap your teacher's shoulder to get attention, or is he or she more likely to tap yours? In a family group, is a child more likely to push a parent, or the parent a child? In each instance, the answer may seem obvious.

However, if you combine these feelings with those we discussed regarding personal space, you can see that we are very careful about whose personal space *we* will violate. We almost *never* violate the personal space of someone superior to us by title, position, or family role. On the other hand, with people over whom we hold a position of responsibility or to whom we feel superior, *we* are most likely to initiate first contact.

skin sensitivity: *in communication, the physical contact permissible between persons of different age, rank, or role*

Drawing by Sam Hunt; © 1967 The New Yorker Magazine, Inc.

"I was supposed to contact you, but I'm not sure I have."

In review . . .

Nonverbal communication cues are part of the total communication process. These cues include paralanguage, proxemics, and skin sensitivity, among others.

kinesics: *"body language" in which body motions and postures communicate feelings*

→ Think about it

The **question**: We shared with you the manner in which a dateless high school senior identified some young women to call for a date. He did so simply by talking with them and watching their behavior, without ever asking them directly whether they had a date to an upcoming dance. How did he do it?

The **answer**: He simply watched for covert signals. Using his knowledge of nonverbal communication, he watched for signs from his female friends that they could be approached or that they liked him. How? In terms of proxemics, he observed which young women stood closest to him when they talked with him. In terms of paralanguage, he listened for the warmest tones. In terms of skin sensitivity, he watched to see who would accidentally bump him, or touch him as she passed. None of these cues alone would be enough, but for the careful, dateless male observer, these cues together gave the information he needed. He could guess who would be most receptive to a call from him. Can you think of any other nonverbal communication not mentioned here?

Chapter Application and Review

In this chapter we discussed a number of nonverbal cues that people use when evaluating or getting a general impression of others. Another such form of communication involves *kinesics*—body placement and motions. For example, on page 258 we asked to which persons illustrated you would be most likely to speak. If you responded only to their body positioning, the person leaning forward with eyes downcast, legs pressed together, and hands clenched almost seems to be saying "Don't bother me!" How could the signs be any more obvious? On the other hand, the persons slouching a little, leaning back with legs crossed loosely, and smiling are clearly approachable.

Think about it. If you are trying to look friendly, your posture alone can say "I'm easy to talk to." So—look everybody in the eye, cross your legs loosely, don't fold your arms, and have a ready smile!

Another point, perhaps obvious, but also very important, is the general impression you make by your choice of cosmetics and clothes. Say you're going to be picked up for a special date on Saturday night. What would you think of your date if he or she showed up smelling of the garden fertilizer shoveled that afternoon? You'd be being told

one thing. On the other hand, if the aroma was perfume or aftershave, the message would be something very different. The same point applies to clothing. You're always advised to dress your finest for a job interview. Why? There are two reasons. First, first impressions last. Second, you're making a nonverbal statement to the person interviewing you that the interview was important enough for you to go out of your way to dress appropriately.

The examples go on and on, but the point is clear. We talk to each other to communicate. At the same time, the way we say our message and the environment in which we speak may make as lasting an impression as the actual words.

One psychologist has suggested that in the communication of attitudes and feelings, only seven percent of the total message may be communicated verbally. It was proposed that 38 percent of the message is conveyed by the tone of voice of the speaker, and 55 percent is relayed by the facial expressions of the one who is talking. That means a total of 93 percent of an emotional or attitudinal message may be nonverbal! So, talk with body language if you want to make yourself heard.

REVIEW QUESTIONS

SECTION 1 (pages 245–258)

1. What are the major benefits to humans of having the ability to use language?

2. Why is memory so important in the use of language? Describe the two major

views of how memory works and illustrate one view.

3. Explain the difference between performance and competence in language and make up a sentence for each concept.

4. List and describe the four characteristics shared by all spoken languages.

5. In order for people to communicate in a given language, with what three aspects of the language must they agree?

6. What four characteristics are required before an organism can develop a language?

SECTION 2 (pages 258–268)

1. Define communication and identify the four elements in most important systems of communication. Choose one system and identify the four elements in that system.

2. Do you consider the patterns of communication used by bees a language? Why or why not?

3. Do you consider the communication established between humans and animal primates a language? Explain.

4. Identify various types of nonverbal communication and provide an example of each type from your own life.

ACTIVITIES

1. To understand the difference between reappearance and utilization concepts of memory, consider how long it takes you to learn the following series of numbers: 010011101001101010001. Now, use the following coding system: 000 = 0, 001 = 1, 010 = 2, 011 = 3, 100 = 4, 101 = 5, 110 = 6, and 111 = 7. Learn the code so you can recall the numbers 0 through 7 easily when given any set of three 0's and 1's, and vice versa. Now have a friend read the series above to you slowly. As your friend reads, translate the triplets of 0's and 1's into single digits between 0 and 7. To recall the original series, simply use the single digits to generate the 0 and 1 combinations. Here you've used a few rules and little memory to store a greater amount of information than you could learn and recall otherwise.

2. Career Search. Advertisers are constantly searching for sign-stimuli. These are the innate releasing stimuli that caused a highly predictable response in any organism. We humans do not react to very many such stimuli. Think of the advantages to advertisers if they could identify sign stimuli that would release buying behavior in us! Any time a product is revised at all it is usually advertised as "NEW." Could this be a sign stimulus? Try to identify as many possible language-based sign stimuli in advertising as you can.

3. Career Search. Psychologists often work with handicapped people, such as the deaf. Invite to your class someone who can communicate using American Sign Language. What are the problems in communicating with someone who is deaf? Are there any

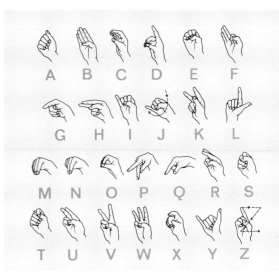

shades of emotion or meaning that cannot be communicated other than verbally? Using the signs on page 270, see if you can communicate in sign language. How much does it slow you down when you must communicate by gesture, rather than by mouth?

4. Career Search. Aphasia involves language difficulties caused by brain damage from war or accidental injury or from illness. Receptive and expressive aphasias involve problems with hearing and expressing language. Aphasias may occur also in writing or in spoken language skills. Ask your school psychologist or some community professional to discuss this condition and some of the difficulties it causes. Find out the various methods used to surmount it.

5. For one day keep track of how many people smile at you when you look at them in your normal way in the hallways of your school. Then, the next day, changing as little of your other behavior as possible, try to smile at every person you meet and keep the same count. How many people smile at you the second day? Is there any difference? What does this tell you about the manner in which your gestures are causing people to react to you?

6. Nonverbal communication plays a large role in the total amount of communicating we do. We rely on a wave of the hand to say "hello" or "good job" or "I'm okay." Make a list of as many gestures as you see used in a day, where the gesture itself communicates an entire message without a word having been spoken. How many different gestures did you find?

7. One of the most important communications we receive as we are driving is the highway-related information relayed to us by signs. What messages are most important to us? In what ways do the highway signs change as the average speed of the cars passing them increases? Identify as many aspects as you can of the ways in which highway signs are designed to communicate the maximum amount of information in the least possible amount of time. What changes would you recommend to increase the impact of the messages being relayed? When your list of answers is complete, select the best and the worst advertising billboard messages that you found.

INTERESTED IN MORE?

DEESE, J. *Psycholinguistics.* Allyn and Bacon, 1970. Will be interesting (but brief) reading. An essay by an experimental psychologist who switched his beliefs about the storage and use of language-based information from a "reappearance" to a "utilization" point of view. Explains his reasons for shifting.

LILLY, J. *The Mind of the Dolphin: A Nonhuman Intelligence.* Doubleday, 1967. This is an interesting case study of how the beliefs of a scientist influence both what he studies and how he studies it. Lilly analyzes the sonar (sound) signals of dolphins and tries to communicate using human sign language. He raises some very challenging issues about subhuman communication skills.

LINDEN, E. *Apes, Men, and Language.* Penguin Books, 1976. Starting with an analysis of how humans have taught sign language to chimpanzees, this author extends these findings to discuss how we believe humans communicate.

MATLIN, M. *Cognition.* Holt, Rinehart & Winston, 1983. A delightful text, covering the traditional topics in learning and memory plus chapters on perceptual processes, problem solving, and language. Activities interwoven with text encourage understanding.

MILLER, G. A. *The Psychology of Communication: Seven Essays.* Basic Books, 1967. A challenging series of essays that examine a wide range of problems involving psychology and communication. Covers topics from automation (humans communicating with machines and vice versa) to the study of psychic phenomena.

POLLIO, H. R. *The Psychology of Symbolic Activity.* Addison-Wesley, 1974. Lightly illustrated, this book discusses a wide range of symbolic activities from thinking to language. Heavy reading, but well written.

REYNOLDS, A. G. & FLAGG, P. W. *Cognitive Psychology.* Winthrop, 1972. Covers many topics, but has especially good sections on models of memory, language development in infants, and problems (as they relate to language) of living in a bilingual home.

TERRACE, H. *Nim: A Chimpanzee Who Learned Sign Language.* Knopf, 1979. Terrace reports on his attempt to teach a chimpanzee sign language. Through use of data, he challenges the conclusions of Beatrice and Allen Gardner on the language ability of chimps.

UNIT FOUR

MOTIVATION AND EMOTION

Sometimes it is difficult to determine by the expression on a person's face which emotion he or she is experiencing. These people, however, appear unanimous in their feelings of joy.

So far we have examined influences, both internal and external, that affect human behavior. In this unit we'll look at why you and other humans behave as you do. How do you know what goals to strive for? Why should you even bother to be active?

Chapter 9, Your Motivations, surveys three types of motivating forces: physiological needs, which you don't control; mixed motives, which involve both physiological and learned responses; and psychological, or learned, motives, which stir you because of prior experience.

In Chapter 10, Your Emotions, we'll look at some of the most complex of human experiences, those feelings that grip and move you, including stress and love. Finally, we'll consider some of the problems psychologists face when trying to bring emotions into the laboratory to be studied and defined.

9 Your Motivations

CHAPTER OUTLINE

WHAT'S THE ANSWER?

☐ "My friend and I went to a party the other night. It was really nice— candle light everywhere and a good time was had by all. And—wow!—what a spread! They even had lobster. I didn't eat too much more than I usually do. My folks had made me eat a huge dinner earlier. But my friend who's staying with me ate like a horse. I don't think she left the area where the food was all night." *Which of these two people probably has better control of her eating habits? Why do you think so?*

☐ "No, Carlita, no. I can't accept the scholarship."

"But, Pam, you earned that scholarship. Your test performance was the best of any senior in the city!"

"I know, Carlita, I know. But Jim didn't get one. I just can't accept mine—it would crush him!" *What motives are operating here? Why is this female refusing the scholarship that was not won by some male she knows?*

1 What Is Motivation?

In the last unit we discussed learning and memory, processes which clearly influence our behavior. We also do many things merely out of habit. However, in this and the next chapter we'll

Most people have heard of the mountain climber's answer to the question "Why do you climb the mountain?"—"Because it's there." Motivation activates behavior and provides the energy to achieve a goal. This person is rapelling off the Devil's Backbone in Alaska.

be looking at another major influence that is always operating in our daily lives—motivation.

Motivation is an intervening variable (see Chapter 1). It does two things. First, it activates behavior, or provides the energy for it. Second, it directs the activated behavior toward a goal. To be true to our earlier definition of intervening variables, we'll need to find out what independent variables cause motivation to occur. *And* we'll need to see how our behavior changes when our motivation increases or decreases.

Why do we need such a concept?

It is obvious that there are many *different causes* of human behavior. We've already looked at two: inherited mechanisms and learned responses. Yet even with inheritance *and* learning held constant, we see differences in behavior. For instance, some Saturdays you go to a movie, other Saturdays you'd rather go to a dance. Some days you eat a sandwich after school, and some days you do not. So your own *behavior varies* from time to time. In addition, your behavior differs from that of your friends, and also from that of your own family. Motivation helps us to explain these variations in behavior both within individuals and among different people in the same situation.

There are also a number of behaviors whose motivations *help us survive*, both individually and as a species. We seek food. We try to avoid pain. As we'll see, motivation involves a very complex combination of internal stimuli—aches, pains, and urges—as well as many external cues.

Lastly, when we talk about behavior being energized or started, we're really talking about *guiding* behavior. Think a moment. When you're out on a date, you're trying to read a very vague set of signals, some of which we were discussing in Chapter 8. Yet, those very weak stimuli may (if you can detect them) unleash very strong responses. In fact, the vigor of the response may be used as a measure of the strength of your motivation. But, what if you encounter aversive stimuli? Then you are likely to stop doing something. So a fourth category of reasons why we need the concept of motivation includes the idea of *efficiency*: we can use weak stimuli to guide strong behaviors. And, we can respond to other stimuli and stop behaviors that might cause us injury.

It should be pointed out that not all psychologists agree on the importance of motivation. For example, those who emphasize operant conditioning really are not concerned with internal processes—which motivation clearly is. Operant conditioners explain "motivated" behavior just on the basis of rewards. Keep these points in mind in the following discussion.

Vital elements

There are three important elements in all motivated behavior. The first element is *the events that cause a need* for the behavior to occur. These events may be inherited, learned, or a combination of both. The second important element is, the *internal result*. This may be a drive or urge, a purpose, or a motive. These words are often used in place of one another—sometimes correctly, sometimes in error.

Goal is the third important factor. This may sometimes be called an incentive. All three of these elements—a need, an internal result, and a goal—are combined in motivated behavior. Let's see how they relate to each other.

Going in cycles

The operation of these three elements of motivated behavior is often said to be circular or repetitive. They operate in a cycle, such as we've shown in the diagram. Right now as you're reading, how hungry are you? Your answer will place your current level of motivation in hunger at some point in the cycle. For our purposes we can jump in anywhere to describe the cycle to you, because the sequence of events is constant—they *always* occur in exactly the same order. Let's use how hungry you are right now to show you what's involved.

Need. This is an internal state that motivates our behavior. In our example, it's called hunger. Such needs are often physiological, but their place in the cycle may also be occupied by learned needs, as we'll see a bit later.

Drive. A *drive* is an aroused state of an organism. Drives are aroused by depriving an organism of the goal object or incentive it needs to satisfy itself. Each need will create specific kinds of drives within us and also give us various cues as to its existence. For example, when you get hungry, you *feel* hungry. If you're thirsty, you experience a different set of cues. These cues guide your responses.

Responses. Any motivated response will be directed toward a particular goal object. However, the specific response you make may be learned or it may be inherited. As we discussed earlier, we humans don't have many inherited responses that we don't control. In fact, the only motivated behavior that causes a rather uncontrolled response is pain. Pain will cause you to withdraw.

Almost all other motivated responses are learned. In our example, we asked you how hungry you were. If you finally decided you were hungry enough to put this book down and go search for food, then you were engaging in learned behavior. And you had a number of options. You could go to your kitchen refrigerator and get something to eat. You might journey to the nearest food machine or to a nearby restaurant. All of these would be responses motivated and guided by your hunger, yet they are learned responses.

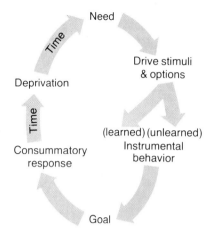

Figure 9-1 The "motivational cycle" showing the continuing series of events and experiences that combine to form a "motive."

drive: *an aroused state resulting from deprivation of some need*

Hunger is a physiological motivation involving a need, a drive, and a response.

Goal. If your responses were successful, you eventually reached the goal object (food) you were seeking. Actually there were two different kinds of goals you might have sought, depending on your needs. Positive goals are those for which you strive, such as food or water. Negative goals are those that you try to avoid or escape, such as pain. The actual goal is always directly related to the need and drive that are operating.

Reaction to the goal. This is more complex. Once you reach your goal, you will change your actions. Having reached the food, you'll now start eating it. If you were thirsty, once you reached water you'd drink it. Yet, if you began to experience pain, you would do something quite different. So, the response or reaction you emit at the goal depends on the nature of the goal itself. Is the cycle now complete? Not yet. Remember, we said the cycle was continuous. Read on.

Deprivation. As soon as you finish consuming, avoiding, or escaping from the goal object, you start into the phase of the cycle called deprivation. Once you've eaten a certain amount you stop; time goes by then as you go on to other things. Between lunch and supper (if you don't have a snack) you may go for six or eight hours without food. In short, you are depriving yourself. The passage of time causes an increase in deprivation. However, what happens during this time can affect the deprivation. For instance, if you are very active or in a very cold climate, you will get hungrier than if you are quiet, or in a warmer environment. In any event, with the passage of time, you become more and more deprived. And the result? Your needs grow again—you grow hungry. More drive, more responses, and so forth. The cycle goes on and on.

Homeostasis

This is a very important concept. What happens when you get hot? You perspire. The air around you then causes the perspiration to evaporate, and the physics involved in that process causes you to feel slightly cooler. You can easily prove this yourself by simply wetting your finger and then waving it in the air. If you move it fast, it will feel cooler than if you simply hold it still.

And what if you feel cold? Obviously, you get goose-bumps. These are actually caused by little muscle cells, each attached to the hairs on the surface of your body. When you feel cool, these muscle cells contract, causing the hairs on your body to stand erect. This takes energy, and to respond to this demand, your sympathetic nervous system diverts blood to the surface of your body to supply these cells. In the process of "burning" the sugar brought by the blood, the surface of the skin heats up.

All of this is by way of illustrating that these two responses—perspiration and goose-bumps—occur automatically. If your body temperature moves too far from the correct temperature, sensors detect the drift and cause corrective processes to occur. This sensing and monitoring, including all of the processes that may be called into action to correct any deviation from a desired norm, is called *homeostasis*.

There are many examples of homeostatic mechanisms within us. Automatically controlled in this way are our temperature, the amount of sugar in our blood, and the ratio of oxygen to waste products which our blood contains. We'll see homeostasis operate a number of times in the processes discussed in this chapter.

Figure 9-2 A household thermostat is similar in function to the body's homeostasis. When the temperature falls below a certain level, the thermostat turns on the heat. In hot weather the thermostat turns on (first) an attic fan and (finally) an air conditioner. In a like manner the body acts to keep itself at a balanced level, or emotional neutral.

In review . . .

Motivation influences many aspects of our life and helps explain different causes of behavior. It aids survival, accounts for variations in any individual's behavior, and guides our actions. Motivation operates in a cycle. Homeostasis involves maintaining various bodily processes within a narrow range of acceptability. Deviations from that norm lead to automatic corrective actions.

homeostasis: *the process of sensoring and monitoring that helps establish and retain balance in body systems*

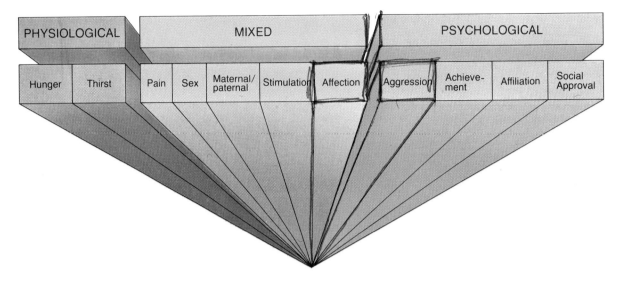

Figure 9-3 Motives range from the most purely physiological, such as hunger, to the entirely psychological, or learned, such as the desire for social approval. In between are a vast array of "mixed motives," involving both physiological and psychological components. The continuum above shows some of the motives we will examine here.

2 Physiological Motives

Responses and the nervous system

This is one of the places where we can apply the knowledge gained from our discussion of the nervous system in Chapter 4. Physiological motives involve actions that are more or less directly related to body responses. What happens if you get very scared? Your heart starts to pound, you start breathing more heavily, and you feel a rush of heat across the surface of your skin. These are normal reactions, but they differ in each of us.

Individual responses when motivated. When each of us gets scared, excited, or angry our body tends to react. The fact is, whatever pattern of stirrings occurs when you get mad is likely to be the same pattern of organ and glandular activity that you'll experience with *any* motivational or emotional experience! That is, whether you're mad, fearful, or excited, the pattern of organ activity will tend to be the same, and may be unlike that of anyone else. Perhaps your heart is most responsive, or your breathing rate, or any of several other body indicators of emotional reaction. This unique pattern of organ responses that each of us shows is called *autonomic response specificity*.

autonomic response specificity: *the unique pattern of organ responses made by each individual in reaction to emotion*

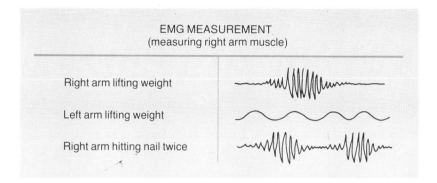

EMG MEASUREMENT
(measuring right arm muscle)

Right arm lifting weight

Left arm lifting weight

Right arm hitting nail twice

Figure 9-4 The EMG, or electromyogram, measures muscular responses of subjects as they *think* about certain activities. In the experiment shown here, the EMG was hooked to their right arm. Subjects were asked to think about the activity at the left. The resulting EMG responses to the right indicated to researchers that minute muscle responses were involved in thinking. Later research showed that muscle movements and thinking were not necessarily connected.

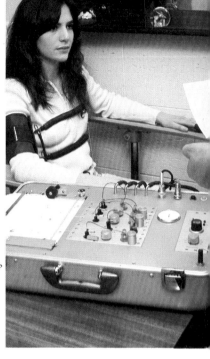

Other clues? Are there other physical changes that may indicate psychological states? It is known that when we are interested in someone or something, the pupils of our eyes tend to get bigger. Other changes are less sure. For instance, many years ago, psychologists thought that thinking might just involve subthreshold muscle movements. They thought that maybe thinking was nothing more than silent "talking." They thought that by measuring minute muscle movements they could tell when thinking was occurring. Things aren't that easy. Later research showed that such small muscle movements—whether of the eyes, the vocal chords, or the voluntary muscles—are neither sufficient *nor* necessary for thinking to occur. Motivation is equally complex.

In review . . .

Human motives range from physiological motives (hunger and thirst) through "mixed" motives, which involve both physiological and learned aspects (pain and sex), to purely learned motives (achievement and fear). Our body reacts as it becomes motivated. For each of us our specific pattern of arousal is the same for any motive. Visible parts of the body, such as our eyes, are also thought to react when we experience stress.

Lie detector tests measure autonomic nervous system responses to various psychological stimuli. The glands and parts of the brain will respond differently when placed under stress. Blood pressure, and heart and respiration rates are among the measures used to detect lying. A neutral series of questions is asked first to establish a *base line*, or normal pattern. Finally, the crucial questions "Did you commit the robbery?" "Do you know who killed Mr. Rodriquez?" or the like, are inserted into the series.

Hunger

To give you some idea of the complexity of our behavior, let's look at the factors we so far know are involved in a very important physiological motive—the human experience of hunger.

We've all experienced it. Several hours of hard dancing, or play at the beach, or hiking in the mountains and what happens? We're starved! There are several aspects of hunger to consider.

What makes us hungry? There are our obvious body needs for growth, repair, and storage of reserves. But even more important are the environmental cues, of which there are several. First, the simple sight and odor of food causes us to get hungry. Experiments have shown data indicating that the larger the stack of feed placed in front of chickens, the more they'll eat! The same tendency, unfortunately, has been found in us humans. In the United States, we eat more at Thanksgiving or at any holiday meal, partly because the amount of food put before us is greater.

Second, our prior experience plays a role. If you decide to skip supper today, you'll find you get hungriest right around the time when you normally eat supper. If you can get past that time, you'll find you begin to feel less hungry even though it's been longer since you ate.

Third, a variety of other environmental conditions also influence how hungry we get. For example, on a hot day our thirst increases, but our hunger drops.

What makes us start eating? It is a fact of biology and physics that our body weight will remain constant only as long as the food we eat (that is, the energy we take in) equals the energy we expend. For example, what do you think would be the result if you simply took a deeper cut into the butter each day and added one extra shake of dressing to your salad each night? If you were already fully matured and on a steady diet, those two changes would add 100 pounds to your body weight in 10 years! We must have very accurate control over how much we eat, but how is that control to be achieved?

Several answers have been suggested, but, first, what makes us decide to eat? Your first guess might be the obvious one; our stomach starts to growl when we get hungry. Do these stomach contractions actually cause us to eat? Enthusiasm for this idea died quickly when it was demonstrated that even with all sensory nerves to the stomach cut, people still got hungry.

Another possibility is body weight reduction. Certainly, if our food intake is reduced for a long period of time—so long that we lose perhaps ten percent of our weight—we are very hungry. Yet, the percent of body weight lost alone will not allow us to predict how hungry we may become. Only four hours may pass after breakfast yet by lunchtime we'll be far hungrier than we might predict given our minor loss in weight.

Hunger may also be caused by a factor in our blood. Hunger may result from a drop in our *blood sugar level*, which (in all but diabetics) is monitored by the amount of *insulin* we produce. Recently, a hormone released by the intestines in response to food intake has been shown to reduce eating. The absence of that hormone may lead to eating.

Finally, the hypothalamus is also involved. The lateral (side) hypothalamus is often called the *eating* center. And the ventro-medial (meaning the bottom, central) portion of the hypothalamus is the satiety ("I'm full!") center. These centers were discovered in studies of brain stimulation, but we still don't know precisely what stimulates them.

And the story isn't finished. Work in the 80's indicates that these centers do not directly control eating. Rather, they are both involved in establishing the *set point* for our body's ideal weight. As our weight falls below that point, we tend to eat more; as we get above it, we tend to eat less. Apparently this balance between eating and not eating is monitored by the two centers in our hypothalamus.

Thus, eating is caused by environmental factors (time of day, smell of food, visible presence of food), deviations from our normal set-point for body weight, and internal factors, such as blood sugar level, the absence (or presence?) of selected hormones, and the lateral and ventro-medial hypothalamus. Much work remains to sort out the relative contributions of these factors. The death from self-starvation of singer Karen Carpenter in 1983 stimulated the study of *anorexia nervosa*, a complex emotional illness most often affecting young women. Some of them have endangered (or lost) their lives by dieting to lose over 60 percent of their normal weight.

How do we stop eating? This is as vitally important an ability as is the fact that we start eating—in some ways even more important. We can do without food for several days, but if we did nothing but eat food for several days we might kill ourselves. Getting ourselves to stop eating is a two-stage process.

First, *head* effects cause us to stop eating. A primary site where this is accomplished is our *mouth*. We know—through practice at least three times a day for most of our lives—about

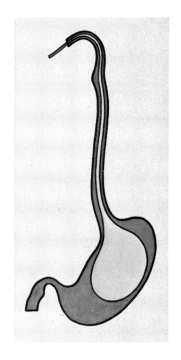

Figure 9-5 Graduate students in one early experiment swallowed a balloon attached to a hose. When the balloon was inflated it was possible to record their stomach contractions by measuring the air pressure. The researchers related these contractions to the feelings of hunger they experienced. However, later research revealed that stomach contractions actually increase after eating. This suggests that these contractions play little or no role in our normal experience of hunger.

how much we should eat. Experiments have been conducted with dogs whose esophagus (the tube connecting the mouth with the stomach) was operated upon. The dogs could chew and swallow their food, but the food was then diverted out of the body through the side of the dog's neck. Such experimental dogs would eat more than they normally would, yet they still stopped eating, only to resume again later when their earlier eating had obviously been of no help to them. It's as if each dog had a "food meter" which allowed it to gauge how much food had passed its mouth. A similar factor causes us to stop eating.

There are also *stomach* factors. The fact that the dogs would eat *more* than normal before stopping when no food at all was reaching their stomach hints at the existence of the other factor. As our stomach fills, this also becomes a cue to stop eating.

In addition, a hormone secreted by the intestines in response to food intake is released into our blood stream as mentioned above. As the body chemical balances begin to correct themselves because we've eaten, monitoring sites in the hypothalamus probably respond to this hormone and control our longer-term ability to keep from eating. One of the major problems we humans face—especially in the food-rich, North American societies—is that of *obesity*, or long-term overweight. Box 9-1 discusses some of the factors that seem to cause some of us to be overweight.

The amount of water in our body cells and in our blood determines when we will feel thirsty.

Thirst

What makes us thirsty? A healthy adult loses more than two quarts of water through natural processes each day. The two great storehouses of water within us are the fluid inside the cells of our body and the fluid outside those cells. The relative amount of salt in these two pools of liquid determines the balance of fluids between them. If there is too little fluid in either reservoir, we become thirsty. This causes us to drink water (if it's available), which makes our kidneys more efficient in reclaiming water as they process waste products.

What makes us start drinking? We can make ourselves thirsty by eating. After a particularly rich, creamy, chocolate milkshake, the first thing you want is a glass of water. Here you've added liquid and made yourself thirsty! Cells in our hypothalamus monitor the amount of water in our cells. The monitors for the amount of extracellular fluids are in our kidneys. Either the hypothalamus or the kidneys can stimulate drinking, but they tend to operate together.

Why do we stop drinking? Deprived of water for 24 hours, humans drink enough in two and a half minutes to replace missing fluids. The relative moistness of the mouth and fullness of the stomach are environmental cues that cause us to stop drinking. A *lack* of fluid can cause severe problems, but *excesses* are simply passed through the system.

Both hunger and thirst share a number of features. Both drives are physiological in nature. However, the environment may to some extent determine how hungry or thirsty a person gets. We may also acquire certain tastes—for hamburgers rather than fish, for instance, or for lemonade rather than tea.

Feature   9–1   OVERWEIGHT? WHAT'S THE PROBLEM?

What keeps people overweight? Three things are involved. First, the more overweight we are, the more overweight we are able to become. Why? Because the larger a fat cell gets, the greater is its capacity to store fat. Bigger leads to even bigger! And overweight people tend to have higher base levels of insulin, which aids in the efficiency of converting sugar into fat. So metabolic changes increase our fat-producing and -storing capacities.

Second, inactivity is often blamed for overweight. But it's not true. Overweight people do seem to move slower the more they gain, but the obesity produced the slowness, not the other way around!

Third, unhappiness is sometimes blamed for overweight. You eat to comfort your miseries, right? Not really. As obesity increases, a person moves more slowly. That person thus needs fewer calories, but eats more to keep the fat cells happy. This vicious circle eventually leads to personal unhappiness, but it's more of a symptom than a cause of obesity. And so to the related question:

What makes people overweight? There's good evidence that a tendency toward obesity is set during the years of infancy, from birth until two. That critical period determines the number of fat cells we have throughout our life. Reducing the weight of obese children over age two reduces the *size* of their fat cells, but not the number of them. As one psychologist has put it, ". . . a fat, bouncing baby may well grow into a fat, lethargic adult."

Obesity is thought to be caused also by environmental factors in early childhood. In one study, among 19 pairs of identical twins split up in infancy and raised separately, the average difference in body weight between the twins in each pair was about 10 pounds. Among 25 pairs not split up but raised together, the average difference was only four pounds. Obviously, environment had an impact on their tendency to gain or lose weight.

One classic study of obesity found that overweight people were very influenced in their desire to eat by the taste, smell, and sight of good food. The obese tend to rely too much on external cues to tell them whether or not to eat. In one experiment a clock indicated that it was "dinner" hour, although it was actually well before the normal eating time for the people participating. They got hungry anyway, just on the cue from the clock!

====== In review . . .

Our body's needs for growth, repair, and storage of resources combine with our prior experiences and many other environmental stimuli to make us hungry. However, our hypothalamus is now thought to set our body weight. Two factors combine to cause us to stop eating. Our head monitors how much we take in, and our stomach registers the amount of food being stored. In the longer run we are kept from eating as unknown body factors restore themselves. Thirst is similar in some ways. The hypothalamus causes us to drink, and the same mixture of factors that stops our eating also stops our drinking.

Think about it

The **question**: At the start of the chapter we described two girls who went to a party. Both had had a big supper beforehand, yet at the party one ate much more than the other. Which of the two do you think is more likely to have better control of her eating habits? Why do you think so?

The **answer**: This question is a little tricky, since you would have had to have read the story carefully to pick up all the hints. It is likely, though, that the girl who ate *more* at the party probably has fewer problems with being overweight. People whose body-weight set-point is moderate and who have little difficulty staying at their desired weight often get trapped at a party.

Without meaning to, they tend to eat too much. Parties are exceptions for most of us. We don't have much practice in standing on our feet with a lot of food and snacks around us. As a result the normal cues as to when we've eaten enough are missing. The conversation quoted mentioned the "huge dinner" that was eaten earlier by the speaker—a person who probably always overeats. We also know that the light was dim (candlelight) and that people who regularly have weight problems tend to respond more strongly to the mere sight of food. Thus, we would guess that the person who was talking (the one who didn't eat as much) is more likely to have trouble with her weight!

3 "Mixed" Motives

Now let's look at some of our motives that have two components. They are partly physiological, yet they are also dependent on certain kinds of environmental stimulation. There are a variety of such motives, including pain and sex. These emphasize the physiological component.

Other mixed motives would include our need for activity, stimulation, and affection. These motives have some physiological basis, but some of their aspects are obviously learned. Mixed motives have the greatest variety and generate the greatest controversy. Very different kinds of evidence are required in their study.

Pain

The experience. Pain has two components. One we discussed earlier—the perception or *feel* of pain. That's the awareness you experience when a doctor injects medication into your arm, or a friend twists your arm too far behind your back. Pain commands your immediate attention. That seems to be one of the purposes of pain. It serves as a warning when we do something—or when something is done to us—that may injure us.

The other component is our interpretation of the pain—our *reaction* to it. This has many aspects of a motivation. We try to avoid it, and we'll work to escape from it once it's there. So, there are two major elements of pain—physiological and learned. Let's examine each of them.

Physiological elements. The gate-control theory of pain suggests there are two systems that carry messages about pain. *Fast* messages to our brain may alert its higher portions to be ready to receive information. Or, they cause messages to be sent back down the spinal cord to inhibit slower incoming messages. The *slow* messages are the actual information about the pain—where it is, how much of the body is affected, and how serious the source of pain is. Thus, if the fast messages have intercepted the slower messages, we may not feel the pain. This would explain how it is that athletes sometimes play for many minutes in a sports contest without even realizing that they have broken a bone.

Learned elements. A number of years ago some small Scottish terriers were raised in a totally isolated cage. They were fed, but they could only hear and smell other dogs and humans. Apparently they grew up healthy in almost every way. When they were tested at the age of 9-12 months, however, it was found that if you struck a match in front of these dogs, they would sniff it, putting out the flame with their wet noses, and burning themselves in the process. Most dogs only need to do that once to learn to stay away from matches. Not so with these raised-in-isolation Scottish terriers. Strike other matches and they'd repeat their painful experience again and again. These animals could perceive pain, but apparently they couldn't interpret it. It was as if they had missed some important learning experiences at an earlier critical period in their lives.

Humans experience pain in somewhat the same way. It's a sensory stimulus that is perceived and interpreted. Physiological elements and prior experience are combined to yield what we label as pain.

Control of pain. If the findings so far are correct, we may have to assume that our normal reaction to pain is an acquired (learned) motivation. Three factors are important in mastering pain.

The first is *anxiety*. It is known that as our anxiety or worry about pain increases, the experienced pain grows worse. That's one reason we always seem to associate trips to the dentist with intense pain—we worry about it too much!

The second factor is *attention*. If our attention is distracted, we can reduce or even almost eliminate our reactions to painful stimuli.

The third factor is *control*. If we control the amount of pain to which we are being subjected, we can tolerate more of it.

So how do we master our reaction to pain? If we can, we should reduce our anxiety and try to pay attention to something else. Also, we should gain as much control as possible over when and how much and how often the pain will be experienced. The Lamaze childbirth method is a good example. A woman in natural childbirth using the Lamaze method is taking part in a planned series of activities to reduce her anxiety. Her attention is diverted, and she is given some activities to gain control over the pain she experiences. The reports from many such mothers who have used the method make it undeniable that the method does work.

The Lamaze childbirth method advocates exercises that divert attention from pain and help the mother-to-be learn how to gain control over painful stimuli.

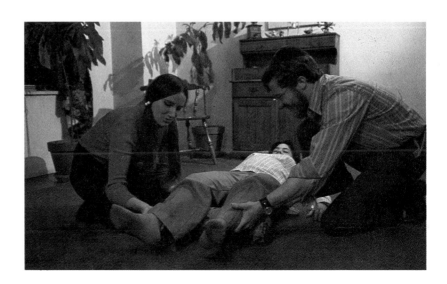

Sexual behavior

Sexual behavior is another mixed motive, drawing on both physiological and learned elements. It's unusual in that it is not at all important to the survival of the individual organism—human or animal. Yet, it is crucially important to the survival of each species.

Physiological elements. Sex as a motive resembles hunger and thirst in two principal ways. It is based on physiological mechanisms and it is an approach motive, not an avoidance motive like pain.

On the other hand, sex is very different from the physiological motives. There is no actual physiological need. Responding to our sex drive *expends* energy, rather than increases it, as happens after we've eaten or drunk needed substances. Finally, sex in humans is much more dependent on stimuli found in our environment.

There are three groups of factors that influence our sexual behavior. First, the *physiological* factors include primitive reflex circuits involving the lower spinal cord. Also the brain, especially our old friend the hypothalamus, plays an important role. And in higher animals and in humans the *cortex* plays an increasingly important role in sexual behavior.

A second set of factors are *hormonal*. However, while hormones cause us to be interested in sexual activities, they do *not* cause sexual behavior itself. As we move up the scale of animals we find that hormones play less and less of a crucial role.

Sexual behavior in humans is a complex "mixed" motive composed of physiological and learned elements. Basic to the adult bond of love is the physical warmth and affection received in childhood.

For us humans, the environmental factors or *learned elements* are the third and most important controllers of our sexual activities. In fact, much of what we call "sex" is learned behavior. Tenderness and affection—so much a part of human sexual activities—are learned responses. In fact, *only* with humans do these learned factors take precedence over physiological factors. For humans, the bond of affection is necessary for a long-lasting and mutually satisfying sexual relationship.

The basic elements on which such a relationship is built are learned during childhood. During this period we learn trust. We learn to accept and enjoy physical contact. We also develop the behaviors that our society considers "male" or "female." And we find pleasure in seeking the company of others.

Current attitudes. In modern society in the 1980's, many people hold attitudes toward sexual behavior different from those held just 20 to 30 years ago when your parents were growing up. Various polls through the 70's and 80's clearly indicate this fact. Of course, there are also people who feel strongly that these changes are undesirable. This is often a source of conflict in society. In some cases a large, highly emotional gap has developed between the adolescent and older fellow humans concerning the issue of sex.

Certain biological facts, however, do not change. Sexual relations can still produce a child. The moral decisions in such matters are serious ones. To enjoy one's own life at the risk of creating another is not a decision to be lightly made. Help may be available from parents, but if not, numerous services are offered by society — from religious counseling centers to social workers' telephone hot lines — to aid you in thinking clearly if you experience problems in this important area of life.

In review . . .

Mixed motives involve physiological components and the influence of learning that has often occurred during critical periods in early life. Pain is one such motive. Experience with pain in the earlier years is important in learning how to react to pain. Sex is another mixed motive. Its physiological aspect has some similarities with hunger and thirst, but otherwise it differs in many ways. Hormones also influence sexual behavior, but human sexuality tends to be dominated by environmental (learned) cues. The moral decisions concerning sex are extremely complex in today's world.

4 Psychological, or Learned, Motives

It's not easy to determine which learned motives are most important. Are we to rank them according to the degree of our psychological need? The satisfaction they provide? We can, perhaps, decide on the basis of the number of people who seem to need to satisfy them, but this does not really provide the answer either.

Physiological processes play only an indirect role here. These learned motives are not aroused by physiological needs but rather by environmental cues. As we talk about these motives, remember that just naming a motive is not the same as explaining it.

Gaining secondary goals

Our primary needs are for water, food, and the avoidance of pain. The importance of secondary goals is learned, perhaps because of their relation to our primary goals. For instance, money gains its power as a secondary or learned goal because it buys us food, drink, and the means to get relief from sickness and pain.

Notice there's been a very important shift here. When the primary needs—hunger or thirst—exist, we are *pushed* by them toward a specific goal. We are driven to find food or water as is our need. On the other hand, the learned goals *pull* us toward them. The value of the goal itself has now become the primary motivating factor.

Expression

Several things determine whether we will respond to a particular learned motive. One is the *availability of the response*. We simply cannot succeed as a bricklayer if we do not know how to mix the mortar. A second important factor is our *expectancy of success*. Very few of us would play basketball against a star of the Boston Celtics in response to our need for achievement. We couldn't possibly expect to win.

Another factor determining how we'll respond is the *value of the goal* itself. Under many circumstances, as the value of the goal increases, so does the amount we'll do to try to achieve it—up to a certain point as we'll discuss shortly.

Finally, the *environment* in which we find ourselves also determines how we'll respond. The stimuli that are present, the tools (and skills) we have, and the social pressures to which we are continually subjected all influence our responses to learned motivation.

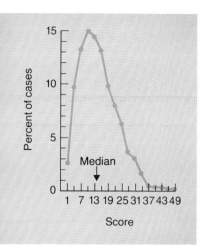

Figure 9-6 This distribution shows how 1,971 university students scored on the Taylor Manifest Anxiety Scale, which has a possible score of 0-50 (Taylor, Janet A. "Drive Theory and Manifest Anxiety," *Psychological Bulletin*)

Measurement

We'll discuss the techniques of testing humans in more detail later, but for now we'll give you just a brief preview of three techniques by which we measure various learned motives.

Projective tests. A projective test uses a neutral stimulus to draw responses from the person taking the test. These responses supposedly indicate the attitudes or feelings that are influencing his or her performance. One example is the Thematic Apperception Test, or TAT. Here the person is shown different pictures of various types of people and asked to make up a story. He or she would tell what led up to the pictured situation, what was going on in the picture, and what the probable results would be.

Inventory. These tests may use multiple-choice questions, true-false questions, or simply a check-list in which you indicate which of the items apply to you. One good example of such a test is the Taylor Manifest Anxiety Scale, or TMAS. Table 9-1 has items drawn from this test—50 true-false statements about things that happen to you or describe you. Answer the questions either true or false as they apply to you. By scoring yourself, you can compare your score with those of 1,971 college students who took the test. See Figure 9-6.

Situation test. Finally, it is also possible to measure your learned motives by creating a situation simply to observe your performance in it. Rather than provide many details of such a testing situation, we'll review recent studies of one learned motive, achievement, since that research has used all three types of tests.

Achievement

Sources. In most North American societies the emphasis on achievement is enormous. It's no wonder we end up highly motivated to achieve as adults. Some people don't, of course,

ANSWERS: Give yourself one point for all of the following statements that you marked TRUE: 2, 5, 6, 7, 8, 10, 11, 13, 14, 16, 17, 19, 20, 21, 22, 23, 24, 25, 26, 27, 28, 30, 31, 33, 34, 35, 36, 37, 39, 40, 41, 42, 43, 44, 45, 46, 47, 48, and 49. Give yourself one point also for all of the following that you marked FALSE: 1, 3, 4, 9, 12, 15, 18, 29, 32, 38, 50. Now total the number of points you have. This is a rough estimate of how anxious you judge yourself to be. The higher you score yourself, the more anxious you think you are. The midpoint for one sample of college students was at about 13.

Table 9-1 **A test of anxiety** 293

Number on a sheet of paper from 1 to 50.
Mark each of the following statements TRUE if it describes you and FALSE if it does not.

1. I do not tire quickly.
2. I am often sick to my stomach.
3. I am about as nervous as other people.
4. I have very few headaches.
5. I work under a great deal of strain.
6. I cannot keep my mind on one thing.
7. I worry over money and business.
8. I frequently notice my hands shake when I try to do something.
9. I blush as often as others.
10. I have diarrhea once a month or more.
11. I worry quite a bit over possible troubles.
12. I practically never blush.
13. I am often afraid that I am going to blush.
14. I have nightmares every few nights.
15. My hands and feet are usually warm enough.
16. I sweat very easily even on cool days.
17. When embarrassed I often break out in a sweat which is very annoying.
18. I do not often notice my heart pounding and I am seldom short of breath.
19. I feel hungry almost all the time.
20. Often my bowels don't move for several days at a time.
21. I have a great deal of stomach trouble.
22. At times I lose sleep over worry,
23. My sleep is restless and disturbed.
24. I often dream about things I don't like to tell other people.
25. I am easily embarrassed.
26. My feelings are hurt more easily than those of most people.
27. I often find myself worrying about something.
28. I wish I could be as happy as others.
29. I am usually calm and not easily upset.
30. I cry easily.
31. I feel anxious about something or someone almost all of the time.
32. I am happy most of the time.
33. It makes me nervous to have to wait.
34. At times I am so restless that I cannot sit in a chair for very long.
35. Sometimes I become so excited that I find it hard to get to sleep.
36. I have often felt that I faced so many difficulties that I could not overcome them.
37. At times I have been worried beyond reason about something that really did not matter.
38. I do not have as many fears as my friends.
39. I have been afraid of things or people that I know could not hurt me.
40. I certainly feel useless at times.
41. I find it hard to keep my mind on a task or job.
42. I am more self-conscious than most people.
43. I am the kind of person who takes things hard.
44. I am a very nervous person.
45. Life is often a strain on me.
46. At times I think I am no good at all.
47. I am not at all confident of myself.
48. At times I feel that I am going to crack up.
49. I don't like to face a difficulty or make an important decision.
50. I am very confident of myself.

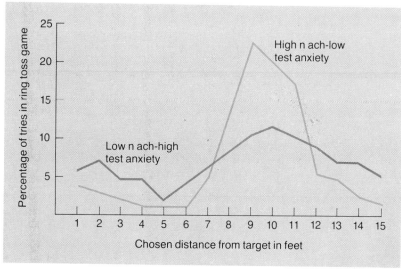

High n ach-low test anxiety

Low n ach-high test anxiety

Percentage of tries in ring toss game

Chosen distance from target in feet

The desire for achievement is a learned motive. Here Martina Navratilova uses the skill that won her the 1982 championship at the United States Open at Forest Hills. Figure 9-7 The graph shows the results of an experiment in which subjects threw rings at a stake, after selecting the distance from the stake at which they preferred to stand. The letters "n ach" refer to need for achievement.

but most do. Children with higher needs for achievement are most often raised in societies that do three things: First, they make early demands on an infant such as toilet training. Second, the child experiences a large number of such demands. Finally, these demands are made with great severity. All of these influence achievement motivation.

Psychologists now believe that this motive to achieve is composed of two subordinate motives—a hope for success and a fear of failure. It is thought that the TAT that we discussed earlier measures our hope for success. The TMAS is thought to measure our fear of failure. So if we give both tests to someone, we should be able to combine the results to predict his or her motivation to achieve.

Look at the graph, which shows the results of one such study. A large number of students were given both the TAT and the TMAS. From this total group were chosen two types of individual. One group was made up of those who scored high on the TAT in need for achievement and low in the TMAS as regards their anxiety. The second was a group that scored low on the TAT (meaning they had a low need to achieve) and high on the TMAS (meaning they were quite anxious). All of these people were then challenged to play a game of ring toss. They could stand anywhere from one to fifteen feet away from the peg on the floor. The independent variable in the experiment was the test score of the subjects—were they of low or high need to achieve? The dependent variable was how far they chose to stand from the peg.

As was expected, those with a high need to achieve stood at moderate distances from the stick. Too close and they could take no credit for any successes. Too far and they weren't likely to have many successes. So, as predicted, they chose the middle range. They could credit their own personal skill for any points they made. And those with a low need to achieve? Very different were they. They tended to stand very close, since they weren't looking for a challenge, or they stood very far away. Standing that far back they clearly couldn't be blamed if they failed to achieve!

It seems that the value of our success goes up as the likelihood of achieving success goes down. Yet as the probability of success goes down, the fear of failure goes up. Work in the late 70s indicates that our own personal standards of excellence also affect the nature and severity of tasks we will choose for ourselves.

Fear of success—a women's problem? Early in the 1970s a challenging piece of research was published, based on a simple projective test of men and women. Participants were asked to complete the sentence seen in Figure a if they were male and that in Figure b if they were female. The resulting stories were scored to indicate attitudes towards success or failure.

Fears of success were measured by expressed fears, by guilt or worry about the success, or by denial of the success. It was found that 65 percent of the females' stories showed a fear of success when writing about Anne, but only nine percent of the males' stories showed fears of success when writing about John. The psychologist who made this discovery suggested that women must deal with success very differently from men. She said that successful women experience much more guilt, worry, or even denial of success than do successful men.

Such controversial results don't usually lie around unchallenged for very long, and these results certainly didn't, either. For example, notice (1) that the stories involve *medical* school, which had—even into the late 60s—been considered a haven for males, not females. Might this not cause some concern for the success of a female? Notice also that (2) there was no comparable group of males and females writing of the successes

Figure 9-8a, 9-8b A projective test of male and female attitudes toward success. Figure a shows the sentence that males taking the test were asked to complete. Figure b shows the sentence given to females. Results seemed to indicate that women deal with success differently from men.

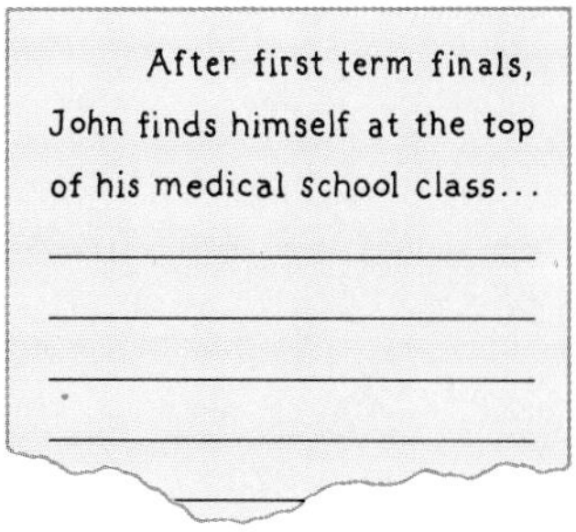

After first term finals, John finds himself at the top of his medical school class...

(a.)

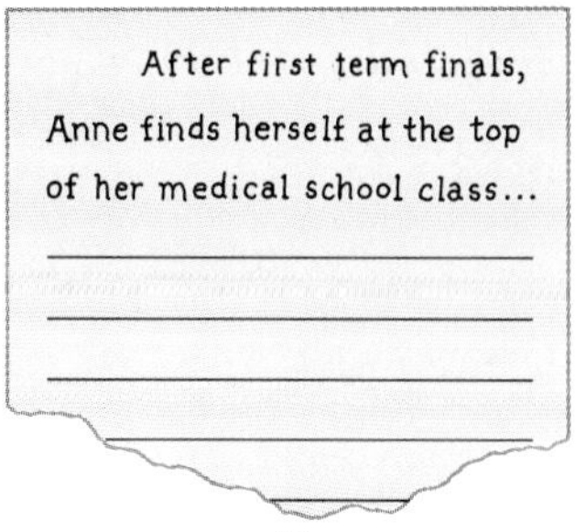

After first term finals, Anne finds herself at the top of her medical school class...

(b.)

Women's motivation for achievement has been under discussion in recent years. Some studies indicate that women may fear success. On the other hand, increasing numbers of women are achieving high positions in communications, business, and other professions formerly considered male domains.

or failures of John and Anne in *nursing* school. Finally, (3) society's values changed rapidly during the 70s as women made a lot of progress toward equal pay for equal jobs.

Moreover, and perhaps in response to social values, females may not fear success itself as much as success gained at the expense of males. Remember our comments in Chapter 3 on females acting inferior sometimes in the presence of males.

→ Think about it

The **question**: Pam had won a scholarship in a city-wide competition. She refused to accept it because Jim, a male friend, had not earned one and she was afraid of upsetting him. What motives might she have had?

The **answer**: This is a very complex area of research, but we're beginning to gain some understanding. For most humans achievement is composed of a hope for success and a fear of failure. Females, however, also seem to fear success—especially if it is achieved at the expense of males. In many societies, females are trained to yield to the male.

What is apparently happening here is that Pam is reacting—perhaps without even being aware of it—to pressures she feels. She places her feelings for Jim and her fear of his reaction above her own opportunity for self-fulfillment. Such attitudes are changing rapidly in modern society.

Fear

Fear's role in human behavior. Are fears inevitable? In some senses yes, they are. Fear is a constant part of the life of many persons. The experiment described in the caption for Figure 9-9 summarizes why fears may be inevitable. Fear, then, seems to be learned. And why? It occurs any time we experience trauma—something we cannot immediately control. It has been suggested that a main purpose of fear is to get us into action to regain control of our environment. Box 9-2 describes an enlightening experiment that has tragic implications. It teaches us that when we have prior experiences with being helpless, we are likely to continue to assume we cannot help ourselves even in situations where we can.

Feature   **9-2 CONDITIONED HELPLESSNESS**

Two groups of dogs—we can call them the Haves and the Have-nots, if you like—took part in an experiment. All the dogs were first put in a simple apparatus. Both groups were then treated identically except for one experience: The Have-nots received an *inescapable* shock to their paws. It didn't matter what the Have-not dogs did, they could not escape that shock to their paws. The Have dogs, in the same apparatus, were able to escape the shock to their paws by pressing or nudging a panel with their head. So the Haves learned they could escape the shock.

Then each dog was transferred for training to a standard-type shuttle box, like the one in the illustration on the following page. A light came on in the chamber where the dog was, and a shock followed. The dog could escape the shock by jumping across the barrier into the other chamber. Or it could avoid the shock entirely by jumping when the light itself came on. The same opportunity was available to all dogs—both Haves *and* Have-nots.

And what were the results? The Haves learned to escape perfectly, and as time wore on and they gained experience, they also learned to avoid the shock completely. Life was tolerable again. Not so for the Have-nots. Less than a quarter of the Have-not dogs learned to escape the shock in the shuttle box, and *none* of them learned to avoid the shock entirely.

It's as if the Have-nots had learned that nothing they could do mattered. In fact, this demonstrated what is now called *conditioned helplessness*. It didn't make the Have-nots feel any better, but at least the scientists can call them something besides confused Haves. They were conditioned helpless. Their prior experience with being helpless generalized (refer back to Chapter 6 if you're bewildered by that term) to situations where they *could* have acted to help themselves.

What do you suppose are the implications of this research in terms of human strivings and ambitions?

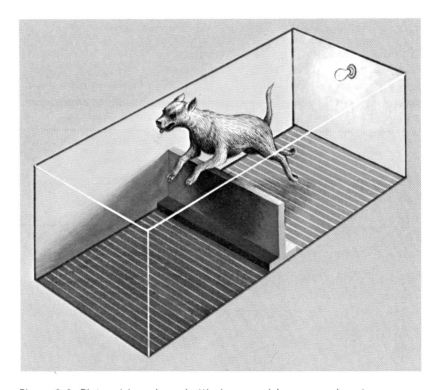

Figure 9-9 Pictured here is a shuttle box, used in an experiment in fear. A dog is placed in one chamber, a light is turned on, and then ten seconds later a shock is given to the dog's feet. This is repeated until the animal learns to jump to the other chamber (escape conditioning). If the experiment is continued, the animal learns to jump as soon as the light appears and before the shock is given (avoidance conditioning). Reduction of fear is the reinforcer. The animal now creates its own fear, responds to it, and reinforces itself by reducing its own fear. Extinguishing fears, in humans or animals, is very difficult to do.

If we *know* we cannot control our environment, it also reduces our attempts to do so. This leads to fear, and that fear gives way to depression. If we *can* control our environment, then fear can aid us in seeking the responses we need to regain that control. In that way, fear is clearly serving as a motivating force.

5 A Theory to Summarize

In the tremendous array of human motives—from hunger to fear, from thirst to achievement—is there any unifying element? How do they all relate to one another? A psychologist named

Abraham Maslow has proposed what he calls a hierarchy of needs. He suggests our needs are organized into five groups, as summarized in the chart. He suggests that most physiological needs must be satisfied before the needs for safety will become of primary importance. All lower level needs must be pretty well satisfied before we can move on to the higher levels. But, of course, these needs can overlap.

Maslow's is not a perfect theory. It's quite global, and it focuses on motivations, not emotions (our subject in the next chapter). Yet, it nicely blends physiological needs with learned ones. It also strikes a good balance between inherited features and environmental ones. And it accurately describes an order of needs that you yourself may have observed. The highest level of need, *self-actualization*, identifies a person's need to express his or her highest human potential. Maslow says not many of us get that far. A look at a few of the people who are considered to have reached a very high level of self-actualization suggests why: Eleanor Roosevelt, Albert Einstein, and Albert Schweitzer among others. It's a select group—but of course your own self-actualization can take place without your aiming quite as high as they did.

Figure 9-10 Abraham Maslow's Hierarchy of Human Needs

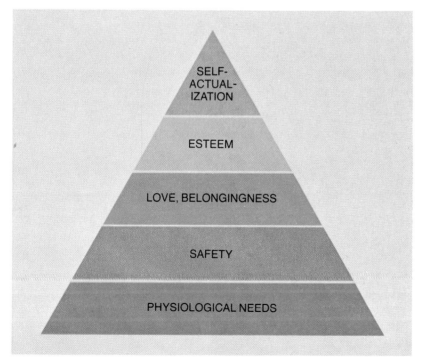

███████   In review . . .

Whereas physiological motives push us toward a goal, in learned motives the attractiveness of the goal pulls us toward it. Expressing learned motives requires the availability of a response, an expectancy of success, a goal worth pursuing, and an environment in which to do so. Achievement is one such motive. One study, now questioned, shows fear of success as mainly a problem for women. Fear is another learned motive and can be demonstrated in animals. If we can control our environment, fear subsides; if we can't, it leads to helplessness and depression. Abraham Maslow has proposed a theory of five major needs, arranged in a sequence in which they arise and can or must be satisfied, the highest being self-actualization.

Chapter Application and Review

USING PSYCHOLOGY   *How can you control your weight?*

In an earlier *Using Psychology* section we discussed ways in which you can break a bad habit. Overeating is a bad habit that many people have in Western society. And being overweight is a major problem. Bad for you physically, those extra pounds can also have ruinous effects upon your social life, not to mention your self-image and getting clothes to fit.

So, if you are slim, how can you stay that way? And if you are overweight, how can you change your ways?

Some tips have been given in this chapter, and we'll summarize these first:

Remember that chickens—and humans—tend to eat more just because more food is put before them. So, obviously, if you keep your portions small, and the table free from full platters and heaped serving dishes, you'll be less tempted to overindulge.

You also read that, as creatures of habit, we get hungry about the same times every day. And if we fail to eat at the usual hours, our hunger will tend to fade, not increase. So, arrange interesting activities to carry you past your meal time, and you'll find it easier to eat less later on.

In addition to avoiding the environmental cues of sight, smell, accustomed times, and large amounts to eat, there is another method that works quite well—that of *increasing toleration*. Increasing toleration involves scheduling exactly when the unwanted response is to occur. For example, suppose you are slowly gaining weight and you wish to cut back on the amount you are eating between meals. Watch yourself and make notes of when—under what conditions and at what time of day—you find yourself nibbling crackers or peanuts or taking that extra soft drink.

If you are able to identify the stimulus that seems to cause you to eat—whether it is another person who eats at the same time, or a particularly stressful situation—so much the better. However, the important point here is that you must make an agreement with yourself. You must agree to wait a short time after you first get the impulse to eat before gratifying your craving. If the craving tends to occur around 4 o'clock, you must decide to wait until 4:01 before going to the kitchen the first day or two.

The trick, once you've got yourself in check that way, is to begin to lengthen the amount of time you must wait. After a cou-ple of days, stretch yourself to 4:02, then 4:03, and so forth. This delay of self-gratification demonstrates to you that you can control your behavior. It also begins to give you more and more practice living with the craving without yielding to it right away. As you achieve success in getting yourself to wait longer and longer, you will begin to find that you're waiting almost until supper, by which time it isn't necessary to nibble at all. The result? Success!—using the method of increasing toleration.

REVIEW QUESTIONS

SECTION 1   (pages 275–279)
1. Why is motivation such an important and useful concept?
2. Identify the six major elements of the motivational cycle and provide an example of each. How are the six elements interrelated?
3. What is homeostasis? Provide an example.
4. What parts of the central nervous system are most important in the normal operation of physiological motives?

SECTION 2   (pages 280–286)
1. What are the body responses during motivational states?
2. What is autonomic response specificity? How does it relate to the study of motivation?
3. Name four or five hunger stimuli. What parts of the nervous system are involved?
4. When you're eating, what factors cause you to stop? What factors keep you from eating again immediately?
5. Name four or five factors that can make you thirsty.

6. What factors cause you to stop drinking?

SECTION 3   (pages 286–290)
1. What does the term "mixed motive" mean as discussed in the text?
2. What kind of a motive is pain? Name the two major components of pain. What purpose does pain serve?
3. What determines the effects of incoming pain messages within the nervous system? What influences the reactions to such messages?
4. Name three means of lessening reactions to pain.
5. What kind of a motive is sex for humans? How does it differ from the sex motive in lower animals?

SECTION 4   (pages 291–298)
1. How do physiological and psychological, or learned, motives differ in their effects?
2. Name four factors affecting whether or not a learned motive will result in action.
3. How can learned motives be measured?

4. What is achievement motivation? What hopes and fears does such motivation seem to involve?

5. What can fear motivate us to do? What are some possible outcomes?

SECTION 5 (pages 298–300)

1. How does Abraham Maslow explain human motivations?

2. What are some possible flaws in Maslow's theory?

ACTIVITIES

1. Have you ever been on a hike or isolated by accident or natural disaster in such a way that you were without food for a while? If so, try to relate your behaviors regarding hunger to the motivational cycle discussed in this chapter. For instance, as your *need* for food developed, how did you experience the *drive?* Your *goal* was food, but what responses did you make to get to food? What was your reaction to the goal of food once you'd reached it? After you ate, did the feeling of hunger take more time than usual to develop again, or did it take less time?

2. Read a book (such as Piers Paul Read's *Alive*) or a poem (such as Samuel Taylor Coleridge's "The Rime of the Ancient Mariner") or go to a movie in which hunger or thirst plays a major part. Trace the development of behaviors that can be credited to increasing hunger or thirst. Identify what the characters do to avoid the ill effects of hunger or thirst, and spell out how and why their behavior becomes more and then less efficient as they become more and more hungry or thirsty.

3. Gather a collection of pictures. These should include an attractive baby, a handsome male, a beautiful female, an automobile accident, and scenery such as a mountain or field. Under conditions of constant lighting, show the pictures one at a time to a friend. Your subject should view the picture for at least 15 seconds, sitting so that you can see the size of his or her pupils. Do you find differences in your viewer's pupils in response to each picture? What can you conclude about picture attractiveness and its relation to pupil size?

4. When you get up some morning, eat a normal breakfast, and then go without eating or drinking anything until supper. If you choose to do this experiment, do *not* read any further until you have done it; then come back and finish reading this. . . .

Now that you've fasted all day, think back. At what time between your normal breakfast and supper times did you feel hungriest? If this period was around your normal lunch time, were these "hunger pangs" caused by physiological needs or learned cues? If there were cues, list them. Did you get hungry any earlier than your usual supper time? If so, what cues made you hungriest?

5. There is a link between hunger and thirst in that you can reduce hunger slightly by drinking. Similarly, some foods make us thirsty. Which make you thirstier, sweet foods or salty ones? As an experiment, at the same time each day for two weeks try alternating between a snack of salted popcorn one day and a snack of vanilla ice cream the next. Follow your snack each day with as much water as makes you feel comfortable, recording the amount consumed. At the end of the two weeks—but not before—total the amounts you drank after eating the salty food and after eating the sweet one. Which food made you thirstier? Why?

6. Choose any learned motive, such as achievement. Over the next week record (a) when and where you display the motive, (b) the particular goal you are seeking at that time, (c) how successful you are, and (d) how you might improve your behavior to advance your goal.

7. Career Search. Persons trained in the psychology of pain reduction can teach others to control pain. Interview the instructor of a Lamaze class to find out the steps taught to prospective parents and the psychological principles involved.

INTERESTED IN MORE?

BECK, R. C. *Motivation: Theories and Principles*, 2nd ed. Prentice-Hall, 1983. This author covers both human and animal motivation. Of interest is the analysis of human motivation in terms of learned and physiological elements.

BOLLES, R. C. *Theory of Motivation*, 2nd ed. Harper & Row, 1975. Has a strong section on physiological aspects of motivation, but this involves heavy reading.

COEER, C. N. *Motivation and Emotion.* Scott, Foresman, 1972. A short but broad introduction to theories and behaviors that involve motivation. Good discussion of the relationship between motivation and emotion.

HOYENGA, K. B. & HOYENGA, K. T. *Motivational Explanations of Behavior: Evolutionary, Physiological, and Cognitive Ideas.* Brooks/Cole, 1984. A well-written, well-illustrated, far-ranging look at motivated behavior—from biology to social psychology. Good reading for the dedicated student.

LEVENKRON, S. *Treating and Overcoming Anorexia Nervosa.* Scribner's, 1982. An excellent analysis of the causes and attempted cures for anorexia nervosa and related problems.

MURRAY, E. J. *Motivation and Emotion.* Prentice-Hall, 1964. Interweaves naturalistic observations with research conducted in both the clinic and the laboratory.

PACKARD, V. *The Hidden Persuaders.* D. McKay, 1967. A classic book that discusses the many and varied "tricks of the trade" used by advertisers to influence people's buying through ads, packaging, and the in-store environment.

WEINER, B. *Human Motivation.* Holt, Rinehart & Winston, 1980. Heavy emphasis on various theories of motivation makes this book tough going, but for those who are interested, it's an excellent introduction to psychologists' views of motivated behavior.

10 Your Emotions

WHAT'S THE ANSWER?

☐ "Cindy, I just *don't* understand it. Sure, I love him. From all I can find out he's told half the basketball team—and they've told *all* their friends—that he likes me, too. You've told me. Rosey's told me. I mean, the message is pretty clear."

"So, what's the problem, Steph?" asks Cindy.

"Well, it just seems to go from bad to worse. I get so nervous when I'm around him. I mean, I've heard *his* voice shake a couple of times, and I know when we're alone he sometimes seems very shaky, really nervous, too. I so want to impress him. And the harder I try, the worse I do." *What is wrong here?*

☐ *Why do professional card-players always seem to wear dark glasses?*

☐ In a sympathetic manner, Chris says, "I was sorry to hear about your grandfather's death, Mort."

"Thanks," replies Mort. "My grandmother really took it hard. I guess you know it happened way back at the beginning of the summer. That's been four months and she's still really depressed. I think it's abnormal. She knew for a year he was going to die." *Is it "abnormal"? Is there another possible explanation for the long-term depression of Mort's grandmother?*

Joy is one of the earliest emotions experienced by humans. Although certain physiological motives are inherited, emotions are entirely learned.

1 What Is Emotion?

The kiss, the face turning red as beads of sweat form on the forehead, and the clenched fist all share at least one thing in common: Each is an outward sign of what is sometimes called inner turmoil or emotion. Unlike motivation, which we were able to define with some precision, emotion is a much more difficult term to narrow down

We *all* know what it's like to feel emotion. Emotion is love and hate, anger and fear, pride and jealousy. It's things we like to do (such as be in love). Yet it's also things we don't like to do (such as be angry or afraid). Emotions sometimes create states within us that we'd do anything to maintain. Other times they create negative feelings that fully occupy us until we can eliminate them. Since emotions are so very diverse, some psychologists wonder whether they share enough in common to be called the same thing.

Yet, as we'll see, all of these emotions—and many others we could suggest—share two things in common. First, they are motivational; they act just like the motives we discussed in the last chapter. And second, they are related to our level of arousal, as we'll be showing you at some length in this chapter.

The effects of arousal

The accompanying illustration depicts Canadian psychologist Donald Hebb's ideas of the relationship between our level of arousal and the ability of that arousal to guide our behavior. It's an important point to consider. Think for a moment about what happens if you become fearful. Let's suppose you are afraid of snakes. We can follow your responses as you become more and more aroused.

First, if your level of arousal in all dimensions is low, you'll be sound asleep. That's like having all your needs fully met. On the motivational cycle, if you have just satisfied all your needs and avoided all threats, you'll probably go to sleep. But time marches on, and at some later point, when your total level of arousal begins to climb, you'll probably wake up. Maybe you'll be hungry, or thirsty, or cold. But if you're camping out and it's

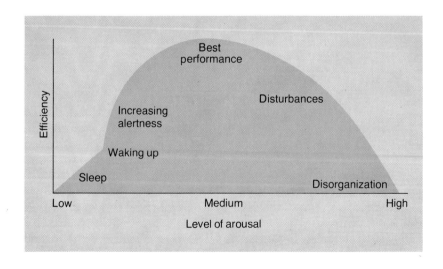

Figure 10-1 Some psychologists believe that our level of arousal has a direct effect on how well we perform. For example, in driving a car our performance will be poor if we are either very sleepy or too highly excited. A moderate level of arousal is best.

a fear of snakes you've got, a *rustling* in the leaves may be enough to awaken you. Now you're *thinking* about snakes, and that raises your level of arousal somewhat more. Then if you *see* a snake at some distance, you'll probably reach a moderate level of arousal. You'll be at your peak of efficiency in finding a stick to use as a weapon, climbing a tree to get away, or crossing a stream to put a barrier between yourself and the snake—whatever it takes to protect yourself.

But then let's suppose that snake comes even closer. Or perhaps hiking in the woods later that day, you come around a corner on the trail and there sunning itself on a rock is a large rattlesnake, now rapidly coiling and shaking its tail. Suddenly, as you are confronted by these signals only three feet ahead, your arousal is boosted to its highest levels. What is the effect on your behavior? You literally may be "paralyzed" with fear.

As we'll see later, it is thought that only about 15 percent of all humans show the correct behavior in dealing with such stressful situations. The middle 70 percent show varying degrees of disorganization. And from 10 to 25 percent (depending on the source of the arousal) may show totally inappropriate behavior. This can range from panic, to incorrect responses, to no response at all.

High levels of arousal can severely disrupt our behavior. For example, if you are deeply in love, you may find that your social interactions with the object of your affections are very strained. You keep thinking that your behavior is very unlike the "normal" you, especially when you are in front of your friends and trying hard to impress him or her.

Efficient behavior

Returning to the illustration, we find that very low or very high levels of arousal provide poor guidance for the situation at hand. With very low arousal the messages are too weak. With high arousal, the signals may be too strong—meaning that there may be too many good responses right at your finger tips. "Watch it! There's a snake by your foot!!" What to do? Jump? Run? Stand very still? Hit it with the stick you're carrying? Look first to see whether it's poisonous? Scream? Spray it with insect repellant? If you start doing all of these things at once it may confuse the snake, but it's not efficient. It does nothing to reduce your arousal.

And a related point, also important, should be mentioned here. We've seen that as our level of arousal increases, our response becomes less efficient. However, notice that a low or moderate level of arousal causes us to be quite efficient in our behavior. In addition, the extent of disruption caused by comparable degrees of arousal may be very different for different emotions. Under some conditions we can tolerate a lot more arousal than others.

Defining emotion

So, how *are* we to define the term *emotion* so that all these intellectual and motivational highs and lows will be encompassed in one concept? Let's try this: *Emotion* is a conscious experience involving subjective (private) feelings, physiological arousal, expressive reactions, and observable activities related to the experience. Emotions play a large role in guiding all our behavior. Inherited inclinations, learning, and reasoning combine with motivated or emotional urges to control much of what we do.

2 How Do We Study Emotions?

When psychologists study emotions, they tend to focus on one of three things. These are (1) observable emotional behaviors (such as facial expressions or words), (2) arousal, and, most recently, (3) verbal labels or explanations attached to aroused (emotional) states.

Genuine emotions are difficult to elicit in the laboratory. You don't fall in love in a lab. You're unlikely to show jealousy or anger. Yet, we have made a lot of progress in the study of human emotions in the past 25 years. Let's examine two different research strategies that have proven very helpful.

Dimensions of emotion

Charles Darwin thought animals used facial expressions to communicate their intent—such as whether they intended to attack or approach. He suggested that human expressions might serve essentially the same purpose. If so, it should be possible for humans to agree in their interpretations of facial expressions.

Faces and emotion. Our faces are always giving us away. A "pokerface" may be the ideal for playing cards, but it's very difficult to achieve. A face is an extraordinary social stimulus. As you learned earlier, at some point in the development of infants the human face is preferred above all other stimuli.

Harold Schlosberg had actors pose for pictures showing a large variety of emotions. Then people were asked to sort the

emotion: *a conscious experience that includes a state of arousal, a label, and a perceived link between the two*

What emotion does the woman at the left seem to be experiencing? Now study the face of the woman on the right. What feelings do you think it expresses? As an experiment, ask your friends the same question about these two pictures. How would you explain the differences and similarities in their replies?

pictures according to a scale that included a number of emotions such as fear, anger, love, surprise, and so forth. What were the results? Using these labels, people tended to sort the pictures into groupings that could be identified along three major dimensions. One was the *pleasantness-unpleasantness* dimension. This put love, mirth, and ecstasy at the pleasantness end and anger and determination at the unpleasantness end.

The second dimension that emerged, an *acceptance-rejection* dimension, was not quite as clear-cut. Surprise, fear, and suffering were at the acceptance or attention end and disgust and contempt at the rejection end.

The third was an activity dimension stretching from *sleep to tension (arousal)*. This showed the importance of arousal, or level of activation, in identifying the emotion being posed.

Only one major concern about these studies could be raised: Would the same dimensions result if different photographs were

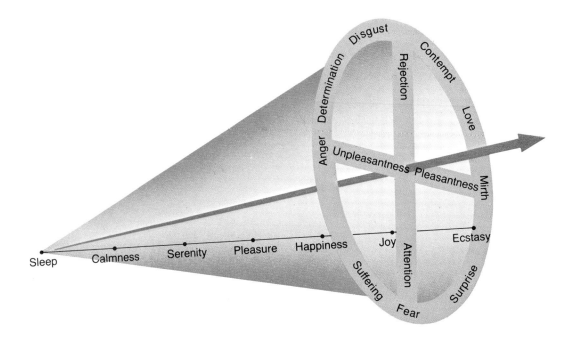

Figure 10-2 A three-dimensional graph showing the relation believed to exist among three dimensions of emotion, including one series of emotions ranging from sleep to ecstasy. Leaf through this chapter and see what emotions seem to be expressed by the faces shown. Where would you place each one on the graph?

sorted? Other studies have since confirmed the importance of the pleasant-unpleasant dimension. On the other hand, photographs in the acceptance-rejection dimension were sometimes identified as belonging to the arousal dimension. So we evaluate emotions good or bad, and at a certain level of arousal. This seems to be as far as posed photographs can take us.

In the early 60's Robert Plutchik tried to find out what would be experienced along a dimension of emotions that stretched from sleep to ecstasy, varying only the level of arousal. The emotion experienced was shown to differ as the subjects' level of arousal changed. Results indicated a series of emotions that started with sleep (no arousal). As arousal increased, the emotion changed from calmness, to serenity, then pleasure, happiness, and joy to ecstasy, the most intense form of emotion on this dimension. Table 10-1 summarizes the most fundamental emotions that appear in a wide variety of theories of emotions. Can you think of any emotional experience that you've had that would *not* fit under one of the emotions listed there?

Table 10-1 **The language of emotions: internal, behavioral, and functional**

INTERNAL FEELINGS	OBSERVED BEHAVIOR	FUNCTION OF EMOTION
Fear, terror	Withdrawing, escape	Protection
Anger, rage	Attacking	Destruction
Joy, ecstasy	Mating, possessing	Reproduction
Sadness, grief	Losing contact	Deprivation
Acceptance, greed	Eating	Incorporation
Disgust, loathing	Vomiting, defecating	Rejection
Expectancy, watchfulness	Sensing	Exploration
Surprise, astonishment	Stopping	Orientation

→ Think about it

The **question**: Why do professional card-players always seem to wear dark glasses?

The **answer**: "Professional" card-players are usually playing cards to make a living, so winning is important. We've just seen that our face may often suggest what our internal emotional state is. Consider the pressure on card-players when they are holding a *very* strong hand. First, their level of arousal will be high, so all their reactions will be emphasized. Second, they are eager to play the hand with strong cards, so they are probably at the extreme acceptance end of the acceptance-rejection dimension. Third, it's very pleasant or good to be in a high stakes card game with a good hand. So on the pleasant-unpleasant dimension, again, the lucky card-holder is at an extreme.

In sum, with a good hand a professional card-player is under high arousal, at the extreme end of the acceptance and the pleasant dimensions. All factors would combine to make such emotions easy to "read," so a card-player does everything possible to hide the signs from careful observers.

Words and emotion. How do we *speak* about our own emotions? A second attempt to label the dimensions of emotion simply studied our language. Interviews were used, and people were asked to write their own definitions of words identifying emotions. More than 550 items were identified. In defining or analyzing certain types of emotions, people tended to use the same cluster of words or phrases. It seems safe to assume that if many of the same words are used to define or describe several emotions, then these emotions are probably related. Thus, a large list of 50 emotions was condensed into four dimensions: hedonic tone (goodness-badness), relatedness, activation, and

Table 10-2 **Comparing underlying dimensions of emotion**

BASIC DIMENSION BEING TAPPED	DIMENSIONS OF EMOTION SUGGESTED FROM THE STUDY OF	
	PHOTOGRAPHS	WORDS
LIKE OR DISLIKE	Pleasant-unpleasant	Hedonic tone
APPROACH OR AVOID	Accept-reject	Relatedness
LEVEL OR AROUSAL	Sleep-arousal	Activation
		Competence

competence. Note that these are similar to the three dimensions based on the study of photographs of posed emotions. Table 10-2 compares the results of the two studies.

We don't yet know exactly what to conclude. However, it does point out that there are some basic dimensions underlying our emotions—our discussions, experiences, and views of them.

In review . . .

Our level of arousal directly affects how we behave. High levels of arousal cause inefficient behavior. An emotion is defined as a state of arousal and an attempt to label it. The study of emotions has included two approaches: studying and labeling photographs of posed emotions or analyzing the words we use in describing emotions. Arguments continue as to how many and what specific dimensions underlie emotional response.

Theories of emotion

Theories and facts sometimes don't seem to agree too well. Notice, as you read, that analyzing how we *talk* about emotion suggests a very different set of organizing principles than some of the theories which follow. We'll discuss three—one developed in the 50s, one in the 60s, and one in the 70s.

Activation Theory: *a basically physiological theory of emotion that stresses the underlying state of arousal*

Activation. Remember our definition of emotion as a state of arousal and the way in which we interpret or label it. The first theory, called the *Activation Theory of Emotion*, stresses that arousal underlies emotion; more arousal means more emotion.

But that rather simple idea is based on a variety of observations—some confirmed, some now disputed.

When we are emotionally aroused, our EEG brain waves (check back in Chapter 4 to review the EEG) show a certain loss of regularity. This irregular EEG pattern of arousal can be produced by stimulating or removing the portions of our central and autonomic nervous systems that help arouse or calm us. Indeed, one of the most startling discoveries came from early studies of electrical stimulation of the brain. What was discovered was a *pleasure center* in the brains of rats. For electrical stimulation in the limbic system, hungry rats would ignore food just to press a bar in a Skinner box as many as 5,000 times per *hour*. Other research found that other parts of the limbic system and hypothalamus are involved in such diverse emotions as aggression and fear.

Advocates of this Activation Theory suggest that emotions are expressed in three ways. First, they are expressed through cortical activity such as thought, worry, or anxiety. Second, they're expressed through body activities such as sweating or crying—actions controlled by the autonomic nervous system. Finally, emotion is also expressed through facial expressions and muscle tension.

Thus, one mode of expressing emotion involves cortical arousal, a second involves brain-stem arousal, and a third involves body motor arousal. The tie between emotion and physiology seems fairly tight. This activation theory places heavy emphasis on physiological activities. However, it doesn't spend much time discussing the "thinking" or "feeling" parts of emotion. That is corrected in the second theory.

Attribution. In his *Attribution Theory*, Stanley Schachter asserts that our emotions result from the joint impact of our *level of arousal* and the *interpretation* we make of an existing situation. More recently, others have added the idea that to experience an emotion, we must also make a *causal link* between the arousal and the label we give it.

In Chapter 9 we mentioned that our body's reaction to arousal—be it loving or lying, fearing or fighting—is essentially the same. We name our response (that is, our emotion) by means of information we pick up from our environment. Thus, a given level of arousal may be labeled anger or love or any of the other emotions we've already identified, based on what we think caused the arousal in the first place.

For instance, what would you predict would happen if you were physiologically aroused but could not explain why? If this theory is correct, you should look for cues from your environment. Thus, as we change the environment (the cues), we ought

Attribution Theory: *a theory of emotion based on the assumption that emotion results from the combined impact of the state of arousal, the interpretation we make of this state, and the causal link we make connecting the arousal and our interpretation.*

Four groups of subjects were invited to receive an injection of a new vitamin substance that was supposed to improve eyesight. Called *Suproxin*, the substance was actually Adrenalin, which is a stimulant. Adrenalin was given to the three experimental groups. As a consequence, their level of arousal was increased. The control group received an injection of a neutral solution.

Next, one group of the subjects was fully *informed* as to what to expect from the injection (increased heart beat, feeling warm, and so forth). Group two was *misinformed* (expect a headache and general numbness). A third experimental group was told nothing; they remained *ignorant*. The *control* group was told nothing, but their injection would not have caused anything noticeable to happen anyway. All subjects were assigned to one of two experimental treatments and then required to wait "for the Suproxin to take effect." While waiting, each person was asked to fill out a very personal, insulting questionnaire.

Also filling out the questionnaire with each person was a confederate of the testers (or "stooge") who pretended to do one of two things: become angry, or become very euphoric (joyous). In the first case the confederate simply got madder and madder at the "insulting" questionnaire. Finally he wadded up the questionnaire, stuffed it into the wastebasket, and left the room. With members of the other group the confederate merely laughed at the more and more insulting questions. Making an airplane of the questionnaire, and cracking jokes, he finally "sank" the questionnaire as a basketball into the wastebasket. Notice that the actual actions were similar for both confederates, but in one case the questionnaire led to euphoria, in the other, anger.

Finally, all subjects were told that since their "mood" might also affect their vision, they should now rate their anger or happiness. At this point the experiment was finished.

Figure a shows the results for the informed, the misinformed, the ignorant, and the control subjects who had waited with the "euphoric" confederate. The informed subjects had expected the physical sensations, and they were least influenced by the cues from the environment (the mood and actions of the stooge). The control group subjects (receiving no Adrenalin) were slightly more influenced. The ignorant, getting the Adrenalin but no explanation, were even more influenced. The misinformed (expecting numbness) were the most influenced. Figure b shows the performance of the three groups in the anger condition. The subjects in the informed group were not influenced at all by the stooge. The control group was slightly affected. However, the ignorant subjects were clearly affected and became much more angry. These people could all be described as experiencing a state of arousal in search of an explanation. Attribution Theory strikes again.

to be able to change the "emotion" you will report you are experiencing. Box 10-1 gives the results of a study that did just that.

Or consider another possibility. If someone *is* aroused, but has a good explanation for it, is he or she likely to be convinced by any other version? That is, is the person likely to accept any

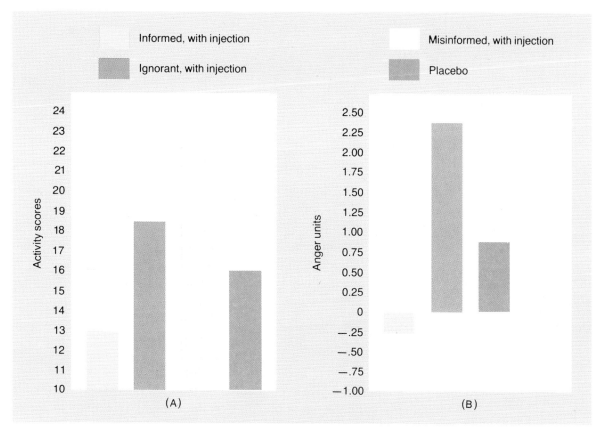

Figure 10-3 Bar graphs of the results of the experiment described in Box 10-1. Figure a shows the activity level of members of each of four groups of subjects who were exposed to an experimental "stooge" who was acting happy. Notice how little the fully informed group was influenced. Figure b: Results from the same experiment for three groups of subjects exposed to an angry stooge. Again notice the lack of impact of the stooge on the behavior of the people in the informed group. (Schachter and Singer, 1962)

more cues from the environment? It's not likely. And what if you merely experience the same *thought* from time to time? Will you always experience it as an emotion? No, you won't. If the theory is right, you'd only call it an emotion if you were also *aroused* when the thought occurred and you linked the thought to the arousal.

These possibilities point to one of the functions of theories in psychology. They organize data, and they generate predictions by which the theory can be tested. And tested it is.

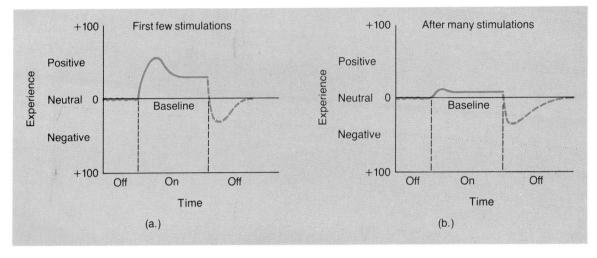

Figure 10-4 The Opponent-process system. Figure a shows emotional arousal after the stimulus of a new, exciting event. Notice what happens when the stimulus is experienced and what happens after it is withdrawn. Figure b shows emotional arousal after a repeated stimulating event. Notice what happens now when the stimulus is experienced and what happens when the stimulus is withdrawn.

Opponent-process. A third attempt to develop a theoretical explanation for emotions tackled the issue by returning to one of the most basic processes of motivation—homeostasis. This theory is based on three assumptions. First, it assumes we try to keep our arousal at a moderate level. We strive to keep it tolerable, and rather constant—kind of an emotional neutral.

Second, it assumes that any change in our level of arousal will bring into action an internal opposing process. That process will return the experienced level of arousal to the tolerable level.

Third, since arousal may increase *or* decrease, it follows that the opposing process can either decrease *or* increase.

Now this leads to a couple of rather interesting predictions. For example, if we can remove from your environment whatever it is that caused you to become aroused, then that should change how you perceive the environment. The theory also implies that your emotional experiences will change over time. Why? Because the opponent process will—through repeated experiences—also change over time.

So what? Well, let's take the matter of love. When you *first* fall "madly" in love, several things happen: (1) You can't concentrate on anything else. (2) In idle moments you find yourself thinking about him or her. (3) You'll go out of your way to "accidentally" run into that person. (4) You'll arrange to spend

Opponent-process Theory: *a theory of emotion based on the principle of homeostasis, or the tendency for any level of arousal to bring into action an opposing process that will restore a balance*

The Opponent-process Theory of emotion maintains that our bodies try to keep our arousal at a moderate level. When we experience a strong feeling, we unconsciously strive toward the opposite feeling to achieve homeostasis, or internal balance.

as much time as possible with or near him or her. And so forth. But if the Opponent-process Theory is correct, then as soon as Mr. or Miss Perfect walks into your emotional life, an opposing internal process is started to bring you back to ground level, to calm you down, to bring your arousal level back to the moderate zone.

But let's go one step further. Suppose your Mr. or Miss Perfect steps in front of a speeding truck soon after meeting you and is annihilated—killed instantly. Removing this arousing stimulus from your environment will expose you to the impact of the second, developing negative state.

Check back in the earlier part of this chapter and you'll see that loneliness is the emotion often located directly across from (or opposite) love. However, although your love may have been very intense, it only existed for a very short period of time. So the rebound or negative feelings you have are relatively mild. Yes, you've lost Mr. or Miss Perfect, but you recover fairly rapidly. Because the positive stimulus is gone, there is no longer a need for the internal, negative force to bring you back to a neutral level of arousal. As the developing internal negative experience wears off, you return to neutral.

But let's suppose a different state of affairs. Let's assume that you and Mr. or Miss Perfect hit it off beautifully—you *are* the chosen parties for each other. Marriage follows, then children, and finally middle age.

Take a moment here to note that it is very difficult both to be intensely in love and still continue to do the normal chores of life. Your mind is constantly wandering. Your working efficiency drops, and you waste incredible hours just thinking of your loved one. So the internal process operates to bring you back to reality—back to a more balanced level of stimulation so you can respond to other cues.

But to return to the story of life with your chosen one, you and your mate eventually retire, and after many happy years, your Mr. or Miss Perfect of years gone by dies. Remember the intense feelings back when you first met? They have dwindled gradually because of the steady, slow development of a negative, internal state.

Now suddenly, your beloved is gone. What will be the result? Read the Think About It that follows.

Think about it

The **question**: In the opener to this chapter Mort was expressing surprise that his grandmother was still depressed four months after the death of her husband. He labeled her response "abnormal." Are there any other explanations?

The **answer**: Clearly, in terms of the Opponent-process Theory, there is another answer. Even though Mort's grandmother might have had a year to prepare herself for her husband's death, that forewarning might actually have made matters worse.

Suppose his grandparents cared very deeply for each other. They probably had built up strong internal responses to keep their emotions at a moderate level when they were together. During the last year of care and caring Mort's grandparents may well have spent even more time with one another than usual. As a result the internal processes keeping them emotionally balanced had a lengthy time to stabilize. Once Mort's grandfather passed on, his wife was now faced with his absence. But she also now had to recover from tremendous internally generated feelings of loneliness and sorrow—made all the more intense by the last year of illness during which they spent so much time together.

A summary of theories of emotion. One theory of emotion concerns physiology, another thinking, and the third internal processes of which we may not even be aware. Are they really addressing the same set of behaviors? Yes, they are. Since emotions are very complex, you are driven to react in many different ways. And a lot of things are going on inside you at the same time. These theories are not mutually exclusive, but they attack the complex issues of emotions from very different angles.

We know that various parts of our nervous system and glands *are* active when we're experiencing an emotion (Activation Theory). We also know the cortex is busy in emotional reactions. From this we can account for the "thinking" portion of emotional experiences identified by the Attribution Theory. Finally, we can combine the physiological and thinking activities with the idea of homeostasis—the need of the body to return the system to some kind of operating middle ground. Hence, the Opponent-process Theory.

3 The Development of Emotions

Anger may drive us into attacking someone. Fear makes us seek to run away. Love causes us to approach someone. Yet, at birth infants are not able to express emotions in our adult sense. Are our emotions inherited? Mostly likely no. Some of the components involving the physiological and bodily responses to emotion *are* inherited, but not the emotions themselves. They're learned. And they develop from the very simple array of human capabilities with which we arrive on this earth.

One of the classic descriptive studies in developmental psychology was done in the early 1930s. It traced identifiable emotions in human infants as they developed. During the first month or so of life an infant has very few response capabilities. He or she can be quiet or scream. Yet even by the age of three months

The ability to feel tenderness is not present in the young child but develops as he or she gets older, if the necessary growth experiences for its appearance have taken place.

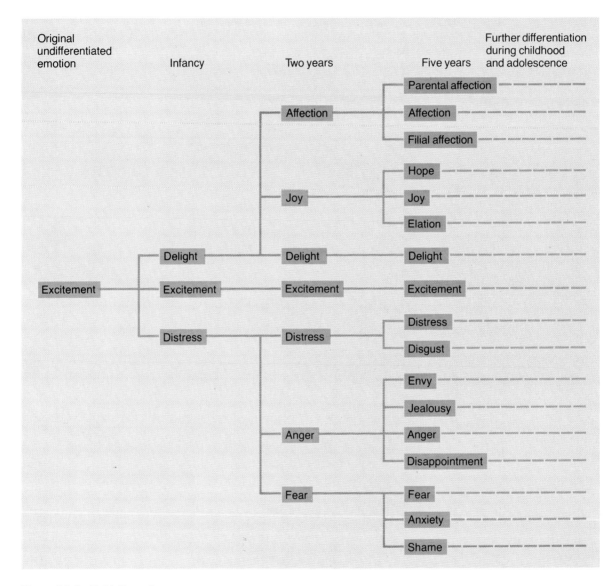

Figure 10-5 At birth an infant has only two possible responses with which to address the world—crying or being quiet. Notice how rapidly these responses develop into a vast array of widely differing emotions.

these early vocal offerings will often cue parents as to what the problem is. Distress—hunger or a wet diaper—yields a distinct cry as compared with other vocal sounds. And soon thereafter the child is cooing when all is well. It is interesting that as infants develop they learn more negative responses. And these they learn more rapidly than they learn positive, other-oriented responses. It is as if humans are concerned with no one but themselves in the first few months. Only during the latter parts of the first year do social and other-oriented responses such as affection begin to emerge.

■■■■■ In review . . .

Many theories of emotion have been developed, but three recent ones are typical. The Activation Theory assumes simply that the level of arousal is crucial to the experienced emotion. The Attribution Theory assumes that emotions result from the combined effects of our level of arousal and the interpretation we make of that arousal. The Opponent-process Theory assumes that we try to keep our level of emotional arousal balanced. Although we inherit a certain number of physiological motives, our emotions are entirely learned.

4 Some Emotions You'll Experience

We're too rich in the emotions we can offer—love and hate, fear and aggression, boredom and joy, depression and anxiety—to discuss all of them. So let's take just a sample of them and study in more detail what they involve. Let's study frustration, stress, and love.

Frustration

From where does it come? You have just enrolled in a judo class that meets Mondays and Wednesdays from five to seven. You've paid your good money for ten weeks of instruction and here you sit in a traffic jam—half a mile from class, ten minutes late, and counting. So the environment has created a situation that can lead to frustration. By now you are probably showing a number of internal symptoms. The motorists around you are glaring at you because of the way you're trying to push your way through traffic. They would agree that you are behaving as if frustrated. All the conditions are present: The environment is creating a blockage to your progress—an independent variable. You are reacting internally—the intervening variable. And your behavior—the dependent variable—indicates your internal state.

Reactions to frustration. The responses to frustration may cover quite a range of possibilities. One response is often anger and aggression. In fact, the *frustration-aggression hypothesis* was suggested many years ago: Frustration leads to aggression. One "cruel" but very well-known experiment was conducted back in the late 1930s to test this hypothesis.

A number of preschool children were allowed time to play with an average set of toys—nothing outstanding, just nice toys.

Everybody faces frustration at one time or another, and daily irritations are especially likely in urban areas. Here a driver experiences stress as she tries to hold in her anger in a traffic jam.

The constructiveness of their play was rated. Then they were given 15 minutes to play with a brand new set of the best toys available. And then—from the children's point of view—tragedy struck. The experimenters asked the children to return to the original average toys. They were now allowed to play *only* with these, even though they could see the brand new toys unused. As you might suspect, there was a marked decline in the constructiveness of the children's play. In short, frustration led to aggression.

Frustration may also lead to a variety of other responses. One of them is fear or anxiety. It may be fear of punishment or of the loss of a desired goal object—whether that be food or judo lessons. Frustration may also lead to withdrawal or apathy, although sometimes that is not available to us as an option. Are you frustrated by the fact that your grades are lower than you *know* you're capable of earning? One solution is to work harder, but if the frustration becomes too much, another (less desirable) solution is available. You could lower your level of aspiration, but that really amounts to withdrawal. Still another response may be physical stress. Since stress, and our reaction to it, can be so complex, we'll discuss that separately.

Control. We all have to deal with frustrations all the time. How do we handle them? It becomes one measure of our total personal adjustment, as we'll discuss in Chapter 12. Our *frustration tolerance* level is the degree of hindrance or threat that we can endure without resorting to deviant or inappropriate modes of responding. Let's examine that in more detail, as we look at another emotional problem with which we sometimes must deal.

Stress

From where does it come?   Stress differs from frustration in that it has much less of a social orientation. We most often experience stress in our usual environment. More extreme than most motivations, it threatens our ability to continue to function normally. However, we must perceive the threat and be unable to handle it before stress will be registered.

Thus, we define stress as our state when we perceive that our well-being is endangered. When this occurs, we must devote all our energies to protecting ourselves and restoring a sense of well-being.

Examples.   Are there examples of stress in your everyday life? Perhaps not. But, there are studies of humans' reactions to the continuing stress in a situation such as war. A study was conducted of more than 2,000 infantry men who fought in the Pacific during World War II. They were asked the question listed at the top of Table 10-3.

Compare the percentage of soldiers who report each of the symptoms listed there with the statements we made early in this chapter about the percentage of people who respond inappropriately.

Control.   In fact, any time our body is stressed, it mobilizes its resources. One of the best analyses of how our body reacts to defend itself was conducted back in the late 40s. What was proposed was the *General Adaptation Syndrome*. It was suggested that when we perceive a stress, we go through three stages of reaction.

The first is the *alarm*, or "oh my gosh," stage. Its first part is the *shock* itself when damage is experienced—be it a cut, a bump, a broken bone, whatever. Its second part is the *countershock*. Here the body resources are called into action. The sympathetic nervous system pumps body resources into the affected area, and the body prepares for resistance.

If the stress continues, the second phase or stage, called *resistance*, occurs. The first reactions of our body that were started during the countershock stage are continued. In effect, our body is attempting to restore an appropriate level of stimulation

stress: *an emotional state that occurs when a person perceives a threat to his or her well-being*

General Adaptation Syndrome: *the three stages of reaction to stress: shock and countershock, resistance, and exhaustion*

by correcting whatever problem has developed. The more serious the problem, the more body resources will be involved in trying to correct it. Temperature may go up, but blood pressure tends to return to almost normal. To the casual observer—not aware of whatever injury or stress you're reacting to—your functions and color may seem almost normal.

→ ## Think about it

The **question**: A skilled driver and her passenger were in a car that rolled over, apparently in a situation that permitted the driver to use skill to minimize personal risk and injury. In describing the accident afterward she related that her passenger got sick to his stomach as a result of the accident. Why—in a motivational sense—did it happen?

The **answer**: There is research available—even with chimpanzees—to suggest that being in control of a situation is much less stressful than being in a position where control is entirely in the hands of another person. Here, though, he had a driver who was very skilled, the passenger recognized that he couldn't do anything to prevent or control the coming accident even if he wanted to. His stress was high. As seen in Table 10-3, while under stress he "emitted" one of the less desirable—but nonetheless predictable—responses.

Table 10-3 Reported "emotional" responses of combat troops while under fire

During World War II 2,095 infantrymen fighting in the Pacific were asked the following question: "Soldiers who have been under fire report different physical reactions to the dangers of battle. Some of these physical reactions are in the following list. How often have you had these reactions when you were under fire?"

PERCENT OF MEN REPORTING THE RESPONSE	SYMPTOM
84	Violent pounding of the heart
69	Sinking feeling to the stomach
61	Shaking or trembling all over
56	Cold sweat
55	Feeling sick at the stomach
49	Feeling of weakness or feeling faint
45	Feeling of stiffness
27	Vomiting

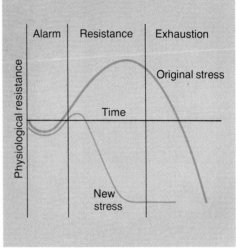

Finally, if the various resistances your body has offered can correct the problem, normal operation is restored. You get over the cold, the wound heals itself, or the broken bone is mended. But, if the stress continues too long, or if it is too severe, then your body gradually moves into the third stage, *exhaustion*, as the body's resources are used up. As a result, many of the reactions seen when the stress first occurred may be seen once again.

Once exhausted, what happens if any additional stressors are encountered? Your body may be able to register alarm and perhaps marshal some resistance, but, since reserves are so low, exhaustion may come much more rapidly. The final result is a collapse of the defenses, and death is very likely to follow.

Figure 10-6 If you find yourself exposed to extreme danger for a long period of time, your ability to resist stress will be roughly as shown. If you overcome the first threat after consuming much of your bodily (energy and emotional) reserves, then a new stress will overcome you much more rapidly. If stress is too acute, it can lead to inappropriate behavior.

In review . . .

We experience a broad variety of emotions, frustration being among the most common. It is generally thought that frustration does lead to aggression, but in some circumstances other responses may also occur. Stress occurs when we perceive that our well-being is endangered and we devote bodily resources to correcting the problem. The General Adaptation Syndrome suggests we proceed through three stages when stressed: alarm, resistance, and exhaustion.

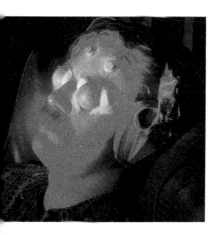

Experiments on the effects of sensory deprivation (conditions of extreme boredom) have shown some startling results. Students with halved ping-pong balls taped over their eyes, kept suspended in a water-bath, with no sound, soon began to lose contact with reality and even to hallucinate.

Are you ever bored with what you're doing? Research indicates that all humans need stimulation and tend to seek it, sometimes in "thrills."

Boredom

From where does it come? The examples we've cited in the chapter so far have always involved what happens when we get too *much* stimulation. We all enjoy moments of quiet, however. We seem to like to get away from the rush of life to dream or daydream—essentially to regain a fresh view of the world and some sense that we control it.

But therein lies an interesting question. We've talked about too much stimulation. If the concept of homeostasis—maintaining a balance—is correct, what happens if we find ourselves experiencing too *little* stimulation? Solitary confinement, involving limited visual and auditory stimulation, no social contact, and a barren environment, is considered a very severe punishment. Why is this so? Examine the illustrations for some interesting studies conducted on boredom.

Control. What do we learn from the experiments? That our development depends on experiencing a normal range of varying events—visual and intellectual. Research seems to demonstrate quite well that we require these stimuli during maturation and development. In addition, we need a diverse world of experiences in order to maintain our own self-concept. It helps us to perceive accurately the world of which we are a part, and to maintain our normal social and personal skills.

If a lecture turns boring, what do we do? We tap our fingers or wiggle in our seat—anything to keep ourselves stimulated. If we lose track of or interest in a conversation at a party, what do we do? We start looking around for someone else to talk with. We are constantly seeking a variety of stimulation. Perhaps amusement park rides push our search to the limits, but in one sense they exist because of our desire for excitement and change.

Love

From where does it come? And now, let's return to a subject we discussed once before in Chapter 3—love. It's an emotion, of course, and one of the most intense that we may experience. But why does it exist? What causes it? What benefits come from it? These are not easy questions, and recently love has become the object of focused study by psychologists. The findings are illuminating.

First, you will remember we suggested love between two adult humans involves three things—attachment, caring, and intimacy.

Think back to the Attribution Theory. It gives you hints on some of the factors influencing all emotions, including love. If you recall, two elements were essential—arousal and mental labeling. But where did it all start? In your mother's lap—literally. A newborn infant is not very beautiful by "baby contest" standards. The love which parents feel tends to be spiritual and protective. However, this early love grows with time—remember the Opponent-process Theory. It has been demonstrated that a major factor in establishing affection and love between mother and child is physical contact. At least in the child's eyes, a mother who supplies comfort is very important. From the rubbing and stroking, the rocking and nursing that are so much a part of the feeding process, grows the emotion we later call love.

We can define *love* simply as feelings of affection for others. The infant's love for its mother is the first such feeling to develop and express itself in humans (see Box 10-2 on page 328).

This is followed later (some psychologists say) by *peer*, or *age-mate love*. Peer love is the first to exist outside the family. It often finds its first expression in the choosing of a preferred or favorite playmate. When we were first let out of the house, this playmate for each of us was just as likely to be male as female—sex really didn't matter. In the later years of childhood, the playmate is very likely to be of our own sex and general age. Play, as we discussed in Chapter 2, is a very important part of this love.

Usually in adolescence, however, the first example of true *heterosexual*, other-directed love develops. This is *romantic* love, which often accompanies the human sexual drive. Romantic love is a powerful motivational force for humans, even capable of overriding the purely sexual drives of motivation. It seems our literature teems with love scenes, yet the objective study of love has begun to emerge only in the past decade or two. One major problem was simply providing an operational definition of love—a problem we face over and over again in the study of all emotions.

Heterosexual love, as we said, usually emerges at puberty. The practice of dating allows a refinement of the skills involved in such love. Romantic love often reaches its fullest expression by late adolescence. It continues to function through most of adulthood and the elder years.

Several factors are important to the full development of our skills in heterosexual love. One of these is trust. A second is the acceptance of heterosexual contact. It's a big step socially and mentally to move from the secure years of late childhood into the adolescent years. As a child we often had the support of a same-sex playmate and the warmth of a home, but in early adolescence more time must be spent outside the home. As this period continues, young men and women gain additional skills

Peer, or age-mate, love is a part of human development according to many psychologists. Bonds of companionship and play experiences are very important to the development of love.

Feature   10–2   IRON MOMS AND OTHER PROBLEMS IN LIVING

Mothers usually seem to be such reliable figures. When we arrive on this earth Mother is already there. She gives us food, warmth, and protection. She coos at us, cleans up our every mess, and always seems to be around when something goes wrong. These facts lead to an interesting question. What causes infants to begin to love their mothers? That is, is "infant love"—the first identifiable human love—innate or learned? Will it occur anyway, or do we learn to love?

Some possible answers were provided by Harry Harlow's classic study of infant-mother love, conducted using monkeys during the 50's. The illustration shows the basic apparatus. One of the first and simplest problems was whether food or creature comforts was more important. After all, we do spend more time sleeping than eating. In one of the very first studies, infant monkeys were isolated just after birth. They were placed in a cage with two kinds of "mothers." The hard-iron mom was made of welded wire. The other "substitute" mom was covered with ter-

rycloth toweling. That was one independent variable.

The other independent variable involved which mother gave milk. In various conditions of the experiment, some monkeys were placed with a milk-giving cloth mother and a non-milk-giving wire mother. Others had a milk-giving wire mother and a non-milk-giving cloth mother.

Note the results. When the monkeys were forced to make an either-or choice, the wire mothers received only about 10 percent as much attention as the comfortable cloth mothers, even if the wire mother gave the milk. Clearly, physical comfort was more important.

Some of the traditional theories about love for our mother growing out of the sight of her face as we're feeding clearly didn't do too well. As one psychologist put it, such explanations of infant-mother love will have to ". . . be fashioned from whole cloth rather than whole milk"! Such love, then, is learned; it is not inherited.

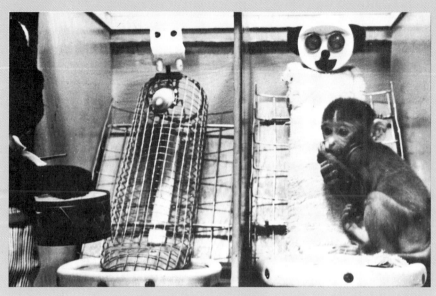

in relating to the opposite sex. Differences in roles help to contribute to developing heterosexual love. Finally, an often overlooked, but very important factor is the social motivation for physicial proximity—that intimacy of which we've spoken.

▦▦▦▦ In review . . .

Boredom is any state in which we seek higher levels of excitation than our current one. Many experiments have shown the importance of varying stimulation to maintain our contact with our physical and social environment. Love is one of our most powerful emotions, yet it is a learned pattern of responses. Search for the brain control center(s) for love continues. Many do not expect a single or a limited number of control centers for "love" to be found.

Chapter Application and Review

USING PSYCHOLOGY   *Love and the theories of emotion*

Is there any way you can apply the theories of emotion to your own life and loves? Well, if emotional experiences are based on a blend of arousal and labeling, then one of the functions of dating is to permit time for the arousal to occur. Dating can provide opportunities to identify and share mutual interests. As fear recedes and common interests are found, the number of shared activities may increase. Certainly the labeling of what you feel as you do things together may be *love* (Attribution Theory).

If a love is to grow between two individuals, it would seem that the intensity of that love would grow with increasing levels of arousal—higher arousal yielding a greater or more rapidly developed love. Some examples suggest themselves. One is to note a

common experience of adolescents who go to summer camp. They meet a young man or young woman with whom they fall in love. Summer camps emphasize activity—horseback riding, swimming, hiking . . . you name it. So if the activity level is high and love does develop between a young man and woman, it follows such a love might have developed more rapidly because of the physical activity. Another possibility is that the feelings under such conditions will be more intense. The social and physical qualities of the "loved other" will be exaggerated and idealized beyond what careful examination will bear.

Using this hypothesis (and focusing on Attribution Theory), what can you do if you are madly in love with someone, but haven't managed to catch his or her eye? Why not try suggesting some activity that will involve physical exertion—skiing or skating, biking or hiking? Run the arousal level up, and if nothing develops . . . go back to studying psychology!

Awareness

The statistics are overwhelming that regardless of how discouraged you may be about *ever* meeting someone you can truly love, it will happen. Being prepared for it, being aware of the things—psychologically, motivationally, and interpersonally—that affect the process is perhaps the only "assistance" you need.

One other set of observations of which to be aware may surprise you. We don't yet know where love comes from. We've identified sites controlling hunger and thirst, and all sorts of sensory and motor activities in the brain. We even know where many of the physiological aspects of sex are monitored and controlled in the brain and spinal cord. But we have not located such things as human will. Nor, for that matter, are we even sure we'll be able to find where "love" is located. Perhaps love will to some degree always remain the "great mystery."

REVIEW QUESTIONS

SECTION 1 (pages 305–308)
1. What happens to the efficiency of behavior as the level of arousal increases? Provide an example.
2. What is emotion?
3. Give examples of an emotion as (a) an independent variable, (b) an intervening variable, and (c) a dependent variable.

SECTION 2 (pages 308–319)
1. Describe two approaches used in studying emotions. What are the findings yielded by each approach?
2. What are the usual "dimensions of emotion"? Provide an illustration for each one.
3. Compare and contrast three major theories of emotion. On what points do these differing theories agree?

SECTION 3 (pages 319–321)
1. Are emotions inherited or learned? Support your answer.

2. Choose an emotion experienced by two-year-olds and list the differentiated feelings that proceed from it during childhood.

SECTION 4 (pages 321–329)
1. What are some possible results if you become frustrated?
2. What is "frustration tolerance"? Give an example of it.
3. What is stress and how does your body react to it?
4. Identify the three stages of the General Adaptation Syndrome.
5. What is boredom and what causes it?
6. Is love an inherited or learned emotion? Describe three different types of love. Is there a brain center for love?

ACTIVITIES

1. Does your family have a large collection of old photographs? If so, go through them and see whether you can sort them into three stacks representing the pleasantness-unpleasantness dimension, the acceptance-rejection dimension, and the passive (sleep) to active (arousal) dimension. To avoid bias, you might find it better to use photographs from a magazine. Whichever source you choose, after you've sorted your photographs, mix them up again and ask a couple of friends to sort them. Do they agree with your classifications?

2. To appreciate the extent to which words can influence emotion, research the speeches of leaders in World War II. Compare the words of a dictator, such as Hitler or Mussolini, with the words chosen by a democratic leader such as Mackenzie King of Canada, Franklin D. Roosevelt, or Winston Churchill. What differences do you find? What motives is each leader appealing to in his people?

3. The text uses falling in love and being in love to illustrate the Opponent-process theory. Pick an emotion-packed activity with which you are familiar, and give an Opponent-process explanation for the emotions you experience during the activity. Or interview someone with a potentially dangerous occupation, such as deep-sea diver or window washer on a high-rise building. See whether you can detect in this person the same shifting emotional experiences over time.

4. What kinds of environmental events are frustrating to you? How do you behave when you are frustrated? In terms of the various theories of emotion, describe some ways in which you might reduce your frustration without giving up your goals.

5. Teenagers report that they tend to fall in love during summer camp, and that their feelings tend to be more intense than love experienced during a regular school year. Which of the three theories of emotion offers the best explanation for this? Using your chosen theory, develop an explanation for this phenomenon.

6. Career Search. Marriage counselors are trained to advise couples whose marriages are causing them emotional problems. Invite a marriage counselor to class to describe the methods he or she uses to try to improve deteriorating marital relationships.

INTERESTED IN MORE?

CANDLAND, D. K., et al. *Emotion.* Brooks/Cole, 1977. Tough reading, but this series of papers reviews at some depth the environmental influences on emotion.

DARWIN, C. *The Expression of Emotions in Man and Animals.* University of Chicago Press, 1972. One of the original detailed studies of the behaviors, facial expressions, stances, and postures by which humans and animals communicate emotions.

DOLLARD, J., et al. *Frustration and Aggression.* Yale University Press, 1939. The original study of the relationships between environmental events indicating success or failure and the behavior that follows the events. Heavy emphasis on learning rather than inherited behaviors.

EKMAN, P., FRIESEN, W. V., & ELLSWORTH, P. *Emotion in the Human Face: Guidelines for Research and An Integration of the Findings.* Pergamon Press, 1972. One of the most up-to-date programs of research emphasizing inherited causes of human emotional behavior.

IZARD, C. E. *Human Emotions.* Plenum, 1977. Reviews a wide array of human emotions from fear to love. Includes related research strategies and important theories.

JACOBSON, E. *Biology of Emotions.* Charles C Thomas, 1967. Offers a very different analysis of emotions than that offered by Dollard and his colleagues in their study. Emphasizes inherited, physiological factors influencing human emotions.

Nebraska Symposium on Motivation. University of Nebraska Press. A yearly collection of six to eight research papers on a wide variety of motivational and emotional topics. Very tough reading, but sometimes has extremely good critical summaries of an area of observation and research.

PLUTCHIK, R. *Emotion: A Psychoevolutionary Synthesis.* Harper & Row, 1980. Not the lightest reading in the world, nonetheless this text offers a good description and analysis of a wide variety of theories of emotion.

UNIT FIVE

PERSONALITY AND TESTING

Being cheerful, energetic, and outgoing are characteristics popularly attributed to people having "a good personality."

In this unit we examine aspects of personality, both normal and abnormal, from theoretical explanations to testing. Since personality is such a complex concept, in Chapter 11 we first tackle the problem of definition. Then we move on to analyze the best theories of personality that have been proposed.

Chapter 12 describes some symptoms and forms of abnormal behavior occurring when inherited and environmental factors go awry. In Chapter 13, we examine some forms of therapy developed to improve problematic behavior, and how each theory of personality indicates which strategy will be used.

Finally, in Chapter 14, we look at the various tests that measure differences in people, including differences in personality but also in human aptitudes, achievements, interests, and intelligence.

CHAPTER OUTLINE

WHAT'S THE ANSWER?

☐ "I'm really jealous of my sister. Here I am about to graduate, and I only made it on to Student Council this year. Sis's a freshman—just a ninth-grader—and she's already been elected."

"Wilma, I know what you mean. My older brother was the same way. You know what your sister and my brother have in common? They've both got a lot of personality. Your sister kind of just radiates charm—even for a ninth-grader! And Kirk's the same way: Everywhere he goes, people smile with him. He gushes at the right time, gets serious when he needs to, and always has a good word for everybody. He's just got a magnetic personality." *How is the term "personality" being used here?*

☐ "I'll never forget that cookie jar. When we were real young, every time we visited my grandmother I used to scheme with my twin sister about how we could get into the jar and get those delicious cookies. Sure we got caught sometimes, but it was well worth it. They were delicious!

"And then all of a sudden one year it didn't seem quite so important to us to get into that jar without anybody knowing about it. Pretty soon we couldn't even bring ourselves to swipe those cookies at all." *How old would you say the twins were when this change in behavior took place? What would Freud say had to happen before it would occur?*

When you mention someone's "personality," you are probably referring
to a specific, obvious trait, like shyness or a bouncy disposition. By studying these children's faces, you might note such individual differences—of
course such differences would have to be consistent in order to be considered part of the child's characteristic "personality."

1 What Is "Personality"?

When you talk about someone's personality, what do you
really mean? Have you ever heard someone say, "She's very aggressive" or "He's so shy—such an introvert!" or "My mother is
really sweet"? Or how about "He's very dependent" or "She's got
a terrific personality—a lot of sparkle!" You may not have heard
exactly those words, but you can see what we're suggesting. The
term "personality" has a variety of meanings, each unique to the
situation in which it appears.

Common usage

Obvious skill. Many different descriptions are possible, but when most people use the term "personality," they are using it for one of two purposes. In several of the examples we just gave you, personality is labeling an obvious feature. Someone is sweet, or introverted, or shy, or aggressive. Of the many things that a person may be, we often identify him or her in terms of the single characteristic that is most obvious. The impression we make on people may be used by them to label our "personality."

Interpersonal skill. But there's another way in which most of us use the term "personality," and that is to indicate a more general kind of skill in representing oneself to others. Someone who works as a receptionist or as a telephone operator or in a front office sales job is often thought qualified for the job because he or she has "a lot of personality." What's really being said here? Maybe it's just that such people can get along well with other people. Some of the traditional ads offering courses in personality are really offering little more than helps in improving your skills in meeting, greeting, and working with others. And yet it's training identified as "improving your personality" or "allowing you to reach your full potential." Here personality is being used as a general label for social skill and finesse.

Psychologists' usage

Multiple definitions. Why does the fact that most people disagree on how to define personality cause us trouble as psychologists? Because psychologists can't (or don't) agree on exactly what "personality" is either! That's not to say we don't define it. In fact, the problem is exactly the reverse—too *many* definitions of personality.

But is there really disagreement? Yes and no. There are a large number of widely differing theories about our human personality. Which theory you're discussing largely determines how you define personality. It's a very complex subject, dealt with and studied in a variety of ways.

But we are not adrift in a sea of confusion. Not only people on the street, but also psychologists show a lot of agreement as to the different uses of the term. What is involved are the critical factors of inherited and learned behaviors. For example, inherited factors in identical twins can explain their similar behavior. On the other hand, two people with different living experiences, heredity, and motivation will respond very differently when given the same stimulus. This is to be expected.

Personality is composed of both inherited and acquired characteristics. Identical twins often show similar responses to a situation, as might be expected. Psychologists are interested in explaining why unrelated people may also behave similarly, and conversely why seemingly similar people often respond differently to the same stimulus.

→ Think about it

The **question**: The skit that opened this chapter described two high school students talking about a sister's and a brother's "personality." What definition of personality were they using in their conversation?

The **answer**: As we've just discussed, "personality" was being used by the high school stu-dents to mean "social skill." Both the sister and brother who were being discussed were given credit for achieving various goals because they were popular or easy to get along with. These are uses of "personality" as social skill. It's one possible use of the term, but not one frequently used by psychologists.

However, how are we to explain situations in which people with different inheritance, experience, and motivation respond *similarly?* How are we to explain when people with essentially identical heredity, experience, and motivation respond *differently* in identical situations? These are the circumstances that cause psychologists to study "personality." In one sense, personality attempts to account for what we cannot predict from our knowl-edge of your prior learning and inheritance as they act in com-bination with your current motivational state.

Personality defined. Having qualified what we're talking about when a psychologist studies "personality," let's see if we can now define it to your satisfaction. *Personality* will be consid-ered here as the dynamic organization within an individual of

personality: *the dynamic or-ganization within an indi-vidual of the systems that determine his or her char-acteristic behavior or thought*

those systems that determine his or her characteristic behavior and thought. That's a complex definition, but so's the concept being defined. First, you'll notice the definition emphasizes that personality is *organized* (the key word is "organization"). Second, *adjustment* is also involved. Here the key word is "dynamic," which means active or changing. Third, notice how the uniqueness of each of us is preserved. Specifically, the definition mentions our "individual characteristic behavior and thought." Fourth, stability is implied. Finally, and perhaps most importantly, by referring to "system*s*," this definition emphasizes that there may be multiple causes of our behavior.

Elements of personality

Of what benefit is this to us? It organizes our thinking about personality. It allows us to suggest that personality—as we'll be studying here—has a number of elements. Let's review each of them briefly.

Characteristic. When we talk about personality, we are talking about those aspects of each of us that are enduring, constant, stable parts of us. If you're aggressive today, the odds are high you'll be aggressive tomorrow. If you're shy now, you'll very likely still be shy when you wake up tomorrow morning. So we *are* talking about stable characteristics, and these are what psychologists study under the heading of personality.

Each individual is unique but in certain situations may respond in the same way as other people. Psychologists study those aspects of personality that are consistent traits, that is, that appear repeatedly, under a wide variety of circumstances.

Consistent. A second aspect of personality, or any trait identified with personality, is that it must occur repeatedly. The response should occur in a wide variety of circumstances. An aggressive person will tend to be so in many different situations—in a restaurant, in the classroom, in most social relationships—essentially everywhere the opportunity arises.

Unique. A third important aspect of our personality is that we are each essentially unique. We each have a certain amount of aggression, malice, humor, virtue, happiness, poise, and so forth. However, the combination that defines *you* is identifiable. Despite the powers of prediction gained from a knowledge of your heredity, your past experiences, and your current environment, there is still enough that is unique about your response capabilities as to warrant the study of your personality.

▓▓▓▓▓   In review . . .

Most people use the term "personality" to identify the most obvious characteristic of a person, or to refer to that person's social skills. Psychologists are mainly interested in personality to (1) explain why people with similar heredity, experience, and motivation may react differently in the same situation; and (2) explain why people with different heredity, past experiences, and/or motivation may nevertheless react similarly in the same situation.

Techniques of study

So far throughout this book we've talked about how the study of groups is used to reach conclusions about individual behavior. Yet, in our discussion of personality you may have noted that we seem to be concentrating on aspects of the individual. How are the individual aspects of personality studied?

Group. In order for an aspect of personality to be of interest, it must occur widely. Psychologists focus on universal characteristics, yet they do so by studying unique examples in an individual case. *Nomothetic* studies are those where a characteristic (such as aggression) is studied in a large number of people who may be similar only in that they share this single trait. There's an obvious problem here. Can we reconstruct a whole personality for any of us simply by reassembling a series of isolated traits or characteristics?

nomothetic studies: *studies in which a particular characteristic is examined in a large number of people*

idiographic studies: *studies in which a single individual is examined as a complete, complex, interacting system*

Individual.   The answer is provided by another technique of study. The *idiographic* technique involves studying a single individual as a complete, complex, interacting system.

This dual approach is much like the nature-nurture argument we discussed in Chapter 1. Neither study technique is enough. The idiographic technique identifies what the important variables seem to be for each individual. The nomothetic technique supplies the group-based data. Both techniques of study are used as appropriate.

2 Theories of Personality

Why are they important?

The reason we have stressed the complexity and vagueness of defining personality is because its definition depends upon which theory you are using. Theories are of central importance in studying personality.

Theories serve several purposes. First of all, they *organize* what is already known or suspected about a total set of data. As new data develop, the theory must often be adjusted.

Second, theories also serve what is called a *heuristic* function. That is, they suggest, by organizing the important facts, exactly what kind of research is needed to fill in missing facts.

Third, theories provide a formal statement of the central principles (here, a view of personality). They identify the important as well as the unimportant.

So theories serve a variety of important functions, not only (or especially) in the study of personality, but also in all areas of psychology.

Changes in our view of humans

We will spend the rest of this chapter analyzing some of the vast array of personality theories that have been developed in the three quarters of a century since Freud's earliest works. These theories will be organized and presented roughly in the order in which they initially appeared. Four major types of theories have been developed, some much more successful than others. Each emphasizes different independent and dependent variables. The types of theories we'll be covering are presented in Table 11-1. Also seen in that table are some of the most

Table 11-1. **Major theories of personality**

TYPE OF THEORY	THEORIST/THEORY	BASIC IDEA
BIOLOGICAL (OR TRAIT)	William Sheldon/Constitutional Psychology Gordon Allport/Psychology of the Individual Raymond B. Cattell/Factor Theory	Human behavior is traced to the joint effects of the organism's inherited capabilities and past experience.
PSYCHOANALYTIC	Sigmund Freud/Psychoanalytic Theory of Psychosexual Development Alfred Adler/Individual Psychology Erik Erikson/Psychosocial Theory of Adjustment Carl G. Jung/Analytical Psychology	Human behavior is determined by a person's past (childhood) experiences, which color his/her perceptions of current events.
(SOCIAL) LEARNING	John Dollard & Neal E. Miller/Reinforcement Theory Albert Bandura/Social Learning Theory B. F. Skinner/Radical Behaviorism	Human behavior results from an organism's past learning, current perceptions, and higher-level processes of thinking and organization.
HUMANISTIC	Carl R. Rogers/Person-centered Theory Abraham Maslow/Holistic Theory	Human behavior can be understood only in terms of the person's internal perceptions of self and others leading toward personal fulfillment.

prominent psychologists associated with each type of theory. We'll examine more closely a sample or two of each of these broad classes of theories.

▬▬▬▬   In review . . .

In studying personality, psychologists may use idiographic or nomothetic techniques. The study of personality involves many aspects of human behavior—almost everything an adult human organism does or can do. Theories of personality organize what we do know, stimulate new research, and formally specify a view of personality. Four groups of such theories have been developed in the past century: trait, psychoanalytic, behavioral or social learning, and humanistic views.

3 Trait Theories

Traits are enduring, stable attributes or characteristics of a person. If our behavior changes, does this mean one of our traits has changed, or has our behavior been influenced by our environment? Trait theorists are still arguing about this point.

Phrenology

You read earlier about phrenology, the study based on the assumption that the lumps on a person's head are related to specific abilities. Although this proved untrue, the notion did introduce the idea that body features might be used to influence and thus predict certain features of personality.

Typology

William Sheldon (1899-1977), an American medical doctor, first offered in the early 1940s one of the most interesting modern views of such a theory of personality. Sheldon identified three different general forms of human physique, or *somatotype* (see drawings). According to Sheldon each of us could be rated as to the amount of each form represented in our body.

In addition, Sheldon also suggested that there is a close relation between our personal temperament (measured by observer ratings) and measures of our physique taken from somatotype photographs. This is, in fact, the single, essential assumption of Sheldon's theory—that a continuity, or a high correlation, exists between physique and behavior. The three personality types identified by Sheldon are also identified in the illustration.

Sheldon's view is intriguing, but it is limited primarily by an obvious problem. How can you rate someone's personality or behavior without seeing him or her behave? In short, raters of behavior must also see the physique of the body that is behaving. The measures and ratings are thus confounded. This alone may account for the high correlations Sheldon reported relating body form and behavior.

On the other hand, there is an inherent logic in the form of our body determining some of our behavior. Maybe stereotypes explain Sheldon's findings. That is, maybe you and I reward someone for behaving according to certain stereotypes. In other words, if we believe that fat people are jolly, we may already be inclined to laugh with them even before they speak.

So it's a low-level, common-sense kind of theory, and it may be dignifying it a bit to label it a developed theory of personality. Certainly few predictions for therapy can be generated!

somatotype: *a form of human physique as identified by Sheldon*

PHYSIQUE		TEMPERAMENT
ENDOMORPHIC soft, round, overdeveloped digestive viscera		**VISCEROTONIC** sociable, relaxed, loves eating
MESOMORPHIC muscular, rectangular, strong		**SOMATOTONIC** assertive, energetic, courageous
ECTOMORPHIC long, fragile, large brain, sensitive nervous system		**CEREBROTONIC** artistic, introverted restrained, fearful

Figure 11-1 Sheldon's body types and the temperaments associated with them.

Factor theory

Raymond B. Cattell (1905-) has developed a different approach to the description and analysis of personality. He relies on data collected from three sources: a person's life record, self-ratings, and objective tests. Drawing from people's life records and self-ratings, Cattell identified major personality factors both within individuals and in people in general. These important factors were identified through complex statistical analyses, and they are listed in common language in Table 11-2.

Cattell distinguishes between *surface* traits, which are observable patterns of behavior, and *source* traits, which he viewed as underlying, internal traits responsible for our overt behavior. He viewed the source traits as more important. Source traits can be identified only by means of computer analysis of all the collected data. Cattell also distinguishes between *general* traits—those possessed by all—and *specific* traits—those typical of only one person.

surface traits: *observable patterns of behavior*

source traits: *underlying internal traits responsible for overt behavior*

general traits: *personality traits possessed by all people*

specific traits: *personality traits typical only of one person*

Table 11-2 **Cattell's factor theory**

MAJOR PERSONALITY FACTORS
outgoing—reserved
more intelligent—less intelligent
stable—emotional
assertive—humble
happy-go-lucky—sober
conscientious—expedient
venturesome—shy
tender-minded—tough-minded
suspicious—trusting
imaginative—practical
shrewd—forthright
apprehensive—placid

Indeed, one of the major criticisms registered against these factor-analysis based theories is that by collapsing so much data they lose the individual person in the process. Yet, if you observe carefully, it *is* possible to trace the increases and decreases in various response styles in a given individual over a period of time. Others—perhaps rightly—criticize the factor and trait theorists for not being theoretical at all. Rather, they are empirical, or data-oriented. This is true enough but not necessarily bad. Any set of theories emphasizing precision is not to be faulted only on that basis.

Sigmund Freud founded the psychoanalytic school of thought, which includes both a theoretical system and a method of therapy.

4 Psychoanalysis

Psychoanalysis must be understood as *both* a major theoretical system and a form of therapy. Here we'll discuss it only as a theory, holding our discussion of psychoanalysis as therapy until Chapter 13. The entire theory is based on only two forms of observations made by Sigmund Freud. He studied deviant, or irrational, behavior of a very small number (less than a dozen) of his own medical patients. He also drew observations from everyday life, such as expression of humor and slips of the tongue.

Central elements

The conscious-unconscious dimension. There are two major elements underlying all of Freud's theory. One of these is his conception of the conscious-unconscious dimension. He suggested that the mind has three subsystems. The *conscious* involves thoughts of which you are aware. Thus, your thinking about psychology and Freud's views of our conscious mind are in your conscious mind right now.

The *preconscious* involves thoughts of which you are not immediately aware. However, they are thoughts you can bring to conscious attention easily and rapidly. Want an example? Who's your best friend of the opposite sex right now? Immediately a picture of somebody flashed into your mind. That person was—if you've been paying attention and not daydreaming!—just in your preconscious.

Your *unconscious* involves the largest source of influences on your overt, conscious behavior, as seen in the diagram. Without our awareness (according to Freud) the conscious becomes a symbol or vehicle of unconscious urges. Thus, by studying such things as slips of the tongue and dreams, Freud would assert we can study unconscious processes.

Libido. Remember that psychoanalysis was first developed in the 1800s, just as physics, chemistry, and biology were making great strides as disciplines. Essentially mimicking the theories of physics and physical energy, Freud proposed that each of us is born with a certain amount of psychic energy, or *libido*. This energy creates inner tensions that we seek to reduce. Freud stressed sexuality in his theoretical statements and analyses, but he used the word "sexual" broadly, as it relates to many different intentions and activities.

Structure

Freud's major contribution was his development of the concepts of the *id, ego,* and *superego*. He viewed them as separate but interacting systems. Freud liked to use analogies when he spoke and wrote. He often compared the id, ego, and superego to a Russian troika. Success in moving this type of vehicle requires contributions by three horses all hitched abreast, and the same idea applies (Freud asserted) in developing a functioning personality.

The *id* is the initial system present at birth. All libidinal energy is deposited there. That is, all the organism's personal activities are at first directed to satisfying the needs of the id. The id has to do with our most basic desires, and it cannot tolerate tension. Functioning completely unconsciously, the id is said to operate in terms of the *pleasure* principle. It seeks pleasure for itself without any regard for the needs, wants, or concerns of others.

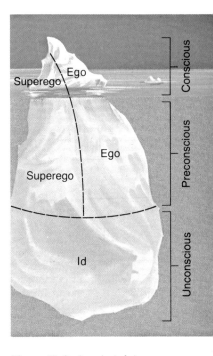

Figure 11-2 One helpful way to remember Freud's view of our conscious-unconscious and our id-ego-superego structures is to think of them as an iceberg. Most of an iceberg is underwater, and most of the influences of our behavior (from the id and superego) are unconscious. Only a little of an iceberg shows, and we are aware (that is, conscious) of only very few of the influences on our behavior.

id: *according to Freudian theory, the source of basic desires operating solely for self-gratification (the pleasure principle)*

Alfred Adler (1870-1937) was a disciple of the Freudian school who contributed the concept of the *inferiority complex*. The feelings of inadequacy experienced by all children in relation to their more powerful and knowledgeable parents must be overcome to achieve full mental health.

And Jung was interested in opposites. His other important contribution was the idea of *introversion* (a turning inward, or seclusiveness) and *extroversion* (outward looking, outgoing). For Jung, the successful person can bring the opposing parts of his person (inclinations toward introversion *and* extroversion, among others) together.

Alfred Adler. The other important person in this group would be Alfred Adler, who assumed that since we have little control over our life in childhood, we grow up feeling inferior. For Adler, the battle to overcome this feeling of inferiority becomes a style of life. Those who fail to master the feelings of inferiority, or who remain overly worried about it even when they have mastered it, are said to have developed an *inferiority complex*.

■■■■■ In review . . .

Three types of trait theories have developed: phrenology, typology, and the factor theory. Psychoanalysis is the original modern theory of personality based on the assumption that there exists an unconscious and a psychic energy (libido). Starting only with the id, we develop an ego and a superego. Life and death instincts show a balance between aggression and a pursuit of pleasure. Both Jung and Adler developed personality theories related to Freud's.

5 Social-Learning Theories

Now let's turn to more modern theories with a different set of emphases. In the early chapters we spoke about the precision of the scientific methods. After those discussions you may have felt slightly uncomfortable as you read about Freud's views of personality. In fact, Freud's theory *is* in many ways his personal statement about how personality may develop and organize itself. One of the major criticisms of psychoanalytic thought was that it did not easily lend itself to tests in the laboratory.

While fascinated with Freud's ideas, a group of American psychologists began, in the early 1940s, to develop what became a theory of personality. Their early theories shared many things in common with psychoanalysis. Both were trying to explain similar patterns of abnormal behavior. Both observed the person and tried to determine what was occurring within. Yet, the new

introversion: *in personality theory (Jung), a turning inward or reclusiveness*

extroversion: *in personality theory (Jung), a turning outward toward others*

inferiority complex: *a failure to master the feelings of inferiority felt by all children in relation to adults*

school—the behavioral theories—emphasized a close tie to scientific methods. They included in their general theory only confirmed and confirmable findings from the psychological laboratory. The result was a much less dramatic theory, but one that yields testable predictions.

Dollard/Miller's stimulus-response theory

Translating Freud's theory into concepts and language that could be studied in the laboratory did not turn out to be as hard as you might suspect. Psychologists John Dollard and Neal Miller developed their theory of personality stressing the importance of learning. It was based on a small number of observable, simple processes and elements.

In their own words "... in order to learn one must want something, notice something, do something, and get something. Stated more exactly, these factors are drive, cue, response, and reward." Let's review each of those factors. According to these men we are born with a set of innate needs—for food, water, oxygen, and warmth, to name but a few. We would have died if these needs had not been satisfied during our early life, yet now we can perform the necessary responses ourselves. Obviously, although the needs may be inherited, the responses to meet them are learned.

Drive. Two kinds of drives operate within us. At birth and while young we may be stimulated into action mainly by *primary drives* such as hunger. As is true of all drives, the stronger the deprivation (for example, hunger), the stronger the drive. Moreover, if some stimulus always occurs when a primary drive is operating, then that stimulus may also come to cause behavior. These are *secondary (or learned) drives* that develop if a stimulus occurs frequently in association with a primary drive. One example is fear.

Cue. Once a drive is aroused, cues guide you. They encourage you to respond, determining when and where you will respond and even which response will be made. How do your parents call you when it's time for a meal? That call or bell or shout is a cue. It guides you to the table, where the appropriate eating responses can be performed.

Response. At birth we have a series of organized (often reflexive) responses we can make. These can be called our *initial response hierarchy*. Learning—which Dollard and Miller view as central to the development of personality—can lead to changes

Drive, cue, response, and reward are factors in the development of personality, according to psychologists Dollard and Miller. Learning is central to their stimulus-response theory.

initial response hierarchy: *the series of responses an infant can make at birth*

in that initial response hierarchy. The latest order—the one you're using now—is called the *resultant hierarchy*. Drives accompanied by cues guide the organism to respond in a particular way and place.

Reinforcement. This is the most controversial portion of this theory, for reasons we developed back in Chapter 6. A response that reduces our drive level is reinforcing; it will tend to occur again. We are likely to do again whatever response reduced our hunger.

Notice how learning is emphasized. You start with an array of organized reflexive responses, but experience and reinforcements soon change that order. These theorists say that your personality is based on your most recent learning experiences. You change from day to day and month to month. Your personality, then, is composed of habits—the learned associations between drives, appropriate cues, and responses. You differ from your friends because your prior experiences differ. Your personality can be expected to change with future experiences.

Unlike psychoanalysis, Dollard and Miller's theory is testable. Although based on the study of how animals work, their conclusions have also been found true of humans.

B. F. Skinner
and behaviorism

Skinner doesn't have a theory of personality. Yet the principles of operant conditioning can be applied to the development of statements about how personality is formed and how it functions. Dollard and Miller emphasize internal processes such as motivation, drive, drive-reduction, and reinforcement. By contrast, Skinner concentrates entirely on observable behavior. For Skinner, nobody is "neurotic"—one simply shows a variety of ineffective modes of escape. You are not "frustrated"—you are simply replacing one response with another.

According to Skinner, much of our behavior—especially in the company of others—involves freely emitted "operants" (see Chapter 6). If an operant is reinforced, Skinner asserts, we will be more likely to emit that operant in a similar situation.

Thus, two important concepts for Skinner are generalization and discrimination. We must learn stimulus generalization so that we will emit responses to a variety of similar, if not identical, situations. For instance, you can eat a hamburger whether sitting in McDonald's or in Burger King. Likewise, we must learn to discriminate when to and when not to emit certain responses. Talking in class is all right, but not when your

B. F. Skinner (right) follows the behaviorist school of psychology, which concentrates on operant conditioning and observable behavior.

teacher has asked for quiet. Talking in church is all right, but not when the preacher is preaching.

And what assures that all these operants will be reinforced? Skinner emphasizes the importance of generalized reinforcers—such things as money and social approval. They are often associated with primary goal objects such as food and water. Yet, on occasion, we can still be controlled by a smile.

Bandura and social learning

Research in the 40s, 50s, and much of the 60s was concerned mainly with animals. You can smile at animals, but that doesn't usually reinforce them. Food does reinforce a hungry animal; water does reinforce a thirsty one. For humans, however, it is the effects of reinforcement that are crucial.

Bandura has a very different view. He maintains that even by observing someone perform a response for which he or she is rewarded, learning will occur. He feels that gaining a reinforcer determines whether or not a response is *performed, not* whether it is learned. So novel behaviors can be acquired just by looking.

We've come quite a way. Notice that the *trait* theories with which we started emphasize how each person is a collection of constant traits, abilities, or responses. Thus different people may respond differently in the same situation because of different traits. Yet Bandura and those endorsing a social-learning theory are saying that the behavior of each of us in the same situation may differ because of conditions. If your aunt kisses you, you're peeved; if your mother does, you're tolerant; if your boyfriend or girlfriend does, you're happy.

Evaluation

And how do we critique these theories? Whereas Freud, Adler, and Jung probably put too much emphasis on heredity, perhaps the behavioral and social-learning theorists have put too little. The theories do offer testable predictions. They offer a lengthy continuity with animal research going back almost 50 years; they're simple, and they generate some immediate and applicable suggestions for therapy, as we'll see in Chapter 14.

6 Self-Growth Theories

As one pair of psychologists has observed, psychoanalysis seems to paint a bleak picture of humans. On the other hand, learning theorists seem to picture us as robots passively reacting to environmental stimuli we don't control. Neither attitude applies to the self-growth theories. These humanistic theories value our human "growth potential," or striving for self-betterment. Carl Rogers and Abraham Maslow assume that we cannot understand a person by examining his or her environment or actions within it. Rather, we must analyze how the person perceives the environment and his or her role in it.

Carl Rogers and person-centered theory

According to Rogers, "... behavior is basically the goal-directed attempt of the organism to satisfy its needs as experienced, in the field as perceived." Two aspects of the person are essential to understanding Rogers' theory: the organism and the self. The *organism* is the focal point of all experience. This experience, defined from the person's own point of view, involves everything that *could* (not is, *could*) be experienced. It changes from moment to moment. The total of this experience is called the *phenomenal field*.

As a person grows from infancy to adulthood and gains experience, what eventually emerges as part of the phenomenal field is the *self*. For you it is composed of all the things you can say or know about "I" or "me," and your relations with your

Carl Rogers regards behavior as the attempt of an organism to satisfy its needs and strive toward self-actualization, or fulfillment.

phenomenal field: *according to Rogers' theory, all the experiences that a person could experience*

According to Carl Rogers, we all seek acceptance and love, or *unconditional regard*, from those in our lives who are most important to us.

environment and the people who are part of that environment. In addition to self, there is also an *ideal self*—what you would like to be.

Rogers assumes we each possess an inherited urge or need for *self-actualization*. This is thought to be a tendency to develop and utilize all of our potential. Self-actualization is a single goal toward which we all strive.

And how do we know when we are advancing toward self-actualization? We assess everything we do and assign a value, positive or negative, to it. If it feels good when we are doing it, or even thinking about it, then it *is* good and should be done. Now the naive might use that as a justification for engaging in almost anything. But remember that in striving toward self-actualization, the value is attached positively only to those activities the self thinks are advancing it toward actualization.

The final concept that is important in Rogers' theory is termed *unconditional positive regard*, or acceptance. It causes us to seek acceptance, warmth, and love from the valued people in our life. If we don't get it, we are not advancing. The organism needs positive regard not only from those around it, but also from the self. Thus, if you feel anger toward a friend, you will tend to deny its existence since you know that in good friendships anger shouldn't exist. In short, we learn to seek positive regard—we try to do things that gain us praise. When we find it, what follows is an improvement in self-regard.

self-actualization: *the process of developing and utilizing all of one's potential*

unconditional positive regard: *approval from valued people in one's life that is necessary for development*

Psychologist Abraham Maslow believes that human beings strive to fulfill a progression, or hierarchy, of needs. Basic psychological needs must be satisfied before a person can move on to the higher needs.

metaneeds: *the need for goodness, order, unity, justice and the like to enrich the individual and the world*

Maslow's holistic theory

Since we discussed aspects of Maslow's efforts in Chapter 9, we won't go into full detail here again. But Maslow clearly objected to studying only a portion of humans, preferring to consider humans as a whole, complete organism. Consistent with our earlier discussion of the cyclical nature of motivation, Maslow didn't believe humans often reached a state where they had no needs. And if they did, it was only for a very short time.

In effect, Maslow proposed a hierarchy of needs—basic needs and what some have called "metaneeds." The basic needs (see page 299) are arranged in a hierarchy in which more basic physiological needs must be satisfied before one can cater to more high-level needs. These are the needs of hunger, affection, security, self-esteem, and self-actualization—the deficiency needs.

Metaneeds refer to needs for goodness, order, unity, justice, and so forth. Clearly more than one of the metaneeds may be operating at any given time. Although these are growth needs, serving mainly to enrich the person and the world, they are, according to Maslow, as inherent as the basic needs.

One of Maslow's major contributions was to suggest that healthy people might *not* simply be the opposite of sick people. He studied a number of people whom he considered to be fully self-actualized in the richest sense of the term—fully effective, mature human beings, some alive when he studied them, some long dead. Listed in Table 11-3 are some of the things he found healthy, self-actualized people to exhibit. It's an interesting list. Are you self-actualized yet? Could you qualify for this list?

Self-esteem and self-actualization are high on Abraham Maslow's hierarchy of needs. Guion Buford and Sally Ride achieved firsts in space—she for women and he for blacks. Such accomplishments enrich both the individual and the world. At right Buford is testing an exercise device designed for space flight.

Table 11-3 **Abraham Maslow's list of behaviors indicating self-actualization**

Self-actualizing people will be:

oriented toward reality
accepting of self, of others, and of nature
more spontaneous
problem-centered (not self-centered)
more detached from others and desire more privacy
self-sufficient and independent
more appreciative and intensely emotional
more likely to have mystical experiences
more identified with humankind
involved in rich interpersonal experiences
more democratic in attitude
markedly more creative
aware of needs for improvements in their culture

Evaluation

How are we to evaluate the self-growth theories? Maslow's theory shares many similarities with Rogers'. We can note the following about both: They stress research, which is a benefit. They have shortened the many years required for psychoanalysis to very short-term efforts designed to solve immediate problems. Although the major concepts are defined, the definitions tend to be abstract, and thus subject to a rich variety of interpretations! The change in approach provided by stressing the person's perspective of his or her environment is interesting intellectually. But Rogers' concept is difficult to measure in the laboratory; there is so much emphasis on current views of and needs from the environment. Rogers and Maslow pay little attention to childhood experiences or unconscious determiners of behavior.

In review . . .

Attempting to express Freud's psychoanalytic theory in terms that could be studied scientifically, a stimulus-response theory was developed. Drive, cue, response, and reinforcement were identified as critical elements in personality, which was viewed as a series of learned habits. The past decade has seen self-growth theories gain more adherents. Rogers developed person-centered theory. Maslow lent even greater emphasis to the wholeness of the person, emphasizing only human needs.

Chapter Application and Review

Did you notice what happened as we progressed from type theories through psychoanalysis and behaviorism to self-growth theories of personality? We retraced steps on a path traveled before in Chapters 2 and 3, for instance. The type theories, and to a very real extent the psychoanalytic theories, give heaviest emphasis to things that we as individuals can't control. Our body shape is largely determined by genetic messages passed on by our parents. Freud made room for learning experiences in childhood in his views of the developing personality. Even so, the person (child) involved did not control the nature of that relationship. Much was determined by heredity.

By contrast, the social-learning and S-R views of personality are not much concerned with developmental factors. Some people have even suggested that Skinner's views would tend to make us robots. In short, in theories developed in the 1930s to 1950s, environment received much emphasis.

Now look at how the humanists have responded. Their theories talk again about free will and the desire or need to achieve as much as we are capable of achieving—self-actualization. What we do with our life is largely up to our own individual initiative. This grants us a chance to improve upon the genetic base we inherited and sidestep the manipulation of the environment. Self-growth theories offer us the hope that we can be masters of our own fate.

Trait or state?

There is a question about personality that may have been bothering you. Our definition at the start of the chapter clearly identifies personality as an attribute of each individual, even though a concession is made in recognition of the impact of the environment. Where *is* personality located? At least three views seem possible. One suggests that each of us is a unique collection of traits. We all are aggressive to a certain extent, sad, humorous, achievement-oriented, and so forth. Thus, personality tests assess the aspects of the individual which will function wherever the individual goes. You can find out which traits apply to you by taking these tests. Then perhaps you can make a conscious effort to modify those traits of which you're not particularly proud.

Yet, there's also a second view. Perhaps, our behavior—and thus our personality—is totally determined by where we are at the moment. You have undoubtedly felt the swellings of pride as you were able to help a younger brother, sister, or friend solve a problem where *you* had the experience needed. Yet another time you stood around with your hands in your pockets, clearly in over your head in an adult conversation—hoping no one would notice you, right? So this second view suggests that personality factors which are supposed to be "constant"—that is, present in all of us—are not there. Rather, our behavior is determined by the situation in which we find ourselves.

A dilemma? Yes, but a third view seems to offer a rational answer. Perhaps the degree to which our behavior is constant (meaning true to alleged "traits" we carry with us) is not fixed. Nor may our behavior vary with each situation in which we find ourselves (meaning that the environment, not us, would be determining our behavior). Rather, behavior may be markedly influenced by even broader social and cultural variables in our environment. Someone with a well-developed sense of self and self-worth—to use Rogers' terminology—may well be honest (for example) in all situations; someone without that sense may be "honest" in some situations, but not in others—that is controlled by the environment. The critical question, then, becomes what is the nature of the environment—familial, social, and cultural—that will foster your sense of self? It is to this topic that we turn in the next two chapters.

REVIEW QUESTIONS

SECTION 1 (pages 335–340)

1. In what ways do people usually define the term "personality"?
2. Why are psychologists interested in the study of personality?
3. Should personality best be viewed as an independent, an intervening, or a dependent variable? Defend your answer.
4. Name and explain the elements of personality.
5. Describe the two approaches most frequently used to study personality.

SECTION 2 (pages 340–341)

1. Why are theories of personality important?
2. Name four types of personality theories.

SECTION 3 (pages 342–344)

1. Describe three trait theories of personality. What do they have in common?
2. What are some major objections to the Cattell theory?

SECTION 4 (pages 344–348)

1. What assumptions did Freud make about personality?

2. Describe the development of personality according to Freud.
3. Name and give examples of the basic human instincts proposed by Freud.
4. Name two personality theorists who based their theories on Freud's. What important contributions did they make?

SECTION 5 (pages 348–352)

1. How and by whom was Freud's theory modified so that it could be studied scientifically? What was the new theory called?
2. Describe the important elements of the theory you just named.

SECTION 6 (pages 352–355)

1. How do the self-growth theories of personality differ from the psychoanalytic and learning theories?
2. Describe the important elements of Rogers' person-centered theory.
3. How does Maslow's theory differ from Rogers' theory?
4. What changes in emphasis have taken place in personality theory over the last 100 years?

ACTIVITIES

1. In terms of the definition of personality that is offered here in this text, write an essay about yourself. Identify those parts of your publicly observable behavior that are *organized*. Show also how you *adjust* to your environment. Identify what is *unique* (that is, without equal) about you. Finally, include in your essay as many factors in your hered-

ity or environment as you can find that affect your daily behavior and thought.

2. If you did the essay in #1 above, ask a friend to write a similar essay about *you*. Once your friend has finished, compare your own essay (the answer sheet!) with that of your friend. How are they similar? How do they differ?

3. If both you and a friend did the essay suggested in #1 above, then compare your essay about yourself with a friend's essay about him- or herself. How many parts of your essays are similar and how many are different? What factors do you both mention as influencing your personality?

4. "Slips of the tongue" happen all the time. Records have even been made of some of the funniest slips of the tongue that occurred back in the early days of radio and television when the broadcasts were "live" and errors couldn't be deleted. Either get a copy of such a record and listen to it, or keep a list of your own of slips of the tongue, or slips that you have heard in the past or that you hear during your daily activities. Freud thought such slips were revealing subconscious urges. If that is correct, can you identify from the circumstances of the slip (whether on the record or from your own experience) what might be revealed about the unconscious of the person who made the slip? Is there any way to confirm your guesses?

5. One of the major elements of Carl Jung's theory of personality was the introversion-extroversion dimension. What is it? Do you think you are introverted or extroverted? In defending your answer, keep a list of your own behaviors for a day or a week when around others. Use that list to identify examples of you behaving as an introvert and/or as an extrovert. For interest, compare your own list with friends who were present at the time mentioned on your list. Did they see you as behaving as an introvert or an extrovert? Do they agree with your own analysis?

6. Career Search. Many high schools offer adult evening courses that aim at developing the individual's self-confidence, feelings of self-worth, and personal assertiveness. Such assertiveness training may also be conducted by various women's groups in the community. Invite a teacher or leader from one of these groups to address the class on techniques used and training required to function in such a role. Ask him or her to give a brief sample of a typical class session.

7. Carl Rogers' person-centered theory is based partly on the concept of an "ideal self" and how similar it is to the "actual self." How about you? Write an essay in which you identify how you would ideally like to be. What friends would you have? How would you behave? Then write another (brief) essay about your actual self. Now compare the two essays. If the description of the ideal self is realistic, but not the same as your ideal, then it should be possible for you to change toward your ideal. Analyze your behavior for the past 24 hours, especially those situations when you did not behave as your ideal self would have. What caused the less than ideal behavior? How can you change so as to behave more and more like your ideal? Compare your answers with trusted friends.

INTERESTED IN MORE?

ALLPORT, G. W. *Letters from Jenny.* Harcourt Brace Jovanovich, 1965. A collection of letters arranged and analyzed to explain the development and operation of a personality.

DiCAPRIO, N. S. *Personality Theories: A Guide to Human Nature,* 2nd ed. Holt, Rinehart & Winston, 1983. Provides expanded coverage of each of the theorists discussed in this chapter, and also discusses a number of related theorists. Well illustrated; written in an engaging, educational style.

HALL, C. S. *A Primer of Freudian Psychology.* New American Library, 1978. A good review of Freud's work, analyzing the impact of psychoanalysis on more modern theories of personality.

HALL, C. S. & LINDZEY, G. *Theories of Personality,* 3rd ed. John Wiley, 1978. A classic reference that devotes a separate chapter to each major personality theory. Includes a look at the influence of Eastern philosophies on theory. Tough reading.

MASLOW, A. *Toward a Psychology of Being.* D. Van Nostrand, 1968. A well-known psychologist emphasizes the importance of creating and maintaining mental health.

MISCHEL, W. *Introduction to Personality,* 3rd ed. Holt, Rinehart & Winston, 1981. Examines trait, psychodynamic, behavioral, and self-growth (humanistic) theories and how these theories are applied in psychotherapy. Covers effects of televised aggression and sex bias on personality.

NYE, R. D. *Three Psychologists: Perspectives from Freud, Skinner, and Rogers,* 2nd ed. Brooks/Cole, 1981. Analyzes the human personality in terms of psychodynamic, behavioral, and trait theories.

ROGERS, C. *On Becoming a Person.* Houghton Mifflin, 1961. Rogers' self-growth theories contrast sharply with psychoanalytic thinking.

ROTTER, J. B. & HOCHREICH, D. J. *Personality.* Scott, Foresman, 1975. A brief paperback discussing various theories of personality and personality measurement.

SZASZ, T. S. *The Myth of Mental Illness.* Harper & Row, 1961. Argues that many of the attempts to diagnose and treat mental disorders are aimed at protecting society rather than helping individuals solve their "problems in living."

WHITE, R. W. *Lives in Progress: A Study of the Natural Growth of Personality,* 3rd ed. Holt, Rinehart & Winston, 1975. A well-written book of case studies that views important events in life as these events relate to various theories of personality.

Personality: Mental and Behavioral Disorders

WHAT'S THE ANSWER?

☐   "Wilma, I just can't go on!"

"What's the problem, Rudy? It seemed to me that you were finally getting things under control."

"True, but I've got all these courses! We've got finals coming up in the next two weeks, and I can't possibly be ready. I'm so nervous my stomach is always in knots. I start studying one thing and then spend half my time worrying about something else I should be doing. Study all this week. Work at my part-time job on Saturdays. Take exams next week. I can't even get to sleep when I go to bed!"

"Why do you suddenly think you can't go on, Rudy?"

"It seems as if it's gotten worse these last two weeks. I get the feeling I'm going to have a nervous breakdown. I've just *got* to drop out of school." *What's going on here? Should Rudy drop out of school? Is he likely to suffer a "nervous breakdown"?*

☐   People who have experienced severe automobile accidents sometimes find that they are unable to recall anything about the accident itself, or of events immediately (sometimes even days) before the accident. *Is this loss of memory abnormal?*

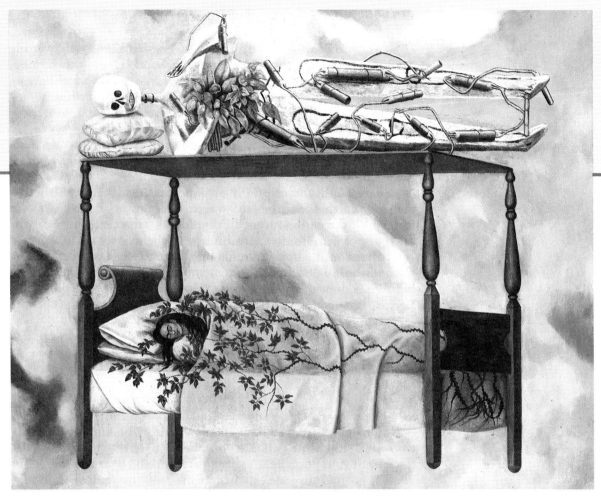

In this painting artist Frida Kahlo captures some of the feelings of mystery, fear, and strangeness we all have experienced at some time in our dreams.

1 Abnormal Behavior

It happened quite rapidly. Maria was a first-year medical student studying some of the wide variety of illnesses medical doctors are now able to diagnose. One morning Maria was reading about lung infarctions (collapses) resulting from impeded blood circulation through the lungs. As she read she thought she was beginning to feel some slight pains in her chest. When she studied rashes, she began to notice some small red spots on her arms.

Usually a family member or close friend first notices a change in behavior that might be considered "abnormal." The border between normal and abnormal is difficult to define.

or family. Yet, even here there are difficulties in definition. The internal discomfort that would cause one person to seek help might be considered normal wear-and-tear by another. And, as we'll see shortly, we've got to exclude organic (physical) causes before we can say a purely psychological problem is involved. Sometimes we may seek professional psychological help because we think we've got an emotional-behavioral problem. Actually, however, there may be a physiological explanation for our feelings—perhaps an internal chemical imbalance or a disease.

Social. We described earlier a situation in which the first judgment of abnormality may be made by our friends. This is an example of where our eccentric behavior, if judged eccentric by social norms, may be called abnormal. If you always go out to water your yard only when it's raining outside, people may begin to watch you more closely. If you act as if you are mortally afraid of some harmless thing, (called having a phobia), again people will call your behavior abnormal.

The major difficulty with such socially based definitions of what is normal and abnormal is that social norms change or differ from place to place. It would not now be normal for a member of Congress to show up in formal suit wearing a powdered white wig for a day's debate. Yet, *not* to have done so would have been considered abnormal 200 years ago. Whereas it might be abnormal to wear a cowboy hat all the time in Boston, it would not be abnormal to do so in Dallas!

Feature 12–2 VOODOO?

The power of the environment in helping each of us maintain contact with reality is often underestimated. One example of the power of purely outside forces to adversely affect us internally is provided by voodoo. Stories of voodoo hexes have been often told in modern times. Probably you have read about voodoo dolls being stuck with pins and of other voodoo practices. What some have called the only complete study of the power of voodoo death cites a number of instances where tribal members were hexed, "boned," or bewitched. The end result was death. But why? Citing a wide variety of scraps and bits of findings that seem to confirm these stories, one investigator has suggested three factors. Notice how each factor is environmental, *not* mysterious in any way.

The three factors are (1) the devastating effects on the body of continuing intense fear—it can have a number of physical effects. (2) The power attributed to the customs (superstitions) of the society. Suppose you've heard of the power of voodoo actions all your life and seen its effects a number of times. If you have the misfortune to be "hexed," then it's likely you will respond as you've seen (or heard of) so many others doing. Finally, (3) each member of the community may aid the effects of voodoo hexes by isolating the victim. Without the benefit of people with whom to talk, friends to offer support, food to eat, or a task to perform, and with everyone treating you as if you were already dead, essentially all emotional and personal support is removed. The effects can be devastating.

Still, there are some other ways to define normal social behavior. In a court of law, your behavior may be declared abnormal simply because of the professional judgment of a psychologist or psychiatrist. In this sense you are abnormal if a professional says you are. Such a judgment is usually based on statistical averages, repeated testings of "normal" performance, and so forth.

Conclusion. As we'll see, there are a number of sources that may lead to abnormal human behavior—environment, chemicals, inherited inclinations. One psychiatrist phrased the dilemma about as well as anyone. He said, "Whenever we try to give a definition of what mental health is, we simply state our preference for a certain type of cultural, social, and ethical order."

One of the best means of identifying abnormal behavior is to start by acknowledging the wide variety of sources of influence of our behavior. This leads to a wide range of human behaviors that are or may be acceptable. Thus, developing a precise definition of abnormal behavior is very difficult. Let's try it this way: Abnormal behavior exists if we find that one or more of three

"Look wh...
did t...

Figure
ple of

Feature 12–5 "THEY" GOT ME!

At age 23 Bill was diagnosed as a paranoid schizophrenic and hospitalized. The youngest of three brothers, he had no friends, little education, and no job skills. He suffered from epilepsy, and he'd always been thought of as an "oddball."

Just before he was admitted, things got markedly worse for him. He started referring to himself in the third person. He gave away his family's money to the church. This left his mother without funds to pay for the winter's heating fuel. As the winter progressed, he became more and more withdrawn and suspicious of others. After planning and starting a trip to Atlanta, he lost his job in a hardware store. Here he converses with his therapist:

Bill: In fact, now that Bill thinks about it, every time he's planned that trip to Atlanta he's lost his job. It's happened four times now. Bill's grandfather was a king. He was a millionaire, but he was cheated and robbed of his life's savings. They took all his money.

That's the reason Bill's family is so poor.

Therapist: Who are "they"?

Bill: They're evil and cunning. They still have all that money and they live in a mansion. Everything they've got came from cheating Bill's grandfather. Bill gave his family's money to the church so they wouldn't get it. Bill *really* outsmarted them!

Therapist: Why do you call yourself "Bill" instead of "I" or "me"?

Bill: It sounds more important that way.

Bill's situation is not an unusual one. His whole family—especially his mother—treated him as they would an invalid. They never demanded much of him, and his family viewed his epileptic seizures as very distasteful. Bill's solution to this atmosphere and his own (understandable) low self-esteem was to project blame for his shortcomings onto external events or other people ("they"). He also developed delusions of grandeur, importance ("Bill said. . .") and persecution ("they stole. . .").

Causes. Some experiments confirm psychoanalysts' views that depression is aggression turned inward, and mania is a defense against depression. Learning theorists think depression may be reinforced by sympathy from others. Other theorists have looked to faulty cognitive processes for an explanation. Evidence suggests that inheritance plays a role—if one identical twin becomes depressed, in 50 to 90 percent of cases studied the other twin will also show depression. Yet, environment is also important. Several factors, such as losing one's mother before the age of 11, have been shown to increase susceptibility to depression. To date there are almost more theories than facts regarding the cause or causes of depression.

Schizophrenia

Schizophrenia is not (as popularly thought) concerned with a "split mind." The closest condition that would lead to an apparently "split" mind is the dissociative disorder called multiple personality that we discussed earlier. We can best view schizophrenia as a collection of disorders, all of which have a number of symptoms in common. Schizophrenics number almost half of the patients confined in state and county hospitals, and of all

state a
ings of
specific

trait an
of anxie

defense
conscio
that hel

repressi
anism i
gets si
cause p

schizophrenia: a disorder of thought involving loss of contact with reality

Table 12-4 **Symptoms of schizophrenia**   **385**

SYMPTOM	EVIDENCE
LACK OF EMOTIONS	Person shows little emotional responsiveness; emotion is absent or inappropriate.
WITHDRAWAL	Little contact with others and with reality.
DISTURBED THOUGHT	Illogical thought sequences, inability to hold a coherent line of thought.
INCOHERENT SPEECH	Speech may wander, seem poorly connected.
DELUSIONS	Shows delusions that are hard to understand: persecution, sexual, religious, grandeur.
HALLUCINATIONS	May show sensory disturbances of hearing or vision; may involve distortions of body sense.
ABNORMAL BEHAVIOR	Behavior may be physically abnormal in showing weird or unusual body positions or gait; lack of facial expressions.
UNRELIABILITY	May show lack of consistency; likely not to be trustworthy regarding responses to questions.

those patients who are middle-aged, about 60 percent are schizophrenic.

Schizophrenia, unlike the affective disorders of mood discussed above, is rather a disorder of thought, involving one or more of the symptoms listed in Table 12-4. The primary symptom of schizophrenia is a loss of prior efficiency in the home, social, and work environment. While some view the subtypes below as distinct disorders with unique causes, most mental health professionals today view them simply as clusters of behavioral symptoms. The labels, however, remain in frequent use.

Undifferentiated (simple). Simple schizophrenia often develops slowly. Gradually retreating from normalcy, the person shows an increasing loss of interest and emotion, of ambition, and of logical thought. Personal health and hygiene are neglected as the person becomes more and more inactive and apathetic. Of all the types of schizophrenics, the simple schizophrenic is most likely to be able to maintain him- or herself in the everyday world. The usual point of onset is early in life—often during adolescence. As a result, the family may

undifferentiated (simple) schizophrenia: *a condition involving loss of ambition, interests, and emotion, to the point where self-maintenance becomes impossible*

Schizophrenia is a disorder of thought, accompanied in many cases by loss of contact with reality. Paranoid schizophrenics may suffer from delusions of persecution, as is implied in this painting by a schizophrenic man.

knowingly or otherwise be pulled into continuing to support a simple schizophrenic as his or her outside contacts with friends, school or job, and reality gradually deteriorate.

Disorganized. The *disorganized* schizophrenic suffers from one of the most severe forms of the disorder. Often having an early onset, it may show up as an inappropriate, overwhelming concern with little things, or with philosophical or religious issues. This focus excludes everything else. As the condition becomes more severe, the thinking patterns become increasingly immature, distractible, or not even related to events in the immediate environment. What follows may be baby talk, incoherent conversation, even silliness, giggling, or babbling. This verbal output has been called "word salad."

Catatonic. The *catatonic* is another severe form of schizophrenia. It takes several forms, but it has been found that about 44 percent are withdrawn catatonics. They will show marked inactivity, even to the extent of demonstrating "waxy flexibility" in which they will hold one body position for hours at a time. If an arm or leg is placed in a new position, they will then continue to maintain that posture. Such a patient will often be mute, yet pass rapidly into an excited state. About 29 percent have been found to swing between states of withdrawal and agitation. The other 27 percent remain mainly excited or agitated.

Paranoid. The *paranoid* schizophrenic is less severely abnormal in his or her behavior, yet severe deficits are still obvious. Paranoid persons often experience delusional or illogical thoughts. They may hallucinate, or they may endure "complexes" of superiority, persecution, or grandeur. Paranoids often retain quite acceptable verbal skills. If you grant their initial assumptions, they may well convince you of the truth of their delusional thoughts!

The process-reactive dimension. In some people schizophrenia develops over a long period, only gradually becoming identifiable. This is a *process schizophrenia*, and it usually leads to lengthy hospitalization and poor likelihood of recovery. Others seem to have a good life history, and then they experience a sudden breakdown, sometimes following an increase in stress. This is a *reactive schizophrenia*, and usually the person recovers and again becomes a contributing member of society.

Causes. What causes schizophrenia? There are several possibilities. One is the environment. Perhaps *conflict* is the key

disorganized schizophrenia: *a condition involving immature, distractible thinking patterns, incoherence, or "word salads"*

catatonic schizophrenia: *a condition involving marked inactivity, rigid postures; may pass into a violent state*

paranoid schizophrenia: *a condition involving delusional or illogical thoughts and "complexes"–of superiority, persecution, etc.*

here. If you view the environment as causing schizophrenia, then the condition can be considered a response to unanswerable pressures. Another explanation involves the *double bind*. (See illustration.) A poorly integrated family with inadequate communications between parents may be involved. Traumatic experiences in childhood may be a cause.

Indeed, a number of theoretical explanations have been offered to explain schizophrenia. Some credit inappropriate reliance on defense mechanisms. Unlike many other personal abnormalities, schizophrenia has even been linked to a variety of inherited factors. There is some evidence that schizophrenia tends to run in families. Yet, while it may be inherited, it may result from successive generations all tending to create environments in which schizophrenia is fostered. There is even evidence supporting biochemical and neuronal explanations of how schizophrenia is caused. In the next chapter we'll talk more about the treatment and prognosis for schizophrenia.

Personality disorders

Many people suffer from one of the numerous *personality disorders*. In such disorders the symptoms have often long been true of the individual. Thus, persons suffering a personality disorder may rationalize that it is "just part of me." Changing their behavior therefore can be very difficult.

Such disorders include *paranoid personality* (being suspicious and mistrusting, but not delusional or psychotic), *schizoid personality* (being a loner), and *schizotypal personality*, which is similar to the schizoid but more severe in showing thought abnormalities and perceptual and speech problems. In these conditions sufferers experience symptoms similar to but less severe than those of schizophrenia. Other conditions include the *narcissistic personality* (having consistent feelings of self-importance and being unable to accept criticism), *compulsive personality* (aiming constantly for perfection), and the *passive-aggressive personality* (showing indirect resistance to normal, acceptable demands at home or work, especially at work), and the *histrionic personality* (experiencing faulty interpersonal relationships or internal distress). Some psychologists have claimed that the assumptions on which the DSM-III is based are male oriented and thus lead to the diagnosis of an artificially large number of women as depressed or having a histrionic personality.

Antisocial personality disorders. Widely studied because of its public, social nature, the *antisocial personality* shows a lack of shame and remorse after committing a bad act. Such persons exhibit a seeming inability to learn from punishment and bad experiences. They suffer no anxiety, which may account for their failure to learn how to avoid punishment.

Do NOT look at this sign!

Figure 12-2 This sign creates a *double bind* by making a demand that has been violated in the act of understanding it.

⬛⬛⬛⬛⬛ In review . . .

The large number of symptoms and the broad variety of forms of psychosis make precise diagnosis of many psychotic disorders very difficult. Psychoses include affective disorders, which influence the mood or emotions, and the schizophrenias: simple, disorganized, catatonic, and paranoid. For both process and reactive schizophrenias there seem to be many complex causes. A wide variety of other enduring personality disorders includes the antisocial personality.

Chapter Application and Review

USING PSYCHOLOGY   *How can you judge what is abnormal?*

What often starts the process of admitting a person to a hospital for observation or analysis of abnormal behavior? The first judgment that the person's behavior *is* abnormal is made, not by a professional, but by the person's friends, neighbors, family, or fellow workers. If one of your friends began behaving strangely, at what point would you decide to encourage him or her to seek professional help? How would you make the judgment that the behavior was abnormal?

A group of psychologists was interested in answering exactly that question. They asked a large number of students, and a similarly large number of public health nurses, police, social workers, ministers, and physicians (*not* psychiatrists) to react to items from a widely used test of normal human behavior. These people were asked to indicate which items identified abnormal behavior. For example, one item usually said, "I have frequent attacks of nausea and vomiting." That item was changed to "He has frequent attacks of nausea and vomiting." People reviewing the 190 statements like that were asked to indicate how concerned they would

be about a person's being psychiatrically disturbed if they observed such behaviors. These people were asked whether they would show no, some, or much concern.

What do you think they found? What would *you* use to judge the behavior of one of your friends as abnormal? Table 12-5 contains the results. Listed there are each of the general types of behavior which this large sample of people watched. As indicated, there are three major types of deviant behavior most people use to judge someone's behavior to be abnormal. The first type concerns social inadequacy, which means behavior contrary to normal moral, social, or legal expectations. The second cluster of symptoms involves personal inadequacy, or being unable to perform at normal levels of personal confidence and ability. The last factor focuses on psychotic tendencies, which involve a variety of abnormal personal actions. They emphasize behaviors not closely related to our normal environment.

If you look at the items being measured in Table 12-5, you will note that they can be grouped into six clusters: (a) drug and alcohol abuse, (b) social maladjustment, (c) destructive tendencies, (d) personal inadequacy, (e) thought disorder, and (f) unusual preoccupations. These are the behaviors to which you should pay attention. They will help you make what is never an easy judgment—deciding when a behavior is abnormal enough to require professional help.

Table 12-5 **Symptoms of abnormal behavior**

SYMPTOM	BEHAVIOR	SYMPTOM	BEHAVIOR
SOCIAL INADEQUACY	Drug abuse	PERSONAL INADEQUACY	Lack of confidence
	Alcohol abuse		Extreme sensitivity
	Sexual deviation		Task incompetence
	Rejection of law		
	Family discord	PSYCHOTIC TENDENCIES	Phobias
	Personal neglect		Fanatically religious
	Dangerous to others		Bizarre sensory experiences
	Self-destructiveness		Lying
	Sadism		Paranoid thinking
			Manic behavior

REVIEW QUESTIONS

SECTION 1 (pages 361–367)
1. What is the "Medical Student Syndrome," and how can you avoid it?
2. Who is usually the first to judge that someone's behavior is abnormal?
3. Name three ways in which abnormality is defined and give an example of abnormality and normality according to each definition.
4. What are three signs that may indicate the need for professional help?

SECTION 2 (pages 367–372)
1. What were the earliest modern systems of classifying mental illnesses?
2. Give some reasons for not using a specific label in identifying someone as abnormal.

3. What two procedures should be included in a full diagnosis of psychological problems?

SECTION 3 (pages 372–381)
1. What are two characteristics of mild behavioral disorders?
2. In what ways are anxiety disorders and phobias "abnormal?"
3. What is meant by a somatoform disorder? Give three examples.
4. Describe the different types of dissociative disorders.

SECTION 4 (pages 382–387)
1. Why is it difficult to make a precise diagnosis of many psychotic disorders?
2. Explain what is meant by "affective disorders." List three specific types.

3. Name the different forms of schizophrenia and describe some symptoms shared by all schizophrenias.

4. What are some suspected causes of schizophrenia?

SECTION 5 (pages 387–388)

1. Describe some personality disorders.

2. What are some characteristics of an antisocial personality?

ACTIVITIES

1. Dress for school in an unusual way for one day. For example, try wearing a suit, or perhaps sandals and white socks. In a brief essay, summarize people's reactions to the change in your clothing.

2. For one day, try changing the way you customarily greet people. For example, if you are usually quiet, give everyone a cheery hello. Describe any changes in the way people react to the "new you."

3. Try another test of the effects of your behavior on others. When you're talking with a friend, stare at your friend's ear instead of looking him or her in the eye. Does this seem to make your friend nervous? What response do you get?

4. Choose a criminal whose crime made him nationally known (such as John Hinckley, who attempted to assassinate President Ronald Reagan) and who was subsequently diagnosed as mentally ill. In an essay, recount all you can find out about the behavior that brought about the diagnosis.

5. **Career Search.** If your community has a psychiatric center, invite a psychiatric nurse to class to describe the types of behavior that require hospitalization and what criteria are used for diagnosis.

INTERESTED IN MORE?

ALDINE, V. M. *Dibs: In Search of Self.* Ballantine, 1976. A paperback describing the life of a seriously disturbed boy, his behavior, and how psychotherapy helps him.

CAMPBELL, R., et al. *The Enigma of the Mind.* Time-Life Books, 1976. Part of the "Human Behavior" series, this paperback focuses on the environment, causes, and treatment of abnormal behavior.

COLEMAN, J. C. *Abnormal Psychology and Modern Life*, 5th ed. Scott, Foresman, 1976. Analyzes the factors—biological, psychosocial, and sociocultural—that cause mental illness. Assesses the methods used to treat abnormal behavior.

DAVISON, G. C. & NEALE, J. M. *Abnormal Psychology.* John Wiley, 1978. A well-written introduction to the basic issues and conditions surrounding abnormal behavior, including social problems. Includes a discussion of treatment.

FREUD, S. *Psychopathology of Everyday Life.* W. W. Norton and Co., Inc., 1971. You may be surprised to find that Freud is a delight to read. Here he analyzes everyday behavior (such as slips of the tongue and dreams) from the psycho-analytic perspective.

MEHR, J. *Abnormal Psychology.* Holt, Rinehart & Winston, 1983. A detailed, well-illustrated text that describes abnormal behaviors and how they relate to normal, everyday behavior.

SCHREIBER, R. F. *Sybil.* Henry Regnery, 1973. The story of a woman with multiple identities. Her problem is unusual, but the treatment is typical.

SIZEMORE, C. C. & PITTILLO, E. S. *I'm Eve.* Doubleday, 1977. The incredible life story of the woman about whom *The Three Faces of Eve* was written. Tells of other personalities she later experienced and their impact on her life.

STONE, S. & STONE, A. *Abnormal Personality Through Literature.* Prentice-Hall, 1966. A paperback describing various mental illnesses, with examples from literature.

THIGPEN, C. H. & CLECKLEY, H. M. *The Three Faces of Eve.* Doubleday, 1957. The book behind the movie. Focuses on "Eve's" early life and the problems of her triple personality.

ULLMAN, L. P. & KRASNER, L. *Psychological Approach to Abnormal Behavior,* 2nd ed. Prentice-Hall, 1975. This behavioral (learning-based) approach contrasts with Freud's *Psychopathology.* Shows how reinforcement and punishment can influence even severely abnormal behavior.

ZAX, M. & COWEN, E. L. *Abnormal Psychology: Changing Conceptions,* 2nd ed. Holt, Rinehart & Winston, 1976. Uses an historical approach to compare and contrast theories of abnormal behavior. Includes a discussion of electroshock treatment and mental health movements.

CHAPTER OUTLINE

WHAT'S THE ANSWER?

☐ *Are the gold stars given to children for good work in school, or as rewards at home toward their weekly allowance, related to any form of therapy?*

☐ It's been 20 years or more since a new large state mental hospital has been built in the United States or Canada. The result is that such facilities are often quite old. *Why is this occurring? Do North American governments no longer care about the treatment of those with abnormal behavior problems?*

☐ "How can it be? I made a deal with my girlfriend. She thought I was gaining too much weight, and I thought she was beginning to look a little plump, too. So we agreed that if I lost ten percent of my body weight and she lost ten percent of her body weight, we'd go to the Senior Ball together. I had to lose 20 pounds, but she had to lose 15."

"So? What's your problem, Jack?"

"Everything was great at first. I love to eat, but I jumped out to an early lead in our race. It was no trouble to keep from eating. But the longer I went with such a strict diet, the tougher it got. And then the dance started drawing closer. She lost more weight, and I *really* started getting worried. Now the date for the dance is almost here, and I'm really getting nervous. I just can't seem to keep from eating. What's wrong with me?" *What is wrong here? What theory of conflict can best explain what is happening? Is there anything that can be done to help this person achieve his goal?*

Psychotherapy was originally designed as a one-to-one relationship between patient and therapist. Now much therapy is accomplished in groups, such as this one, in which a nonthreatening environment encourages people to share their problems under the guidance of skilled personnel.

1 Models of Abnormal Behavior

We start this chapter with a problem. We've talked about many different theories of personality and the wide range of mental disorders that can occur. It seems natural now to review the various treatments or therapies that are being used to "cure" or control the various abnormal behavior patterns. But it's not that easy, and therein lies our problem.

Abnormal behavior has *many* different causes. If you have a behavior disorder, the theory of personality selected by your therapist has a direct impact on what he or she will identify as the "cause" of your problem. Likewise, which theory your therapist selects also largely dictates the form of therapy that will be used. Let's go back through that one part at a time to show you the "problems."

Multiple causes

Inherited/biological factors. There are several inherited or biological factors that influence your behavior. These would include the *genetic messages* inherited from your parents. One study of genetic factors and schizophrenia reported that among 24 pairs of identical twins, if one twin was diagnosed schizophrenic, 42 percent of the time the other later experienced the same disorder. For 33 pairs of fraternal twins, this happened only 9 percent of the time. Genetic messages also cause differences in our biochemistry. There is indirect evidence that the excessive presence of *dopamine* in the central nervous system leads to schizophrenic-like behavior. Unusually low levels of the neurotransmitters serotonin, norepinephrine, and dopamine may be involved.

Of course, there are other biochemical factors, including hormones. We saw earlier that certain physiological factors such as nutritional and vitamin deficits can seriously influence our behavior. So can other essentially physiological stresses, such as isolation for long periods of time in solitary confinement.

Psychological factors. There are three major groups of psychological or environmental factors that can affect your behavior. For instance, *developmental* events may affect you even in the first year of life—problems in feeding, or stressful patterns of behavior by your mother. The early childhood years—according to some theories and research—are especially critical ones for normal development. And problems you first experience as a child may cause later problems. The worst effects of these early difficulties may not be felt until late adolescence or even full adulthood.

A second set of psychological factors are *family* pressures and events. You control some of these; others you don't. You don't control the order in which you are born into your family, nor do you control your family's ultimate size. If you're an only child, you gain certain social and interpersonal skills. But what if you are the fourth-born with three older brothers who are four, seven, and ten years old when you arrive? Obviously, your social training would be very different. The patterns of communication

The family life you experience as a child is a strong factor in your psychological development and in your chances for good mental health.

developed and used within your family also influence your adult behavior. Suppose one of your parents tells you how much you are loved, but always seems too busy to work or play or learn with you. If you are constantly subjected to "mixed signals," it may have adverse effects on your adult personality.

Finally, throughout our adult life we are all constantly subjected to *conflicts and stresses* over which we may have very little, if any, control. The effects of these stressors upon ourselves depends on our genetic make-up, our childhood successes and failures, and our most recent experiences. A specific event such as a frustration may vary widely in its impact upon us depending upon our current emotional balance.

Cultural factors. Finally, there is a third set of factors that influence our likelihood of showing abnormal behavior. These cultural factors are less personal, less controllable, less immediate, and generally more permanent aspects of our environment. Your *age* is one good example of such a factor. You're probably a late teenager right now. You'll change with age, but very little this week or next. The social class of your parents or your beliefs about religion will not be easily or quickly changed either. Yet, the beliefs and expectations of others about individuals who are teenagers, or males, or females, and so forth will affect your behavior and your mental health.

Models for change

There are two major groupings of factors that are the most widely cited in explaining behavior—both normal and abnormal: the *medical* model and the *psychological* model. Let's review the important parts of each model of abnormal behavior.

Medical model. Suppose you smash your foot against a leg of your desk. Anxiously you look down but see no broken skin; then, suddenly, your second toe HURTS. When you lift your foot, it hangs down toward the floor. It hurts even worse if you try to wiggle it. Very simply, you—and a bit later, your doctor—assume you've broken your toe.

This is a situation in which an external behavior—a dependent variable or response, if you will—is "determined," or explained, by an internal cause. The underlying assumption is a simple (medical) one: If a symptom shows up, then there is an internal cause of that symptom. And therapy is quite simple: Find that internal cause, fix it, and the symptom will go away because the "cause" has gone away. In this model abnormal behavior is viewed as an illness. Professionals who use such a theory as the basis for treating abnormal behaviors refer to people with problems as "patients"—just as a medical doctor does. Wouldn't Freud's theory of psychoanalysis qualify as being based on a medical model? Of course. But there's another and very different view.

Psychological model. Let's suppose that "abnormal" behavior is learned. Let's continue to suppose that we can learn new responses—from eyeblinks to word lists. Now extend that logic to offer an explanation for abnormal behavior. In short, let's assume that we *learn* to behave abnormally.

This *is* a very different view. For instance, people believing in this model would feel that there is not an internal cause, but rather that the behavior itself *is* the abnormality. Change the behavior and you've solved the problem—*if* you have changed the behavior back into the normal, acceptable range. Therapy, then, is very different too. Now our goal is to change the reinforcers so as to reinforce those behaviors we want the client (note the change in terminology?) to exhibit. Treat the symptom(s) and you've treated the problem. If you think back to the theories of personality you've studied, these two models were obvious everywhere.

Resolution? As you might suspect, there is strong disagreement among people endorsing each of these models. What if someone came in to a therapist wanting a cure for the tendency to bite fingernails?—his or her own, of course! A medical-model therapist would assume there was an internal problem that was showing up as fingernail biting. That therapist would help the patient look for, identify, and understand the internal stresses.

A therapist endorsing the psychological model would take a very different approach. He or she would be concerned with what reinforcers are maintaining the behavior. Once identified, they could be changed, *or* more powerful reinforcers could be implemented to increase the frequency of other more desirable behaviors. Using this approach, the medical-model therapist would be sure the internal cause would simply show up as a different symptom (symptom substitution). The psychological-model therapist would assume the behavior, once cured, was just that—cured.

How does theory affect therapy?

By now the answer to that question is probably obvious. There are two major views, as there have been in many of the psychological processes we've studied so far, as to the actual cause(s) of mental disorders. The therapist's views on this determine how he or she will perform psychotherapy. Moreover, which theory of personality is endorsed will also affect the choice of psychotherapy. Table 13-1 lists the types of mental health professionals who can offer psychotherapy as well as the types of therapy they are typically best trained to perform.

Different abnormalities are best treated in different ways. Some therapies are best with milder disorders. Other therapies—and sometimes other assumptions about cause—are more effective in handling more severe forms of mental disorder.

Therapy format

Group versus individual. The original forms of psychotherapy (for instance, psychoanalysis) were designed entirely to involve one therapist and one patient. But that can be very expensive. The pressures of expense were among several that aided the development of forms of therapy that could treat several people at once. It was cheaper, but it also had some other benefits.

Alcoholics Anonymous is a good example of such a program. It offers group support and understanding. It provides group pressure to keep the person aware of and trying to exercise control over his or her problem. It provides a nonthreatening environment that encourages each person to share problems, fears, successes, and failures.

Table 13-1 **Mental health professionals: title, training, and task**

TITLE	TRAINING AND TASK
CLINICAL PSYCHOLOGIST	Doctoral degree (Ph.D) in psychology involving 3-5 years of graduate school followed by a one-year supervised internship (mental hospital or other clinic) involving additional research and/or clinical experience. Uses talking and social learning/behavioral therapies.
COUNSELING PSYCHOLOGIST	One-year internship in counseling situation (e.g., marital or family). Uses same therapies as clinical psychologist.
PSYCHIATRIST	Doctoral (M.D.) degree involving 4 years plus 1 year internship and up to 3 years of residency—the primary source of training in mental disorders. Mainly uses physical therapies.
PSYCHOANALYST	Doctoral (Ph.D. or M.D.) degree and extensive training in psychoanalytic theory/practice including the psychoanalysis of the therapist him-herself. Relies on psychoanalysis, often combined with other therapies according to training.
PSYCHIATRIC NURSE	Usually includes a bachelor's (R.N.) degree involving special training with mental patients. Supervised services, often in hospital setting.
(PSYCHIATRIC) SOCIAL WORKER	Master's (M.A. or M.S.W.) degree involving 1-2 years of graduate work, often including some supervised training in social service programs. Usually deals with people in their home.
PSYCHIATRIC AIDE	No formal academic training is necessary beyond high school, although an Associate of Arts (A.A.) degree is now offered by some colleges for general training/experience in mental health. Work limited to supervised direct contact with inpatients.
PARAPROFESSIONAL	Mature and well-adjusted people are now being trained to provide specific services under direct supervision, especially in crisis intervention (e.g., crisis hotline) situations. No formal education necessary.

A team approach. One response to the problem of choosing personnel has been to develop a team approach. A treatment team might be composed of a neurologist, a psychiatrist, a clinical psychologist, and perhaps a counseling psychologist and a psychiatric nurse. The range of talents and experiences represented by such a team greatly increases the diversity of treatments that can be offered to a client or patient. But it can also be a very expensive approach.

exude p
tion. (2
your th
are try
genuine
in his
"expert
therapi

consist:
shock,
which :
of chilc
tered t
client c

Soc
the

So
vironm
we lea
behave
ogist's
simply
ent ev

Sy:
noted
can't t
anxiou
ious, v
Let
proced
things
thinkir
tests—
listed.
to the
gives y

patients do seem to improve. For others, the shoc
render the person more receptive to other forms of

Several different sources may be used to cause t
instance, *Electroconvulsive Shock (ECS)* involves :
powerful electric current through the brain. The sl
massive neuronal firing and body convulsions. *Insi*
is another, even less frequently used way of proc
Such an injection will put a person into insulin sh
its more severe forms, also involves convulsions.

Chemotherapy. You've probably taken aspirir
drug to relieve cold or allergy symptoms or for ot
That's *chemotherapy*—the use of drugs to treat un'
toms. Chemotherapy for psychological problems is
use of drugs to cure physical ills, except the syr
"treated" are behavioral or emotional.

The difficulty with drugs—and an objection
against them—is that they don't usually solve p
may make the problems seem to go away, and th
the anxiety caused by problems, but they don't s
lems themselves. Some drugs, then, are most freq
solve temporary problems such as anxiety assoc
proaching final exams or getting married. The dar
is that drug reliance will simply be substitutec
problem was previously causing the difficulties.

Are there benefits to using drugs? Yes. Such n
increase reaction to other forms of therapy. They
the intensity of many symptoms. They have als
duced the number of persons residing in mental

Surgery. Surgery as a therapy is often the tr
choice. Use of surgery in order to create behavi
never been in wide favor. As our knowledge of tl
organization improves, our use of surgery may pc
Nowadays surgery is limited almost entirely to
tumors or blockages that are influencing normal
ing. *Lobotomy*, once used to calm violent patiel
vering the front portion of the brain from inte
centers. It is occasionally used now in termir
people who are suffering unbearable pain.

Talking therapies

These are a very diverse lot of psychothera
number of differing assumptions. They make di
on the therapist and client alike, and they o
techniques. If you were to agree to undergo one

Mental health clinics often use the team approach to diagnose and treat clients. The personnel discussing a patient here include a neurologist, a psychiatrist, a clinical psychologist, and a social worker.

Offering psychotherapy. In the sections to follow we'll examine three different forms of psychotherapy in this order. First, *physical* therapies assume there are internal causes of mental disorder and that these causes are often physiological. Thus, these forms of therapy may involve shock, drugs, or even, in extreme cases, surgery. Second, the *talking* therapies are of two types. Some assume the medical model view of behavior, others assume the psychological model view. These are therapies that stress the correction of mental disorders by talking about them. Finally, the *social learning and behavioral* therapies assume mainly the psychological model view of mental disorder.

In review . . .

At least three possible causes of abnormal behavior can be identified: inherited or biological factors, psychological or learned factors, and cultural factors. There are two major models to explain abnormal behavior: the medical model and the psychological model. A psychotherapist chooses therapy based mainly on which theory of personality he or she endorses.

2 Forms of P⁣

What is psychot

Psychotherapy
therapy is the use c
of mental or behav

At the time of t
1692-3, abnormal l
thought to be due
possession of the a
that view.

In 1792 Pinel s
patients in hospitα
treat the mentally

More recently,
titled *A Mind Tha*
years he spent in
The horrors he de
the modern menta

Finally, World
large number of
given—psychologic
first time a federal
ioral problems as
achieve that treat⁣
tion of the forms

Physical thera⁣

Obviously, the
for each disorder.
for use mainly ir
marily psychiatri⁣
medical procedur
forms are much ı
are a mild form
tion drugs adds
therapies—in the
form of therapy.

Shock. The
patient's physiol
This may lead to
and then a perio
largely unknown

psychotherapy: *the use of psychological techniques for the treatment of mental or behavioral disorders*

A "behavior modification" teaching box is supposed to help keep a child's attention from wandering.

implosive therapy: *a counterconditioning therapy in which great amounts of anxiety are aroused and "conquered"*

contingency contracting: *an operant conditioning technique in which the behavioral goal is spelled out and steps toward its achievement are rewarded*

token economy: *an operant conditioning technique in which tokens are used to reward proper behavior*

In the final portion of this therapy, you go back to the items on your list of test-taking fears and start with the least anxiety-causing stimulus. Your therapist will have you continue to think about that stimulus, but if you start feeling tense, you're instructed to practice relaxing. Eventually what happens is that whatever stimuli—whatever aspects of test-taking—made you nervous become counterconditioned (unlearned). These stimuli now cause you to relax. You emit a response that is incompatible with the anxiety that tests once aroused in you. Moreover, your self-concept actually seems to improve. You've mastered a fear!

Implosive therapy also relies on counterconditioning, but it's not a therapy for the "faint of heart." It relies on arousing a tremendous amount of anxiety and then pointing out to the client that neither the worry nor the source of the anxiety had any ill effects.

Operant therapies. Operant therapies emphasize the results of behavior—that is, the reinforcements that can be gained. They rely on positive reinforcers and shaping techniques, as shown in Box 13-2.

One interesting use of these principles involves *contingency contracting*. This is the principle influencing any child who "earns" an allowance. The contract exists between family members (or between client and therapist). Conditions to be met are spelled out, as are the reinforcements to be gained for the contracted behavior. For instance, contingency contracting can be used to reduce marital discord by listing the responsibilities of each partner in areas causing difficulties. Another example of contracting involves an agreement with oneself. Keeping track of your own behavior is called *charting*. Evaluation of your own performance and reinforcing yourself are both necessary to achieve success with this procedure.

Another system of therapy involves setting up a *token economy*. The important element is having a token (for instance, poker chips, M & M candies, or something else) that can easily be awarded for proper behavior. These systems rely on the secondary reinforcing qualities of the tokens. The method works best when a parent or therapist has absolute control over the reinforcers so that the rules of the economy system can be enforced. Clients or mental hospital patients must make the link between gaining tokens and being able to turn them in for desired things. Once it's realized that an extra dessert, the opportunity to play with special toys or games, a trip to movies, or the like can be earned, changes in behavior often begin to occur rapidly. Such therapeutic programs have been used in treating a wide range of behaviors, from simple problems in reading to

| Feature | 13–2   **THERAPIST-POWER** |

Dr. Z: Well, Clarissa, what was it that you wanted to talk with me about?

C: Well . . . It's hard to put it in words . . . I guess just the way I've been feeling lately . . . (pause) . . .

Dr. Z: I'm not sure I understand. How have you been feeling?

C: Well . . . confused, I guess. And sort of hopeless about college. I start thinking about whether I want to go or not and get so bogged down. . . . (pause) . . .

Dr. Z: So you think about it some, and that gets you worrying. What do you do then . . . once you're worrying about it?

C: Well . . . I do something else . . . to take my mind off it. Like watching TV or calling my boyfriend. Just anything to get it out of my mind.

Dr. Z: I guess in the short run that helps you handle it . . . you can stop yourself from worrying about the decision when you think about it. But I wonder it if really helps you in the long run?

C: I'd never looked at it that way, but I guess you're right. I can stop myself from worrying when I stop thinking about it, but that way I never think about it enough to make the decision . . . so it's always there to worry some more about later.

Dr. Z: That's exactly what I meant. So can you see a way to handle the decision that will involve less worrying?

C: I think so . . . I just need to get it over with . . . I mean really think it out and decide. I've been avoiding it and that's been keeping me worried.

Dr. Z: I think you're right on target.

C: But, whew! It's such a big decision! I may not worry as much once I've decided, but I sure am gonna be worrying when I sit down to do it!

Dr. Z: Well, it seems to me you need some systematic way of trying to decide, because it *is* a big decision with lots of different sides to it.

C: Yeah . . . some organized way to think it through, but how?

Dr. Z: One thing you might try is to simply list out all the pros and cons you can think of . . . that way you can take everything into consideration, and weigh it out . . .

C: That makes sense! I'll give it a try!

This is behavioral therapy. Notice that Dr. Z plays an active role in leading the client from problem to solution. It's more task-oriented than is person-centered therapy. It focuses on the problem at hand, without being so concerned with internal feelings of worry.

some forms of schizophrenia. Of course, there may be a problem in keeping clients from backsliding once they are no longer earning tokens for their desirable behaviors.

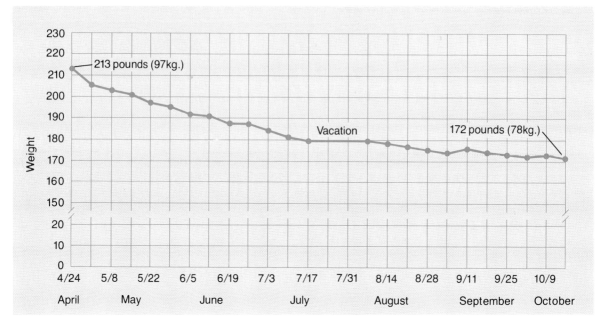

Figure 13-1 An example of charting. Starting on April 24th at a weight of 213 pounds (97 kg.), this person started plotting his weight as he got up each morning. In just under six months, his weight dropped to 172 pounds (78 kg.), a loss of 41 pounds (19 kg.)

The **question:** Are the gold stars used in school and at home with children related to any form of therapy?

The **answer:** Most definitely, yes. The gold stars, and the allowance given to children by their parents for household tasks performed or behavior maintained or exhibited under certain circumstances are both "tokens." These are unimportant in themselves except for the fact that they can usually be swapped for things—for higher grades in school, for time with a favorite game, for a trip to a movie, for additional food in a mental hospital, for savings or new stereo equipment at home—whatever is desired by the person earning the tokens. These tokens are an obvious representation of the kinds of reinforcements on which much of society works. Sometimes people with behavior problems need to be reminded of what is obvious to most of us—that good behavior gains us things we desire. So the gold stars are "tokens," or secondary reinforcers, that can be swapped for things that are important to anyone participating in such a system.

Cognitive therapies. Evidence is growing that much human behavior *is* voluntarily controlled, and that we do often retain an ability to correct the "problems in living" that we may experience.

One example of new forms of therapy that emphasize cognitive aspects is Albert Ellis' *Rational Emotive Therapy* (or RET).

Ellis assumes the client is rational and able to control his or her thoughts and behavior. In RET, three steps are examined: A is the *activating* experience—you flunked a test. C is the *conse-*quences, emotional and behavioral—you go to your room, become depressed, and feel your self-esteem drop disastrously. B is your *belief* about A—if you loved the subject, you feel depressed; if you hated the subject, you could even feel relieved. Ellis says A does *not* cause C. Rather, B causes C; beliefs cause the consequences. As a therapist, Ellis works to convince you that abnormal behavior results from faulty thinking (cognitive) processes. Correct the thinking and you've corrected the behaviors.

Which theory is right? Maybe all of them. Notice how the last several theories (except RET) strike somewhat of a balance between the biologically determined views of a psychoanalyst and the environmentally based views of the traditional learning theorist. The newer theories and therapies recognize the joint impact of both biology and environment. However, they stress that each of us maintains rational control of our own life.

Rational Emotive Therapy (RET): *a cognitive therapy devised by Ellis in which the therapist challenges the client's irrational beliefs*

13-3 **"A SUPERFLUOUS SUPEREGO AND OTHER PROBLEMS IN LEARNING TO LOVE YOUR THERAPIST"**

Here's a problem that might not have occurred to you. You're a *very* aggressive person. In fact, you've decided you're so aggressive that it would be a good idea to visit a psychotherapist. But what kind do you choose?

What if you and your concerns about being aggressive run headlong into a Rational Emotive Therapist—one who actively *tells* you in no uncertain terms that *your* thinking is wrong? Well? Are you going to sit there and take that? No, it's not likely.

The problem here—and it *is* one—is a mismatch between client and therapist. It happens. In fact it happens often enough that in the 1970s people began to study the results of different choices. We can now offer tentative advice on what kind of client and behavior problem can best be handled by what kind of psychotherapist.

For instance, person-centered therapy works better with introverted clients than with extroverted clients. The reverse is true for Rational Emotive Therapy. By contrast, systematic desensitization works equally well with both types. In the treatment of mild disorders, clients tend to improve with both psychodynamic kinds of therapy and behavioral therapies, but in different ways. Psychodynamic therapy is most effective with patients having higher income, more intelligence, and more education, who are younger and married. On the other hand, patients with behavioral abnormalities may be better treated with behavioral therapies. The behavioral therapies seem to work fairly successfully with a much greater variety of clients.

Now, what kind of therapy would you choose?

3 Conflict—A Theoretical Analysis

Now let's take one common human problem with which we all have to deal. Let's review that problem—conflict—in terms of how each theory interprets it. We'll then look at the various therapies that each theory suggests.

Trait theory

This section is easy. Trait theories, such as Sheldon's, don't deal directly with conflict. Such theories don't offer specific suggestions for change to conquer conflict.

Psychodynamic theories

Conflict is a central part of these theories of personality. In psychoanalysis, the balance struck between the life instincts and the death instincts is rooted in conflict. The balance of psychic energy struck among the id, ego, and superego is at heart a conflict. Conflict is stirred, according to Freud, by instinctual urges fighting with the sources of punishment and guilt buried within us.

One form of therapy encourages children to "act out" their anger as an aid to relieving behavioral symptoms.

How are we to solve or control these conflicts? Freud suggested the defense mechanisms. Their main goal is to satisfy the instincts while reducing—or, if we're lucky, avoiding—the punishment and guilt. If we express our instinctive urges, we'll often be punished by society for breaking its laws. If we recognize those instinctive urges and never act, we feel guilty.

And the therapy? As we learned some pages back, psychoanalysis tries to get the patient to review earlier moments in life. It attempts to increase his or her understanding of the urges within. In theory, this will then release the psychic energy that was previously devoted to controlling earlier psycho-sexual conflicts.

Social learning/behavioral theory

One of the best theoretical treatments of conflict explains its operations in terms of five basic assumptions, listed in Table 13-2. Using these assumptions, we can identify several common forms of conflict with which we all must deal day by day.

Approach-approach. Suppose you've just dropped your coins into a food machine. You can't decide between an apple and a sandwich. That's really conflict in name only. There's no

Table 13-2 **Social learning/behavioral theory assumptions about conflict**

ASSUMPTION	EXPLANATION
APPROACH GRADIENT	Our tendency to *approach* a positive goal or stimulus *increases* as we get nearer to it.
AVOIDANCE GRADIENT	Our tendency to *avoid* a negative stimulus or goal also *increases* as we get nearer to it.
RELATIVE INTENSITY	Our tendency to avoid increases faster than our tendency to approach as we get nearer the goal or stimulus.
DRIVE LEVEL	Increasing our drive level (or level of arousal) associated with a goal will increase the overall tendencies to approach and/or avoid the goal.
CONFLICT	When conflict exists between two response tendencies (either to approach or to avoid), the stronger of the two tendencies will occur.

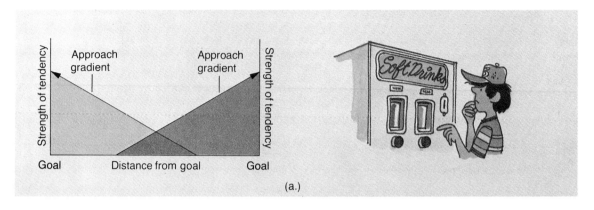

(a.)

Figure 13-2A An approach-approach conflict.

reason to avoid either one, as seen in Figure A. As soon as you start leaning toward (preferring) one or the other, the approach gradient will take over and you will approach (select) whichever you desire at the moment.

Approach-avoidance. You've been gaining weight recently, so you decide to go on a diet. So far, so good, but the thing that made you gain was your love of eating. If you've been on your diet just a week, you will still be faced with an approach-avoidance conflict when you sit down to eat. As diagrammed in Figure B, the approach tendency is to eat; the avoidance tendency is to cut down on the food you're eating. You will experience the point of maximum conflict when the tendency to approach is exactly countered by an equal tendency to avoid. At that point you will show indecision ... Should I eat? Or shouldn't I eat?

Figure 13-2B An approach-avoidance conflict.

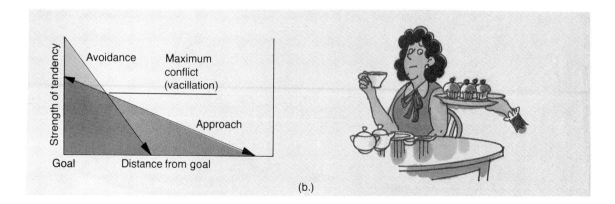

(b.)

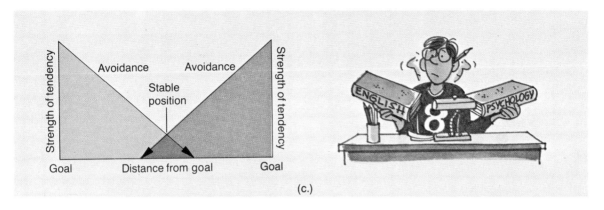

Figure 13-2C An avoidance-avoidance conflict.

Avoidance-avoidance.   Suppose you had to study for both a psychology and an English exam, as seen in Figure C. If you were doing poorly in both courses, then you might want to avoid both of them. In this conflict you'd tend to remain about halfway between the two decisions. Here we often see a response called "leaving the field." Are you having tests in both psychology and English? Do you need to study for both? Well, let's go to a movie! ... It's called "caught 'twixt the devil and the deep blue sea"!

Multiple approach-avoidance.   This is a very common conflict. Suppose you want to buy a car. You have two choices, and each has strengths and weaknesses. One car is cheap to run but looks terrible; the other is expensive but good-looking. If you choose one of them, you lose the other—a common problem when faced with a double approach-avoidance problem.

Figure 13-2D A multiple approach-avoidance conflict.

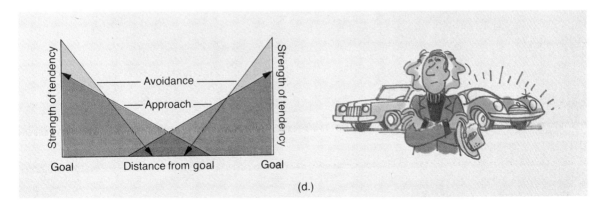

State and County Mental Hospital Patients per 100,000 Population

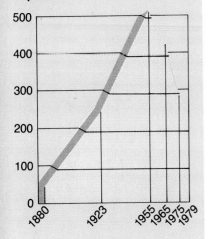

Source: *Statistical Abstract of the United States*

Figure 13-3 Since shortly after the development and widespread availability of tranquilizers, the number of patients being housed in state and county mental hospitals has been dropping steadily. The trend started just after World War II in 1945 and continued through 1979, the last year for which figures are available.

What therapy would be used in this situation? In addition to aiding a client in understanding the sources of his or her conflict, a therapist would attempt to reduce the drive level or desire associated with each choice. Although the conflict may still be experienced, it wouldn't be so intense.

Person-centered theory

Conflict plays an unusual role in Carl Rogers' person-centered theory. You may perceive your *self* as being happy and carefree. Conflict—called *incongruence* by Rogers—may be encountered when you notice through your experiences that you are really feeling sad, and that your perception of being carefree is only a way of protecting yourself from hurt.

Rogers' theory describes a search for authenticity as an attempt to resolve any such conflict. For Rogers, therapy is a place where it is safe to explore our genuine feelings and experience them appropriately. When our experience is consistent with our feelings, and we are able to communicate those feelings, "congruence" has been achieved.

In review . . .

The third class of psychotherapies is the most diverse. These are the social learning and behavioral therapies, including systematic desensitization and implosive therapy. Other such therapies include operant therapies, cognitive therapies, and psychodynamic therapies. One social-learning theory has developed a number of principles for analyzing and controlling conflict situations. Person-centered therapists help people avoid conflict situations.

Think about it

The **question:** We noted at the start of the chapter that large state mental institutions are no longer being built. Do North American governments no longer care about the treatment of those with abnormal behavior problems?

The **answer:** No. Rather, the type of treatment that is being offered is now more than just custodial. When mental patients were simply being cared for before tranquilizers were available, it was thought necessary to have large (efficient) treatment facilities. The more modern use of tranquilizers and the emphasis on community mental health centers and preventative mental health measures have markedly reduced the need for large mental institutions. Changes in the nature of therapy itself are responsible for the change in the nature of the institutions being used.

4 Evaluation of Therapies

Common elements

The major underlying element common to all therapeutic techniques is the recognition that human behavior *can* be changed. The means for changing behavior may vary, but not the most basic assumption that the task is achievable. Another similarity is that client and therapist are seeking information about the source of a problem and/or how best to change abnormal behavior. From this knowledge, ways to alter behavior are developed.

Other factors. The following elements occur widely enough to be thought of as common to all forms of therapy:

(1) *Acceptance* by the therapist of the client as a human. The client is valued as a person and is provided assistance in solving a behavioral problem. The only exception to this is the Rational Emotive therapist, who accepts the client as a person but actively rejects the client's faulty beliefs.

(2) *Guidance* is offered by the therapist in seeking the source of the difficulties and/or changing the abnormal or troublesome behavior.

(3) The psychotherapist maintains *encouraging detachment*. The therapist is accepting of you as a person, nonjudgmental of your actions, fears, dreams, and behaviors. The therapist is not emotionally involved in your despair or your concern with your problem. Again, the possible exception is the Rational Emotive therapist, who may be disagreeing violently with some of your beliefs.

⟶ Think about it

The **question**: We described someone who had made a bet with a good friend about losing weight. As time went on the person found it harder and harder to continue losing weight, and the more he tried the jumpier he got. How can this be explained? Can anything be done to get back on the track toward losing weight?

The **answer**: The behavioral theories seem to offer the most direct explanation for what's occurring here. Obviously, for the person described there is an approach-avoidance conflict situation. Eating has long been a favorite activity, so food is an attractive goal for him. Yet, losing the body weight is also an attractive goal. The thought of not being able to go to the dance with his girlfriend is boosting his motivation to try to achieve his half of the bargain. Thus, his drive level is steadily increasing.

The best favor he could do for himself would be to reduce his anxiety. He should tell his girlfriend that the bet is off. That will reduce the intensity of the approach-avoidance conflict he's experiencing, and let him concentrate more on the more important task of losing weight.

(4) Your psychotherapist is ethically bound to maintain a proper *social distance* from you. The client-therapist relationship is a professional one. In fact, the relationship between client and psychotherapist is governed by ethical and legal restrictions very similar to those that exist between patient and medical doctor.

(5) Finally, all of the psychotherapies assume psychotherapy is a *cognitive activity*. With the possible exception of certain operant-conditioning procedures, all therapies involve talking, thinking, verbal skills, and analysis.

Evaluation

Problems with evaluation. One of the continuing problems in evaluating the effectiveness of various forms of psychotherapy is an inability to identify an agreeable *basis for evaluation*. Should we judge by a client's own reports of improvement? Disappearance of symptoms? The efficiency of various therapeutic techniques?

Another problem involves *theoretical differences*. A behavioral therapist would be satisfied to show the removal or blockage of a symptom, whereas a psychoanalyst would feel that without the patient's gaining insight, the symptom must reappear.

A third problem is finding *objective judges*. Who can best judge the effectiveness of a therapy? The *client* may unconsciously want rapid or delayed recovery. No *therapist* would devote his or her life to a therapeutic technique and then

Many communities in the United States have established ''hotline'' centers, to which people experiencing mental stress can appeal for help. Such centers are instrumental in counseling potential suicides, people with drug-related problems, and others facing crisis situations. Some communities have established call-in services for children needing reassurance or aid while their parents are at work.

acknowledge it doesn't work. How about asking the patient/client's *family?* They may be the best judges because they will continue to live with the person and thus be able to detect a return to normal behavior.

Is psychotherapy effective?   Essentially, yes. After very pessimistic reports in the early 1960's about the apparent lack of effectiveness of traditional forms of psychotherapy, the results in the past decade have been much more encouraging. A new statistical technique called *meta-analysis* permits effective, controlled comparisons of therapy and non-therapy groups.

How effective is psychotherapy? First, as one psychologist has suggested, psychotherapy in almost any form is more effective than unplanned help or no help. Second, no particular technique seems consistently best in treating disorders; however, other psychologists would argue that more intense forms of therapy are most likely to lead to permanent improvements. Third, clients who show early improvement tend to retain that improvement. Finally, the personal characteristics of the client and the therapist and the nature of their interaction are more important than the form of psychotherapy; most effective is an *eclectic* approach in which these personal factors are all considered in choosing a form of therapy.

5 Mental Health

At this point we've spent almost three chapters talking about mental disorders from theory to therapy, yet these problems affect only a minority of people. Now it seems fitting to take a moment to mention mental health, which concerns all of us, and what we can do to maintain it.

What is
mental health?

What are the things a professional psychologist might look for in deciding if you *are* mentally healthy? There are at least seven factors that can be identified. These are listed with a brief description in Table 13-3 on the next page.

Today we are seeing more emphasis on mental health and on efforts designed to prevent emotional breakdowns. More emphasis is being given to psychology in high schools, and to education about mental health in the home, the school, and the community. Churches, in particular, are offering programs to help people handle problems and crises in their lives.

Table 13-3 **To be mentally healthy is to be . . .**

CHARACTERISTIC	HOW TO IDENTIFY IT
EFFECTIVE	Behavior is goal-directed, intended to reduce problem sources by direct attack. Attempts are made to overcome sources of tension and fear.
EFFICIENT	No time is wasted in meeting one's responsibilities. Undue effort is not spent on hopeless tasks. This leads to a savings of energy and effort used otherwise in erecting defenses to justify an inability to achieve what couldn't be achieved anyway. Use of energy thus becomes efficient.
APPROPRIATE	Thoughts, feelings, and actions are adjusted to situations and include a recognition of the age, level of maturity, and skills of another person. Fear, worry, and tension are experienced, but don't become the focus of all an individual's efforts.
FLEXIBLE	Adaptation is a key to mental health. When facing conflict or frustration, the person recognizes the problems and deals with them by seeking alternate routes or means to the goal.
ABLE TO LEARN	The mentally healthy person continually adjusts to his or her environment and profits from each experience. There is no intent to commit the same mistake over and over again, but rather to adjust behavior in light of past experience.
INTERPERSONALLY EFFECTIVE	Can deal successfully with other people; such a person strikes an appropriate balance between give and take—yielding neither to personal greed nor the whims of others.
SELF-SECURE	Has a firm sense of self and of security based on realistic assessment of strengths and weaknesses.

(Adapted from Coleman, 1975, pp. 48-49.)

The personnel. Psychology is now among the most popular subjects offered in college, and greatly increased numbers of people are taking graduate training. These students, as they complete their work, are moving out into the community and increasing the breadth and depth of psychological services that are available. In addition—parallel with efforts in medicine—*paraprofessionals* are being used in supervised roles in counseling, in telephone advice services, and in a widening range of public outlets.

▒▒▒▒▒▒   In review . . .

All psychotherapies share in common the assumption that behavior can be changed and that the therapist and patient/client are interested in a common "problem." Evaluating the success of psychotherapy is difficult because of the problem of defining the basis for evaluation, the differences among various theories, and the difficulty of finding impartial judges of success. Our current definition of "mental health" is undergoing change in the places, the processes, and the personnel assisting in achieving it.

───

How should you handle frustration?

Even with relatively good mental health many of us behave in certain ways that don't really do us much good. At times these behaviors can even be self-destructive. One feeling that often provokes unusual behavior in ordinary situations is that of frustration.

We spoke earlier about the many different forms of frustration with which we must deal. The "frustration" may actually be something beyond our control. Sometimes we simply feel frustrated internally, but at other times we act frustrated—angry, withdrawn, stressed. What is our most likely response? Unless we're prepared for the frustration, we are inclined to fight back, to be aggressive. However, there are several better responses we could make. Following are some suggestions as to how you can handle the problem of frustration when you face it.

Channel the aggression. Aggression isn't a very effective response to frustration. Rather, the energy being spent on aggression should be redirected. Seek additional help. For instance, if you have a big job to be done and a fast-approaching deadline, then contact some friends and get the extra help you need to get the task finished. Sometimes frustration comes because we're "too close" to the problem. The old saying of "not being able to see the forest for the trees" applies here. If someone insults you, it's quite "natural" to want to lash back, but pause for a moment first and ask yourself what led that person to insult you. "Counting to ten before screaming" has much the same effect. It allows you a moment to consider a more rational plan of action.

Work around anxiety. Defense mechanisms are usually bad, especially if they encourage you to continue your day-to-day activities without assessing the cause of your problem. However, as a means of dealing with occasional frustrations, the defense mechanisms may have something to recommend them. For instance, *rationalization* involves justifying your actions somehow in such a way that you don't feel guilty about the way you're behaving. If such behavior is not at the expense of others, then rationalizing what you are doing to keep from being frustrated may yield mental health, without qualifying you as mildly disordered.

The same logic can also be applied to *compensation*. In certain situations, when we realize our shortcomings—and those usually *are* frustrating—it may cause us to try all the harder to achieve and excel in another activity. In that sense, if frustration leads to compensating activity in another arena, no damage is done and considerable progress can result.

Withdrawal with a difference. A third way to respond to frustration is to back away. *Flexibility* in achieving one's goals may often yield far greater returns than rigid adherence to what may later prove to be the wrong set of intentions. Finally, if it is true that your progress toward a legitimate goal has been blocked, then frustration might be the logical response. But it may be a lot wiser to look for alternative paths by which to achieve the desired goal. Are your parents forbidding marriage right now? Consider enrolling in the same college as your boy- or girlfriend, or one nearby. It'll get you educated, keep you together, and allow you to share a lot more experiences with which to demonstrate to parents and self alike that the love *is* genuine. Make a short-term sacrifice for a long-range gain. We're probably the only organism in existence that really understands that concept.

In review . . .

Frustration is one feeling that can cause certain behaviors, which sometimes can be self-destructive. In attempting to handle it in our daily problems of living, aggression, itself, is not an effective response. But frustration can be reduced by channeling the aggression into new compensating activities, and working around the anxiety and the tension created. Maintaining a flexible approach to life's problems may be a better response, and at the same time, a way of achieving one's goals with a minimum of frustration.

Chapter Application and Review

USING PSYCHOLOGY   *Some common problems*

In the text above we examined frustration, a problem that most of us experience many times in our lives. Here we'll discuss certain areas of mental health that are often of special concern to adolescents.

Daydreaming

First, let's consider daydreaming. Do you daydream? Daydreaming seems to be a carry-over from childhood. What exactly causes it? There are several possibilities. For one, despite your increasing skills, as an adolescent you sometimes may not be given responsibilities and challenges that match what you can do. The result is boredom and idle time on your hands. Any boring environment, at any age, is likely to encourage daydreaming. In addition, some adolescents may not have had a childhood that led to interpersonal contacts and the development of friendships. Encouraged to play alone, such children come to rely on self-generated activities, conversations, and imagined events.

The effects of daydreaming are fairly obvious. You seem to lose track of ongoing events, and fail to pay attention to your immediate environment. Too much daydreaming may lead you to rely too much on imaginary solutions to everyday problems. Dreams may be entertaining and self-serving, but they are not functional solutions.

What to do? First, reach a specific decision as to how much is an acceptable amount of daydreaming. Second, change the environment that leads to daydreaming. Where do you find yourself daydreaming more than you think you should? In your bedroom? Then study at the dining room table. In school? Then consider changing subjects or rearranging your study schedule. There's nothing wrong with an active imagination, but excessive daydreaming—if that becomes a problem—can be controlled.

Feelings of inferiority

Alfred Adler saw each of us as striving to overcome the weaknesses we perceive in ourselves. His was an optimistic revision of Freud's psychoanalytic theory. As children learning to talk we gain a certain control over our environment, and this sets a pattern of striving to conquer the feelings of inadequacy we all share. However, if not controlled, this striving may lend too much emphasis to the "problems" or inadequacies being overcome. Such a person then, according to Adler, develops an *inferiority complex*. Have you ever felt that you suffer from such a complex? It can be caused by excessive adult expectations. It can also result from being relatively immature and identifying with childhood skills (or a lack of them) rather than realistically assessing your new adolescent skills.

A difference in your rate of physical maturation may have caused you to develop much later than your friends. To note some of the advantages of this, you might review Chapter 3. Some feel inferior, however, if their body is not as fully developed as that of the "typical teenager." Finally, your friends and/or a lack of status in your school may encourage—rightly or wrongly—feelings of inferiority. As someone has pointed out, thank goodness there *is* life after high school!

The problem of feelings of inferiority is not one to be ignored. It can lead to a self-fulfilling prophecy: I feel inferior, therefore I will act inferior. That leads others to think the one who acts inferior must be inferior. Again, the solution is close at hand. First, and most important, an accurate assessment of your strengths should be undertaken. What *are* you good at? What *do* you enjoy doing? List these strong points. You may be pleasantly surprised. Second, identify with positive role models (of which we'll speak more in a later chapter). That is, choose successful friends to imitate. Finally, try to change not only your mental environment (or attitude), but, as much as possible, your physical environment as well.

Shyness

Shyness is another common problem that many of us must learn to handle. In a survey of almost 2,500 American college-age students, one researcher found 73 percent—almost three-quarters—felt that at some point in their life they had been shy. In fact, at the time they were surveyed (around the age of 20), 44 percent of the men and 39 percent of the women still labeled themselves as shy.

What, exactly, is shyness? It's not easy to identify since it takes many different forms.

Outward signs. There are several different behaviors that seem to shout "I'M SHY!": not speaking up in groups; looking down; standing or sitting at the back of a group out of the focus of attention, to name a few.

Physiological symptoms. Perspiring and blushing are physical signs of anxiety that are detectable by anyone paying attention to the shy person. Butterflies in the stomach, pounding heart are internal symptoms similar to what happens any time any of us experiences a general arousal. If you are shy, you know the sense of self-consciousness that accompanies the condition. Am I sweating? Do my trembling hands show? Is it obvious I'm standing here in the corner?

Reducing shyness. Overcoming shyness is not easy. However, it *can* be achieved if a person starts with a commitment and a willingness to make several major changes in his or her style of living.

The factors that have influenced anyone to learn to be shy can just as well be *un*learned. Activities that you control can be used to change your self-image, your behavior, and the way other people think about your shyness. In one sense, the attitude you have toward your shyness is the most important aspect. For example, if you are going to a dance, then where do you sit (or stand)? If you behaved in your usual way, of course, you'd sit in a remote location. That would ease your embarrassment, and reduce the amount of contact you have with others at the dance. However, sitting in an out-of-the-way place would also make it difficult for anyone even to ask you to dance, and create in others the impression that you really *don't* feel like dancing. Thus, to get rid of your shyness you must deliberately take steps to change (1) the way you think about yourself, and (2) the way you behave. This will help people change the way they think about you and make it easier for you to be less shy next time. Shyness is a problem that is learned. Positive steps can be taken to reduce it.

REVIEW QUESTIONS

SECTION 1 (pages 393–399)

1. Name some of the possible causes of abnormal behavior and provide examples.

2. Compare and contrast the two major views of abnormal behavior. Describe the approaches each recommends.

3. Why is personality theory important in treatment?

4. Describe some of the varying formats in which therapy may be given.

5. What are some of the advantages of a team approach to treatment?

SECTION 2 (pages 400–409)

1. How have public attitudes toward abnormal behavior changed over the past several hundred years?

2. Describe the advantages and disadvantages of the different physical therapies.

3. What is involved in psychoanalysis?

4. Describe three important qualities of person-centered therapists. What influences do these qualities have on the progress of a client in therapy?

5. Name and explain the types of social learning or behavioral therapy that are based on classical conditioning.

6. What techniques in therapy are based on operant conditioning?

7. Name a type of cognitive therapy and describe the view its proponents take on how abnormal behavior develops.

SECTION 3 (pages 410–414)

1. Describe how the different personality theories view conflict.

2. Name and explain the types of conflict described by social learning/behavioral theorists.

SECTION 4 (pages 415–417)

1. What assumptions do all the therapies described in this chapter have in common?

2. Name four or five common characteristics of therapists in their client-therapist relationships.

3. What are some of the difficulties in evaluating the effectiveness of psychotherapy?

4. Is there any "best" therapy? Why or why not?

SECTION 5 (pages 417–420)

1. How is our concept of mental health changing?

2. Describe some constructive ways to handle frustration.

ACTIVITIES

1. Many times when people tell us about problems they are having, we have been trained (often without our awareness) to play down the problem. Someone says she feels terrible because she did poorly on a test. The reply you often hear is, "Oh, don't worry about it." A more supportive response would be, "You seem worried . . ." Keep a record for a week of conversations you overhear or take part in where a problem is mentioned and immediately glossed over or minimized. Identify examples where a more supportive comment might have been more appropriate. What do you find? Do people tend to respond to one another only socially, without really helping to solve one another's problems?

2. **Career Search.** There are many different groups to help people who have a behavioral problem. Examples include Alcoholics Anonymous, Weight Watchers, Gamblers Anonymous, Al-Anon (for the families of alcoholics), Parents Anonymous (for those with

problems involving child abuse or parenting), Barriers for Free Living (for those who are partially disabled), and Lighthouse for the Blind. Invite a representative from such a group to come into your class to talk about the kinds of problems-in-living the group is intended to handle, and what treatment or therapeutic strategies it suggests.

3. Systematic desensitization involves learning how to relax. This is done first by learning how to sense when you are tense, and then practicing strategies for relaxing. Pick a muscle group (such as your jaw muscles) and clench them as tightly as you can. Continue to do so until your muscles ache, *really* ache. Then relax your jaw, and let your mouth hang down on your chest. Concentrate on what you do in order to relax those muscles; learn relaxation as a new response. Repeat this process with every muscle group you can think of, starting from your head and moving toward your feet. It may take an hour or more to do all of them. Tense, create the pain, and then relax, concentrating on what you do in order to relax—your main goal. Then, the next time you feel yourself getting tense—as you start an exam, perhaps—practice your new relaxation skills. It should help your performance, and certainly your endurance.

4. Try taking a poll of your parents, your neighbors, and your friends who are not in this class. Ask them to define what they consider to be normal, healthy behavior. Record their definition and list each behavior they mention.

5. Career Search. Join the volunteer program of a local mental hospital conducting work, physical, or play therapy programs. Talk with a staff member about the limits imposed by the patient's right to privacy, and about how those rights are respected. Write a summary of your experiences. Consider: What impact did your visit have on the patients? What examples did you see of the application of psychological principles in the wards? Do you think the environment of the mental hospital itself causes people to behave abnormally? If you found yourself in a mental hospital, how would you try to behave in order to be released?

INTERESTED IN MORE?

BANDURA, A. *Principles of Behavior Modification.* Holt, Rinehart & Winston, 1969. Discusses how to change behavior, from a social-learning point of view. Stresses the roles of observation and self-regulation.

COLEMAN, J. C. & GLAROS, A. G. *Contemporary Psychology and Effective Behavior,* 5th ed. Scott, Foresman, 1983. Examining social and personal environments, these authors suggest ways to achieve maximum personal growth and effectiveness.

COREY, G. *Theory and Practice of Counseling and Psychotherapy.* Brooks/Cole, 1977. An excellent source describing how various theories can be applied to a specific behavior problem. Shows how various psychotherapies derive from personality theories.

LAZARUS, R. S. *Patterns of Adjustment,* 3rd ed. McGraw-Hill, 1976. Includes a discussion of successful adjustment to stress. Reviews various models of success and failure of adjustment and gives a brief analysis of failure.

MARKS, J. *Help—A Guide to Counseling and Theory Without a Hassle.* Messner, 1976. Writing for students, the author describes forms of psychotherapy and tells how to go about getting help.

MARTIN, G. & PEAR, J. *Behavior Modification: What It Is And How To Do It.* Prentice-Hall, 1978. Presents the principles of behavior modification, from basic concepts to their application to complex problems. Includes discussion of observation skills.

PERVIN, L. *Current Controversies and Issues in Personality.* John Wiley, 1978. A short, challenging book that discusses a wide range of problems, from caring for the mentally ill to analyzing why people don't offer help. To guide the reader, a series of questions opens each chapter.

PRICE, R. H. & DENNER, B., eds. *The Making of a Mental Patient.* Holt, Rinehart & Winston, 1973. Traces the stages of mental illness from first detection to hospital commitment. Gives strategies for survival.

SCHULTZ, D. *Growth Psychology: Models of the Healthy Personality.* D. Van Nostrand, 1977. This short book picks up on Maslow's concept of a healthy personality. Covers various theories about how a person can develop one.

SZASZ, T., ed. *The Age of Madness.* Anchor Books, 1973. Szasz suggests that society decides what is "normal" to protect itself and fails to recognize the needs of the involuntarily committed "mentally ill." He uses literature and personal stories to support his position. Interesting reading.

VISCOTT, D. S. *The Making of a Psychiatrist.* Arbor House, 1972. Light reading on a heavy subject. Presents an overview of one psychologist's training and experience.

14 Testing

CHAPTER OUTLINE

WHAT'S THE ANSWER?

☐ *In career counseling, what's wrong with just asking people what they'd like to be? Why wouldn't they know best what their own interests are?*

☐ "My grandfather was 63 last year. He got laid off from his job when his company lost a big contract. The dumbest thing happened to him. One place where he went for a job interview asked him to take an intelligence test before they'd hire him. He didn't get that job. He found out later that his intelligence rating wasn't high enough on that test to handle the job he wanted. Can you imagine that? I've lived with him all my life. He's raised three kids. He's been a construction foreman. He's done everything. The person he talked to said older people's IQ drops with age. The older they get, the dumber they get is what I guess he meant. I don't believe it. Gramps is too smart for that." *What is the truth here? Will your intelligence grow, remain constant, or drop as you get older?*

The Rorschach is a projective test consisting of a series of formless but symmetrical ink blots. The client is asked to tell what each form represents. Interpreting the results can be subjective and requires considerable skill.

1 The Makings of a Test

> *... no two persons are born exactly alike, but each differs from each in natural endowments, one being suited for one occupation and another for another.*

This statement is one of the first times society recognized what is now widely accepted fact: there *are* individual differences among people. What is so interesting is that it was written some 2,400 years ago! It's contained in Plato's *Republic*. Plato identified three kinds of people, as seen in Table 14-1 on the next page. He suggested that the way in which men performed certain actions that were requested of them indicated which ones would

Individual factors. A third view is exactly opposite the original general-factor proposal. This suggests that each test by its very content determines what is being measured. One theory states that our intellect is composed of 120 mental abilities, composed of three types of factors. These include four kinds of contents, five kinds of mental operations, and six resulting products. If this assumption is true, there'd be little correlation between the results on any of these tests—we might be very high on some and still be quite low on other subtests.

Summary. Which theory is correct? No simple answer will do. One psychologist has even suggested aspects of all three views are correct! Argument is fruitless. Intelligence tests should be chosen—as is true of any test—with an eye toward the ultimate use of the results.

Tests of intelligence

Alfred Binet, in France, was the first person to develop a test of intelligence. The original work was based on two assumptions, both of which later proved to be true. First, it was assumed that to test intelligence it would be best to present problems which allowed the children to function normally. Second, it was also assumed that all else being equal, as a child got older he or she should be able to solve a broader, more complex variety of problems.

Figure 14-3 A sample question from the Progressive Matrices Test, a culture-free intelligence test.

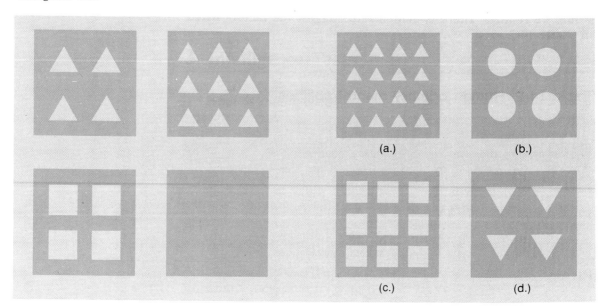

(a.) (b.)

(c.) (d.)

or indeed retarded
ing have been mac
of training best s
tarded must be c
retarded can (with
level. The modera
do semiskilled or ;
dates are only mi
function reasonab

What causes
Functional retarda
known organic ca
conditions such ;
and cretinism (or
can be caused by
natal environmer
cause retardation
ences on the deve

Known influen
intellectual de

What's your I(
hood who is the s
people at random
tween their IQs. `

Heredity. If
formation. There
same house. If yo
you, your IQs wi
you have an iden
more likely to be
tionship increases
But since children
gether will have
we've also confir

Aging. One (
or not it changes
chologists gave so
test. Seven years
cent) many of th
longitudinal study
52.)

Does IQ chan
study. Read the

Alfred Binet (above) designed the first intelligence test in France in 1903. The Stanford-Binet Intelligence Scale is still in use today. Manipulative tests, like the one this man is taking, measure one aspect of intelligence. Manual dexterity and aptitude are often tested by companies seeking employees who excel in certain skills.

The result of all this work was a 30-item test—the predecessor of the still-available Stanford-Binet Intelligence Scale. To administer the Stanford-Binet test requires a highly trained examiner. For each age level up through early adolescence there are tests of varying content, but roughly equal difficulty. More and more challenging tests are offered as age level increases.

Other popular tests are the Wechsler Adult Intelligence Scale (WAIS) and the Wechsler Intelligence Scale for Children (WISC). The Wechsler tests were initially designed for adults, rather than children as was the Stanford-Binet test. Both the WAIS and the WISC have separate verbal and non-verbal performance scales.

The Intelligence Quotient

The intelligence test probably most familiar to you is the "IQ" test. What is an IQ, or Intelligence Quotient? Three terms are important. The first is *mental age* (MA), or the average age, expressed in months, of children who answer correctly certain items on a standardized test. For example, if a girl exactly eight years old passes those items passed by the average ten-year-old,

Stanford-Binet Intelligence Scale: *six tests, at each age level, of varying content and increasing difficulty*

Wechsler Intelligence Scale: *tests using verbal and performance scales, for adults and children*

Interviews are a form of test situation which all of us must face at one time or another.

Many mentally re
ple enjoy the cha
comradeship of c
in the Special Ol

Another is the *structured* interview that covers a specific series of questions and topic areas—the interviewer may even be working from a sheet of questions. It reduces biases—both yours and the interviewer's—but it may be stressful if it doesn't allow you to expand on your answers.

A third type is the *unstructured* interview, where you can ask questions of whoever is conducting the interview. Of interest here is how the interview is controlled. A skillful job applicant may manage to talk only about those abilities in which he or she excels, especially if interviewed by an inexperienced personnel manager.

The fourth type of interview is the *exhaustive* interview, where you may be interviewed for many hours and/or by more than one person at a time. This can also be very stressful, but not unlike the type of day that would be faced by a very busy business or academic person.

Errors. All these interview and observation techniques tend to be subject to certain types of errors of assessment. One such error is *stereotyping*, which is attempting to fit the applicant's performance into categories so broad as to be ineffective. As we discuss later, not *all* redheads have fiery tempers, not all Chinese are earnest and loyal only to family ties.

A second problem is *insensitivity*. Sometimes an interviewer may not interpret an applicant's answer correctly. Thereby the interviewer misses an opportunity to pursue what might otherwise be a fruitful line of questioning or observation.

A third problem is the *halo effect*—meaning that prior knowledge of the applicant (good *or* bad) influences interviewers' observations. They may record data only so as to confirm opinions and beliefs formed before the interview and contrary to answers or evidence being offered by the applicant.

Because of these potential error sources, there has been a long effort to try to render the assessment of personality more objective and precise.

Quantifying behavior

As we discuss two means of collecting data for assessing personality, we'll describe each procedure briefly. Then we'll select a test or two to show you the concepts that apply. Two major types of such personality tests exist.

Questionnaire/self-report tests. Tests of this type are easy to give to large groups of people. Most such personality tests involve a large number of questions, each of which can be answered yes/no or true/false. These test results are often used as an initial screening device—a rough indicator of present or possible future problems. Tests such as these are usually supplemented by additional tests. They are used to verify the initial findings, or follow-up to find more information about conditions revealed by the first tests.

Probably the most widely known of all personality tests is the Minnesota Multiphasic Personality Inventory, or MMPI. There are now more than 6,000 references to and studies of the MMPI published. The MMPI is composed of 550 statements about you—simple statements about aspects of you, to which you can easily respond "true," "false," or "cannot say."

These statements can be scored and analyzed by computer in terms of 10 scales of tendency toward such disorders as hypochondriasis (Hs, or health anxiety), depression (D), and Schizophrenia (Sc, suggesting withdrawal into a private world). Buried within the 550 statements are some items used to detect lying or faking socially desirable answers—the Lie (L), Faking (F), and Correction (K) scales. An example? Responding "true" to "I like everyone I know" will elevate your score on the Lie scale.

Although the MMPI has rather poor reliability, it is still a critical tool used in assessing personality. Other tools include the interview, the intelligence test, and the projective test. The MMPI identifies possible diagnoses to be verified or rejected using other sources of data.

Projective tests. The last major group of tests is the projective tests. These offer the person taking the test a seemingly formless, unstructured task. Very few cues are offered as to what is expected or what is a "good" or "correct" answer. The theory

Happy

So-So

Sad

Think about coming to school in the morning. Which face shows how you feel when you think about coming to school in the morning?

Figure 14-5 The "Faces" Attitude Inventory asks children a number of questions related to their feelings about themselves, learning, school, and peer-group status. They respond by indicating which of the three faces most clearly reflects their attitude toward each item.

projective tests: *seemingly formless and unstructured tests that offer stimuli aimed at revealing our unconscious feelings and views*

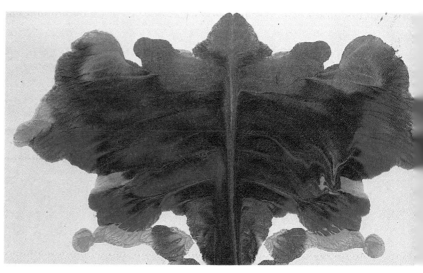

The picture of women above (left) is from the Thematic Apperception Test—a well-known subjective test consisting of a number of cards showing pictures of people. The person being examined is asked to make up a story about each picture, telling what is happening, what the people are thinking, what they are feeling, what led up to the present situation, and what happens next. (Right) Rorschach test blots are supposed to trigger images. What do you see in the Rorschach-type blot above?

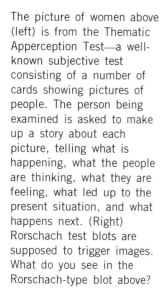

behind these tests suggests that given a specific, but vague stimulus, subjects will have to draw on their own perception of the situation to respond. It is thought that when we are forced to do this, it will cause us to reveal our own personality or views of the important controlling events in the world.

The theory seems sound, but there are some problems. Projective tests are subjective. Their validity and reliability have been questioned by some psychologists because of the limited number of norms provided for some of these tests. As a result, psychologists tend to use these types of tests only for guidance, not as a sole source of information about a client or patient.

One classic projective test is the Thematic Apperception Test (or TAT), which has also been available since the early 40s. The TAT consists of detailed pictures that are open to different interpretations. Persons taking the test are asked to make up a story about each one. They are to relate what led up to the situation, what is going on, what the characters are thinking or feeling, and what is likely to follow.

Scoring is not standardized. However, the examiner might be looking for themes that keep appearing in the stories. There may be a tremendous range of responses, but the results for the TAT are often determined by the examiner's experience with giving the test. For any individual, it is the unusual responses—those that depart from the expected—that are most important.

Projective tests—how good? How are we to evaluate the projective tests? The underlying assumption is that unstructured test situations can be used to detect enduring personality traits. Especially with the TAT there is evidence that it may be affected by temporary, everyday things. Hunger, lack of sleep, or social factors such as frustration or failure in other test situations may affect the results. Perhaps the most effective use of projective tests is as an "ice-breaker" early in the therapeutic situation.

▬▬▬ In review . . .

Personality is measured most often in one of two ways: by direct observation, or by questionnaire/self-report tests, such as the MMPI or various projective tests. The projective tests (Rorschach, TAT) present the person taking the test with an ambiguous stimulus. In theory the person must inject his own perceptions into the situations to provide a response. Such projective tests can be subjective and thus not too valid.

Chapter Application and Review

USING PSYCHOLOGY   *Can you improve your IQ?*

Within limits, yes, it is possible to improve your IQ. Several factors are involved, since your intelligence is determined by both heredity *and* environment. Thus, it is possible to create an environment that will do the most for your intellectual development. Since intelligence is most often measured in a formal testing situation, experience with the testing format is clearly helpful. It pays to know what kind of testing procedure will be used.

A second factor concerns motivation. Prior classroom experiences may sometimes discourage you from trying to do your best in a formal testing situation. A relaxed, confident attitude is helpful. Keep in mind that no test at any time in your life is an absolutely critical event from which there is no recovery if things don't go well. An error some students make is to get too keyed up for the tests. They run their motivation level up so high that they are beyond their peak performance range. Do something you enjoy the night before the examination!

Third, some might hope to "cheat" on the tests by trying to find out beforehand what questions will be asked. Of course, that isn't really raising your IQ. The tests are given on the assumption that you are a "naive" subject. This means that you've not already seen the specific problems being posed for you in the test. If that's not true, then the test is not a valid one.

Finally, most commonly used intelligence tests in North America are based on middle-class values and typical experiences. Anything that will increase your exposure to such an environment is likely to increase your measured IQ. Friends, clubs, social organizations, and participation in community affairs are some examples. So, it *is* possible to affect your IQ within a limited range by focusing on environmental factors affecting your experience and performance in the test.

While you may not be concerned with this matter now, there is also some helpful information available about how you may be able to maximize (when the time comes) your *children's* intelligence. This involves many factors in development (Chapter 2). Also review the interesting facts about birth order, which are summarized in Table 14-3.

Table 14-3 **Factors affecting your intelligence***

FACTOR	IMPACT
BIRTH ORDER	Earlier born tend to be smarter (because they are in a richer intellectual environment).
FAMILY SIZE	Larger total family size tends to mean lower IQ for comparable birth order (#2 child of 2 siblings smarter than #2 child of 7 siblings).
SPACING	More distance between children means less adverse effects of later birth order (because the average intellectual climate is richer).

*Note: The studies on which this table is based involved differences in IQ of only 1-2 points through an entire generation.

REVIEW QUESTIONS

SECTION 1 (pages 427–437)

1. What is the purpose of tests? Why have they been developed?

2. What is "normal distribution"?

3. Why are standardized norms for tests important?

4. What is meant by saying a test is "reliable"?

5. What is "test validity?" Explain three ways in which a test may be shown to be valid.

6. Compare and contrast the scoring of objective and subjective tests.

7. If a test is efficient, what do we know about it? Why is efficiency important in Testing?

8. What precautions help assure that tests will be administered and interpreted in an ethical manner?

SECTION 2 (pages 437–440)

1. What types of tests are used in career and vocational counseling? On what are such tests based?

2. Compare and contrast achievement and aptitude tests.

SECTION 3 (pages 440–447)

1. Give at least two definitions of intelligence.

2. Describe three different views concerning the nature of intelligence.

3. Name and describe briefly the most commonly used intelligence tests.

4. How is IQ calculated?

5. What is now known about retardation?

6. Why is creativity difficult to measure?

7. What are some influences on the development of intelligence?

SECTION 4 (pages 447–451)

1. Describe briefly how your behavior in an interview might be used to evaluate your personality. What errors of assessment might be made and why?

2. What are projective tests? Name those most commonly used.

3. Are projective tests well validated? Are they reliable?

4. What would you want to know about any test you took?

ACTIVITIES

1. Examine back issues of *Reader's Digest, Family Circle,* or any magazine that is likely to run "tests" of marital happiness or personal adjustment. Select a test and list for yourself what skills you think are being tested. Then take the test, score your performance, and see how well the article says you did. Now, reread the article closely and see if you can find out how the "normal" performance was defined. What group of people was used to standardize the test? How well did the article and test specify the norms, reliability, validity, objectivity, and efficiency of the test?

2. **Career Search.** If your school has a school or counselling psychologist, find out whether you can take either of the traditional tests of vocational interest (the Strong-Campbell or Kuder tests). If you take a test, make an appointment with the psychologist to have your scores interpreted. Did you find any interest revealed that you hadn't known you had? If this service is not available, colleges and universities often teach a course on "tests and measurement." Students in the course are learning how to administer and interpret vocational interest tests. Through your teacher you might contact a nearby college to find out if they need volunteers to take these tests.

3. **Career Search.** Does your school district or county use an achievement test such as those available from Iowa, California, or Stanford? If so, invite one of the school psychologists or central-administration personnel to your class. Ask him or her to bring along the national norms for the test as well as the performance data for the students in your grade from the whole district or county. Discuss the tester's interpretation of the data, including any explanations for the performance of the local students as compared with the national norms.

4. **Career Search.** Sit down with someone who loves you—a friend, parent, brother, or sister. Have this person help you analyze what things you do best. Are you superquick in mathematics? Fast with a smile? Easy to get along with? Do you work especially well with people in a noisy or crowded situation? Find out your strengths. Then decide how you can best convince an interviewer of those strengths. Now you're ready. Do you need a job for next summer? Start making contacts now. See how many times you can get yourself interviewed. If you don't get a particular job, try to find out why.

5. In cooperation with your teacher, make some symmetrical inkblots. Fold a piece of heavy white construction paper in half. Into the crease drop several drops of ink; now press the two halves together so as to squeeze the ink out into a variety of symmetrical forms. You may have to do quite a

number before you get a satisfactory variety of forms. Now show each form, one at a time, to the class. Ask those classmates who wish to participate to write down two or three things that they see in the form—either in its parts or as a whole. Then collect the papers and share the responses with the class. How much agreement is there? Why might people respond very differently to the same form?

INTERESTED IN MORE?

ANASTASI, A. *Psychological Testing*, 5th ed. Macmillan, 1982. A classical text covering many aspects of testing. Describes limits on procedures, and gives examples of intelligence, achievement, aptitude, and personality tests.

COON, K. *The Dog Intelligence Test*. Avon, 1977. Don't take this one too seriously. Gives instructions for administering and scoring ten dog intelligence tests. Fun to read.

CRONBACK, L. J. *Essentials of Psychological Testing*, 3rd ed. Harper & Row, 1970. Thorough coverage of all the major issues involved in developing and administering a test of skill or potential. Includes a wide array of tests.

EYSENCK, H. J. *Know Your Own IQ*. Penguin, 1968. Eight tests, with answers and scoring instructions, that allow you to make an estimate of your IQ as it might be measured on the major standard tests.

KAMIN, L. J., ed. *The Science and Politics of IQ*. Halsted Press, 1974. Gives a variety of views on a series of controversial aspects of intelligence: its existence, causes, and assessment.

THORNDIKE, R. L. & HAGEN, E. P. *Measurement and Evaluation in Psychology and Education*, 4th ed. John Wiley, 1977. Heavy reading. Covers the basics of testing and some related social and political issues.

TYLER, L. E. *Tests and Measurements*, 2nd ed. Prentice-Hall, 1971. A brief, tough, solid review of the assumptions underlying tests. Includes a review of test development, statistics, and a discussion of issues of fairness and accuracy.

WHIMBEY, A. & WHIMBEY, L. S. *Intelligence Can Be Taught*. Bantam, 1975. Suggests that many abstract skills measured by tests can be improved with training. Thus, you can raise your IQ.

UNIT SIX

SOCIAL PSYCHOLOGY

People become a "group" when they interact and share desires, goals, and a program for action.

In previous units you read about the development of the individual and the many and varied physiological and psychological aspects of that growth. This unit, however, turns outward from the single organism to examine how individuals change and respond when in a group. In Chapter 15 we discuss how groups operate, how they benefit their members, and how their members communicate within them. We also look at some of the problems groups may face.

Chapter 16 focuses on the social interactions that we all experience as part of our personal development. It offers you guidance in such areas as making friends, falling in love, changing attitudes, avoiding aggressiveness, and learning skills of altruism and leadership. When you finish this unit you should be better equipped to understand your relationships with others.

15 Social Behavior of Groups

WHAT'S THE ANSWER?

☐   Imagine that you're walking along the sidewalk minding your own business—all alone as far as you know. You're happy because your teacher just praised you in class for a project you'd turned in. You're headed home, by way of your best friend's house. Things are going well. In this mood you see a squirrel near the edge of the sidewalk in the grass. For no apparent reason you strike up a conversation with the squirrel. Not expecting an answer, you say, "Good afternoon, squirrel. How's your day been?"

You're just about to ask a second question when you see someone leaning against the tree beyond the squirrel. You hadn't realized anyone was there. What happens? You blush. You get nervous. You walk a little faster to get away as fast as you can. And you avoid looking the person in the eye if you can. *What's happening here? Why?*

☐   "I really don't understand it, Denise. How could it have happened? You know I'm the quiet type, and I don't even like football that much."

These Californians are members of a cooperative group that shares interests and norms.

"What happened, Yvette?"

"Well, I went to Saturday's championship game with my brother and his friends, but I mean they practically had to *drag* me to get me to go. Then I met the kids from my movie maker's club there and we all sat together. Our crowd filled up a whole section of the grandstand. We were all yelling and jumping up and down every time the team made a good play."

"That sounds pretty usual to me, Yvette."

"But that's not it. When we won the game, I ran out on the field with everyone and helped tear down the enemy goalposts! I can't believe I did it. Something must have happened to me."

Is this an example of a group mind at work? Is there such a thing as a group mind? Does it exist, for example, when a group becomes a mob?

457

8. Pick a group of which you are a member that has a leader who impresses you very positively. Analyze his or her style of leadership in terms of the points about leadership that you have now read about. Pick another group of which you are also a member but one that has a leader with whom you are *not* very impressed. Also analyze his or her style of leadership. Now compare the analyses you've made. What similarities are there in the two styles of leadership? What differences? What changes in the style of a poor leader would be necessary to make him or her a more effective leader?

INTERESTED IN MORE?

ARONSON, E. *The Social Animal,* 4th ed. W. H. Freeman, 1984. A short, interesting introduction to the principles and practical applications of social psychology.

EVANS, R. I. & ROZELLE, R. M., eds. *Social Psychology in Life,* 2nd ed. Allyn and Bacon, 1973. Contains many fundamental social-psychological studies. Includes articles on measuring and experimental techniques.

FISHER, J. D., BELL, P. A., & BAUM, A. *Environmental Psychology,* 2nd ed. Holt, Rinehart & Winston, 1984. Introduces a concept not heavily covered in this chapter: how environmental factors such as weather, crowding, architecture, and the city influence our social behaviors.

FREEDMAN, J. L., SEARS, D. O., & CARLSMITH, J. M. *Social Psychology,* 3rd ed. Prentice-Hall, 1978. A well-written general text that covers many areas in social psychology, from attitude to conformity, from attraction to the impacts of an urban environment.

GOLDING, W., *Lord of the Flies.* Coward, McCann, 1954. A novel about the development of social structure among castaway preadolescent boys. A good study of the formation of groups.

HOLLANDER, E. P. *Principles and Methods of Social Psychology,* 3rd ed. Oxford University Press, 1978. Case histories illustrate social-psychological principles and methods used in studying socialization. Examines leadership, interaction, and the operation of groups.

ITTELSON, W. H., et al. *Introduction to Environmental Psychology.* Holt, Rinehart & Winston, 1974. Explores how physical environment affects social interactions. Heavy reading but interesting material.

KIESLER, C. & KIESLER, S. B. *Conformity.* Addison-Wesley, 1969. A good introduction to social-psychological processes and how people are influenced by those around them. Focuses on conformity and nonconformity.

KORDA, M. *Power: How to Get It, How to Keep It.* Random House, 1975. An analysis of how to restructure your life and environment to gain power in any large organization or group.

MALCOLM X & HALEY, A. *The Autobiography of Malcolm X.* Grove Press, 1965. In the real world, this is a very good example of the limits imposed by social class and the struggle and success of one person to exceed those socially-imposed limits; fascinating reading as you follow Malcolm X from ghetto to national power.

MARTINEZ, J. L., ed. *Chicano Psychology.* Academic Press, 1977. Discusses research on Chicanos in such areas of social psychology as bilingualism, testing, and mental health.

Murphy, R. W., et al. *Status and Conformity*. Time-Life Books, 1976. A richly illustrated look at the ways in which social status affects behavior. Includes many examples of conformity.

Raven, B. H. & Rubin, J. Z. *Social Psychology*, 2nd ed. John Wiley, 1983. A wide-ranging, challenging introduction to social processes that includes both effective pictures of humans in action and challenging summaries of human behavior.

Secord, P. F., Backman, C. W., & Slavitt, D. R. *Understanding Social Life: An Introduction to Social Psychology*. McGraw-Hill, 1976. A brief, well-written introduction to the wide range of behaviors studied by social psychologists—how we learn to be human, how we watch and judge each other, our behavior in small and large groups, and other topics ranging from crime to role-playing.

Worchel, S. & Cooper, J. *Understanding Social Psychology*, 3rd ed. Dorsey Press, 1983. A wide-ranging introduction to social psychology—from attribution to falling in love, from attitudes to group dynamics, from aggression to helping behavior. Many helpful illustrations of social processes.

Wrightsman, L. S. *Social Psychology*, 2nd ed. Brooks/Cole, 1977. A comprehensive introduction to the theories and methods of social psychology. Covers attitudes and attitude change, social behavior, relationships, and environmental influences.

CHAPTER OUTLINE

WHAT'S THE ANSWER?

☐   "It was really a surprise! Laurie and I were the very best friends all the way through high school. Then she went west to college, and I went south, and what a difference there was when we met last week!"

"How could you tell, Diane?"

"Well, there isn't any one thing I can point to. It was just that we hadn't seen each other for nine months. When we got back together again she was almost like a different person. Now she's into painting while I've started pursuing music. We both still love football, but she's also into photography. I don't even own a camera! I just don't know what that school did to her!" *What happened here? Can you explain why two best friends seem to be drifting apart?*

☐   *To change people's attitudes, is it better to stir their emotions, or to hit them with facts?*

☐   Suppose you're driving along at the speed limit and suddenly you look up into your rear view mirror. So close behind you that you see only two hands on the steering wheel and a heavy set of eyebrows is another driver. You're immediately furious. You slow down, and sure enough, the fellow passes you and immediately starts tailgating the car ahead. You get even madder.

Part of everyone's socialization comes from membership in groups. Friends
and fellow workers make important contributions to an individual's personal
development.

At the next traffic light you pull up beside this dangerous driver, all set to
give him a piece of your mind. As you roll down your window, he looks over at
you and yells, "Hey, thanks for pulling over. If you see a cop, would you get
him for us? We need an escort. My wife's in labor . . . . I hope we make it!"
Now aren't you ashamed?

☐   "Hold on, we've just had a flat!"
"The road's clear. You can pull over. What a day for a flat tire!"
"I'll pull in right next to that car there. They've got a flat too."
"No! We'll need help. Keep going farther down the road. If it won't hurt
your car, get several hundred yards past them before you stop; they've already
got someone helping." *Who's right here?*

1 Your Socialization and Personal Development

Socialization is the word that describes the development of social skills, as we discussed in Chapter 15. By high school age you have already learned a lot of personal skills—from math to language, from how to write and mail a letter to how to open and read one. Yet all this training will be of little use to you if you are unable to establish and maintain contact with family and friends.

Socialization is a non-stop process. Experience is constantly being enlarged upon as you move from childhood through adolescence into adulthood. Indeed, much of your life, at least up through young adulthood, is spent preparing to move from currently existing roles into new ones. The changes usually involve more responsibilities and increased social contacts.

Personal development, or the development of the "looking-glass self" of which we also spoke briefly in Chapter 15, leads to the development of poise and confidence. This assumes, of course, that your impact on the members of your family is positive and that they "reflect" a good image back to you. Moreover, most of the theories of development and personality assume that you will gain skills and abilities as you age. Maturity comes slowly; it can't be rushed. As you mature, you gain what might best be called *perspective*, or a view of self and others. This perspective lends stability to your social interactions. You come to understand your own strengths and weaknesses as well as those of others. Understanding both yourself and others is crucial to your success as an adult.

Family experience, then, provides an environment in which you can find comfort and support. Yet your parents (as a favor to you) will usually keep urging you to step out into the world. Try new things, they will say, gain "experience." This world of experience, once gained, is reflected in several ways. It will show up in your *attitude*. You'll have a certain degree of confidence in yourself and an awareness of your limits. It will show up in your *appearance*—a *very* important factor, as we'll see shortly. And it will show up in a growing, expanding appreciation for what might be called your *inner* self as opposed to your *outer* self. You'll do things in public that are not "really you." You'll gain a collection of inner thoughts, desires, and dreams that you'll not share with just everyone. Yet as that inner reservoir develops, what is really developing is the personality upon which you'll draw in establishing friendships and in finding, perhaps, the mate with whom you'll wish to share your life.

Finally, from the lessons of home life, from childhood experiences at school and at play, and from early adult experiences as a teen-ager, there will come a proper balance of *give and take.* There will be a sense of knowing when to assert self, and when to hold back and give others an opportunity. This description probably sounds rather blissful and ideal. It is, but then that is what *theory* usually is! The *facts* are what we turn to now, and they are not quite so easy to organize and interpret.

2 Interpersonal Attraction

Whether it concerns becoming "teacher's pet," finding a friend, or falling in love, the issue of interpersonal attractiveness is of central importance.

Relations with friends

Why are friends needed? Your friends make up the society of which you are a part. With contributions from you, they set social norms by which you are judged "normal" or "abnormal," acceptable or unacceptable. This society is a *reference group*—the group whose values, actions, and goals you accept. In the late 1950s such a group considered it best to wear white (athletic) socks to school. In the early 1970s (where school dress codes would permit it) it was fashionable to wear sandals and *no* socks. But consider the group with whom you would like to be associated now. What would happen to your chances of joining that group if you started wearing white socks . . . or sandals and no socks??

reference group: *any group whose values, actions, and goals an individual accepts*

The friends you associate with make up your *reference group.* Their values and attitudes will tend to be very like your own.

Friends also form a valuable source of information on some subjects. Adolescents learn much about social values from friends. It is from this group that they are likely to draw a future partner with whom they'll wish to live. So the more experience gained in working and socializing with friends, the better your interpersonal skills and abilities will become.

Are there limits to who can be a "friend"? We humans often tend to divide ourselves along arbitrary lines. North American societies tend to be divided into old and young. We sometimes divide ourselves by race or by national origin, or even by sex. Often these divisions make no sense in terms of the purposes of a group. The result is often to limit the groups from which we can draw friends.

In response to this tendency our society sets up rules and situations in which exchanges across these boundaries can occur. A dance allows sexes to mix. Scouting codes that encourage helping the elderly allow young to mix with old. Work situations can mix all age levels. Yet when we emphasize our differences and the means by which we can overcome them, we may raise doubts about whether the "real" self or the "social" self is being seen. "Did that 'nice young woman' help me across the street because she *is* nice, or because I'm old?"

How is a friendship formed? Because of the limits imposed by our society, friendships usually form in situations where you believe you're getting to see the "true self" of an acquaintance. If this is so, then how is the friendship formed?

Friendships are usually based upon common interests and goals. They rely to some extent upon frequency of contact and tend to fade with distance or change.

Figure 16-1 A drawing of one apartment house in a 17-building complex used in a study of the impact of distance upon the choice of friends. It turned out that the closer people lived to one another, the greater the likelihood that they would become friends.

For one thing, your behavior must be seen as voluntary. It must not appear that you have any higher or hidden goal in mind. Thus, the things you must reveal about yourself in an involuntary setting such as the principal's office would not qualify here.

Another strategy is to be constantly in the vicinity of the friend-to-be. The fact that high frequency of exposure leads to positive feelings is one of the most basic assumptions of advertising agencies. The same may be true with friends.

How can we analyze the forming of a friendship in terms of the strength that a happy family life gives to you? Friendship is established on the basis of (1) shared confidences and (2) aid rendered when it was not necessary—perhaps even at some cost to yourself. It should also involve (3) high frequency of contact, and (4) the absence of alternative explanations for your behavior. In terms of yourself, friendship is the revelation to another of some of your inner self, based on confidence both in yourself and in the trusted "other."

Ending it. Alas, even as we strive to start some friendships, we find it necessary to terminate others. The loss of a friend is often caused by the entrance of another even more valued person into the life of one of the friends. Or it can be caused by an increased distance between good friends—you or your friend move across town, county, or country. Or, gradually as you continue to mature, you change both socially and individually. What attracted you to your friend may no longer exist.

▬▬▬ In review . . .

Developing your social skills starts as you gain poise and confidence within the family. Maturity leads to perspective, and your social skills are practiced first in the home and then among friends who form your peer group. Revealing your "true self" is important in forming any friendship, as are sacrifices made without thought of personal gain. Friendships last as long as each friend gains from the relationship, but they are often ended by distance and changing values.

→ Think about it

The **question**: Have you ever had a friend go away as described at the start of the chapter? And, if so, have you ever visited that friend later and felt less comfortable with him or her than when you were neighbors? How do you explain what's happened?

The **answer**: One of the major factors that determines who will be our friends and best friends is where we live and where our friend lives. When you and a friend live near each other, you will usually have a lot of contact with each other. You'll share a lot of activities and interests. This means you'll see each other quite a bit and feel comfortable since each of you can predict the likes and dislikes of the other.

Generally, the farther away a friend moves, the less likely it is that you will remain good friends. As time passes, distance prevents you from seeing the interests of your friend change. Each of you finds other friends with different interests, and you develop along different paths. It's somewhat like watching a child grow up. If you don't see the child for a year or more, the changes are very obvious to you. The same is true of a friend. As the environment of each of you changes, your interests may grow apart.

Likability and agreement. In the long run you will be best friend (and, later on, a better husband or wife) to someone who likes you and agrees with you. It's the reason parents and "experts" are always stressing that you should "marry your own kind." Of course there are exceptions that have worked out well, but they're just that, *exceptions*. A very clever study of this has been made that may give you some insight into what we've been saying for several pages now.

Picture this: You agree to participate in an experimental study of problem-solving with another student at your school. It involves seven sessions of one hour each, working with a person whom you don't know. But, just before the experiment starts, you overhear your new coworker talking about you to the experimenter. The other person comments on what a lazy worker they know you are, and says some other nasty things about you.

Now the experiment starts. You do your best. Each day (you really don't quite understand why the person talks so loudly) you overhear your coworker talking about you to the experimenter, but the comments get better and better. By the last day the other person is very positive in his or her comments about you. After the last session is completed you're asked how well you like the other person in the experiment.

Once you've finished your rating, you are told that this person (the stooge) was cooperating with the experimenter. The stooge's comments about you were designed to change gradually from very negative to very positive. If your rating of the stooge resembled those ratings of others who participated in a similar experiment, the person's final comments were *most* important in influencing the rating you made. It turns out that if a stooge's rating of his coworker (in this case, you) goes from low to high, the subject will rate the stooge higher than if the stooge's rating begins and remains high throughout.

How do we explain this? If the ratings are good all along, the subject may come to question the person's skills in judgment. The subject "knows" that not very solid evidence was used at the start. If the high initial ratings drop, the subject tends to blame the other person.

In your case, the person's comments about you steadily improved, so you would be inclined to take (at least most of us would have!) full credit for the improvement. "Obviously" that person had watched you perform and had realized how good you really were! That shows up in the highest ratings in the − to + category—the one you experienced. In short, we like people who like us, but it isn't only the liking itself that's important, rather the context in which that liking develops. Moreover, if people agree with you, it reinforces your own opinions that you—and they—are right. This strengthens even more the bond between you.

Birds of a feather and other factors.   I expect you've heard the old sayings "Birds of a feather flock together," and "Opposites attract." Which is right?

Some data will help lead you to the answer. In the early 1970s, if men and women married without taking into consideration the religious preferences of either, we could expect that 56 percent of all married couples would be of the same religion. Actually, it was almost 94 percent. Also, whites married whites and blacks married blacks more than 99 percent of the time.

There are two hypotheses that capture the spirit of the sayings in the first paragraph. One could be called the *similarity* hypothesis: in predicting friends and marriages, similarities are of greatest importance. The *complements* hypothesis could be the

Although there are exceptions, staying with "your own kind" is most likely to provide stable relationships. When they marry, most people tend to choose mates who share their religion and have other cultural similarities. In the United States, the Amish are a group that follows this tendency very strictly, adhering to their own distinct values in conduct and dress.

second one: strengths in one person may make up for lack of similar strengths in the other member of a friendship or marriage. However, as some have pointed out, these two hypotheses are not really the opposites of one another.

Think back to the barriers we were talking about: old-young, black-white, and so forth. Similarity seems to be very important, if we use the way people actually behave (statistically) as the basis for our judgment. Issues of race and religion, perhaps even of age and social class, seem to be very important. Crossing those barriers for friendship is difficult and for marriage almost never done. Here the complements can become very important. A person weak in personal or family economics marries someone who understands banking. A leader and a follower may find happiness. In short, satisfying many other interpersonal needs can be very important in the establishment of a successful friendship or marriage. Collective ability—where one or the other member of a couple has the required skill—is important. How is all of this to be handled by an eager young adolescent? The secret is intelligent selection.

Romantic love

In Chapter 3 we defined love as involving three components: a sense of attachment, a sense of caring, and an intense bond of affection and shared interests. Another important element of love is that it provides a sense of security. We all are happier when we have someone caring for us and someone worth caring for. Yet, despite the advantages of being in love, it doesn't happen often in a lifetime.

Romantic love involves a complex array of human responses, including some negative feelings such as jealousy, anxiety, and even fear. You read about love in Chapter 10, in the theories of emotion.

As age approaches: Love companion. We've spoken of passion as too intense an experience to last a lifetime, and true that is. What follows, then? In our society divorce has become one way by which couples respond to altered feelings. The nature of love changes during the course of a shared life. An *equity principle* might well describe the actions of a married couple. The principle sometimes applies even to who marries whom. The well-to-do, ruggedly attractive person may seek and hold a well-to-do and attractive partner. In addition, within a marriage itself, a certain balancing of responsibilities and a meeting of the needs of the other partner must take place.

Should I marry? No amount of advice can help you make that personal decision. Parents sometimes try to discourage a child from marrying a specific partner of whom they don't approve. The usual strategy for this is to point out that the relationship is "infatuation," not true love. Time will tell, but the child to whom that advice is being given really won't know until that time has passed.

Marriage, generally, is the formation and acceptance by both parties of a moral, religious, and legal commitment. Yet, those making such a commitment do not always recognize the years of sacrifice and common toil to which they may be actually committing themselves.

Romantic love is a very complex human emotion involving attraction, attachment, and caring, but it often includes negative feelings, such as jealousy, as well.

In review . . .

Interpersonal attraction is caused by many factors, most of which we can control. Living or working close together is a very important factor. Once contact is established, we tend to remain attracted to those who like us and agree with us. Similarities in race, religion, amount of education, and interests are important in predicting success in marriage, but vast differences in abilities and interests may complement one another in some marriages.

equity principle: *in marriage, the balancing of responsibilities and needs as a couple*

3 Attitudes

Attitudes make up a part of human social behavior that is very important to the proper functioning of society. Understanding how attitudes are formed may well be crucial to the ultimate success of human existence.

What are they?

"I don't like your attitude!" "Don't mind her. She's just got a bad attitude." "His whole attitude changed when I told him that." Attitudes are everywhere. We all have them. We see them in others. They affect how we behave, and how we behave seems to indicate something about our attitude(s). What are attitudes, exactly? Can we study them? Do attitudes actually have much of an affect on our day-to-day life?

An *attitude* is a readiness to respond in a positive or a negative way to a class of people, objects, or ideas. Attitudes are often used to convey in a few words an analysis of many different behaviors. If you say you're angry, it may refer to past events that happened to you, current belief, and even possible future actions. Attitudes are sometimes thought to cause our behavior. Some people even go so far as to say that *all* our behavior is caused by attitudes.

Elements of attitudes

It is assumed that attitudes are composed of three parts: (1) belief, (2) like or dislike, and (3) behavior.

Cognition (value), the belief dimension. This is the total knowledge or information that a person has which bears on the attitude. For instance, are there such things as Unidentified Flying Objects (UFOs) visiting our planet from outer space? A belief about UFOs might take the form of a statement—"UFOs appear only at night and are most likely to be seen in isolated places by single humans or very occasionally by two people at the same time." That is a belief, pure and simple—one part of an attitude.

Emotion, the like or dislike (affective) dimension. This is the emotional aspect of your attitude. If you believe in UFOs, then you may also have an emotional reaction to them, expressed as "The thought of ever seeing a UFO makes me feel very uncomfortable."

Action, the behavior dimension. Here your readiness to respond is stressed. "If I ever saw a UFO, I would try to get on

attitude: *a readiness to respond in a positive or negative way to a class of people, objects, or ideas*

board," would be an action statement about UFOs. Public opinion pollsters sometimes have trouble with the action component of an attitude. Why? Because it's very easy to say certain things, but much harder to do them. Actions *do* speak louder than words, but not always in the same way!

Forming attitudes

In forming an attitude the first shift you make is from having *no* attitude to having *some* attitude, either positive or negative. Your environment is the main influence on the attitudes you form.

Personal experience. If an incident is important to you, then your own early reactions to it are likely to color your attitude toward similar experiences later. If you're hot, thirsty, and uncomfortable the first time you drink papaya juice, and are immediately refreshed, you're likely to form a positive attitude toward it. Repeated exposure is likely to intensify your good (or bad) feelings toward an object. The *mere-exposure hypothesis* suggests that repeated exposure to neutral objects or situations will increase your liking of them.

Parents. The basic needs—for food, warmth, protection and security, cleanliness, and training in respecting the rights of others—are universal. These needs are met almost without exception by parents, who come to be viewed by their children as

Feature   **16–1   FIRST IMPRESSIONS LAST**

In a study of first impressions a lecturer was described beforehand to one class as follows: "People who know him consider him to be a *rather cold* person; industrious, critical, practical, and determined." To another very similar class the lecturer (dressed identically and giving the same lecture) was called "a *very warm* person" instead of "rather cold." The rest of the descriptive words applied to him were exactly the same. Do you think that the changes of only two descriptive words would influence how the students reacted to the visiting lecturer?

It certainly did. The group to whom he was introduced as cold rated him as being more self-centered, formal, unsociable, unpopular, irritable, and humorless than the group that was told he was warm. In addition, in the "cold" class only 32 percent of the students made a comment or asked a question during his lecture. In the class where he was introduced as warm, a full 50 percent participated.

Are first impressions important? You bet!

all-knowing authority figures. Thus, children turn to their parents for guidance when more subtle issues develop. Religion, political party affiliation, and attitudes toward strangers or members of other racial or ethnic groups are areas in which parents train children in their mold. Having reached their own decisions based on past experience, they then relay these attitudes to their children. And the evidence is overwhelming that on these issues the training is quite effective.

Other groups. Schools, the peer group, and the mass media (radio, television, magazines, and newspapers) have an important influence on your attitudes. It has been demonstrated that children's television programs, such as *Sesame Street*, have a major impact when they reach the very young. In most other cases it was found that the mass media reinforce existing attitudes.

Attitudes gone awry: Prejudice

Definition. *Prejudice* is an attitude formed prior to or without taking into consideration any examination of the objective facts. One example is *racism*, which involves judgments about all members of a race by a member of another race. It is a widespread form of prejudice, common to many forms of human society. The same factors that influence the formation of attitudes also influence the development of a prejudice. Associating with people who are racists will encourage such prejudices. Even the mass media may unwittingly encourage maintaining such attitudes.

prejudice: *an attitude formed prior to or without taking into consideration any examination of objective facts*

racism: *prejudicial judgments about all members of a race by a member of another race*

stereotype: *a rigidly held, usually oversimplified, and often negative belief about most members of an identifiable group*

discrimination: *prejudice in action; the rejection or acceptance of someone solely because he or she belongs to a specific identifiable group*

Stereotypes. A *stereotype* is a rigidly held, usually oversimplified, and often negative belief about most members of an identifiable group. Stereotypes are simple: The Irish are quick-tempered. Germans and Japanese are industrious. Politicians are crooked. Parents are conservative. Stereotypes have developed to help us simplify the amount of information we must process. One psychologist has described them as a kind of social shorthand that helps us organize our perception of people. We then ignore their individual differences.

Discrimination. Prejudice is an attitude; discrimination is a behavior. *Discrimination* involves accepting or rejecting someone solely because he or she belongs to a specific, identifiable group. Discrimination can take many different forms. For instance, institutional policies, such as quotas, may preserve the attention directed to the issue of race. We discussed in Chapter 14 how tests of intelligence must be standardized very carefully so as not to be applied in a racist manner.

Even the definition of race has been disputed. As recently as 1960, the census considered a person to be of the black race if he or she had any black ancestors. The problems in desegregating United States schools, even a quarter century after the first Supreme Court rulings to do so, show how slowly attitudes change.

Changing attitudes

How do attitudes change? Persuasion is one method of attempting to change an attitude. Carl Hovland and Irving Janis have identified four crucial elements of persuasion.

Source. Several factors can influence whether a source will be able to change your attitude. You would be most likely to follow the advice of a person who was both *knowledgeable* about the subject and apparently *trustworthy*. Sources most *similar* to you are often most effective in changing your opinion. For example, young women, not elderly men, appear in soap commercials. They are trying to appear as similar as possible to the ideal consumer of such products.

The *power* of the source is also important. If you work in an office and your boss recommends a new brand of ballpoint pen, you're much more likely (in most cases) to try it than if a file clerk recommends it.

People are most likely to be persuaded when the person trying to influence their opinion is knowledgeable, trustworthy, and powerful.

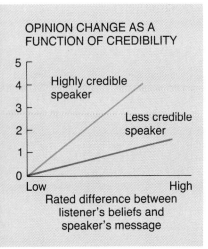

OPINION CHANGE AS A FUNCTION OF CREDIBILITY

Figure 16-2 When a highly credible person tries to change your opinion on an unimportant matter, the more his or her opinion differs from yours the more your attitude is likely to change.

Message. Several aspects of the message and how it's presented will affect whether people's attitudes change. If an audience is opposed to the message you want them to hear, you should present *both* sides of the argument. And in what order should they be presented? Give *your* views first if the other views will follow immediately. However, if there's a long period of time between the two, then present your views last.

Audiences you address may be in marked disagreement with you, or they may hold opinions only slightly different from yours. How should you move an audience toward your point of view—by giving them a message similar to their viewpoint, or by giving a markedly different one? A little of both is best. And how much arousal should you attempt to stir up? Too little arousal (or fear) encourages people to ignore the message; too much causes them to become defensive and reject it. Again, a balance is best.

Channel. Which has a more powerful effect, advertising on television or in newspaper ads? Think about your own behavior. You're used to having the radio or television on. You may or may not pay attention to it. However, when you read a newspaper or a magazine, you've made a commitment to pay attention to the incoming information. Printed advertising may reach a more receptive audience.

Recipient. There are a number of facts about *you* that will influence whether someone can change your mind. Your own internal needs and goals clearly have an impact. Most of us are concerned about our personal success—some more so than others. Advertisers often try to relate their products to youthful men and women who are obviously successful.

Think about it

The **question:** To change someone's attitude, is it better to stir that person's emotions, or to just give facts?

The **answer:** If the people to whom you are speaking are opposed to your views, use an emotional appeal when you first present your views. This procedure allows you to get their attention, so you can then hit them with the facts!

Cognitive dissonance

We've considered how to influence a person. Now let's consider how people can handle conflicts between their attitudes and actions or between two conflicting beliefs.

Leon Festinger developed a theory of cognitive dissonance to explain relationships between cognitions (pieces of knowledge). Such relationships may be *irrelevant*. (Knowing that snow is cold doesn't affect your knowing that basketball is exciting.) They may be *consonant*, which means that one cognition follows from another. (Since you know that rain makes you wet, you seek protection when it rains). Or they may be *dissonant*, or conflicting. (You participate in a boring experiment and then are asked to tell the next subject how interesting and valuable the study is.)

Cognitive dissonance is considered to be an unpleasant experience, one which we all work to reduce or eliminate. We have three choices: we can (1) *change* our cognitions, (2) *add* new cognitions, or (3) *alter* the importance of various cognitions.

A much discussed study on obedience by Stanley Milgram illustrates cognitive dissonance. Milgram set up an experiment in which a subject was to serve as "teacher" to monitor the performance of a "learner" trying to master new information. Milgram instructed the teacher to apply an electric shock of increasing severity with each error the learner made. As the severity of the shock was increased, the subject (a stooge out of sight of the "teacher,") gave responses indicating increasing pain, eventually screamed, and fell silent. Many of the teacher subjects protested, but they obeyed—continuing to boost the shock level.

Milgram's study illustrates obedience to authority, but it also shows the creation of cognitive dissonance. People were able to overcome their dissonance about inflicting pain or harm on a helpless stranger by rationalizing that (a) they had been paid to be a "teacher," (b) they had agreed to perform, and therefore (c) they felt obligated to do as they were told. In short, they shifted blame to Milgram as the responsible "authority."

In review . . .

Attitudes include three types of components: Cognitive (value), affective (emotional), and action (behavioral). Attitudes are based on our personal experience and are usually influenced by our family, friends, and society (especially through television). Prejudice is an attitude formed without reference to facts, often involving stereotypes; discrimination may result. Persuasion is an attempt to change someone's attitude. The source of persuasion, the message, the channel, and aspects of the recipient can all influence success in changing an attitude. Attitude change can result from cognitive dissonance. People find it necessary to reconcile conflicting attitudes or to justify acts that conflict with their beliefs.

An example of cognitive dissonance.

4 Aggression

Of all the behaviors in which we humans may engage, the most sinister is aggression. *Aggression* is behaving with the intent to inflict harm or injury on other humans. What causes it? Can we control it? Let's look at the evidence.

Causes

Inherited? Freud thought that aggression was an inherited, natural instinct of humans. If so, then channeling the aggression to positive acts would be the best we could hope to achieve. But other views have gained popularity in the last decade. They stem from research about observational learning.

Learned. Aggression can be viewed as a learned behavior that responds to the same reinforcers and the same controlling stimuli as other learned behaviors.

Frustration can lead to many forms of behavior, among which is aggression (see Chapter 10). Discovering that someone is willing to do you harm is another important cause of aggression. The same result occurs whether someone actually strikes out against you physically or just does so verbally.

A third cause of aggression is to observe models like yourself get caught in situations similar to the one you're in. If they become aggressive—and get away with it—you, too, will tend to become aggressive. This is one of the reasons why people are worried about the level of aggression on television.

In addition, there are other causes. One is the "long hot summer" effect. We tend to be more aggressive in hot weather than in cool. However, the causes of aggression are seldom if ever that simple. For instance, in cities there's another obvious factor also operating—crowding, as discussed in Box 16-2.

And don't forget the Attribution Theory of Emotion. That suggests that environmental cues can cause you to interpret your level of arousal as anger. If crowding is stressful, it's likely that your anger will increase when you are in crowded situations. A city near riot in the summer would first have symptoms that included heat, crowding, role models of aggression, and rising levels of arousal. Small wonder that riots occur!

Control of aggression

Since we've assumed that aggression is a learned behavior, four different possibilities might be considered as providing the best way in which to control it.

Feature   **16–2   HIGHWAYS AS "BYE"-WAYS**

LOS ANGELES (Chicago Tribune Service)—War has broken out on Southern California freeways. The antagonists are packs of frustrated motorists no longer able to cope with traffic congestion. Their weapons, according to the Los Angeles Police Department, are their cars.

In the past nine months, authorities have recorded almost 400 "vehicular assaults with a deadly weapon" on the 650 miles of heavily traveled freeways that slice through the hills and deserts of greater Los Angeles.

(The) director of behavioral sciences and psychology for the Los Angeles Police Department (says), "They get frustrated at the stackups on our freeways, they get angry at other inconsiderate drivers, and their tolerance level overflows. They explode. Their car becomes a weapon, and they strike out with it."

"In one case, four different cars were involved and they battled each other for 50 miles," recalls an accident investigator.

"People tend to elongate their body and personal territory to include their cars," (says the L.A.P.D. director). "Then they take it as a personal assault when someone enters their space. They see it as an attack on their person.

"For many people, cars are extensions of their egos. . . . If somebody hits you, you either run away or strike back. It works the same way on the Freeway." (June 1978).

You've now read enough psychology to interpret the behavior discussed here. We've spoken of nonverbal communication and the importance of the distance between people who are talking. Here we see the results when people feel that their personal space has been violated. In addition, apart from license plates, no way existed to identify anyone. The tools were at hand with which to be aggressive. All these factors created the conditions for freeway warfare.

Modeling. If observational learning is effective, then exposing people to unaggressive models should lead to a lower tendency to aggress. This is much more effective in preventing aggression if some other positive responses can also be offered. There's little evidence that punishing aggression will prevent it from occurring at the next opportunity.

Explanation. If the reason for aggression can be justified, a person is less likely to be aggressive in return. The success of such efforts, however, depends on a rational exchange of information. That's something that can't always be done in aggressive situations!

Catharsis. Freud's theory suggests that aggression may result from high levels of internal arousal. If this arousal can be "taken out" harmlessly to release the built-up energy, then less aggression should occur. This has *not* been supported by recent research. Providing other ways to be aggressive appears to calm people down at first, but later seems to cause even more aggressive behavior.

Incompatible response. It seems that aggression can be controlled by creating incompatible responses to the stimuli that cause aggression. One incompatible response is *humor*, which often works well in defusing aggression.

➡ **Think about it**

The **question**: Earlier we described what might happen if you were tailgated too closely on the highway. What would've happened if the person tailgating had been able to explain to you that he was rushing someone to the hospital? What would your reaction have been?

The **answer**: You would probably have felt ashamed. Aggression without apparent cause will cause others to be aggressive in return, but if behavior that seems aggressive can be explained, it is less likely to cause aggression in return.

5 Altruism, the Principle of Concern for Others

Offering help

The decision to offer help to a fellow human in distress is a complex one, more so than it might seem at first look. Many people, perhaps most, hold back. Those who do act must make five decisions, often in rapid order. Only if the correct decisions are made will the help be offered.

Notice the situation. First, the would-be helper must notice the situation. The easiest way to avoid "getting involved" is not to notice a problem.

Interpret: Emergency! Second, the passerby must interpret the situation as an emergency. Two things seem to influence whether or not this occurs. One is correctly perceiving a situation. Haven't you ever noticed the difficulty of separating the sound of a shot from that of a car backfiring? Can you tell the difference between a scream and a laugh? The other is that the helper-to-be must have the motivation to get involved. There are real reasons to avoid becoming involved. These range from potential danger to the threat of a lawsuit if inappropriate help is rendered.

Assume responsibility. This was where the breakdown occurred in the "Genovese incident," when 38 people watched from windows as a young girl was murdered. *Diffusion of responsibility* might have led everyone watching to assume someone else had taken care of the problem. If so, then the more people watching an apparent emergency, the *less* the likelihood any one of them would call for help.

In one experiment a number of people were called together to sit in separate rooms and discuss problems they were having in adjusting to college life. First time around each person simply introduced him- or herself through the speaker system and stated the problem. A stooge of the experimenter stated that he had troubles with epilepsy.

On the second round (you guessed it) this person staged an attack. The result was that the greater the number of people who participated in the experiment, the less likelihood there was of his being helped. Now, it turns out that the critical factor in the failure to offer aid was the isolation of each person in the group. When people *can* communicate, the odds of getting help actually go up as the size of the crowd increases, as they do with the obviousness of the problem.

Identifying how to assist. Fourth, a person will offer help only if he or she is able to identify how help should be offered. Many fail to do so simply because they don't know how. If someone even in your own family stopped breathing, would you know how to administer artificial respiration? What if he or she had a heart attack? Can you perform cardio-vascular resuscitation?

Implement the decision. Finally, suppose the helper-to-be has wended his or her way through all these decisions and has decided to offer help. The decision must still be implemented: the helper-to-be must become a helper.

Obtaining help

The people who most frequently get help are likeable. They are most likely to be helped if they're similar to us. You're much more inclined to help someone start his or her car in your own school's parking lot than on a similar lot downtown. Finally, people are more likely to be helped if they are *truly* in need, where the problem can't be handled alone but the costs of helping are not too great.

If people have been reinforced for helping previously, your odds of gaining help go up. If they're in a positive mood, and especially if they've viewed a model offering similar help, the same holds true. When social norms permit or encourage helping, when the helper is not preoccupied or busy, and when he or she may be returning a favor, the odds increase even further that you'll get the help you need. The most important factor here is that the helper-to-be interpret the need correctly.

▓▓▓▓▓   In review . . .

Aggression can have several causes. It can be caused by being frustrated or attacked by others, or by seeing others aggress. Aggression can be controlled by modeling, by having the basis for someone else's attack explained, or by catharsis. Eliciting an incompatible response is the most successful control. Offering to help somcone requires that you notice the situation, interpret it as an emergency, assume responsibility for acting, identify how to give aid, and act. Help is most often offered when "costs" are low, the person is similar to us, the need for help is obvious, and we've just seen others give help.

➡ Think about it

The **question**: To get help when you get a flat tire while driving on a freeway, should you pull in near someone else who is getting help fixing a flat or should you stop farther down the highway?

The **answer**: You should stop several hundred yards down the highway, for two reasons. First, having someone up the highway from you who is already getting help will expose passing motorists to a model who is helping someone in the same situation. Second, the time between seeing the model and noticing your problem will be enough for potential helpers to make and act on a decision. They must notice the situation, identify it correctly, realize (if true) that they have the skills and tools to help you, *and* still have time to slow down. A quarter mile should be enough!

Chapter Application and Review

USING PSYCHOLOGY   *How can you attract people?*

How do we attract people, particularly members of the opposite sex? Common sense, combined with a little experience, has a lot to do with it. There are two assumptions that are commonly made about attraction. One assumption can be called the Principle of Least Interest. In any relationship the fate of the couple will be determined by the person who is *least* interested.

The second assumption can be called the Principle of Playing Hard to Get. If you make yourself difficult to approach, or if you remain stand-offish to the person in whom you are interested, it will make him or her try harder to "get" to you. How valid are these assumptions? Research has indicated that the first principle is *true;* but the second one is *false!*

A team of social psychologists have studied many aspects of what falling in love involves. They suggest that "What ... men and women fail to realize is that any time a person's total hopes for happiness depend on the whim of one, ... that person is in trouble .... In every case, men and women would do far better if they converted the energy they normally spend on attracting one partner, who may or may not be interested in them, to devising ways to meet twenty potential partners." The message is simple: The most stunning person in the world meets no one by sitting home.

Attention-getters. All you have to do is to apply what we've already discussed elsewhere in this book. How about showing your interest in attracting others without seeming to do so? You could wear a button supporting some activity or group you favor. If it has small print, people will have to stand very close to read it. Since it's not easy to read without seeming obvious, you've got the perfect opener for a conversation. Or, carry a recent bestseller; many will have read it, and others will want to. They may ask your opinion. By the way, don't carry it until you've read enough of it to be involved!

Of course, physical attractiveness can also be a help. Remember, in Chapter 5 we mentioned some ways in which clothing can be used to emphasize your strengths or reduce the impacts of your problems. Chapter 9 gave hints on how you can lose some weight, if that's a problem.

Establishing contact. Contact with others is very important, too. The key, again, is to get out and *do* things. Try to join the "Y" or some other social or athletic club. Go where people are, and natural social processes will take their course. Learn to be friendly without being forward. The genuinely offered compliment has a way of gaining you many new friends.

And how about getting involved in your community? Probably your parents have already encouraged you along these lines. From snorkeling to photography, from Scottish country dancing to hiking, there must be something that interests you. Sink time into it. Without interests of your own, you'll not appear very interesting to others. And remember the lessons of high frequency of contact.

What do you say after (s)he's said hello? An error some people make is offering complete statements that tend to end a conversation. View conversation more as a volley in tennis: if you drop the ball, your partner has nothing to return! Has something funny happened to you? Talk about it. When responding to a question, finish with one of your own. You *love* to talk about yourself, of course. But think about the other person, too, because most of us *love* to talk about *us*. It's the subject we each know best. Once started, a conversation is kept going simply by keying your reactions—good, bad, or indifferent—to what's happening. And we already know what's going to keep a conversation, and ultimately the date, going: common interests, mutual support, and skills offered by each person to benefit the other.

Setting the limits. Parents are rightfully concerned about their children. They hope their training of a child during his or her childhood was appropriate. If it was, then by the time adolescence rolls around and social contacts start increasing, there may be little for them to worry about. But that's a lesson most parents learn hard, if at all. They know that by the time most adolescents start dating, the standards of friends tend to replace those of home.

For that reason alone it is important for you as an adolescent to set your own limits on what activities you will participate in, even before the opportunities present themselves. The decisions you make reflect your past upbringing and the environment in which you find yourself, but you'll need to think about your personal values and how you feel about yourself. Some rational planning will make it easier to draw the necessary lines.

REVIEW QUESTIONS

SECTION 1 (pages 488–489)
1. How do people develop social skills?
2. What is meant by "maturity"?

SECTION 2 (pages 489–495)
1. What factors are important in forming friendships? Which are important in ending friendships?
2. List some of the factors thought to be important in interpersonal attractions. Which of these are important early in the relationship, and which become important later on?
3. Do "birds of a feather flock together" or do "opposites attract?" Explain your answer.
4. What is "puppy love"? How can you tell if a relationship is only "puppy love"?
5. How often do people experience love as passion? What happens to passionate love in marriage?

SECTION 3 (pages 496–501)
1. Name and explain the three components of attitudes.
2. What forces in our lives influence and shape our attitudes and opinions?
3. What are some of the problems encountered in measuring attitudes?
4. What is prejudice? Can it be controlled or eliminated?
5. What is persuasion? Name some of the factors that determine whether or not persuasion will be successful.
6. Explain cognitive dissonance, giving an example from everyday life.

SECTION 4 (pages 502–504)
1. Is aggression learned or inherited? Explain your answer.
2. Describe several ways of controlling aggression.

SECTION 5 (pages 504–506)
1. What are the five steps involved in offering to help someone?
2. What aspects of a situation increase the likelihood that help will be offered?

ACTIVITIES

1. Who was your best friend in sixth grade? Describe how the friendship formed with that person (if you can remember), or with a more recent best friend. What needs of each person were served by the friendship? What benefits were gained by each person? If the friendship is over now, what factors finally led to its decline or end?

2. As a class project, identify on a map of your city where each student in the class

lives. Have each student name one other person in school with whom he or she has done something outside of school hours. Consult the map. On the average, how many blocks or miles does each student live from other students in the class? Is the distance greater or lesser than the average distance between the homes of persons who get together outside of school? What other factors can influence who does what activities with whom?

3. Scan your local newspaper or any family magazine to find advertisements that use facts to appeal directly to the cognitive part of a reader's attitude. Also find ads that appeal directly to the affective, or emotional, part of an attitude, as well as ads that appeal for action. Which techniques are most often used? For which type of appeal was it hardest to find examples? To what component of a buyer's attitude are advertisers most likely to appeal? Do advertisers of different products try to appeal to different parts of buyers' attitudes?

4. Identify an attitude of one of your friends—perhaps a religious attitude, a political party preference, or an opinion regarding taxes or war or some national issue. Do you agree or disagree with your friend on that attitude? Has your position on the subject changed within the past couple of years? Why? Has your friend's opinion changed? Why? How important has your family been in shaping the attitudes you now hold?

5. In your community pick a group—a racial group, a religious denomination, a political organization, or even people just living in a certain part of town. Interview a number of the students in your school about their attitudes toward the group you've chosen. Assess how much they know about the feelings of that group and their general awareness of the situation of the group. Then also interview members of the group you've identified concerning their own views on how other citizens in the town view them. Assess their feelings and their awareness of others' opinions. What evidences of prejudice, "halo effect," discrimination, or stereotyping do you find? Can any such errors be corrected? How?

6. Career Search. Invite a member of your local police department into your classroom to talk with you about the tactics used by police to handle aggression. On a separate occasion invite a psychologist from a prison or from your community to talk about personal strategies for controlling one's own aggression or aggression directed at oneself by others. Compare and contrast the points made by these different speakers.

7. Have you ever offered help to someone in an emergency situation? Describe the situation in terms of the series of decisions you had to make before deciding to offer help. What aspects of the situation influenced your decision? Have you ever offered help that turned out not to be needed? Analyze that situation in the same way.

INTERESTED IN MORE?

BAILEY, R. H. *Violence and Aggression.* Time-Life Books, 1976. From the "Human Behavior" series, a well-illustrated volume that examines human urges to hurt others. Shows many forms of aggression and examines possible means of curbing these impulses.

BECK, R. C. *Applying Psychology: Understanding People.* Prentice-Hall, 1982. Examines learning and remembering, job performance, emotion, attitude, and communication, among other topics. The emphasis is on practical applications for living that can be drawn from psychology.

BERSCHEID, E. & WALSTER, E. *Interpersonal Attraction.* Addison-Wesley, 1969. Examines a wide variety of factors that may determine how attractive you are or how attractive you find someone else to be. Covers both romantic love and acceptance or rejection by a group.

EVANS, R. I. *The Making of Social Psychology: Discussions with Creative Contributors.* Gardner Press, 1980. An unusual book of interviews with top-name theorists and researchers in social psychology. An insider's view of how social psychology has grown and changed over the past half century.

FISHER, R. J. *Social Psychology: An Applied Approach.* St. Martin's Press, 1982. Heavy reading, but a nice social-psychological analysis of humans in social situations—everything from small groups to international relations. Also offers comments on social conflict, environment, and law.

JONES, J. M. *Prejudice and Racism.* Addison-Wesley, 1972. A far-ranging review of a complex subject. Dissects the social psychologist's view of racial prejudice.

LATANE, B. & DARLEY, J. M. *The Unresponsive Bystander: Why Doesn't He Help?* Prentice-Hall, 1970. A classic study of the factors that influence when help will be offered in emergencies.

McGINNISS, J. *The Selling of the President.* Trident, 1968. A paperback that takes a United States tradition (electing the President) and shows how it is influenced by another United States tradition (advertising). An exercise in practical attitude change.

RUBIN, Z. *Liking and Loving: An Invitation to Social Psychology.* Holt, Rinehart & Winston, 1973. Uses personal relationships as a means of presenting theories and findings of social psychology.

ZIMBARDO, P. G. *Shyness: What It is, What to Do About It.* Addison-Wesley, 1977. More than 80 percent of an international sample of over 5,000 people say they are or were shy at some point in their life and 40 percent of the same group see themselves as shy now. This book has a lot to offer—to about 4 out of 10 readers! It gives constructive suggestions on how to manage or reduce shyness.

UNIT SEVEN

RESEARCH PROCESSES AND CAREERS

As they pursue research goals, psychologists must protect their subjects by following strict professional and ethical standards.

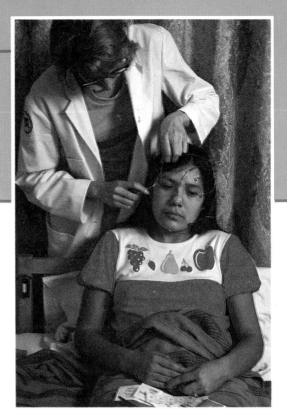

In Chapter 17 of this unit we'll examine the research processes that were used in the various experiments described throughout this book. We'll examine how experiments are put together. We'll also look in more detail at how psychologists design and run experiments, the very heart of data-gathering. Numbers and nuances, or data and how we understand them, are our subject. We'll look at how numbers are used not only to design experiments, but also to summarize, interpret, and communicate the results. As a conclusion to the text, in the Epilogue, we'll discuss some of the many career opportunities in the expanding field of psychology.

17 Methods and Numbers

WHAT'S THE ANSWER?

☐   *Why is it not enough for an advertiser to say "Washing with Ripsnort yields a 16 percent cleaner wash"?*

☐   "Sheila, I don't think I'll ever forget an argument I heard when I visited the Canadian Parliament during the Spring of 1979. Two Members of Parliament (MPs) were arguing on the floor about the average annual income for Canadian households."

"What's so memorable about that, Bart?" asks Sheila.

"A Liberal MP said something like, 'The average annual income is 16,000 Canadian dollars (CD) per household throughout Canada!' Another MP who was a Conservative got up and—in fact, he interrupted—to point out 'Nonsense! The *average* Canadian household earns *less* than $12,000 (CD) per year!' What made it so interesting is that both MPs were right."

"That can't be," replies Sheila. "One of them has to be wrong!"

Who's right here, Sheila or Bart? Why?

1 Experiments and Controls

The "What's the Answer?" section shows you two ways in which statistics are used in our everyday world. We're surrounded by statistics. There seems to be no way to avoid them.

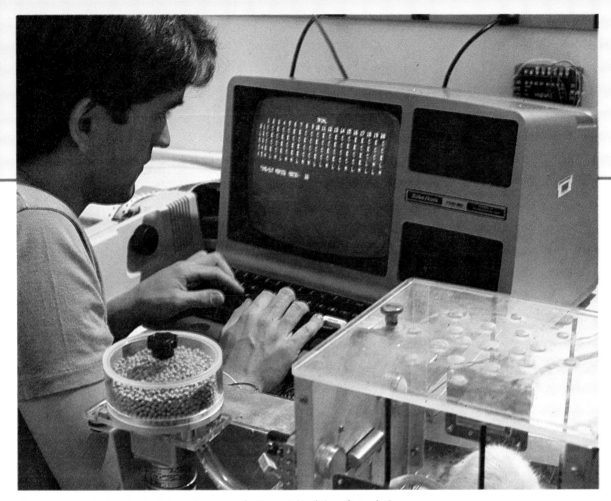

Research psychologists test hypotheses and attempt to determine what stimulus causes what response. Using experimental methods in a laboratory is one way to gather data.

We're tempted to say that past studies have shown average North Americans to be 21 percent confident of their knowledge of statistics, 38 percent worried about it, 16 percent uncertain, and 25 percent eager to forget the whole thing! Do statistics scare you? They shouldn't. The only thing you ought to be worried about is how people *use* statistics to try to convince you of something, because statistics can "lie."

The fear of statistics that many people have is based on a lack of understanding. Statistics themselves are not difficult to understand. Psychologists use statistics in everything from testing intelligence to basic research. To help you understand statistics, let's first talk about how psychologists conduct research. From that we can show you how statistics are used.

What is an experiment?

Reviewing briefly what we discussed in Chapter 1, do you remember what an experiment is? It's an attempt to establish a functional relationship between independent and dependent variables. In short, it's an effort to find out what stimulus causes what response. We suggested that to do that you could gather data using experimental (laboratory) methods or naturalistic (field-research) observations. You could also conduct interviews or surveys. A number of examples of such procedures for gathering data have been given throughout this book.

Ideas for experiments. From where do ideas for experiments come? That's a problem you may have already faced when your teacher asked you to "do an experiment studying behavior"! As you might suspect, most experiments don't occur "out of the blue." Thomas Edison once said, "Genius is 5 percent inspiration and 95 percent perspiration!" He's not far from right, but the ideas for experiments come from a number of sources. One is the "I wonder what would happen if ... " process. Have you ever been curious as to why people almost always walk in the right door when a building has two doors, even without signs telling them to do so? Observing our environment, noting something that usually happens, and then trying to develop an explanation for it is one ready source of ideas.

Another source is the research that some other person has done in the past. Many psychologists engage in what is called "programmatic" research. This means that each study may be but a small part of an ongoing research program. One psychologist published almost 30 studies back in the 1950s and 1960s. They were attempts to explain why it is that distributed practice is better than massed practice, as we discussed in Chapter 7!

A third source is to test hypotheses derived from a theory. If a theory is correct, it ought to be possible to extend it and make predictions about what should happen in situations never tested before. A fourth related source of ideas is simply to review the research literature. Checking recent publications—journals, magazines, books or texts—is a good way to discover the latest findings on current topics. Regardless of the source of the ideas, once the question is posed, the difficulties of finding the right answer have only begun.

Reviewing the literature is one good way to locate a research topic of interest. Current findings are often reported in recent publications and can suggest the need for a related investigation.

Controls

We have stressed right from the start how important it is to have control groups. Do you remember why? In order to establish a functional relationship between an independent and a dependent variable, we must isolate the effect of the independent variable. So we establish a situation in which subjects experience every important variable. That's our control group. In addition, then, we have a second group that experiences all of the normal variables *plus* the independent variable in which we're interested. That's our "experimental" group. If differences occur between what our experimental group does and what our control group does, what can we conclude? It must be due to the effects of our independent variable. Statistics help us decide whether such differences are important.

One important alternative must be considered when we set up our control. Should we use two separate groups—one experimental, one control? Or, should we use one group for both experimental and control conditions and let each person experience both conditions? There are a number of guidelines to help us make that decision.

Between subjects. In Chapter 15 we talked about leadership and about what makes people attractive to us. In order for any group to operate effectively, it must include people with good ideas—new views, ways to achieve a group's goals, and so forth. Often the leader is such a person, yet it has been observed that frequently the most intelligent person in a group is neither the most popular nor the leader. Might leadership be better if an intelligent person could be made more attractive, and thus better liked?

Box 17-1 describes a piece of research intended to measure exactly ·this effect. It was suggested that smart people may (sometimes) simply seem less attractive. How could you make such a person appear more approachable? Why not have him or her make a mistake—something that could happen to any of us? Read Box 17-1 on the next page to see how this was done.

Have you read Box 17-1? All right, now think about it for a moment. Why couldn't we just let one group listen to the smart person, rate him, and then collect the ratings again after the smart person had committed the blunder of spilling the coffee? Because the group has been permanently altered by listening to the first tape. They've already formed an impression and then committed themselves to paper. They are no longer "naive"—meaning that they now "know" something about the person. Thus they do not have the necessary qualifications any more to

Feature **17–1   FALLING ON FACE TO GAIN FACE**

Thirty-six 19-year-old males were recruited to listen to one of three tape recordings. Each recording contained a taped interview consisting of 50 difficult questions and the replies to them. One control group of 12 heard the person being interviewed answer 15 of the questions correctly. This was considered an average response. Another 12 control subjects heard the person answer 48 of the questions correctly. During the taped interview, the person being interviewed also made statements about his high school activities to reinforce the impression of his being of superior ability. The 24 subjects who served in the control groups heard only this conversation.

The 12 subjects serving as the experimental group also heard, near the end of this last interview, sounds of coffee being spilled. There was much noise and clatter and the person being interviewed was heard to say, "Oh, I've spilled coffee all over my new suit."

After listening to the interview, each subject was himself interviewed by one of two interviewers, who did not know which tape the subject had heard. The subjects were questioned about their feelings concerning the ability and attractiveness of the person interviewed on the tape. The person who gave the superior performance was rated significantly smarter by his listeners than was the person giving the average performance. But what is more interesting, the person of superior ability was considered to be more attractive if he had made the social blunder of spilling his coffee!

Thus, in this particular experiment the hypothesis was confirmed. A person thought to be of high ability was seen as more attractive, and thus more approachable, when other behavior made him more human.

---

serve as the experimental group in our experiment. This important change is the main reason why the experiment described in Box 17-1 was conducted using three separate groups. It's called a *between-subjects* design. Experimental and control group ratings are being compared here *between* groups.

Another example may help you. Suppose we're interested in learning how the lighting in your schoolrooms influences your ability to learn material by reading. We might set the lights at some level, give you a piece of material to learn, and then test to see how much you'd learned. But now we can't use you again, because you've already learned the material! If we set the lights at another level and gave you the same material, you'd instantly know it as well as the first time you'd learned it! Instead, a between-subjects comparison—using similar, but different students—is needed.

between-subjects experiment: *an experiment that compares ratings between control and experimental groups*

Within subjects. Have you ever said a word or a phrase over and over again out loud? Remember how the phrase "toy boat" became very hard to pronounce if you repeated it out loud as rapidly as possible? Soon you couldn't pronounce it correctly. One thing that might have happened to you when you said the word over and over again is that the word began to lose some of its meaningfulness for you.

When what is being measured is the loss in meaningfulness of individual words, the same measures can be made over and over again within the same person. You could say "toy boat" many times and then rate it. You could then say "putrid" many times and rate it, and so forth. The loss of meaningfulness is not influenced by the fact that the same person is saying and rating many words. Here, then, a *within-subjects* experimental procedure could be used.

Throughout this book there are examples of both types of research, some within-subjects and some between-subjects designs. The effects of the experiment itself on the subject are what force us to use one or the other procedure.

Sources of error

We all make errors. Sometimes they're deliberate, and sometimes they're totally unintentional. There are three types of error that psychologists must always be on guard against in running experiments.

Demand characteristics. Psychologists sometimes forget that humans are human. Humans are smart; they're (almost) always thinking; and they're usually trying to please each other. So when an experiment is conducted, the people who serve as subjects are going to be guessing about *everything* that happens to them. That includes the instructions, the room, the task, and even the smile on the researcher's face. They may develop hypotheses (guesses) about what's being studied that have absolutely nothing to do with the real purpose of the study. Yet those guesses may cause the subject to behave other than naturally. Such changes in behavior may influence the conclusions that the researcher is trying to reach.

Demand characteristics are those aspects of an experiment that influence a subject's responses unintentionally. Every time you get an injection of medication to cure an illness, the drug itself is probably causing changes in your body. But what else is involved? Calling for the appointment, driving to the doctor's office, waiting, being examined, rolling up your sleeve, and feeling the pin-prick of pain are also part of the total "treatment." They're irrelevant to the effects of the drug; they're demand characteristics. They must be controlled in an experiment, to be sure that they are present and alike in both the experimental and the control group.

demand characteristics: *those aspects of an experiment that unintentionally influence a subject's responses*

within-subjects experiment: *an experiment that compares ratings made by the same subject on different occasions*

To control demand characteristics, researchers use a *single-blind* technique. Here the experimenter knows what group a subject is in, but the subject himself or herself does not.

→ **Think about it**

The **question**: Why is it not enough for an advertiser to say "Washing with Ripsnort yields a 16 percent cleaner wash"?

The **answer**: Because no control-group data has been reported. It's *possible* that washing with something else would yield a 28 percent cleaner wash. To be expressed properly, *any* statistic should include enough information to allow it to be properly analyzed. Aren't you better informed if you're told, "Washing with Ripsnort yields a 16 percent cleaner wash than no washing at all," or "Washing with soap yields only a 13 percent cleaner wash than no washing at all"?

Experimenter bias. We humans smile when we're pleased. And it pleases researchers to have their theories confirmed in the laboratory. So it would be natural for a researcher to smile when subjects perform correctly and to frown when they don't. Since subjects notice how the experimenter reacts, they may try to guide their responses in order to receive that smile. In short, unless care is taken to make sure every subject is treated exactly the same in an experiment, it's possible for experimenter biases to influence the results of an experiment unintentionally.

Experimenters need to be alert and honest in the collection and analysis of data. A scientist might communicate his or her biases to research assistants, so care must be taken to prevent this. For instance, in Chapter 8 you learned that only seven percent of an emotional message may be communicated by the verbal portion of that message. The other 93 percent may be communicated nonverbally by a tone of voice, a frown or smile, or even a delay in responding.

Such errors are almost always unintentional; one estimate is that about one percent of data may be incorrect. Thus, one of the best controls is simply to make everyone *aware* of them. In addition, in some experiments it's possible to use a *double-blind* technique. Here neither the experimenter nor the subject knows the experimental conditions to which a subject has been assigned. The experiment we described in Box 17-1 involved a double-blind procedure. Each subject knew only about the one tape to which he had listened. Each interviewer did *not* know which tape the subject had heard. Since no one participating in the interview knew enough about the experiment to bias the results, it was a double-blind.

double-blind experiment: *an experiment in which neither the experimenter nor the subject knows the experimental conditions to which a subject has been assigned*

Errors caused by measuring.   Any time a psychologist wants to measure someone's behavior, he or she must do so without interfering with the behavior being measured. In Chapter 6 we said that one of the measures of the strength of a learned response was how long it took to extinguish the response. The problem, of course, is obvious: By the time we know how well-learned the response was, we've destroyed it! Naturalistic observation offers possibilities for watching and recording natural behavior without influencing it at all.

Psychologists must always be on guard to assure that their methods don't influence the behavior being measured, and to assure this they've developed a number of protective ways. We've already reviewed two of them—single- and double-blind techniques of data collection. *Deception* is a third way; subjects are not informed until after the experiment about what the true purposes of the experiment were. A fourth way involves assessing a subject's *awareness*. This is done by asking the subject a series of questions after the experiment in order to learn whether he or she has detected what was being done. In this way adjustments can be made if they are needed. In addition, subjects who knew (or guessed correctly) what was being measured can be compared with those who remained naive. This will reveal whether or not knowledge of being measured influenced anyone's behavior.

After an experiment it is often necessary to assess a subject's awareness of what behavior was actually being measured. Any necessary adjustments can then be made in the results.

Table 17-1 **The rights of research subjects**

SUBJECT HAS A RIGHT TO:	WHICH MEANS:
Give informed consent	The decision to participate should be based on all relevant information that can be released before the experiment.
No pressure to participate	Psychologists must be sure their subjects are not forced to participate.
An honorable "contract"	Both psychologist and subject should perform as if morally and ethically bound to a clearly stated series of mutual obligations upon agreeing to participate.
Freedom from physical and mental stress	Any possible psychological or physical harm should be fully explained before the start of an experiment to assure the subject understands any risks.
Complete debriefing and follow-up	Once the experiment is completed, the subject should be fully informed of all relevant aspects. The psychologist assumes a responsibility to correct any possible physical or mental damage.
Anonymity and confidentiality	The subject's individual data will be held in secret and never reported in a form allowing identification of a specific subject's performance without prior permission from the subject.

(Adapted from APA, 1973).

Ethics in research

What happens to a subject? There are some very strict ethical guidelines that are endorsed by psychologists through their American Psychological Association. Table 17-1 lists the "rights" of anyone who is asked to participate in an experiment. One of the most important rights is that of *informed consent*. Few experiments would be destroyed by telling the subjects beforehand what is going to be done to them.

But what if we're studying honesty, for instance, as it is shown by response to finding money on a sidewalk? Suppose we're interested in what you'd do when (1) alone, (2) with a friend, or (3) as part of a large crowd of people. Clearly, we couldn't tell you beforehand that we were studying your honesty! If we'd told you, then of course you'd try to return the money. But what if you didn't know you were being watched?

So there are situations where the experiment could be conducted before your permission to use the results would be asked. This, however, is done *very* rarely! All of us have a right to know the benefits and dangers that might result from any experiment before deciding whether or not to take part in it.

In addition, some experiments—you read about several in Chapter 6—involve animals. Again, there are very strict ethical rules describing the care that must be taken of research animals. These rules provide specific guidance as to what can and cannot be done.

How are these human and animal-care decisions reached? This question must be asked: Are the benefits to society as a whole greater than any potential (or actual) harm that might be done? If the answer is yes, then the research should be done. However, reaching that decision is not always easy. And the responsibility for making it is an important factor in designing any experiment.

═══════ In review . . .

Ideas for experiments come from curiosity, past research, and theory. To establish a functional relationship between a cause and an effect, psychologists use control groups. They compare experimental- and control-group behavior between subjects or within subjects. In doing research psychologists must be on guard against demand characteristics, experimenter biases, and errors caused by the process of measuring behavior. All psychological research is done following a strict set of ethical guidelines for treatment of subjects.

2 The Importance of Statistics

So far we've been talking about the basic principles by which psychologists design experiments and specify their independent and dependent variables. We've seen how they create their control and experimental groups and how they collect their *data*, or results.

Such procedures usually lead to numbers. Numbers lead to confusion. Confusion leads to mistakes. To prevent mistakes we've got to reduce confusion. To reduce confusion we've got to reduce the number of numbers. To reduce the number of numbers we've got to have a system. That system is statistics! Sometimes they can be misused, but most often that happens only because they are misunderstood. They should be considered as an *aid* to, *not* a substitute for, common sense. A *statistic* is a numerical fact or datum. *Statistics* has to do with the collection, arrangement, and use of those numerical facts or data.

statistics: *numerical facts or data, or their collection, arrangement, and use*

Important terms

In doing an experiment we are usually trying to reach conclusions about a much larger group of people than the ones we are actually studying. In Chapter 1 we were trying to decide whether it was true that blonds have more fun. Obviously we couldn't study *all* blonds. Instead we drew a sample. Doing so immediately involved us in some very basic statistics.

Population. The *population* in psychological research is any group of people, animals, concepts, or events all of which are alike in one respect. In our study the population was all blonds. But we might study all automobile accidents, or all salespeople, or all males weighing less than 130 pounds. All of these are populations. We almost never know something for sure about a population, because we can never study all members of a population—it's usually too large a group.

Sample. Because of this problem we study a *sample*, which is any subgroup drawn by a nonbiased method from a population. A sample is *always* a subgroup. Thus, it is always smaller than the population.

Obviously, the method by which we draw our sample from the population is *very* important. The usual method is to draw a *random sample*. That's a sample for which every member of a population has an equal chance of being chosen.

population: *in doing an experiment, any group comprised of people, animals, concepts, or events that are alike in one respect*

sample: *in doing an experiment, any subgroup drawn by a nonbiased method from the population*

random sample: *a sample in which every member of a population has an equal chance of being chosen*

It is very important to draw an accurate sample if results are to have validity. In a random sample every member of the population has an equal chance of being chosen.

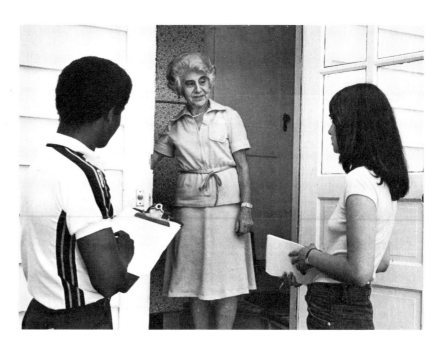

Estimate. An *estimate* is any characteristic of a sample. In selecting your sample of blonds you might have been interested in the age of your sample. That average age would be an estimate. Clearly, the "fun" they reported would be another estimate.

Parameter. A *parameter* is any characteristic of a population. What is the average age of all blonds in North America? We have no way of knowing for sure, but we can estimate it by calculating that age for our sample of blonds. Thus, a sample average is an estimate of a population parameter. We hope our sample has been drawn at random—that is, without bias—from the population. If it has, then our estimates should also be true of the population from which that sample was drawn.

Descriptive statistics

To summarize and analyze any data, three types of statistics can be used. The simplest are the descriptive statistics. Inferential statistics are used for making decisions, and they can be much more complex. More on that type later on. Correlational statistics are also descriptive, but they can also be used to make certain kinds of decisions. Let's look at each form.

Descriptive statistics, as we said, are the simplest ones. Their main use is to collapse large amounts of data into a few numbers. These numbers will convey an impression about—a description of—the whole group of numbers.

Frequency distribution. For example, if you scored 45 on a test in a high school psychology class, would you be happy? If you've been paying attention so far, then you should have mumbled to yourself that we haven't told you enough yet. A *frequency distribution* will list all the possible scores (the distribution), and show how many people gained each possible score (the frequency). This is the simplest data analysis we can perform.

One of the most common forms of such distributions is called a *normal* distribution, as seen in Figure 17-1 on the next page. However, in addition to how you placed in the distribution, you'd also want to know some other information.

Averages. The first piece of information most people would want to know is the "average" score for the class. That's not an easy question to answer—there are several "averages." The average may be a point around which scores are grouped, or the most typical score, or sometimes the most frequent one. Different distributions yield different averages.

estimate: *any characteristic of a sample*

parameter: *any characteristic of a population*

frequency distribution: *a list of all possible scores that includes a count of the number of times each score appears*

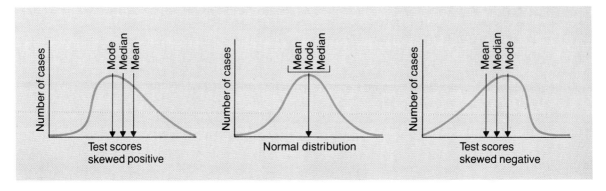

Figure 17-1 In a normal distribution all measures of the mid-point (mean, median, and mode) fall at the middle. However, when most of the data is skewed, (more at one end of the distribution) the mean is "pulled" furthest from the "tail," while the mode is least affected.

The *mode* is the simplest. It's the score that occurs most often. To calculate it just develop a frequency distribution and then report the most common score. When would you use it? When the data are grouped mainly at one end of the distribution of scores. For example, giving the mode would be the most revealing way to show the salary structure of a company. This would show the salary that most people earn.

The *median* is slightly more complex. It is the score that is the midpoint of the distribution; half the scores are above it and half below. How do you find the median? Just count all the scores and divide in half. Then start at the top or bottom and count halfway.

The *mean* is the average you're probably most used to. To find the mean you just add up all the scores and divide by the number of scores. It's the most sensitive measure of "average," because every score affects the mean.

When should we use the mean, the median, or the mode? If your distribution is normal, then the mode, median, and mean are identical—right at the mid-point. As the scores shift so that more and more scores fall at one end or the other, the mean is most affected.

Inferential statistics

You've just gotten a new car. Just as you drive up in front of your best friend's house to show it off, your friend backs out of the driveway in her family's brand new car. The two of you are planning to go somewhere together, but whose car are you going to use? Naturally, an argument follows. The two of you finally

the mode: *the score that occurs most frequently in a distribution*

the median: *the score that is the midpoint of a distribution, arrived at by counting all the scores and dividing by two*

the mean: *the average score in a distribution, arrived at by adding all the scores and then dividing by the number of scores*

decide to flip a coin. It's an arbitrary but fair decision, since it leaves the "decision" up to the laws of chance. Your friend loses, so she suggests, "Two out of three?" She wins the next flip, but you win the third one. As she asks, "Three out of five?" we hope the impossibility of it is beginning to occur to you. How many times will you get a "head" if you flip a coin 100 times? Fifty, we hope. So we always resolve arguments by an odd number of random events.

What if you flipped coins with her 100 times and you won 60? Would you worry about the coin? What if you won 70 times—always guessing "heads"? How about 80? When *would* you start to worry that your coin was biased, or that something other than chance was causing the results? In resolving that question you will make an inferential decision. If extreme things happen too often, then we assume it was not chance that was operating. *Something*—probably your independent variable in an experiment—was causing the data to behave other than randomly.

➡️ **Think about it**

The **question**: We reported to you a conversation in which two members of the Canadian Parliament were said to be arguing about the average annual income for Canadian households. The Conservative MP reported the average was less than $12,000 (CD); the Liberal MP indicated it was more than $16,000 (CD). Who was right, and why?

The **answer**: Both were. Remember, the Conservative party was *not* in power at the time. Thus a Conservative MP would wish to select "averages" that would not make Canadians seem well off. The Liberal Party *was* in power at the time, so one of its MPs would select figures suggesting great progress by Canadian citizens. Since they were both working with the same set of data, the Conservative MP chose to report *median* income, while the Liberal MP chose to report *mean* income.

Any distribution of a nation's annual income by household is not normally distributed. Most citizens make adequate salaries, but a few make *very* high salaries—meaning the mean is most increased. Thus, the median will be somewhat lower, but the mean will be higher because of the few extremely positive earnings figures. Without identifying their "averages" each was correct—but only partly so.

What about that coin? Table 17-2 on the next page shows you how likely it is that you would by chance flip 100 coins and end up with various ratios of heads to tails.

Inferential statistics are used to help scientists make decisions. Could the differences that occur between an experimental group's performance and that of the properly matched control group occur by chance? The less the likelihood that a chance event could have occurred, the more the likelihood that your independent variable *is* having an effect on your dependent vari-

Table 17-2 **The laws of chance in tossing 10 coins**

If you tossed 10 coins in the air 100 times, then you would find at least:		
_____ heads and	_____ tails about	_____ times
10	0	0.1
9	1	1.0
8	2	4.4
7	3	11.7
6	4	20.5
5	5	24.6
4	6	20.5
3	7	11.7
2	8	4.4
1	9	1.0
0	10	0.1

able. A *significant difference* is simply a statement that the difference between two (or more) groups' performances is too great to be thought due only to chance factors.

3 Correlation

A *correlation* indicates the amount of variation in one variable (such as your weight) that can be predicted from knowledge about another variable (such as your height).

A correlation is always reported as a number that can vary from −1.00 to +1.00. The *size* of the number tells you how strong a correlation exists between two sets of data. A correlation of 0 means that there is no relation. And remember the laws of chance. Just by chance there might be a slight correlation in two sets of data even when no actual relationship exists. Thus, a correlation smaller than ±.40 is seldom of interest to a psychologist. A correlation of 1.00 means there is a perfect correlation—every change in one variable can be predicted exactly by a change in the other variable. Obviously, we don't find correlations that big very often—and when we do, we usually call them *laws*, not correlations!

A correlation also tells us something about the nature of the relationship—whether positive, negative, or zero (meaning nonsignificant).

correlation: *a correlation indicates that amount of variation in one variable that can be predicted from knowledge about another variable*

Positive. A positive correlation usually exists between your salary and the amount of income tax you have to pay. As your salary goes up, your taxes also tend to go up. Positive correlations can range from +.01 to +1.00.

Here are some examples of statistics being used to confuse, not to communicate. Can you find the flaws?

First, "With proper treatment, a cold can be cured in seven days, but left to itself a cold will hang on for a week!" All that's happened here is a change of terms, *not a* change of message!

Second, "80 percent of all fatal accidents occur within five miles of home." But, then, how many trips have you ever taken where the first and last five miles weren't within five miles of home? Here's another view of the same situation: How much of your driving is done within five miles of home?

Third, and this one is a bit tricky, "If I buy an article every morning for $.99 and sell it for $1.00 every afternoon, then I make only one percent on total daily sales." *However*, we should point out that the same merchant is making 365 percent annually on the money he or she has invested in the business!

Fourth, read carefully: "For every VW sold in Italy, three Fiats are sold in Germany!" Does that mean Fiat is three times as popular? Where? In Germany? In Italy? The important missing fact here is the absolute number of cars that Germans and Italians buy. If Germans buy *more* than three times as many cars as Italians, then the Fiat is actually a *less* popular car in Germany than the Volkswagen is in Italy! Without all the data, we can't make a decision.

Finally, "The more races Wally Booth runs on Pennsyl Motor Oil, the more he wins!" Does that mean we should buy Pennsyl Motor Oil? Another equally true statement would be, "The fewer races Booth runs on *any* motor oil, the fewer he wins!" Sometimes statisticians simply seem to be assuring our firm grasp of the obvious!

Zero. A zero, or nonsignificant correlation means simply that it is of no help to you to know anything about one variable if you must predict the other. An example of a zero correlation would be an attempt to use the speed of a truck to try to predict the height of its load. They simply are not significantly related.

Negative. A negative correlation means that as one variable increases, the other is actually decreasing. A fall in one is associated with a rise in the other.

In review . . .

The simplest type of descriptive statistic is a frequency distribution of the raw data. Averages (mode, median, or mean) can also be calculated. Inferential statistics are used to help a scientist decide whether experimental-control differences could occur by chance or are more likely due to the effects of the new independent variable. Correlations summarize the size and nature (positive, zero, or negative) of a relation between two sets of data. A high correlation does not mean one variable has caused the other.

Chapter Application and Review

By now you've probably been able to guess for yourself: Correlation research is usually passive. This means that the researcher simply watches and records—height, speed through a stop sign, or whatever. Such data simply report the extent to which two sets of data are related to each other. Doing experiments, on the other hand, involves actively changing the independent variable to note changes in the dependent variable. We've already discussed the importance of control groups, but the key to good research is keeping accurate, detailed, readable records. Without them, a researcher is lost.

So now you've finished your research, and you've got this huge stack of data. What next? In Chapter 1 we said that one part of the total activities of a scientist is communication. In some ways, it's the most vital activity of all. No research can have an impact until it's been published or word of it has spread around. There is general agreement on the form in which reports should be written. Moreover, a lot of help is available to anyone wishing to write a research report. So here we will just briefly outline the essential elements of a report in the order in which they generally should appear.

Abstract. A single issue of a research journal may have from three to fifty research reports in it! No scientist is interested in all of them. The abstract is where you lay out the skeleton of your research—your hypothesis, the design (method) of your experiment, the very basics of what you found (or, alas, failed to find), and what you conclude. Each fact is given in no more than one sentence. The goal is not to relay all the information, but to mention the essential parts.

Introduction. Why did you do this research? In this section, you summarize (1) what has already been found out about what is being studied, (2) any conflicts in previous research (which may be noted or commented upon), (3) hypotheses (guesses) about what may be occurring, and (4) the specific factors to be studied and how they will be investigated. The goal here is simply to tell the reader what you're studying and why.

Method. Here you should have three or four separate sections. (1) *Subjects* will describe the population you were studying and the sample you drew from that population. (2) *Design* will describe how many groups were involved. You will identify the independent and dependent variables, as well as the relationship of the control group to the experimental group. (3) *Apparatus* will include a description of any unusual equipment used for the experiment. Everyone knows what a slide projector is, so naming it is enough. However, if you're using a "modified one-way platform avoidance chamber," you'll want to describe it in more detail.

Finally, (4), *procedure* will explain what the subjects were asked to do, and often will include the various activities of the experimenter. The instructions you gave to your subjects may be included; if not, the reader should at least know what each subject was told.

In fact, one good way to check on how good your method section is, is to give it to a friend. Let him or her read it, and then ask your friend to explain it to you—with *no* hints from you! If he or she can't accurately describe your experiment, then you should add to or change the information you've included (or find a smarter friend)!

Results. Finally, you get to report what you actually found. Don't interpret it in this section, just report the findings. Here you would include tables of numbers such as averages and measures of variation. In addition, any graphs of the subjects' behavior would also be included. In this section you might also add any other descriptive, inferential, or correlational statistics you have calculated. Also report the values showing the probability your differences (between experimental and control groups) could have occurred just by chance. You do *not* usually show the calculations themselves, just the results.

Discussion. Bad experiments are not usually reported. That's an indirect way of saying the discussion section should not simply be a list of apologies! Here you analyze what you've found in your experiment. You talk about how your results confirm the hypotheses you developed in the introduction, or how they fail to do so.

References. One famous research psychologist once commented that *"plagiarism* is stealing from one person without credit; *scholarship* is stealing from many without credit"! There's a nugget of truth to the statement, one not easily learned by young scientists. Very few original pieces of research are done. There's only been one Freud in the world of psychoanalysis. Others have built on his work. It's the same in most fields of research.

Always include in your references the work of others from which your research is being drawn. It is not uncommon even for short research reports to contain as many as 100 references. You'll notice the many references cited at the end of this book.

REVIEW QUESTIONS

SECTION 1 (pages 513–521)

1. From where do scientists get their ideas for experiments?

2. Why are control groups necessary in experiments?

3. Compare and contrast "between-subject" experiments and "within-subject" experiments.

4. What are "demand characteristics," and how do we keep them from influencing the results of experiments?

5. What is "experimenter bias," and how can it be prevented?

6. What kinds of errors can be caused by the processes of measuring behavior?

7. What ethical restrictions limit experimentation?

SECTION 2 (pages 521–526)

1. Define and give an example of each of the following: population, sample, estimate, parameter.

2. Name and distinguish among the three most common types of statistics.

3. What is a frequency distribution?

4. How are the mode, the median, and the mean of a set of data similar and how are they different? When will their numerical value be closest to equal?

5. How do inferential statistics differ from descriptive statistics?

SECTION 3 (pages 526–527)

1. Name and describe two types of information given by a correlation.

2. What does it mean when two variables in an experiment are found to be highly correlated?

3. Describe the standard format in which most reports of psychological experiments are presented.

ACTIVITIES

1. Career Search. Write to the Publications Office, American Psychological Association, 1200 Seventeenth Street, N.W., Washington, D.C. 20036, for a copy of their ethical standards that apply to research conducted with animals. Before the publication arrives, imagine that your class is a group of research psychologists. From what you've learned in this book, develop your own set of standards. When the APA standards arrive, compare them with yours.

2. To watch the laws of chance and the principles of sampling in operation, find a supply of marbles—red ones, white ones, and blue ones. Place sixty marbles of one color, thirty of another, and ten of the third into a box. Allow a number of your friends to draw one marble at a time without looking into the box. After you have recorded which color marble each one drew, have them replace the marble in the box. Shake the box and allow them to draw again. Do this ten times and then ask each of your friends to guess how many marbles of what color there are in the box. Keep track of all the data you collect, and after ten or more friends have drawn their marbles (and replaced them), see what your totals are for each color of all the sets of ten marbles. How accurate would your own guess be, based on the repeated sets of ten that were drawn? Identify the population, the sample, the estimate, and the parameter in this experiment. And . . . don't lose your marbles!

3. Run an experiment to develop a frequency distribution. Does the main entrance to your school have at least four doors? If so, get some friends to help and then observe for fifteen minutes one morning. Record how many people enter each door and (on a separate distribution) how many leave. Or you could ask as many people as possible to choose their favorite number between zero and nine, inclusive. Is there a favorite?

4. If you ran the experiment in Activity 3 in the morning, as suggested, try repeating it for the same length of time in the afternoon. Compare the two frequency distributions. Is there a difference in the number of people entering as opposed to leaving? Now, look only at those who enter in the morning, and those who leave in the afternoon: Is there any difference in the frequency with which they choose to use each door? What can you conclude from this?

INTERESTED IN MORE?

AGNEW, N. M. & PYKE, S. *The Science Game: An Introduction to Research in the Behavioral Sciences*, 2nd ed. Prentice-Hall, 1976. Discusses how to design, conduct, and write a research report on an experiment in psychology.

BRADLEY, J. I. & McCLELLAND, J. N. *Basic Statistical Concepts: A Self-Instructional Text*, 2nd ed. Scott, Foresman, 1978. A programmed-learning text introducing descriptive, inferential, and correlational statistics.

CAMPBELL, S. K. *Flaws and Fallacies in Statistical Thinking.* Prentice-Hall, 1974. A painless and funny look at how statistics can be used to misrepresent the data they are summarizing. Includes examples from research and advertising.

DOHERTY, M. E. & SHEMBERG, X. M. *Asking Questions About Behavior: An Introduction to What Psychologists Do*, 2nd ed. Scott, Foresman, 1978. Shows how to develop a question and design a simple experiment to answer it. Emphasizes the study of stress.

DOWNIE, N. M. & HEATH, R. W. *Basic Statistical Methods*, 5th ed. Harper & Row, 1983. A good means of mastering introductory statistics independently: includes 3 to 16 problems per chapter, with answers listed in the appendix.

HUFF, D. & GEIS, I. *How to Lie With Statistics.* W.W. Norton & Co., Inc., 1954. An old book but still an excellent source of funny examples of the use and misuse of statistics. Nine out of ten people like it.

LOVEJOY, E. P. *Statistics for Math Haters.* Harper & Row, 1975. Approaches the introduction of statistics as a logical exercise, rather than a series of mathematical techniques. Not light reading, but interesting.

MOSTELLAR, F., et al. *Statistics by Example.* Addison-Wesley, 1973. Designed for high-school students, this four-volume series covers exploring data, designing patterns, finding models, and weighing chances. Uses real data to show the value of statistics in clarification.

REED, J. G. & BAXTER, P. M. *Library Use: A Handbook for Psychology.* American Psychological Association, 1983. An excellent guide to the use of library resources to find published information on psychology. Written by a psychologist and a librarian, it conducts the reader through all major reference resources for psychological literature.

SARBIN, T. & COE, W. *The Student Psychologists' Handbook: A Guide to Sources.* Schenkman, 1969. Shows how to locate sources, use a library, and organize, write, and reference a research paper.

SPENCE, J. T., et al. *Elementary Statistics*, 4th ed. Prentice-Hall, 1983. A well-written introduction to standard statistical techniques. This classic text is accompanied by a workbook that helps students determine the type of statistical test most appropriate.

WOOD, C. *Fundamentals of Psychological Research*, 2nd ed. Little, Brown, 1977. Analyzes the major research strategies, with heavy emphasis on statistical analysis.

Psychology and Careers

CHAPTER OUTLINE

1 Psychology: Problems and Potentials

By now you know that psychology is a profession as well as a science. Clearly, a need exists for psychological services in many areas of current concern, both scientific and therapeutic. The treating professional offers therapy to individuals with problems requiring immediate attention. The research professional has the more long-range goal of understanding underlying processes—those involved in schizophrenia, for example—in order to develop better therapy.

Research experiments often involve control-group subjects, who receive no treatment for their problems. Yet control groups are necessary, for without them there is no assurance that the experimental treatment does make a difference. Box E-1 gives an example of the ethical dilemma posed by such research. It illustrates how the goals of research-oriented psychologists may conflict with those of therapeutically oriented psychologists.

If you are considering a career in psychology, you will need to decide on which side you prefer to contribute—theory and research or practice and applications. Here, however, we are going to consider not only those careers in psychology that require specialized knowledge but also some jobs requiring less education, where skills in psychology can also make a significant contribution.

Animal research provides professional opportunities for psychologists to use experimental methods or naturalistic observation.

2 Psychology: Jobs and the Future

Reports in the mid-1980's indicate that unemployment among psychologists with a Master's degree or a Ph.D. is well below the national averages. At that time 8 to 10 percent of the country's workforce was unemployed, but less than two percent of the Ph.D.-holding psychologists were looking for work.

One reason for this is that psychologists are needed to solve new problems facing society. For example, people are living to older ages, and the fraction of the world population made up of elderly people is growing. What do we know about the aging

Feature   **E–1   ETHICAL DILEMMAS**

Consider the following newsstory from The Houston Post:

Placebo Study has Scientists in Quandary

Boston (UPI)—In a recent study showing the ability of aspirin to prevent fatal or crippling stroke in men with stroke symptoms, some volunteers died.

They died not because they were taking a dangerous drug, but because they were taking something worthless, a placebo.

If they had been taking aspirin, they might have lived. But if no one in the study had taken the placebo, the researchers could not have found out that aspirin cuts the risk of death or paralyzing stroke in half for men who've had minor strokes.

The *placebo* is an ineffective substance given to a control group when testing is being done on the effects of taking a drug. Why is such a control necessary? Some drugs may influence our health or behavior only because we *think* they will, not because of any actual physiological effect.

This poses a problem for researchers. They must be able to state that a drug or therapy can and does help humans before it will be authorized or accepted for general use. And that leads to a difficult ethical dilemma. Who should be in the "control" group that will receive worthless substances that are known *not* to influence the condition being studied? If a drug does turn out to be successful in the experimental group, the people in the control have not been given a treatment that would have helped them.

But what happens if the drug or therapy turns out to have unanticipated bad side effects? Under these conditions, the subjects in the experimental group may be worse off than those in the control group. Yet, researchers cannot know whether a drug or therapy will help until it has been compared with a no-treatment and a placebo control. In this conflict, which point of view do you think should prevail?

process? How can we understand the elderly—their needs and concerns, joys and life styles? Another problem concerns the rise of technology in the modern world. How will people learn to handle the greater amounts of free time that technology is creating? What new benefits (or problems) will this new technology create for us? Problems like these will cause the range of job opportunities for psychologists to expand in coming years.

But even with these opportunities, is psychology the field for you? Interest tests—such as those reviewed in Chapter 14—may give you the answer. However, there are other ways you can assess your interests. Even while you are going to school, you can gain some experience in the work world, *before* you are committed to a particular career path. The more career options you examine, the more likely you are to be happy with your ultimate choice. How can you accomplish this?

Human relationships in all careers can be beneficial when people have an understanding of psychological principles. If you want to be a youth group leader, you must understand developmental psychology and be skilled in communication techniques. If you want to work on a one-to-one basis with the handicapped, qualities of empathy and warmth are essential. Here a specialist teaches language to a deaf child.

One strategy is to *volunteer* in an organization where the principles of psycholgy are—or should be—applied. Such agencies include psychiatric, emergency, or outpatient wards in a local hospital, nursing homes for the elderly, hospices for the dying, or agencies sponsoring visitation programs for the elderly. You can offer your help to child-care centers, a baby-sitting service, or an elementary school teacher. What if you think you're interested in a career in research psychology? Once you have completed your first psychology course, consider volunteer-

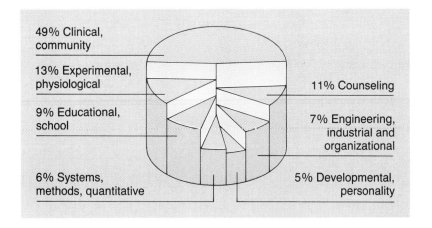

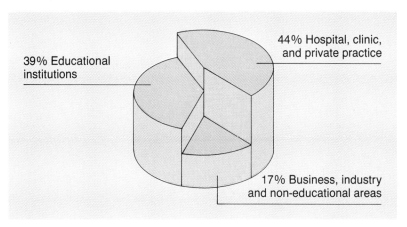

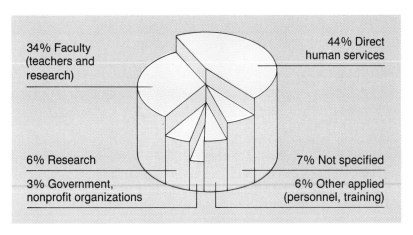

Figure E-1 Graph of replies by Ph.D.-level psychologists to the question "What kind of psychologist are you?"
Figure E-2 Main source of employment of the psychologists surveyed.
Figure E-3 Nature of work they performed.

Biofeedback is currently of interest to psychologists as a means of reducing tension in an increasingly stressful society. Here a psychologist records the degree of psychokinetic activity being experienced by a subject (out of view).

ing your time at a nearby college to work with a professor and his or her graduate students, helping them with their research. These are some of the more obvious possibilities, but don't ignore other options that may be available to you.

A second strategy involves how you spend your summers. What kind of a *summer job* might teach you something about psychology? Psychology is applied in a variety of settings. How about working for an advertising agency? Or in the personnel department of a large store or company? How about accepting a sales position? The park department in many cities hires a number of teenagers to run recreational and learning programs for children during the summer. You might try working for your state or federal government. The opportunities in states will vary, but the federal government has an astounding array of agencies and departments that utilize the strategies and principles of psychology.

In the following section we briefly describe a few of the jobs that involve psychology—starting with some volunteer positions, and continuing through careers requiring higher education. But we can only suggest the range of occupations in which knowledge of psychology is helpful or required—to cover them all might fill another book this size!

Table E-1 **Jobs to consider for gaining experience where principles of psychology can be applied**

JOB	EXAMPLES
POLICE WORK	Traffic counter Front office work; public relations
HOSPITAL	Community-based, volunteer service groups Recreational worker
COMMUNICATIONS	Newspaper advertising department Radio or television commercial sales Billboard company
COMMUNITY	Organizer for youth groups Coordinator of volunteer services
PERSONNEL WORK	Test monitor for industry Personnel office of industry or educational institution
EDUCATION	Teacher's aide Library aide
CHILD-CARE	Child-care center Babysitting

Chapter Application and Review

USING PSYCHOLOGY *Jobs requiring a knowledge of psychology*

Job: crisis hotline advisor

Employer. A large county hospital.

Can you do it? A person holding this job might well be in his or her senior year in high school. For most such crisis intervention programs, applicants must complete a training program. A county hospital, for instance, might offer such training over three weekends. A typical assignment would involve two four-hour shifts a week.

What's involved? Crisis hotline personnel respond primarily to two kinds of problems. One involves the immediate, possibly life-threatening situation that can arise as a result of a personal or family crisis—perhaps an argument, or the unexpected death of a loved one. Drugs or drug overdoses can also bring about an immediate need for help. The other type of problem is the crisis evolving from long-term stress, such as that experienced in the family, on the job, or in a failure to develop one's career. Crises like these are not quite so life-threatening but still need to be resolved.

A person handling a hotline will have a list of psychologists and psychiatrists as well as information about a wide array of treatment facilities and programs operating in the vicinity. The skill in this job is being able to calm the caller, identify what his or her problem seems to be, and help that caller in seeing the wisdom—once the immediate crisis has been dealt with—of contacting the most appropriate agency for long-term follow-up.

Job: word processor salesperson

Employer. A local computer dealer.

Can you do it? People with an interest in psychology are likely to have a higher-than-average interest in behavior—both theirs and others. That interest—even if only backed by a high school diploma—is a vital element of the successful salesperson. One recent report suggests that the best salespersons are motivated by the need for status, control, respect, routine, accomplishment, stimulation, and honesty. With those needs met, a salesperson—regardless of level of education—will feel happy. A basic understanding of people's driving forces—their needs for achievement, affiliation, and safety—is but one aspect of psychology that would aid someone seeking a career in sales.

What's involved? The key requirement may be experience. One psychologist has suggested that you cannot educate someone to be good in sales—but sensitivity to others can be improved by training. One must also be dominant, persistent, skillful at language, able to query prospective customers and relate their needs to those answered by the product you are offering—and it wouldn't hurt to have a high level of energy.

Job: ward attendant

Employer. A state mental hospital.

Can you do it? The successful applicant need not have a high school diploma, but he or she should have a stronger-than-average commitment to helping people often not able to help themselves. Simple concern for humanity may be the key ingredient.

What's involved? On a typical day the attendant helps the ward staff run the basic hospital facilities and programs. This means making beds, bathing patients, and cleaning the recreational and living areas. Also, the worker might participate in recreational activities with the patients, such as music, art, or sports events, or visits outside the hospital.

Job: mental health assistant

Employer: A senior citizen service center.

Can you do it? This is a new career field, usually requiring at least an associate degree. An associate degree is awarded after a two-year course preparing for paraprofessional occupations in nursing homes, community mental health centers, centers dealing with mental retardation, or even special-education centers for the variously disabled in public schools.

What's involved? Typically supervised by a staff psychologist, an assistant helps with or conducts admission interviews. He or she may be responsible—under supervision—for administering various psychological tests, either to new patients or to assess the progress of those already admitted.

Job: high school psychology teacher

Employer: The local Board of Education.

Can you do it? What's required is a commitment to teaching. Since teaching is not a source of great financial reward, it is important to be able to find rewards in the job itself. Teaching requires a bachelor's degree, and current rules (and the recent pressures for competency testing) make it likely you will continue your education, working gradually toward a master's degree over the first 7 to 10 years or so in this position.

What's involved? A high school teacher has total responsibility for teaching five or six courses, but rarely are all six courses in the same subject area. Thus a student planning to teach psychology would do well to develop another major teaching strength—perhaps in sociology, economics, computers, or biology.

Job: personnel director

Employer: A large department store.

Can you do it? The successful applicant is likely to have a bachelor's degree in psychology, having concentrated on courses involving interviewing, test construction and interpretation, statistics, and—perhaps surprisingly to you—law. Such a person might also have taken a minor in management courses in a university's College of Business Administration. He or she would stress organizational and quantitative skills. This is not an entry-level job, however. Some prior experience with the employer's policies is a definite requirement.

What's involved? A personnel director may participate in a wide array of activities, depending on the nature and interest of his or her employer. Clearly, the decisions to hire and fire would be this person's responsibility, especially for the support staff in any organization. Such a person might also develop programs to improve or maintain staff skills—in sales, interpersonal sensitivity, or any other skill involved in conducting the company's business.

Job: school psychologist

Employer: A city school system.

Can you do it? A master's degree is a must for this position; an undergraduate major in psychology is desirable. In addition, most school psychologists must be licensed or certified in their state of employment, which involves taking a test.

What's involved? In bigger districts, you might stay in one school, but many school psychologists divide their time among a number of schools. They are usually working with children experiencing the normal array of problems in school. A school psychologist might give reading, aptitude, interest, or intelligence tests, and must be skillful in interpreting them. At other times he or she might work directly with the children or young adults in school or with the family of those students.

Job: clinical psychologist

Employer: Yourself.

Can you do it? To use this title in most states requires a Ph.D. (a Doctor of Philosophy) or a Psy.D. (a Doctor of Psychology). The Psy.D. is a new degree, developed in the 1970's. In a Psy.D. program, a student gains skill in psychotherapy, undergoing intensive training in testing, interviewing, giving supervised therapy, and using all the tools of the clinical psychologists.

What's involved? A practicing clinical psychologist is often self-employed. Thus, required skills include those needed to run any business, in addition to knowledge of testing and practical experience with the limits and strengths of various forms of therapy. He or she must develop working relations with other clinicians in the area—psychiatrists, medical doctors, and other contacts in local hospitals and mental health facilities. From such sources come the patient/client referrals that are vital to one's success as a psychotherapist.

A typical day might involve 8 to 10 hours in various stages of psychotherapy with different individuals. The hours have to be offered at times when clients are free to visit, so this may not be a traditional 9-to-5 job. Other types of therapy a clinical psychologist might offer are group therapy or consultaion with other therapeutic organizations such as Alcoholics Anonymous. It is also possible, of course, to utilize these same skills as a clinical psychologist in a state-supported mental hospital, a Veterans Administration hospital, or a community mental health center.

Job: consulting psychologist

Employer: A management consulting firm.

Can you do it? A Ph.D. is required for this job. Such a person might spend graduate school in an industrial/organizational psychology program learning management practices, testing strategies, interpersonal behavioral strategies, and intervention techniques in complex organizations.

What's involved? A consultant—by the very nature of his or her job—must offer an array of skills not normally represented among the full-time employees of companies that hire consultants. Thus, a consultant's job, by its very nature, tends to be short-term. A consultant might, for instance, advise a company's top management on how to take human performance limits into account in the design of a control board for a nuclear power plant. He or she might be involved in all aspects of the design of an interstate highway—signs, bridges and cross-over devices, and lane-flow control.

In conclusion

Employers are most likely to hire someone who offers special skills. In psychology, as in many other career fields, job choices are limited if you have only a high school diploma. Surprisingly, when you have a Ph.D. you also have relatively few choices, but by that time you have chosen to "fine-tune" your educaton and experience to a specific kind of job—you are a specialist.

Those with a bachelor's degree in psychology may have the most options, with the widest array of possible employers. Moreover, psychology is a logical undergraduate major for those planning graduate work in such fields as sociology, social work, law, medicine, or education. Human behavior plays a key role in all these areas.

The bibliography that follows lists a variety of resources—some free, all valuable—to help guide you in your preparation for the future.

ACTIVITIES

1. What do you view as the most important unanswered problem or challenge still facing psychologists? Defend your answer.

2. Career Search. Invite several graduate students in psychology from a local college or university to speak to your class about how they got to their current positions in graduate school. Ask them to indicate some of the details of their undergraduate years in college, especially what parts of their curriculum they have found most valuable. What changes would they make in their own preparation if they had it to do all over again? For a more balanced series of advisory presentations, you might invite some students training to be clinical psychologists, others training to teach or do research.

3. Career Search. Write a brief essay on your own career goals. Sit down with your teacher or a career guidance person at your school to go over your plans. Ask this person to react with his or her best judgment to your plans.

INTERESTED IN MORE?

Careers in Psychology. American Psychological Association, 1978. Single copies of this document are free on request from the APA. Discusses what psychology is, and includes descriptions of jobs held by various psychologists.

FRETZ, B. R. & STANG, D. J. *Preparing for Graduate Study in Psychology: Not for Seniors Only.* American Psychological Association, 1980. Aimed at college students but interesting reading for high school students considering an advanced degree in psychology. Reviews the steps in and makes helpful suggestions about identifying and guiding your own interests.

GRASHA, A. *Practical Applications of Psychology*, 2nd ed. Little, Brown, 1983. Leads the reader through an array of psychological principles as they apply to such problems as how to study more effectively and how to improve communication skills.

SKINNER, B. F. *Beyond Freedom and Dignity.* Knopf, 1971. Raises some important issues about control of human responses through positive reinforcement of desired behaviors.

SUPER, D. E. *Opportunities in Psychology: Careers Today.* National Textbook, 1976. Reviews employment prospects, the likely pay for various jobs, and the education that is required.

TOFFLER, A. *Future Shock.* Random House, 1970. A challenging look at modern industrial society and its impact on our lives. The new emphasis on service industries creates a potential impact on psychology as the science of human behavior.

WILLIAMS, R. L. & LONG, J. D. *Toward a Self-Managed Life Style.* Houghton Mifflin, 1975. Designed for students who would like to use the techniques of behavior modification to change their own behavior. Shows how we can act upon our environment and exercise self-control.

WOODS, P. J., ed. *Career Opportunities for Psychologists: Expanding and Emerging Areas.* American Psychological Association, 1976. Does an excellent job of analyzing present and future job prospects in the field of psychology.

WOODS, P. J., ed. *The Psychology Major: Training and Employment Strategies.* American Psychological Association, 1979. Although targeted at college students, this text includes an excellent analysis of how to identify your own interests, how to shape your education, and how to present yourself to a potential employer. Includes a wide-ranging analysis of job opportunities for those interested in psychology.

ADLER, ALFRED (1870–1937) is credited with founding the "school" of individual psychology, the theory that the individual's need for power and superiority are the driving forces of his/her personality. He introduced the concept of the inferiority complex.

ALLPORT, GORDON (1897–1967) American psychologist who is noted for his studies of personality. He was especially interested in the phenomenon of prejudice.

ANASTASI, ANNE (1908–   ) is known for her work in measurement and intelligence testing and the investigation of individual differences. Among her most important works are *Differential Psychology* and *Psychological Testing*.

BANDURA, ALBERT (1925–   ) Well-known for his work in demonstrating the importance of observation and imitation in learning, he believes reinforcement only becomes important in strengthening and maintaining a new behavior pattern but not in acquiring it.

BEKESY, GEORG VON (1899–   ) Hungarian-born physicist who became an innovator in the field of perception. His research in hearing won him the Nobel Prize in 1961 for his discoveries concerning the physical mechanisms of stimulation within the cochlea.

BINET, ALFRED (1857–1911) is considered the most important French psychologist of his time. He took special interest in the varying mental capacities of humans and, with Theodore Simon, developed tests to measure human intelligence levels.

BOWER, GORDON H. (1932–   ) has carried on a wide-ranging program of research on the underlying processes of learning and memory. His *Theories of Learning* (coauthored with E. R. Hilgard) is considered a classic text. As editor and writer, he has been a leading authority on learning for several decades.

CLARK, KENNETH B. (1914–   ) An educator and psychologist who has studied the psychology of prejudice and racial problems. Among his writings are *Prejudice and Your Child, Dark Ghetto,* and *Desegregation: An Appraisal of the Evidence.*

EBBINGHAUS, HERMANN (1850–1909) originated memory studies and invented the nonsense syllable as a means of studying learning and memory supposedly not influenced by the mate-

SOME SIGNIFICANT PSYCHOLOGISTS

rial's meaning. His studies of long-term memory are still cited.

ELLIS, HAVELOCK (HENRY) (1859–1939) Noted for his research in the psychology of sex, he examined this topic from a biological and anthropological viewpoint and set down his findings in seven volumes called *Studies in the Psychology of Sex.* Ellis also studied the psychology of dreams.

ERIKSON, ERIK (1902–   ) A German psychoanalyst who migrated to the U.S. in 1933. Erikson proposed that people pass through certain developmental stages that must be successfully completed in order to move successfully to the next stage.

ESTES, WILLIAM K. (1919–   ) was primarily responsible for developing a statistical approach to learning theory. He has developed a number of influential mathematical models of learning processes—an analysis of stimuli, responses, and how they are associated. He has also edited a number of influential journals in experimental psychology, most recently the *Psychological Review.*

FREUD, SIGMUND (1856–1939) is considered the father of psychoanalysis. His writings and work stemmed from his theory that the development of personality depends on basic sexual and aggressive drives. He stressed the person's past in analyzing his or her present. Freud also studied the nature of hysteria and wrote works including *Civilization and Its Discontents* and *The Psychopathology of Everyday Life.*

GIBSON, ELEANOR J. (1910–   ) studied perceptual learning and perceptual development in children; her study of the "visual cliff" is among her best-known works. She has also extended those early studies into an analysis of reading and how it relates to and influences learning.

HALL, G. STANLEY (1846–1924) An American psychologist whose achievements include founding one of the first psychology laboratories in the U.S. and publishing pioneering studies in childhood, adolescence, and human genetics. Hall's studies of children are considered his most important work. He is also a founder of the *American Journal of Psychology,* the *Journal of Applied Psychology,* and the American Psychological Association.

HARLOW, HARRY F. (1905–1981) An American psychologist well-known for thirty-five years of research with monkeys and the effects of surrogate (substitute) mothers on these animals. Through his experiments, Harlow investigated neurophysiology, motivation, and love.

HORNEY, KAREN (1885–1952) A German-born psychoanalyst who stressed the social rather than the biological influences on human behavior. Unlike Freud, Horney believed that society is largely responsible for causing women to feel inferior to men. Her significant publications include *The Neurotic Personality of Our Time, Self-Analysis,* and *Our Inner Conflicts.*

HULL, CLARK (1884–1953) An American psychologist known for his concern with understanding the learning process. His behavioral studies resulted in a book, *Principles of Behavior,* in 1943 in which he proposed a theory of learning and behavior that had a major influence on American psychology for two decades.

JAMES, WILLIAM (1842–1910) American psychologist and philosopher who was a major influence in establishing the functional school of psychology. He taught at Harvard University for many years and founded the first psychology laboratory in the U.S.

JUNG, CARL (1875–1961) Swiss psychologist and psychiatrist who broke with Freud in 1913 to found analytical psychology. Jung introduced the concepts of introvert and extrovert, as well as the collective unconscious (human memories of which we are unaware) and archetypes (universal symbols in art, literature, and religion).

KOFFA, KURT (1886–1941) An American psychologist and researcher and one of the founders of Gestalt psychology. He is considered an innovator in the study of perception of movements and in problems of seeing.

KOHLBERG, LAWRENCE (1927–   ) Known for his studies on the development of moral reasoning in children. The three major developmental levels he proposes share some similarities to Piaget's stages in human development.

KOHLER, WOLFGANG (1887–1967) A founder of Gestalt psychology along with Koffa and Wertheimer. Unlike his colleagues, he took special interest in animal behavior and learning.

LACEY, BEATRICE C. and JOHN I. (1919– and 1915–   ) were among the early workers to identify and document the importance of underlying physiological processes to the phenomena studied by psychologists. They studied physiological arousal and demonstrated its uniqueness in each of us, its stability over time, and its importance to many of our environmental interactions.

LAING, R.D. (1927–   ) A psychiatrist whose views of mental illness are revolutionary. He feels that mental "illness" is not necessarily abnormal but is instead a defense against external stresses. Laing is credited with helping to organize therapeutic communities in Great Britain.

LEWIN, KURT (1890–1947) A German social psychologist of the Gestalt school. He studied the effect of authoritarian and democratic behavior on groups.

LORENZ, KONRAD (1903–   ) A founder of ethology—the study of animal behavior—and one of three recipients of the 1973 Nobel Prize in physiology and medicine. He is particularly well-known for his concept of imprinting and for studying animal behavior by observing animals in their natural environment rather than in the laboratory.

MACCOBY, ELEANOR (1917–   ) In studying child growth and development, she has observed the effects of praise, love-withdrawal, reward, and physical punishment on the socialization of children. In addition to studying the effects of differing child-rearing techniques, she has focused in recent years on sex differences among children. She is author of *Development of Sex Differences* and co-author of *Patterns of Child Rearing* and *Experiments in Primary Education.*

MASLOW, ABRAHAM (1908–1970) studied human motivation and developed a personality theory centered around basic human needs—the hierarchy of needs. One of his most important writings is *Motivation and Personality.*

MILGRAM, STANLEY (1933–   ) is known for his experiments in obedience to authority, conformity, and crowd behavior. His best-known and widely controversial experiment on obedience to authority was published in 1963.

MILLER, NEAL E. (1909–   ) His earliest works center on learning. He and John Dollard developed a theory of personality that attempted to convert Freud's Psychoanalytic Theory into a series of testable assertions based on learning principles. In recent years his investigations of conditioning and the autonomic nervous system

have established an entirely new field—biofeedback.

PIAGET, JEAN (1896–1980) A Swiss psychologist who had pioneered in the study of the thought processes of children. His early interest in biology was balanced by an uncle's encouragement to study philosophy, leading ultimately to his being among the first in this century to stress the way children think rather than what they think. He viewed intelligence as involving adaptation to the environment and stressed the importance of the child's actions in moving him/her through the various stages of thought.

ROGERS, CARL (1902–   ) Introduced the concept of client-centered therapy to the traditional doctor-patient role relationship. His interest in using scientific methods in psychotherapy led him to record, transcribe, and publish a verbatim account of a psychotherapy case thus paving the way for making his theory of the self testable.

SCHACHTER, STANLEY (1922–   ) A social psychologist known for his studies of group behavior, social influence, and dependency needs. He helped develop the theory of cognitive dissonance and was one of the first to examine dependency and also the impact of the environment on our interpretations of emotion.

SIMON, HERBERT A. (1916–   ) is famous for his studies in human information-processing and computer simulation of those human behaviors. Outside of psychology he is best known for his organizational theory and decision-making in complex organizations which gained him the 1978 Nobel Prize in Economics.

SKINNER, B.F. (1904–   ) An American best known for his development of the basic principles of operant conditioning. He has extended his studies of learning and his belief in behaviorist principles into such areas as programmed learning and into controversial views on how society should be organized, as discussed in his best selling books *Walden Two* and *Beyond Freedom and Dignity.*

SPERRY, ROGER W. (1913–   ) has performed classic studies of sensory and motor integration. His studies of patients whose corpus callosum has been severed opened up whole new research areas on the "splitbrain," and contributed to the understanding of vision and cognitive functioning.

THORNDIKE, EDWARD LEE (1874–1949) An educational psychologist who contributed to the study of learning and teaching. Also interested in mental testing. Thorndike invented the puzzle box as a means of investigating how animals solve problems. These studies led to his integrated learning theory and had a strong influence on the development of modern principles of operant conditioning.

TULVING, ENDEL (1927–   ) has spent almost a quarter century studying the input and retrieval aspects of human memory, including subjective organization, available versus accessible memory, and episodic versus semantic memory—a concept he introduced.

WATSON, JOHN B. (1878–1958) held that behavior should be studied in an objective, experimental manner, and that psychology was thus an experimental science. He established a new area of psychology called behaviorism which emphasizes the role of the environment and the observable behavior of an organism in the development and understanding of humans.

WECHSLER, DAVID (1896–   ) started his study of cognitive growth in the 1920's. The entire series of Wechsler Intelligence tests grew out of this early work—tests that affected the lives of millions of people worldwide.

WERTHEIMER, MAX (1880–1943) A founder of the Gestalt school of psychology, which disputes the traditional psychologists' efforts to analyze experience into its individual parts. He asserted experience must be examined in its totality.

WUNDT, WILLIAM (1832–1920) Often called the father of modern psychology, he founded the first modern psychological laboratory for the study of behavior. His laboratory experiments contributed greatly to the establishment of psychology as an experimental science.

The page number following each definition refers to the page on which the word or term is first discussed.

absolute refractory period: the short time period after firing, during which the neuron can't fire no matter how stimulated (p. 119) [Compare *relative refractory period*]

absolute threshold: the smallest amount of a stimulus that can be detected by an organism (p. 151) [Compare *difference threshold*]

abstract: a report in which the skeleton of a body of psychological research is laid out, including the hypothesis, the design of the experiment, the results, and the conclusion drawn (p. 528)

achievement test: a test aimed at assessing how much of a given subject has been learned (p. 438) [Compare *aptitude test*]

action potential: the reaction of the neuron to stimulation that is above threshold (the point at which it will fire) (p. 119) [Compare *resting potential*]

Activation Theory: a basically physiological theory of emotion that stresses the underlying state of arousal (p. 312) [Compare *Attribution Theory, Opponent-process Theory*]

adolescence: the span of years between the onset of puberty and the completion of bone growth (p. 85) [Compare *puberty*]

afferent neurons: cells that conduct nerve impulses from the receptors toward the brain or spinal column (p. 124)

altruism: placing others' needs above one's own; offering help to another person (p. 504)

Ameslan: American Sign Language of the deaf (p. 262)

amnesia: loss of memory from physical causes or as a defense mechanism against anxiety-provoking situations (p. 375) [See also *defense mechanism*]

amplitude: measure of the intensity of a sound wave; perceived as loudness (p. 158)

anthropomorphism: attribution of human characteristics to animals (p. 34)

anxiety: diffuse feelings of fear and inadequacy (p. 374) [See *trait anxiety, state anxiety*]

aptitude test: a test that assesses knowledge with the goal of predicting performance (p. 439) [Compare *achievement test*]

association (contiguity): the principle stating that a stimulus and a response become connected if they occur close together in time and space (p. 186)

association cortex: the part of the brain that stores, processes, and retrieves words and thoughts (p. 256)

association value: in relation to words, the degree to which a word can bring to mind other words (p. 222)

associative neurons: see *internuncial neurons*

attitude: a readiness to respond in a positive or negative way to a class of people, objects, or ideas (p. 496)

Attribution Theory: a theory of emotion based on the assumption that emotion results from the combined impact of the state of arousal, the interpretation we make of this state, and the causal link we make connecting the arousal and our

GLOSSARY

interpretation (p. 313) [Compare *Activation Theory*, *Opponent-process Theory*]

auditory cortex: the part of the brain that provides feedback from our ears to monitor our speech (p. 255)

auditory nerve: relays information from the ear to the brain (p. 159)

autonomic nervous system: the system controlling the glands and organs (p. 126)

autonomic response specificity: the unique pattern of organ responses made by each individual in reaction to emotion (p. 280)

average: in statistical data analysis, a point around which frequencies are grouped, the most typical frequency or the highest frequency (p. 523) [See also *mode, median, mean*]

axon: that part of a neuron through which impulses travel away from the cell body (p. 121)

behaviorism: a school of psychology that studies only observable behavior, omitting any concern with "mind" (p. 24)

between-subjects research design: a procedure in which experimental and control-group ratings are compared between groups (p. 516) [Compare *within-subjects research design*]

biofeedback: the use of electronic instruments to register bodily processes (heart beat, etc.) in observable form as an aid in learning to control them (p. 137)

bipolar affective disorder: a mental disturbance involving exaggerated moods—elation, agitation, and depression (p. 383)

brightness: perception of the intensity of light waves (p. 153)

catatonic schizophrenia: a condition involving marked inactivity, rigid postures; may pass into a violent state (p. 386)

catharsis: in psychoanalysis, the release of emotional tension (p. 402)

centrality: with regard to communication, the number of links from any one position in an ordered group to another position (p. 467)

central nervous system: the brain and spinal cord (p. 126) [Compare *peripheral nervous system*]

cerebellum: hindbrain part that controls posture, balance, and the muscle tone of voluntary muscles all over the body (p. 129)

channel: in communication, the medium by which the signal is carried away from the transmitter (sound waves, wire, paper, etc.) (p. 260)

charting: in operant therapy, keeping track of your own behavior (p. 406)

chemotherapy: the use of various drugs to treat emotional and behavioral symptoms of psychological problems (p. 401)

chemtrode: hollow tube implanted in brain permitting the delivery of small amounts of chemicals to specific points (p. 122) [Compare *electrode*]

classical conditioning: a learning process in which a stimulus that reliably produces a response is paired repeatedly with a neutral stimulus (one that doesn't produce the response). In time the neutral stimulus will cause the response when presented by itself. (p. 188)

clustering: grouping similar items together to aid in their recall (p. 225)

cochlea: tightly coiled, liquid-filled inner ear part where hair cells stimulate the auditory nerve (p. 159)

cognitive theories: explanations stressing mental operations, mainly in the fields of language and development (p. 40)

cognitive therapy: therapy that emphasizes voluntary control of behavior (p. 408)

collective unconscious: according to Jung, the accumulated memories and urges of the whole human race (p. 347)

communication: the passing of information from one organism to another via signals (p. 258)

complements hypothesis: the belief that strengths in one person may make up for a lack of those strengths in the other member of a friendship or marriage (p. 493) [Compare *similarity hypothesis*]

compulsion: see *obsession/ compulsion*

concurrent validity: in testing, how well scores on a new test correlate with scores on a test with previously established validity (p. 433) [See also *predictive validity, content validity, face validity*]

conditioned response (CR): any behavior that resembles the unconditioned response but is caused by the conditioned stimulus after conditioning (p. 189)

conditioned stimulus (CS): any event which is "neutral" and doesn't elicit a desired response at the start of classical conditioning but comes to produce a conditioned response (p. 189)

conditioning: in psychological research, the modification of an experimental subject's behavior in such a way that an act or response previously associated with a given stimulus becomes associated with a formerly unrelated stimulus; also, the modification of human behavior by life experiences (p. 188)

conductivity: the ability of the neuron to relay impulses or stimulation from one point to another in the body (p. 119)

cone: receptor element in the retina of the eye which is sensitive to color but needs a certain amount of light to function (p. 154) [Compare rod]

congruence (genuineness): in person-centered therapy, the therapist's willingness to be authentic in his or her relationship to the patient (p. 405)

conscious, the: according to Freud, the thoughts of which a person is aware (p. 345) [Compare preconscious, unconscious]

content validity: in testing, how well the test covers the topic under study (p. 433)

contiguity: see association

contingency contracting: an operant conditioning technique in which the behavioral goal is spelled out and steps toward its achievement are rewarded (p. 406)

continuous reinforcement (CRF): in conditioning, reinforcing every correct response (p. 197) [See partial reinforcement]

control group: in an experiment, the group of subjects exposed to the same condi-

tions as the experimental group except that the independent variable is not applied (p. 32) [Compare experimental group]

conversion disorders: physical manifestations such as paralysis, blindness, deafness, or tics (twitching) with no apparent physical cause (p. 379)

corpus callosum: brain part connecting the two halves, or hemispheres, of the cortex (p. 131)

correlation: in psychological research, the amount of variation in one variable that can be predicted from knowledge about another variable. (Correlations are always reported as a number ranging from −1.00 to +1.00 and can be positive; negative; or nonsignificant, that is, zero). (p. 526)

correlational statistics: in psychological research, a group of procedures used to determine the amount of variation in one variable that can be predicted from knowledge about another variable (p. 526)

cortex: highest part of the forebrain, composed of two halves, or hemispheres; controls most complex sensory-motor reactions and is the seat of thought, memory, and language (p. 129) [See motor cortex, auditory cortex, association cortex]

counterconditioning: the re-modification of behavior to overcome the results of earlier conditioning (p. 208)

CR: see conditioned response

CRF: see continuous reinforcement

critical period: a period in maturation during which particular events or behavior must take place in order for

certain skills to be accomplished properly (p. 66)

cross-modal transfer: taking one form of stimuli and translating it mentally into another form (e.g., sight into touch) (p. 78)

cross-sectional study: a study in which two or more groups of different age are observed for an identical, one-time-only period using the same measures for each group (p. 52) [Compare longitudinal study]

CS: see conditioned stimulus

dark adaptation: the process of becoming more and more sensitive to dim flashes of light after coming out of the daylight (p. 155)

Death instincts: according to Freud, the instincts which surface mainly as aggression (p. 346) [Compare Life instincts]

decoder: see receiver

defense mechanism: an unconscious, adaptive maneuver that helps prevent anxiety (p. 374) [See repression, amnesia, denial, rationalization, reaction formation, projection, phobia]

deindividuation: loss of identity (p. 471)

delusion: a false belief regarding the self or persons or objects outside the self that persists despite the facts (p. 386)

demand characteristics: aspects of an experiment that influence a subject's responses despite the experimenter's intentions (p. 517)

dendrite: the branched part of a neuron that carries impulses toward the cell body (p. 121)

denial: a defense mechanism in which a person rejects intolerable reality (p. 375) dependent variable: the factor, chosen by the experimenter, that may or may not change when the independent variable is changed. Its actual value is determined by the subject being tested (p. 31)

depressant: any drug that reduces activity in the nervous system or slows down some body function (p. 142) [Compare *stimulant*]

descriptive statistics: group of procedures used to collapse large amounts of data into a few numbers to convey a clear impression (p. 523)

development: the systematic, orderly changes organisms experience as they live and either gain or lose abilities (p. 53)

developmental psychology: the area of psychology that studies changes in human behavior as they relate to age (p. 50)

difference threshold: the amount of change in a stimulus necessary in order for the change to be detected half the time (p. 151) [Compare *absolute threshold, just noticeable difference*]

discrimination: (1) prejudice in action; the rejection of someone solely because he or she belongs to a specific identifiable group (p. 498) (2) response that permits an organism to emit different responses to similar situations that differ in crucial ways (p. 204) [Compare *generalization*]

dissociative disorders: disorders involving a sudden but temporary change in the memory or knowledge of one's identity (p. 379)

disorganized schizophrenia: a condition involving immature, distractable thinking

patterns, incoherence, or "word salads" (p. 386)

distributed practice: practicing or studying in blocks of time separated by periods of rest or other activities (p. 226) [Compare *massed practice*]

distribution: in statistical data analysis, all possible results (p. 429)

DNA: deoxyribonucleic acid, the master key to the genetic code (p. 68)

dominant gene: an information code that exerts its full effect over the effect of a passive gene with which it is paired (p. 68) [Compare *recessive gene*]

double bind: situation in which a person is given two sets of cues which contradict one another (p. 387)

double-blind technique: an experimental procedure in which neither the experimenter nor the subject knows whether a given subject is a member of the control group or the experimental group proper (p. 518) [Compare *single-blind technique*]

drive: an aroused state resulting from deprivation of some need (p. 277) [See *primary drive, secondary drive*]

eclectic: as applied to psychology, using ideas and techniques derived from a variety of different theories (p. 25)

ECS: see *electroconvulsive shock*

EEG: see *electroencephalogram*

efferent neurons: cells that conduct nerve impulses from the brain or spinal cord to the muscles or glands (p. 125)

effectors: muscles or glands to which the nervous system connects (p. 124)

ego: according to Freud, the rational, aware self operating in terms of the reality principle (p. 346) [Compare *id, libido, superego*]

electroconvulsive shock (ECS): a treatment for psychosis that provides a brief, powerful electrical shock to the brain (p. 401)

electrode: brain implant permitting the stimulation of specific parts of the brain by very slight electrical charges (p. 122) [Compare *chemtrode*]

electroencephalogram (EEG): machine used to measure the electrical activity of the nervous system (p. 124)

emotion: a conscious experience that includes a state of arousal, a label, and a perceived link between the two (p. 308)

empathy: in person-centered therapy, the therapist's willingness to identify with and understand the patient (p. 405)

encoder: see *transmitter*

endocrine (ductless) glands: glands producing hormones that affect organs and other glands, or directly influence behavior (p. 133)

equity principle: in marriage, the balancing of responsibilities and needs, as a couple (p. 495)

eros: see *Life instincts*

estimate: in psychological research, any characteristic of a sample (p. 523)

ethology: branch of zoology which applies the principles of naturalistic observation to the study of animals' behavior in their natural environment (p. 65)

exocrine (ducted) glands: glands producing secretion (sweat, tears, etc.) that can influence behavior but doesn't tend to alter it (p. 133)

experiment: in psychological research, an attempt to establish a functional relationship between independent and dependent variables (p. 514)

experimental group: in an experiment, the group of subjects to whom the independent variable is applied (p. 32) [Compare *control group*]

experimental method: any data collection technique in which control is exercised over as many variables as possible that might influence the behavior being studied (p. 33)

extended family: a family that includes grandparents and other relatives, often residing together or in close proximity (p. 478) [Compare *nuclear family*]

extinction: the decrease in the frequency of a behavior until it is eliminated because it is no longer reinforced (p. 203)

extroversion: in the personality theory of Jung, a turning outward toward others (p. 348) [Compare *introversion*]

face validity: in testing, how well a test appears to be measuring what it's supposed to be measuring (p. 433)

field-research methods: in psychological research, the collection of data about naturally occurring behavioral phenomena in a non-laboratory setting (p. 514)

firing: the process in which chemicals enter and leave

the neuron, causing a change in its electrical charge (p. 118)

fixation: according to Freud, the arrested development of the personality at a less-than-mature stage (p. 347)

Fixed Interval Schedule: a schedule of reinforcement in which the first response after a definite period of time is reinforced (regardless of the number of responses between times (p. 198) [Compare *Variable Interval Schedule*]

Fixed Ratio Schedule: a schedule of reinforcement in which the reward always follows a fixed number of responses (p. 197) [Compare *Variable Ratio Schedule*]

forebrain: of the three principal brain sections, the largest and most complex; controls some unconscious, automatic activities, such as those of the body's organs, as well as complex voluntary processes (p. 128) [Compare *midbrain, hindbrain*]

fovea: focal point of the eyes (p. 155)

frame of reference: a set of values, customs, and attitudes that make up a particular approach to a subject (p. 20)

fraternal twins: twins created from two separately fertilized eggs (p. 57) [Compare *identical twins*]

free association: in psychoanalysis, speaking freely of whatever thoughts or feelings occur (p. 402)

frequency: (1) in statistical data analysis, the number of times a result occurred (p. 523) (2) number of sound-wave cycles occurring per second (p. 158)

frequency distribution: statistical data analysis show-

ing how many times each possible result occurred (p. 523)

frustration-aggression hypothesis: the notion that frustration leads to aggression (p. 321)

frustration tolerance level: the degree of hindrance or threat a person can endure without resorting to deviant or inappropriate modes of responding (p. 323)

fugue state: a state in which amnesia is combined with a move to a new environment (p. 379)

functionalism: a school of psychology in which the function, purpose, or goal of a behavior is stressed, and behavior is studied directly (p. 24)

functional relationship: the manner in which changes in an independent variable influence the value of a dependent variable (p. 32)

General Adaptation Syndrome: the three stages of reaction to stress: shock and countershock, resistance, and exhaustion (p. 323)

generalization: response that causes an organism to emit similar responses to a variety of similar but not identical stimuli (p. 203) [Compare *discrimination* (2)]

generalization gradient: the decrease in the conditioned response as the test stimuli become less and less like the original stimulus (p. 203)

general traits: personality traits possessed by all people (p. 343) [Compare *specific traits*]

genetic code: the form in which molecules transmit genetic information. Those characteristics within the genes that are passed on from one generation to the next (p. 68)

geotaxis: characteristic orientation of an organism to gravity (p. 64)[See *taxis*]

Gestaltism: a school of psychology that concentrates on the study of total figures, or whole patterns of experience (p. 24)

gonads: the sex glands of both sexes (p. 134)

grammar: a system of rules governing the use of a language (p. 247) [Compare *semantics, syntax*]

group: two or more persons who communicate and who share a number of goals, desires, or targets for common action (p. 458)

groupthink: a decline of group members' mental efficiency, reality testing, and moral judgment, resulting from in-group pressures and producing faulty group decisions (p. 474)

hallucination: perception of objects with no reality; experience of sensations with no external cause (p. 142)

hallucinogens: any drug producing changes in the normal senses, particularly hallucinations (p. 142)

halo effect: the effect of prior knowledge upon current observations (p. 448)

hedonic tone: the goodness-badness dimension people use to help label their emotions (p. 311)

hemisphere: one of two equal halves of the cortex controlling responses on one or the other side of the body (p. 131)

heuristic: serving to discover or find out (p. 340)

hindbrain: of the three principal brain sections, the one closest to the spinal cord;

performs a number of reflex actions, including such responses as blinking the eyes (p. 128) [Compare *forebrain, midbrain*]

homeostasis: the process of sensoring and monitoring that helps establish and retain balance in body systems (p. 279)

hormone: a specific organic product of human and animal cells, transported by body fluids, which produces a specific effect on the activity of cells remote from its point of origin (p. 133)

hue: identifies the perceived color of a light wavelength (p. 152)

hypnosis: an alerted state of consciousness, the exact nature of which is still in dispute (p. 140)

hypothalamus: important part of the forebrain controlling eating, drinking, and certain sexual activities as well as more fully automatic adjustments such as temperature (p. 129)

hypothesis: in psychological research, a prediction of experimental results which is derived from a theory; an educated guess (p. 514)

id: according to Freud, the source of basic desires operating solely for self-gratification (the pleasure principle) (p. 345) [Compare *ego, libido, superego*]

identical twins: twins created from a single fertilized egg (p. 57) [Compare *fraternal twins*]

identity crisis: search for an answer to the question "Who am I?" (p. 98)

idiographic studies: studies in which a single individual is examined as a complete, interacting system (p. 340) [Compare *nomothetic studies*]

imagery rating: in relation to words, the degree to which a word can bring to mind a concrete picture (p. 222)

implosive therapy: a counter-conditioning therapy in which great amounts of anxiety are aroused and "conquered" (p. 406)

imprinting: a process in which the young of an animal, at a particular and limited time after birth, form a strong attachment to any moving person or object (p. 65)

incidental learning: learning that occurs without intent (p. 221)

inaccessible memory: the apparent forgetting of previously learned material (p. 235)

independent variable: the factor, chosen by the experimenter, that is changed or varied in a psychological experiment; the cause (in a functional relationship) of change (p. 30)

inferential statistics: group of procedures used to estimate how often something might happen by chance (p. 524)

inferiority complex: a failure to master the feelings of inferiority felt by all children in relation to adults (p. 348)

informed consent: an agreement to participate in an experiment based on information released before the experiment is conducted (p. 520)

initial response hierarchy: the series of responses an infant can make at birth (p. 349) [Compare *resultant hierarchy*]

instinct: a complex pattern of response that is unlearned and present in all normal members of a species (p. 64) [Compare *reflex*]

instrumental conditioning: see *operant conditioning*

intelligence quotient (IQ): a score arrived at by dividing mental age (as determined by testing) by chronological age, and multiplying by 100 (p. 443)

internuncial (associative) neurons: cells that transfer incoming messages to outgoing neurons (p. 125)

interval schedule: in conditioning, a partial reinforcement schedule which gives reinforcement for the first correct response after a certain amount of time has passed (p. 197) [See *Fixed Interval Schedule; Variable Interval Schedule*]

intervening variable: a non-observable process within the experimental subject proposed to explain the observed relationship between an independent and dependent variable (p. 31)

intimacy: intense bond between two people seen in a variety of behaviors (p. 97)

introspection: in psychology, a technique in which a subject reports his or her thoughts (p. 23)

introversion: in the personality theory of Jung, a turning inward or reclusiveness (p. 348) [Compare *extroversion*]

inventory tests: measurement technique using multiple-choice questions, true-false questions, or simple checklists; those being tested indicate which items describe their learned motives or personality attributes (p. 438)

irritability: the ability of a neuron to respond to stimulation (p. 118)

jargon: a special vocabulary shared with other members of a group to which one belongs (p. 89)

just-noticeable-difference (j.n.d.): the amount by which a stimulus must be changed in order for that change to be detected (p. 151) [Compare *difference threshold*]

kinesics: "body language" in which body motions and postures communicate feelings (p. 268)

Kuder Occupational Interest Survey: a test that forces choices along certain scales such as Mechanical, Artistic, to determine the most suitable occupation (p. 438)

language: an abstract system for communication composed of symbols and meanings set down according to certain rules (p. 247)

larynx: the voice box, or vocal chords (p. 256)

law: in psychological research, a perfect correlation of 1.00, meaning that every change in one variable can be predicted by a change in another variable (p. 526)

Law of Effect: the principle stating that reinforced responses will increase in frequency (p. 187)

leadership: process in which one person exerts influence or control over others (p. 481)

learning: a relatively permanent change in a behavioral tendency that occurs as a result of practice or observation (p. 184)

lesioning: cutting or otherwise destroying a part of the nervous system (particularly the brain) (p. 123)

libido: according to Freud, an amount of inner psychic energy each person is born

with (p. 345) [Compare *ego, id, superego*]

Life instincts: according to Freud, the instincts which seek pleasure in a variety of ways (p. 346) [Compare *Death instincts*]

lobotomy: severing the front portion of the brain from the internal processing center; formerly used to calm chronically violent mental patients (p. 401)

longitudinal study: a study in which one group of subjects is observed over a long period of time (p. 52) [Compare *cross-sectional study*]

long-term memory: memory lasting 120 seconds or more (p. 216) [Compare *sensory store, short-term memory*]

looking-glass self: the self we see in others' reactions to us (p. 479)

malleability: the quality in humans that allows changes in environment to cause changes in behavior (p. 54)

manic depressive psychosis: a mental disturbance involving exaggerated moods—elation, agitation, and depression (p. 383)

massed practice: practicing or studying material from start to finish without a break (p. 226) [Compare *distributed practice*]

maturation: those changes in the behavior of an organism that can be traced directly to physical growth (p. 54)

maturational readiness: the first time an organism is physically ready and able to respond correctly in a particular situation (p. 66)

median: in statistical data analysis, the result occurring at the midpoint of the distribution (p. 524) [Compare *average*]

meditation: a state of deep, concentrated thought that aims to expand human consciousness (p. 139)

mean: in statistical data analysis, an average obtained by dividing the sum of all results by the number of results obtained (p. 524)

metaneeds: the needs for goodness, order, unity, justice, and the like to enrich the individual and the world (p. 354)

method of loci: a device to help recall by mentally connecting items to be remembered with other bizarre items, which are often arranged in a series (p. 230)

Method of Successive Approximations: operant conditioning method which results in a final complex behavior achieved through rewarding a series of responses more and more like the desired behavior (p. 192) [Compare *shaping*]

midbrain: one of the three principal brain sections located just above the hindbrain; controls some of the same reflex responses as the hindbrain but also controls more complex responses such as walking (p. 128) [Compare *hindbrain, forebrain*]

Minnesota Multiphasic Personality Inventory: a test composed of 550 items designed to detect abnormal response patterns (p. 449)

mnemonic: any device that aids in the learning, storage, and/or recall of information (p. 229)

mode: in statistical data analysis, the result occurring most frequently (p. 524) [Compare *average*]

motor cortex: the part of the brain that controls vocal cords, tongue, and mouth movements (p. 255)

multiple personality: a condition in which one person has two or more separate personalities and consciousnesses (p. 380)

negative reinforcer: any event the decrease or removal of which leads to an increase of the organism's behavior preceding it (p. 187)

negative transfer: hindrance of new learning that results from similar previous learning (p. 236) [Compare *positive transfer*]

neuron: the basic cell of the nervous system; a cell body with one or more axons and one or more dendrites (p. 118)

nomothetic studies: studies in which a particular characteristic is examined in a large number of people (p. 339) [Compare *idiographic studies*]

nonverbal communication: transmission of information by means other than language in its spoken, written, or otherwise coded form (p. 266)

norm: a standard of behavior established and maintained by the way people actually behave (p. 462)

normal distribution: in testing, a range of scores in which most people's results are grouped near the middle; more precisely, a frequency distribution in which the mode, the median, and the mean are identical, occurring at the mid-point (p. 429)

nuclear family: a family group consisting of mother, father, and children (p. 478) [Compare *extended family*]

object constancy: see *object permanence*

objective test: a short-answer test in which each person giving the test reaches the same conclusion about the person taking the test (p. 433) [Compare *subjective test*]

object permanence (constancy): according to Piaget, the sense developed by children that physical objects persist and remain constant even if no longer seen or seen in different perspective from different points of view (p. 91)

observational learning: learning by imitation (p. 195)

obsession/compulsion: the need to repeat in inappropriate action or thought to the point where it interferes with normal activities (p. 378)

olfactory epithelium: smell receptor site located on the roof of the nasal cavity (p. 161)

operant (instrumental) conditioning: altering the frequency of a response by giving a reinforcement whenever that response is given (p. 192)

operational definition: a definition in which the concept is identical to the operations used in measuring the concept (p. 29)

operant therapy: therapy emphasizing the reinforcement that can be gained by changing and reshaping behavior (p. 406)

Opponent-process Theory: a theory of emotion based on the principal of homeostasis, or the tendency for any level of arousal to bring into action an opposing process that will restore a balance (p. 316) [Compare *Activation Theory, Attribution Theory*]

optic nerve: relays visual information to the cortex (p. 154)

otolith organs: organs in the head which respond to static position to help a person maintain balance (p. 163) [Compare *semicircular canals, vestibular sense*]

papillae: bumps on the tongue; taste cells are clustered on those at the surface and sides of tongue (p. 162)

paradoxical sleep: see *REM sleep*

paralanguage: nonlinguistic aspects of speech that can affect interpretation, such as tone of voice, pauses, and emphasis (p. 266)

parameter: in psychological research, any characteristic of a population (p. 523)

paranoid schizophrenia: a condition involving delusional or illogical thoughts and "complexes"—of superiority, persecution, and the like (p. 386)

parasympathetic nervous system: the system that conserves energy and restores resources after strenuous action (p. 126) [Compare *sympathetic nervous system*]

partial reinforcement: in conditioning, reinforcing only some correct responses (p. 197) [Compare *continuous reinforcement*]

Partial Reinforcement Effect: resistance to extinction of a behavior acquired under other than continuous reinforcement (p. 203)

peer group: friends of generally the same age and life experience (p. 62)

PEG system: associating numbers to be remembered with a familiar item that rhymes with them (eight is gate, etc.) (p. 230)

perception: what occurs when you apply our experience to interpret sensations (p. 150)

peripheral nervous system: all neurons in all systems other than those in the brain and spinal cord (p. 126) [Compare *central nervous system*]

personality: the dynamic organization within an individual of the systems that determine his or her characteristic behavior or thought (p. 337)

person-centered therapy: the non-directive therapy of Carl Rogers which places emphasis on the patient's current life situation (p. 403)

phase difference: difference in perception of sound waves received by each ear when sound originates on one side (rather than directly in front of) the head (p. 173)

phenomenal field: according to Rogers' theory, all the experience that a person could experience (p. 352)

phi phenomenon: an optical illusion of motion occurring when side-by-side lights flash alternately (p. 172)

phobia: an inappropriate, exaggerated fear of an object or situation (p. 375) [See *defense mechanism*]

physiological: having to do with the chemical and physical functions and activities characteristic of living organisms and of living matter such as organs, tissues, and cells (p. 116)

physiological zero: the temperature of the surface of the skin (p. 162)

placebo: substance taken by the control group when testing for all the social and other events that are involved in taking a drug (p. 534)

plagiarism: a failure to include in a research report references to the work of others from which the research is drawn (p. 529)

population: in psychological research, any group of people, animals, concepts, or events which are alike in one respect (p. 522) [Compare *sample*]

positive reinforcer: any event the presence or increase of which leads to an increase in the preceding behavior of the organism (p. 187) [Compare *negative reinforcer*]

positive transfer: ease in new learning that results from similar previous learning (p. 236) [Compare *negative transfer*]

power: influence or control exerted over others (p. 481)

preconscious, the: according to Freud, the thoughts of which a person is not immediately aware that can be brought to conscious attention easily and rapidly (p. 345) [Compare *conscious, unconscious*]

predictive validity: in testing how well a test accurately predicts what you already know (p. 432)

prejudice: an attitude formed prior to or without taking into consideration any examination of objective facts (p. 498)

pressure wave: also called sound wave; sound source vibration travelling through a gaseous or solid medium (p. 158)

primary drive: drive to satisfy innate need for life necessity such as food, water, oxygen, or warmth (p. 349) [Compare *secondary drive*]

primary reinforcement: a stimulus that is naturally (innately) reinforcing (such as food, water) (p. 198)

[Compare *secondary reinforcement*]

proactive interference: what occurs when previously learned material interferes with more recently learned material (p. 232) [Compare *retroactive interference*]

programmatic research: a research study that is part of an ongoing research program (p. 514)

projective tests: seemingly formless and unstructured tests that offer stimuli aimed at revealing unconscious feelings and views (p. 449)

projection: attributing one's own personality traits or attitudes to others (p. 375) [See *defense mechanism*]

proxemics: the study of the distance maintained between humans in the course of daily life (p. 266)

psychoanalysis: a school of psychology founded by Sigmund Freud. As theory, it stresses unconscious conflicts (p. 25); as part of a therapeutic technique, it stresses bringing these conflicts into consciousness (p. 402)

psycholinguist: a scientist who studies the psychological aspects of the acquisition and use of language (p. 252)

psychophysics: the branch of psychology that studies the relations between physical events and the related psychological experiences (p. 150)

psychoses: a group of disorders that involve extensive and severe disintegration of the personality (p. 381)

psychotherapy: the use of psychological techniques for the treatment of mental or behavioral disorders (p. 400)

puberty: sexual maturity (p. 86) [Compare *adolescence*]

Purkinje shift: the shift from cone to rod vision at sunset, which makes you perceive more blues and purples (p. 155)

racism: prejudicial judgments about all members of a race by members of another race (p. 498)

random sample: in psychological research, a sample for which every member of a population has an equal chance of being chosen (p. 522)

Rational Emotive Therapy (RET): a cognitive therapy devised by Ellis in which the therapist challenges the client's irrational beliefs (p. 409)

rationalization: a defense mechanism in which a person substitutes a more acceptable reason than the true one for his or her behavior (p. 375)

ratio schedule: in conditioning, a partial reinforcement schedule which gives reinforcement for a fixed or average number of responses (p. 197) [See *Fixed Ratio Schedule, Variable Ratio Schedule*]

reaction formation: the modification of an anxiety-causing impulse by performing in ways opposite to one's true feelings (p. 375) [See *defense mechanism*]

receiver (decoder): in communication, the intake system for the signal (p. 260)

receptors: a variety of cells that react to stimuli in the environment (touch, sight) (p. 124)

recessive gene: an information code that exerts its full effect only if paired with another recessive gene; its full effect will be masked if it is paired with a dominant gene (p. 68) [Compare *dominant gene*]

reductionism: reducing the principles and explanations of any discipline to some science that is considered more basic (p. 40)

reference group: any group whose values, actions, and goals an individual accepts (p. 489)

reflex: unlearned response to a stimulus; usually does not involve the whole organism (p. 64) [Compare *instinct*]

reinforcement: anything following a behavior that causes an increase in the frequency of the behavior (p. 187) [See *primary reinforcement, secondary reinforcement*]

relative refractory period: the time periods after firing during which a neuron can fire but only if it receives extra strong stimulation (p. 120) [Compare *absolute refractory period*]

reliability: in testing, the ability of a test to give consistent, stable, constant results each time it is given (p. 431)

REM (paradoxical) sleep: a stage of sleep in which *r*apid *e*ye *m*ovements indicate that a person is dreaming (p. 135)

repression: a defense mechanism in which a person forgets situations which would cause painful emotions (p. 374)

resistance: in psychoanalysis, a reaction identified by what a person avoids talking about or by the obvious conclusions a person avoids making (p. 402)

response: any observable activity of a human or animal (p. 186) [See *stimulus*]

resting potential: the normal electrical charge of the neuron when not firing (p. 119) [Compare *action potential*] resultant hierarchy: the development of personality that results from learning (p. 350) [Compare *initial response hierarchy*]

RET: see *Rational Emotive Therapy*

retina: eye part whose function is similar to that of the film in a camera (p. 154)

retroactive interference: what occurs when new learning interferes with previously learned information (p. 232) [Compare *proactive interference*]

risky-shift phenomenon: the tendency of a group to endorse a riskier policy than its members would if acting alone (p. 469) [Compare *stingy-shift phenomenon*]

rod: receptor element in the eye's retina used to see in poor light (p. 154) [Compare *cone*]

role: a pattern of behavior that is expected because of membership and position in a group (p. 462)

role conflict: the situation experienced when role demands in one group seem in opposition to role demands in another group to which an individual belongs (p. 463)

Rorschach Inkblot test: ten inkblots, symmetric but formless, which are used to elicit free association responses and thus reveal abnormalities (p. 450)

sample: any subgroup drawn by a nonbiased method from a population (p. 522)

saturation: degree of purity of lightwaves of a given wavelength (p. 153)

schizophrenia: a disorder of thought involving loss of contact with reality (p. 384) [See *undifferentiated schizo-*

phrenia, catatonic schizophrenia, paranoid schizophrenia, disorganized schizophrenia]

scientific method: a formal, orderly set of procedures used to arrive at facts and laws, classify things, and test hypotheses (p. 20)

secondary drive: drive to satisfy need that develops in response to a stimulus occurring in association with a primary drive (p. 349)

secondary reinforcement: a stimulus which gains reinforcing properties through prior association with a primary reinforcer (p. 199)

selective breeding: breeding used to "purify" a characteristic or trait under study (p. 55)

self-actualization: the process of developing and utilizing all one's potential (p. 353)

semantics: the study of word meanings (p. 252) [Compare *syntax, grammar*]

semicircular canals: organs connected to the inner ear and filled with hair cells which respond to changes in the head's rotation to help a person maintain balance (p. 163) [See *otolith organs, vestibular sense*]

sensation: what occurs when a stimulus activates a receptor (p. 150)

sensory store: very brief memory span (0-1 second) (p. 215) [Compare *short-term memory, long-term memory*]

shape consistency: the perception of items as square, round, or whatever, no matter what the angle from which they are viewed (p. 169)

shaping: in operant conditioning, reinforcing successive steps toward a desired

behavior (p. 193) [Compare *Method of Successive Approximations*]

short-term memory: memory lasting 1-120 seconds (p. 215) [Compare *sensory store, long-term memory*]

signal: in communication, the form in which the message is produced, such as speech, or the dots and dashes of Morse code (p. 260)

significant difference: in psychological research, a difference between two groups' performances too great to be thought due only to chance factors (p. 526)

similarity hypothesis: the notion that in predicting friends and marriages, similarities are of great importance (p. 493) [Compare *complements hypothesis*]

single-blind technique: an experimental procedure in which the experimenter knows whether a given subject is a member of the control group or the experimental group, but the subject does not know (p. 518) [Compare *double-blind technique*]

skin sensitivity: in communication, the physical contact permissible between persons of different age, rank, or role (p. 267)

simple schizophrenia: see *undifferentiated schizophrenia*

socialization: training in the general values of a society and the specific beliefs or biases of a family (p. 488)

social learning theories: psychological explanations predicated on environmentally based principles (p. 348)

somatic nervous system: the system responsible for bodily sensation and movement (p. 126)

somatoform disorders: disorders that involve physical symptoms where no physical cause can be found (p. 378) [Compare *conversion disorders*]

somatotype: a form of human physique as identified by Sheldon (p. 342)

source traits: underlying internal traits responsible for overt behavior (p. 343) [Compare *surface traits*]

specific traits: personality traits typical only of one person (p. 343) [Compare *general traits*]

SQR3 approach: a strategy for learning that involves five steps: *S*urvey, *Q*uestion, *R*ead, *R*ecite, and *R*eview (p. 240)

standard deviation: in statistical data analysis, a measure of variability (using square-root calculations) which accurately determines how widely results deviate from a mean (p. 429)

Stanford-Binet Intelligence Test: six tests, at each age level, of varying content and increasing difficulty (p. 443)

state anxiety: temporary feelings of anxiety related to a specific situation (p. 374) [Compare *trait anxiety*]

statistic: a numerical fact or datum (p. 521)

statistics: the collection, arrangement, and use of numerical facts (p. 521) [See also *inferential statistics, correlational statistics, and descriptive statistics*]

status: a role or position that identifies differences important to the group in exchanging goods and services (p. 464)

stereotype: a rigidly held, usually oversimplified, and often negative belief about most members of an identifiable group (p. 498)

stereotyping: in testing, attempting to fit a tested person's performance into too broad categories (p. 448)

stimulant: any drug that increases activity in the nervous system or in any function of the body (p. 142) [Compare *depressant*]

stimulus: anything that can produce a change or sensation in an animal or human sense organ; anything that causes a response (p. 186)

stingy-shift phenomenon: the tendency of a group to take a more extreme conservative position than its members would if acting alone (p. 470) [Compare *risky-shift phenomenon*]

stress: an emotional state that occurs when a person perceives a threat to his or her well-being (p. 323)

Strong-Campbell Interest Inventory: a test inventory of some 325 items to determine career interests (p. 438)

structuralism: a school of psychology in which subjects use introspection and analyze their experiences (p. 23)

subjective test: a test, such as an essay test, in which the examiner's skills play a large part in assessing the results (p. 433) [Compare *objective test*]

superego: according to Freud, the conscience and ego ideal based on the values of one's parents (p. 346) [Compare *ego, id, libido*]

surface traits: observable patterns of behavior (p. 343) [Compare *source traits*]

symbol: something that stands for something else (such as a cross symbolizing Christianity) (p. 247)

sympathetic nervous system: the system that prepares body resources (organs and glands) for strenuous action (p. 126) [Compare *parasympathetic nervous system*]

synapse: the junction between any two neurons, through which chemicals relay messages from one neuron to the next (p. 121)

synergism: the multiplying effect on individual ideas of challenge and examination by others (p. 481)

syntax: the order of words in a sentence (p. 251) [Compare *semantics, grammar*]

systematic desensitization: a counterconditioning technique for training patients to relax in the presence of fears and anxieties (p. 405)

tachistoscope: apparatus used by psychologists to present visual images for very brief time periods (p. 214)

taxis (TACKsis): the response or orientation of a whole animal either toward or away from some physical stimulus (p. 64) [See *geotaxis*]

telegraphic speech: form of speech prevalent in late infancy composed mainly of two-word phrases in which substantive words are used without connectors (p. 75)

test: in psychology, a systematic procedure for comparing the responses of two or more persons to the same series of stimuli (p. 429)

thalamus: in the forebrain, major "switching point" for messages from all senses except smell (p. 129)

Thanatos: see *Death instincts*

therapy: see *psychotherapy*

threshold: the minimum level of stimulation at which a neuron will fire (p. 121)[See *absolute threshold, difference threshold*]

timbre: perception of the complexity of a sound, its mixture of tones and overtones (p. 158)

token economy: an operant conditioning technique in which tokens are used to reward proper behavior (p. 406)

trait anxiety: chronic feelings of anxiety (p. 374) [Compare *state anxiety*]

transfer: the effects of past learning on the ability to learn new materials or tasks (p. 236) [See *positive transfer, negative transfer*]

transference: in psychoanalysis, the reenactment with the analyst of a frustrating relationship from childhood (p. 402)

transmitter: in communication, the source that produces a message (p. 260)

unconditional positive regard: (1) approval from valued people in one's life that is necessary for our development (p. 353) (2) an element in person-centered therapy (p. 404)

unconditioned response (UR): any behavior predictably caused by an unconditioned stimulus (p. 189)

unconditioned stimulus (US): any event that reliably pro-

duces a predictable response (p. 188)

unconscious, the: according to Freud, the urges and thoughts of which a person is not aware that largely influence conscious behavior (p. 344) [Compare *conscious, preconscious*]

undifferentiated (simple) schizophrenia: a condition involving loss of ambition, interests, and emotion to the point where self-maintenance becomes impossible (p. 385)

unipolar depression: feelings of apathy or sadness so pervasive that a person's ability to function is affected (p. 382)

UR: see *unconditioned response*

US: see *unconditioned stimulus*

variable: factor which changes or causes change in an experiment (p. 30) [See *dependent variable, independent variable, intervening variable*]

Variable Interval Schedule: a schedule of reinforcement in which the first response following a changeable, average period of time is reinforced (p. 198) [Compare *Fixed Interval*]

Variable Ratio Schedule: a schedule of reinforcement in

which the reward is given after a variable number of responses (p. 198) [Compare *Fixed Ratio Schedule*]

vestibular sense: sense which responds to rotation and tilt of the head to provide the balance necessary for correct posture, walking, and running (p. 163) [See *semicircular canals, otolith organs*]

Weber's Law: the law stating that the stronger or greater the stimulus, the larger the amount of change required before an observer can detect any difference (p. 151)

Wechsler Intelligence Scale: tests using verbal and performance scales, for adults and children (p. 443)

within-subjects research design: a procedure in which experimental data are repeatedly collected from the same individuals (p. 516) [Compare *between-subjects research design*]

X-axis (abcissa): in graphs used to record the results of psychological research, the horizontal axis along which the independent variables are plotted (p. 32) [Compare *Y-axis*]

Y-axis (ordinate): in graphs used to record the results of psychological research, the vertical axis along which the independent variable is plotted (p. 32) [Compare *X-axis*]

REFERENCES

Chapter 1

Boring, E.G. **A History of Experimental Psychology,** 2nd ed. New York: Appleton-Century-Crofts, 1957.

Bridgman, P.W. **The Logic of Modern Physics.** New York: Macmillan, 1927.

Deese, J. **Psychology as Art and Science.** New York: Harcourt Brace Jovanovich, 1972.

Fossey, D. "Close Encounter with Great Apes," **Science Digest,** 1983 (August), 67–71, 105–106.

Garner, W.R. "The Acquisition and Application of Knowledge: A Symbiotic Relation," **American Psychologist,** 1972, 941–946.

Hebb, D.O. "What Psychology Is About," **American Psychologist,** 1974, **29,** 71–79.

Marx, M.H. & Hillix, W.A. **Systems and Theories in Psychology,** 2nd ed. New York: McGraw-Hill, 1973.

McInish, J.R. & Coffman, B. **Evaluating the Introductory Psychology Course.** Menlo Park, California: Addison-Wesley, 1970.

Ramsey, N.F. **Science as an Art.** Middlebury, Vermont: Middlebury College Publications Department, 1969.

Rosenthal, R. **Experimenter Effects in Behavioral Research,** Enlarged Edition. New York: Irvington Publishers, 1976.

Singer, E., Blane, H.T., & Kasschau, R.A. "Alcoholism and Social Isolation," **Journal of Abnormal and Social Psychology,** 1964, **69,** 681–685.

Chapter 2

Bell, S.M. & Ainsworth, M.D.S. "Infant Crying and Maternal Responsiveness," **Child Development,** 1972, **43,** 1171–1190.

Bower, T.G.R. **Development in Infancy,** 2nd ed. San Francisco: W.H. Freeman & Company, 1982.

Butler, R.N. **Why Survive?: Being Old in America.** New York: Harper & Row, Pub., 1975.

Carmichael, C. **Nonsexist Child-rearing.** Boston: Beacon Press, 1977.

Cooney, J. "Sesame Street," **PTA Magazine,** 1970, **64,** 25–26.

Elkind, D. & Weiner, I.B. **Development of the Child.** New York: John Wiley, 1978.

Evans, E.D. & McCandless, B.R. **Children and Youth: Psychosocial Development,** 2nd ed. New York: Holt, Rinehart & Winston, 1978.

Fein, G.G. **Child Development.** Englewood Cliffs, New Jersey: Prentice-Hall, 1978.

Fischer, K.W. & Lazerson, A. **Human Development: From Conception Through Adolescence.** New York: W.H. Freeman & Company, 1984.

Fishbein, H.D. **Evolution, Development, and Children's Learning.** Pacific Palisades, California: Goodyear, 1976.

Haaf, R.A. & Bell, R.Q. "A Facial Dimension in Visual Discrimination by Human Infants," **Child Development,** 1967, **38,** 893–899.

Hamilton, M.L. **Father's Influence on Children.** Chicago: Nelson-Hall, 1977.

Hess, E.H. **Imprinting: Early Experience and the Developmental Psychobiology of Attachment.** New York: Van Nostrand Reinhold, 1973.

Hess, E.H. "Imprinting in a Natural Laboratory," **Scientific American,** 1972, **277** (August), 24–31.

Ilg, F.L. & Ames, L.B. **School Readiness.** New York: Harper & Row, Pub., 1966.

Ingle, D.J. **Who Should Have Children?** Indianapolis: Bobbs-Merrill, 1973.

Kagan, J. "The Baby's Elastic Mind," **Human Nature,** 1978, **1(1),** 66–73.

Lamb, M.E. **The Role of the Father in Child Development.** New York: John Wiley, 1976.

Lewis, A. **An Interesting Condition.** New York: Doubleday, 1950.

Lorenz, K.Z. **The Foundations of Ethology.** New York: Springer-Verlag, 1981.

Lowrey, G.H. **Growth and Development of Children,** 7th ed.

Chicago: Yearbook Medical Publishers, Inc., 1978.

McFarlane, A. "What a Baby Knows," **Human Nature,** 1978, **1(2),** 74–81.

Murray, A.D. "Infant Crying as an Elicitor of Parental Behavior: An Examination of Two Models," **Psychological Bulletin.** 1979. **86.** 191–215.

Mussen, P.H., Conger, J.J., & Kagan, J. **Child Development and Personality,** 4th ed. New York: Harper & Row, Pub., 1974.

Newman, B.M. & Newman, P.R. **Infancy and Childhood: Development and Its Contexts.** New York: John Wiley, 1978.

Newton, N. & Modahl, C. "Pregnancy: The Closest Human Relationship," **Human Nature,** 1978, **1(3),** 40–49.

Ostwald, P.F. & Peltzman, P. "The Cry of the Human Infant," **Scientific American,** 1974, **230** (March), 84–90.

Papalia, D.E. & Olds, S.W. **A Child's World: Infancy Through Adolescence,** 3rd ed. New York: McGraw-Hill, 1982.

Pearl, D., Bouthilet, L., & Lazar, J. (Eds.). **Television and Behavior: Ten Years of Scientific Progress and Implications for the Eighties** (Vols. 1 & 2). Washington, D.C.: U.S. Government Printing Office, 1982.

Piaget, J. & Kamii, C. "What Is Psychology?" **American Psychologist,** 1978, **33,** 648–652.

Rubinstein, E.A. "Television and Behavior: Research Conclusions of the 1982 NIMH Report and Their Policy Implications," **American Psychologist,** 1983, **38,** 820–825.

Scarr, S. Development in Lindzey, G., Hall, C.S., & Thompson, R.F., **Psychology,** 2nd ed. New York: Worth Publishers, 1978.

Scarr, S. & Weinberg, R.A. "Attitudes, Interests and IQ," **Human Nature,** 1978, **1(4),** 29–36.

Solley, C.M. & Murphy, G. **Development of the Perceptual World.** New York: Basic Books, 1960.

Sontag, L.W. "Implications of Fetal Behavior and Environment for Adult Personalities," **Annals of New York Academy of Sciences,** 1966, **134,** 782–786.

Tryon, R.C. "Genetic Differences in Maze Learning Ability in Rats," **The Thirty-Ninth Yearbook, National Society for the Study of Education.** Bloomington, Illinois: Public School Publications.

Wenner, W.H. & VanderVeer, B. "Infancy: The First Two Years," in Smith, D.W. & Bierman, E.L. (Eds.), **The Biologic Ages of Man.** Philadelphia, Saunders, 1973.

Chapter 3

Allport, G.W. **Pattern and Growth in Personality.** New York: Holt, Rinehart & Winston, 1961.

Amster, L.E. & Krauss, H.H. "The Relationship Between Life Crises and Mental Deterioration in Old Age," **International Journal of Aging and Human Development,** 1974, **5,** 51–55.

Benbow, C. & Stanley, J. "Sex Differences in Mathematical Ability," **Science,** 1980, **210,** 1262–1264.

Biller, H.B. "Fatherhood: Implications for Child and Adult Development," in Wolman, B.B. (Ed.), **Handbook of Developmental Psychology.** Englewood Cliffs, New Jersey: Prentice-Hall, 1982.

Binstock, R.H. & Shanas, E. (Eds.) **Aging and the Social Sciences.** New York: Van Nostrand Reinhold, 1976.

Bronfenbrenner, U. **Two Worlds of Childhood.** New York: Simon & Schuster, 1970.

Botwinick, J. **Cognitive Processes in Maturity and Old Age.** New York: Springer Publishing, 1967.

Conger, J.J. **Adolescence and Youth.** New York: Harper & Row, Pub., 1973.

Curtis, J. **Working Mothers.** Garden City, New York: Doubleday, 1976.

Dale, P.S. **Language Development: Structure and Function.** Hinsdale, Illinois: Dryden Press, 1972.

Fromm, E. **The Art of Loving.** New York: Bantam, 1965.

Hoffman, L.W. & Nye, F.I. **Working Mothers.** San Francisco: Jossey-Bass, 1974.

Horn, J. "Physical Fitness, 10 Years Later," **Psychology Today,** 1976, **10(2),** 26, 30.

Kubler-Ross, E. **On Death and Dying.** New York: Macmillan, 1969.

Levinson, D.J. **The Seasons of a Man's Life.** New York: Knopf, 1978.

Leibert, R.M. & Wirks-Nelson, R. **Developmental Psychology,** 3rd ed. Englewood Cliffs, New Jersey: Prentice-Hall, 1982.

Loehlin, J.C. & Nichols, R.C. **Heredity, Environment, and Personality.** Austin, Texas: University of Texas Press, 1976.

Lowenthal, M.F., Thurnher, M., & Chiriboga, D. **Four Stages of Life.** San Francisco: Jossey-Bass, 1976.

Lugo, J.O. & Hershey, G.L. **Human Development: A Multidisciplinary Approach to the Psychology of Individual Growth.** New York: Macmillan, 1974.

Maccoby, E. & Jacklin, C. **The Psychology of Sex Differences.** Stanford, California: Stanford University Press, 1974.

Moody, R.A., Jr. **Life After Death.** Atlanta, Georgia: Mockingbird Books, 1975.

Rice, F.P., **The Adolescent.** Boston: Allyn & Bacon, 1975.

Schafer, A. & Gray, M. "Sex and Mathematics," **Science,** 1981, **211,** 231.

Shock, N.W. & Norris, A.H. "Neuromuscular Coordinating as a Factor in Age Changes in Muscular Exercise," in Brunner, D. & Jokl, E. (Eds.), **Medicine and Sport, Vol. 4: Physical Inactivity and Aging,** 1970.

Sommer, B.B. **Puberty and Adolescence.** New York: Oxford University Press, 1978.

Tanner, J.M., Whitehouse, R.H., & Takaishi, M. "British Children, 1965," **Archives of Diseases of Childhood,** 1966, **41.**

Weg, R.B. "Changing Physiology of Aging: Normal and Pathological," in Woodruff, D.S. & Birren, J.E. (Eds.), **Aging: Scientific Perspectives and Social Issues.** New York: Van Nostrand Reinhold, 1975.

Chapter 4

Bailey, R.H. and the Editors of Time-Life Books. **The Role of the Brain.** New York: Time-Life Books, 1975.

Barber, T.X. **Hypnosis: A Scientific Approach.** New York: Van Nostrand Reinhold, 1969.

Boring, E.G. **A History of Experimental Psychology,** 2nd ed. New York: Appleton-Century-Crofts, 1957.

Brecher, E.M. and the Editors of **Consumer Reports. Licit and Illicit Drugs.** Mount Vernon, New York: Consumers Union, 1972.

Brecher, E.M. and the editors of **Consumer Reports.** "Marijuana: The Health Questions. Is Marijuana as Damaging as Recent Reports Make It Appear?" **Consumer Reports,** 1975, **40,** 143–149.

DeCoursey, R.M. **The Human Organism,** 4th ed. New York: McGraw-Hill, 1974.

Delgado, J.M.R. **Physical Control of the Mind.** New York: Harper & Row, Pub., 1969.

Gardner, E. **Fundamentals of Neurology,** 6th ed. Philadelphia: Saunders, 1975.

Grossman, S.P. **Essentials of Physiological Psychology.** New York: John Wiley, 1973.

Groves, P.M. & Schlesinger, K. **Introduction to Biological Psychology,** 2nd ed. Dubuque, Iowa: Wm. C. Brown, 1982.

Hilgard, E.R. **Divided Consciousness: Multiple Controls in Human Thought and Action.** John Wiley, 1977.

Holmes, D.S. "Meditation and Somatic Arousal Reduction: A Review of the Experimental Evidence," **American Psychologist,** 1984, **39,** 1–10.

Holmes, D.S., Solomon, S., Cappo, B.M., & Greenberg, J.L. "Effects of Transcendental Meditation Versus Resting on Physiological and Subjective Arousal," **Journal of Personality and Social Psychology,** 1983, **44,** 1245–1252.

Jones, K.L., Shainberg, L.W., & Byer, C.O. **Drugs and Alcohol,** 2nd ed. New York: Harper & Row, Pub., 1973.

Kay, E.J., Lyons, A., Newman, W., Mankin, D., & Loeb, R.C. "A Longitudinal Study of the Personality Correlates of Marijuana Use," **Journal of Consulting and Clinical Psychology,** 1978, **46,** 470–477.

Miller, N.E. "Biofeedback and Visceral Learning," **Annual Review of Psychology,** 1978, **29,** 373–404.

Miller, N.E. & Brucker, B.S. "A Learned Visceral Response Apparently Independent of Skeletal Ones in Patients Paralyzed by Spinal Lesions," in Birbaumer, N. & Kimmel, H.D. (Eds.), **Biofeedback and Self-regulation.** Hillsdale, New Jersey: Erlbaum, 1979.

Milner, B., Branch, C., & Rasmussen, T. "Evidence for Bilateral Representation in Non-right-handers," **Transactions of the American Neurological Association,** 1966, **91,** 306–308.

Noback, C.R. & Demarest, R.J. **The Nervous System: Introduction and Review.** New York: McGraw-Hill, 1977.

Ornstein, R.E. "Right and Left Thinking," **Psychology Today,** 1973, **6**(May), 86–92.

Ornstein, R.E. **The Psychology of Consciousness,** 2nd ed. New York: Harcourt Brace Jovanovich, 1977.

Peele, S. "Addiction: The Analgesic Experience," **Human Nature,** 1978 **1**(9), 61–67.

Rose, S. **The Conscious Brain,** Updated edition. New York: Vintage Books, 1976.

Schwartz, G.E. "Biofeedback, Self-regulation, and the Patterning of Physiological Processes," **American Scientist,** 1975, **63,** 314–324.

Schwartz, M. **Physiological Psychology,** 2nd ed. Englewood Cliffs, New Jersey: Prentice-Hall, 1978.

Sperry, R.W. "The Great Cerebral Commissure," **Scientific American,** 1964, **210** (January), 42–52.

Thompson, R.F. **Introduction to Physiological Psychology.** New York: Harper & Row, Pub., 1975.

Wallace, R.K. & Benson, H. "The Physiology of Meditation," **Scientific American,** 1972, **226** (February), 85–90.

Chapter 5

Amoore, J.E. **Molecular Basis of Odor.** Springfield, Illinois: Chas. C. Thomas, 1970.

Brown, T.S. "Olfaction and Taste," in Scharf, B. (Ed.) **Experimental Sensory Psychology.** Glenview, Illinois: Scott, Foresman, 1975.

Geldard, F. **The Human Senses,** 2nd ed. New York: John Wiley, 1972.

Goldstein, E.B. **Sensation and Perception,** 2nd ed. Belmont, California: Wadsworth, 1984.

Gregory, R.L. **The Intelligent Eye.** New York: McGraw-Hill, 1971.

Hochberg, J.E. **Perception,** 2nd ed. Englewood Cliffs, New Jersey: Prentice-Hall, 1978.

Ludel, J. **Introduction to Sensory Processes.** San Francisco: W.H. Freeman & Company, 1978.

McBurney, D.H. & Collings, V.B. **Introduction to Sensation/Perception,** 2nd ed. Englewood Cliffs, New Jersey: Prentice-Hall, 1984.

McBurney, D.H. & Gent, J.F. "On the Nature of Taste Qualities," **Psychological Bulletin,** 1979, **86,** 151–167.

Mueller, C.G. **Sensory Psychology.** Englewood Cliffs, New Jersey: Prentice-Hall, 1965.

Scharf, B. "Audition," in Scharf, B. (Ed.), **Experimental Sensory Psychology.** Glenview, Illinois: Scott, Foresman, 1975.

Wade, N. **The Art and Science of Visual Illusions.** London: Routledge & Kegan Paul, 1982.

Chapter 6

Adams, J.A. **Learning and Memory: An Introduction.** Homewood, Illinois: Dorsey Press, 1976.

Bandura, A. **Social Learning Theory.** Englewood Cliffs, New Jersey: Prentice-Hall, 1977.

Cofer, C.N. (Ed.). **The Structure of Human Memory.** San Francisco: W.H. Freeman & Company, 1976.

Edson, L. and the Editors of Time-Life Books. **How We Learn.** New York: Times-Life Books. 1975.

Ferster, C.B., Culbertson, S., & Perrott, M.C. **Behavior Principles,** 2nd ed. Englewood Cliffs, New Jersey: Prentice-Hall, 1975.

Garry, R. & Kingsley, H.L. **The Nature and Conditions of Learning,** 3rd ed. Englewood Cliffs, New Jersey: Prentice-Hall, 1970.

Hergenhahn, B.R. **An Introduction to the Theories of Learning.** Englewood Cliffs, New Jersey: Prentice-Hall, 1976.

Houston, J.P. **Fundamentals of Learning.** New York: Academic Press, 1976.

Hulse, S.H., Egeth, H.E., & Deese, J. **The Psychology of Learning,** 5th ed. New York: McGraw-Hill, 1980.

Kimble, G.A. **Hilgard and Marquis' Conditioning and Learning,** 2nd ed. Englewood Cliffs, New Jersey: Prentice-Hall, 1961.

Logan, F.A. & Ferraro, D.P. **Systematic Analysis of Learning and Motivation.** New York: John Wiley, 1978.

Mackintosh, N.J. "Imitation and Observational Learning," in Harre, R. & Lamb, R., **The Encyclopedic Dictionary of Psychology.** Cambridge, Massachusetts: MIT Press, 1983.

Mackintosh, N.J. "Theories of Learning," in Harre, R. & Lamb, R., **The Encyclopedic Dictionary of Psychology.** Cambridge, Massachusetts: MIT Press, 1983.

McFarland, D.J. "Reinforcement,'" in Harre, R. & Lamb, R., **The Encyclopedic Dictionary of Psychology.** Cambridge, Massachusetts: MIT Press, 1983.

Pavlov, I.P. **Conditioned Reflexes.** New York: Dover, 1960.

Peterson, L.R. **Learning.** Glenview, Illinois: Scott, Foresman, 1975.

Reynolds, G.S. **A Primer of Operant Conditioning,** revised edition. Glenview, Illinois: Scott, Foresman, 1975.

Tarpy, R.M. **Basic Principles of Learning.** Glenview, Illinois: Scott, Foresman, 1975.

Tarpy, R.M. & Mayer, R.E. **Foundations of Learning and Memory.** Glenview, Illinois: Scott, Foresman, 1978.

Chapter 7

Adams, J.A. **Learning and Memory: An Introduction.** Homewood, Illinois: Dorsey Press, 1976.

Bahrick, H.P, Bahrick, P.O., & Wittlinger, R.P. "Fifty Years of Memory for Names and Faces: A Cross-sectional Approach," **Journal of Experimental Psychology: General,** 1975, **104,** 54–75.

Bower, G.H. "Improving Memory," **Human Nature,** 1978, **1(2),** 64–72.

Bower, G.H. & Hilgard, E.R. **Theories of Learning,** 5th ed. Englewood Cliffs, New Jersey: Prentice-Hall, 1981.

Brown, R. & McNeil, D. "The 'Tip-of-the-Tongue' Phenomenon," **Journal of Verbal Learning and Verbal Behavior,** 1966, **5,** 325–327.

Cofer, C.N. "Properties of Verbal Materials and Verbal Learning," in Kling, J.W. & Riggs, L.A. (Eds.), **Woodworth and Schlosberg's Experimental Psychology.** New York: Holt, Rinehart & Winston, 1971.

Craik, F.I.M. & Lockhart, R.S. "Levels of Processing: A Framework for Memory Research," **Journal of Verbal Learning and Verbal Behavior,** 1972, **11,** 671–684.

Craik, F.I.M. & Tulving, E. "Depth of Processing and the Retention of Words in Episodic Memory," **Journal of Experimental Psychology: General,** 1975, **104,** 268–294.

Ebbinghaus, H. **Memory: A Contribution to Experimental Psychology** (1885). Roger, H.A. and Bussenius, C.E. (translators). New York: Teachers

College, Columbia University, 1913.

Luria, A. **The Mind of a Mnemonist.** New York: Basic Books, 1968.

Matlin, M. **Cognition.** New York: Holt, Rinehart & Winston, 1983.

Morgan, C.T. & Deese, J. **How to Study,** 2nd ed. New York: McGraw-Hill, 1969.

Paivio, A. **Imagery and Verbal Processes.** New York: Holt, Rinehart & Winston, 1971.

Peterson, L.R. & Peterson, M.J. "Short-term Retention of Individual Verbal Items," **Journal of Experimental Psychology,** 1959, **58,** 193–198.

Tarpy, R.M. & Mayer, R.E. **Foundations of Learning and Memory.** Glenview, Illinois: Scott, Foresman, 1978.

Thorndike, E.L. & Lorge, I. **The Teacher's Word Book of 30,000 Words.** New York: Columbia University Press, 1944.

Tulving, E. & Madigan, S.A. "Memory and Verbal Learning," **Annual Review of Psychology,** 1970, **21,** 437–484.

Zajonc, R.B. & Rajecki, D.W. "Exposure and Affect: A Field Experiment," **Psychonomic Science,** 1969, **17,** 216–217.

Chapter 8

Berko, J. "The Child's Learning of English Morphology," **Word,** 1958, **14.**

Bolles, R.C. **Theory of Motivation,** 2nd ed. New York: Harper & Row, Pub., 1975.

Bray, J.H. & Howard, G.S. "Interaction of Teacher and Student Sex and Sex-roles and Student Ratings of College Instruction," **Contemporary Educational Psychology,** 1980, **5,** 241–258.

Brown, R. **A First Language: The Early Stages.** Cambridge, Massachusetts: Harvard University Press, 1973.

Brown, R. "The First Sentences of Child and Chimpanzee," in Brown, R., **Psycholinguistics.** New York: Free Press, 1970.

Chomsky, N. **Aspects of the Theory of Syntax.** Cambridge, Massachusetts: MIT Press, 1965.

Ciolek, T.M. "Communication, Human General," in Harre, R.

& Lamb, R. (Eds.), **The Encyclopedic Dictionary of Psychology.** Cambridge, Massachusetts: MIT Press, 1983.

Ciolek, T.M. "Communication, Non-verbal," in Harre, R. & Lamb, R. (Eds.), **The Encyclopedic Dictionary of Psychology.** Cambridge, Massachusetts: MIT Press, 1983.

Clark, H.H. & Clark, E.V. **Psychology and Language: An Introduction to Psycholinguistics.** New York: Harcourt Brace Jovanovich, 1977.

Cofer, C.N. (Ed.), **The Structure of Human Memory.** San Francisco: W.H. Freeman & Company, 1976.

Dale, P.S. **Language Development: Structure and Function.** Hinsdale, Illinois: Dryden Press, 1972.

Deag, J.M. **Social Behavior of Animals.** London, England: Edward Arnold, 1980.

Deese, J. **Psycholinguistics.** Boston, Massachusetts: Allyn & Bacon. 1970.

Duncan, S., Jr. "Nonverbal Communication," **Psychological Bulletin,** 1969, **72,** 118–137.

Dyer, F.C. & Gould, J.L. "Honey Bee Navigation," **American Scientist,** 1983, **71,** 587–597.

Dyer, F.C. & Gould, J.L. "Honey Bee Orientation: A Backup System for Cloudy Days," **Science,** 1981, **214,** 1041–1042.

Foss, D.J. & Hakes, D.T. **Psycholinguistics: An Introduction to the Psychology of Language.** Englewood Cliffs, New Jersey: Prentice-Hall, 1978.

Frisch, K.V. **The Dance Language and Orientation of Bees.** (Chadwick, L.E., trans.) Cambridge, Massachusetts: Belknap Press, 1967.

Gardner, B.T. & Gardner, R.A. "Two-way Communication with an Infant Chimpanzee," in Schrier, A.M. & Stollnitz, F. (Eds.), **Behavior of Nonhuman Primates: Modern Research Trends (Vol. IV.)** New York: Academic Press, 1971.

Gardner, R.A. & Gardner, B.T. "Teaching Sign Language to a Chimpanzee, **Science,** 1969, **165,** 664–672.

Graham, J. (Ed.). **Great American Speeches: 1898–1963.** New

York: Appleton-Century-Crofts, 1970.

Grier, J.W. **Biology of Animal Behavior.** St. Louis: Times Mirror/Mosby, 1984.

Hall, E.T. **The Silent Language.** Garden City, New York: Doubleday, 1959.

Hall, E.T. **The Hidden Dimension.** Garden City, New York: Doubleday, 1966.

Hamilton, A. "What Science Knows About Dolphin 'Talk,'" **Science Digest,** 1965 (May), 9–13.

Hintzman, D.L. **The Psychology of Learning and Memory.** San Francisco: W.H. Freeman & Company, 1978.

Hayduk, L.A. "Personal Space: Where We Now Stand," **Psychological Bulletin,** 1983, **94,** 293–335.

Kahananui, D. & Anthony, A.P. **Let's Speak Hawaiian: A Comprehensive Classroom Text for Language Learning,** 2nd ed. Honolulu, Hawaii: University Press of Hawaii, 1974.

Keller, H. **The Story of My Life.** New York: Doubleday, 1903.

Lachman, R., Lachman, J.L., & Butterfield, E.C. **Cognitive Psychology and Information Processing: An Introduction.** Hillsdale, New Jersey: Erlbaum, 1979.

Leiber, J.F. "Meaning," in Harre, R. & Lamb, R. (Eds.), **The Encyclopedic Dictionary of Psychology.** Cambridge, Massachusetts: MIT Press, 1983.

Lilly, J.C. & Miller, A.M. "Sounds Emitted by the Bottlenose Dolphin," **Science,** 1961, **133,** 1689–1693.

Limber, J. "Language in Child and Chimp?" **American Psychologist,** 1977, **32,** 280–295.

Matlin, M. **Cognition.** New York: Holt, Rinehart & Winston, 1983.

Mehrabian, A. "Nonverbal Communication," in Arnold, W.J. & Page, M.M. (Eds.), **Nebraska Symposium on Motivation.** Lincoln, Nebraska: University of Nebraska Press, 1971.

Menyuk, P. **The Acquisition and Development of Language.** Englewood Cliffs, New Jersey: Prentice-Hall, 1971.

Palermo, D.S. **Psychology of Language.** Glenview, Illinois: Scott, Foresman, 1978.

Reynolds, A.G. & Flagg, P.W. **Cognitive Psychology.** Cambridge, Massachusetts: Winthrop, 1977.

Sapir, E. "The Unconscious Patterning of Behavior in Society," in Dummer, E.S. (Ed.), **The Unconscious: A Symposium.** New York: Knopf, 1927.

Terrace, H.S. **Nim.** New York: Knopf, 1979.

Chapter 9

Birney, R.C., Brunswick, H., & Teevan, R.C. **Fear of Failure.** New York: Van Nostrand Reinhold, 1969.

Blass, E.M. & Hall, W.G. "Drinking Termination: Interactions Among Hydrational, Orogastric, and Behavioral Control in Rats," **Psychological Review,** 1976, **83,** 356–374.

Casey, K.L. "Pain: A Current View of Neural Mechanisms," **American Scientist,** 1973, **61,** 194–199.

Crouch, J.E. & McClintic, J.R. **Human Anatomy and Physiology.** New York: John Wiley, 1971.

Davis, J.D. & Levine, M.W. "A Model for the Control of Ingestion," **Psychological Review,** 1977, **84,** 379–412.

Harlow, H.F., McGaugh, J.L., & Thompson, R.F. **Psychology.** San Francisco: Albion, 1971.

Hess, H.E. "Attitude and Pupil Size," **Scientific American,** 1965, **212,** 46–54.

Hoffman, L.W. "Fear of Success in 1965 and 1974: A Follow-Up Study," **Journal of Consulting and Clinical Psychology,** 1977, **45,** 310–321.

Honrer, M.S. "Toward an Understanding of Achievement-Related Conflicts in Women," **Journal of Social Issues,** 1972, **28,** 157–175.

Hoyenga, K.B. & Hoyenga, K.T. **Motivational Explanations of Behavior: Evolutionary, Physiological, and Cognitive Ideas.** Monterey, California: Brooks/Cole, 1984.

Keesey, R.E. & Powley, T.L. "Hypothalamic Regulation of

Body Weight," **American Scientist**, 1965, **63**, 558–565.

Klein, S.B. **Motivation: Biosocial Approaches.** New York: McGraw-Hill, 1982.

Kuhl, J. "Standard Setting and Risk Preference: An Elaboration of the Theory of Achievement Motivation and an Empirical Test," **Psychological Review**, 1978, **85**, 239–248.

Lacey, J.I. "The Evaluation of Autonomic Responses Toward a General Solution," **Annals of the New York Academy of Sciences**, 1956, **67**, 123–163.

Levinthal, C.F. **Introduction to Physiological Psychology,** 2nd ed. Englewood Cliffs, New Jersey: Prentice-Hall, 1983.

Logan, F.A. & Ferraro, D.P. **Systematic Analysis of Learning and Motivation.** New York: John Wiley, 1978.

Lykken, D.T. "Psychology and the Lie Detector Industry," **American Psychologist**, 1974, **29**, 725–739.

Mednick, M.T.S. & Puryear, G.R. "Race and Fear of Success in College Women: 1968 and 1971," **Journal of Consulting and Clinical Psychology**, 1976, **44**, 787–789.

Melzack, R. "The Perception of Pain," **Scientific American,** 1961, **204(2)**, 41–49.

Melzack, R. & Wall, P.D. "Pain Mechanisms: A New Theory," **Science**, 1965, **150**, 971–979.

Plotnik, R. & Mollenaucr, S. **Brain & Behavior: An Introduction to Physiological Psychology.** San Francisco: Canfield Press, 1978.

Podlesny, J.A. & Raskin, D.C. "Physiological Measures and the Detection of Deception," **Psychological Bulletin**, 1977, **84**, 782–799.

Schachter, S. & Rodin, J. **Obese Humans and Rats.** New York: Halsted Press, 1974.

Seligman, M.E.P. **Helplessness.** San Francisco: W.H. Freeman & Company, 1974.

Seligman, M.E.P. **Helplessness: On Depression, Development, and Death.** San Francisco: W.H. Freeman & Company, 1975.

Smith, G.P. & Gibbs, J. "Brain-gut Peptides and the Control of Food Intake," in Martin, J.B., Reichlin, S., & Bick, K.L. (Eds.), **Neurosecretion and Brain Peptides.** New York: Raven Press, 1981.

Spence, J.T. & Helmreich, R.L. **Masculinity and Femininity: Their Psychological Dimensions, Correlates, and Antecedents.** Austin, Texas: University of Texas Press, 1978.

Taylor, J.A. "A Personality Scale of Manifest Anxiety," **Journal of Abnormal and Social Psychology**, 1953, **48**, 285–290.

Tresmer, D. "Fear of Success: Popular but Unproven," in Travis, C. (Ed.), **The Female Experience.** Del Mar, California: CRM Books, 1974.

Chapter 10

Bridges, K.M.B. "A Genetic Theory of the Emotions," **Journal of Genetic Psychology**, 1930, **37**, 514–527.

Cofer, C.N. **Motivation and Emotion.** Glenview, Illinois: Scott, Foresman, 1972.

Darwin, C. **The Expression of Emotion in Man and Animals.** Chicago: University of Chicago Press, 1965.

Dienstbier, R.A. "Emotion-attribution Theory: Establishing Roots and Exploring Future Perspectives," in Dienstbier, R.A. (Ed.), **Nebraska Symposium on Motivation** (Vol. 26). Lincoln, Nebraska: University of Nebraska Press, 1979.

Ekman, P. **Darwin and Facial Expression: A Century of Research in Review.** New York: Academic Press, 1973.

Ekman, P. & Friesen, W.V. **Unmasking the Face.** Englewood Cliffs, New Jersey: Prentice-Hall, 1975.

Gordon, R.M. "Emotion Labelling and Cognition," **Journal for the Theory of Social Behaviour,** 1978, **8**, 125–135.

Harlow, H.F., McGaugh, J.L., & Thompson, R.F. **Psychology.** San Francisco: Albion, 1971.

Hebb, D.O. **Textbook of Psychology,** 3rd ed. Philadelphia: Saunders, 1972.

Izard, C.E. **Human Emotion.** New York: Plenum, 1977.

Leventhal, H. "Toward a Comprehensive Theory of Emotion" in Berkowitz, L., (Ed.), **Advances in Experimental Social Psychology** (Vol. 13). New York: Academic Press, 1980.

Reisenzein, R. "The Schachter Theory of Emotion: Two Decades Later," **Psychological Bulletin**, 1983, **94**, 239–264.

Rinn, W.E. "The Neuropsychology of Facial Expression: A Review of the Neurological and Psychological Mechanisms for Producing Facial Expressions," **Psychological Bulletin**, 1984, **95**, 52–77.

Rubin, Z. "Measurement of Romantic Love," **Journal of Personality and Social Psychology,** 1970, **16**, 265–273.

Sackheim, H.A., Gur, R.C., & Saucy, M.C., "Emotions are Expressed More Intensely on the Left Side of the Face," **Science.** 1978. **202**. 434–436.

Schachter, S. "The Interaction of Cognitive and Physiological Determinants of Emotional State," in Berkowitz, L. (Ed.), **Experimental Social Psychology,** Vol. I. New York: Academic Press, 1964.

Schachter, S. & Singer, J.E. "Cognitive, Social, and Physiological Determinants of Emotional State," **Psychological Review**, 1962, **69**, 379–399.

Schlosberg, H. "Three Dimensions of Emotion," **Psychological Review**, 1954, **61**, 81–88.

Solomon, R.L. & Corbit, J.D. "An Opponent-process Theory of Motivation: I. Temporal Dynamics of Affect," **Psychological Review**, 1974, **81**, 119–145.

Stanley-Jones, D. "The Biological Origin of Love and Hate," in Arnold, M. (Ed.), **Feelings and Emotions: The Loyola Symposium.** New York: Academic Press, 1970.

Strongman, K.T. **The Psychology of Emotion,** 2nd ed. New York: John Wiley, 1978.

Chapter 11

Campbell, R. and the Editors of Time-Life Books. **The Enigma of the Mind.** New York: Time-Life Books, 1976.

Dollard, J. & Miller, N.E. **Personality and Psychotherapy: An**

Analysis in Terms of Learning, Thinking, and Culture. New York: McGraw-Hill, 1950.

Feshbach, S. "The Environment of Personality," **American Psychologist,** 1978, **33,** 437–446.

Fisher, S. & Greenberg, R.P. **The Scientific Credibility of Freud's Theories and Therapy.** New York: Basic Books, 1977.

Hall, C.S. & Lindzey, G. **Theories of Personality,** 3rd ed. New York: John Wiley, 1978.

Harmatz, M.G. **Abnormal Psychology.** Englewood Cliffs, New Jersey: Prentice-Hall, 1978.

Hartshorne, H. & May, M.A. **Studies in the Nature of Character. I: Studies in Deceit.** New York: Macmillan, 1928.

Hogan, R., DeSoto, C.B., & Solano, C. "Traits, Tests, and Personality Research," **American Psychologist,** 1977, **32,** 255–264.

Maddi, S.R. **Personality Theories: A Comparative Analysis,** 3rd ed. Homewood, Illinois: Dorsey Press, 1976.

Maslow, A.H. **Toward a Psychology of Being.** New York: Van Nostrand Reinhold, 1968.

Mischel, W. **Introduction to Personality,** 3rd ed. New York: Holt, Rinehart & Winston, 1981.

Mischel, W. "On the Future of Personality Measurement," **American Psychologist,** 1977. **32,** 246–254.

Mischel, W. **Personality and Assessment,** New York: John Wiley, 1968.

Mischel, W. & Mischel, H.N. **Essentials of Psychology,** 2nd ed. New York: Random House, 1980.

Nye, R.D. **What is B.F. Skinner Really Saying?** Englewood Cliffs, New Jersey: Prentice-Hall, 1979.

Nye, R.D. **Three Psychologies: Perspectives from Freud, Skinner, and Rogers,** 2nd ed. Monterey, California: Brooks/Cole, 1981.

Rogers, C.R. **Client-centered Therapy: Its Current Practice, Implications, and Theory.** Boston: Houghton Mifflin, 1951.

Rotter, J.B. & Hochreich, D.J. **Personality.** Glenview, Illinois: Scott, Foresman, 1975.

Wertheimer, M. "Humanistic Psychology and the Humane but Tough-minded Psychologist," **American Psychologist,** 1978, **33,** 739–745.

Wiggins, J.S., Renner, K.E., Clore, G.L., & Rose, R.J. **The Psychology of Personality.** Reading, Massachusetts: Addison-Wesley, 1971.

Chapter 12

Abramson, L.Y. & Sackeim, H.A. "A Paradox in Depression: Uncontrollability and Self-blame," **Psychological Bulletin,** 1977, **84,** 838–851.

Adams, V. and the Editors of Time-Life Books. **Crime.** New York: Time-Life Books, 1976.

Agras, S., Sylvester, D. & Oliveau, D. "The Epidemiology of Common Fears and Phobias," **Comprehensive Psychiatry,** 1969, **10,** 151–156.

Brown, G.W. & Harris, T. **Social Origins of Depression: A Study of Psychiatric Disorder in Women.** New York: Free Press, 1978.

Campbell, D.E. & Beets, J.L. "Lunacy and the Moon," **Psychological Bulletin,** 1978, **85,** 1123–1129.

Coleman, J.C. **Abnormal Psychology and Modern Life,** 5th ed. Glenview, Illinois: Scott, Foresman, 1976.

Cox, G., Costanzo, P.R., & Coie, J.D. "A Survey Instrument for the Assessment of Popular Conceptions of Mental Illness,"**Journal of Counseling and Clinical Psychology,** 1976, **44,** 901–909.

Davison, G.C. & Neale, J.M. **Abnormal Psychology: An Experimental Clinical Approach,** 2nd ed. New York: John Wiley, 1978.

Dougherty, F.E. "Patient-therapist Matching for Prediction of Optimal and Minimal Therapeutic Outcome," **Journal of Counseling and Clinical Psychology,** 1976, **44,** 889–897.

Gynther, M.D., Fowler, R.D., & Erdberg, P. "False Positives Galore: The Application of Standard MMPI Criteria to a Rural Isolated Negro Sample," **Journal of Clinical Psychology,** 1971, **27,** 234–237.

Harmatz, M.G. **Abnormal Psychology.** Englewood Cliffs, New Jersey: Prentice-Hall, 1978.

Kaplan, M. "A Woman's View of DSM-III," **American Psychologist,** 1983, **38,** 786–792.

Kesey, K. **One Flew Over the Cuckoo's Nest.** New York: Signet—The New American Library, 1962.

McCary, J.L. **Freedom and Growth in Marriage.** Santa Barbara, California: Hamilton, 1975.

Mehr, J. **Abnormal Psychology.** New York: Holt, Rinehart & Winston, 1983.

Rosenhan, D.L. "On Being Sane in Insane Places," **Science,** 1973, **179,** 250–258.

Rowe, D. **The Experience of Depression,** New York: John Wiley, 1978.

Sarason, I.G. & Sarason, B.R. **Abnormal Psychology: The Problem of Maladaptive Behavior,** 4th ed. Englewood Cliffs, New Jersey: Prentice-Hall, 1984.

Schact, T. & Nathan, P.E. "But Is It Good for the Psychologists? Appraisal and Status of DSM-III," **American Psychologist,** 1977, **32,** 1017–1025.

Shakow, D. "Segmental Set: The Adaptive Process in Schizophrenia," **American Psychologist,** 1977, **32,** 129–139.

Smith, D. & Kraft, W.A. "DSM-III: Do Psychologists Really Want an Alternative?" **American Psychologist,** 1983, **38,** 777–785.

Spitzer, R.L., Williams, J.B., & Skodol, A.E. "DSM-III: The Major Achievements and an Overview," **American Journal of Psychiatry,** 1980, **137(2),** 151–164.

Srole, L., Langner, T.S., Michael, S.T., Opler, M.K., & Rennie, T.A.C. **Mental Health in the Metropolis: Midtown Manhattan Study,** Vol. I. New York: McGraw-Hill, 1962.

Strauss, J.S. & Docherty, J.P. "Subtypes of Schizophrenia: Descriptive Models," **Schizo-**

phrenia Bulletin, 1979, **5,** 447–452.

Watson, C.G. & Buranen, C. "The Frequencies of Conversion Reaction Symptoms," **Journal of Abnormal Psychology,** 1979, **88,** 209–211.

Wilner, A., Reick, T., Robins, I., Fishman, R., & Van Doren, T. "Obsessive-compulsive Neurosis," **Comprehensive Psychiatry,** 1976, **17,** 527–539.

Woodruff, R.A., Goodwin, D.W., & Guze, S.B. **Psychiatric Diagnosis.** New York: Oxford University Press, 1974.

Chapter 13

Albee, G.W. "The Protestant Ethic, Sex, and Psychotherapy," **American Psychologist,** 1977, **32,** 150–161.

Auerbach, S.M. & Kilmann, P.R. "Crisis Intervention: A Review of Outcome Research," **Psychological Bulletin,** 1977, **84,** 1189–1217.

Bergin, A.E. & Lambert, M.J. "The Evaluation of Therapeutic Outcomes," in Garfield, S.L. & Bergin, A.E. (Eds.), **Handbook of Psychotherapy and Behavior Change: An Empirical Analysis,** 2nd ed. New York: John Wiley, 1978.

Carlsson, A. "Antipsychotic Drugs, Neurotransmitters, and Schizophrenia," **American Journal of Psychiatry,** 1978, **135,** 164–173.

Coleman, J.C. **Abnormal Psychology and Modern Life,** 5th ed. Glenview, Illinois: Scott, Foresman, 1976.

Coleman, J.C., Butcher, J.N., & Carson, R.C. **Abnormal Psychology and Modern Life,** 7th ed. Glenview, Illinois: Scott, Foresman, 1984.

DiLoreto, A. **Comparative Psychotherapy.** New York: Aldine-Atherton, 1971.

Ellis, A. **Humanistic Psychotherapy: The Rational-Emotive Approach.** New York: McGraw-Hill, 1973.

Eysenck, H.J. "The Effects of Psychotherapy," in Eysenck, H.J., (Ed.), **Handbook of Abnormal Psychology: An Experimental Approach.** New York: Basic Books, 1961.

Gomes-Schwartz, B. & Schwartz, J.M. "Psychotherapy Process Variables Distinguishing the 'Inherently Helpful' Person from the Professional Psychotherapist," **Journal of Consulting and Clinical Psychology,** 1978, **46,** 196–197.

Harmetz, M.G. **Abnormal Psychology.** Englewood Cliffs, New Jersey: Prentice-Hall, 1978.

Jacobson, N.S. "Problem Solving and Contingency Contracting in the Treatment of Marital Discord," **Journal of Consulting and Clinical Psychology,** 1977, **45,** 92–100.

Kilbourne, B. & Richardson, J.T. "Psychotherapy and New Religions in a Pluralistic Society," **American Psychologist,** 1984, **39,** 237–251.

Lazarus, A.A. "Has Behavior Therapy Outlived its Usefulness?" **American Psychologist,** 1977, **32,** 550–554.

Miller, N.E. "Behavioral Medicine: Symbiosis between Laboratory and Clinic," in Rosenzweig, M.R. & Porter, L.W., (Eds.), **Annual Review of Psychology** (Vol. 34). Palo Alto, California: Annual Reviews, 1983.

Phares, E.J. **Clinical Psychology: Concepts, Methods, and Professions.** Homewood, Illinois: Dorsey Press, 1984.

Ryan, V.L., Krall, C.A., & Hodges, W.F. "Self-concept Change in Behavior Modification," **Journal of Consulting and Clinical Psychology,** 1976, **44,** 638–645.

Sarason, I.G., & Sarason, B.R. **Abnormal Psychology: The Problem of Maladaptive Behavior,** 4th ed. Englewood Cliffs, New Jersey: Prentice-Hall, 1984.

Sarbin, T.R. & Mancuso, J.C. **Schizophrenia: Medical Diagnosis or Moral Verdict?** New York: Pergamon Press, 1980.

Shean, G. **Schizophrenia: An Introduction to Research and Theory.** Cambridge, Massachusetts: Winthrop, 1978.

Sloane, R.B., Staples, F.R., Cristol, A..H., Yorkston, N.J., & Whipple, K. "Patient Characteristics and Outcome in Psychotherapy and Behavior Therapy," **Journal of Consult-**ing and Clinical Psychology, 1976, **44,** 330–339.

Strupp, H.H. "The Outcome Problem in Psychotherapy: Contemporary Perspectives," in Harvey, J.H., & Parks, M.M., (Eds.), **The Master Lecture Series (Vol. 1), Psychotherapy Research and Behavior Change.** Washington, D.C.: American Psychological Association, 1982.

Sue, S. "Clients' Demographic Characteristics and Therapeutic Treatment: Differences That Make A Difference," **Journal of Consulting and Clinical Psychology,** 1976, **44,** 864.

Suinn, R.M. **Fundamentals of Behavior Pathology,** 2nd ed. New York: John Wiley, 1975.

Szasz, T.S. "The Ethics of Therapy," **National Forum: The Phi Kappa Phi Journal,** 1978, **LVIII(2),** 25–29.

Szasz, T.S. **The Myth of Mental Illness.** New York: Harper & Row, Pub., 1961.

Turkewitz, H., O'Leary, K.D., & Ironsmith, M. "Generalization and Maintenance of Appropriate Behavior Through Self-control," **Journal of Consulting and Clinical Psychology,** 1975, **43,** 577–583.

Wolpe, J. "Cognition and Causation in Human Behavior and Its Therapy," **American Psychologist,** 1978, **33,** 437–446.

Zimbardo, P.G. **Shyness: What It Is. What to Do About It.** Reading, Massachusetts: Addison-Wesley, 1977.

Chapter 14

Anastasi, A. **Psychological Testing,** 4th ed. New York: Macmillan, 1976.

Campbell, D.P. & Hansen, J.C. **Manual for the SVIB-SCII Strong-Campbell Interest Inventory,** 3rd ed. Stanford, California: Stanford University Press, 1981.

Coon, K. **The Dog Intelligence Test.** New York: Avon Books, 1977.

Flynn, J.R. "The Mean IQ of Americans: Massive Gains 1932 to 1978," **Psychological Bulletin,** 1984, **95,** 29–51.

Kaplan, R.M. & Saccuzzo, D.P. **Psychological Testing: Princi-**

ples, Applications, and Issues. Monterey, California: Brooks/ Cole, 1982.

Loehlin, J.C., Lindzey, G., & Spuhler, J.N. **Race Differences in Intelligence.** San Francisco: W.H. Freeman & Company, 1975.

Mednick, S.A. "The Associative Bases of the Creative Processes," **Psychological Review,** 1962, **69,** 220–232.

Mischel, W. "On the Future of Personality Measurement," **American Psychologist,** 1977, **32,** 246–254.

Raven, J.C. **Progressive Matrices.** London, England: H.K. Lewis, 1956.

Schmidt, F.L., Hunter, J.E., McKenzie, R.C., & Muldrow, T.W. "Impact of Valid Selection Procedures on Work-force Productivity," **Journal of Applied Psychology,** 1979, **64,** 609–626.

Sternberg, R.J. "What Should Intelligence Tests Test? Implications of a Triarchic Theory of Intelligence for Intelligence Testing," **Educational Researcher,** 1984, **13(1),** 5–15.

Thorndike, R.L. & Hagen, E.P. **Measurement and Evaluation in Psychology and Education,** 4th ed. New York: John Wiley, 1977.

Torrance, E.P. **The Torrance Tests of Creative Thinking.** Princeton, New Jersey: Personnel Press, 1966.

Tyler, L.E. & Walsh, W.B. **Tests and Measurements,** 3rd ed. Englewood Cliffs, New Jersey: Prentice-Hall, 1979.

Velandia, W., Grandon, G.M., & Page, E.B. "Family Size, Birth Order, and Intelligence in a Large South American Sample," **American Educational Research Journal,** 1978, **15,** 399–416.

Watson, P. "I.Q.: The Racial Gap," **Psychology Today,** 1972, **6(4),** 48–50, 97, 99.

Zajonc, R.B. & Markus, G.B. "Birth Order and Intellectual Development," **Psychological Review,** 1975, **82,** 74–88.

Chapter 15

Asch, S.E. "Studies of Independence and Conformity: A Minority of One Against a Unanimous Majority," **Psychological Monographs,** 1956, **70**(9, Whole No. 416).

Back, K.W. (Ed.). **Social Psychology.** New York: John Wiley, 1977.

Bardwick, J.M. **Psychology of Women.** New York: Harper & Row, Pub., 1971.

Baron, R.S., Roper, G., & Baron, P.H. "Group Discussion and the Stingy Shift," **Journal of Personality and Social Psychology,** 1974, **30,** 538–545.

Belsky, J., Lerner, R.M., & Spanier, G.B. **The Child in the Family.** Reading, Massachusetts: Addison-Wesley, 1984.

Bem, S.L. "The Measurement of Psychological Androgyny," **Journal of Consulting and Clinical Psychology,** 1974, **42,** 155–162.

Bowlby, J. **Attachment and Loss: Volume 1—Attachment.** New York: Basic Books, 1969.

Bowlby, J. **Attachment and Loss: Volume 2—Separation, Anxiety, and Anger.** New York: Basic Books, 1973.

Bowlby, J. **Attachment and Loss: Volume 3—Loss, Sadness, and Depression.** New York: Basic Books, 1980.

Haney, C., Banks, C., and Zimbardo, P.G. "Interpersonal Dynamics in a Simulated Prison," **International Journal of Criminology and Penology,** 1973, **1,** 69–97.

Herbst, P.G. "The Measurement of Family Relations," **Human Relations,** 1952, **5,** 3–35.

Hollander, E.P. **Principles and Methods of Social Psychology,** 3rd ed. New York: Oxford University Press, 1976.

Howell, W.C. & Dipboye, R.L. **Essentials of Industrial and Organizational Psychology,** rev. ed. Homewood, Illinois: Dorsey Press, 1982.

Janis, I.L. **Groupthink: Psychological Studies of Policies, Decisions, and Fiascoes,** 2nd ed. Boston, Massachusetts: Houghton Mifflin, 1982.

Lorenz, K. **On Aggression.** New York: Bantam, 1966.

Perry, J. & Perry, E. **Face to Face: The Individual and Social Problems.** Boston, Massa-

chusetts: Little, Brown (Educational Associates), 1976.

Rather, D. & Gates, G.P. **The Palace Guard.** New York: Harper & Row, Pub., 1974.

Raven, B.H. & Rubin, J.Z. **Social Psychology,** 2nd ed. New York: John Wiley, 1983.

Schjelderup-Ebbe, T. "Social Behavior of Birds," in Murchison, C. (Ed.), **A Handbook of Social Psychology.** Worcester, Massachusetts: Clark University Press, 1935.

Shaw, M.E. "Communication Networks," in Berkowitz, L. (Ed.), **Advances in Experimental Psychology,** Vol. 1. New York: Academic Press, 1964.

Spence, J.T. & Helmreich, R.L. **Masculinity and Femininity: Their Psychological Dimensions, Correlates, and Antecedents.** Austin, Texas: University of Texas Press, 1978.

Weick, K.E. "Small Wins: Redefining the Scale of Social Problems," **American Psychologist,** 1984, **39,** 40–49.

Wrightsman, L.S. **Social Psychology,** 2nd ed. Monterey, California: Brooks/Cole, 1977.

Chapter 16

Bandura, A. **Aggression: A Social Learning Analysis.** Englewood Cliffs, New Jersey: Prentice-Hall, 1973.

Berkowitz, L. "Some Determinants of Compulsive Aggression: Role of Mediated Associations with Reinforcements for Aggression," **Psychological Review,** 1974, **81,** 165–176.

Brigham, J.C. "Ethnic Stereotypes," **Psychological Bulletin,** 1971, **76,** 15–38.

Cann, A., Sherman, S.J., & Elkes, R. "Effects of Initial Request Size and Timing of a Second Request on Compliance: The Foot in the Door and the Door in the Face," **Journal of Personality and Social Psychology,** 1975, **32,** 774–782.

Centers, R., Raven, B.H., & Rodriques, A. "Conjugal Power Structure: A Re-examination," **American Sociological Review,** 1971, **36,** 264–278.

Darley, J.M. & Latane, B. "Bystander Intervention in Emergencies: Diffusion of Responsibility," **Journal of Personality and Social Psychology,** 1968, **8**, 377–383.

Davis, M. **Intimate Relations,** New York: Free Press, 1973.

DeJong, W. "Consensus Information and the Foot-in-the-Door Effect," **Personality and Social Psychology Bulletin,** 1981, **7**, 423–430.

Dutton, D.G. & Aron, A.P. "Some Evidence for Heightened Sexual Attraction under Conditions of High Anxiety," **Journal of Personality and Social Psychology,** 1974, **30**, 510–517.

Feldman, M.P. **Criminal Behaviour: A Psychological Analysis.** New York: John Wiley, 1977.

Harmatz, M.G. & Novak, M.A. **Human Sexuality.** New York: Harper & Row, Pub., 1983.

Harrell, T.W. & Harrell, M.S. "Army General Classification Test Scores for Civilian Occupations," **Educational and Psychological Measurement,** 1945, **5**, 229–239.

Hepner, H.W. **Psychology: Applied to Life and Work,** 4th ed. Englewood Cliffs, New Jersey: Prentice-Hall, 1966.

Hornstein, H.A. **Cruelty and Kindness: A New Look at Aggression and Altruism.** Englewood Cliffs, New Jersey: Prentice-Hall, 1976.

Karlins, M., Coffman, T.L., & Walters, G. "On the Fading Social Stereotypes: Studies in Three Generations of College Students," **Journal of Personality and Social Psychology,** 1969, **13**, 1–16.

Klapper, J.T. **The Effects of Mass Communication.** Glencoe, Illinois: Free Press, 1960.

Kleinke, C.L. **First Impressions: The Psychology of Encountering Others.** Englewood Cliffs, New Jersey: Prentice-Hall, 1975.

Levinger, G. "Toward the Analysis of Close Relationships," **Journal of Experimental Social Psychology,** 1980, **16**, 510–544.

Levinger, G. & Snoek, J.D. **Attraction in Relationship: A New Look at Interpersonal Attraction.** Morristown, New Jersey: General Learning, 1972.

Lofland, J. **Doing Social Life: The Qualitative Study of Human Interaction in Natural Settings.** New York: John Wiley, 1976.

Moyer, K.E. **The Psychobiology of Aggression.** New York: Harper & Row, Pub., 1976.

Oskamp, S. **Attitudes and Opinions.** Englewood Cliffs, New Jersey: Prentice-Hall, 1977.

Raven, B.H. & Rubin, J.Z. **Social Psychology: People in Groups.** New York: John Wiley, 1976.

Rokeach, M. **Beliefs, Attitudes, and Values: A Theory of Organization and Change.** San Francisco, California: Jossey-Bass, 1968.

Rubin, Z. **Liking and Loving: An Invitation to Social Psychology.** New York: Holt, Rinehart & Winston, 1973.

Stewart, E.W. **The Human Bond: Introduction to Social Psychology.** New York: John Wiley, 1978.

Tiefer, L. "The Kiss," **Human Nature,** 1978, **1**(7), 28–37.

Walster, E. & Walster, G.W. **A New Look at Love.** Reading, Massachusetts: Addison-Wesley, 1978.

Walster, E., Walster, G.W., Piliavin, J., & Schmidt, L. "Playing Hard-to-get: Understanding an Elusive Phenomenon," **Journal of Personality and Social Psychology,** 1973, **26**, 113–121.

Worchel, S. & Cooper, J. **Understanding Social Psychology,** 3rd ed. Homewood, Illinois: Dorsey Press, 1983.

Zajonc, R.B. "Attitudinal Effects of Mere Exposure," **Journal of Personality and Social Psychology,** 1968, **9**, 1–20.

Chapter 17

Aronson, E., Willerman, B., & Floyd, J. "The Effect of a Pratfall on Increasing Interpersonal Attractiveness," **Psychonomic Science,** 1966, **4**, 227–228.

Ethical Principles in the Conduct of Research with Human Participants. Washington, D.C.: American Psychological Association, 1973.

Hebb, D.O. "What Psychology Is About," **American Psychologist,** 1974, **29**, 71–79.

Kasschau, R.A. "Semantic Satiation as a Function of Duration of Repetition and Initial Meaning Intensity," **Journal of Verbal Learning and Verbal Behavior,** 1969, **8**, 36–42.

Psychology Teacher's Resource Book: First Course. Washington, D.C.: American Psychological Association, 1973.

Rosenthal, R. "How Often Are Our Numbers Wrong?" **American Psychologist,** 1978, **33**, 1005–1008.

Williams, B. **A Sampler on Sampling.** New York: John Wiley, 1978.

Epilogue

Bolles, R.N. **What Color Is Your Parachute?** Berkeley, California: Ten Speed Press, 1972.

Careers in Psychology. Washington, D.C.: American Psychological Association, 1980.

Fretz, B.R. & Stang, D.J. **Preparing for Graduate Study in Psychology: Not for Seniors Only!** Washington, D.C.: American Psychological Association, 1980.

Johnson, D.W. **Human Relations and Your Career: A Guide to Interpersonal Skills.** Englewood Cliffs, New Jersey: Prentice-Hall, 1978.

Korten, F.F., Cook, S.W., & Lacey, J.I. **Psychology and the Problems of Society.** Washington, D.C.: American Psychological Association, 1970.

Moine, D.J. "Going for the Gold in the Selling Game," **Psychology Today,** 1984, **18**(3), 36–39, 42–44.

Sheehy, G. **Passages.** New York: Dutton, 1976.

Skinner, B.F. **Beyond Freedom and Dignity.** New York: Knopf, 1971.

Woods, P.J. (Ed.). **The Psychology Major: Training and Employment Strategies.** Washington, D.C.: American Psychological Association, 1979.

INDEX